Dave Slibsager
641 B St
Hollister, CA 95023
637-5467

Economic Issues
for
Consumers

Economic Issues for Consumers

SECOND EDITION

ROGER LeROY MILLER
UNIVERSITY OF MIAMI

WEST PUBLISHING COMPANY
ST. PAUL   NEW YORK   LOS ANGELES   SAN FRANCISCO

CREDITS

Photography by Susan Miller.

Other credits are as follows:

Page 177 Reprinted with permission of Sears, Roebuck and Co. **Page 189** With permission of Budget Control Services, Inc., of Shelburne, Vermont. **Page 225** Copyright 1975 by Consumers Union of United States, Inc., Mount Vernon, N.Y. 10550. Excerpted by permission from Consumer Reports, May, 1975. **Page 287** Chart reprinted with the courtesy of Insurance Information Institute, 110 William Street, New York, New York 10038. **Page 397** Reproduced by courtesy of *Consumer Views*, published by Citibank. **Page 493** Reprinted with permission of the copyright owner, Sandoz Pharmaceuticals, Division of Sandoz, Inc.

Library of Congress Cataloging in Publication Data

Miller, Roger LeRoy.
    Economic issues for consumers.

    Includes bibliographies and indexes.
      1. Finance, Personal. 2. Consumer education.
I. Title.
HG179.M48 1978   332'.024   77–16218
ISBN 0–8299–0151–5

Contents in Brief

Contents

CHAPTER 14: GETTING THERE BY CAR IS HALF THE WORRY

315

CONSUMER ISSUE L: BUYING TRANSPORTATION

328

CHAPTER 15:   THE HEALTH CARE DILEMMA

Preface

Inflation continues. Consumer products become more complex. None can deny the validity of these two statements. Nor, do I believe, that any of us are willing to deny that inflation coupled with our complex goods-oriented society means that knowledge of consumer economics is more imperative now than ever before. The quest to become a rational consumer continues into the 1980s.

THE FORMAT OF THE BOOK—CHAPTERS AND ISSUES

You will notice a somewhat unusual format throughout the following pages. I have attempted to present the major areas of consumer economics in chapter form. At the end of many of these chapters, a consumer issue has been presented. For example, after an explanation of what inflation is and how it affects the consumer, an issue follows that outlines how the individual can best protect himself or herself against the ravages of inflation. As another example, after the chapter on food, a consumer issue outlines the steps that the individual can take to become a better food-shopper. To a large extent, the consumer issues offer more practical advice than do the chapters.

PEDAGOGICAL AIDS

Students will find a number of pedagogical aids in both the chapters and the consumer issues. Each chapter starts off with a chapter preview that indicates to the reader what will be covered. Then, to "ease the blow" of the new terminology, a Glossary of Terms that might not be known to the reader is presented before the actual text begins. At the end of each chapter, there is a point-by-point Summary that can be used for review. Then, Questions for Thought and Discussion that follow the Summary may be used as the basis for class discussion or as the basis for individual thought or even discussion in groups of students without the aid of an instructor. Things to Do gives some projects that a class can do as a group or that individuals can do at the request of the professor or on their own. Lastly, Selected Readings are presented. This list is not merely a rundown of academic articles that students can never hope to understand. Rather, it presents some alternative sources of reading for those students who wish further explanations of certain sections of the chapter.

The consumer issues have basically the same pedagogical devices, except that there is no preview and the issue Summary gives more practical hints on certain consumer decision-making problems.

ILLUSTRATIVE MATERIALS

You will notice a wide use of illustrative materials—photographs, charts, and cartoons. In my experience, visualization of certain ideas not only aids the student in understanding the material but also makes the task of reading the text more enjoyable.

THE ORDER OF CHAPTERS AND ISSUES

In no way is it necessary to follow exactly the order in which I have presented the chapters and issues in this book. Some instructors may even eliminate specific chapters that they feel they do not have time to cover. Also, issues can be eliminated, particularly where extensive audio-visual materials are used to illustrate practical applications of the principles within the chapters.

KEY CHANGES IN THE SECOND EDITION

Because of the many excellent comments, criticisms, and reviews that I have received on the First Edition, I have altered somewhat the materials in this new Second Edition.

NEW CHAPTERS AND ISSUES

Chapter 13—The Appliance Society
Chapter 19—Leisure, Recreation, and Travel
Chapter 20—Retirement and the Golden Years
Issue J—Renting a Place to Live
Issue K—Buying and Servicing Your Consumer Durables
Issue Q—Before You Spend Your Vacation Dollar
Issue R—When the Alternative Is a Nursing Home

Other Chapters and Issues That Were Reworked   Many chapters were reorganized to be more consistent with the flow of the concepts, e.g., the chapters on housing and life insurance were extensively reorganized.

An expanded treatment of home insurance has been added.

The chapter sequence in the book has been altered to reflect more accurately the way in which the course is taught.

The chapter and issue on inflation have been moved to the front of the book in order to emphasize the problems of inflation facing today's consumer.

There has been an extensive addition and updating of tables and exhibits.

References have been updated and added where necessary.

SUPPLEMENTARY MATERIALS

A practical and easily understandable *Student Workbook* has again been provided by Dr. Phillis Basile. Students using it will find the text material more interesting and understandable. Moreover, they will be better able to apply the principles of rational decision making to practical problems.

The *Instructor's Manual* has also been expanded and proved by Dr. Basile. She has added and changed test items where necessary. Those test items have the answers included.

ACKNOWLEDGEMENTS

Major reviewers who offered detailed criticism for the First Edition were as follows:

Professor Howard Alsey
Department of Home Economics
Arkansas State University

Professor Jean S. Bowers
Department of Home Economics
Ohio State University

Professor Judy Ferris
College of Home Economics
South Dakota State University

Professor Barbara Follosco
Department of Home Economics
Los Angeles Valley College

Professor Ron Hartje
School of Business
SOUK Valley College

Professor James O. Hill
Department of Economics
Vincennes University

Professor Eugene Silberberg
Department of Economics
University of Washington

Professor Nancy Z. Spillman
Department of Economics
Los Angeles Trade-Technical College

Professor Faye Taylor
Department of Home Economics
University of Utah

Professor Margil Vanderhoff
Department of Home Economics
Indiana University

Professor Joseph Wurmli
School of Business
Hillsborough Community College

A large number of extremely conscientious instructors helped me with the Second Edition revision. They are, in alphabetical order, as follows:

Professor Phillis B. Basile
Department of Economics
Orange Coast College
California

Professor Joseph E. Barr
Department of Economics—Chairman
Farmingham State College
Massachusetts

Professor Harold R. Boadway
Department of Economics
Moraine Valley Community College
Illinois

Professor Margaret Jane Brennan
College of Home Economics
Western Michigan University

Professor Judy Ferris
Department of Home Economics
South Dakota State University

Professor Linda Graham
Department of Economics
Wichita State University
Kansas

Professor Hilda Jo Jennings
Department of Home Economics—Chairman
Northern Arizona University

Professor Ann Lawson
Department of Marketing/Economics
Thomas Nelson Community College
Virginia

Professor Geraldine Olson
Department of Home Economics
Oregon State University

Professor James Poley
Department of Business
City College of San Francisco
California

Professor Rose Reha
Department of Business Education
St. Cloud State University
Minnesota

Professor Shirley Schecter
Department of Home Economics
Queens College
New York

Professor Jolene Scriven
Department of Business Education
Northern Illinois University

Professor Frank A. Viggiano Jr.
Department of Economics
Indiana University of Pennsylvania

Professor Joseph Wurmli
School of Business
Hillsborough Community College
Florida

I am deeply indebted to the countless hours that the above individuals spent reviewing my proposed changes. Without their help, I could not have completed this project in its current form. Their input, I believe, will be obvious when comparing this edition with the First.

Susan Vita Miller provided all photographs.

I have found through the years that the best way I can improve on what I write is by soliciting the comments of those who use my texts. I therefore stand ready to answer any and all comments, criticisms, or questions relating to what follows in this book. It is with the help of those who want the best for their students that I can find out what is best for the ultimate reader of *Economic Issues for Consumers*.

ROGER LeROY MILLER
Coral Gables, 1978

GLOSSARY OF TERMS

Consumers

Individuals who purchase, use, maintain, and dispose of products and services.

Standard of Living

Usually defined as the amount of goods and services that a person or a family is capable of purchasing and consuming (and saving) in one year. The per capita standard of living in the United States equals the total amount of income divided by the number of people in the country, then corrected for any changes in prices over the years.

Capitalist

An individual who owns all or part of an income-producing asset.

The Age of the Consumer

CHAPTER PREVIEW

☐ What are the characteristics of our consumer-oriented society?
☐ Were we really better off in the "good old days"?
☐ What rights do consumers have today?
☐ Is there a need for consumer education?

1 You consume. I consume. Your friends consume. We all consume in one way or another. As **consumers**, we number at least 216 million in the United States alone. And the dollar value of what we consume is staggering—in 1978 an estimated $1,250 billion. That comes out to over $5,750 for every household in the United States.

What do we buy as consumers? A grab bag of goods as varied as 18-carat gold toothpicks, toothpaste, five-bedroom houses, movie cameras, TVs, hamburgers, hot dogs, and terrariums. Table 1-1 lists some of the broad categories of goods and services on which we spend billions of dollars.

A MORE COMPLEX LIFE

Certainly, today's consumer products, and hence today's living experience, seem incredibly more complex than those of our ancestors. At the beginning of the United States, although life was hard, it certainly did not appear to be as complicated as it does today. For almost everyone, it was either do or die—eke out a bare existence tilling the ground or forget about staying around. Back then, over 90 percent of the population was engaged in agriculture. One of the most complicated things about living then was coping with the vagaries and vicissitudes of the weather. Of course, all of the day-to-day problems involved in human relationships existed then as they do now and as they will in the future. But as both consumers and producers, Americans had much less choice and, hence, faced less complicated decision making. Times have changed. Today, less than 5 percent of the population is engaged in agricultural production, and the **standard of living** is many times higher than it was at the beginning of this country. The number and variety of products available to us seems to approach infinity. And the number of different types of economic pursuits we can engage in seems overwhelming.

THE NOT SO GOOD OLD DAYS

Many people contend that America should go back to the good old days, when we were happier and less alienated from our environment. Many believe that during its beginnings this nation was composed of happy farmers who owned their own land and shared equally in the economic pie, but that somehow things have changed. Today there is, according to many, an extreme maldistribution of income

---

Table 1-1
Personal Consumption Expenditures by Major Type, 1977

This table shows an actual tabulation of the billions of dollars that are spent by American consumers on various categories of goods and services. (The last category, "All others," includes everything that was not listed specifically.) You can check the latest issue of the *Survey of Current Business* to find out how much personal consumption expenditures have grown since 1977.

Source: *Survey of Current Business.* October 1977.

TOTAL	**$1,159.1**
SUBCATEGORIES:	
Automobiles and parts	83.6
Furniture and household equipment	66.6
Food and beverages	236.4
Clothing and shoes	78.9
Gasoline and oil	44.2
Housing services	187.4
Household operation services	80.2
Transportation	42.8
All others	339.0

and wealth compared to those good old days. To be sure, the obvious inequality in income today is undeniable. But does the past in fact resemble our description? Only when we have answered this question can we determine whether we are now better or worse off.

Go back, for example, to the year 1800 or to any year before the Civil War. There was certainly much more inequality in income then, partly because many people in the South were slaves. Their income was in fact very, very small. If you go back as far as colonial days, you find that over half of the working members of the population were either slaves or indentured servants (persons whose labor was contracted for a length of time to pay the cost of their immigration to this country). When you look at the wealth statistics—that is, information on how much of the property was owned by what percent of the population—you get a striking picture. In 1860, the top 1 percent of families held 24 percent of the total wealth in the U.S., the top 5 percent held 53 percent, and the top 10 percent held almost 75 percent. That picture seems to have very little room for many self-employed farmers all getting their little share of the action. Today we actually see much less wealth distribution inequality.

INCOME UNCERTAINTY

Something else not so good in the good old days was the extreme variability in the income of farmers. After all, farmers were at the mercy of pestilence, drought, bumper crops (with their resultant low prices), competition in the world market from farmers of other countries, floods, hailstorms, frosts, and every other conceivable natural calamity that could greatly affect income from year to year. Today, a smaller portion of our population is subject to such variability in income because only 4 percent of the population is engaged in farming.

AND LIFE ITSELF

Not only has income become more certain for the vast majority of Americans, but today life itself has become a more certain prospect; that is, people are more likely to live longer than their ancestors. Back in the so-called good old days at the turn of the century, expected lifetime was about 47 years. By the beginning of the 1970s, it had risen to about 71 years. Certainly not all Americans benefit equally from improved health conditions, but even those who benefit least still lead healthier lives than most of their ancestors did.

OUR COMPLEX SOCIETY

Although longevity and income have become more certain, the living process appears, as we stated above, to have become more complex. Technology changes every day and, according to some, at such a rapid pace that it has made day-to-day living more difficult. If you do not know from one minute to the next what technological advance is going to alter your optimal choices as a consumer, then you are obviously in a fix. One thing to remember, however, is that in the United States technology responds not to the absolute dictates of some higher power, but rather to the profit incentives that rest on the desires of consumers taken as a whole. Technology will develop products that it hopes consumers will buy; but if no consumer wants to buy them, then there is no profit in continuing production (unless the government decides to subsidize such technology).

Individually, we may be confused by the mass of products that modern technology puts before us. But on the whole we are getting what we want, because in fact we are buying these new products voluntarily.

If you were able to choose products only out of either a 1908 Sears and Roebuck catalog or a current one, most of you would probably pick a current one because the choices would be so much greater and so much closer to your tastes and preferences. Today you cannot buy many of the things listed in the 1908 catalog—buggies, horseshoes, tapeworm remedies, and so on. However, there are even more things that you can buy today that you could not buy in 1908. Technology is obviously both a curse and a blessing.

It is not, however, an uncontrolled monster. As a matter of fact, technology has often simplified rather than complicated our lives.

For example, the newest jet airplanes are extremely complex compared to airplanes of, say, 20 years ago. However, have you ever seen what a pilot must do to control a 747? Today, pilots do little more than make certain that the computer that runs the plane is working right. The machinery they are operating is extremely complex, and of course their responsibilities for lives and expensive machinery are great but their work tasks are not that complicated once they have mastered them. In other words, technology can provide us with very complex and sophisticated products that are not difficult to use. Is our life more complicated or less complicated because we have these products? Only you, of course, can ultimately decide.

One thing you can be sure of: the more complicated consumer products become, the more incentive there will be for information agencies to tell you what the best buys are. It is predictable that we should see more organizations like Consumers Union selling information about consumer products as (or if) the products get more complicated.

WE ARE NOT JUST CONSUMERS

We do not usually get something for nothing. Hence, most of us are more than consumers. At one time or another we have to work; we have to act as employees, or producers. In fact, there are about 95 million of us in the measured labor force, earning incomes as professors, stewards/stewardesses, truck drivers, typists, engineers, artists, construction workers, businesspersons, fashion consultants, or any of the other ways for making a living. Additionally, many, such as homemakers, work to provide services for family members but are not given monetary payment. Those of us who are paid to work for a living receive wages, or salaries, that account for about 75 percent of all of the income generated in any one year in the American economy. The other 25 percent of that income goes to those of us who are owners of things like land, stocks, bonds, oil wells, and apartment buildings.

Most of us are, therefore, consumers, employees, and/or **capitalists**, for we consume in order to survive and be happy; we work in order to receive the income necessary to buy what we want; and often we obtain income from our savings, whether in the form of stocks or houses. In fact, more than 35 million Americans have directly purchased shares in American corporations; another 80 million indirectly own shares through their pension plans.

The picture of Americans painted above is not yet complete. We are also citizens. We vote on public issues and we consume goods and services that are provided by federal, state, and local governments.

A GROWING NATION

We are a growing nation: while the population is rising at a slower rate than in the past, it is still in fact rising, as can be seen in Figure 1-1. And we have a dynamic economy. Our standard of living has risen almost continually. Figure 1-2 shows the rising per capita standard of living in the United States over the last several decades.

THE PROBLEMS FACING TODAY'S CONSUMER

Our consumer society is a problem-solving society because consumers are constantly faced with problems that they must solve one way or another. It is not enough to think in terms of getting the best deal with one's income. There are a multitude of factors that enter into every buying and saving decision. In this book, we will look at a wide variety of areas where consumer decision making is critical. These include purchases of major items such as food, clothing, housing and equipment, transportation, and medical care. We will look at insurance, saving and investing, as well as retirement and the leisure society. The responsibilities of the business community and the government to you the consumer will be stressed throughout. And we will look at the responsibilities that you have as a consumer.

**Figure 1-1
Population in the
United States**

We see that from 1920
on, population has
been growing quite
steadily, and it is
projected to reach
about 225 million
Americans by 1985.
(Before 1940, the data
does not include
Alaska and Hawaii.)

Source: Bureau of the
Census, *Current Population
Reports.*

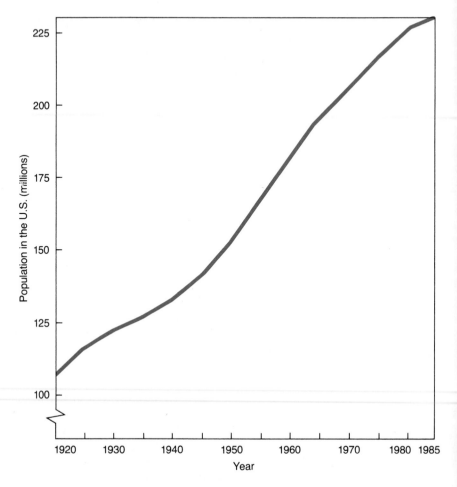

CONSUMER RIGHTS

As we will see in the following chapter, consumers have recently obtained rights never before enjoyed. In our complex consumer-oriented society, we have witnessed a consumerist movement that has involved governments at all levels. It has even been stressed by recent Presidents. In 1962, President John F. Kennedy sent the first consumer protection and interest program to Congress. In that message, he stated four consumer rights:

1. The right to safety—a protection against goods that are dangerous to life or health.
2. The right to be informed—not only to discover fraud, but also to make rational choices.
3. The right to choose—a restatement of the need for many firms in a competitive market and for protection by government where such competition no longer exists.
4. The right to be heard—the right of consumers to have their interests heard when governmental policy decisions are being made.

To these four rights most consumer representatives would add a fifth:

5. The right to redress for reasonable damages incurred when dealing in the marketplace.

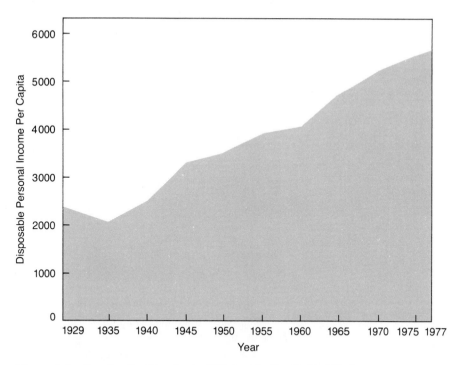

Figure 1-2   Per Capita Standard of Living in the United States

In the United States the amount of income available for spending per person, after taxes, has been growing quite steadily from just before the Great Depression in 1929 until today. Of course, there was a severe downturn during the Depression, but that can be considered an unusual occurrence in this nation's history. Note that the dollars here are expressed in terms of 1972 purchasing power. If they were expressed in terms of 1978 purchasing power, the figures would be quite a bit higher. The data before 1960 exclude Alaska and Hawaii.

Source: U.S. Bureau of Economic Analysis, *National Income and Product Accounts of the United States, 1929-65*, and the *Survey of Current Business*, various issues.

CONSUMER
PRINCIPLES

Throughout the text a number of principles will be repeated over and over. They are important enough to be presented here without further explanation.

1. Your time is scarce and valuable.
2. Information about products and services is valuable and important, but costly to obtain.
3. Every choice that you make necessarily means that you give up something, whether it be in the use of your time or the use of your income.

THE NEED FOR CONSUMER EDUCATION

Reading this text involves an investment in learning to be a rational consumer. Will the investment pay off? It would be presumptuous for the author to categorically tell you yes. Nonetheless, it is rational consumers who can best manage their economic affairs in a complex consumer society. In the case of consumer economics, a little knowledge is not a dangerous thing for it goes a long way.

The level of consumer "literacy" in the United States must improve if we are to benefit fully from a growing standard of living. A few years ago, a study done by the National Assessment of Educational Progress under the auspices of the Education Commission of the United States found some shocking statistics on the American population. Some of these statistics follow:

1. Eight out of ten Americans between the ages of 25 and 36 cannot balance a checkbook; only 1 percent of the 17-year-olds tested could balance a checkbook.
2. Fifty percent of those between the ages of 25 and 36 are unable to fill out a simple income tax form without making a mistake.
3. Given the dimensions of a carpet in feet and its price per square yard, only two out of five young adults can compute the carpet's cost.
4. Only half the adults and the 17-year-olds tested could correctly pick out the most economical box of a particular product based on unit price.
5. Only 10 percent of the 17-year-olds and 20 percent of the adults could calculate a taxi fare correctly.

What does all this mean? It means that many consumers are wasting hundreds of dollars a year. It also means that the more one learns about consumer economics and how to apply it to day-to-day living, the fewer mistakes one will make out in the real world marketplace where dollars are exchanged for goods and services.

The age of the consumer is indeed upon us. Hopefully, the age of the informed consumer is not too far away.

SUMMARY

1. We are all consumers who purchase a variety of goods and services.
2. Life today differs from life in the good old days in many ways: (a) we are no longer an agricultural society, (b) our standard of living is many times higher than it was when this country first began, (c) most of us face much more cer-

tainty in our income flow than in the past, (d) both wealth and income are more equally distributed today, and (e) our life expectancy is much greater.
3. We are not just consumers; we are also employees, producers, capitalists, and citizens who vote and enjoy publicly offered goods and services.
4. Consumers have rights today relating to safety, information, choice, and the ability to be heard by policymakers.
5. Studies show that there is a need for increased consumer education.

QUESTIONS FOR THOUGHT AND DISCUSSION

1. Can you think of any individuals in our society who are not consumers?
2. Why is there so much nostalgia about the good old days?
3. Does the fact that we have increased unemployment today compared to a few years ago mean that we face the same kind of income uncertainty as our ancestors who worked on farms?
4. Is there a limit to how complex consumer products can become?
5. Do you think that the average standard of living will continue to rise throughout your lifetime in this country?

THINGS TO DO

1. See if you can add to the list of consumer rights given in this chapter.
2. Find out if the average per capita standard of living has continued to rise in the United States (Hint: Look up the current issue of the *Survey of Current Business*, which gives income corrected for price changes).
3. Keep a running tabulation on general consumer principles that will be presented throughout this book.

SELECTED READINGS

Clark, Lincoln H., ed. *Consumer Behavior—The Dynamics of Consumer Reactions.* New York: New York University Press, 1958.

"Consumer in the Marketplace." *Consumers' Research Magazine*, October 1976, pp. 3-8.

"Consumer Information; Federal Agencies and Information Centers." *Consumer Reports*, December 1976, pp. 342-347.

Forum: Can Consumers Face the Challenge of a Changing World? New York: J. C. Penney Co., Spring/Summer 1977.

Markin, R. J., Jr. *Consumer Behavior: A Cognitive Orientation.* New York: Macmillan Publishing Co., 1974.

Miller, Roger LeRoy. *American Economic Life: Yesterday and Today.* San Francisco: Canfield Press, 1974.

Mohr, Lillian H. *A Proposal for 1977: A National Foundation for Consumer Education.* Washington, D.C.: U.S. Government Printing Office, 1977.

Weiss, Roger. *The Economic System.* New York: Random House, 1969.

*

GLOSSARY OF TERMS

Antitrust Policies

Government policies to prevent business monopoly. Antitrust policies are aimed at establishing and maintaining competition in business to assure the consumer fair prices and goods of adequate quality.

Common Law

The unwritten system of law governing the rights and duties of persons from decisions based on custom and fixed principles of justice. Common law is the foundation of both the English and U.S. legal systems (excluding Louisiana).

Monopoly

A form of market structure in which one or only a few firms dominate the total sales of a good or service.

Legal Clinic

A group practice concept applied to a law office.

The Consumer Gets a Voice[1]

CHAPTER PREVIEW

☐ Is the consumer movement a new one?

☐ What are antitrust policies all about, and how do they affect the consumer?

☐ How do state and local consumer protection agencies compare with federal ones?

☐ Can the private sector do anything to protect the consumer?

☐ What is the essence of consumer activist groups?

☐ What are the new innovations in providing legal assistance to consumers?

[1] I am deeply indebted to Professor Phillis Basile for her help on this chapter and the following issue. She is responsible for much of what follows.

11

2 Like the police officer who tries to break up a family fight and suddenly finds himself the target of both the husband and the wife, the concept of consumer protection is constantly in the middle of an argument. On one side of the argument are those who believe that the only consumer protection needed arises out of competition in the marketplace, and that consumer protection insults consumers by implying that they are helpless. On the other side are those who believe that consumerism, or consumer activism, is needed to counteract the lack of competition in the marketplace. Although most people have become aware of consumer protection only in the last ten years, it has a long history.

A HISTORY OF CONSUMER PROTECTION

The earliest forms of consumer protection were really attempts to make market protections effective. Because there are many buyers and sellers in a competitive market, no one buyer or seller can individually influence the price of a particular good. We assume that buyers and sellers know what they are doing and the product for which they are bargaining. But even if they know what they are bargaining for, it may be difficult to determine exactly how much they are bargaining for and how much they are getting. And so from earliest recorded times, we have found ourselves involved in the setting of standards of weights and measures.

POLICING STANDARDS

As you might expect, once the standards of weights and measures were established, the next problem was to make sure they were being met. So the second development in consumer protection was policing the standards of weights and measures. Once fraud in the marketplace had been made illegal, the market had to be policed and the police work had to be evaluated. Thus, the courts and administrative bodies came into the consumer protection system. The principle that was and is being supported here is the principle of competition. If enough consumers have enough information, they can protect themselves in the marketplace.

BUSINESS WANTED THEM, TOO

But, of course, even this system was not purely a consumer protective system. Consumers did not work the hardest for standards of weights and measures, police work, and courts. Rather, producers found themselves engaged in competition that they deemed detrimental to their own interests. Remember, *everyone* is a consumer. We tend to think of consumers in supermarkets, department stores, car showrooms, and so on; that is, we think of the consumer role only at the retail level. But businesses are also consumers when they buy goods and services to be used in further production. Businesses, then, have two reasons for being interested in the enforcement of standards:

1. To protect themselves when they go into the market to buy, and
2. To protect themselves against fraudulent competitors who may be more successful in selling to the individual consumer than the traditional business.

ANTIMONOPOLY POLICIES

At the same time that standards were being set and enforced, another concept was becoming prominent—the concept of antimonopoly, or **antitrust policies** on the part of the government. The rights of buyers and other competitors had long been protected in **common law** because the courts refused to enforce monopolistic contracts. But before the Sherman Antitrust Act was passed in 1890, there had been no stated public policy that **monopoly** and price fixing were unacceptable in the American economy. Although this legislation was designed to protect the interests of all competing producers in the market, it had consumer implications as well because in order for competition to exist there must be many buyers and sellers in the markets so that no one alone can influence price.

At the turn of the century, consumer protection as we mean it today did not really exist. The set of rules to provide the seller protection as a competitor in the marketplace had only an incidental effect on consumers because the information and antimonopoly requirements might make it easier for consumers to operate in the market. In the years between 1900 and World War I, however, there was a distinct change not only in the consumer area, but throughout the social and economic concerns of the period. This was the period of the "muckrakers"; the period of the first wage and hour laws; the period of the first women's and minors' protective legislation; and the period in which the first federal law designed specifically to protect consumers was passed. This was the Food and Drug Act of 1906 dealing with the production, transportation, and sale of foods, drugs, and medicines.

FOOD AND DRUG ACT

Although 30 years earlier Congress had rewritten the postal laws to make fraud through the mails illegal, the emphasis was still on the transaction at the retail level of the marketplace. The Food and Drug Act of 1906 began to look behind the practices in the retail market and into how food actually was being produced and sold. Upton Sinclair's book *The Jungle* awoke the general public to the fact that consumer protection meant more than information at the point of sale. In that book, Sinclair graphically presented the buying public with the squalor that existed in the meat packing business. Groups began seeking some form of "consumer protection" in products that were processed before they arrived at the marketplace.

But the Food and Drug Act of 1906 was not the beginning of a strong, continuous surge in consumer interest or in consumer protection. Not until 1914 was the Federal Trade Commission Act passed to provide administrative machinery to enforce antitrust laws and to spell out unfair methods of competition, including deceptive advertising. And it was fully 32 years later that the 1938 Food, Drug and Cosmetic Act was passed to enlarge the protective features of the 1906 legislation.

The passage of the 1938 legislation was the last significant federal activity on the consumer protection issue until 1958, 20 years later. But unlike the earlier period, the federal interest in consumer issues in 1958 was a beginning, not an end. And in the following years a flood of legislative activity resulted not only at the federal but also at the state and local levels. In the 10 years between 1965 and 1975, more than twice as many laws were passed in the consumer area than had been passed in the previous 90 years.

WHY THE RENEWED
INTEREST IN THE
CONSUMER?

What happened to make the interest in consumer protection, which had flared and died in earlier periods, become a strong continuing flame of concern?

Some people have pointed to Ralph Nader, whose 1965 book *Unsafe at Any Speed* brought to public attention the issue of automobile safety. But Upton Sinclair's *The Jungle*, which preceded the passage of the Food and Drug Act of 1906, and Stewart Chase's *Your Money's Worth*, which preceded the sporadic consumerist activity in the 1930s, had not led to continuing consumer protection activity. Something else was operating in the system, and that something else, according to some, was the complexity of modern economic life. By the early 1960s, the explosion in technology, in production, in transportation, and in information systems had been fully felt by the American consumer. The developments in plastics, frozen foods, and dried foods had made preprocessing and prepackaging an everyday fact of American life. The American automobile had become a complex, accessory-loaded machine that could no longer be easily understood by the buyer. Consumers found themselves at the center of an increasing mass of information—so much information, in fact, that now they not only had to look for the information, but had to discriminate among all of the kinds of information available. In addition to all this was the impersonality of the modern American marketplace. The small community has been replaced by the large city; most of our goods are moved by mass marketing techniques, are prepackaged, and even machine-delivered; and markets have extended to a national and even an international scope. All of this has left us, the individual consumers, in a complex world feeling helpless as we attempt to determine what to buy, how to use it, and to whom to complain if the product fails us.

Moreover, in making buying decisions, consumers spend much time seeking and evaluating information. In a relatively simple system, consumers may know enough about the products they are buying and enough about the people from whom they purchase them to feel that they need to spend little time to make a good decision. But in the complex technology of today, seeking information may become a very time-consuming job. To know enough to make completely satisfactory consumer decisions in every field takes a lifetime. This, by the way, is not a new thought: Wesley Mitchell, a prominent economist of the turn of the century, in a 1912 article, "The Backward Art of Spending Money," pointed out the difference between a business firm, which hires experts to carry out its many functions, and the family unit, which makes all of the same and even more complex decisions through a single buyer or two. Mitchell concluded that if the family had developed as well as the production unit, by now we would have homemakers who specialize in each of the different aspects of family buying. In effect, consumers in the 1960s began to ask government to perform some of these specialist functions by establishing standards of packaging and disclosure that would enable them readily to compare claims from many sellers. There was also a strong movement to provide government standards of safety so that consumers could eliminate such concerns from their information-gathering task.

**PROTECTION
AFTER THE FACT**

The legal system that had developed over the years was not geared to handle the problems of millions of individuals with small sums of money at stake, each sum important to the individual but no one large enough to pay for the costs of litigation.

The mounting sense of helpless frustration led consumers to look for a new form of consumer protection: protection *after* the fact. The new emphasis in consumer protection became consumer redress: the right of every consumer legitimately to air grievances and to seek satisfaction for damages incurred through a system that would not penalize us because the individual sum involved was small. This was not the same as the earlier consumer protection against fraud. We consumers now asked for redress, not because we had been deliberately defrauded, but because the complexity of the marketplace had made it impossible, in our eyes, for us to protect ourselves adequately before the fact of purchase.

THE PRESIDENTS SPEAK UP

We pointed out in Chapter 1 that President Kennedy sent a consumer protection program to Congress in 1962. Presidents Johnson and Nixon reaffirmed the consumer rights stated by President Kennedy, and the strong tide of consumer legislation at the federal level continued. In 1977, President Carter asked for more legislation.

Legislation, of course, is not the end of the story. Legislation must be administered and the administration must be efficient if the concept of consumer protection is to be effective. In 1964, President Lyndon B. Johnson made a gesture in this direction when he appointed the first Special Presidential Assistant for Consumer Affairs. Although this person, a member of the staff of the Office of the President, had no direct authority, the fact that such a position existed made certain that consumer interests would have some representation at the federal policy level. The office was continued by President Nixon until 1973, when it was transferred to the Department of Health, Education, and Welfare. The transfer of the office from the direct contact of the President appeared to some consumer activists to be a sign of weakening federal support.

STATE AND LOCAL GOVERNMENT AND PRIVATE CONSUMER PROTECTION

We have spent a good deal of time detailing the history and developments in federal consumer protection in the United States. While federal action is important because once adopted it expresses the policy of national importance in the field, the policy is often the result of prolonged activity at the state and local government level or in the private sector of the economy. This has been especially true of consumer protection policy. In fact, some states, localities, and private groups have gone far beyond the limits now set by federal policy.

State and local governments have always been involved in setting standards, weights and measures, and marketing standards, as well as standards that define the term *fraud*. Even today, enforcement of consumer fraud statutes is left largely to state and local governments. Many of the areas of fraud are commonly dealt with under criminal fraud statutes arising out of the criminal fraud case decisions of earlier years. And these are primarily state and local law. Furthermore, in the areas of credit, insurance, health and sanitation, and all issues dealing with contract rights, primarily state governments have enacted legislation dealing with consumer problems. In fact, state response has sometimes been much earlier than federal response. For example, as early as 1959, both New York and California had legislation on the books to protect the rights of consumers in credit transactions. And not until Massachusetts passed the first truth-in-lending law was federal action on this important issue likely to succeed. The federal Consumer Credit Protection Act (truth in lending) was passed in 1968. Massachusetts, in effect, became a pilot case for the national legislation.

THE PRIVATE SECTOR

How does the private sector of the economy fit in with the public activities for consumer protection? As you might expect, activity in the private sector has been varied and, in many cases, short-lived and uncertain in its effect. But in some specific areas, private activities have been most important. The first of these is product testing. Although the federal government has only very recently begun to test products and reveal the results of those tests in a way that makes it possible for consumers to use the information in making their own purchases, private product testing groups have been around for a long, long time. Consumers Union and Consumers' Research, Inc., exist primarily for the purpose of providing consumers with information on products they may buy.[2]

There are other product testing groups whose interest is not directed toward consumers but whose activities produce information that consumers can use. The American Standards Association is an example of this kind of private agency. The ASA, organized in 1918, exists primarily to develop standards and testing methods that may be used by manufacturers. By setting a common level of performance, these standards and testing methods can protect manufacturers against unfair competition. But, of course, they also provide protection to consumers who are buying products, the safety of which may be important. Using the standards developed by the ASA, other private laboratories or testing groups certify the efficiency and/or safety of such items as electrical appliances, gas appliances, textiles, and many other products. In addition to the product testing that takes place at the manufacturing level, a wide range of product testing is done by retailers who wish

[2]We discuss them on pages 60–61.

to perform a consumer service and to provide themselves with a competitive advantage.

One must be wary, however, of the "seals of approval" that appear on numerous products. Here we can discuss two of the most well known seals: the Underwriter's Laboratory, or UL label, and the Good Housekeeping "Seal of Approval."

Underwriter's Laboratory. Most household appliances display the UL label, and many manufacturers boast of it in their advertising. The UL label, however, only certifies that the product or appliance does not have the potential of causing fire, electric shock, or accident. Underwriter's Laboratory does not undertake any evaluation of the actual quality of the appliance you are purchasing. The UL label does not mean that the product has been compared to its competitors and proven better. Moreover, the only way the UL label can be obtained is by the manufacturer either submitting the product and paying a fee or agreeing to a specified control procedure. In order to keep the UL label, a fee must be paid every year. Some companies decide not to pay that fee and may, therefore, have perfectly sound products without the familiar UL label.

Recently, the Underwriter's Laboratory has been branching out into the testing of marine equipment (e.g., life preservers); medical equipment (e.g., adjustable hospital beds); and others. UL has also entered the area of general safety hazards. For example, it might test a particular electric coffee pot to see if the lid falls off when it is tipped, although this has nothing to do with the electrical part of the product. Recently, UL has required manufacturers to include safety tips in the use and care manuals for products it approves.

Good Housekeeping Seal. It has been over 35 years since the Federal Trade Commission required Good Housekeeping to eliminate the term "seal of approval." Nonetheless, for many consumers, the seal does denote approval. Good House-

"It's my observation that more and more consumers are looking after their own interests these days."

DRAWING BY BOOTH; © 1972 THE NEW YORKER MAGAZINE, INC.

keeping does not test whether a product is good or bad; presumably, it only sees whether the product or service submitted by a manufacturer, who plans to advertise in *Good Housekeeping* magazine, will live up to all the claims made for it in the advertisement.

In principle, if the Good Housekeeping seal is on a product, you can receive a refund or replacement if the product or performance is defective. Take note that no product is tested by the Good Housekeeping Institute Laboratories in New York City unless there is a possibility of it being advertised in the magazine. Before a manufacturer can use this Good Housekeeping seal, it must guarantee to the magazine that the volume of advertising placed in *Good Housekeeping* is the same as that which it places in other media (or, at least two columns a year).

RECOVERY OF DAMAGES

Recovery of damages for the individual consumer is a major issue in the consumer protection movement today. States have generally provided this kind of service only in special types of sales that have presented special problems. For example, in California the state has provided for registration, for disclosure standards, and for administrative procedures on consumer grievances about service and repair for radios and TVs, automobiles, and major appliances. In cities and counties all over the country, the concern with consumer damages has been expressed more broadly as agencies of the local government are acting as the mediators in disputes between consumers and sellers.

The makeup and the authority of these local agencies vary dramatically. In some areas, the authority is lodged in an "old line" agency, such as the Bureau of Weights and Measures, which already has operations in the consumer field. In other cases, the agency is made part of a department of social services. But in its most effective form, the local consumer agency is independent and owes responsibility to no one but consumers and the public at large.

PRIVATE AGENCIES

Local government agencies are new participants in the public area of consumer protection, an area that has traditionally belonged to the private sector. Probably the best known of such private agencies is the Better Business Bureau. The National Better Business Bureau has been in existence since 1916 and has local affiliates in all major cities and counties. The Better Business Bureau has a multiple purpose:

1. To provide information on products and selling practices to consumers.
2. To provide businesspeople with a source of localized standard setting as to acceptable business practices.
3. To provide a technique for mediating grievances between consumers and sellers.

Because the Better Business Bureau has no enforcement powers, all actions must be voluntary. And because the Better Business Bureau is dependent on the business community for its membership, it cannot afford to antagonize those in business more than it antagonizes consumers. The weaknesses in the voluntary system were felt most strongly when the consumerist movement began to press for protection, not only against the fly-by-night, illegal, fraudulent firm, but against marketing practices that were generally accepted by the business community. Once consumers began to seek redress for damages suffered from exaggerated advertising, ineffective warranties and guarantees, safety hazards, and poor choices made by consumers because of the structure of the market in which goods were sold, the private business organization was unable to police its members effectively. But the Better Business Bureau continues to survive and to thrive as it seeks to improve communication with the consumer. For example, the Better Business Bureau's arbitration program has been expanding. It is attempting to deal more formally with the issue of consumer redress for grievances with sellers and producers of goods and services.

Although the Better Business Bureau is the oldest of the private agencies that seek to mediate grievances, it is by no means the only one. As consumerism has grown, the media have been both criticized for their performance and mobilized for consumer protection. The media have been criticized for the type of advertising they have carried and for their lack of interest in providing time for countercommercials, or public service consumer information. But newspapers, radio stations, and TV stations have all been in the forefront of attempts to help consumers who have legitimate complaints; these media have provided column space or air time for "consumer action." These programs have been highly successful in obtaining results for those consumers who are able to make use of them. Affiliates of both the ABC and NBC networks have run regular consumer report and consumer action series, as have many of the independent television stations. These programs typically use publicity as the powerful weapon to resolve the consumer's grievance.

Thus, looking back, we can see that the concept of consumer protection started as a set of standards necessary to protect both buyers and sellers in a fair exchange; next, standards were set for health and safety, primarily to protect consumers; later, both consumers and businesses were protected against fraud; finally, the concern became the techniques of marketing and the problems of consumers in finding their way through the maze of technological detail in a highly industrialized society. No longer are consumers to be protected only up to the point of purchase; protection past the point of purchase is now a goal. This new area of consumer protection involves groups that seek, both publicly and privately, to provide mechanisms for settling consumer grievances without the need for going to court.

ACTIVE CONSUMER GROUPS

We noted at the beginning of the chapter that many people find the term "consumer protection" insufficient, if not downright insulting; they seek consumer policy participation. While Ralph Nader, through both his own activity and the activities of the organizations founded through his energies, has become the symbol of consumer activism in the 1960s and 1970s, consumer organization at the state and local level actually began long before Ralph Nader appeared on the scene. It is well to remember that the consumer cooperative movement began many years ago. And although it has never successfully defeated the corporation as a business form, it has succeeded in helping some consumers solve some of their problems.

During the 1930s, consumer groups sprang up over the country as many people found it necessary to stretch precious few dollars to cover basic living needs. The burst of consumerism, of course, occurred in the 1960s, and by the early 1970s organizations existed at state and local levels throughout the country. And in 1967, the Consumer Federation of America was formed to coordinate the efforts of such groups at the national level. Local consumer activist groups have been in the forefront in pressing for legislation on credit, packaging, no-fault insurance, and adequate labeling of food and drugs. They have been active as well in seeking protection of consumers in such fields of major abuse as automobile and appliance repair services.

While acting at their own levels to seek redress for consumers who felt that they have been damaged in private transactions, the state and local groups have also worked to provide education and representation to consumers in hearings before government legislative and administrative bodies. The ultimate goal of these groups is to have consumer participation in the policy decisions made by government. In addition, they seek for consumers the strength to participate indirectly in the policy decisions of business firms by their power in the marketplace by acting as a single group. Thus, at least some consumers seek to participate in the functioning of the marketplace in the same way that large corporations and major trade unions do.

The development of this kind of consumer activism is significant because it illustrates that consumers can also have points of view. In any public policy issue, there may be a business interest; there may be a labor interest; there may be a consumer interest. The price of food, for example, is a major issue that has involved all of these interests in recent years. The question is: What is the public interest? From this point of view, where is consumer protection heading? What issues must be resolved as we expand, or try to expand, the concept of consumer protection?

PROVIDING LEGAL ASSISTANCE

Many consumers feel that they would like to sue for improper services performed or defective products purchased. However, high legal fees have often kept many consumers from getting their "day in court." One alternative that we outline in detail in Consumer Issue B following this chapter is a small claims court. The other option is to go to a **legal clinic**.

LEGAL CLINICS

A legal clinic is a group practice concept. A group of lawyers share office space and facilities; they use paralegal personnel for routine work that does not involve actual law practice. They standardize their procedures and are able to reduce fees anywhere from 25 percent to 50 percent below what one would normally pay to a regular attorney working in a normal law firm. Legal clinics will even teach you to help yourself in traffic courts or small claims courts for a fee of $10 to $25. However, they will not take cases requiring extensive litigation. As of 1976, there were clinics in Los Angeles, Phoenix, Denver, and Washington, D.C.

PREPAID LEGAL SERVICE

It is now possible for some individuals, particularly in California and in New York, to subscribe to a prepaid legal plan just as they subscribe to prepaid health and automobile insurance. A subscriber to such a plan pays an annual flat fee that entitles him or her to an array of legal services. For example, Group Legal Services, Inc., in Los Angeles charges $25 a year. For that fee, subscribers have the privilege of dialing a toll-free number 24 hours a day for advice. If the problem cannot be easily resolved on the telephone, the subscriber is referred to one of 500 participating attorneys. There the subscriber gets a 25 percent discount from the prevailing local rate. A pilot plan was started in New York by New York County Legal Services Corporation. Initially it was restricted to people with annual incomes between $6,000 and $20,000. The membership cost was a flat fee of $100, plus $25 a year for a spouse and $10 for each child under 21.

There are many ways to obtain satisfaction when you the consumer feel you have been wronged in the marketplace. In Consumer Issue A we outline the steps you should take and the agencies you can go to for help.

SUMMARY

1. Among the first consumerist activities ever engaged in was the formation of standards of weights and measures. Following this was the policing of these standards.
2. Businesses were interested in enforcing such standards to protect themselves when they were buying materials or products and also to protect themselves against fraudulent competitors.
3. Among the first purely consumer-oriented activites were antitrust or anti-monopoly policies aimed at preventing or breaking up existing monopolies that fixed prices at higher than competitive levels to the detriment of the consumer.
4. Although the first food and drug act was passed in 1906, not until the 1938 Food, Drug, and Cosmetic Act did consumer protection become a strong aspect of federal government activity. The most recent development in the consumerist movement is consumer redress after a wrong has been committed.
5. In the 1960s and 1970s, starting with President Kennedy and extending through the present, the rights of consumers and the need for increased consumer protection have been popular executive topics.
6. Consumer protection continues to exist at the federal, state, and local levels of government, as well as being maintained by private agencies.
7. The best-known private agencies are Consumers Union and Consumers' Research, Inc., both meant chiefly to provide information to consumers. In addition, branches of the Better Business Bureau attempt to help consumers as well as businesspeople. There are also private testing agencies such as the American Standards Association and Underwriter's Laboratory.
8. State and local agencies have recently set up numerous devices to help consumers recover damages for fraudulent business activities. At the very minimum, local government mediators act in disputes between consumers and sellers and will often refer both parties to an appropriate agency if specific laws have in fact been violated.
9. Recently, activist consumer groups have engaged in consumer advocacy at all levels of government. The ultimate goal of consumer participation in the policy decisions of business firms, at least indirectly by their power in the marketplace, has been sought through the formation of certain segments of the marketplace into a single advocacy group.
10. Consumers can now purchase lower priced legal services from legal clinics or subscribe to prepaid legal service plans.

QUESTIONS FOR THOUGHT AND DISCUSSION

1. Why is the consumerist movement thought to be relatively new even though it started many years ago?
2. Exactly what are antimonopoly policies? Why do monopolies hurt the consumer? (Hint: Look up the Sherman Act.)
3. What is the difference between consumer protection before the fact and consumer protection after the fact?
4. If you had to set up a model consumer protection act, what would you include in it?
5. What do you think the current administration's stand on consumer protection is?
6. Do you think the consumerist movement is still as strong as it was a few years ago?
7. Should the government engage in product testing and present the results of those tests to consumers?
8. What private sources of consumer information do you use in making your decisions about what to buy?
9. Do you think that legal services should be provided to low-income individuals free of charge or at prices below cost?

THINGS TO DO

1. Engage in a research project in which you outline the history of consumer activism back to its origins in England. What groups have been around longest? What principles of consumerism have been with us longest?
2. If you happen to know a lawyer, talk to him or her about recent developments in laws affecting the consumer and the "sanctity" of contracts entered into by both consumer and seller.
3. Call your local Better Business Bureau and ask for its booklet describing the bureau, its activities, and all of the areas in which it is active. If there is no Better Business Bureau in your area, contact the local chamber of commerce.
4. Obtain a list of the books put out by Ralph Nader and his associates. Read one or two of them and then read Upton Sinclair's *The Jungle*. Do you see any similarities? Have things gotten better or worse in the United States?

SELECTED READINGS

Aaker, David A., and Day, George S. *Consumerism: Search for the Consumer Interest*. New York: The Free Press, 1974.

"Consumer Is Paying Plenty: A Critical Report on Government Regulation." *U.S. News & World Report*, November 4, 1974.

"Consumers Are Rewriting the Rule Book." *Fortune*, March 16, 1974, p. 41.

"Consumers Aren't Angels Either." *duPont Context* 2 (1973): 9-10.

"Consumers May Get a Break." *Nation*, May 4, 1974, pp. 550-551.

Faber, Doris. *Enough! The Revolt of the American Consumer*. New York: Farrar, Strauss & Giroux, 1972.

Gaedeke, Ralph M., and Etcheson, Warren W. *Consumerism: Viewpoints from Business, Government, and the Public Interest*. San Francisco: Canfield Press, 1972.

Levy, R.. "Metamorphosis in the Marketplace?" *Duns Review*, February 1977, pp. 65-67.

Magnuson, Warren. *The Dark Side of the Marketplace*, 2d. ed. Englewood Cliffs, N.J.: Prentice-Hall, 1972.

Mead, W. B. "Help from a Consumerist Congress." *Money*, April 1975.

Nader, Ralph, ed. *The Consumer and Corporate Accountability.* New York: Harcourt Brace Jovanovich, 1973.

"New Interventionists." *Time*, April 18, 1977, p. 64.

Peterson, E. "Consumerism as a Retailer's Asset: Program at Giant Foods." *Harvard Business Review*, May 1974, pp. 91-101.

Scrag, Philip G. "Consumer Rights." *Columbia Forum*, Summer 1970.

Scrag, Philip G. *Counsel for the Deceived.* New York: Pantheon, 1972.

"Things Are Getting Better Faster for Consumers." *Changing Times* 31 (February 1977): 17-18.

"U.S. Consumer Groups: Livelier than Ever." *U.S. News*, December 6, 1976, pp. 90-91.

How to Get Help for Consumer Problems

Knowing what kind of services are available is the first step in taking advantage of consumer service agencies. Generally, government agencies and private voluntary and business groups provide the following four consumer services:

1. Information to consumers before purchase is made. This service, designed to help you the consumer help yourself, includes standard setting, inspection, investigation of marketing techniques, product testing, labeling and other disclosure legislation, publication of results, and formal teaching.

2. Aid to consumers after purchase is made, generally through the enforcement of public policy to prevent unsatisfactory or fraudulent practices from being repeated. This service includes accepting complaints, investigating the complaints, possibly instituting legal proceedings followed by a judgment, and imposing either injunction against the action or penalty for breaking the law. This kind of action does not help individual consumers make up their own losses.

3. Redress to individual consumers for their individual losses as a result of purchases. Now we are involved with a complaint, an investigation, possibly publicity or mediation,

sometimes settlement, or legal action followed by a judgment and enforcement of the judgment.

4. Representation of consumers in issues with a consumer interest before a legislative body, government administrative agencies, and private business leadership. Here again we are generally concerned with the complaint, with investigation and research regarding the complaint and the problem that it reflects, and developing and publicizing plans for remedy; often these result in changes in legislation.

WHERE TO GO?

Knowing when, where, and how to go for consumer services may turn out to be just as big a job as learning how to buy in the first place. There are at least 37 federal agencies involved in consumer issues, and even more state, local, and private agencies with which you might have to deal. We will be primarily concerned with the problems that you face when something goes wrong, rather than how you get information before you buy a product. But even this limitation does not significantly reduce the number of agencies or organizations with which you will have to contend, for many of the agencies that provide in-

formation before you buy are the same ones that provide the protection after you buy. And, of course, when you are concerned with complaints about products, you are most likely going to be dealing with a business firm, and there are some 12 million business firms in the United States. Thus, if you are going to deal successfully in the market and with consumer service agencies, you will have to develop a strategy.

A STRATEGY

You should always first figure out a strategy for trying to get your grievances straightened out without going to an outside party. After all, it takes additional time and effort to get somebody else involved in your disputes with a seller. Thus, whenever you buy anything, *keep a receipt* if you are worried that there may be problems later. But before you make the purchase, be certain to *have everything put in writing* about any take-back provisions, warranties, or guarantees.

Say you buy something and it falls apart a week later. A call to the store, and preferably a talk with the person you bought it from, will tell you immediately whether you will have problems. Many times reputable stores will either give you an identical article that is in good working condition, repair the one you have, or refund your money. If the salesperson does not agree, then you look higher up: find the manager or the owner. If you still do not get satisfaction and you are dealing with a nationally advertised product or with a large chain store, you may want to find the address of the president or the chairman of the board and write him or her directly to complain.[1] In Exhibit A-1 on page 26, you can see a sample copy of a letter that might be appropriate. Personal letters to the presidents of large companies get quick responses surprisingly often. But sometimes they do not. If your effort fails, where to next?

To answer this question, you may also have to decide how much you want to put into it. Do you just want your money back, or your own satisfaction, or do you want to make sure that this never happens again? Some states have special catalogs put out that tell you what to do with your complaint. For example, California has the *Complete California Consumer Catalog* available for $1.50 from the California State Government Publications Section, P.O. Box 20191, Sacramento, California 95820. By the time you read this, other states may have made up similar booklets.

GETTING YOUR MONEY BACK

If getting your money back or solving your own problem is your primary goal, then you will

[1]In your local library you can look at *The Consumer's Register of American Business* and *The Directory of Foreign Manufacturers in the United States.*

probably do best to work with those at the local level who are also concerned with that. So you should see whether there is a local consumer affairs agency or a consumer affairs office in your local government. The telephone book is probably your nearest source of information. In most major cities today, there is a yellow pages listing under consumers of the major public agencies that provide consumer services. A call to the administrative officer of the county or city in which you live should quickly give you the information on the availability of public consumer services.

In some areas of the country you can lodge your consumer complaint via videotape. This is actually happening in Pitkin County, Colorado. A caucus of consumers who are concerned about a specific problem usually obtain 15 minutes of videotape time to present their concern. The tape is then shown on TV at a commissioner's meeting, and the commissioners' responses are videotaped. The

requests and responses are then compiled into one tape which is shown in the rural area where it originated and also in Aspen, Colorado.

If you find no local consumer agency, look under the state listings; if no listing looks promising under the state, call the state attorney general's office. If there is a consumer agency in the state, the attorney general's office will be sure to know. That office and such agencies work closely together because a large amount of consumer fraud that is uncovered by the consumer agency is prosecuted through the attorney general's office. In Table A-1 we present the addresses of state consumer protection agencies.

Private Organizations

While your state and your community may have no public consumer affairs agency or office, there may be a private organization—whether an organization of consumers, a local newspaper, radio, or television

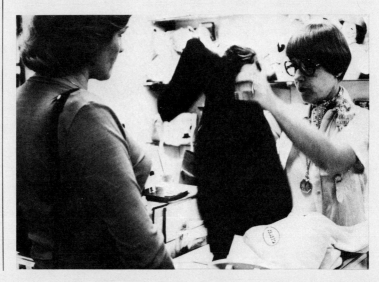

EXHIBIT A-1   How to Lodge a Complaint

Your address
Date

Addressee
Company Name
Street Address
City, State, Zip Code

Dear Sir or Madam:

I am writing this letter to inform you of my dissatisfaction with (name of product with serial number or the service performed) which I purchased (the date and location of purchase).

My complaint concerns (the reason(s) for your complaint). I believe that in all fairness you should (the specific action you desire for satisfaction) in order to resolve this problem.

I sincerely look forward to your reply and a speedy resolution to my complaint. I will allow two weeks before referring this complaint to the appropriate consumer agency.

Yours truly,

Your Name

Enclosures (include copies, not originals, of all related records)

---

station—that provides a consumer service. It usually is not hard to find out about the newspaper, radio, and TV services because they are advertised over the media that perform them, although it may be more difficult to learn about a private consumer organization. But if a private organization is having any success at all, you probably will have read about it in the newspapers and you will find it listed in the telephone book. If you have to hunt too hard for it, it probably is not yet an effective group. If so, it may not be too helpful in getting your money back, but you should probably consider joining it if you want to make sure that your problem does not happen again. Finally, getting your own money back may depend on private legal action. We discuss the use of the small claims court later. If you find that you have to go to a higher court, you will have to face the fact that legal fees must be paid. However, even if you are unable to pay them, you need not give up; in many cities, the traditional legal aid society has been augmented by special legal services for low-income families, and these services often have a strong emphasis on consumer problems. In some states, too, group legal practices have been approved, and you might obtain help through your union or some other organization that has contracted with such a group legal service. On some college campuses, the student body government has set up or arranged for legal services to be available to students; these may permit students to pursue some of the consumer problems that beset them.

Specific Industry Agencies

There are some specific industry programs to help resolve disagreements between buyers and sellers, as in the dry cleaning industry and in the appliance industry, for example. In your area, the local chapter of the American Medical Association and the American Dental Association may also provide such a mediation service. Generally, these professional associations provide for some form of self-discipline, either through a county committee of physicians or dentists or through the appointment of independent arbitrators. Remember, however that like the Better Business Bureau, the professional or industrial policing organization often finds that it can police

Table A-1
State Consumer
Protection Agencies

Alabama. Consumer Protection Office, Office of the Governor, 138 Adams Bldg., Montgomery 36104

Alaska. Attorney General of Alaska, Pouch "K" State Capitol, Juneau 99801

Arizona. Consumer Fraud Division, 159 State Capitol Building, Phoenix 85007

Arkansas. Consumer Protection Division, Justice Building, Little Rock 72201

California. Consumer Protection Unit, Office of the Attorney General, 600 State Bldg., Los Angeles 90012

Colorado. Office of Consumer Affairs, 112 E. 14th Avenue, Denver 80203

Connecticut. Dept. of Consumer Protection, State Office Bldg., 165 Capitol Ave., Hartford 06115

Delaware. Division of Consumer Affairs, 704 Delaware Avenue, Wilmington 19801

Florida. Division of Consumer Affairs, Dept. of Agriculture and Consumer Service, 106 W. Pensacola Street, Tallahassee 32301

Georgia. Georgia Consumer Services Program, 15 Peachtree Street, Room 909, Atlanta 30303

Hawaii. Director of Consumer Protection, Office of the Governor, 250 S. King Street, 602 Kamamalu Bldg., Honolulu 96811

Idaho. Consumer Protection Division, State Capitol, Boise 83702

Illinois. Consumer Fraud Section, Office of the Attorney General, 134 N. LaSalle Street, Room 204, Chicago 60602

Indiana. Office of Consumer Protection, 219 State House, Indianapolis 46204

Iowa. Consumer Protection Division, Office of the Attorney General, 220 E. 13th Court, Des Moines 50319

Kansas. Consumer Protection Division, Office of the Attorney General, State House, Topeka 66612

Kentucky. Office of the Attorney General, 309 Shelby Street, Room 109, Louisville 40601

Louisiana. Office of the Governor, Office of Consumer Protection, 1885 Wooddale Boulevard, Suite 1218, P.O. Box 44091, Capital Station, Baton Rouge 70804.

Maine. Consumer Protection Division, Office of the Attorney General, State House, Augusta 04330

Maryland. Consumer Protection Division, Office of the Attorney General, One South Calvert Street, Baltimore 21202

Massachusetts. Consumer Protection Division, State House, Boston 02133

Michigan. Assistant Attorney General in Charge of Consumer Protection, Law Building, Lansing 48913

Minnesota. Office of Consumer Services, 5th Floor, Metro Square Bldg., 7th & Robert, St. Paul 55101

Mississippi. Consumer Protection Division, Office of the Attorney General, State Capitol, Jackson 39201

Missouri. Consumer Protection Division, Office of the Attorney General, P.O. Box 899, Supreme Court Bldg., Jefferson City 65101

Montana. Consumer Protection Division, Office of County Attorney, 155 W. Granite Street, Butte 59701

Nevada. Deputy Attorney General for Consumer Affairs, Supreme Court Bldg., Carson City 89701

New Hampshire. Assistant Attorney General, State House Annex, Concord 03301

New Jersey. Director Division of Consumer Affairs, Room 504, 1100 Raymond Boulevard, Newark 07102

New Mexico. Consumer Protection Division, Supreme Court Bldg., Box 2246, Santa Fe 87501

New York. Consumer Frauds and Protection Bureau, 80 Centre Street, New York 10013

North Carolina. Consumer Protection Division, Office of the Attorney General, P.O. Box 629, Raleigh 27602

North Dakota. Consumer Protection Division, Office of the Attorney General, State Capitol, Bismarck 58501

Ohio. Administrator, Division of Consumer Protection, Dept. of Commerce, 275 E. State Street, Columbus 43215

Oklahoma. Assistant Attorney General for Consumer Protection, 112 State Capitol, Oklahoma City 73105

Oregon. Consumer Protection Division, Office of the Attorney General, 555 State Office Bldg., Portland 97201

Pennsylvania. Bureau of Consumer Protection, Department of Justice, 25 S. Third Street, Harrisburg 17101

Rhode Island. Chief of Consumer Affairs, Rhode Island Consumers' Council, 365 Broadway, Providence 02909

South Carolina. Office of Consumer Affairs, Governor's Office, State House, Columbia 29201

South Dakota. Secretary, Dept. of Commerce and Consumer Affairs, State Capitol, Pierre 57501

Table A-1 Continued

Texas. Antitrust and Consumer Protection Division, Capitol Station, P.O. Box 12548, Austin 78711

Utah. Assistant Attorney General for Consumer Protection, State Capitol, Room 236, Salt Lake City 84114

Vermont. Consumer Protection Bureau, Box 981, Burlington 05401

Virginia. Consumer Affairs, Dept. of Agriculture and Commerce, 8th Street Office Bldg., Richmond 23219

Washington. Consumer Protection and Antitrust Division, 1266 Dexter Horton Bldg., Seattle 98104

West Virginia. Consumer Protection Division, Dept. of Agriculture, Charleston 25305

Wisconsin. Director Bureau of Consumer Protection, Dept. of Agriculture, 801 W. Badger Road, Madison 53713

Wyoming. State Examiner and Administrator, Consumer Credit Code, State Supreme Court Bldg., Cheyenne 82001

District of Columbia. Department of Economic Development, Consumer Retail Credit Division, Room 306, 614 "H" Street, N.W., Washington 20001

Commonwealth of Puerto Rico. Director of the Consumer Services Administration, P.O. Box 13934, Santurce 00908

Virgin Islands. Consumer Services Administration, P.O. Box 831, Charlotte Amalie, St. Thomas 00801, or Vitraco Mall, Christiansted, St. Croix 00820

only some of its members, or can police them only to a point acceptable to the members of the organization. For if the organization ceases to exist, the policing effect of the organization will also die.

In Chapter 12 on housing, Chapter 13 on equipment and appliances, and Chapter 14 on transportation, we give the specific names and addresses of industry organizations that help solve consumer problems.

WHAT HAPPENED TO ME SHOULDN'T HAPPEN TO ANYBODY

If you feel strongly enough not only about getting your own satisfaction but also about making sure that nobody else suffers your experience, then you will find yourself involved with a whole series of additional service organizations. Sometimes, unfortunately, this is the only satisfaction that you, the consumer, can get—or at least your only satisfaction without spending endless sums of money for private lawyers. Most of the federal and state agencies are designed not to provide help to the individual consumer, but rather to make sure that the laws on the books are properly enforced. In making this kind of a complaint, it is again important that you have a record of your purchase and your payment. And if you are complaining about the performance of a product, you should have the product itself or the container in which you purchased it. If your problem arose from a service that was provided, you must have your records of the service, the name of the person or firm that provided it, and some evidence for your claim that the service was unsatisfactory. Although states and localities have used an infinite variety of ways to deal with these problems of enforcing the rules of the marketplace and protecting the general welfare, they have relied most heavily on four types of agencies:

1. The state department of agriculture: Important in consumer protection because it deals with food. Many departments of agriculture also are concerned with the problem of weights and measures, with pesticides, and with the setting of prices at which some commodities, such as milk, are sold.

2. The public health department: concerned with the safety of food and the sanitation in its handling, processing, and display for sale, and whether or not any of its contents might sicken or kill humans.

3. The state agency or agencies that license occupations and professions: may be called by different names. And some licensing boards, such as those for medicine and the law, may be entirely separate from each other.

4. The state attorney general's office or the local district or state's attorney's office: concerned with practices that are illegal through fraud or deceptive advertising.

If your problem with a product or a service involves food, health, licensed services, or possible fraud, you can start with these four kinds of agencies, which you will find at every local and state level.

Remember, though, that all of these agencies have many duties not specifically oriented to serving a complaining consumer. Obviously, the DA's office considers violent crimes more serious than problems of small fraud carried out against consumers. In health and agriculture, the agencies have to be concerned with issues that may affect the health of the industry or the public health in an emergency situation; they also provide services to others of the public besides consumers. Licensing agencies have to maintain standards that have been set to protect not only consumers but also other practitioners in the same industry. In recent years, however, most of these agencies have assigned at least one unit to consumer complaints. These are typically called consumer affairs offices; and you usually will find someone who is willing to listen to you and who is responsible for taking some action on consumer complaints. Even in the energy crisis in 1974, the office of the energy "czar" set up a consumer services section. And that

brings us to the federal government.

THE FEDERAL GOVERNMENT

If your problem is with a product that is sold nationally, or if your problem is large enough that it affects people all over the country, you will want to go to a federal agency.

Office of Consumer Affairs

The Office of Consumer Affairs, which once advised the president directly, is now within the Department of Health, Education, and Welfare. It analyzes and coordinates all federal activities on behalf of consumers. To this purpose it, among other things, conducts investigations and surveys and holds conferences. It also supplies policy guidance to the General Services Administration in its role of making consumer product information publicly available. The Office of Consumer Affairs is also involved in a consumer education program. Any time you have an inquiry, comment, or suggestion, send it to the Director, Office of Consumer Affairs, Department of Health, Education, and Welfare, Washington, D.C. 20201. Although the agency has no power to redress grievances, if enough letters are sent about the same problem, the Director will try to do something about it by suggesting government policy changes or new legislation. Usually, though, if you think you have a grievance worth being taken care of, you should direct yourself to one of the many federal agencies. As a

help in this task, it might be worth your while to send away for a booklet called "Consumer Information," catalog number PL86, from the Superintendent of Documents, U.S. Government Printing Office, Washington, D.C. 20402. It costs 10¢. We list below some of the agencies you may have occasion to complain to.

When you write, direct your letters, to the chairperson, the agency's name, Washington, D.C., and the zip code, which we give after each of the agencies.

THE OLD GUARD

The Office of Consumer Affairs in the Department of Health, Education, and Welfare performs a relatively new function at the federal level. But the "old guard," the agencies that have been around the longest, fall into the same general categories as those we mentioned for states and local governments: agriculture, health, antifraud, and licensing. Although we call them the old guard, many of these agencies have dramatically changed in the last few years. Once agencies that typically represented the interests of the industries they regulated, they have begun to see themselves as champions of the consumers who buy the products or use the services the agencies oversee. Some have been much more responsive to consumers than others, not always because they chose to be, but because they have been forced to be by consumer activists. For example, a survey of the Federal Trade

Commission by Ralph Nader and his associates was the reason the FTC changed its attitude. When the Nader survey was reinforced by a survey made by the American Bar Association, the change in the Federal Trade Commission was assured. Changes in the Food and Drug Administration reflected not only changes in the attitude of the agency, but changes in the laws under which it operated as well. Several events and changes—passage of the Truth in Lending Act in 1968, revision of the meat packing regulations in 1967, requirements for nutritional labeling, introduction of care labeling on garments in 1973, and creation of the Consumer Product Safety Commission—provided a whole new framework within which the old guard agencies and the new agencies would operate. Let us take a look at some of these agencies from the point of view of the consumer who has a complaint to make. How do you make it? Where do you make it? And what can you expect to happen?

The Food and Drug Administration (5600 Fishers Lane, Rockville, MD 20857)

The Food and Drug Administration has regional offices in many cities. In each of these offices there is a person who is specifically charged with consumer services. Many of the FDA's 5000 employees are technical experts working in specific fields under FDA jurisdiction. Any complaint about a food, drug, or cosmetic that you purchased should be made either to your regional office or directly to Washington, D.C. The agency will ask for as much information as you can give them, and they are particularly interested in seeing the container or the food or drug about which you are complaining. If they believe your complaint is justified, they will have a member of their staff visit the firm in question to observe and to check out its production and packaging procedures. They will check the labeling on the container and the contents of the product to determine whether or not it meets all of the legal requirements. If you do not have the product—because you used it up or it was destroyed—you may still make your complaint. The FDA will seek additional supplies of the product on which to base its decision. The FDA is always very interested in receiving reports of consumers even though the complaints may not turn out to have legal standing. Through such consumer reports, the FDA often discovers new problems developing in foods and drugs and new instances or new outbreaks of old problems. In those areas in which the FDA sets and/or enforces standards, consumers can play a very important role because it is for them that these standards are ultimately set. Unless the agency is hearing from consumers, it may be making avoidable mistakes.

Federal Trade Commission (Washington, D.C. 20580)

The FDA largely enforces standards of product and performance. But the Federal Trade Commission standards are essentially those of practice— competition in the marketplace; false, misleading, and deceptive advertising by sellers to buyers; and packaging and labeling of firms engaged in nonfood sales. In recent years, the FTC has become quite demanding in its rulings on advertising practices: it has begun to require more than merely stopping deceptive practices and sometimes requires the seller of a deceptively advertised product to make a positive public statement on the product's limitations. To assure competition in the marketplace, the FTC has in recent years looked hard at merchandising methods long considered fair and competitive. For example, the FTC has studied whether or not the control of advertising and the resultant brand loyalty of consumers can be grounds for an antitrust suit in the cereals industry. It has also been interested in the general effect of advertising on consumer buying habits. This is a whole new approach, for in earlier years the FTC looked only at specific advertising issues and only after consumers or another seller or advertiser had complained.

The FTC has regional offices and consumer service representatives in major U.S. cities It has established a special office to serve consumers and provides a wide range of informative pamphlets for consumers. If you have a complaint for the FTC, you may make it to a regional office or to the Washington, D.C., headquarters office. If it believes you have a valid complaint, the FTC will send an investigator out to check with both you and the firm. Typically, the FTC works in two ways: first, it investigates whether or not a particular seller or advertiser has violated a particular law that the agency enforces and, if so, takes action to stop the practice by the single firm. Second, the agency looks for new patterns of practice or new areas that may mislead consumers. If it finds any such patterns or areas, the FTC may act against an entire industry rather than a single firm to stop the practice altogether. Sometimes such investigation leads to a new interpretation of an old law; other times it leads to information on which new legislation will be based. Individual consumers can play an important role in the work of the FTC just as with the FDA, because consumers are the persons for whom their work is ultimately carried out.

U.S. Department of Agriculture (Washington, D.C. 20250)

Although the U.S. Department of Agriculture primarily provides services to farmers, it also protects consumers in very important ways, notably by inspecting and grading meat, poultry, and fish. In recent years, the agency has also become a primary source of information for consumers on the best ways to spend their food dollars. The USDA does this through its Cooperative Extension Service, operated in conjunction with land grant universities throughout the United States. Any complaint you have on the grades of meat you buy or the quality of the poultry that is shipped interstate is best reported to your local health department or your local department of agriculture.

The USDA has long operated on a federal, state, and local cooperative basis. On the other hand, if you are a militant consumer who wishes to change the entire framework within which meat grading is carried on, then you will want to join an organization and attack the entire USDA head on. In 1971, and again in 1973 and 1974, when meat prices soared to new highs, consumers around the country organized in many groups to pressure the market to bring meat prices down. Because of the many levels of industry involved in bringing meat from the farmer to the consumer, these consumer efforts generally failed. Through it all, the USDA played the role of the farmers' advocate rather than the consumers' advocate—an excellent example of the conflict of interest that can arise when a government agency is expected to represent more than one interest group.

U.S. Postal Service (Washington, D.C. 20260)

This agency is responsible for investigating mail fraud, unordered merchandise, obscenity, and other mail-related problems that you might encounter.

Department of Housing and Urban Development (Washington, D.C. 20410)

This agency is responsible for numerous federally subsidized housing programs. There is a consumer affairs coordinator whom you can contact.

Interstate Commerce Commission (Washington, D.C. 20523)

Any complaints that you have regarding moving companies, truck shipments, or railroads can be addressed specifically to this agency.

CONSUMER PROTECTION BY THE CPSC

One of the newest federal agencies designed to protect the consumer is the Consumer Product Safety Commission. It was set up in 1972 and given sweeping powers to regulate the production and sale of consumer products that are potentially hazardous. The agency will eventually have a staff of over a thousand, which will make it one of the major federal regulatory agencies for consumer protection.

Creating the Agency

Consumer product safety legislation began in 1953 with the enactment of the Flammable Fabrics Act (see page 239) designed to protect consumers from hazards created by the use of consumer products. Between 1953 and 1972 Congress enacted legislation regulating specific classes rather than broad categories of consumer products. Finally, as a result of 1970 recommendations of the National Commission on Product Safety, the Consumer Product Safety Act was passed in 1972 creating the CPSC to regulate all potentially hazardous consumer products.

Products Subject to the Act

The 1972 Act states that ". . . any article, or component part thereof produced or distributed for sale to a consumer for use in or around a permanent or temporary household or residence,

a school, in recreation or otherwise, or for the personal use, consumption or enjoyment of a consumer" shall be subject to regulation by the CPSC. As further evidence of how comprehensive the Act is, the authority to administer other Acts is transferred to the CPSC. These Acts include the Federal Hazardous Substance Act, the Child Protection and Toy Safety Act, the Poison Prevention Packaging Act, the Flammable Fabrics Act, and the Refrigerator Safety Act.

Purposes of the Act

As stated in the Act, the CPSC was created:

1. To protect the public against unreasonable risk of injury associated with consumer products;
2. To assist consumers in evaluating the comparative safety of consumer products;
3. To develop uniform safety standards for consumer products and to minimize conflicting state and local regulations; and
4. To promote research and investigation into causes and prevention of product related deaths, illnesses, and injuries.

Form and Functions of the CPSC

To achieve all of these purposes, an independent regulatory commission was set up consisting of five commissioners appointed by the President and subject to Senate confirmation for 7 year terms. Not more than three of the commissioners can be of the same political party. The President decides which one of the commissioners will be chairperson. Most of the early commissioners have been

persons with scientific training or with previous experience in consumer protection activity.

The commission was set up to conduct research on product safety and maintain a clearinghouse to "collect, investigate, analyze, and disseminate injury data, and information, relating to the causes and prevention of death, injury, and illness associated with consumer products . . . " To this end, the CPSC immediately started gathering data on the two hundred most hazardous consumer products in the nation. The data have been obtained by requiring hospital emergency wards to indicate the particular cause of any injury, illness, or death related to a consumer product. After the initial CPSC survey, the most hazardous consumer product was found to be the bicycle.

It was hoped by the CPSC that the data obtained and the resulting hazard index for consumer products would move manufacturers to improve voluntarily the most hazardous products and forewarn consumers about which products to be most careful.

POWERS OF THE CPSC

Not only can the CPSC set safety standards for consumer products, it can also ban the manufacture and sale of any product deemed hazardous to consumers. It has, for example, temporarily banned some adhesive sprays and other such consumer items as well as imported items.

The commission also has authority to seize products from the market that are deemed "imminently" hazardous. The process of seizure resembles that provided for under the Food, Drug, and Cosmetic Act discussed on pages 204–208.

The CPSC also has made use of its power to require manufacturers to report information about any products already sold or intended for sale that have proven hazardous.

Impact of the CPSC

Congress sought to create an agency with broad powers to regulate the sale and manufacture of all consumer products. The CPSC is likely to have increasingly profound effects upon the consumer products industry. At the very least, we can expect that the CPSC, if it continues its present effectiveness, will give consumers more certainty about the safety of products they buy. That is, the CPSC may increase the amount of information available concerning consumer products.

Regulations set by the CPSC, however, have resulted in safer but more expensive products. Recently regulations for power mowers were challenged by certain government agencies because they would raise the price of the mowers "too" much. This involves the thorny issue of weighing the costs of safety against the benefits. In other words, how much safety do we want to pay for?

HOW TO GET IN TOUCH WITH THE CPSC

If you think that there is an unsafe product on the market, or if you have any questions about product hazards and safety, you may want to get in touch directly with the CPSC hot line. That number is toll free from anywhere in the United States, (800) 638-2666; or, in Maryland, (800) 492-2937. You can also write to the Consumer Product Safety Commission in Washington, D.C. 20207, and explain your concern over a particular product or products.

OBTAINING MORE INFORMATION ON FEDERAL CONSUMER SERVICES

The first thing you can do to obtain more information on the availability of federal consumer services is send away for *Guide to Federal Consumer Services*, publication number (OS) 76-512, from the Superintendent of Documents, U.S. Government Printing Office, Washington, D.C. 20402. You can also write to the Consumer Information Center, Pueblo, Colorado 81009, and subscribe to *Consumer News*, which is published twice monthly by the Office of Consumer Affairs. The cost is $4 a year (stock number 057D). You can also ask them to put you on their mailing list to re-

EXHIBIT A-2   Today's Top Hazards.

SOURCE	NUMBER OF REPORTED ACCIDENTS
Stairs, ramps, landings (indoors, outdoors)	543,105
Bicycles and bicycle equipment	447,279
Football-related equipment and apparel	384,502
Baseball-related equipment and apparel	355,898
Basketball-related equipment and apparel	343,973
Nails, carpet tacks, screws, thumbtacks	290,845
Chairs, sofas, sofa beds	213,286
Architectural glass	182,220
Tables (nonglass)	166,947
Skates, skateboards, scooters	156,471
Swings, slides, seesaws, playground equipment	152,057
Beds and bunk beds (including springs, frames)	132,270
Floors and flooring materials	101,590
Bathtub and shower structures, nonglass shower enclosures (except doors and panels)	60,467
Fuels, liquid, kindling, illuminating	59,192
Swimming pools and associated equipment (in-ground only)	57,323
Power lawn mowers	57,155
Bleaches and dyes, cleaning agents, caustic compounds	34,844
Cooking ranges, ovens, and equipment	28,148
Furnaces, floor furnaces	11,585

Source: Consumer Product Safety Commission, 1976

ceive a free booklet, *Consumer Information*, which is a catalog of approximately 250 selected government publications of consumer interest. It is published quarterly.

If you do not know which way to turn, you may wish to write or visit a Federal Information Center. You will find a person trained with information about the vast number of federal agencies and programs. Below we list the Federal Information Centers in thirty-seven cities.

ARIZONA
Phoenix
(602) 261-3313
Federal Building
230 N. 1st Ave. 85025

CALIFORNIA
Los Angeles
(213) 688-3800
Federal Building
300 N. Los Angeles St. 90012

Sacramento
(916) 449-3344
Federal Building
U.S. Courthouse
650 Capitol Mall 95814

San Diego
(714) 293-6030
202 C St. 92101

San Francisco
(415) 556-6600
Federal Building
U.S. Courthouse
450 Golden Gate Ave. 94102

COLORADO
Denver
(303) 837-3602
Federal Building
U.S. Courthouse
1961 Stout St. 80202

DISTRICT OF COLUMBIA
Washington
(202) 755-8660
7th & D Sts. S.W. 20407

FLORIDA
Miami
(305) 350-4155
Federal Building
51 S.W. 1st Ave. 33130

St. Petersburg
(813) 893-3495
William C. Cramer
Federal Building
144 1st Ave. S. 33701

GEORGIA
Atlanta
(404) 526-6891
Federal Building
275 Peachtree St. N.E. 30303

HAWAII
Honolulu
(808) 546-8620
U.S. Post Office
Courthouse & Customhouse
335 Merchant St. 96813

ILLINOIS
Chicago
(312) 353-4242
Everett McKinley
Dirksen Building
219 S. Dearborn St. 60604

INDIANA
Indianapolis
(317) 269-7373
Federal Building
575 N. Pennsylvania St. 46204

KENTUCKY
Louisville
(502) 582-6261
Federal Building
600 Federal Place 40202

LOUISIANA
New Orleans
(504) 589-6696
Federal Building
701 Loyola Ave. 70113

MARYLAND
Baltimore
(301) 962-4980
Federal Building
31 Hopkins Plaza 21201

MASSACHUSETTS
Boston
(617) 223-7121
John F. Kennedy
Federal Building
Government Center 02203

MICHIGAN
Detroit
(313) 226-7016
Federal Building
U.S. Courthouse
231 W. Lafayette St. 48226

MINNESOTA
Minneapolis
(612) 725-2073
Federal Building
U.S. Courthouse
110 S. 4th St. 55401

MISSOURI
Kansas City
(816) 374-2466
Federal Building
601 E. 12th St. 64106

St. Louis
(314) 425-4106
Federal Building
1520 Market St., 63103

NEBRASKA
Omaha
(402) 221-3353
Federal Building
U.S. Post Office & Courthouse
215 N. 17th St. 68102

NEW JERSEY

Newark
(201) 645-3600
Federal Building
970 Broad St. 07102

NEW MEXICO

Albuquerque
(505) 766-3091
Federal Building
U.S. Courthouse
500 Gold Ave., S.W. 87101

NEW YORK

Buffalo
(716) 842-5770
Federal Building
111 W. Huron St. 14202

New York
(212) 264-4464
Federal Office Building
U.S. Customs Court
26 Federal Plaza 10007

OHIO

Cincinnati
(513) 684-2801
Federal Building
550 Main St. 45202

Cleveland
(216) 522-4040
Federal Building
1240 E. 9th St. 44199

OKLAHOMA

Oklahoma City
(405) 231-4868
U.S. Post Office Building
201 N.W. 3rd St. 73102

OREGON

Portland
(503) 221-2222
1220 S.W. 3rd Ave. 97204

PENNSYLVANIA

Philadelphia
(215) 597-7042

Federal Building
600 Arch St. 19106

Pittsburgh
(412) 644-3456
Federal Building
1000 Liberty Ave. 15222

TENNESSEE

Memphis
(901) 534-3285
Clifford Davis Federal Building
167 N. Main St. 38103

TEXAS

Fort Worth
(817) 334-3624
Fritz Garland Lanham
Federal Building
819 Taylor St. 76102

Houston
(713) 226-5711
Federal Building
U.S. Courthouse
515 Rusk Ave. 77002

UTAH

Salt Lake City
(801) 524-5353
Federal Building,
U.S. Post Office & Courthouse
125 S. State St. 84138

WASHINGTON

Seattle
(206) 442-0570
Federal Building
915 2nd Ave. 98174

If none of the above-mentioned centers is nearby, you may call one of the following local numbers and ask to be connected by a toll-free tie line to a Federal Information Center.

ALABAMA
Birmingham 322-8591
Mobile 438-1421

ARIZONA
Tucson 622-1511

ARKANSAS
Little Rock 378-6177

CALIFORNIA
San Jose 275-7422

COLORADO
Colorado Springs 471-9491
Pueblo 544-9523

CONNECTICUT
Hartford 527-2617
New Haven 624-4720

FLORIDA
Fort Lauderdale 522-8531
Jacksonville 354-4756
Tampa 229-7911
West Palm Beach 833-7566

IOWA
Des Moines 282-9091

KANSAS
Topeka 232-7229
Wichita 263-6931

MISSOURI
St. Joseph 233-8206

NEW JERSEY
Trenton 396-4400

NEW MEXICO
Santa Fe 983-7743

NEW YORK
Albany 463-4421
Rochester 546-5075
Syracuse 476-8545

NORTH CAROLINA
Charlotte 376-3600

OHIO
Akron 375-5475
Columbus 221-1014
Dayton 223-7377
Toledo 244-8625

OKLAHOMA
Tulsa 548-4193

PENNSYLVANIA
Scranton 346-7081

RHODE ISLAND
Providence 331-5565

TENNESSEE
Chattanooga 265-8231

TEXAS
Austin 472-5494
Dallas 749-2131
San Antonio 224-4471

UTAH
Ogden 399-1347

WASHINGTON
Tacoma 383-5230

WISCONSIN
Milwaukee 271-2273

DO YOU WANT TO DO IT YOURSELF?

Finally, a consumer complaint —a problem with a faulty product or an unsatisfactory service, or a feeling that there is no way that you can make a good bargain for yourself in the marketplace—may lead you to feel that changes must be made. Such changes may have to be accomplished by yourself. But it can be done.

FCC Reacts

An example of what we can do individually has been demonstrated by John Banzhaf, a professor of law at George Washington University in Washington, D.C. In 1967, Banzhaf took advantage of the Federal Communication Commission's "equal time" doctrine, which the television industry

must follow. Since the doctrine requires that equal time be given to opposing sides of controversial issues, Banzhaf requested the FCC to require television stations and cigarette advertisers to provide time for antismoking commercials in response to cigarette commercials. For many years, there had been controversy over cigarette advertising on television; the evidence was mounting that lung cancer was associated with heavy cigarette smoking and that advertising cigarettes on TV encouraged more people to smoke.

The Federal Communications Commission ruled that for every three cigarette commercials shown, one antismoking commercial should be shown free. The FCC ruling was challenged, but it was upheld in court; and the antismoking ads are thought to have reduced cigarette sales significantly. Finally, as a result of the changing attitudes brought about in some part by the antismoking ads on television, Congress required in January 1971 that advertising of cigarettes on television be dropped nationwide.

National Activist Organizations

Although Banzhaf's efforts had dramatic effects, he did not really act entirely alone. Before 1967, many organizations had been involved in the controversy over the association between cancer, smoking, and cigarette advertising. One of these was Consumers Union. You can join Consumers Union simply by participating in the annual voting for its directors, or by informing CU that you want to join. Subscribers to

Consumer Reports automatically become members. Becoming a member of CU does not necessarily involve you directly in active consumer advocacy, but it does enable you to help choose the future directions of this large organization. In recent years, Consumers Union has broadened its concerns; in addition to product testing, it now studies problems affecting consumers generally. In 1973 Consumers Union opened an office in Washington, D.C., with the special responsibilities of watching over the activities of federal administrative agencies and the Congress, and of keeping in touch with the participants.

Another national organization is the Consumer Federation of America, which represents almost 250 national, state, and local consumer groups, unions, churches, and farm organizations. The goal of the CFA is to build a unified effort toward a threefold aim: to foster consumer education, to gain consumer legislation, and to encourage consumers to actively affect consumer-related decisions. Although you cannot become an individual member of the CFA, you can consult it for information on state and local consumer organizations and activities throughout the country. It is a good source of information if you are interested in becoming active in your own area.

SUMMARY

1. When you have purchased a faulty product or been given inadequate services for money spent, you should develop a strategy for your redress of grievance. That strategy will involve the following: (a) before you purchase any good or service, make sure that all guarantees, warranties, and take-back provisions are in writing; (b) if you are dissatisfied after purchase, speak with the person who sold the good or service to you; (c) if no satisfaction is obtained there, speak with the manager or owner; (d) if still no satisfaction is obtained, contact the president or chairman of the board if your purchase was a nationally advertised product or one from a large chain store; (e) when you cannot obtain satisfaction directly from the company, you may wish to seek out a local consumer affairs agency or an office of consumer affairs from your local or state government. In the yellow pages, look under consumer to find out if there is one in your area, or call the state attorney general's office to get information on the possibility of contacting a particular agency in your local or state government.

2. Private organizations may help you. These are difficult to find, however, in certain areas. If there is a college campus in your area, a call to the home economics department may be useful.

3. Certain specific industries have consumer-oriented agencies, such as the American Medical Association, the American Dental Association, the American Bar Association, the Association of Home Appliance Manufacturers, the Gas Appliance Manufacturers Association, and the National Retail Merchants Association. Directly contacting one of these associations might be your best step when you seek redress for an applicable grievance.

4. Each state has the following departments that you can contact directly for specific areas of help: agriculture, public health, occupational licensing, and attorney general's office. In addition, your local district attorney's office may be helpful in cases of fraud or deceptive advertising.

5. The federal government may be of assistance to you or can refer you to the appropriate agency at the state or local level. You may wish to contact one of the following: the Office of Consumer Affairs in the Department of Health, Education, and Welfare; the Federal Trade Commission; the Food and Drug Administration; the U.S. Department of Agriculture; the Consumer Product Safety Commission; the Federal Communications Commission; U.S. Postal Service; the Department of Housing and Urban Development; and the Interstate Commerce Commission.

QUESTIONS FOR THOUGHT AND DISCUSSION

1. Who do you think benefits most from consumer protection agencies?

2. Should there be an agency to inform low-income consumers that other agencies exist to help them?

3. If you were head of the Consumer Product Safety Commission, how would you determine which products should be banned from the market?

4. When do you decide it is time to seek help for a consumer grievance?

5. How do you decide when to seek help against fraudulent activity on the part of businesses?

6. What is the difference between consumerism and consumer advocacy?

THINGS TO DO

1. Draw up a list of consumer affairs agencies in your area. First look in the yellow pages under consumer to see what is listed there. Then contact the district attorney's office. Next contact the state attorney general.

2. Write to various industry organizations such as the National Retail Merchant's Association. Find out what kind of grievance procedure is set up for consumers who feel they have been wronged.

SELECTED READINGS

Campbell, S. R. "Consumer Complaints: What to Do If You Don't Get Action." *Better Homes and Gardens*, April 1974.

"Consumer Agency's Targets." *Business Week*, March 30, 1974, p. 29.

"Got a Complaint? Call your State Consumer Office." *Changing Times*, April 1975.

"Help for Consumers: Government Agencies." *Today's Health*, April 1974, pp. 64-65.

Karpatkin, R. "Advocate's Advance." *Time*, June 28, 1974, p. 66.

Louviere, V. "Getting Relief from Consumer Headaches." *Nation's Business*, June 1974, p. 40.

How to Use a Small Claims Court

Do you think that your former landlord gypped you by keeping your security deposit when you moved out? Did a dry cleaner ruin or lose your clothes? Did you make a claim to your insurance company that it refused to pay? Did a company issue you a warranty on one of its products and then charged you for a repair job while it was still covered?

If you felt helpless when any of these things happened to you, you need not have. To right such wrongs, you could have used the small claims court in your area. However, before you use a small claims court, you may first want to exhaust some of the available alternatives, which include such things as the consumer hot lines available in many states and cities; consumer advocates, who will take up your gripes with the appropriate people and print the results in newspaper columns; and, in some cities, radio and TV newspersons who narrate complaints over the air. They are often very effective. We discussed some other ways you can complain and get redress of your consumer grievances in the last Consumer Issue. If you still feel you need judicial help, then you might want to use a small claims court. Before you do that, you should know what a small claims court is all about.

WHY WERE THEY FOUNDED?

In 1913, a noted professor of the Harvard Law School, Roscoe Pound, gave a justification for small claims courts. He said, "It is a *denial of justice* in small causes to drive litigants to employ lawyers, and it is a shame to drive them to legal aid societies to get as charity what the state should give as a right." In most states today you have the right to use the services of small claims courts to litigate, usually, claims under $500.

CRITICISM OF THE COURTS

Small claims courts are not appreciated by everyone. Former Federal Trade Commissioner Mary Gardner Jones once said:

Our courts are for all practical purposes foreclosed to the individual citizen with the typical grievance involving nondelivery or unsatisfactory service of goods, landlord defaults or indifferent performance under a lease, or even personal injury or property claims which involve relatively minor amounts.

She apparently does not believe that small claims courts usually serve these purposes. Neither does Judge J. Shelly Wright of the U.S. Court of Appeals in Washington, D.C. He contended that "the promise of the small claims courts has not been ful-filled, for in actual operation there is little correspondence between the professed aims of these courts and the ends they serve." Judge Wright believes that most small claims courts have been used as collection agencies by businesspersons.

Businesspersons are indeed the plaintiffs in many cases; they bring suit against consumers who have defaulted in payments for goods already delivered. In 1966, for example, 11 ghetto retailers in Washington, D.C., reported 2690 court judgments, one for every $2200 of sales that year. Things are changing, however, mainly because consumers are becoming aware of their rights in small claims court proceedings, and they are using small claims courts today in order to right their grievances. A 1970 study by Consumers Union showed that the small claims courts in the four cities investigated did indeed help consumers. For example, of the 153 suits filed by consumers against landlords, repair shops, stores, car dealers, and other businesses, 100 were definitely settled in favor of the plaintiff. However, not all consumers have small claims courts available. Ralph Nader's researchers estimate that 41 million Americans have no access to small claims courts, particularly in rural areas.

BUT YOU HAVE TO WATCH OUT

Complications can arise in any small claims court proceedings. In many states, the defendant can automatically and routinely have a case transferred to a regular civil court. In most civil courts, without an attorney your efforts are worthless. So, if a case in which you are plaintiff is transferred to the civil court, you must incur the expense of an attorney or drop the suit.

Further, a small claims judgment in your favor does not mean you will get full satisfaction for your loss. The judge may tell the defendant to pay you $100 on a $150 claim (which, of course, is still $100 more than you started with). But no matter what the defendant is told to pay you, the small claims court does not act as a collection agency. You do not always collect when you win. For example, in the 1970 study by Consumers Union, of the 62 cases which the consumer plaintiff won, 13 proved uncollectable. You must realize that a defendant who does not show up in court is not likely to pay. You may be able to obtain a so-called "writ of execution" from the small claims court if you can show that the defendant is not paying you. But this writ of execution against the defendant's property, bank account, or wages is often not effective.[1]

[1]Note that even if a debt is not collectable now, it stays on the records. Thus, if the person who owes you money (who lost the judgment in small claims court) comes into some assets in the future, you can activate the judgment at that later time.

Additionally, you must realize that you probably will have to make several trips to the courthouse and, if the court has no evening session in your area, you may miss time from work.

HOW THEY WORK

The first thing you do is find the small claims court in your area. Ask the court clerk whether the court can handle your kind of case. For example, some large cities have special courts to handle problems between renters and landlords. While you are at the courthouse, it is probably not a bad idea to sit in on a few cases. That will give you an idea of what to expect when your day in court arrives. Then make sure that the court has jurisdiction over the person or business you wish to sue. Usually the defendant must live, work, or do business in the court's territory. If you are trying to sue an out-of-town firm, you may run into real problems. You probably should go to the state government, usually the secretary of state, and find out where the summons should be sent. Remember that since the small claims court is not a collection agency, if you are filing suit against a firm that is no longer in business, you will have a very difficult time collecting.

Make absolutely certain that you have the correct business name and address of the company being sued. Frequently, courts require strict accuracy; and if you do not abide by that requirement, the suit is thrown out.

Once you file suit, a summons goes out to the defending party, either by registered mail or in the hands of a sheriff, bailiff, marshal, constable, or sometimes a private citizen. Once a company receives the summons, it may decide to resolve the issue out of court; about one-quarter of all cases for which summons are issued are settled this way. Many times, however, the defendant company may not even show up for the trial, in which case you stand a good chance of winning by default. (But, as we said, no-shows are usually also hard to collect from.)

PREPARING FOR TRIAL

How should you prepare for trial? Obviously, if you know a lawyer, you can get some quick advice. In any event, you should have all necessary and pertinent receipts, canceled checks, written estimates, contracts, and any other form of documentary evidence that you can show the judge. Have the entire affair set down in chronological order with supporting evidence so you can show the judge exactly what happened. Make sure that your dates are accurate; inaccurate dates would prejudice your case against you.

If you are disputing something like a repair job, you may have to get a third party as an "expert." Generally, this third party will be someone in the same trade. It is often difficult to get persons to testify against their fellow workers in the same trade. He or she may, however, be willing to give a written statement. Sometimes this is viewed as acceptable evidence. If possible, when you are suing

Table B-1

Small Claims Courts Characteristics in Selected States

STATE	NAME AND LOCATION OF COURT	MAXIMUM AMOUNT OF SUIT	ARE LAWYERS ORDINARILY ALLOWED?	WHO CAN APPEAL? Plaintiff	WHO CAN APPEAL? Defendant	WHAT IS THE INITIAL COST TO SUE?
California	Small Claims Branch of Municipal Court, Sacramento	$ 750	No	No	Yes	$2.00+
District of Columbia	Small Claims Branch of Superior Court, Washington, D.C.	$ 750	Yes	Yes	Yes	$1.00+
Florida	Civil Division of the County Court, Miami	$2,500	Yes	Yes	Yes	$3.50+
Georgia	Small Claims Branch of Civil Court, Atlanta	$ 300	Yes	Yes	Yes	$7.00+
Illinois	Circuit Court, Springfield	$1,000	Yes	Yes	Yes	$0-$500-$11.00 $500-up-$26.00
Iowa	Small Claims Div. of Municipal Court, Des Moines	$1,000	Yes	Yes ($5.00)	Yes	$9.00+
Maine	Small Claims Div. of District Court, Augusta	$ 800	Yes	Yes	Yes	$5.00
Massachusetts	Small Claims Div. of Municipal Court, Boston	$ 400	Yes	No	No	$3.98
Michigan	Small Claims Div. of District Court, Lansing	$ 300	No	No	No	$5.00+

Table B-1 Continued

STATE	NAME AND LOCATION OF COURT	MAXIMUM AMOUNT OF SUIT	ARE LAWYERS ORDINARILY ALLOWED?	WHO CAN APPEAL? Plaintiff	Defendant	WHAT IS THE INITIAL COST TO SUE?
Minnesota	Small Claims Div. of Municipal Court, St. Paul	$1,003	Yes	Yes	Yes	$3.00
New Jersey	Small Claims Div. of District Court, Trenton	$ 500	Yes	Yes	Yes	$2.70+
New York	Small Claims Div. of Civil Court, New York City	$1,000	Yes	Yes	Yes	$4.48
North Carolina	Small Claims Div. of District Court, Raleigh	$ 500	No	Yes	Yes	$10.00
Pennsylvania	Small Claims Div. of Municipal Court, Philadelphia	$1,000	Yes	No	No	$11.00
Texas	Justice Court, Houston	$ 150	Yes	Yes	Yes	$7.00
Virginia	Civil Div. of District Court, Richmond	$5,000	Yes	Yes (if over $50)	Yes (if over $50)	$5.50
Washington	Small Claims Div. of Justice Court, Seattle	$ 300	No	No	Yes (if over $100)	$1.00
Wisconsin	Small Claims Div. of County Court, Madison	$1,000	Yes	Yes	Yes	$7.50

over disputed workmanship, bring the physical evidence of your claim into court. If your local dry cleaner shrunk that wool sweater of yours to a size 3, do not fail to show it to the judge.

WHAT HAPPENS IN COURT

The judge will generally let you present your case in simple language without the help of a lawyer. In fact, in many states neither you nor the defendant may bring a lawyer to help you. You may get the judge's decision immediately or by notice within a few weeks. In some states, you can appeal the case, but in many situations the small claims court plaintiff does not have the right to appeal. Remember, whatever action you decide to take after the judgment should be weighed against the costs of that action. Your time is not free, and the worry that may be involved in pursuing a lost case further might not be worth the potential reward of eventually winning.

If your opponent tries to settle the case out of court, make sure everything is written down in a manner that can be upheld if the offer is reneged. Anything that is written should be signed by both of you and filed with the court so that the agreement can in fact be enforced by the law. It is best to have your opponent appear with you before the judge to tell of the settlement terms. Generally, if you win or if you settle out of court, you should be able to get your opponent to pay for the court costs, which range from $3 to $20, depending on the state.

WHERE, WHAT, AND HOW MUCH?

On pages 40 and 41 in Table B-1, we give you a brief rundown of the name of the court in selected states, where the court is located, the maximum amount of the suits, and some other information such as the costs to you of filing a small claims suit. Remember, you want to be a rational consumer decision maker. Weigh the potential benefits of going to court against the potential costs. If the potential gain to you is less than the value you place on your time and the worry and fear that will be involved when you in fact get before a strange judge in a strange setting, it may be just best to forget the whole thing. On the other hand, if you are convinced that your case is just, that you have indeed been gypped, and the sum of money involved is not insignificant, by all means take advantage of the information presented in this consumer issue and start the proceedings.

SUMMARY

1. If you feel that a local retailer has cheated you out of more than a few dollars (but less than $500 to $1000, depending on your state of residence), you might find it worthwhile to go to a small claims court.

2. A judgment in your favor from a small claims court does not guarantee payment of the claim. Many successful suits lead to uncollectable payments.

3. If you decide to file suit in a small claims court, ask the clerk of your local small claims court

whether your kind of case can be handled there—that is, whether the court has jurisdiction over the person or business you wish to sue.

4. Once a summons is issued to whomever you are suing, you may find that the person or company will decide to resolve the issue out of court.

5. If you go to court, make sure you have the events and actions of the entire affair set down in chronological order with supporting evidence so that you can show the judge exactly what happened. Supporting evidence includes receipts, canceled checks, written estimates, contracts, and correspondence.

6. When you enter a dispute over workmanship, bring physical evidence of your claim into court, if possible.

QUESTIONS FOR THOUGHT AND DISCUSSION

1. In your opinion, who makes the most use of small claims courts?

2. Why should you decide in some cases not to go to a small claims court?

3. Do you think that small claims courts should take on bigger cases? That is, do you think that the maximum amount of money at issue in a suit should be raised in many states? Why or why not?

THINGS TO DO

1. Find out the current maximum amount of money that it is permissible to enter a suit over in the small claims court in your

state. Are lawyers allowed in small claims courts in your state today? Can both plaintiff and defendant appeal? What does it now cost to sue?

2. Go to a local small claims court and observe some of the action. Do you think that all of the cases should have been brought into court? What would determine whether some of them should not have been brought into court?

3. Talk to a lawyer about the advisability of using the small claims court in your area.

SELECTED READINGS

"Caveat Venditor; Suing in Small Claims Court; Advice of D. Matthews." *Time*, September 10, 1973, p. 70.

"Could the Small Claims Court Settle Your Beef?" *Better Homes & Gardens*, April 1977, p. 52.

Cratchit, B. "Tell Us about Small Claims Courts." *Ramparts*, September 1972, p. 47.

MacDonald, S. "Sue Me, Said Mr. Kass to Mrs. Blustein; New York's Small Claims Court." *New York Times Magazine*, April 7, 1974, p. 32.

Price, Howard, et. al. *The California Handbook on Small Claims Courts*. Sacramento: Hawthorne Books, Inc., 1972.

"Small Claims Courts." *Consumer Reports* 38 (December 1973): 383–385.

Steinberg, A. "Needed: Peoples Courts that Work for People." *Reader's Digest* 105 (July 1974): 39-40.

GLOSSARY OF TERMS

Comparison Shopping

A shopping technique that involves comparing values of different products both from the same retailer and from different retailers. Comparison shopping involves using time to acquire information about different sellers and different products.

Informative Advertising

Advertising that gives information about the suitability and quality of products. To be contrasted with competitive advertising.

Competitive Advertising

Advertising that contains basically little information and is used only to allow a producer to maintain a share of the market for that product. An example is cigarette advertising.

Comparative Advertising

Advertising that specifically compares the advertised brand with other brands of the same product.

Bait and Switch

A selling technique that involves advertising a product at a very attractive price; then informing the consumer once he or she is in the door that the advertised product is either not available, of poor quality, or not what the consumer really "wants"; and finally, promoting a more expensive item.

The Information Glut

CHAPTER PREVIEW

☐ Has there been an advertising explosion?

☐ Who pays for advertising?

☐ What are the characteristics of informative versus competitive advertising?

☐ What are some of the forms of false advertising and how is it being regulated?

☐ How can door-to-door salespersons be handled?

☐ How does the Federal Trade Commission operate?

☐ Why are radio and TV advertising the way they are?

☐ How do you go about obtaining privately produced information?

3 Whether you like it or not, you are subjected to about $40 billion of advertising every year: whether you like it or not, every time you turn on a commercial TV channel, you are treated to some sort of ad at least every ten minutes; when you turn on a commercial radio station, the melodious sounds of advertising strike your ears at least every five minutes; every time you open your local newspaper, advertisements cross your field of vision. And if that is not enough, you can purchase more information about every good or service you might want to buy: you can buy books on how to invest money in the stock market; how to buy a house, real estate, a car; how to keep fit and trim; how to avoid being defrauded. You name it, and you can buy or get free some bit of information on it. Information is all around us, bombarding us every second of every waking hour— or so it seems.

Obviously some of this information is useful to us and some of it is not. And just as obviously, more information might sometimes be useful to us if we could get it at a "reasonable" cost. Information, however, is a valuable commodity, generally requiring resources to provide and to obtain. As a result, we never have *perfect* information about any of the products we buy because it would be too costly for anybody to provide.

There is a tremendous variety of sources of information about goods and services. They include:

1. Personal selling by individuals.
2. Packaging, advertising, and broadcast promotions.
3. Expert professional organizations.
4. General news media.
5. Friends, relatives, and acquaintances.
6. Government standards (for example, grading of meats and vegetables).
7. Nonprofit rating organizations, such as Consumers Union and Consumers' Research, Inc.
8. Private industry rating and evaluation systems.

In this chapter, we will examine many of these different sources.

HOW MUCH INFORMATION SHOULD WE ACQUIRE?

What we want is good information at the "right" price. In our daily lives we *acquire information up to the point where the cost of acquiring any more would outweigh the benefits of that additional information.* In other words, we engage in rational decision making, which we will talk more about in the next chapter. When we decide to go shopping for food, we may look at advertisements for only a few supermarkets instead of trying to find out the price of specials at all 46 stores in our city. Why do we look at only a few? Because we have found that it does not pay to look at any more than those few pieces of information. When we go shopping for a new car, we may go to only a few dealers within our immediate area. Why go to only a few and not all? Because, again, we have found that it does not pay to go to all of them.

Some of us may not do any **comparison shopping** at all. We may not even bother to read advertisements or to seek out additional information about the goods and services we wish to purchase. Instead, we may decide to shop at a very expensive store where only the most expensive brands are carried. Why? Perhaps we are "status-seeking," or perhaps we consider our time too valuable to spend in comparative shopping, in acquiring additional pieces of information. We may believe that high price means high quality, which is possible but not necessarily true. If we shop in this manner, we are not necessarily poor shoppers; we may simply have determined that it is not worth our while to acquire quantities of information. We are then essentially nonshoppers.

Information in the form of advertisements relating to products in our economy has been on the upswing, as can be seen in Figure 3-1, which shows the expansion of U.S. advertising. A detailed look into advertising will show why it pays sellers to advertise, who pays for it, and the problems of false advertising.

THE ADVERTISING EXPLOSION

There must be a fairly good reason why we are subjected to so much advertising and why the amount of it is increasing each year. Look at it from the advertiser's point of view. Most businesspeople are in business for one reason and one reason only—to make money. Obviously they would not advertise if they did not think advertising could make them more money, or at least maintain their current sales and level of profits. Thus, by common sense alone, we can assume that they believe the additional sales they will make through advertising will at least cover the costs of advertising. In this sense, advertising can be treated like any other expenditure. If it fails to pay for itself, it will be reduced. If it more than pays for itself, it will be expanded. So the advertising explosion can be attributed to the

**Figure 3-1
Advertising
Expenditures in
the United States**

Source: McCann-Erikson
Advertising Agency, Inc.

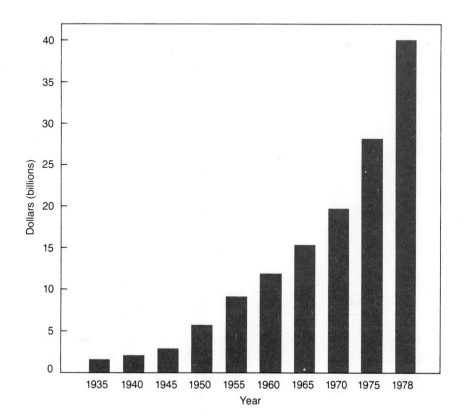

realization by businesses that more advertising yields them more than enough additional sales to justify the expenditure. Of course, when you look at it this way, you also come to a startling realization about who ultimately pays for advertising.

WHO PAYS?

Since businesses are out to make money for themselves and are not necessarily altruistic, you can be certain that if they can help it they are not going to lose money by advertising. Only when they make a mistake about the profitability of a particular advertising campaign do they pay for it themselves, by taking a loss on that particular expenditure. In general, however, the cost of advertising is built into the price of the products we buy. After all, the costs of labor expenses are built into the price of the products we buy. So are the costs of buildings and machines. So why shouldn't the cost of advertising be built into the price of advertised products? Well, it is, and there is very little you can do about it, except, of course, to purchase nonadvertised items that are similar in quality to advertised ones and are lower in price. This can be done in supermarkets with nonnational brands of food products, and with a number of other products that you come across elsewhere while shopping. But here we reach a dilemma; if it is possible to purchase nonadvertised products at lower prices than advertised products and get an equal product, why are any of us so stupid as to buy nationally advertised brands?

THE VALUE OF BRAND NAMES

Obviously, many of us have decided that brand names have value in and of themselves. There must be a few reasons why at least many of us purchase brand names.

1. **Brand names may mean less variance in quality:** If we generally have learned that brand name products vary less in quality than other products, then obviously the brand name has a value, for it tells us to anticipate fewer problems. This may be true, for example, with electronic equipment: you may decide to purchase, say, Sony stereo components because you have found out, or have heard from your friends, that the brand name "Sony" gives you a lower probability of having to take the equipment in for repairs. Therefore, if you go to a stereo shop and see two amplifiers next to each other, one by an unknown company and the other by Sony, you may be willing to pay a higher price for the brand item.

    The same is true for food or services. People sometimes prefer to pay slightly more for nationally advertised products because they have more confidence in them. Whether or not national brand names and quality are always related is a moot point. Advertisers have been selling brand name reliability for years. Only recently has brand name reliability been questioned, and from most of it has come a denial that brand name and reliability are associated. However, many consumers are still willing to pay more for brand name products.

2. **Brand products may offer better warranties:** When something goes wrong with the national brand product you bought, it may have a superior warranty and the service you can get on it may be quicker and less of a hassle than for a nonnational brand. Hence, you may decide to pay more for the national brand.

3. **National brand products may have a larger number of repair facilities:** It may be difficult to get nonnational brand products repaired as easily as those of a national brand. This fact is quite obvious with automobiles, especially with

an exotic foreign job. How many gas stations can help out when a Maserati refuses to start? And even if they knew how, how quickly would they be able to get the parts?

BRAND NAME LOYALTY

The discussion above illustrates the reasoning behind brand name loyalty, which is fostered by national advertising. Brand name loyalty is rational for some people and not rational for others. It is up to you to decide whether you wish to pay the higher price for nationally advertised items. If none of the above considerations seems important, then perhaps you should not. This might be particularly true with nonnational brand foodstuffs, like canned peas and carrots and such products. At least it is obvious that much advertising is done merely to establish brand name loyalty.

The question remains, of course, whether such loyalty actually helps the consumer. Many critics of advertising contend that such advertising does nothing for the consumer, and in fact ultimately does nothing for the producer. To understand this argument, we have to look at the various kinds of advertising.

TYPES OF ADVERTISING

Basically, its critics and students place all advertising into two categories, which, however, sometimes overlap. The first category is **informative advertising**, which is presumably always good; and the second is **competitive** (persuasive) **advertising**, which presumably is always bad. (Of course, there is also false advertising, which we treat in the following section.)

INFORMATIVE ADVERTISING

Informative advertising is just what the term says: it informs and nothing else. You can think of a tremendous amount of informative advertising you see all the time: supermarkets advertise their prices; stereo shops advertise the brands they sell and their prices; producers advertise new products that were not previously available. In other words, you the consumer are being informed about prices, products, and availability. You can take that information for what it is worth and use it in any way you want. You are not asked to believe that a product is better or worse than another one, or that a company does a good or a bad job. Rather, you are simply given the relevant information about the key aspects of a good or service, and those key aspects are price and availability.

In the United States, there is a tremendous amount of informative advertising, advertising that even the critics of advertising would not suggest we get rid of. There are some very unusual products you would never expect to be advertised because the market is so specialized. Did you know, for example, that the producers of multimillion-dollar steam electricity generators send salespeople around to various electric utilities to inform them about the availability and the costs of different types of steam generators? Did you know there are hundreds of specialized trade magazines that treat very narrow fields of interest, and that companies in those fields subscribe to them just to find out what is happening and what products are available? There are journals for printing, publishing, electric utilities, leatherworks, paper producers, flour millers, and so on. In fact, most industries have a trade magazine or two in which very specialized informative ads can be found.

COMPETITIVE
ADVERTISING

Another kind of advertising is called competitive and, again, it is just what the name implies. It comes about through brand name competition. Cigarettes are a good example. Cigarette companies advertise a tremendous amount. Until recent legislation, they spent millions of dollars a year to advertise on television. The question is: What good is this type of advertising? If you look at it from the consumer's point of view, perhaps none at all. Ultimately each of the large tobacco companies puts out a tremendous amount of advertising, and no single one of them gets the edge on all the others through this advertising. In other words, they reach a stalemate. Although if any one of them stopped advertising it would lose sales, it gains no more by advertising than it would if *none* of them advertised at all. This is what competitive advertising is all about.

Any time we try to regulate competitive advertising, we run into a problem: the risk of eliminating informative advertising. Who is going to be wise enough to decide what is competitive and what is informative? Where does the cut off point lie? How would advertising actually be regulated? For example, if you were in charge of deciding about car ads, what would you let manufacturers say? Could they list only the obvious, such as horsepower and the size of tires? Or would you let them say that their new model "handled better" because of an improved suspension system? You would have a hard choice to make, indeed. The Federal Trade Commission has begun to specify what is and what is not informative advertising, but its rulemaking procedures are not yet settled.

Recent years have seen the growth of a kind of competitive advertising that approaches informative advertising in certain respects—at least if it is done honestly.

COMPARATIVE
ADVERTISING

Until the last few years, there was very little **comparative advertising**—that is, advertising that actually names competitor brands when making comparisons between them and the advertised brand. This is a change from the standard comparison between something and "Brand X." For example, Volvo compared itself with other brands of cars, like Saab and Mercedes. Numerous other examples of comparative advertising should come readily to mind. Although many people had thought that such advertising was illegal, it never actually was; but in the past, radio and television stations were either reluctant to take it or refused it altogether. When properly and honestly done, comparative advertising is obviously a benefit to us consumers, for it saves us the time of doing the comparisons ourselves.

FALSE ADVERTISING

One type of advertising that everyone agrees about is false advertising, for fraudulent information dissemination is certainly not in the public interest, particularly if it can be stopped without spending too many resources. There are many types of false advertising. An example of it should give you the flavor of what you have to watch out for.

BAIT AND SWITCH—
THE CASE OF BEEF

Perhaps you have had the joy of reading some of the great beef baiting ads, such as "government inspected, tender, delicious beef sides, only 90¢ a pound, including all the cuts of beef steak, roasts, etc." Well, what may await you if in fact you are dealing with a false advertising claim is diagrammed in Figure 3-2.

As soon as you walk in the door of the meat store that advertised the beef side, you are met by the friendly and persuasive salesperson. You ask to see the 90¢ a pound beef advertised in the local paper. You are shown it, and obviously you would not feed it to your dog, let alone your family. The salesperson agrees, stating that this "is the type of meat they use in institutions." Next, you are shown an extremely good-looking side of beef. It has little fat and is exactly what you had in mind. In fact, it looks a lot like the picture in the ad you saw in your local

Figure 3-2
Bait and Switch

Advertised meat at 90¢/pound

Actual edible meat available at
$1.60/pound

Trimmed meat at $2.00/pound

Additional trimming if dishonest
dealer

True cost $3.10/pound

newspaper. But, of course, this beef is going to cost you $1.60 a pound. If you agree to buy, you sign a contract.

But $1.60 per pound isn't actually what you end up paying for the beef, because the butcher is going to have to trim away about one-fifth of the beef side's hanging weight in fat and bone; a more dishonest "beef baiter" may trim away as much as one-half. However, the price you pay is for the *gross* weight, the weight *before* trimming. And if you do not stay around to look at the cutting and packaging of your meat, a dishonest dealer may give you a side that you did not select, one of a lower quality. Even if you do make sure that you are given the side of beef you chose, if you have no freezer of your own and use his "freezer plan," you may ultimately get lower quality cuts, anyway, as he replaces the beef you left with him.

Beef baiters practice a classical variety of a standard fraudulent practice called **bait and switch**. When you, the buyer, take the bait from an advertisement and go to buy the advertised item, the advertiser gets you to switch to a higher-priced quality or brand. The key to never being tricked by one of these schemes is to learn how to recognize the pattern of a bait and switch scheme and to walk out when you think you're being had. No one forces you to take the bait and then accept the switch. The Federal Trade Commission puts bait and switch at the top of its list of common fraudulent practices or deceptions on the part of businesses. Other deceptions include:

1. **Contest winner:** You are told you have won a contest, but it turns out you must buy something in order to receive your prize.
2. **Free goods:** You presumably will get something free if you buy something else. But you may be paying a higher price for that "something else" than you would have otherwise.
3. **Merchandise substitution:** In place of what you thought you were buying, the seller substitutes a different variety, make, model, or quality of a good.

Again, you do have ways to avoid deceptive practices by sellers, or at least to reduce their probability. One way is to establish yourself as a steady customer of reputable sellers in your area. Once sellers know you are a steady customer, even if they are tempted to cheat you, they would realize its unprofitability, since they rely heavily on your repeat purchases for their business.

DOOR-TO-DOOR SALESPERSONS

There are probably more fraudulent practices used in door-to-door sales than in any other aspect of product selling. You would probably be appalled if you looked at the methods used by salespersons for encyclopedias, vacuum cleaners, land, and even Bibles. Their sales pitches range from quoting phony list prices of their products in order to make their own price look like a bargain, to getting people to sign a questionnaire that is really an installment credit contract. So notorious are their techniques that it is not worth our while to go into detail about how door-to-door salespersons ply their trade. Suffice it to say that again you have the option of escaping their grasp. One way you can make sure you never get taken by some-one peddling at your door is by never letting them *in* the door. You have that choice. If this fails, you can always call the police to get rid of an unwanted sales-person at your door.

It should not be forgotten, though, that sometimes door-to-door salespersons may provide you with a product or service that is useful and is a good deal. In fact, certain products are sold only door to door and cannot be gotten anywhere else— for example, special types of household cleaning aids and certain cosmetics and toiletries like Avon products. If you happen to like these special products, you have no choice but to accept a door-to-door salesperson. However, in these cases you are not dealing with someone trying to sign you to a 36-month installment contract on a set of 58 books at a total price of $650. Rather, you deal with smaller sale prices and, hence, less risk of really getting taken.

COOLING OFF
PERIODS

Many states now have a "cooling off" law that must be applied to many if not all installment contracts. For example, Ohio has a three-business-day cooling off period. Say a door-to-door salesperson gets you to sign a contract to purchase a set of encyclopedias and pay for it over 36 months; during a three-day period, you can renege on that contract. Essentially, you are given three days in which to think over what you have committed yourself to, and also to acquire information about alternative means of purchasing the product you contracted for. That is, you have time to investigate to make sure that you did not in fact get taken by a high pressure door-to-door salesperson.

This cooling off provision was adopted as a rule in 1972 and 1973 by the Federal Trade Commission. Exhibit 3-1 on page 54 is a typical "Notice of Cancellation" that should be available from any door-to-door salesperson.

DIRECT MAIL ADVERTISING

Most of us receive large quantities of direct mail advertising every year. This is third class mail that sellers of goods and services and fund raisers use. A lot of people consider it junk mail. It is a big business whatever it is called. Your name is probably on at least 150 lists, which are rented or exchanged for other lists. Which list you are on depends on where you live, what type of car you drive, what your occupation is, what magazines you receive, what charities you contribute to, and so on. It is used heavily by nonprofit organizations, such as educational and public interest groups, which raise 80 percent of their contributions through the mail.

Commercial supporters of direct mail contend that it permits more informative advertising because those who write the ads can deal with the subject in more detail than they can in a one-minute TV commercial.

Some companies receive large revenues from renting their lists. It is asserted that American Express Company gets over $2 million a year from its list rentals. The magazine *Psychology Today* apparently gets over $1 million a year from its list rentals. Thus, unless you request otherwise, whenever you sign up for an American Express card or buy a subscription to *Psychology Today* you are having your name added to a mailing list that will be subsequently rented or exchanged.

Perhaps this is an invasion of privacy; perhaps you should be given an option. When you subscribe to something or buy something from an organization that rents lists, it would not be too difficult for that organization to allow you to say no to having your name rented or exchanged with other firms. *Consumer Reports* told its subscribers in 1976 that they could have their names removed from any list that CU exchanges. American Express, *MS* magazine, and Diner's Club also offer this

EXHIBIT 3-1   **Notice of Cancellation**

(enter date of transaction)

_____
(date)

You may cancel this transaction, without any penalty or obligation, within 3 business days from the above date.

If you cancel, any property traded in, any payments made by you under the contract or sale, and any negotiable instrument executed by you will be returned within 10 business days following receipt by the seller of your cancellation notice, and any security interest arising out of the transaction will be canceled.

If you cancel, you must make available to the seller at your residence, in substantially as good condition as when received, any goods delivered to you under this contract or sale; or you may, if you wish, comply with the instructions of the seller regarding the return shipment of the goods at the seller's expense and risk.

If you do make the goods available to the seller and the seller does not pick them up within 20 days of the date of your notice of cancellation, you may retain or dispose of the goods without any further obligation. If you fail to make the goods available to the seller, or if you agree to return the goods to the seller and fail to do so, then you remain liable for performance of all obligations under the contract.

To cancel this transaction, mail or deliver a signed and dated copy of this cancellation notice or any other written notice, or send a telegram, to

_____
(name of seller)

at _____ not later than midnight of _____
(address of seller's place of business)   (date)

I hereby cancel this transaction.

_____   _____
(date)   (buyer's signature)

option. If you are truly interested in getting your name removed from lists, you can do the following:

1. Write to any organization that uses your name and ask for it to be removed from that list.
2. Complain to the post office about the receipt of mail that you consider pandering. This can be done by filling out form 2150. By law, any mailer listed on that form must drop your name from its mailing list.
3. Write to Direct Mail/Marketing Association, Inc., 6 East 43rd Street, New York, New York 10017. Ask for a Mail Preference Service form. Once filled out and returned, your name will be removed from lists used by over 400 cooperating mailers who account for 70 percent of direct mail advertising.

THE FEDERAL TRADE COMMISSION

There are government agencies, both state and federal, that are making an attempt to control advertising. More than half of all advertising is national in its coverage. Since it therefore involves interstate commerce, the Federal Trade Commission has control over that advertising. The FTC is organized into two principal operating bureaus—the Bureau of Consumer Protection and the Bureau of Competition. The former has chief responsibility for "monitoring advertising, labeling and deceptive practices, reviewing applications for complaints, drafting proposed complaints concerning . . . practices and, of course, prosecuting cases after the commissioner issues a formal complaint." The FTC has 12 regional offices in various parts of the country. At each regional office, a staff of attorneys and specialists in consumer protection has the responsibility of monitoring advertising and competitive practice in an area of several states. The staffs also conduct investigations of complaints and suspected violations and will try cases concerning alleged unfair practices in that particular geographical area.

The FTC receives letters or other communications complaining of violations from many sources, including competitors of alleged violators, consumers, consumer organizations, trade associations, better business bureaus, other government organizations, and state and local officials. In addition, the commission staff has a large program for monitoring radio and TV commercials, national advertising media, and, through field offices, local advertising media. In the last few years, the FTC has created in major cities consumer-protection coordinating committees that attempt to bring local, state, and federal consumer protection officials in a particular geographical area together in an attempt to provide a coordinated one-stop consumer complaint service.

The statutes administered by the FTC are many. Those that more specifically involve advertising are the Wool, Fur, and Textile Fiber Products Labeling Acts of 1939, 1951, and 1958, respectively. (We treat these in detail on pages 240–241.) In addition, a 1938 amendment to the original FTC Act of 1914 specifically prohibits false advertising of food, drugs, cosmetics, and devices. The lending provisions of the Consumer Credit Protection Act of 1968, administered by the FTC, requires full disclosure in advertising that makes representations about credit terms.

CORRECTIVE ADVERTISING

Lately, the FTC has stepped up its rulings against what it considers to be false advertising. In a famous case, Profile bread was required to eliminate its advertising claim concerning the weight-reducing qualities of its product. It turned out that the reason Profile bread has fewer calories per slice than other breads is because it is sliced thinner. The FTC has also stepped in to stop a number of companies from advertising claims that it considers fallacious or misleading. The most controversial aspect of this campaign is the requirement by the FTC that certain companies spend a specific amount of money advertising the fact that they did indeed present false information.

Sometimes the FTC's attempt at **corrective advertising** has shocked much of the industry in question. For example, the FTC claimed that Wonder Bread was wrong in advertising its nutritive value because the implication was that Wonder Bread is unique. The FTC reasoned that it was not unique because other enriched loaves had the same nutritive value. Notice that the FTC did not claim the ads were *false*, or that they misrepresented the product. It simply said that what was claimed was not unique to that product.

It is also possible for information about the falsity of advertising itself to be misleading. For example, a product named Zerex was advertised as an effective stopper of radiator leaks. The TV ad showed a puncture in a can of Zerex being sealed over from within by the coagulating action of the contents of the can. The FTC charged that Zerex's advertising was false and publicly maligned the company for using deceptive illustrations, threatening, in addition, to remove the product from the market altogether. However, a few months later, the FTC withdrew its charges; it admitted that the ads in question were not actually deceptive. The FTC unfortunately was not financially accountable for the sales lost by the Zerex company. We can hope that no federal, state, or local agency charged with protecting you, the consumer, will again be so hasty in its judgment of deceptive advertising. On the other side of the coin, even when the FTC does apparently prove its case against deceptive advertising, some companies are allowed to continue that advertising. An example is the case that the FTC initially won against Preparation H; because of the time-consuming judicial appeal procedure, the company has been able to continue its ads for years despite rulings against them.

THE FTC AND RALPH NADER

Ralph Nader and his associates issued a report in 1969[1] recommending a complete overhaul of the FTC's staff, practices, and policies. Their findings and recommendations included, among others:

1. There has been too much secrecy about what the FTC is doing.
2. The FTC has been preoccupied with the trivial while ignoring large-scale deceptions.
3. The FTC "fails woefully to enforce its laws properly. It relies too heavily, nearly exclusively, on voluntary non-binding enforcement tools. These cannot be expected to work at all unless backed up by stricter coercive measures, which are almost completely lacking now."

[1]Edward F. Cox, Robert C. Fellmeth, and John E. Schultz, *"The Nader Report" on the Federal Trade Commission* (New York: Richard W. Baron, 1969).

4. The FTC essentially "proceeds in purely random fashion" in seeking out improper or illegal business behavior.

The chairman of the FTC at the time, P. R. Dixon, was accused by Nader and his associates of having "institutionalized mediocrity, rationalized a theory of . . . inaction, delay and secrecy, and transformed the agency into the government's Better Business Bureau."

Basically, the Nader report indicated that the federal government organization with the most responsibility for protecting consumers from deceptive and unfair selling practices was wasting too much effort on trivial matters that merely gave the impression that it was vigorously policing the American economy. The American Bar Association panel that studied the FTC, at the request of President Nixon, came up with many of the same criticisms that Ralph Nader's associates did. In the late 1960s, the FTC took account of both Nader's and the American Bar Association's criticisms. However, despite its "new look," it still does not move very fast and still suffers from many of the criticisms outlined above.

You may wish to write to the Federal Trade Commission, Washington, D.C. 20580, and ask for a free copy of their booklet, *List of Publications*. Of particular interest is a listing of consumer education, instructional aids, and consumer information. Many of the booklets are free or cost from 10¢ to 25¢.

OTHER AGENCIES HELPING YOU OUT

The FTC is not the only agency charged with controlling advertising. There is also the Food and Drug Administration, the U.S. Postal Service, the Federal Communications Commission, and the Securities and Exchange Commission. Their basic laws result in some overlapping jurisdiction. Consequently, for example, the FDA and the FTC operate under a voluntary agreement giving specific areas of authority to each agency and responsibility for policing local advertising problems to state attorney general's offices.

THE WHY AND WHERE OF RADIO AND TV ADVERTISING

At the beginning of this chapter we asked a question: Why are you subjected to so much advertising on radio and TV? Well, now we can answer it. There is no basic reason why you should not be able to purchase the services of radio and TV signals without paying the cost of watching sometimes deceptive, sometimes disturbing, but also sometimes entertaining advertisements. I personally find it annoying (and this is, of course, a value judgment) that in order to watch a full-length movie on commercial (nonpublic) television, I must be subjected to an advertisement every time the plot gets good and thick. That may not bother you. But I do not have a choice—at least not in most states. Neither do you. Why? Because TV and radio are regulated by the Federal Communications Commission (FCC). Television and radio waves are emitted within a publicly controled monopoly franchise. If you do not have a license from the FCC, you do not have the right to transmit TV or radio signals.

WAY BACK WHEN

This was not always so. When radio first came into being, anybody who could set up a transmitter could in fact transmit. But soon the government decided to regulate what was occurring. To ensure that whoever owned a particular airwave frequency was not bothered by someone else's pirate transmission, the FCC was set up to allocate a certain number of radio frequencies to the people who wanted to transmit. However, the rights to transmit radio waves were not sold to the highest bidder. Rather, they were allocated in some "fair" manner to a more-than-willing set of demanders. Since the FCC can rescind valuable licenses, it eventually got control over the content of radio and TV transmissions. That is why the FCC can now set rules for how much and what kind of sex or violence can be exhibited on TV and radio.

More important for us, however, in relation to the amount of advertising we see, is the fact that the FCC has refused for many, many years to issue licenses to pay-television stations, thus creating government franchise monopolies. Although for a long time pay-TV was technologically impossible, it is now a technological reality. But this presents a problem to the owners of commercial television stations. As you can imagine, they would prefer not to have competition; and, in fact, the FCC has been more than willing to help them fight the competition of pay-TV. Pay-TV was also a threat to theater owners, who apparently banded together with commercial television stations in the early 1960s in an attempt to outlaw pay-TV. A referendum was passed in California that "permanently" did just that. It was later declared unconstitutional by the state's Supreme Court, but, in any event, it effectively killed pay-TV in that state for at least a number of years.

THERE IS NO SUCH THING AS FREE TV

Of course, the fact is that you do not get free TV even on commercial channels. You pay for the TV both in the time you spend watching advertising and by purchasing advertised products. Any products you purchase that are advertised on TV include in their price the cost of that TV advertising. If, however, you buy products that are not advertised on TV but you do watch television, you are getting a subsidy from those who buy the TV-advertised products. Now, when you purchase pay-TV—that is, in the six or seven states that now have it—you buy a program by paying $2 or $3 each time you want to watch it. You have chosen to see no commercials, but you certainly pay a higher dollar price for the program. In future years, pay-TV may arrive in most states. You will find much more diversity in the program material you can purchase than you now subsidize on commercial television.

You may have wondered why television has been so "mediocre" in the past, why it has catered to the lowest common denominator. To begin with, the number of television channels, particularly in the earlier years of television, was severely limited by the FCC's caution in granting TV licenses. Those monopoly holders of TV licenses made their money by advertising. The larger the TV viewing audience, the more advertisers are willing to pay for a minute of advertising. For example, one minute of advertising time during the Super Bowl may cost $275,000, whereas during a Monday night pro football game it only (!) costs $125,000.

How do you expect the commercial television program to get the largest audience? Easily: by catering to the average viewer with average tastes.

It should be pretty easy to figure out why television was once called a "wasteland." The average viewer's desires (when considered by academics, government officials, intellectuals, and so on) are pretty "common." What would you expect?

**Figure 3-3
Alphabet Soup**

Not everybody can like opera, sophisticated drama, symphonies, and foreign films. The cards were stacked against the TV station owners (who respond to advertisers who want their products seen by the largest possible audience) when the FCC started looking into the content of television. For TV was a "wasteland" because the Federal Communications Commission had in fact taken upon itself the duty of restricting the number of TV stations in any particular city. In addition, the FCC had helped cause this problem by helping the existing commercial television station owners and movie theater owners fight pay-TV. Although the FCC may contend that it regulates the air waves in the public's interest, it would be hard for us, using any form of dispassionate analysis of the FCC's actions, to reach a similar conclusion. Recently, for example, the FCC stalled the growth of cable TV basically because it was supporting the self-interest of existing TV stations and networks. The actions of the FCC, however, are not unusual for a regulatory agency. If one thing has become clear from the numerous studies by Ralph Nader and his "raiders," it is that regulatory agencies end up serving the interests of the regulated instead of the interests of you and me, the consumers.

COMPARISON OF TV, RADIO, AND OTHER MEDIA

When you think about it, there is little difference in principle between radio and television and all the other information/entertainment media. Newspapers and magazines can influence the American public as much as radio and TV can. Nonetheless, print is very little censored, while radio and TV are very much censored. Perhaps it is true that spoken and visual media face a problem with children's education. However, some might say that such a problem is for parents to handle and not for a federal agency.

BUYING PRIVATELY PRODUCED INFORMATION

If you want to buy a product but are not quite sure which brand to purchase, you need not rely only on the advertisements by the various manufacturers. You can purchase product brand information; you can, for example, purchase *Consumer Reports* or *Consumers' Research Magazine*.

CONSUMER REPORTS

Consumer Reports is the publication of Consumers Union, chartered in 1936 as a nonprofit organization under the laws of the State of New York. The object of Consumers Union has been to bring more useful information into the seller/buyer relationship so that consumers could buy rationally. The first issue of *Consumer Reports*, in May 1936, went to three thousand charter subscribers. They were told about the relative costs and nutritional values of breakfast cereals, the fanciful claims made for Alka Seltzer, the hazards of lead toys, and good buys in women's stockings, toilet soaps, and toothbrushes. Consumers Union's policy has always been to buy goods in the open market and bring them to the lab for testing.

Now approximately two and a half million subscribers and newsstand buyers read *Consumer Reports* every month. Consumers Union accepts no advertising in its magazine and tries to test various types of consumer products objectively. In addition, it gives advice on purchasing credit, insurance, and drugs. One of the major aspects of Consumers Union's testing involves automobiles: which are the best buys, which are safe, which have good brakes, which have safety defects, and so on. Recently, Consumers Union has published articles on ecological topics such as pesticides, phosphates in detergents, and lead in gasolines. It also strongly criticizes government agencies when they act against consumer interests.

If you decide to rely on the recommendations of *Consumer Reports*, you have to realize that it is difficult for even highly objective researchers to present purely objective results. That is not to say that you will get misinformation, but you may sometimes get emphasis on certain aspects of products that are consistent with the tastes of the researchers but not with your own. For example, recommendations about cars may give more weight to safety, gas mileage, or comfort than you personally want to give. You may opt for a different car because you prefer styling or low cost as opposed to safety. Even though the occupants of VWs face a higher probability of serious injury in an accident than do occupants of bigger cars, people continue to buy VWs, presumably because they are cheaper. But you will face this problem of acceptance with any information you obtain either free or at a price. In the last analysis, only you can make a decision, and it has to be based in part upon your personal value judgments. If you are a lazy shopper, you can probably get away with looking at *Consumer Reports* for whatever you want to buy, picking either the "best buy" or the top of the line, calling up your local dealer, and having it delivered. You may get some products you dislike, but on average, if your tastes correspond with those of the persons running Consumers Union, you will save much time searching and will probably avoid basically defective products.

CONSUMERS'
RESEARCH MAGAZINE

Consumers' Research, Inc., founded in 1929, puts out a monthly *Consumers' Research Magazine*, similar to *Consumer Reports*, with a readership of several hundred thousand. It gives product ratings, as well as ratings of motion pictures and phonograph records, and gives short editorials, just like *Consumer Reports*. No advertising income is permitted. The product testing policy of Consumers' Research often involves its borrowing test samples of large, expensive items from manufacturers who sign affidavits that the goods are typical and were selected at random. Sometimes the goods are rented—for example, typewriters—for testing. Consumers' Research often restricts its tests to brands or goods that are nationally distributed, while *Consumer Reports* sometimes tests brands that are distributed in various high-density localities. It is Consumers' Research policy to service their national and international audience rather than give any special attention to products or brands sold in specific geographical areas. Further, *Consumers' Research Magazine* does not give brand names as "best buys" as does *Consumer Reports.* Both organizations pride themselves on stressing safety and efficiency in products. Both have found potentially unsafe products long before any government agency.

BUYING GUIDES

Consumer Reports puts out an annual *Buying Guide* in December; *Consumers' Research's* annual guide appears in October. Both contain a wealth of information on such things as food and nutrition, energy saving ideas, and the like. They both suffer from a problem that is impossible to avoid in a dynamic economy: certain models that are listed may no longer be available by the time you decide to make a purchase.

At any one time, you will be able to pick from at least a half dozen other buying guides, such as the *Consumers' Handbook*, edited by Paul Fargas, or *Better Times*, edited by Francis Cerra. The Department of Agriculture puts out a *Shoppers' Guide.* All suffer from being uneven in coverage, so that none can be recommended in its entirety.

OTHER INFORMATION SOURCES

There are an increasingly large number of privately produced information sources in addition to those mentioned above. For example, a monthly magazine by Time-Life, called *Money*, is aimed at families of middle income and above. Nonetheless, even for low-income families, it often has valuable information about making better consumer choices, such as articles about deceptive selling practices, better nutrition for your family, and so on. A less well researched, but perhaps still useful, alternative private source of information is the magazine *Moneysworth.* However, *Changing Times*, the magazine published monthly by the Kiplinger Service for Families, is perhaps a better source of consumer information. Any given issue may provide information on gimmick reducing machines, how to buy insurance like an expert, new tax rulings that might affect you, how to get interest on your checking account, and why extra long auto loans are bad deals. Most major newspapers carry a column by Sylvia Porter or another consumer information specialist, and there are less traditional sources of information, such as *Mother Earth* magazine. In different parts of the country, specialized regional consumer information sources are available.

Better Homes and Gardens, *Good Housekeeping*, *Sunset*, *Family Circle*, *Women's Day*, as well as other magazines, give helpful consumer information on such things as money-saving recipes, furniture maintenance ideas, and do-it-yourself projects.

SUMMARY

1. Comparative shopping involves acquiring information about alternative sources for a particular product. The acquisition of information, however, requires the use of your time and perhaps other resources, such as gas for your automobile. Therefore, there is a limit to how much comparative shopping you will want to engage in.

2. There has been an advertising explosion in the United States. Expenditures have increased to an estimated $40 billion in 1978.

3. Ultimately, the consumer pays for advertising in the form of a higher-priced product. This is also true for products advertised on television and radio.

4. Individuals often associate brand names with (a) less variance in quality, (b) better warranties, and (c) a larger number of repair facilities.

5. The way to avoid the undesirable consequences of deceptive selling practices, such as bait and switch, contest winner, free goods, and merchandise substitution, is to know before you shop what you are looking for. When a salesperson attempts to sell you something you do not want, be insistent or leave. Generally, you do not get anything free; and if one retailer is selling an item at a drastically reduced price, you should be suspicious unless you know why.

6. Make sure that if you ever decide to buy something from a door-to-door salesperson you receive a Notice of Cancellation, which gives you without any penalty or obligation three business days from the date of the transaction to decide whether you want to cancel the contract.

7. The Federal Trade Commission is empowered to monitor advertising and deceptive practices of businesses. If you think that you have been the victim of deceptive advertising, you might want to contact the local bureau of the FTC. The field office can be located in the telephone directory of the closest big city in your state.

8. Ralph Nader recommended that the Federal Trade Commission undergo a complete overhaul. Among other things, his group of researchers pointed out that the FTC "proceeds in purely random fashion" when it seeks out improper or illegal business behavior.

9. You end up paying for "free" radio and TV when you buy the products advertised in those media, for those products are relatively higher priced in order to pay for radio and TV commercials.

10. There are numerous places where you can obtain privately produced information about products and services you might want to buy. For example, subscribe to *Consumer Reports*, *Consumers' Research Magazine*, *Money*, *Changing Times*, *Moneysworth*, *Better Homes and Gardens*, *Good Housekeeping*, and *Sunset*.

QUESTIONS FOR THOUGHT AND DISCUSSION

1. Who do you think should bear the responsibility for honest advertising? The manufacturer? The advertising agency? The government? The consumer?

2. Do you think that all corrective advertising is necessary?

3. Can advertisers regulate themselves? Is there any evidence that mass advertising has become a less effective marketing device?

4. Do you think there is any end in sight to the advertising explosion?

5. Why do consumers still prefer brand names?

6. Can you distinguish between informative and competitive advertising?

7. Listed in the text are several deceptive advertising techniques. Can you think of any others?

8. Why would a manufacturer want to have its product sold door to door rather than in a retail outlet?

9. Do you think that there should be an increased amount of noncommercial—that is, public—television? Who should pay for it?

10. Why are there more privately produced sources of information, such as magazines of the *Consumer Reports* type, on the market today than there were, say, 50 years ago?

11. Do you think parents do—or should—monitor or censor the TV viewing of their children? Or should national or state government guidelines be set?

THINGS TO DO

1. Read the Nader Report on the Federal Trade Commission. Find out from your local FTC field office whether any of the recommendations in the Nader report have been taken to heart.

2. Examine some marketing journals, such as the *Journal of Marketing* and the *Journal of Advertising Research*. See what some of the authors writing in those magazines believe is necessary for successful advertising.

3. When you see what you believe to be a false or misleading ad, write the manufacturer of the product being advertised asking for an explanation. If you are not satisfied with the explanation, ask your local FTC office if the advertising is in fact deceptive.

4. Experiment with some potential bait-and-switch ads. These are especially prevalent for appliances and locker meat. For example, if you see an appliance ad in your local newspaper, cut it out and go down to the store offering that product at that specified price. See if the salesperson attempts to get you to buy a higher-priced product. If that happens, ask that salesperson if he or she is aware of the FTC's rulings on bait-and-switch cases.

5. Write a list of products that you buy mainly because of the brand name. Then decide which of those products can be bought at a lower price by going to a nonbrand name. Why have you been choosing a brand name for so long?

6. Make a list of products for which competitive advertising is the norm. You can start the list with cigarettes and go on to toothpaste, and then add all the others you believe fall into this category.

7. Take note of the corrective advertising you see on television. Analyze it from the point of view of the consumer. Does the corrective advertising give you information that will change your buying behavior with respect to the product in question?

8. Do research on the argument by commercial television companies against pay-television. Do you think you would be better off if pay-television were allowed throughout the United States? Why or why not?

9. Compare the various informative consumer magazines, such as *Consumer Reports* and *Consumers' Research Magazine*, as well as *Money* and *Changing Times*. If you had a limited amount of time, which one or ones would you read most often? Why?

SELECTED READINGS

Advertising Age (various issues).

Allen, Frederick Louis. *Only Yesterday.* New York: Harper & Row, 1931.

Buxton, Edward. *Promise Them Anything.* New York: Stein & Day, 1972.

"Buy the Product, Not the Package." *Changing Times* 31 (April 1977): 21.

"Caveat Vendor; FTC Crack Down on Advertising for Children." *Newsweek* 83 (June 17, 1974): 69.

Cohen, Dorothy. "The Federal Trade Commission and the Regulation of Advertising in the Consumer Interest." *Journal of Marketing*, January 1969, pp. 40-44.

Consumer Reports (various issues, "The Docket" section).

Cox, Edward F.; Fellmeth, Robert C.; and Schulz, John E. *"The Nader Report" on the Federal Trade Commission.* New York: Richard W. Baron, 1969.

Hearings Before the Senate Committee on Commerce on Truth and Advertising Act, 1971. Washington, D.C.: U.S. Government Printing Office, October 4, 1971.

"How Justice and the FTC Compete." *Business Week*, March 23, 1974.

Levitt, Theodore. "The Morality (?) of Advertising." *Harvard Business Review*, July/August 1970.

Moskowitz, D. B. "Are Unreliable Data Better than None?" *Business Week*, May 25, 1974.

Packard, Vance. *The Hidden Persuaders.* New York: David McKay Co., 1957.

"Sears Agrees to Stop Using Bait-and-Switch Tactics." *Consumer Newsweek* 6 (October 25, 1976).

Telser, Lester G. "Advertising and Cigarettes." *Journal of Political Economy* 70 (1972): 471-499.

"Those Ads that Promise You Riches." *Changing times*, November 1976, p. 17.

Ward, Scott. *Effects of Television Advertising on Children and Adolescents.* Cambridge, Mass.: Marketing Science Institute, July 1971.

GLOSSARY OF TERMS

Barter

The exchange of goods or services without the use of money. If I give you two pencils for one eraser, you and I have exchanged by way of barter.

Credit

A loan that someone offers to you in exchange for a payment, usually called interest.

Conspicuous Consumption

Consumption of goods more for their ability to impress others than for the inherent satisfaction they yield; buying and using consumer goods in a flashy or noticeable manner.

Consumer Sovereignty

A situation in which consumers ultimately decide which products and styles will survive in the marketplace, that is, producers do not dictate consumer tastes.

Rational Consumer Decision Making

Deciding how to buy, where to buy, and what to buy in such a manner that the highest satisfaction is obtained from the consumer's use of resources, including both time and money.

Sunk Costs

Costs that have been incurred already and that cannot be changed. An example of sunk costs is the initial cost of buying a television set. That cost never changes after purchase, but the cost of running it can change— the longer it is kept on, the higher your electricity bill will be.

Parkinson's Law

Work will expand to fit the time allowed.

Making Up Your Mind

CHAPTER PREVIEW

☐ What is involved in rational decision making?

☐ How do goals affect your consumer choices?

☐ Why is value clarification important?

☐ What else determines how you act?

☐ What determines your buying habits?

☐ How much information should you seek before you make a purchase?

☐ What are some of the aspects of alternative life styles?

4 Even if you were the wealthiest person on earth, you would still have to make decisions. Even if all your material wants could be satisfied at the touch of a button, one valuable resource would still be scarce for you, and that resource is your time. You have only so much time in a day and so many days in a life. Even in that nirvana of total abundance, you would still be faced with making a choice about the use of your time: you would have to learn the art of decision making.

We know that in the real world, in which we are all more or less distant from being the richest person on earth, the art of decision making applies to the use not only of our time, but of our other resources as well. Intelligent, rational consumer decision making thus becomes all the more important. We are all faced with a budget problem. We cannot have everything we want, so we must make choices. And once we make them, we must also carry them out in a rational manner. We cannot simply decide to buy a new car. We must also decide what kind of new car —foreign or domestic, small or large, luxury or economy, sedan or station wagon, and so on. We must then decide where to look for the car of our choice and whether to pay cash or buy it on credit. If we use credit, we must decide where to obtain that credit. Decision making never seems to stop.

EXCHANGE AND RATIONAL DECISION MAKING

All consumer decision making ultimately results in a choice that is carried through by exchange. When we decide to enter a certain occupation and take a job with a particular firm, we exchange our labor services for that firm's payment of wages. When we decide to buy a TV, for the set itself we exchange the purchasing power implicit in the money paid for it. When we decide to put our savings into a savings and loan association, we exchange the purchasing power implicit in those savings for shares in the savings and loan association. Actually, we expect to receive at a later date what we put into the savings and loan plus a reward, which is the interest on our savings.

There are many ways in which exchange can be facilitated. In a market economy such as ours, these ways include the use of money instead of trading goods for goods **(barter)**, the use of **credit**, the branding of particular products to give certain types of information, the use of media to transmit product information, and so on. As rational consumers, we may attempt to facilitate our transactions in the marketplace as much as is economically worthwhile: we may sometimes attempt to acquire information that is not provided to us by the seller of the product. Or we may sometimes want private or government agencies to facilitate the exchanges we like to make. A national job market bank might be one means of getting such information; a rental agency listing the available apartments in an entire city might be another means. A magazine that presents test results is yet another. The list could go on and on.

Rational consumer decision making generally involves seeking out those exchanges that are most beneficial to you, the consumer (or that are most beneficial for another person or group if you happen to be the decision maker with that responsibility). But determining the most beneficial choice for yourself presupposes the ability to analyze the benefits (and costs) of alternative choices. This is sometimes impossible, or at best extremely difficult. Whenever your personal values or feelings enter into your decision making, you may have a difficult time in quantifying them sufficiently to make a rational choice. Or you may even have a difficult time putting priorities on the different values you have.

We can generalize the decision-making process into several steps:

1. Define the problem in light of goals and values.
2. Select and explore possible alternatives, that is, collect information.
3. From these, select one alternative.
4. Proceed to accept and evaluate your responsibilities after having selected this one alternative.

What happens after you have selected the alternative should be fed back into future decision-making processes as additional information, not only about what you might have purchased, but also about what your true values and goals really are. This last step is important because many persons have a tendency to blame others when things fail to work out.

WHAT DETERMINES YOUR CHOICES?

There are many determinants of the choices we make in our day-to-day living. If this were a book dealing exclusively with the principles of economics, we could talk about how our choices are governed by our income and the prices of various goods and services. For example, we would find out that, in general, as the price of one product goes up relative to all others, a smaller quantity of the product will be demanded. We would find that as people's income goes up, so, too, does their demand for most goods and services.

But more generally, the choices we make can be looked at as also depending on the values we hold, the goals we set for ourselves and our family, and the customs already laid out before us in our society.

| Should I buy a new car? | What size should I buy? | What body style should I buy? | Automatic or manual transmission? |
| Yes | Compact | Station wagon | Manual |

Figure 4-1 A Typical Decision-Making Process

CLARIFYING OUR VALUES

From the time you were around five years old, people probably started asking you what you wanted to be in life. You might have said a musician, a mother, a father, an artist, a scientist, a doctor, a lawyer, a flight attendant, a fire fighter, or any one of the numerous occupations you might have been aware of at that time. Later on, however, you had to start making some hard-nosed decisions.

It starts for many of us in high school: should we drop out or stay in? Should we be a vocational education major? Should we be a precollege major? Should we take more math or less? Once we have decided to stay in high school, we face another choice: should we go on to college after high school or get a job? In either case, we have to start deciding what we really want to do. Once in college, we have to decide what we want to specialize in. When we get out (if ever), we again have to decide where we want to work and how, the amount of free time we want to have, what kind of risks we want to take, what kind of people we want to be with, and so on.

Often, however, many of us let ourselves be drawn along by whatever happens to come our way—the "path of least resistance," we might call it. And just as often, when this happens we look back and think we made a mistake. We realize we did not clarify our values about life and how to live it. For this reason, career guidance counselors, psychologists, and sociologists increasingly stress the need for individuals to engage in their own soul searching, their own value clarification.

Clarifying our values is an ongoing process. All of us change throughout our lives (or at least we think we do). You are probably not the same person you were five years ago in your values and your view of the world. Sometimes just a round-table discussion with your family or friends or even a career guidance counselor is useful to point out in which directions you have actually moved in the last few years.

What we are all striving for is easy to say—happiness. The way we get there is another matter. Continued value clarification is possible, but how each of us does it might be difficult for someone else to dictate. What is important is that you do not wait until you have a nervous breakdown to decide that your values have changed and are no longer in line with your life style. Gradual change is generally less painful and less costly than abrupt change. For example, if you have spent the last six years as a homemaker and you had not given a thought to what your values are and what you are doing, but now suddenly realize that you are tired of washing dishes, you might become so disapproving of your current situation that the decisions you make will mean an abrupt and painful change in your life. If, on the other hand, all along you had occasionally clarified your own values and related them to your actual living conditions, you could have gradually changed your life style to suit your changing values. The mental and emotional costs to yourself and to other members of your family would probably be lower.

GOALS

Everybody has goals, whether or not they are well defined. To start off, we know that except for pathological cases, the main goal of most individuals is to be happy, however each of us defines it. But to attain that goal, we make numerous subgoals. Yours may be to finish college or to get a good job or to play the guitar well; you may have goals set for your children, if and when you have them; you may have a goal set in your job or your business. These goals will often determine your consumption behavior. If one of your goals is to be relatively well off by the time you are 50, you may then decide to work hard, spend little, and save a lot. That means you will not be tempted to take long vacations or buy higher-priced housing, at least not in the earlier stages of your career. On the other hand, if your goal is different, you may take those longer vacations. You know that you will pay for them later on in the sense that your savings will be smaller.

Individuals change their goals all the time. In fact, experts who specialize in helping people plan for the future often advise that goals should be made for the immediate or short run, intermediate run, and long run, and be revised often. You might have a goal for the next two months of finishing a particular project, doing well in certain classes, or increasing your sales. Obviously, at the end of the stipulated period, you will see if you attained those goals and you will make new ones for the next immediate time period. In the intermediate run, your goals may involve improving your tennis game, painting the house, or getting a new car. And then there are the long-run goals, five-year, ten-year plans, even twenty-year projections into the future. As most people find out, these are often revised according to new information on where you are going in your job, on the size and circumstances of your family, and on your own thinking. Just look back at what you thought five years ago you were going to do. Did you actually end up doing it? Some of you have, but many others have not. Does that mean you planned wrong? It certainly does not. When you make decisions for the future, you use the information presently available. But information is not perfect, or complete. If you used the information rationally and economically, then the goals you set would be rational also; but they will not be unchangeable, because you will continuously acquire new information about yourself and the world around you.

Goals and planning go hand in hand. Consumer decision making is sometimes based on plans that are themselves based on goals. Planning is sometimes a painful procedure, particularly when a family is involved and numerous diverse interests within it must be considered. Compromises must be reached. Compromises must also be reached within one's own mind. People often have a tendency to "want the stars," but since scarcity still hangs heavy, they cannot have it all.

Consumers who plan in a rational manner may be accused of lacking spontaneity. Certainly that is one of the costs of planning; but one of the benefits is that goals can often be met through proper planning and adherence to those plans. To be sure, you must decide. If, indeed, you do decide to become a consumer who plans, then you may be able to satisfy many of your desires and needs. If spontaneity is important in your life, then a set of plans will not be your only way to happiness.

CUSTOMS

Primitive societies are usually ruled by custom. Even modern societies have customs that determine people's choices. In the United States custom plays less of a role in our decision making than it does in many other nations. Nonetheless, if you examine your own behavior as a consumer, you may be surprised at how much you do depends on customs already established. Here are just a few of the things we do that are controlled more or less by custom:

1. The types and combinations of food we eat
2. The exchanging of Christmas cards

3. The style of clothes we wear
4. How we dispose of the dead
5. The type of marriage ceremony we use

Take, for example, clothes. The two or three buttons on the sleeve of a man's suit jacket are there by custom; they are totally nonfunctional otherwise. You can probably think of numerous other features of clothing that have no function other than to fit the dictates of custom. The fact that men in our society do not wear skirts is also dictated by custom, for we partly identify sex role by established dress.

Many of our food-buying habits certainly are affected by our culture. What we consider acceptable for eating may not be considered acceptable in other cultures, and vice versa. What some of us would consider exotic foods with premium price tags others might consider high cost essential foods.

Customs do serve a useful purpose: without them, we could not predict behavior; the result would be considerably more confusion than now exists in our society. Note further that by following customs that are in line with our values, we reduce both time and search costs in determining what our behavior should be.

Your consumption patterns may also be determined by your desire to influence others' opinions of you. Many years ago, a famous American economist, Thorstein Veblen, gave a name to this pattern.

CONSPICUOUS CONSUMPTION

Professor Veblen pointed out, in his *Theory of the Leisure Class*, that many people desire to consume in a conspicuous manner. **Conspicuous consumption** is the use of the goods and services we can afford to show what our social worth is, on the implicit assumption that the more we can afford, the worthier we are. Such consumption is based on conformity—the conformity that one wishes to have, at least in appearance, to the consumption practices of one's neighbors and friends. This type of behavior, also known as "keeping up with the Joneses," is familiar to all of us and is considered by many to be undesirable behavior because it shows a lack of individuality. Although individuality carries high praise in American society, it is not an overriding characteristic of *any* society. Even if individuality is more preached than practiced in our society, the theory of conspicuous consumption still fails to adequately explain people's consumption activities; for as the old adage has it, "one man's meat may be another man's poison." Tastes do indeed differ, as do people's values. Today, motivational psychologists no longer place overriding emphasis on Veblen's theory to explain consumption patterns in our economy.

In fact, there is some evidence to suggest that many individuals practice what might be called inconspicuous consumption. This presumably is particularly so with individual families that have had wealth for many generations. Rather than attempting to show off how much wealth they have, they underplay it, purchasing relatively inexpensive cars, inexpensive clothes, and inexpensive houses. Some individuals may also display, with pride, their conspicuous nonconsumption, such as faded and patched jeans and holey tennis shoes.

BUYING BEHAVIORS

In one respect, there are as many buying behaviors as there are consumers. But in other respects, for the purposes of analysis and to better understand our own buying behavior, we can categorize them into several broad groups, the three most obvious being impulse buying, habit buying, and planned buying.

IMPULSE BUYING

Impulse buying is just that—buying on a whim, walking into a store, seeing something we like, and purchasing it. Obviously, impulse buying cannot explain all of our buying habits because we have certain needs that must be met if we are to survive, the most obvious being minimum amounts of food and shelter. Thus, at least part of what we consume has to be in some way planned. The rest, however, could conceivably be based on pure spur-of-the-moment impulses. Nonetheless, there is a limit to impulse buying. That limit is our income plus our available credit. Scarcity exists everywhere and it starts right at home. Once we run out of income, plus our credit line, we can no longer buy on impulse. Most consumer economists argue against impulse buying because it often wrecks a well thought through budget and may lead to financial difficulties.

HABIT BUYING

Many purchases are made based on habits acquired through years and years. No plans are involved and no impulses, either, just the force of habit. A person might stop at a tavern on the way home from work every Friday night. That person doesn't even have to think about such a consumer activity because it is already a habit. An individual might continue subscribing to, say, a photography magazine just out of force of habit, even though that person has long given up the hobby and doesn't even own a camera any more. Consider, also, that habit buying may be necessary in order to free up time for other buying that requires time and thought. In other words, habit buying isn't necessarily bad.

PLANNED BUYING

Planned buying is also sometimes called **rational consumer decision making.** While it may lack spontaneity, planned buying does have the virtue of safety if it is consistent with available resources. Consumers will generally not overstep their income if they plan carefully to keep in line with available or anticipated income. But even the best laid plans can go awry. And, to top it all off, some motivational psychologists believe that businesspersons can affect our plans, and certainly our impulsive buying sprees, by using effective advertising campaigns.

CONSUMER SOVEREIGNTY VERSUS PRODUCER SOVEREIGNTY

Every day in every way we are bombarded with advertisements as producers attempt to manipulate us into buying their products. How successful are they? Some say very successful; others say not so much. The saving rate in the United States at least gives some evidence that producers have not made us spend any more now than we did in the past, measured as a percent of our total income.

But from there it does not necessarily follow that producers have not encouraged us to buy a bundle of goods we would not have bought without their sometimes hard sell or style techniques. For example, John Kenneth Galbraith, the noted Harvard economist and author, has often maintained that American consumers have been persuaded to consume too many private goods and not enough public goods, such as schools and parks. His conclusion is that the government should step in to wrest away part of consumers' incomes and direct it to public enterprises such as those just mentioned.

In the ideal world where the consumer is sovereign, we consumers, through our dollars, vote for the products or services we want most. Those products that get the most votes yield the highest profits and therefore attract the businesspersons' money from other areas in the economy where dollar votes are smaller. In this manner, the profit system directs resources to areas in the economy where they yield the highest value to the population.

However, even in this ideal world, income may be so maldistributed that very few people are commanding large amounts of resources; hence, the dollar voting system does not distribute goods and services in the way that society deems best. But, setting aside for the moment the problem about distribution of income, the consumer sovereignty issue also rests on an assumption about the economy itself.

That assumption has to do with the degree of competition within the system. If there are many monopolistic practices and restrictions of entry into various industries, a high price may not in fact cause resources to flow into those industries because outside resources are not *allowed* to enter. This is the age-old problem of monopoly. To be sure, if you believe that the United States is made up of monopolies, then you may have some serious doubts about the validity of the consumer sovereignty principle.

One thing we have to remember about this entire unsettled issue is that even if producers as a whole want to influence our buying habits, they must somehow get together to decide how to influence our habits in unison. Otherwise, competition among them (except in the case of monopolies) will not necessarily lead to any predictable conclusion. Even with sophisticated marketing techniques and heavy doses of advertising, consumers, at least on occasion, have demonstrated their desire to be sovereign. Witness the failure of the Edsel in the 1950s, which cost the Ford Motor Company a quarter of a billion dollars because consumers refused to buy it. Witness also the reluctance of the American woman to accept the midi-length skirts, even though the fashion industry pushed them hard. It has been estimated that nine out of every ten new products fail within one year. This comes to a huge number when you consider that thousands of new products are put on the market every year in the United States.

DISTINGUISHING BETWEEN CONSUMER CHOICE AND CONSUMER SOVEREIGNTY

If the consumer has the freedom to decide what to buy and how to use it, then there is consumer choice. In other words, so long as the consumer is presented with a series of options, he or she has choice. On the other hand, **consumer sovereignty** implies that consumers are the ones who determine what those options are. A self-sufficient family living in the middle of the wilderness obviously has both. It alone decides what to grow, how to make things, and how to divide its time between work and play. It directs the use of the resources it has available and makes choices among what is produced. In our society, the richest that the world has ever seen, there is no question that consumers have choices, literally millions of them. But, economists such as John Kenneth Galbraith, as well as more radical Marxists, such as Paul Baran, believe that consumer sovereignty is essentially dead.[1]

We must also point out that even if consumer choice exists, there are a number of things that individuals are forced by law to buy. For example, in certain states, it is illegal to drive a car without also purchasing automobile liability insurance. To be sure, we could say that individuals in such circumstances could

[1]Paul Baran, "A Marxist View of Consumer Sovereignty," *The Political Economy of Growth* (New York: Monthly Review Press, 1957).

**Figure 4-2
The Range of
Consumer Choice
and Sovereignty**

At one extreme, no
one forces us to buy
anything; at the
other, we are required
to purchase an item
whether we like it or
not. Generally,
depending on the
situation, we are
somewhere in
between.

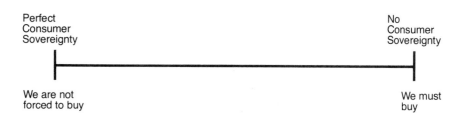

Perfect
Consumer
Sovereignty

No
Consumer
Sovereignty

We are not
forced to buy

We must
buy

always choose *not* to drive, but that is really begging the issue. In essence, then, there is a gray area where we are in effect "semi" forced to purchase certain items. You might say that there is a range of situations facing consumers, such as the one shown in Figure 4-2. We are somewhere in the middle, depending on the situation.

BUYING AND SEARCHING

All consumer decision making generally rests on information, which must be acquired through some searching procedure. What is the best search procedure? Of course, for each person it will be different, but a general rule for rational consumer decision making can be made:

The larger the expected payoff from searching for better information in the market-place, the greater the cost that should be incurred to acquire the information.

What does that mean? In plain language, we probably will spend considerably less time trying to get the best deal on a tube of toothpaste than we will spend trying to get the best deal on a new car. The expected gains from getting a good deal on toothpaste may be at most a few cents; but on a car the gains may be a few hundred dollars. What separates rational from so-called irrational buying habits is that in the former, we look at the expected costs and benefits of seeking out the best deal.

Some people, such as doctors, lawyers, and top executives, consider their time so valuable that they seek out very little information. They may, for example, find a very expensive store in their neighborhood where they buy many products. They may be willing to pay the higher price because they have found that the store carries relatively higher quality brand names, and they make no attempt to gain more information about other sources of the products because they consider the time involved better spent on their careers.

For any one of us, it is not *always* beneficial to spend more time trying to get a lower price or higher quality in a product. At some point, we have to stop our search. We will not search *every* store in our city for the lowest toothpaste price, even though we know that the next store might be the one with the lower price. The point at which we stop searching is determined by the information we already have, and a comparison of what it will cost to acquire new information against what we expect the benefits to be from that new information. A study done in Chicago revealed that when buying a car most people sampled no more than two car dealers. We also have to realize that searching for the best deal may not mean searching everywhere in a large geographical area. Would you buy a new car at a dealer

30 miles away because it is a hundred dollars cheaper than at the dealer two blocks away? If you happened to have warranty or service problems and must take the car back to the dealer who is 30 miles away, you will incur time costs, additional gas costs, and probably car rental costs that you would have been spared had you purchased from your local dealer.

Expected potential benefits must be weighed against actual and expected costs. That is the rule by which you can become a rational consumer decision maker.

YOU'RE THE BOSS

Remember in all of this discussion that you're the boss: you determine your values and make decisions based on those values. Think about that when you analyze the behavior of others, too. If you think somebody is stupid because he or she purchased a product for a price that you thought was too high, you may be trying to impose a low time value on that person just because *you* have a low time value. That person may not like to spend the time looking for deals, although you may like to. Also, you are generally imposing your values on other people if you consider what they bought to be in poor taste. Their taste is merely a reflection of a value system that is different from yours. Thus, while the tenets of rational consumer decision making as outlined above are universal, one person's decision making may be rational for him or her but not for someone else. Do not fall into the trap of trying to apply the rules of others to your behavior, or your rules to the behavior of others.

ALTERNATIVE LIFE STYLES

Whenever you compare yourself with others, you will find contrasts. You may often ask yourself, why does so-and-so seem to have so much free time? How does your best friend manage to work on that TV course you always wanted to take? Or you may find instead that *you* seem to go on vacation all the time and your friends stay around in the city fixing up the house on all their free days. You may come home exhausted at the end of every workday. Or you may be able to take your work in stride and fit in many gratifying extra-household activities. Or you may be the type who constantly complains that "my work is never done."

What we have said in a roundabout manner is that all of us have different life styles. In fact, we can and often do choose among life styles. You may be making that choice right now. And you may want to reconsider it later. You make the choice whether or not you want to, and whether or not you are aware that you are making it. What may be important for you, however, is to be aware of all the decisions you are actually making. Look at a few different life styles to see what they have in common and how they differ.

THE FRUSTRATED INSURANCE SALESMAN: Joe Smith went to college and majored in business administration. He was not a particularly conscientious student, and consequently when placement time came around before his graduation, not too many firms were interested in him. He did like to talk, though, and an insurance company recognized this ability and offered him the best job at that time. He took it, all the while thinking he would eventually find something better.

Marriage came and somewhat altered his outlook about changing jobs, at least for the time being. He felt obliged to make sure he provided for his wife and coming child. A job change would come later. That was 15 years ago. He never did get around to looking for another job. He makes good money now, but keeps telling himself he should have done something else after a few years. He keeps telling himself that he actually could be doing something more exciting with higher pay. But Joe Smith will be a disgruntled insurance salesman until he retires. (He nonetheless might be a good one, as reflected in his high income.)

THE SATISFIED EDITORIAL ASSOCIATE: Sue Jennings majored in English when she went to college. She was always excited about books and writing and thought someday she could be a writer. In the meantime, when she got out of college she took a low-paying job in a New York publishing firm as a copy editor. Eventually she worked her way up in the highly competitive publishing world with much overtime and many frustrating moments to an editorial associate working directly under the executive editor of the whole company. She still thinks that she will someday write a book. In the meantime, she's happy. In fact, she's ecstatic. She has a job with much responsibility; her husband doesn't try to dictate her career plans; and she feels that she is indeed independent and is in the right job, even though her life appears to be hectic with little time for long vacations and leisurely three-day weekends.

THE OVERWORKED COUPLE: Sharon and John Halsing did not finish college. They got married when they were both sophomores and decided they wanted to see the world. So together they "bummed" around Europe for a couple of years taking odd jobs. Finally, when they came back to the States, they both realized, after three or four years of changing jobs, that they could not be happy working for somebody else. So they had a plan. They were going to go into business for themselves. They were both art "freaks," spending many leisure hours in museums. So what was more natural than to start an art supply store which could eventually become a place selling lithographs and paintings? John borrowed some money from his life insurance policy. Sharon took out all of her savings from the bank, and they also got a loan from the Small Business Administration. They started a small store selling art supplies near a local university. The hours they worked were tremendous, but they kept telling themselves that they at least were not working for somebody else. Raising a family was going to have to wait; it just would not fit in right now.

Eventually, the store caught on and students from other universities were even coming there to buy their art supplies. The lithograph section grew by leaps and bounds, and so, too, did the small medium-priced painting gallery. And they were still working long hours six days a week, and had not yet taken more than three or four days off at a time in all the years they had had the store. Were they happy? They could not quite tell. When they were working, they were happy, but when they thought about all those missed vacations, they sometimes got morose. They finally decided that it was too late to raise a family and often regretted that decision. But they certainly weren't unhappy, as all their customers could tell you, for they were served with a smile and good

cheer. Did Sharon and John make the right decision? Sometimes they think they did; sometimes they think they didn't.

THE IDENTITY-CRISIS HOUSEWIFE: Lana Stellen got married even before she finished high school. The kids came fast and furiously: there were four at the end of seven years. Her husband, backed by his father, slowly built up an extremely profitable dry cleaning company with franchises throughout the city. He provided well for her. She was even able to hire help to come in and clean the house once in a while. She thought she was happy, and in fact motherhood suited her well, at least for the time being. Her kids sometimes gave her problems; she spent many a sleepless night with them, and she often had to arbitrate the fights among them. But they did give her a constant source of joy. As they started to grow older, Lana and her husband were able to take three-day weekends, leaving the children with babysitters. Soon they were able to take longer vacations, and often the family went camping weeks on end. Lana had not stopped learning just because she did not go to college. She watched a lot of talk shows on TV, read nonfiction best sellers, and discussed politics with her husband and friends.

At some point in her life, however, she started getting a vague feeling of uneasiness; a feeling of incompleteness sometimes overcame her, especially when she saw newscasts about prominent women in the United States and the rest of the world. Every once in a while she would get a letter from her former best high school friend who had not gotten married until much later in life. This friend had developed a promising career in interior design. Lana started going through periods of moroseness and depression. Finally it hit her. She had to get a job. She had to get out of the house and do something on her own. It turned out after she figured the costs of babysitting, transportation, and taxes she would have to pay that no matter what she did, she would not end up adding much money to the family income. Nonetheless, she had to do it and she did. Many adjustments had to be made in the family at that time, but after the initial shock and disappointment, her husband made a sufficient number of compromises so that it all worked out. Lana had become aware of her frustration and acted on it. She still was not perfectly happy, but of course no one ever is. She did think, however, that she was a better person, and of course that is what counts.

The different life styles above should enable you to realize quickly that what is appropriate for one person may not be appropriate for someone else; and the criterion for appropriateness is simply that which makes you happy. Even before experimenting, though, you can figure out some of the boundaries within which you have to work. For example, Joe the insurance salesman had a steady income, but he felt that there was not much excitement or much challenge after a while. But that feeling is common. The more risky and challenging a job, the greater the chance of not having any income at all in certain years. Whenever we decide on a life style that has security, we are generally choosing, at least in our work, a life style that has less excitement, perhaps, than some other life style. If we want to be sure that the paycheck will always come in, we can get a government job that has tenure after 12 months' work. We may never make a fortune, but neither will we ever starve. If we want to take a chance on hitting it rich, we may pass a good part of our lives never knowing how we will feed ourselves from one day to the next. Such a decision we have to make ahead of time. After the fact, we might say we made a mistake, but we cannot change what has already happened. Ultimately, any decision on life style is intimately tied up with a decision about a career or a field of occupation.

FORESIGHT AND HINDSIGHT

When you decide on your life style you have to make a decision with incomplete information. You will never have perfect information; you can never know how you will feel in the future, what your values will be, and what your job situation will be. You nonetheless have to make a decision. Little did you know that you were going to get tired so fast of sitting at a desk, or that your business was going to go bankrupt, or that what you really needed was an extra year of bumming around the country before you started to work. Had you known it, you would not have done things the way you did.

When you look back five years later, if you want to kick yourself, remember that hindsight is always more reliable than foresight. The best thing you can do with hindsight is perhaps to use it in making a decision about what to do in the future. Since there is no way to reverse your *past* life, you will only cause yourself untold grief if you bemoan the decisions you made then. As trite as it may sound, the saying "let bygones be bygones" is appropriate. To express this fact about the past, we can use the economists' term, **sunk costs**: sunk costs are forever sunk. Assume they have sunk to the bottom of the ocean. Stop worrying about them and look to the future. If you can extract some information from mistakes you made in the past, it is all the better. But do not think you were stupid simply because you disapprove of what has happened to your life through a decision you made five years ago if you based it on the best information available at the time.

TIME, TIME, TIME

In every possible alternative life style, one element remains constant: the amount of time you have available. The question you must answer is how you want to use that time. One life style you choose may involve being always busy, with no time to be with your family or friends and no time for vacations. Most likely you see this all around you; your husband or wife or brother or sister or father or mother or friends may fit into this category. Successful businesspeople are often like this. They use every second of their time to maximize their prestige, income, or fame. These people may work so much that they have little time to spend their large incomes. Compare such persons with men and women who decide to work on a factory assembly line. Their jobs last seven hours a day and may seem boring. But when those seven hours are over, they need not use their remaining hours thinking about the job. After 4:30, their time is their own, as are their weekends and vacations. Their lives are quite a bit different from those of executives who never leave their jobs no matter where they are because they are always thinking about problems. Assembly line workers certainly will never make as much money as the busy executive, but they will have a freedom from worry that makes free time truly free.

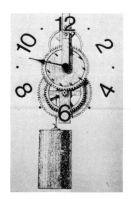

It is important to look at time as a commodity that you purchase. It is also important to judge the quality of that time. Say, for example, you are a busy executive; if when you go home, no matter what anybody says to you, you are still thinking about your work, that time may be of low quality to you as leisure. It is not of the same quality as the time you might have at home were you to devote yourself to your own interests or those of your friends or family. Once in a while you might find it a good idea to take stock of how much time is actually your own in your own life style. You might decide that you need a change in life styles. It need not be of the abrupt kind you read about every once in a while when a company president chucks it all at age 42, buys a house in Mexico, and lives on $100 a month for the rest of his life, which he spends fishing in the harbor. It might instead simply involve going to another firm or working for another person and starting out with the expressed understanding that the amount of time you will spend on that new job will be limited to 35 hours a week instead of 60 as in your old job.

The same is true for those who decide to devote much of their time to the household. Specialization of tasks may be fine for some, but perhaps not for you. Maybe you want to have a part-time job and let others in the family share with you the responsibility for household chores while you share with them responsibility for earning family income. Such possibilities all involve a decision about how you, and the others affected, want to use your time. You can wisely make this kind of decision only if you have some general notion about what your values are.

PARKINSON'S LAW

Whatever our values may be and whatever our life style becomes, most of us share a certain psychological trait commonly known as **Parkinson's Law.** Parkinson made an observation that unfortunately seems to have universal validity: work expands to fit the time allowed. If you are aware of Parkinson's Law, you can fight it. If you are not, it sometimes will overtake you. Say you have allotted yourself four hours to write a report. You had better believe that the report will take you *at least* four hours. However, had you allotted yourself, say, three hours, it would have taken only three hours and probably would not have been any better or worse. In fact, it might have been better because you would have started in earnest right off the bat instead of twiddling your thumbs, sharpening pencils, and looking at additional reference materials for the first two hours. If you have spent much of your time taking care of your children and cleaning house, you know what Parkinson's Law is. If you do not believe it, just see what happens when you take a part-time job and find half of your day is taken away from household tasks. You probably end up doing exactly the same amount in half the time. But when you have the full day, you can be extremely inefficient and essentially make the job full time, yet still feel an awful lot is left to do.

BREAKING THE LAW

Personal Time Plan.   One way that some people get around Parkinson's Law is to plan and draw up lists of things they have to do. The more specialized and specific the lists are, the more efficient they become. Of course, this can be carried too far and we can become fanatical about it. But for many people this is the only way to do enough things so that they feel satisfied with how they spend their lives. Instead of telling yourself that you really ought to read more books, one way to make sure you do it is to chart out book time every day. It does not have to be five hours at a sitting, because you know that is impossible. It might be 15 minutes at a time, four different times during the day. You will be surprised how many books you will have read that way. If you really would like to keep up correspondence with old friends, stop putting it off: set up a specific time and do it. Another way of making sure you get things done and use your time efficiently is to reward yourself. A famous writer once had a plan: because he was an avid smoker and craved nicotine, when he had a contract to fulfill he would reward himself with one cigarette after he finished each page. That way he never missed his deadlines. You may not make the same use of cigarettes, but you might find another self-reward that is appropriate to you.

Such a technique can be extended to lifetime planning, by which you have goals for each day, each week, each month, each year, each five-year period; and you keep redefining these goals. Some extremely efficient people always put down more goals each day than they know they can possibly do. But sometimes they do more than they thought they could because they had set such goals for themselves.

SUMMARY

1. Because we live in a world of scarcity, we are forced to make choices and therefore must involve ourselves in decision making.
2. Rational consumer decision making involves seeking out exchanges that are most beneficial to you.
3. Decision making involves: (a) defining the problem in view of goals and values; (b) selecting and exploring possible alternatives; (c) selecting one alternative; and (d) accepting and evaluating consumer responsibilities after selection has been made.
4. Your goals generally determine the choices you make, and these goals change from time to time.
5. Goals and planning occur together through feedback during and after decision making.
6. Many of our actions and habits are determined by custom, such as the style of the clothes we wear.
7. Consumers generally engage in impulse, habit, or planned buying.
8. Information must be acquired before purchases can be made. However, it is only useful to acquire information up to the point where the expected payoff from searching for more information is not as great as the expected costs of that additional search: the larger the purchase contemplated, the more one should spend seeking information on the best product and the best financial deal.
9. Hindsight is always 20/20, but what has happened in the past cannot be reversed. However, it is useful to analyze past decisions and actions to make better decisions in the future.
10. Even if you have decided to accomplish certain goals because they fit in with your values, you may not be successful if you fall prey to Parkinson's Law—work will expand to fit the time allowed. That is where your personal time plan comes into play.

QUESTIONS FOR THOUGHT AND DISCUSSION

1. Can you think of any product, service, or resource that is actually free? Is your time valuable?
2. Why does scarcity force you to make decisions?
3. How do your goals determine your choices?
4. What are some of the customs of your family or your community that influence your expenditures? How do they differ from the customs of other groups that you have observed?
5. Look around you. Do you think most people engage in some forms of conspicuous consumption? Why?
6. Are there any psychological benefits that individuals might obtain from allowing themselves to impulse buy once in a while?
7. The debate is still raging about whether or not you, the consumer, determine what you buy. Do you feel you have any effect on what producers are willing to produce and offer you for sale?
8. What determines the life styles that different people choose? What determined your life style?
9. What does the statement "sunk costs are forever sunk" have to do with consumer decision making?
10. Why do you think Parkinson's Law seems to work all the time?
11. What have been some of the influences helping you to clarify your own values? What are those values? Are they the same as your parents', your friends', your neighbors'? If they are different, why do you think they are different?

THINGS TO DO

1. Go back to a recent consumer decision that you made—say in the purchase of an article of clothing, a book, a record, a TV, a radio, or whatever. Outline the steps you undertook to reach your final decision. How did you decide when to buy it, what to buy, where to buy, how much to pay, what brand, what quality, and so on? See if you can draw a chart showing the step-by-step progression of your consumer decision making. Now see if there is anyplace within that process where you should have (looking now after the fact) obtained more information? Why did you neglect or fail to obtain more information? After reviewing your decision-making process, do you think it can be improved? In what ways? Do you see a general behavioral pattern that you want to change?
2. Read Vance Packard's *The Hidden Persuaders.* Do you think that book, written a number of years ago, is still valid today? If not, why? Has the world changed so much, or have we become smarter consumers? Has legislation affected anything in advertising that Packard talked about?
3. Write down a set of short-term, intermediate, and long-term goals. Are these the same goals that you had last year, the year before, or the year before that? Do you think you will have the same long-term goals five years from now? If not, why do your goals change? Is there any way you can predict how they will change?
4. Draw up a list of consumer actions that you engage in that are at least in part determined by customs in your family or community. We mentioned five within the text itself.

5. Draw up a list of those things that you purchase on an impulse and those that you plan to purchase very carefully. If the impulse list is very long, does that bother you? How could you change your buying behavior? Do you limit impulse buying to low-cost items?

6. Try to determine the way you decide how many places to shop for any particular item. Does it depend on the price of the item? Does it depend on your knowledge or lack of knowledge of alternative sources of that item? Is there any way you could make a rule that would tell you when to stop looking for a better deal?

7. List the times when you are most likely to suffer from Parkinson's Law.

8. Recall the last time you went window shopping. What kinds of information did you find (and store) in your mind as a reference point for further decisions? Do you think this is a good way of acquiring information about the goods and services available in your community? Why or why not?

SELECTED READINGS

"Bargain Hunting: Enough Is Enough." *Money*, March 1977.

Feldman, Saul D. *Life Styles—Diversity in American Society.* Boston: Little, Brown & Co., 1972.

Hamilton, David. *The Consumer in Our Economy.* Boston: Houghton Mifflin Co., 1962. See especially Chapters 2 and 3.

Katona, George. *The Powerful Consumer.* New York: McGraw-Hill, 1960.

Packard, Vance. *The Hidden Persuaders.* New York: David McKay Co., 1957.

Packard, Vance. *The Status Seekers.* New York: Pocketbooks, 1959.

Paolucci, Beatrice; Hall, Oliva; and Axinn, Nancy. *Family Decision Making: An Ecosystem Approach.* New York: John Wiley & Sons, 1977.

Robertson, Thomas S. *Consumer Behavior.* Glenview, Ill.: Scott, Foresman & Co., 1970.

Scholz, Nelle Tumlin; Price, Judith Sosebee; and Miller, Gordon Porter. *How to Decide: A Guide for Women.* New York: College Entrance Examination Board, 1975.

"Values and Decision Making." *Home Economics Research Abstract*, No. 6 (1968), Washington, D.C.: American Home Economics Association.

Veblen, Thorstein. *The Theory of the Leisure Class.* New York: Macmillan Publishing Co., 1899.

Ward, Scott. *Effects of Television Advertising on Children and Adolescents.* Cambridge, Mass.: Marketing Science Institute, July 1971.

*

GLOSSARY OF TERMS

Patriarch

The male head of a family or clan in which he takes on an authoritarian role that generally extends not only to his own immediate family but also to the families of his sons.

Pair Bonds

Generally, male-female relationships in which the two persons involved share in significant mutual activities and life planning.

Specialization

The dividing up of various tasks so that one individual concentrates only on certain tasks while leaving the other individual or individuals time to concentrate on the remaining tasks. Also called the division of labor.

Crypto-servant

John Kenneth Galbraith's name for the woman's role in America. Women are, he says, secret or nonseeming servants, but servants nevertheless to the males in the society.

The Economics of Love and Pain

CHAPTER PREVIEW

☐ What is the history of marriage in the Western world?

☐ What are the economic costs and benefits of marriage?

☐ Are women "crypto-servants" in our society?

☐ What are the economic aspects of women's liberation?

5 Let us look at the life cycle of the average person in American society. For about the first three years of life you are totally dependent on adults for your care and feeding. If left alone, you could not survive. After a while, however, you become increasingly self-sufficient: you can feed yourself, dress yourself, and make your wishes known in ways other than crying or laughing. All the while, you are being formed by your environment—friends, family, surroundings. When school starts for you, the family takes on less importance. Environmental stimuli outside the family may be more important in formulating the values you will have throughout the rest of your life. If you are the typical American, you will finish high school and go on to some form of higher education. Today, more than 60 percent of high school graduates go on in their schooling. Also, if you are typical, you will eventually get married. For women, the average age of first marriage is 21; for men, 24.

The life cycle starts over again for your offspring when you begin to raise a family, and raising that family will occupy a large percentage of your time and money for the next 20 years or so. What does this mean? Simply that a tremendous part of the average person's lifetime is involved in family activities. It is not surprising, then, that the family occupies a key role in the study of economic and consumption decision making in general. However, the family is not the unique spending unit in this country. Today there are 12 million one-person households. The vast majority of college-age students live with roommates or in dormitories, fraternities, sororities, rooming houses, or communes. No matter what your present or contemplated living arrangement might be, the principles and rules outlined in this text for your personal economics are going to be valid. Nonetheless, it might be useful to look into the economic aspects of marriage, and its counterpart, the dissolution of marriage.

STATE SANCTIONED LOVING

Marriage is an old institution. The form that it takes in our modern Western civilization is the product of a long development in which Greek, Roman, Hebrew, and Christian traditions were combined. Before the rise of Christian notions of marriage, the Germanic peoples and the Jews had a type of marriage similar, it seems, to that of the Greeks and the Romans. It fitted well into a society composed of kinship groups headed by patriarchal chiefs, fathers with great authority over their grown sons and unmarried daughters, and over their sons' families. Every person, male or female, belonged to a clan dominated by a **patriarch**. When a woman married, she was allowed to leave the clan of her birth and enter her husband's clan. However, marriage was not a transaction between the two partners involved but between the chiefs of the two clans, as was the dissolution of a marriage. By the time of Jesus, custom and law allowed a marriage to be terminated arbitrarily by the husband, but not by the wife.

Some contemporary observers maintain that the institution of marriage is dying out. Divorce statistics indeed indicate a slight downward trend in the percentage of young adults remaining married. In addition, the average age at which people first get married has been increasing throughout the history of the United States. But marriage is not yet a dead institution. Since it is not, we might investigate why the marriage contract is such a customary arrangement. Perhaps we might better observe that the "traditional" marriage contract is undergoing a transition; it is being modified by changing motives and roles.

ESTIMATING
ECONOMIC VALUES

It is of course easiest for us to look at marriage as an institution in which love plays a primary role. This view reflects our modern culture; in the marriage institutions of past societies, particularly in the East, love had little if anything to do with getting married. But today, at least for most people in this country, love plays a role. In fact, we might consider the major benefit of marriage to be a reduction in the search costs for love and companionship. Once a mate is found and a marriage made, love and companionship (sexual and otherwise) can be obtained with much less effort than must be expended by single individuals in search of the same goals. Of course, long-term **pair bonds** need not always be legalized by the state in order for people to obtain the mutual benefits. Whatever the reason, however, most persons seek legal bonds. Perhaps the state sanctioning of the marriage contract and the difficulty of reneging on that contract give a sense of security to the partners involved. More importantly, perhaps, there are definite materialistic reasons for legalizing marriage: to establish clear lines of inheritance of material property; and to establish legal responsibility for the care of any children resulting from the marriage (although marriage is not necessary, only legally admitted paternity).

MARRIAGE: COSTS
AND BENEFITS

If we are willing to make some fairly general assumptions, we can estimate the economic value of marriage to both men and women. In 1884, long before today's feminist and liberation movements, Friedrich Engels maintained that monogamous marriage as it had developed in the West was little more than a contractual system by which men exploited women.[1] This argument, of course, ignores some of the important features of marriage today. For one thing, the marriage contract is usually voluntary; hence, both parties can be presumed to be better off married than unmarried (at least for a while). Marriage also involves **specialization**; members of the family specialize in individual endeavors in order to increase the general welfare of the family unit. Moreover, the female member of the family unit, *particularly if she does not work for wages or salary*, receives at least part of the income that is *not* spent on goods and services that only benefit the male. In other words, the nonemployed wife obtains services from jointly consumed goods, such as houses, cars, and stereo systems, in addition to making her own personal consumption expenditures, such as on food and clothing. Of course, she does not obtain these goods and services free of charge, because the specialization aspect of the marriage may require that she do certain tasks. (This situation is reversed, obviously, for young, married, college student families in which the female partner works while the male partner continues higher education.)

Although people certainly would not marry if the benefits were not at least equal to the costs, the benefits of marriage most often mentioned are such non-monetary ones as love, companionship, and children. But there are also economic benefits; most obviously, to a nonemployed woman the economic benefit of marriage is total family income minus the specific personal expenses of other family members, representing the income available for her benefit.

We can obtain a rough approximation of the average lifetime income available for the benefit of a wife by looking at Bureau of the Census data on lifetime income. We take those data and adjust them for taxes paid and then subtract the personal consumption expenditures of other members of the family unit. If we are considering a two-person family, then we subtract the personal expenditures of the husband. When these calculations are done, over the lifetime of the woman in the average two-person family, $382,423 is usable by the wife. In other words, this is the average net economic benefits from marriage. We therefore might conclude that marriage is a valuable economic alternative for many women, viewed only from a dollars and cents point of view, of course.

**CRYPTO-
SERVANTS**

This number may be large, but certainly does not tell the true story. In fact, the women's liberation movement today is attempting to make known the true costs of marriage to the female partner and, even more, the benefits of marriage to the male. Economist John Kenneth Galbraith believes that a large amount of social anxiety has arisen from the conversion of women to the role of **crypto-servant** (*crypto* meaning "secret, not seeming"). That is, women are consigned to the function of managing and executing for their families the high level of consumption

[1]Friedrich Engels, *The Origin of the Family, Private Property and the State* (New York: International Publishers, 1942).

"Henry, I've gone as far as I can in this field. I'm leaving you."

the modern economy permits. Galbraith considers this to be a degrading exploitation:

> *The conversion of women into a crypto-servant class was an economic accomplishment of the first importance. Menially employed servants were available only to a majority of the preindustrial population; the servant-wife is available, democratically, to almost the entire present male population. Were the workers so employed subject to pecuniary compensation, they would be by far the largest single category in the labor force. The value of the services of housewives has been calculated somewhat impressionistically at roughly one-fourth of total Gross National Product.[2]*

Dr. Galbraith has a strong point, but at least some facts contradict the notion that there is an *increasing* amount of female exploitation within the family unit. For example, from 1950 to 1977 the proportion of married women working or seeking work outside the home rose from 24 to 45 percent. (Of course, this does not mean that women are not exploited outside of the family; but we will say more on that later.)

In much the same way that we earlier estimated the value of marriage to the women, we can numerically show the value of marriage to the man.

[2]John Kenneth Galbraith, *Economics and the Public Purpose* (Boston: Houghton–Mifflin, 1973).

MEASURING THE VALUE OF HOUSEWIVES' SERVICES

In numerous tragic accidents every year, women who are both wives and mothers are taken away from their families, most commonly in automobile accidents. When a negligent party is at fault, the husband and family often sue to recover the lost economic value of the wife. Added up, the numbers are indeed startling. To replace a wife and mother requires housekeepers, tutors for the children, extra repair services around the house, extra gardening services, and, of course, some sort of compensation for the "loss of consortium" (affection, companionship, etc.) suffered by the husband. In a sample calculation, it was found that to compensate the family for lost housekeeping services alone (with no allowance for tutoring, love and affection, etc.) would cost over $100,000 for a 37-year-old wife and mother until age 65.

It is certainly not clear who is getting the better deal in marriage because, at least economically, the man and the woman both benefit.

The data also clearly show that specialization vis-a-vis housework and household obligations, including child care, still enters into the structure of a family in which both the husband and the wife work. In a study done in France, Poland, Russia, and the United States, it was found that the average employed women spent over two hours a day doing housework, compared to the less than one-half hour a day that men spent doing the cooking, home chores, laundry, and marketing. Employed men and women seem to spend about the same amount of time doing other household chores, such as gardening, animal care, errands, and shopping. Except for the Soviet Union, employed married women spent more time than men in child care. Since it was presumed that the women worked the same number of hours as the men, it is interesting to note what the women had to give up in order to devote more time to housework and child rearing. They spent less time participating in mass media, such as radio and television, and also less time participating in study and religion.[3] In other words, they seem to have less choice in the things they do. It will be interesting to see if similar studies done in the future will show the same pattern of role-*playing* rather than role-*sharing* in the typical household where both parents work. Will the man and woman be true equals?

EMPLOYED WIVES AND THEIR CONTRIBUTION

There has been a distinct change in the proportion of wives employed outside the home. Today, it is probably in excess of 45 percent. Their contribution to the family income has increased almost as dramatically. From 1960 to 1970, it jumped from 21 percent to 26 percent. Today, the estimate is that 28 percent of all family money income is earned by wives. We can surmise that wives work not only because of financial need, but also for personal fulfillment. Financial need can be caused by (a) getting started in a home, (b) paying extra bills, (c) financing a husband's education, and (d) paying for children's education. With respect to personal fulfillment, it is due to both the increased percentage of women today who are trained for work and of the increased desire by women to have a career of their own.

[3]Alexander Szalai, *The Use of Time* (The Hague: Mouton & Company, 1972), pp. 584-588.

**VOLUNTARY
MARRIAGE
DISSOLUTIONS**

In some cities in the United States, there are more divorces than marriages on any given day. Look at the vital statistics page in the Los Angeles *Times*, for example. The trend is obvious: divorces are increasing not only in the United States but also in the rest of the world. Figure 5-1 shows the per thousand number of divorces in this country over the past half century.

The dissolution of a marriage is, of course, an economic as well as a noneconomic act. Divorce may occur for any number of reasons. And those reasons may not correspond very well with the legal reasons given in court: couples wishing for more than just a friendship may decide to divorce after they "fall out of love"; marriages often dissolve because of money problems or the simple incompatibility of two human beings. When children are involved, they, too, partake in any of the costs and benefits of the decision. Child psychologists have recently discovered that children are often better off living with a single parent than living with both parents in an uncomfortable, disruptive family situation.

The upsurge in divorces may be accounted for by two key changes in American society, one economic, the other social. In the first place, the cost of divorce has fallen as the legal fees have dropped and the courts have become more lenient on the grounds for divorce. Of course, many states still recognize only such things as provable adultery as grounds for divorce; but others, such as California,

Figure 5-1 U.S. Divorces Per 1,000 Females 15 Years or Older

Before World War II, the average was fewer than 9 divorces per 1,000 females. The half decade right after the war saw a rise in divorce rates, which settled down to an average figure of fewer than 10 per 1,000 females from 1950 to about 1963. (Beginning in 1960, figures include Alaska and Hawaii.) Then the rate started rising again, reaching over 15 per 1,000 in the 1970s. (The 1978 figure is an estimate.)

Source: *Current Population Reports, Series P-120.*

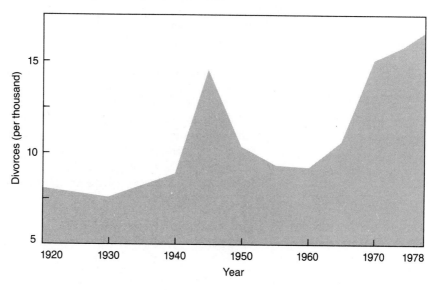

Ohio, and Washington, have essentially eliminated the need for seeking any grounds at all when both parties involved are mutually agreeable to the divorce settlement and there are no children. In other words, "no fault" divorce is in the process of being legalized in more and more states.

Divorce "by mail" is becoming increasingly popular throughout the United States. A number of enterprising companies are even offering do-it-yourself divorce kits. For example, a number of Divorce Yourself franchises have sprouted up in New York. The kit costs less than $100 and theoretically saves on lawyer's fees, which can, even in an uncontested divorce in a no-fault state, be in excess of $500. According to an article in *New York Magazine*, the kits sometimes work and sometimes don't.[4] Many people, especially lawyers, do not approve of these kits.

The act of divorce has become more acceptable and the treatment of divorcees by friends, in general, more favorable and, hence, less costly. Divorcees may not be treated in exactly the same way by all of their friends as they were when they were married, but the social stigma once attached to divorce is slowly but surely dying out.

Another reason for relatively high divorce rates in recent years has often been placed at the feet of the women's liberation movement, an important subject to which we now turn.

THE LIBERATION OF WOMEN

The women's liberation movement is not new. The first women's rights convention was held in 1848 in Seneca Falls, New York, with Elizabeth Cady Stanton and Lucretia Mott its promoters. The purposes of that convention included expanding women's employment and educational opportunities.

Today's women's movement is referred to by its members as the Second Wave, coming after a 50-year pause following the passage of the Nineteenth Amendment and the achievement of suffrage for women in 1920. The current movement can be said to have begun with Betty Freidan's book, *The Feminine Mystique*, which detailed "sexism," or the "disease which has no name" in the suburbia of the 1950s.

Though often identified as a middle-class movement, the women's liberation movement seeks to define and eradicate sexism from all spheres of life for all women. Although the movement seems to be centered in the United States, demands of women in many other countries for such things as safe and legal abortions are rising. In this country, such organizations as the National Organization for Women (NOW) seek to promote equal opportunities for women in employment, education, obtaining credit, and so on. They seek equality largely through the courts and by lobbying legislatures. In addition, local organizations focus on such issues as eliminating sexism from grade school textbooks (in which Dick runs and Sally watches him) and challenging sexist advertisements. Apart from such attempts to alter the institutional framework of American society—including a national campaign to ratify the Equal Rights Amendment to the U.S. Constitution—there is widespread use of "consciousness raising" groups to foster communica-

---

[4]William Flanagan, "You Don't Need a Lawyer to Get a Divorce . . . But It Helps," *New York Magazine*, December 6, 1976, pp. 107-108.

tion among women who sometimes feel isolated in their homes, and to develop an alternative to the sex role conditioning that the women's movement sees as the root of sex bias in society.

Today's women's liberation movement has succeeded in creating an awareness of discrimination in the labor market based on sex, as indicated in Table 5-1. A few years ago, through the efforts of the federal Equal Employment Opportunity Commission, the movement obtained a $50 million settlement against AT&T for alleged sexist practices. Though it presents many diverse demands and speaks with no single voice, the effects of the women's movement are being felt in every household in America.

SPECIALIZATION AND LIBERATION

We should note that if in fact women wish to have complete equality within marriage, then one of the reasons for marriage as it exists in our culture is thereby attenuated. That reason is specialization. For those who wish to specialize in specific activities such as earning income or raising children, *complete* equality of work load within the family unit may not allow for this specialization. The general economic welfare of the family unit may fall. Of course, despecialization within the family unit is not necessarily bad, for if it brings more emotional harmony to the household, then even though the household may be worse off in economic welfare, it may be better off overall. Specialization does not imply that it is necessarily the female who should specialize in housework. Nor does liberation necessarily imply total sharing of *all* tasks; only that an element of choice be available for the female. This element, of course, should be discussed before the two parties enter into a marriage.

Table 5-1

Median Wage or Salary Income of Full-Time Year-round Workers, by Sex and Selected Major Occupation Group, 1975.

Here we present the median wage or salary income of men and women in various occupational groups. Women's median wage or salary income expressed as a percent of men's reaches a high of 70.9 percent for service workers down to a low of 39.7 percent for sales workers.

Source: The Conference Board.

MAJOR OCCUPATION GROUP	MEDIAN WAGE OR SALARY INCOME		WOMEN'S MEDIAN WAGE OR SALARY INCOME AS PERCENT OF MEN'S
	Women	Men	
Professional and technical workers	$10,980	$16,450	66.7
Nonfarm managers, officials, and proprietors	9,008	16,540	54.5
Clerical workers	7,140	12,101	59.0
Sales workers	5,520	13,914	39.7
Operatives	5,417	11,471	47.2
Service workers (except private household)	6,433	9,075	70.9

NONMARRIAGE AND THE OUTSIDE WORLD

For those women who decide not to marry, or are widowed or divorced, important social and economic pressures await them. Even though the Civil Rights Act of 1964 specifies that it is illegal to discriminate by sex (as well as by race or national origin), not all groups will necessarily be treated equally in the job market or the marketplace in general; nor will they be treated equally by their peers or society in general. Until recently, single women generally had an extremely difficult time obtaining credit—purchasing houses, cars, etc., on time. In many places, divorced women with children have had, and still have, difficulty renting houses or apartments. Because the single, widowed, or divorced woman has been considered less "stable," entrepreneurs in their role as profit-makers have sought to treat these groups of potential buyers differently from other groups. Prejudice is difficult to eliminate. In the job market, a single woman often faces tremendous barriers, not the least of which are created by the past behavior of single women taken as a whole. In the past, the life cycle of a woman generally involved getting married and having children, for whom she was expected to care full time. Employers have often been reluctant to hire a young single woman at the same wage rate at which they would hire a man for fear that the woman would eventually quit to get married and raise a family, thus taking with her all of the specific training that the employer had invested in her. This reason for giving less pay for equal work to women is, of course, slowly changing as more and more women continue to work throughout their married and child-rearing years. At most, such women are gone from the job market only during the pregnancy and nursing period, but then reenter the market, giving the child or children to babysitters or child care centers during working hours. Men are also given leave during temporary physical disabilities. (Recently it has been suggested that *both* men and women be given pregnancy leaves!)

A NEW BENEFIT OF STAYING SINGLE

The facts and figures above should not be your only guides for decisions about marriage. We have simply attempted to point out both the costs and the benefits of marriage and divorce. One fairly new hidden cost of marriage is worth mentioning to conclude this chapter. Getting married used to lower your tax burden because Uncle Sam treated married people differently from single people. But single people got together and lobbied to have the taxes changed. Now the law has gone the other way. Table 5-2 shows the tax savings that can be had today if you decide to live together and not get married. If the income of both parties is relatively high, the savings can be quite considerable. You might question what Congress is up to, for, usually, when the benefits of doing something increase, more people want to do it. Should we conclude that Congress is trying to break up the institution of marriage and promote legally unsanctified cohabitation?

THE FUTURE OF THE AMERICAN FAMILY

We have seen in this chapter that divorces are on the rise in the United States. Indeed, marriages end in divorce more often in the United States than anywhere else in the world. Does this mean that the institution of marriage is actually disappearing and with it the American family? Some experts believe that this is indeed the case. They point out that in the past, "extended" families provided each generation with economic security, emotional nourishment, and social activities. At the beginning of this nation, Americans made their livings largely from farming, and they often traveled great distances in groups to seek better farming conditions. Males traditionally labored in the fields; females in the home. As we became a more industrialized nation, men left the home to work in factories, thus reducing contact with family members. Finally, wives and mothers also began to take jobs outside the homes. Statistics confirm that even our traditional idea of a family of a husband and wife and children, let alone an extended family, seems to be deteriorating. By 1980, almost 20 percent of all school age children will be with one parent (and not always the mother since recently more men are taking custody). By that same time, 15 percent of all families will be headed by a woman.

Table 5-2

Personal Income Tax Reform, 1973

	TAX* ON BASIS OF		
Family Income	Joint Return	Two Unmarried Persons	Saving from Remaining Unmarried
$10,000	$ 1,257	$ 1,114	$ 143
15,000	2,298	2,136	162
20,000	3,582	3,192	390
25,000	5,068	4,356	710
30,000	6,794	5,738	1,056
40,000	10,858	8,902	1,956
50,000	15,635	12,640	2,995

*Assumes standard deduction throughout.

In spite of what we see happening, interview surveys constantly show that individuals rank "family" near the top in terms of important sources of personal satisfaction.[5] Thus, for those who believe that family life is indeed important, the future may be less grim than recent trends would lead us to believe.

THE FAMILY—
ANOTHER VIEW

If we compare the family structure of American society today, not with what we think it was in the past, but with what it actually was, we get a different picture. A recent study by Mary Jo Bane, associate director of the Center for Research on Women at Wellsley College, points out that:

1. *The extended family never really existed in the United States on a wide scale. In colonial America, only 6 percent of U.S households had children, parents, and grandparents. The latest figures early in this decade show that it's still 6 percent.*
2. *More families have two parents now (84.3 percent) than there were in colonial days (70 percent).*
3. *Divorce may be disrupting families today; death did it in colonial times. As the death rate has dropped, the divorce rate has increased, but not at the same rate.*
4. *Mothers during colonial times, laboring from dawn to dusk doing housework without today's labor-saving machines, apparently did not spend any more time in raising their children than working mothers do today.*

Professor Bane tells us that yesterday's family was much like today's: "The nuclear family, consisting of parents living with their own children and no other adults, has been the predominant family form in America since the earliest period on which historians have data. . . ." Relationships among relatives appear to have been historically what they are now: "Complex patterns of companionship that only occasionally involve sharing bed and board."[6]

SUMMARY

1. Our Western view of marriage should be contrasted with the view of past Mideastern and European societies, in which love had little to do with the act of getting married. Rather, marriage was a type of economic arrangement negotiated by a family patriarch.
2. Friedrich Engels once said that marriage developed in the West was little more than a contractual system whereby men exploited women.
3. Specialization within a household may allow for both the wife and the husband to have a higher standard of living.
4. If we measure the value of wives' services to their husbands and families, the number becomes very large very quickly. For example, some economists believe that the typical wife's services would cost her husband at least $5,000 to $10,000 a year to replace.
5. There has been an increase in women working outside of the home. Their contribution is almost 30 percent of all family income. Liberation may lead to less specialization in the household. However, it may merely mean more freedom of choice for the female in a pair bond situation.

[5]See "What Future for the American Family?" *Changing Times*, December 1976, p. 9.
[6]Mary Jo Bane, *Here to Stay: American Families in the Twentieth Century* (New York: Basic Books, 1977).

6. Latest statistics show increasing divorce rates, a larger fraction of children living with only one parent, and a reduction in the importance of the family. Comparisons of current data, however, with data from colonial times show that the nuclear family is just as strong today as it was then.

<table>
<tr><td>QUESTIONS FOR THOUGHT AND DISCUSSION</td><td>

1. Do you think it is appropriate to study consumer economics within the framework of the family unit? Or would it be better to discuss it for a one-person household?
2. Do you think that costs outweigh the benefits of any marriage? Why?
3. Does specialization necessarily imply that women should do housework and men should work outside the home for money income?
4. Do you think Professor Galbraith's contention that women are crypto-servants in the United States is a valid one? Why?

</td></tr>
<tr><td>THINGS TO DO</td><td>

1. Look at the vital statistics page of your local newspaper and see what the ratio is of marriages to divorces in your community. Go to the library and look at that same page, say, 30 years ago. Has there been any change?
2. Try to figure out how you would measure the implicit—that is, unstated—value of the services of a homemaker. What would you add to the normal things, such as housecleaning and preparing meals? Would companionship be included? Would gardening activities? Would your computations change if the person in question enjoyed doing those things?

</td></tr>
</table>

SELECTED READINGS

Cotton, Dorothy W. *The Case for the Working Mother.* New York: Stein & Day, 1965.

Engels, Friedrich. *The Origins of the Family, Private Property and the State.* New York: International Publishers, 1942.

Galbraith, John Kenneth. *Economics and the Public Purpose.* Boston: Houghton Mifflin, 1973.

Gross, A. "Marriage Counseling for Unwed Couples." *New York Times Magazine*, April 24, 1977, p. 52.

Grossman, Allyson Sherman. "The Labor Force Patterns of Divorced and Separated Women." *Monthly Labor Review* 100 (January 1977): 48-53.

Horn, J. "Life-Giving Properties of Marriage." *Psychology Today*, January 1977, p. 20.

Horner, Matina. *Femininity and Successful Achievement: A Basic Inconsistency.* Lansing, Mich.: University of Michigan Research Study, 1972.

Konopka, Gisela. "Social Change and Human Values." *Journal of Home Economics*, September 1974, pp. 12-14.

"The Legal Side of Living Together." *Changing Times*, May 1976, pp. 27-29.

Mead, Margaret. "Too Many Divorces, Too Soon." *Redbook*, Fall 1974, p. 72.

Roszak, Betty, and Roszak, Theodore, eds. *Masculine/Feminine: Readings in Sexual Mythology and the Liberation of Women.* New York: Harper & Row, 1969.

"Teaching about Divorce." *Todays Education*, January 1977, p. 31.

Making a Decision about Children

GLOSSARY OF TERMS

Productive Asset

Anything that you own that produces income or satisfaction for you. A productive asset might be, for example, a tractor that you would use on a farm.

Consumption Good

A nonincome producing good or service that you use up in a very short period of time, as opposed to a productive asset. A movie, for example, is a consumption good. So are food and similar products.

Opportunity Cost

The true cost of any action you take. For example, the opportunity cost of your reading this book could be measured possibly by the wages you would receive if you were working during the same time instead of reading the book. The opportunity cost of your education could be measured by what you might have been able to make at a full-time job.

In the "model" situation, once a new family unit is formed, its members initially are the husband and wife. The decision whether to enlarge the family unit must be faced from the very beginning. Long ago, when there was little knowledge about conception and the possibility of its

prevention, this decision usually was not even considered: the children came when they did and there seemed little way to stop them. Of course, men and women always had the choice of forestalling marriage to a later date, and abstinence has always been, and continues to be, an effective means of preventing conception. However, things have changed, at least for most people in the United States.

Decisions about when to have children and how many to have can now be considered by both parties in the pair bond. This is a particularly relevant decision to be made in an era in which children are not the **productive asset** they used to be. On the farm in the old days, raising children was a means of obtaining needed workers. But today, with less than 5 percent of the population working on farms, children are raised mainly as a **consumption good**; that is, not as an investment that will yield income for the parents later on.

THE COST OF CONSUMING

To figure out rationally the size of family desired, a couple might be interested in knowing the expected costs of raising children. The estimates of these costs range from about $70,000 to $150,000 per child! The costs,

of course, are dependent on the income level of the parents: an upper-class family spends more on clothing and education than a lower-class family. If, however, you expect to be a middle-class family in which all of your children go to college, be prepared to come up with the upper end figure for each child. Many families start providing for college education as soon as their children are born, by way of trust funds and insurance programs.

Using family budget studies prepared by the Bureau of Labor Statistics, we can come up with an average figure for raising a child to age 21 in a family with an annual income of between $17,000 and $19,000. Table C-1 gives expenses for the first 18 years of life, plus 4 years in a public college or university. A private college would cost quite a bit more.

More Costs Involved

None of the cost estimates of raising children take account of the *time cost* for the parents. When the wife or husband is prevented from working or from doing other things she or he would rather do because the child or children must be cared for, a cost is incurred. Generally, this cost is called the **opportunity cost** of raising children.

If the mother or father must give up the opportunity to pursue a career, to get more education, to learn ceramics or photography or whatever, then these foregone alternatives are obviously a real cost. Boone A. Turchi, a population specialist at the University of North Carolina, estimated that a woman working in a family with total earnings of $12,000 a year today will give up approximately $100,000 in terms of the 12,900 salaried hours that she must lose because of her children. However approximate such an estimate is, it gives us an indication of how expensive the opportunity cost is of raising children.

Often forgotten in discussions of whether or not children are advisable in a marriage are the problems that children bring into the family unit. A recent survey by the University of Michigan Institute for Social Research discovered that most women seem to identify the time before the arrival of their first child and after the departure of the last grown child as the happiest times of their marriage. Some sociologists and marriage counselors maintain that childless couples have happier marriages than do parents.

At the very least, the married couple can expect the birth of the first child to create difficulties in their relationship with one another. In this period, the sexual life of the couple is disrupted; and in this period there is potential for jealousy, since the new mother spends a large amount of time either being with or thinking about her child that she probably once spent with her mate. Not every husband adjusts gracefully to such a change.

It must be anticipated, also, that with the arrival of a new child or more children, considerably more housework has to be done. This is particularly true during the first six or so years of each child's life, when it is difficult to get the child to clean up after himself or herself, or to assume responsibility for his or her own personal care. Couples who are used to immaculate households often have difficulties readjusting to the disorder brought by children's playthings scattered throughout the home.

A GRAVE DECISION

The decision to become a parent is the decision to bring into the world other human beings who must be cared for and loved and for whom the parents will feel a responsibility to raise in a suitable manner. To become parents is to take on the responsibility of fostering a suitable environment for their children, that is, of creating an economic, social, and moral foundation for each new member of the family. This task is generally not taken lightly and, hence, is a subject of numerous soul-searching sessions between the parents and later among the parents and children. It is particularly true when children get to be teenagers and reach the stage at which they rebel against their parents. In any event, in the United States decisions about having children are certainly changing. In 1970, the birth rate was 88 per 1,000 women age 15 through 44. By 1973, it had dropped to 69 per 1,000, and is estimated to be about 66 per 1,000 in 1978. A recent survey conducted by the U.S. Department of Commerce indicates that young married women between 18 and 24 plan to have an average of fewer than 2.3 children. Contrast this with the 1965 planned average of 3.1.

WHEN IS THE BEST TIME TO HAVE CHILDREN?

If you ask a random sample of people when the best time to have children is, you will usually get three answers: never, right away, and later. Let us look at the two answers in which it has been decided to have children. (We will discuss below the people who answer "never.") If pregnancy and childbearing

Table C-1

The Cost of Raising a Child

The calculations presented in the table are based on the assumption that the annual rate of inflation will average 4 percent per year. It is also based on the assumption that college costs will climb at 8 percent a year

Food	$14,100
Clothing	7,300
Housing	7,000
Medical Expenses	4,500
Recreation	2,700
Miscellaneous	15,000
College	24,000
TOTAL	$74,600

occur at the very beginning of a marriage, the benefits are that the parents are younger while their children are growing and can perhaps relate to them more easily than if they waited. Moreover, by the time the children leave home, parents are still relatively young and can enjoy an active child-free marriage for a good number of remaining years.

On the other hand, the costs of early pregnancy and childbearing are just as important. The sooner children come into the family unit, the less time the couple has to be alone with each other. One thing that new parents are amazed at is the lack of privacy and spontaneity in their life once they have children. Unless you find yourself in a pretty unusual situation, you cannot do everything you want to do once you have children, particularly when they are small. Also, because most couples are financially less well off when they are young and just married, the financial burden of children is heavier. Older couples may have larger and more stable incomes to support children.

At the other extreme, waiting until the family is financially secure to have children presents problems of its own. The costs of waiting are, of course, the benefits of not waiting: the parents are older while the children are growing up and therefore (although no generalization is certain) may be less able to relate to their children; by the time the children leave home, the parents may think they are too old to enjoy an active child-free life themselves. An important medical consideration is that

the higher the age of the mother at conception, the higher is the probability of mental retardation. New mothers over 40, for example, run an 18,000 percent greater risk of having a Mongoloid infant than do new mothers under 25.

Obviously, discussions about deciding when to have children imply the ability of the parents to control conception. It may be

useful, then, to outline the available information centers where prospective parents—or even nonparents—may seek information.

FAMILY PLANNING INFORMATION

Of course, a couple seeking family planning information can look first to their private doctor. If the private doctor is a

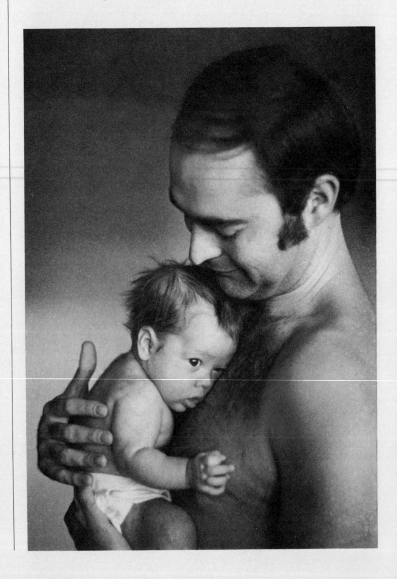

general practitioner or internist, he or she will usually recommend that the woman see a gynecologist who specializes in these matters. He or she will usually require a complete physical examination and will learn about her medical history in order to choose the most suitable birth control technique, whether it be pills, intrauterine device, diaphragm, condoms, or some other method. Or the man can have a vasectomy; but this method is advisable only if the couple wants to remain permanently childless, for the rate of successful reversal of vasectomies is extremely low. (Of course, if an unwanted conception has occurred, abortion is an alternative, although for many, an unacceptable one.)

A couple who feels that they cannot afford the services of a private medical practitioner has an alternative in most states. They can go to Planned Parenthood centers where, after the couple attends a class on birth control, volunteer doctors provide the contraceptive of their choice at a nominal fee, often no more than the supply cost.

SOCIAL PRESSURES TO BECOME A PARENT

Besides the tax deduction that every child gives to parents, there seems to be in much of American life a bias in favor of having children. It can be expected that about after two years of marriage, outsiders to the family unit will start to wonder —discreetly, of course—when the children are coming. According to Ellen Peck, author of *The Baby Trap* (New York: Bernard Geis Publishers, 1971), people "exert ingenious pressures on you to have children. People say your're selfish, that you're missing the greatest things in life or that you're denying your maternal instinct. And the smuggest threat: 'You'll be sorry when you're old.' " To fight against this bias in America, a group has been founded called the National Organization for Nonparents (NON). It has linked itself with Planned Parenthood and Zero Population Growth (ZPG). Whereas Planned Parenthood and ZPG recommend that all couples limit themselves to one or two children, NON is asking whether it would not be preferable if some couples had no children at all and others had six or seven. Anthropologist Margaret Mead contends that "childbearing will become a vocation to be pursued by a diminishing group of people who really want to become parents."

Whether NON and Margaret Mead are right remains to be seen, but the pro-child bias in America today is obvious, at least to any married couple who has put off having children for a while or who seeks permanent contraception.

THE JOYS OF PARENTHOOD

When all the cards are counted, however, and even after looking at all the costs we outlined above, couples become parents because of the expected joy of raising a child, of watching him or her grow and develop into a young adult. But while it is difficult to put in monetary terms the benefits of having children, the *costs* remain and must be reckoned with, and the distribution of those costs within the family unit must also be understood. That is why the decision to have children generally works out for the best when both the man and the woman can agree as to the advisability, the number, and the timing. The decision to get married, as well as the decision to have children, must rank highest among the lifetime decisions that most of us must face. It can be hoped that the information contained in the previous chapter and in this consumer issue will help you make the right decision for you. (If you are already married and/or have children, they may have given you some retrospective insight into your decisions and their consequences.)

SUMMARY

1. Children are no longer the productive asset they used to be when we had a predominantly agricultural society and they could work on the farm.

2. The costs of raising children include not only all the actual money spent, but also the time involved in their upbringing. This time is called the opportunity cost of child raising.

3. The birth rate in the United States has been falling dramatically in the last couple of decades. Its present level will probably give us zero population growth in the not-too-distant future.

4. Family planning information can be obtained from a general practitioner or internist, specialists such as gynecologists and urologists, and Planned Parenthood centers.

QUESTIONS FOR THOUGHT AND DISCUSSION

1. What would happen to birth rates if families were taxed on

the number of children they had?

2. Would it be possible for our society to die out because of an insufficient birth rate?

3. Is there any way you could ever determine whether child-free couples have happier marriages than other couples?

4. When do you think is the best time to have children?

5. Do you think that the social pressures to become a parent are increasing or decreasing?

THINGS TO DO

1. Try to figure out the costs that your parents incurred in raising you to age 18.

2. Is there any way you could figure out the time cost that your parents incurred in your upbringing? If you have children, what are your time costs?

3. Find out the latest U.S. Department of Commerce, Bureau of Census statistics on birth rates. Have our rates actually dropped below those that produce zero population growth? What are the Bureau's projections for the future?

SELECTED READINGS

"Abortion Battle." Newsweek, February 4, 1974.

Bettelheim, B. "Look into Your Future: Child Raising." Today's Health, April 1973, pp. 56-57.

Brenton, M. "Families Anonymous: Help for Distressed Parents." Good Housekeeping, May 1977, p. 94.

Cutright, P. "Timing the First Birth: Does It Matter?" Journal of Marriage and Family, November 1973, pp. 585-595.

"Fertility Rates; Federal Programs." New Republic 171 (July 6, 1974): pp. 7-8.

Gutmann, D. "Men, Women, and the Parental Imperative." Commentary 47 (April 24, 1974) p. 4.

Hoover, Mary, and Modsen, Charles Jr. The Responsive Parent: Meeting the Realities of Parenthood Today. New York: Parents Magazine Press, 1972.

Maddsen, Clifford K. Parents/Children/Discipline: A Positive Approach. Boston: Allyn & Bacon, 1972.

Myrdal, K. G. "Birth Control and Poverty." Current 167 (November 1974): 42-44.

Peck, Ellen. The Baby Trap. New York: Bernard Geis Associates, 1971.

Sklar, J., and Berkov, B. "Abortion, Illegitimacy, and the American Birth Rate." Science 185 (September 13, 1974): 909-915.

Smith, James D. "Birth Control and Economic Well-Being." In Human Behavior in Economic Affairs, ed. by Strumpel Burkhard, et al., San Francisco: Jossey-Bass, 1972, pp. 501-522.

Special Issue on Working Mothers. Parents Magazine, April 1977.

Vahamian, T., and Olds, S. W. "Will Your Children Break . . . or Make . . . Your Marriage?" Parent's Magazine 49 (August 1974): 33-35.

GLOSSARY OF TERMS

Investment in Human Capital

Any activity that makes you more productive. You as an individual can produce just like a machine, which is physical capital. You are, on the other hand, human capital; and when you go to school, you make an investment in yourself because you make yourself better able to perform on the job.

On-the-Job Training

Training that you receive while you are working on a particular job. On-the-job training will raise your productivity and therefore your value to your employer.

Age-Earnings Profile

The profile of how earnings change with your age. When you are young and just starting out working, your earnings are low; as you get older, your earnings go up as you become more productive and work longer hours; and then your earnings start to fall.

The percentage of any given group who participate in the labor force. If, for example, 50 million of the 75 million females between the ages of 16 and 65 are working or looking for a job, then the female labor force participation rate would be two-thirds, or 66.67 percent.

The Consumer as Wage Earner

CHAPTER PREVIEW

☐ What does investing in yourself mean?

☐ What determines how productive you are and, therefore, how much you earn?

☐ What is the payoff to going to school?

☐ What are the differences between wages made in the various occupations?

6 The amount one spends often depends on decisions made about education, training, and occupation. To be sure, there are many different causes of differences in our incomes. Some persons are more clever than others, and so in a similar situation might make more income than others. Some persons have more artistic ability than others, and this, too, can cause a difference in income. Some persons prefer riskier jobs at higher rates of pay than others do: if you are willing to work as a welder on the tops of high-rise buildings, you will certainly make more money than you would as a welder in a very safe ground-floor welding shop. And some people end up making more money because they inherit a fortune from their parents or are put in a well-placed position by a close relative.

But more important, at least for those of you who are now making the investment (right: I said you are making an investment), is your decision to go to school. That decision will permanently affect the level of your command over goods and services in your role as a consumer. Now, what could this possibly mean? You may think you have never made an investment in your life, but you will soon see that you did and, for most of you, not a bad one either.

INVESTING IN YOURSELF

Few persons think it strange or unfair that somebody with an M.A. degree is paid more than somebody with a grade school diploma. In the first place, the M.A. has spent a long time acquiring his or her specialized knowledge; in the second place, the grade school graduate probably could do little of the work the M.A. does (and vice versa). And a basic fact of life is that individuals are generally paid only what they are worth to employers. Education can be looked at, then, as a process of making workers more productive. That is why we could say that you were making an investment in yourself: Going to school is an **investment in human capital**, as it is called, an investment in human beings. Usually, the longer you go to school, the more new skills you learn. You may become a better thinker; you generally become a more responsible person, at least in working situations. Why otherwise would businesses pay more for college grads than for high school grads when they could get the less-educated people to work for them for less money?

Do not get the mistaken impression, however, that going to school will automatically guarantee you a higher income. If you specialize in an activity or a field that no one cares about, the *demand* for your services is going to be quite small. No amount of services you could supply would induce others to hire you at high wages, because what ultimately determines the individual's wages or income is the supply and demand for different types of labor.

WAGES AND PRODUCTIVITY

For any given specialty, the more trained you are, the more productive you will be and, therefore, the higher will be the demand for your services. One way to predict your future income is to analyze how productive you can be in doing something. Employers have a tendency to end up paying workers their exact worth, no more, no less. (Of course, like any general rule, this one has a few exceptions.) Thus, anything you can do to make yourself more productive will result in a higher wage rate and a higher total lifetime earnings.

Formalized schooling is not the only way to invest in yourself; you can learn on your own by reading and practicing skills, or you can learn on the job. In fact,

on-the-job training is one of the chief means by which individuals increase their productivity, by which individuals invest in themselves. (Persons engaged in on-the-job training—for example, as apprentices—are usually paid less than after that training is over.) However, productivity cannot occur in a vacuum. You could be very productive at something that nobody values highly. That means that unless you choose wisely, your area of specialization may be something that society does not value highly and, hence, for which you will be relatively poorly paid. Very few would now think of specializing in learning how to make horseshoes. But, of course, some people were doing just that right at the time when horseshoes were no longer worth very much because of the introduction of mass-produced automobiles. Most of those people who spent time learning how to make horseshoes, after the fact, had made a mistake.

Ultimately, then, investing in yourself requires careful planning. That is to say, you must invest in yourself in a way that increases your productive capacities in areas that are demanded by the economy. If it looks like computer keypunch operators will be unneeded in the future because of optical scanning techniques, then you certainly do not want to specialize in computer keypunching. Choosing an occupation that benefits you most may require an investment in acquiring information about future demands for different types of jobs.

THE RATE OF RETURN TO EDUCATION

Although the evidence is overwhelming that an education is valuable, the old saying, "Get all the education you can get" does not apply equally to everybody; and it certainly is not meaningful without qualification, because you could be acquiring formal education for the rest of your life (as some perennial students do). We can give a general rule, though, and one that will be familiar to you: acquire more education as long as the expected benefits at least cover the costs. As to some of the expected benefits, Figure 6-1 shows the **age-earnings profile** for

**Figure 6-1
Age-Earning Profile
for Selected Degree
Holders**

Source: U.S. Department of
Commerce, Consumer
Income Series P—60, No. 74.

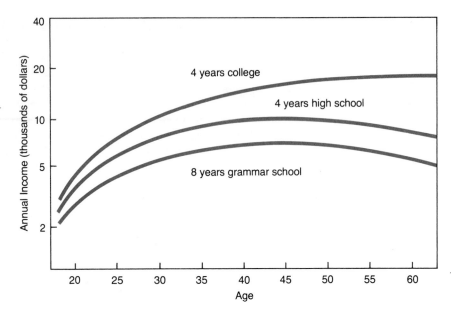

three levels of degree holders—grade school, high school, and college. Note that the more education you get, the higher the curve is. For example, the average high school graduate at 40 years of age may be earning 40 percent more than the average grade school graduate at 40 years of age. In dollars and cents, the figures are even more impressive. Table 6-1 shows the average lifetime earnings of various degree holders: college degree holders obviously make more than grade school degree holders.

What is often ignored in the discussion of college, or of higher education in general, is the noneconomic aspects of the whole process. Individuals change in some ways when they go to college: their tastes change; they are exposed to a broader array of possible life styles; and so on. How does one measure the value of these noneconomic goods? It isn't easy. Ultimately, only you, the individual, can measure that for yourself.

Table 6-1

**Average Lifetime Earnings
of Selected Degree Holders**

The average lifetime earnings of selected degree holders are given in this table. The difference between eight years of grammar school and four years of college is over $500,000. These figures are averages only and are not corrected for the timing of the income received. (Strictly speaking, these figures should be corrected [discounted] for timing, and all made comparable on a present value basis.)

Source: U.S. Department of Commerce.

LEVEL OF EDUCATION	AVERAGE LIFETIME EARNINGS
8 years of grammar school	$1,241,361
4 years of high school	1,574,280
4 years of college	1,800,413

COSTS, TOO

Of course, our general rule has its limits, because it might be more expensive to acquire the higher amount of education; and in fact it is. The main cost of going to college is *not* tuition and books; this cost ranks second, although we see in Table 6-2 that college is not cheap. The main component is the cost of foregone income —that is, the *opportunity cost* of not working. In other words, had you not gone to college, you could be working full time at some average salary for the four years you are in college and out of the job market. But even with the costs of foregone earnings, tuition, and books, the rate of return of investing in education is at least as good as the rate of return of investing in something like the stock market, and certainly higher than putting your savings into a savings and loan association account.[1]

It may be true that in certain years some college graduates cannot get jobs. But, rather than meaning that going to college is a bad deal, it means only that during up-and-down movements in business activity the demands for different types of college degree holders shift. Although you may be caught unaware and out of a job in your area of specialization during college, you still may have made the right choice.

Some of you, however, will have made the wrong choice. In fact, according to the Carnegie Commission, 300,000 to 900,000 students of the 8½ million enrolled should not be in college. Apparently, these students are attending college mainly because of social and parental pressures, rather than from personal choice.[2]

There are now several books backing up the Carnegie Commission's report, one by Caroline Bird entitled *The Case Against College* (New York: David McKay, 1975). She believes that going to college may well be "the dumbest investment" people can make. Ms. Bird contends that a Bachelor's degree doesn't help in obtaining a job and that college training doesn't enable a graduate to earn more money or live a more satisfying, "richer" life. Ms. Bird emphasizes luck and the right idea at the right time as contributing to the success for many people as opposed to the amount of advanced education that they have received. She doesn't even believe college "broadens" students or teaches them to think. What is college then? For all except about 25 percent of the students who love to learn, Ms. Bird believes that it is "at best a social center, a youth ghetto, an aging vat, and at worst a young folks' (rhymes with old folks') home, a youth house (rhymes with poor house) or even a prison . . . a place where young adults are set apart because they are superfluous people who are of no immediate use to the economy. . . ." Ms. Bird may be overstating her case, but she certainly has started a raging debate in academe throughout the country. In response to the book, the executive director of the Association of Independent California Colleges and Universities, Morgan Odall, states that within three years after graduation, more than 70 percent of those who graduated from college occupy jobs that they consider appropriate. He also states that one cannot deny U.S. census data, which show college graduates earning 40 percent more than nongraduates throughout their lifetime. Moreover, during downturns in the economy, unemployment is lowest among college graduates.

[1]This is obviously true for some people only; the statistics reflect only those who were successful at college. For computation, see Gary Becker, *Human Capital: A Theoretical and Empirical Analysis, with Special Reference to Education* (New York: Columbia University Press, 1964).

[2]*More Effective Uses of Resources: An Imperative for Higher Education* (The Carnegie Commission on Higher Education, June 1972).

Table 6-2

Costs of Attending Certain Public and Private Universities and Colleges, 1977

Source: New York Life Insurance Company, *College Costs Today.* (Available free; write to 51 Madison Avenue, New York, New York 10010.)

	UNDERGRADUATE ENROLLMENT	TUITION, FEES, ROOM AND BOARD	ADDITIONAL FOR OUT-OF STATERS
Alabama U	13,800	$1,845	$ 595
Amherst	1,450	5,676	—
Antioch	1,725	4,741	—
Auburn	14,580	1,809	525
Ball State	12,780	1,944	720
Bennington	595	6,550	—
Bowling Green	13,200	2,211	1,200
Brandeis	2,800	5,825	—
Brigham Young	27,000	2,165	360
Brown	5,150	6,297	—
Colorado U	16,800	2,210	1,542
Columbia	2,800	5,587	—
Delaware U	11,350	2,447	1,235
Earlham	1,200	4,805	—
Florida State	18,000	2,130	1,035
Georgia U	17,900	1,923	951
Harvard	5,600	6,430	—
Hofstra	5,000	4,888	—
Illinois U	24,900	2,002	860
Indiana State	11,000	1,869	990
Iowa U	13,000	1,986	1,410
Johns Hopkins	2,100	5,575	868
Kent State	16,000	2,265	—
Kentucky U	21,500	1,890	1,200
LSU	20,000	1,346	730
Massachusetts U	19,800	2,077	1,205
MIT	4,435	6,528	—
Michigan State	35,700	2,173	945
Michigan U	19,655	2,456	1,958
Missouri U	16,950	1,804	1,080
NYU	6,770	5,550	—
North Dakota U	8,375	1,627	728
Northeastern	14,000	4,327	—
Notre Dame	7,000	4,290	—
Ohio State	37,700	2,210	1,050
Penn State	49,000	2,484	1,200
Princeton	4,420	6,130	—
Purdue	24,300	2,140	950
Sarah Lawrence	775	6,690	—
Temple	14,000	2,830	1,200
Texas Tech.	23,000	1,381	1,080
Texas U	31,000	1,872	1,080
Tufts	3,925	5,997	—
UCLA	19,850	2,130	1,500
Virginia Polytech.	17,200	1,671	630
Western Michigan U	13,900	2,058	960
Yale	4,950	5,920	—

THE CHANGING WORLD OF FEMALE ENDEAVORS

Numerous data have been collected to show that women earn less than men. In fact, we commonly hear that women on average earn 60 percent of what men make. Although this figure does not in itself prove that discrimination and sexism operate in the labor market, it does indicate the prospects facing women in the labor market. What we want to look at is the changing characteristics of female labor market participation. In the first place, the **participation rate** of females has been rising steadily from 18.2 percent in 1890 to around 46 percent by 1977. That is, by 1977, 46 percent of females over the age of 16 were in the labor force.

With the new women's awareness in the air, it is not surprising that labor force participation has increased for women as a whole. Civil rights legislation and changing views on the role of women in society have opened to women an increasing number of occupations once restricted to men. Merely a partial listing of women workers in New York City alone now yields women carpenters ("Women's Woodwork"), movers ("Mother Truckers," "Tinkerbell Memorial Trucking Company"), restauranteurs ("Mother Courage," "Food Liberation Inc."), bar owners ("Bonnie and Clyde"), acting companies ("New York Tea Party"), housepainters ("Women Can Do"), and paperhangers ("Paper Hanging Lady"), as well as electricians, landscape artists, structural draftswomen, stock brokers, sound engineers, and recreational consultants. Elsewhere, the advertising of large firms is beginning to feature women in atypical occupations, such as Bell Telephone's female linepersons. (Note that these jobs are still very atypical. The vast majority of women still have a "traditional" woman's occupation.)

Sexism has worked two ways, though, and males have been discriminated against in certain occupations; there used to be few if any male telephone operators, airline stewards, or high school home economics teachers. We are finally hearing male voices when we call the operator, and being served by male stewards on airplanes—although women are not yet in evidence as pilots, air-traffic controllers, etc. In spite of the complaints that many males have lodged against the women's liberation movement, at least some of them have benefited, because the Civil Rights Act of 1964 has been used to eliminate discrimination against males in many occupations.

OCCUPATIONAL WAGE DIFFERENTIALS

Among the incomes of different occupations, at the top of the ladder, as we see in Table 6-3, are the so-called professions—medicine, dentistry, and law. Does that mean you should automatically go out and start studying medicine, dentistry, or law? Obviously not. You could be wasting your time. For example, unless you are able to get into an accredited medical school (and, of course, graduate from it), you cannot legally practice medicine in the United States. The ratio of applicants to acceptances in most medical schools is astounding. Therefore, unless your father is a doctor or you are an extremely good student in an extremely good school, the odds are against your admission to medical training.

The same is not true of law, however. There are numerous law schools that you can attend; you can even learn law at home by mail. Of course, you should not look only at the high salaries in law. To obtain a law degree, you must take three additional years of training after college, three more years of not earning any income. This additional cost of becoming a lawyer means that the rate of return of becoming a lawyer may be no higher than your doing something else.

Table 6-3 **Median Earnings** **by Occupation** **and Sex, 1974** Source: U.S. Bureau of the Census, *Current Population Reports*, Series P-60, Nos. 41, 53, 80 and 97.	**MALE**	**FEMALE**
TOTAL	$11,835	$6,772
Professional, technical, kindred workers	14,873	9,570
Self-employed	21,501	(B)
Physicians and surgeons	25,000+	(B)
Salaried	14,661	9,600
Engineers, technical	18,230	(B)
Physicians and surgeons	24,267	(B)
Teachers, primary and secondary	12,392	9,537
Farmers and farm managers	5,459	(B)
Managers and administrators, exc. farm	15,425	8,603
Self-employed	12,795	4,175
In retail trade	11,723	4,457
Salaried	16,079	9,151
Clerical and kindred workers	11,514	6,827
Secretaries, stenographers, typists	(B)	6,955
Sales workers	12,523	5,168
In retail trade	9,125	4,734
Craft and kindred workers	12,028	6,492
Blue-collar worker supervisors	13,452	6,823
Craft workers	11,772	6,290
In construction	12,142	(B)
Private household workers	(B)	2,676
Service workers, exc. private household	8,638	5,046
Farm laborers and supervisors	5,097	(B)
Laborers, exc. farm	8,145	5,891

(B) Not computed; base less than minimum required for reliability.

Moreover, you may "starve" for a number of years before you become a junior partner in a law firm, for at the start of your age-earnings profile, you will be getting relatively low salaries. Even doctors start their practices at low wages. So, even though the average salary for the occupation is very high, you should not anticipate that your impressive amount of schooling will start making you a nice sum of money right away. To see why this is not necessarily "unfair" or "unjust," we must look at the reasons behind the shape of the typical age-earnings profile as represented in Figure 6-2.

WAGES AND AGES

Look at it this way: when you first start a job, you are inexperienced (you might even need on-the-job training). Your employer will not be inclined to pay you as much as a more experienced worker who can be more productive. Gradually, as you become more productive, better trained, and as the number of weekly hours you work increases, so does your wage rate (even corrected for inflation). Your employer gets more and more information on your productivity and your reliability from all of your previous employment.

You may peak out at age 45 to 55, and then slowly come down until retirement when you cease work altogether. The slow downturn in the age-earnings profile has several causes, one being that older people generally work fewer hours per week and are generally less productive than middle-aged people.

OCCUPATIONAL CHOICE

Not only are there vast differences among the wages for different occupations, as shown in Table 6-3, there are also vast differences in the qualifications, the amount of training, and the type of work required in each occupation. In an occupation that has highly variable periods of employment, the average wage rate is

Figure 6-2 Typical Age-Earnings Profile

Within every class of incomes earned, there is usually a typical age-earnings profile. Earnings are lowest when starting out to work at age 18, reach their peak at around 45 to 55, and then taper off until retirement at around 65 when they become zero for most people. The rise in earnings up to age 45 to 55 is usually due to more experience, working longer hours, and better training and schooling (abstracting from general increases in national productivity).

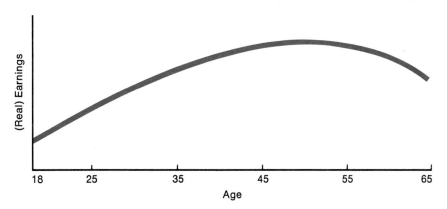

relatively higher than similar work with steadier employment; all this means is that the wage rate is higher to compensate for the periods of unemployment. You must also remember that wages alone are not going to determine whether you made the right choice. If you have a spirit of independence, you will certainly not be satisfied in a large insurance office doing paperwork; if you have a spirit of adventure, you will not be happy as a sales clerk. Therefore, you may finally choose an occupation that promises you a lower wage rate than some others but a more acceptable work situation. After all, most of us work most of our lives; and if we hate our work, we will not be very happy, even if we make quite a bit of income. In other words, the total income you make from an occupation includes more than just money income. It includes psychic income, or the satisfaction derived from one's work situation or occupation. Psychic rewards from a job can be more important for some people than monetary payment.

You also have to decide whether or not you want to live in one area for a long period of time. If you become a junior executive in a company that has a history of switching its executives around the country every 18 months, you will be very unhappy if you dislike moving. On the other hand, you might be very happy if indeed you want to see the country while you are young.

Your choice of occupation in some ways depends on your values and your desired life style. The occupation you choose may even determine the nature of your consumption—that is, the house you live in or the clothes you wear. It also will determine how much leisure you will have. As you have already seen, very few things come free of charge. If you want a job with more leisure, you will generally have less income to spend than from a job with less leisure. If you want a job that is highly stable and risk free, you will pay for it in the form of a lower income.

NONMONEY INCOME

In figuring out what your standard of living will be in different types of occupations, you must also look at the nonmoney income that might be available. We are referring to goods and services that individuals can obtain without the use of money. Nonmoney income can make our lives more satisfying or comfortable. The various sources of nonmoney income are:

1. Material goods produced at home, such as those that come from gardening, sewing, or cutting firewood from the family lot.
2. Income from services in the form of food, clothing, or housing. For example, farm laborers may receive housing accommodations in addition to their money income. Ministers are often given food and housing. In fact, the whole category of fringe benefits for wage earners is covered under nonmoney income.
3. Services provided by family members. Full-time homemakers provide services to other members of the family for which they do not pay directly. Certain members of the family may do auto repairs, chores around the house, and lawn mowing without pay, thus providing nonmoney income to other family members.
4. Service income from owned consumer durable goods. Those who own furniture, a house, equipment, or a car obtain an implicit service income stream from those durable goods.

5. Social income. Such income is available largely at public expense and in-
    cludes public health clinics, libraries, parks, public education, roads, fire, and
    police protection.

    In order to estimate one's total income, it would be necessary to add up
monetary income, the value of psychic income, and the value of all of the nonmoney income you receive.

**WHAT JOBS WILL
PAY IN 1985**

To get some idea of potential income if you successfully enter a specific occupation in the next few years, consider Table 6-4. Here we show estimates of what
jobs will pay in 1985. The data were compiled by the Conference Board, a nonprofit business research organization. The figures are median earnings, meaning
that half the workers will earn more and half will earn less than the dollar figures
expressed here.

**Table 6-4
What Will You
Earn in the Future?**

Source: U.S. Department
of Labor

	1970	1980	1985
Professional and technical workers			
computer programmers	$13,600	$23,712	$26,637
designers	14,260	25,116	28,015
drafters	11,200	21,073	23,530
electrical and electronic engineering			
technicians	11,200	20,111	22,633
personnel and labor relations workers	13,820	24,531	27,690
recreation workers	9,330	16,237	18,044
registered nurses	8,090	13,429	15,561
therapists	9,630	15,626	17,966
Managers and administrators			
bank officials and financial managers	15,990	29,380	29,302
wholesale and retail buyers	12,780	21,736	24,037
building managers and superintendents	9,500	17,550	19,864
farm managers	10,210	19,760	24,973
restaurant, cafeteria, and bar managers	11,230	19,786	22,152
retail sales managers and department heads	12,780	21,736	24,037
Sales workers			
insurance agents, brokers, and underwriters	11,010	19,383	21,619
real estate agents and brokers	12,820	23,777	26,936
manufacturing sales representatives	15,540	29,588	33,943
wholesale sales representatives	13,690	24,635	27,339
retail sales clerks	6,470	10,894	12,324
stock and bond sales agents	23,070	42,380	47,892
Service workers			
firefighters	11,610	20,800	23,569
hairdressers and cosmetologists	5,770	10,101	11,245
health aides (except nursing)	5,440	8,749	10,036
police and detectives	11,100	19,851	22,490
practical nurses	5,870	9,945	11,585

(continued on page 112)

**Table 6-4
Continued**

	1970	1980	1985
Clerical workers			
billing clerks	7,500	12,805	14,287
bookkeepers	6,530	11,180	12,480
computer operators	9,170	15,821	17,459
insurance adjustors, examiners,			
and investigators	10,920	19,214	21,437
real estate appraisers	15,450	28,652	32,461
secretaries	6,860	11,752	13,130
statistical clerks	8,230	14,047	15,669
stenographers	7,520	13,247	14,937
typists	6,070	10,361	11,557
Craftspersons			
air-conditioning, heating, and			
refrigeration mechanics	10,760	18,512	20,540
auto mechanics	9,070	15,561	17,251
carpenters	9,720	16,822	18,707
electricians	11,780	20,397	22,685
supervisors	12,320	22,126	24,908
machinists	10,400	19,409	21,632
plumbers and pipefitters	11,570	20,137	22,438
printing and press operators	10,580	17,680	19,760
radio and TV repairers	9,520	16,419	18,239
telephone repairers and installers	11,150	19,851	23,855
Operatives			
bus drivers	8,950	16,367	18,603
truck drivers	9,640	18,265	21,008

SUMMARY

1. Many income differences are caused by inherent differences in human beings, but they are also caused by the amount of training and education an individual has obtained, the amount of on-the-job training, and the riskiness of the occupation.

2. Going to school is an investment in human capital because it makes you, the human, more productive in the future. Generally, your investment in human capital should pay off in the form of a higher wage later on.

3. However, you must specialize in an activity that is in demand and for which there is not a surplus of supply. Hence, choosing your occupation requires predicting both the demand and the supply for that particular occupation in the future.

4. Generally, individuals are paid according to their productivity. Therefore, anything that raises an individual's productivity may ultimately lead to a higher income.

5. The rate of return of education is as high as the rate of return of investing in other things. A college degree holder may make as much as a half a million dollars more on average than a grade school degree holder.

6. The greatest cost of going to college is the opportunity cost of not being able to work and make an income during those years.
7. A number of studies have appeared showing that a large percentage of students now in college would be better off if they went to work instead.
8. The female labor market role has been changing.
9. An individual's wages (corrected for inflation) are usually lowest when the individual first enters the labor force. That's because the individual is least productive then.
10. In determining one's standard of living, it is important to figure nonmoney income, which includes, but is not limited to, goods produced at home, services produced at home, and social income from government-provided goods and services.

QUESTIONS FOR THOUGHT AND DISCUSSION

1. What are some of the most important factors that contribute to differences in income?
2. Have you ever considered going to school as an investment in your own human capital?
3. Is the act of going to college pure investment or not?
4. Does it seem fair that some students specialize in areas in which they cannot get a job once they get a degree? What would you do about that situation?
5. Why does the government subsidize much of higher education?
6. Do you think college is a good investment?
7. What is the highest cost of going to college?

THINGS TO DO

1. Go to the career guidance center of your college or university. Look at the books on occupations that you could enter. Make a list of the highest paid occupations. Then ask someone in the center whether or not you would be eligible for those occupations. Try to determine why you would or would not.
2. Get the latest data from the Department of Commerce on lifetime earnings of various degree holders. Is it still worthwhile for individuals to complete college?
3. Check the latest edition of the *Occupational Outlook Handbook* (issued quarterly by the Bureau of Labor Statistics, U.S. Department of Labor) for a forecast of your chosen career.

SELECTED READINGS

Becker, Gary. *Human Capital: A Theoretical and Empirical Analysis with Special Reference to Education.* New York: Columbia University Press, 1964.

Berg, Ivar E. *Education and Jobs; The Great Training Robbery.* New York: Center for Urban Education, Praeger, 1970.

Brown, Gary D. "How Type of Employment Affects Earnings Differences by Sex." *Monthly Labor Review*, July 1976, pp. 25-30.

"Career Education: A Whole New Focus for Schools." *Changing Times*, April 1974, pp. 37-39.

Carey, Max L. "Revised Occupational Projections to 1985." *Monthly Labor Review*, November 1976, pp. 10-22.

Erlick, A. C. "Youth, Education and Jobs." *Intellect*, October 1972, p. 10.

Gordon, Margaret S. *Higher Education and the Labor Market.* New York: McGraw-Hill, 1974.

"How Workers Are Faring in Wage-Price Race." *U.S. News & World Report*, June 17, 1974, pp. 47-48.

Howe, H., II, and Freeman, R. B. "Does It Pay to Go to College?" *U.S. News*, January 24, 1977, pp. 59-60.

Iris, B., and Barrett, G. V. "Some Relations between Job and Life Satisfaction and Job Importance." *Journal of Applied Psychology*, August 1972, pp. 301-304.

Jencks, C., et al., *Inequality.* New York: Basic Books, 1972.

Johnson, L., and Johnson, R. H. "High School Preparation, Occupation and Job Satisfaction." *Vocational Guidance Quarterly*, June 1972, pp. 287-290.

Juster, F. P., ed. *Education, Income, and Human Behavior.* New York: McGraw-Hill, 1975.

Michael, Robert T. *The Effect of Education on Efficiency in Consumption.* New York: Columbia University Press, 1972.

Miller, Herman P. *Rich Man, Poor Man.* New York: Thomas J. Crowell Company, 1971.

Mincer, Jacob. *Schooling, Experience, and Earnings.* New York: National Bureau of Economic Research, 1974.

Mooney, Thomas J., and Tschetter, John H. "Revised Industry Projections to 1985." *Monthly Labor Review*, November 1976, pp. 3-9.

Owen, John D. "Workweeks & Leisure: An Analysis of Trends, 1948-1975." *Monthly Labor Review*, August 1976, pp. 3-8.

Ryscavage, P. M. "Measuring Union-Nonunion Earnings Differences." *Monthly Labor Review*, December 1974, pp. 3-9.

Sommers, Dikie. "Occupational Rankings for Men and Women by Earnings." *Monthly Labor Review*, August 1974, pp. 34-51.

Von Hoffman, N. "What Price Education?" *Progressive*, February 1977, p. 55.

"When College Graduates Enter the Real World." *U.S. News*, March 14, 1977, pp. 79-80.

GLOSSARY OF TERMS

Scarcity

The limit that prevents us from having everything we want. Nature creates this limit. Most goods that we want are scarce. That is, there is not an unlimited quantity available at a zero price. Scarcity causes us to make choices.

Trade-offs

The realistic choice that one must make between alternatives. For example, if you buy a couple of new books, by necessity you must trade off that purchase with something else—say, a night out on the town. All choices involve trade-offs between alternatives. A synonym for opportunity cost.

Transfer Payments

Payments made by the government to individuals for which no services are rendered. A transfer payment might be a Social Security check or an unemployment check.

Luxury Good

A good, the purchase of which increases more than in proportion to increases in income. Jewelry, gourmet foods, and sports cars usually fall into this category.

You Have to Live with What You Have

CHAPTER PREVIEW

☐ Why do we budget?

☐ How can a budget work into democratic decision making for the family spending unit?

☐ How important is teenage spending in our economy?

☐ What do typical family budgets look like?

☐ How can one fit a budget into a lifetime plan?

7 We American consumers are rich. That is, we are rich by comparison with the British consumer, the Indian consumer, the African consumer, the Spanish consumer, or the Venezuelan consumer. Table 7-1 shows that the average per capita income in the United States is considerably higher than in most other countries of the world.

But per capita income does not tell the story we want to tell. Table 7-2 shows the different percentages of U.S. families who make particular amounts of income, ranging all the way from poverty to extreme opulence. Most of us, as you can well imagine, find ourselves somewhere in the middle of income earners: we are not absolutely broke, because we do have some form of income, but, on the other hand, we are not Nelson Rockefeller or Hugh Hefner.

However, all of us, whether we are rich or poor, have something in common. You may not want to believe it, but no matter how rich you are, you still have a problem: you cannot buy everything you would like to buy. The problem is universal—a problem we call **scarcity**. All of us are faced with a limited budget, even the Shah of Iran: for if he wanted to buy every single jet in the world, he would not have enough money to do it. Because we all face this universal problem of scarce resources, we can better understand why personal money management is important for all of us, no matter what our income level.

WHY FIGURE OUT A BUDGET OR SPENDING PLAN?

If you find yourself at either end of the income spectrum, you may think it a waste of time to formulate a budget. Obviously, if you have no income, a budget is not what you should be looking for. If you have a seemingly infinite amount of income, you need not formulate a budget with respect to your usual purchases. Most of us, however, lie somewhere in between, right? Because we have limited incomes, every action of ours that involves spending part of that income means we sacrifice something else. Economists term this the opportunity cost of spending. If you decide to spend more on entertainment, you have less left over for all the other things in your budget. Or if you decide to spend more on transportation, you have less for all other things. In other words, every spending decision that you

Table 7-1

Per Capita GNP, 1975, U.S. Dollars

These figures give the total amount of income divided by the population, or per capita GNP. They are corrected for relative cost-of-living differences in the different countries.

Source: U.S. Department of State, Bureau of Intelligence and Research, *Statistical Abstract of the U.S.*, 1976, p. 87; Statistical Office of the United Nations.

	CORRECTED PER CAPITA GNP
Canada	$8,064
United States	7,716
Switzerland	6,948
Australia	6,359
Denmark	6,126
West Germany	5,898
France	5,150
The Netherlands	4,905
England	4,493
Japan	4,023
Italy	3,270
Turkey	1,239

Table 7-2

Money Income of Families by Income Level, 1975

The largest percentage of families earned between $9,000 and $12,000 in 1975. Only 5% earned above $50,000 while less than 5 percent earned under $3,000.

Source: U.S. Bureau of Census, *Current Population Reports*, Series P-60, No. 105, 1-4.

TOTAL MONEY INCOME	NUMBER (THOUSANDS)	PERCENT DISTRIBUTION
Under 2,999	2,565	4.5
3,000-5,999	6,511	11.6
6,000-8,999	7,290	12.9
9,000-12,999	10,048	17.8
13,000-15,999	7,323	13.0
16,000-19,999	8,058	14.3
20,000-24,999	6,518	11.6
25,000-49,999	7,148	12.7
50,000 and over	783	1.4
TOTAL	56,245	100.0

make involves an opportunity cost: you are giving up the opportunity of spending that income on something else. Why? Simply because you have a limited budget; simply because you face a problem of scarcity.

Planning a budget and attempting to stick to it forces the issue of scarcity and opportunity cost out into the open. You cannot deny the fact that you are giving something up when you decide, for example, to take that trip to Mexico. For if you plan it in your budget, you will realize that somewhere else along the line something has to be cut out of the budget. A budget, then, is a way of managing your money in a more or less systematic and rational manner. It is also, however, a control mechanism that causes you to be aware of decisions you are actually making—decisions that are there even if you do not wish to make them an obvious part of your decision-making process. Some of you may be gifted with the ability to determine instantaneously the **trade-offs** involved every time you make a purchase. But most of us would be helped out by a budget. With it, we may be able to hold in check undirected spending activities that can lead to unhappiness and, occasionally, financial disaster when the household must declare bankruptcy.

Budgets are generally planned around a pay period, perhaps a month and sometimes as short a time as a week. Budgeting to this extent is time consuming and often too complicated because it requires individuals to look into the future as well as the past and estimate both income and expenses. For those who are willing to sacrifice the time and overcome the difficulties, it can be a useful financial tool. To be most helpful, budgets should be set up for a year at a time (allowing ample opportunities for revisions during the year). On a yearly basis, one is able to:

1. Anticipate and prepare for changes in one's financial situation.
2. Set aside money for large expenses.
3. Plan for seasonal changes, for example, greater clothing needs in the fall or spring and higher utility bills during winter.

Understanding the "why" behind budget formulation is also linked to value clarification, which we discussed in Chapter 4. A budget can be a basic part of putting into play values that have been clarified as part of lifetime goals in a consumer's lifetime planning process. A budget is also useful for bringing harmony into a household in which money may be a sore point.

DEMOCRATIC DECISION-MAKING

If in your situation more than one person is affected by the way each month's income is spent, then you have to make a choice as to how decisions are to be made. Will decision making be unilateral or dictatorial? Will decision making be democratic, in which case everybody participates? This problem comes up not only in traditional family situations, but also in communal and group-living situations. The principles are the same: if you decide that one person is going to make unilateral decisions, then those whose lives are affected may at one time or another feel cheated, left out, or trod upon. It is important to work out money problems within the family unit, because many families fight about money. A recent survey by Yankelovich, Skelly & White found that 54 percent of the families interviewed argued about money. Families who were hard-pressed by financial problems argued about money 65 percent of the time. The study showed that families who fought a lot about money were unable to communicate freely and frankly on money matters.

The formulation of a spending plan can (if you wish) become an integral part of increasing harmony within any living situation by bringing into light everyone's desires, needs, preferences, and complaints. Each time a major economic decision has to be made, a democratic decision-making unit will involve everybody in the process. On the other hand, situations more akin to tyranny will involve only one person in the decision. In most families today, the so-called male breadwinner is no longer freely allowed all the decision-making powers simply because he brings home the "bread." After all, the housewife also contributes to the total implicit income of the family, to the tune of at least $6,000 to $8,000 a year in a family of four. If she is contributing income, even though it is not in the form of dollars brought home in a paycheck, she too will want to take part in the formulation of the budget, and therefore in the formation of the lifetime goals and plans of the family unit. In some states, such as Washington, the wife has a legal right to share in controlling family finances. That is, either partner is empowered to act independently on behalf of the "community," except for a few specified instances in which the signatures of both spouses are required, such as the signing of a mortgage when a house is purchased.

Our discussion above also applies to such nontraditional spending units as groups and communes.

THE FAMILY COUNCIL

Often, in truly democratic households, there is a meeting of a family council when budget-making time comes around. At this time, everybody airs his or her desires; and everyone, including children, faces the problem of scarcity and the trade-offs that have to be made with a fixed income. Everybody must realize at the onset that no one person's every desire will be satisfied. This is so because many decisions are mutually exclusive; if, for example, a new TV is purchased, it may be impossible to buy a new 10-speed bike. If the family unit decides to trade in the old clunker for a brand new sedan, there may be no vacation in the mountains this year. The beauty of the democratic family-council budget-making process is that everybody's cards can be laid on the table—and the biggest card of them all, of course, is the fixed amount of income that the family has to spend. Even the parents may have much clearer notions of the opportunity costs of their actions and the effects of these trade-offs on other members of the family. Moreover, differences in values often surface during family discussions of money management. It is important for all concerned to understand (and respect) other family member's values.

Viewed in this light, the budget-making process has another, separate goal: not only can it hold in check undirected spending and prevent financial crises, it can also help to solidify family relationships. Lack of money is the basic cause of so many marital squabbles that democratization of the spending process would seem a natural desire of all families who wish to have unity, tranquility, and harmony within the household.

A number of marriage counselors have come up with even more specific ideas about how money matters should be handled within a family. They are as follows:

1. Try the democratic decision-making meeting on an informal basis. If the casual approach doesn't work, have a formal meeting held at a set time and place. The meeting should be presided over by different family members. Such meetings only work if the children are young. Adolescents are likely to be scornful (unless they have grown up with such meetings).

2. Write it down. Communication on paper may be easier than verbally. A bulletin board would be a good way to put messages about desires and financial planning. If there is a quarrel about family spending priorities, have each family member write down the list of priorities in descending order and then compare them.

3. Record the family money fights on cassettes, then listen. Frequently those who are fighting don't really hear themselves.

4. Negotiate a contract; for in so doing, you will find that everybody gives a little and takes a little. Bargains can be struck.

No matter how democratic the process may be, however, there will always be problems with children, particularly when they get to be teenagers and want to assert their own independence (and with adults, too, who wish to assert *their* independence).

COPING WITH THE
TEENAGE CONSUMER

As a group, teenagers form a powerful consumer bloc. Did you know that in 1977 there were 30 million teenagers in the United States, and they spent an estimated $27 billion? That means that every one of them spent on average $900 a year on records, tapes, cosmetics, etc. It is not surprising that advertising agencies have increasingly focused their attention on the teenage market. Teenagers, of course, get much of their money from their parents in the form of an allowance or payment for household chores. Many of them also do work on their own—paper routes, part-time sales jobs, and so on. In one survey, over half of the high school students questioned reported at least two sources of income. Quite a large percentage of teenagers have their own savings accounts, have their own U.S. Savings Bonds stashed away, and belong to Christmas or vacation clubs; some of them have even already obtained insurance.

To a large extent, teenagers pick up the spending habits of their parents. Hence, if the parents are always complaining about never having enough money to finish the month out, if the parents are always fighting about money worries

between themselves, then the teenage children cannot very well be expected to act differently in their own spending. Hence, it may be useful to look at the teenage years as a time when parents can engage in money training. The best teaching method is setting a good example. But more than that, parents can engage in a subtle form of money training that will prepare their children for adulthood.

Of course, most important in money training is to make the teenager realize that everything in life involves a trade-off, spending money being no exception. This realization can be encouraged in a variety of ways. If the teenager is made part of the democratic family council in which budget formulations are made during the year, then he or she is given first-hand knowledge of how painful trade-off decisions might sometimes be and what the trade-offs actually involve. If the parents then want to spend a little more time with their teenager, they can try to get him or her to formulate a personal budget. In this way, the teenager sees in black and white the trade-offs that he or she faces with this very limited income. It is a wise parent who informs a teenage child that even though the teenager's income will be larger later on in life, he or she will still be faced with the same basic problem of scarcity. Many teenagers believe that it is irrelevant to learn good spending and budgeting habits during the teen years because they are convinced that later on they will have "so much money" they will have no worries about how they spend it. We all know, painfully so, that this is wrong; our wants and desires seem to be always one step ahead of our incomes. Hence, we are always faced with the problem of figuring out how to allocate our limited budget to a large number of competing desires and needs. The transition from childhood to adult-

---

EXHIBIT 7-1   **A Child's Allowance Shouldn't Be Hit-or-Miss**

Some families are free and loose about children's allowances. Others play it tight and hold the kids accountable for every dime. Both ways work.

Psychologists and educators point out that there are no hard-and-fast rules. Any sensible approach is good if it is in line with the family's income and mode of living and is followed consistently. "Trouble comes when the allowance is hit-or-miss," says a top New York child psychologist. He adds: "What's really important to understand is that *your* attitude toward money rubs off on the kids. They'll tend to do with pennies or a dollar what you do on a bigger scale."

A Connecticut educator and psychologist who specializes in teen-age problems notes that "a parent's feeling of confidence about money is soaked up by the kids very early—or the parent's feeling of fear and doubt."

A small child should be given a dime or so once or twice a week but never more money than can be managed easily. By 10, the child should be getting a regular weekly amount of pocket money—maybe $1 or a bit more—to provide some spending options.

The habit of saving requires some excess cash that makes it possible.

Pre-teenagers, say psychologists, develop confidence by having more money in hand, but it should still be on a weekly basis. Starting at 13 or 14, a monthly allowance should teach the youngster something about budgeting. But here the advice comes full circle: The parents' spending habits are what the kids really see.

By 15 or 16, the child should have at least some idea of family finances, though too much information may be worse than too little. "Give them a clear, honest understanding if they question you," says a Harvard University psychologist. "But don't make a big thing of it. Don't impart anxiety by forcing the issue."

An obvious blunder at any age is to give a youngster more than friends get. "He should be in line with his peers," says a specialist. "If he gets too much, he may waste it and feel guilty about it in the bargain." Giving too little in the hopes of instilling a sense of frugality is equally bad.

---

hood certainly will be less painful if the teenager understands that the budget problems he or she faces as a teenager are no different in principle and in practice from those he or she will face as an adult member of a family or living unit, even if this living unit consists of one person—himself or herself. For some thoughts on allowances, see Exhibit 7-1.

HOW DOES THE TYPICAL HOUSEHOLD ALLOCATE ITS INCOME?

Averages can sometimes be deceiving. But it may be instructive for you to see how typical households in the United States allocate their fixed incomes to the many competing demands. The U.S. Department of Labor, Bureau of Labor Statistics, has for some time obtained survey data on the spending patterns of households of various income levels. Figure 7-1, a pie graph, shows how an average American family spends its income. A large chunk usually goes for housing services (which include utilities and maintenance). Equal to that expenditure, and sometimes even larger, is the chunk of income that goes for food. Food and housing often account for over 50 percent of the average American family's expenditures in any one year.

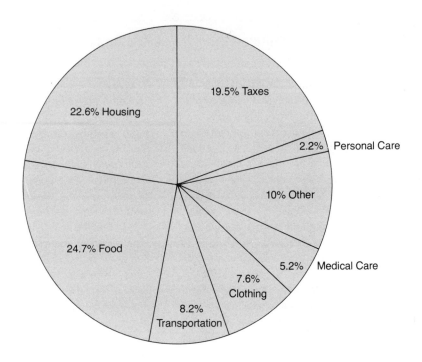

Figure 7-1
Average American Family Budget (based on annual budgets for a four-person urban family, intermediate level of living).

The average American family spends at least one-fourth of its income on housing, and almost one-fourth on food. The rest is divided among transportation, clothing, medical care, personal care, taxes, and other.

Source: U.S. Department of Labor, Bureau of Labor Statistics.

This may seem to be a frighteningly large percentage, but it is not when compared with those of other countries. Table 7-3 shows the percentage of total income spent on food in different countries of the world. Notice that there seems to be a relationship between the percentage of income spent on food and the level of development of the country. In fact, for an accurate measure of how well off a country is, all you would have to look at is what percentage of each family's budget goes for food. The larger the percentage, the less developed the country. (Of course, there will be exceptions to this.)

Clothing, personal care, and medical care take up another large chunk of each family's budget in the United States. Medical care itself has been taking up an increasingly large percentage of total U.S. consumption spending. The reasons why, and what to expect in the future, will be treated when we study medical care in detail, in Chapter 15. Taxes, unfortunately for many of us, take up an ever-increasing amount of our income. (See Chapter 18.) For the average American, over 40 percent of every dollar earned goes to federal, state, and local taxes. Some of those tax monies are returned in the form of **transfer payments**, such as Social Security benefits and unemployment compensation, but the remainder, which is almost 25 percent, is still a large fraction of our total income in the United States. Again, this percentage is not as large as in most other countries of the world, where taxes are higher and total government expenditures as a percentage of total income are also higher. (These countries also, however, may provide more transfer payments in the form of medical services, public housing, and so on.)

DIFFERENT LEVEL BUDGETS

The makeup of the various budget categories change as we go from lower income to higher income spenders. Table 7-4 shows the U.S. Department of Labor's esti-

Table 7-3

Percentage of Total Income Spent on Food in Selected Countries

The U.S. spends the smallest percentage of total income on food of any nation in the world. As much as 60 or 70 percent, or more, of total income is spent on food by some less developed nations, such as Uganda, which spends 79 percent of total income on food.

Sources: FAO Review of Food Consumption Surveys, 1970, and Fortune Magazine, February 1974.

COUNTRY	PERCENT Total Food Expenditures/ Total Income
Argentina	40
Brazil	37
Chile	64
France	36
Honduras	41
Hungary	42
Indonesia *	60
Japan	27
Kenya	38
Korea	49
Malawi *	40
Netherlands *	29
Pakistan	51
Philippines	63
Poland	45
Saudi Arabia	74
Somalia *	60
Spain *	49
Sudan *	70
Switzerland *	21
Thailand	55
Tunisia *	50
Uganda	79
United Kingdom	28
United States	15
Venezuela	25
Yugoslavia	35

*Percent of total expenditures.

mates of what it takes to live on a low-, medium-, or high-income budget for a hypothetical urban family of four. (Note that these estimates say nothing about what the incomes in the United States actually are.) As income goes up, food spending falls and housing expenditures rise as percentages of total income. That means that as our incomes go up, we buy proportionally more housing and proportionally less food. Housing, then, is often considered after a certain point to be a **luxury good**, for people buy a disproportionate amount of it as they get wealthier, as they earn more income. Food, on the other hand, has the opposite character-istic and is often called a necessity.

We have to be careful of such labels as luxury and necessity, however, because they have some subjective connotations. Remember that one person's meat is often another person's poison, so it is not really enough to talk about luxuries and necessities. One person's luxury may be another person's necessity, and vice versa. Most of us have a hard time deciding our own values and goals, let alone deciding for other people. But that is exactly what we do when we consider some-

Table 7-4

Summary of Annual Budgets for a Four-Person Family at Three Levels of Living, Urban U.S., Autumn 1976

Source: U.S. Department of Labor, Bureau of Labor Statistics.

Component	LOW BUDGET Lower	MEDIUM BUDGET Intermediate	HIGH BUDGET Higher	ITEM AS PERCENTAGE OF TOTAL BUDGET Lower	Intermediate	Higher
Total budget	$10,041	$16,236	$23,759			
Total family consumption	8,162	12,370	17,048			
Food	3,003	3,859	4,856	30%	24%	20%
Housing	1,964	3,843	5,821	20	24	25
Transportation	767	1,403	1,824	8	9	8
Clothing	799	1,141	1,670	8	7	7
Personal care	265	355	503	3	2	2
Medical care	896	900	939	9	6	4
Other family consumption[1]	468	869	1,434	5	5	6
Other items[2]	451	731	1,234	4	5	5
Taxes and deductions	1,429	3,134	5,476	14	19	23
Social Security and disability	604	898	911	6	6	4
Personal income taxes	825	2,236	4,565	8	14	19

[1]Other family consumption includes average costs for reading, recreation, tobacco products, alcoholic beverages, education, and miscellaneous expenditures.
[2]Other items includes allowances for gifts and contributions, life insurance and occupational expenses.
NOTE: Because of rounding, sums of individual items may not equal totals.

body else's spending to be wasted on so-called luxury items or frivolous consumption. After all, we purchase "satisfaction," not the items per se: who can judge what another's derived satisfaction is?

CITY VERSUS COUNTRY

Not only are there differences in budget allocations among low-, medium-, and high-income families, there are also differences in typical income levels between urban and rural areas. The costs of living in cities differ from those of living in the country. And the costs of living in a large city differ from those of living in a small city. The U.S. Department of Labor has come up with indexes of relative living costs in different parts of the country. In Table 7-5 we show these indexes. The average of urban areas with populations in excess of 2500 has a base index of 100. If a particular city has an index of 110, then to find out what an intermediate budget would cost in that city, increase the total budget figure under the column "medium" in Table 7-4 by 10 percent. If the area you are living in or wish to live in has an index in Table 7-5 that is less than 100, you must reduce the corresponding budget figure in Table 7-4 accordingly.

A low-income family budget in New York City may be the equivalent of a high-income family budget in Podunk, Somewhere. But, of course, people are generally paid more if they work in big, expensive cities. In fact, you would not expect that moving to a city would necessarily make you better off just because you were offered a higher salary.

Of course, such a comparison is only part of the information you need to decide whether or not to move from one city to another, or from the country to the city or vice versa. A move to the city involves a move to an area where a tremendous amount of cultural activity can be found that is unavailable in less-populated areas. "Specialization is a function of the size of the market," said Adam Smith, the father of modern economics. That means that the larger the size of the city, the more specialized services you will be able to buy. Just think of how many movies, restaurants, theaters, operas, and concerts you can go to in cities of five thousand compared to cities of five million. Many people are willing to pay a relatively high cost in such things as increased congestion, increased living expenses, and increased pollution and crime in order to have available the numerous recreational activities found in large metropolitan areas but not in small rural areas. All of us would certainly like to be able to have the benefits of big cities without paying the costs, but so far nobody has figured out how that can happen. Again, we live in a world of scarcity where, generally, every benefit has a cost. You have to decide whether the benefit is worth the cost. And, of course, in deciding that, you have to bring into play your goals and values.

BUDGET-MAKING, GOALS, AND VALUE CLARIFICATION

Remember that in Chapter 4 we talked about value clarification, about how you decided what your goals were, what your values were, and what they meant in respect to how you should spend your time. Ultimately, this all related to what kind of life you want to lead. Now you can put this more-or-less abstract problem into perspective by applying it to an actual dollars-and-cents decision-making process —budget formulation. When you sit down alone or with the other members of your spending unit, you have to consider the values that you place on the various things you want to do with the income available. To be able to have a clear idea of your values, you first have to have formulated your goals and those of the spending unit

Table 7-5

Relative Cost of Living Indexes for Selected Cities (U.S. City Average = 100)

Source: *Monthly Labor Review*, May 1977.

	RELATIVE COST OF LIVING INDEX		RELATIVE COST OF LIVING INDEX
Atlanta, Georgia	99	Minneapolis-St. Paul, Minnesota	100
Baltimore, Maryland	102		
Boston, Massachusetts	102	New York, New York- Northeastern New Jersey	103
Buffalo, New York	100		
Chicago, Illinois- Northwestern Indiana	97	Philadelphia, Pennsylvania- New Jersey	101
Cincinnati, Ohio-Kentucky	100	Pittsburgh, Pennsylvania	99
Cleveland, Ohio	99	Portland, Oregon- Washington	98
Dallas, Texas	98		
Detroit, Michigan	99	St. Louis, Missouri-Illinois	97
Honolulu, Hawaii	95	San Diego, California	100
Houston, Texas	104	San Francisco-Oakland, California	98
Kansas City, Missouri- Kansas	98	Scranton, Pennsylvania	100
Los Angeles-Long Beach, California	98	Seattle, Washington	96
Milwaukee, Wisconsin	98	Washington, D.C.- Maryland-Virginia	100

as a whole. Then you must set *priorities* among your goals. These priorities will be linked to the three types of goals that you probably will set for yourself or your household, which might be set under the headings:

1. Short-term
2. Intermediate
3. Long-term

If, for example, one of your main long-term goals is to have a super-athletic family in which all members are as physically fit as possible, this will have strong implications for how you spend your income. The decision may be that the family will go to a tennis camp or join a tennis club, or that jogging uniforms for wet weather running will be purchased for the family.

On the other hand, if one part of your goals for your family or yourself involves the appreciation of the arts, a large part of your budget may be allocated to the purchase of books; records and tapes; and theater, opera, and concert tickets.

More basically, you may have the goal of a well-nourished and adequately housed family, or one that is medically protected or has adequate transportation. Here, however, your goals may involve choices. To have a well-nourished family, you may have to stint on housing; to have medical protection, you may have to stint on transportation needs.

Everybody's main goal, of course, can be subsumed under one heading—to be happy. The problem is clarifying your values enough so that you can establish goals that taken all together will spell happiness for you and those around you. When you formulate a budget, you can see exactly what these goals cost. You force yourself to rethink and to reformulate your values when you realize that either they are unattainable or extremely costly in the sense that you must give up the opportunity to do numerous other desired or necessary things.

TRADE-OFFS

Any seeming overemphasis here on the problem of trade-offs should not upset you, for trade-offs are the key to understanding why families and other spending units often run into so many problems. Frequently, it is not realized that trade-offs must be made; hence, when they come unexpectedly, they seem to be someone's fault when in fact no one is at fault. Rather, nature is at fault, because nature is so stingy and does not give us everything we want. That is, nature makes things scarce for us, and ultimately the scarcity reflects itself in the income of the spending unit—an income that is insufficient to satisfy everyone's desires and wants and needs.

For example, assume that you and the other members of the spending unit have decided that physical fitness is an important value you wish to maintain so that your goal for the next several years is good health, stamina, and athletic prowess for the children and the adults in the family. There are many ways you can accomplish this goal. Jogging is probably the cheapest way of building stamina; after the initial outlay for warm, weatherproof suits for the winter and sturdy running shoes, there is nothing else to buy. But not everybody can be satisfied with jogging; and even if they are, they may want to engage in more competitive sports. While the children may be able to engage in more competitive sports that require no additional outlays in the family's budget plan, the parents might be less fortunate. If they wish to engage in sports such as tennis or golf, equipment might have to be purchased, fees might have to be paid for the use of courts or greens, and so on.

The benefit of laying budget-making out on the table is that it becomes difficult to escape knowing the actual cost of attaining the goal that came from clarification of the family's values. Those members of the spending unit who will feel cheated if the parents decide to play tennis indoors during the winter can express their feelings and perhaps a compromise can be reached. In this method of formulating a budget, individual values can come into conflict and must be compromised. If compromise is accomplished in a democratic way through the formulation of monthly budgets, then those in conflict may be willing to compromise because they know that in future months they will gain.

Goal definition and value clarification are integral parts of budget formulation and may be considered the only way to arrive at a good budget. A good budget, of course, is one that works, and a budget itself has many tasks to accomplish besides keeping a family's spending in line. No one should try to overwork that poor budget, however. It will not miraculously bring family happiness to the unhappy family. It will also not work if it lacks an equal chance of being an underestimate as well as an overestimate of the family's spending. In fact, if the budget is made always to be broken in the upward direction, then for many families it is just as bad as having no budget at all. The accusations start coming fast and furiously; fingers are pointed at the person who may have overspent in a particular budget category. Such a spending unit is right back where it started from without any budget at all.

A budget is merely a tentative allocator to be constantly corrected. It should not be considered a straightjacket, but rather an indication of direction that will change depending on changes in individual and family situations. A budget also cannot be considered a cure-all in times when there are big changes in income.

WHAT HAPPENS WHEN INCOME SUDDENLY CHANGES

Often families experience windfall gains and losses in their incomes. You are all aware of the plight of families whose breadwinner is suddenly out of work. Spending must be drastically reduced, if the spending unit is to escape financial ruin. Here a budget is necessary. If a family finds itself in financial straits, a well-constructed budget that has been followed over many months or many years can in fact present the family with categories where they know they can cut back. And when the cutback has to come, again it probably is best to involve the entire family. Unilateral decisions will not be any more appreciated in this situation than in any other.

Every year, many U.S. families suffer a generally unanticipated decrease in income. When this happens, there is a high probability of family discontent. Fights will break out among members more frequently when income has dropped below normal without warning than when such a drop was expected. Unanticipated income drops may also require otherwise nonworking members of the spending unit to seek employment if the income level is to be kept high enough to satisfy the basic wants of the family. In such a situation, it is helpful to be psychologically prepared for the increased discord that will come about from a big drop in income. Also, the budget itself, as mentioned above, can help pinpoint the areas of least need where expenditures can be cut back.

There is a general tendency for families to continue spending at the same level when income drops. The family assumes that the decrease will be temporary, even if it isn't. Savings are used and credit is relied on in order to maintain what the family considers its "rightful" standard of living. In such circumstances, many families can save themselves later grief if they respond quickly to a drop in income. An explicit budget is one place to look for the first place to cut. (Having an emergency or contingency fund available for such unexpected drops in income is also helpful.)

Also, during any one year many families find themselves with more income than they anticipated. Would that all of us found ourselves in that situation often! Unfortunately, not too many of us do. But when it happens, a budget can again be useful, for without it, unilateral decisions on how to spend the extra income may be made to the detriment of some members of the spending unit; discord may again occur because some people will think they are being cheated. Moreover, without budgets, families who discover they will have a higher income in the next 12 months may end up in financial distress by overcommitting themselves. Each member of the spending unit individually starts making plans on how he or she will spend the extra money, but when all those individual increments are added up, the sum is greater than the increment in income. The result is disaster—financial hardship through overspending when income is rising. The way to avoid this is to expand the budget process in the democratic spending unit council to anticipate the problems inherent in a sudden, unpredicted rise in income.

LETTING THE COMPUTER TELL YOU WHERE YOU'RE AT

A number of banks and firms are offering computerized financial evaluations through the mail, along with a consumer finance course covering such subjects as budgeting, insurance, and investment. For example, Responsive Communications, Inc. (RCI) of Newton, Massachusetts, markets its program through the following banks: First National Bank of Boston, First National Bank in Dallas, Continental Illinois National Bank & Trust Company of Chicago, First National Bank of Denver, Manufacturers Hanover Trust Company in New York, and Fidelity Bank in Philadelphia. Residents not served by those banks can write directly to RCI at 430 Lexington Street, Newton, Massachusetts 02166. For a fee ranging from $25 to $50, you receive six booklets, six lessons, and exams to take after reading the booklets. You send in the exam answers and a computer sends back an analysis of your answers with accompanying comments. If the student has any questions, a telephone number is given for the course administrator. At the end of the sixth lesson, the student is asked to fill out a "computerized financial analysis" booklet that asks questions about Social Security contributions, whether you have a will, whether you are retired, if you own your own home, the total of your outstanding debts, the insurance coverage you have, your assets, and so on. The information is fed into a computer and you receive a confidential analysis based on your answers. It is all run by computer, which has stored thousands of paragraphs applying to different situations. You get back approximately 15 pages of single-spaced information that may include how much you should be saving to send your kids to college, how much life insurance you should buy, and other useful pieces of advice. Undoubtedly, other companies and banks will be offering similar financial planning courses that you can take advantage of. You can write RCI for more information.

Alternatively, you might wish to write COAP Planning, Inc., 21 Alberton Avenue, Albertson, New York 11507, for their computerized materials. There are also a number of other firms catering to insurance company investment advisors and brokers that offer computerized individual financial presentations. These services are generally free to customers of the insurance or brokerage companies and are used as promotional devices.

FITTING IT ALL INTO A LIFETIME PLAN

Today there is much talk about early retirement and the decisions that must be made if it is to be a happy period; there is also much talk about more leisure time to be spent and the need to purchase more leisure-related products. These matters should be considered as part of a lifetime plan, one that is revised periodically to take account of changing values, income, and consumption situations. To some extent, lifetime planning can involve taking the spontaneity out of life. But spontaneity need not be lost. Nobody said lifetime plans could not be altered. Their purpose is to rationalize your behavior as a consumer in the most fundamental meaning of the word. If you have certain values and goals and you set them out clearly for yourself and your family, then you can work toward them and have ways of measuring your progress. This can give you a sense of satisfaction that enables you to feel tranquil about life itself. If, however, you are maniacal about your plans, any failure to meet them may cause grief. Therefore, if you can use plans to mold your decisions so that no important elements of your values or goals are omitted, then by all means sit down right now and figure out where you are and where you want eventually to be. As we mentioned before, such a method is a very effective way to give you motivation, if motivation is what you want. It is also a very effective way to get things done instead of having them hang over your head and make you miserable. Below are a few hints about how you can make lifetime planning work for you. Of course, there are no cut and dried rules, and you may not even want to bother with such methods. It is for you to decide.

Important to you as a consumer are monthly and yearly lists of goals, tasks, and ideas. The monthly list, for example, would tell you when to have scheduled maintenance on your car, when to have services performed on household appliances, what days sales are coming up at various stores, and so on. The yearly list, of course, can do the same thing but with an even greater scope. This list will tell you what goals you want to have attained by the end of the year, what purchases you would like to make, and other such items. This way you can decide well in advance the kind of savings program you have to undertake and the composition of your spending program in order to maximize your happiness from your income. If you keep telling yourself, "I really wish I could get around to affording a new camera or a new stereo," you can stop complaining about never getting the things you want by being realistic, making these part of your yearly goals, and saving toward them so that in fact you buy them by a specific date. When you are working toward a goal, it is easier to make the appropriate decisions and take the appropriate actions.

Your goals can be stretched to five years, ten years, and even fifteen years, but, of course, they will be much broader and will be revised every year. Your five-year goal may be to acquire a Bachelor's degree, to learn how to ski better or to play tennis better, to become fluent in Spanish, or to become an active participant in a minority affairs program. You have to work out a program to attain those goals, and here your yearly plans come in; next you go to your monthly plan, weekly plan, and daily plan. Every once in a while you have to take stock of where you are and of your progress toward all of these different goals for the different time-period plans. You will probably want to do this with those around you who would be most affected by these different plans. In fact, it would not be a bad idea to have a family planning period whereby the family council gathers to decide where the family stands and where it wants to be a year from now, five years from now, and so on. If a new house with a view of the ocean is really strongly desired by everyone in the family, then a program to attain that goal can be worked out. That program might require sacrificing many consumption expenditures over the next few years in order to save up the down payment on that house.

Long-range planning is quite simple in concept but sometimes difficult to put into operation, mainly because people do not always like to face up to the difficulties of attaining certain goals. For example, the only way to attain a higher level of consumption activities is to make more income, and the only way you can generally make more income is to become more productive in your job or to change jobs. That may involve going to night school, taking additional training or working on weekends. If you are aware of such requirements, then you know the cost of getting to your goal for yourself and/or your family.

SUMMARY

1. Even the richest among us do not have an unlimited budget and must therefore make choices.
2. Budgeting or making a spending plan forces you to realize that you do face the constraint of a limited income and that you must make trade-offs among those things you desire to purchase.
3. Democratic decision making within a spending unit can involve a family council in which the budget is decided upon.
4. Teenagers represent an important spending group in our society. Teenage spending habits are usually acquired from parents' spending habits. Therefore, the way to have a teenager become a rational consumer is to set a good example and perhaps to get him or her to formulate a personal budget.
5. A typical household in the United States spends about one-quarter of its budget on housing and about one-quarter on food. As a family's income goes up, the percentage spent on food goes down and the percentage spent on housing goes up.
6. Before deciding to live in different cities or areas in the United States, it is worthwhile to check with U.S. Department of Labor statistics on the cost of comparable levels of living in these areas, for they vary widely. An income of $200 a week means a different standard of living in New York City than in Ames, Iowa, because prices are generally higher in New York City.
7. When setting your goal structure, it is important to put in priorities. These can be worked into short-term, intermediate, and long-term goals. These goals must be made consistent with reality, and that is where trade-offs come in to play.

QUESTIONS FOR THOUGHT AND DISCUSSION

1. Do you know anybody who does not face a budget constraint?
2. Do you think citizens of the United States have different problems in meeting their budget constraints than do citizens of India or Turkey?
3. It is sometimes argued that budget making and time plans cut down on one's spontaneity. Do you agree or disagree? Is there any way the two can be reconciled?
4. Democratic decision making by way of a family council sounds old-fashioned to many individuals. What might be a more modern alternative if this is indeed the case?
5. How much voice do you think a teenager should have in family budget making?
6. Why do Americans spend more on housing as their incomes go up than on food?
7. Can you explain why the cost of living is higher in the city than in the country?
8. Why must trade-offs be made?
9. "If I only had 50 percent more income, I could buy everything I wanted." Evaluate this statement. Have you ever made it? Has it proven to be true?
10. Although very few people do serious lifetime planning, don't most individuals implicitly have a "plan"?

THINGS TO DO

1. Make a list of the typical items that a teenager might buy. Do the consumer choices that have to be made by a teenager differ from those that have to be made by an adult?
2. With the help of your reference librarian, go back to the earliest publication you can find from the Department of Labor, Bureau of Labor Statistics, and see what the average American family budget looked like then. How has it changed over the years? Are we spending more or less on food? On housing? What about taxes?
3. Make a detailed list of your short-term, intermediate, and long-term goals. How do these goals fit in with your overall values?
4. Send away for literature on the consumer finance course offered by Responsive Communications, Inc. Do you think it is worth its cost?

SELECTED READINGS

A Guide to Budgeting for the Family, HG-108. Washington, D.C.: U.S. Department of Agriculture, Office of Information.

Dowd, M. "Managing Money in the First Year of Marriage." *Money*, September 1973.

"Guidelines for Updating the Family Budget." *Changing Times*, November 1974.

Helping Families Manage Their Finances, HERR #21. Washington, D.C.: U.S. Government Printing Office.

"How Does Your Spending Compare?" *Changing Times*, October 1976, p. 6.

Margolius, Sidney. *How to Make the Most of Your Money*. New York: Appleton-Century-Crofts, 1969.

Morse, Richard L. D. *Money Management Process*. Manhattan, Kansas: Department of Family Economics, Kansas State University, 1966.

Mumey, Glen A. *Personal Economic Planning*. New York: Holt, Rinehart and Winston, 1972.

Smith, Carlton, and Pratt, Richard P. *The Time-Life Book of Family Finance*. Boston: Little, Brown, 1970.

"Teaching Your Kids to Manage Money." *Changing Times*, September 1976, pp. 39-41.

Thal, Helen M. *Your Family and Its Money*. New York: Houghton–Mifflin, 1973.

"They Help You Budget and Manage Your Money." *Changing Times*, July 1974.

"When Your Budget Signals Danger." *Changing Times*, February 1977, pp. 33-35.

How to Budget Your Limited Income

GLOSSARY OF TERMS

Fixed Expenses

Expenses that occur at specific times and cannot be altered after the fact. A house payment would be considered a fixed expense once the house is purchased or rented. A car payment would be thought of similarly.

Flexible Expenses

Expenses that can be changed in the short run. The amount of money you spend on food can be considered a flexible expense, for you can buy higher- or lower-quality food than you are now doing. Also known as variable expenses.

Once you decide to do some positive money management, you have to get practical: you have to figure out a budget, and then you have to stick to it. The budget, remember, is a planning tool to help you hold in check undirected spending. In this consumer issue we will look at two different types of budgets for two different situations; one is for college students, and the other is for nonstudent spending units.

STEPS IN BUDGET MAKING

Very briefly, after your goals are determined, the following basic steps can be followed in creating a spending plan. Goals are implicit in the Table D-1 budget sheet.

1. Keep records for a month or two to begin with.

2. Determine **fixed expenses**. These include rent and any other contractual payments that must be made if they come infrequently, such as insurance and taxes.

3. Determine **flexible expenses**, such as food and clothing.

4. Balance your fixed plus flexible expenditures with your available income. If a surplus exists, you can apply it to your goals. If there is a deficit, then you must reexamine your flexible expenditures. You can also reexamine fixed expenses in view of reducing them in the future.

Note that fixed expenses are perhaps only philosophically fixed in the short run. In the longer run, everything is essentially variable. One can adjust one's fixed expenses by changing one's standard of living, if that has to be the case.

THE IMPORTANCE OF KEEPING RECORDS

Your budget making—whether you are a college student, a single person living alone, or the head of a family—will be useless if you do not keep records. The only way to make sure that you are carrying out the plans implicit in your budget is by having records to show what you are actually spending. The best way to have records is to write everything down, but that becomes time consuming and time is costly. Another way to keep records is to write checks for everything. That way at the end of each month you can put the checks into different categories. (Many banks offer no-cost checking accounts if you keep a certain minimum balance.) Records are also important in case of hassles with faulty products, services, or the IRS! Thus, you serve two goals by keeping good records. Now let's go on to some specific budgets that you might wish to work out.

GENERAL BUDGETING

Table D-1 is a monthly general budget form that encompasses both estimated and actual cash available and fixed and variable payments. You will note that the category of savings is located under the Fixed Payments heading. This is because the money in your savings account may be used to pay fixed annual expenses—for example, auto, fire, or life insurance—and it is

Table D-1

A General Way to Budget*

CASH FORECAST, MONTH OF _____	ESTIMATED	ACTUAL
Cash on hand and in checking account, end of previous period		
Savings needed for planned expenses		
Receipts		
net pay		
borrowed		
interest/dividends		
other		
TOTAL CASH AVAILABLE DURING PERIOD		
Fixed Payments		
mortgage or rent		
life insurance		
fire insurance		
auto insurance		
savings		
local taxes		
loan or other debt		
children's allowances		
other		
TOTAL FIXED PAYMENTS		
Flexible Payments		
water		
electricity		
fuel		
telephone		
medical		
household supplies		
car		
food		
personal expenses		
clothing		
nonrecurring large payments		
contributions, recreation		
other		
TOTAL FLEXIBLE PAYMENTS		
TOTAL ALL PAYMENTS		
Recapitualtion		
total cash available		
total payments		
cash balance, end of period		

*For more specific categories see Tables D-3 and D-4.

necessary to plan to save in advance for these fixed annual expenses. The key to making it work for you is to go over it every month to see how close your spending is to your monthly estimate.

COLLEGE STUDENT BUDGETS

There are approximately eight and a half million men and women in American universities and colleges. While many students live at home, many others live in dormitories, fraternity and sorority houses, rooming houses, and apartments. Students who live away from home can rely only on themselves to make decisions about how to spend their limited incomes, whether those incomes are obtained from parents, scholarships, or part-time jobs.

Table D-2 presents a suggested budget form for college students. Expenses are anticipated both for the college year and for each month. College students have many expenses that other people do not, such as tuition, fees, books and supplies, and dues to fraternities, sororities, and honorary societies. But students can also anticipate income that most others do not: gifts from parents and others, and scholarships and prizes. All of these have to be taken into account, or else the budget content will prove to be fairly inaccurate and of less value than it could be.

You can alter the budget form to fit your particular situation. What is important is that all categories be arranged in fixed and/or flexible categories. For example, tuition is fixed in the cost per credit hour, but flexible in terms of the number of hours you may wish to take each semester. The key to making it work for you is to go over it every month and see how close to your budget specifications you actually came in your spending. If you really are out of touch with reality, this is how you can find out, and the sooner the better. How many of you in college have friends who continuously come around to you at the end of each month for a "light touch" so they can buy food until their next check comes at the first of the following month? Such spending behavior is generally due to an inability to realize that a limited budget means you just cannot buy everything you want when you want it. A more-or-less permanent budget program that is reviewed every month is one solution to such a problem.

Of course, a budget is not for everybody. You may decide that budgeting your limited income is not worthwhile. You can buy so few things that it really does not matter. You know you have to eat and pay for a room, but in addition to that you do not spend enough money to bother figuring out what you can and cannot buy. Thus, for many of you it may be quite rational to get by without drawing up a budget because the time spent in budgeting would be in excess of the potential benefits. However, you might want to consider a budget and planning program as an investment in money management skills for later years when you will have a lot more money than you need to just cover basic necessities. Often the rate of return on such an investment can be high indeed.

BUDGETING FOR THE NONSTUDENT SPENDING UNIT

Those of you in family units face a slightly different problem from the unmarried college student's. Your income is generally more predictable and is less a function of the generosity of

Table D-2 Suggested Budget Form for College Students

	ANNUAL TOTAL (estimated)	MONTH 9	10	11	12	1	2	3	4	5	6	ANNUAL TOTAL (actual)
Income												
Current earnings												
Drawn from savings												
Gifts from parents												
Gifts from others												
Grants												
Sale of assets (e.g., used textbooks)												
Scholarships, prizes												
Tax refund												
Other												
TOTAL												
Personal Expenses												
Food away from "home"												
Recreation and entertainment												
Tobacco												
Personal care												
Clothing purchases												
Clothing upkeep												
Sending messages (telephone, postage)												
Receiving messages (subscriptions)												
Medical and dental												
Transportation												
Insurance (life, health, auto)												
Gifts and donations												
Loan repayments												
Taxes												
Bank charges												
Vacations												
Fraternity/sorority												
Honorary societies, clubs												
Professional memberships												
SUBTOTAL												
College Expenses												
Tuition												
Fees												
Board												
Room												
Books												
Supplies												
Other												
TOTAL												

others. But your expenses are also generally much higher and involve payments on life insurance policies and mortgages. Naturally, you would have to expect a slightly different set of classifications for your budget than does the college student. Tables D-3 through D-7 are examples of possible budget sheets you might want to use every month. These budget sheets, remember, would be worked into a yearly expenditure tally. And this expenditure tally for the year fits in with a lifetime plan, which you, of course, have decided on with the other members of the spending unit; and which you change as your values, goals, and economic situation change.

Notice that there are entries for savings in the budget sheets. Savings are necessary to optimize your level of consumption throughout your lifetime. In other words, you save to provide for those periods when your income is very low so that your consumption—that is, your expenditures for things you like to buy—does not have to fall drastically. Saving allows you to smooth out your consumption expenditures even though your income may be variable. We all realize that we have to save for the day when, as older persons, we can no longer work. But what we do not realize is that we also save for the day when something happens to us as younger persons that temporarily keeps us from working. Saving for a rainy day is a trite but true analysis of the act of saving. The savings umbrella allows you to keep dry during the storm. After the storm is over, you start again to repair

---

Table D-3

Suggested Monthly Budget Form for Family Units

Does not include fixed monthly major contractual obligations, important future expenses, or savings and investments.

Market purchases: food, beverages, sundries	$_____
Automobile: operation, servicing, minor repairs	_____
Utility bills: electricity, fuel, water, garbage, telephone, cable TV	_____
Laundry and cleaning	_____
Clothing	_____
Incidental expenses	_____
Medical and dental expenses, prescription drugs (not covered by insurance)	_____
Adult allowances	_____
Children's allowances	_____
Family recreation: eating out, hobbies, movies, home entertainment	_____
Miscellaneous labor: babysitter, housecleaning	_____
Subscriptions: newspapers, magazines	_____
Dues: union, lodge, club (other than deducted from paycheck)	_____
Education: evening courses, school charges and fees, special lessons	_____
Religious contributions	_____
Charity contributions (other than deducted from paycheck)	_____
Unexpected expenses	_____
Other expenses	_____
TOTAL MONTHLY LIVING EXPENSES	$_____

Table D-4

Fixed Monthly Payments

Fixed by lease, mortgage, contract, court order or conscience. Does not include fixed annual or semi-annual payments, such as insurance or taxes.

Rent or mortgage payment on home	$_____
Auto loan payment—car no. 1	_____
Auto loan payment—car no. 2	_____
Appliance, TV, furniture loans	_____
Personal loans	_____
Other loans	_____
Credit card payments	_____
Major store installment debt	_____
Other contract debts or payments	_____
Regular contributions to others—parents, etc.	_____
Alimony or child support	_____
TOTAL FIXED MONTHLY PAYMENTS	$_____

that umbrella for the next time you need it. We will cover savings in more detail in Chapter 17.

Certain banks now offer monthly computerized budget accounts for a fee ranging from $3 to $6 per month. One such service is called "Money Minder" and is offered by the United States National Bank of Oregon (P.O. Box 3460, Portland, Oregon 97208). All such computerized systems offer major budget classifications with a specific code number that you mark on each check and each deposit slip. For a higher fee, you can choose up to one thousand individually selected income and expense categories. The monthly report will give you, at a minimum, the following information:

1. Total income and expense by category.

2. Number of items in each category.

3. Percentage of total income and expense by category for month.

4. Percentage of total income and expense by category year to date.

Some systems even allow you the option of budget comparisons, which will compare, for example, a fixed amount you had budgeted to a particular category compared with what you actually spent. Also, after you have used the system for at least thirteen months, you can request a previous year comparison, which permits you to see the change from last year's totals

to this year's totals for each classification. Such automated budgeting systems certainly do take away some of the drudgery that is often associated with financial planning.

If you don't wish to use a bank, you can use a separate computerized budgeting service. We give an example of the output of one such service in Exhibit D-1 on page 142. It is from Budget Control Service, Inc. (P.O. Box 105, Shelburne, Vermont 05482). The sample budget report shows how much "John Doe" spent in various categories that he chose for June 1975. The column marked YTD is how much money has been spent year-to-date for each of the expense categories. The column marked DIFF indicates whether John Doe spent more or

Table D-5

Important Future Expenses

Divide total of yearly expenses by twelve for average amount to be saved each month for big payments to come. (Of course, if you are starting your budgeting on January 1 and the car insurance is due June 30, you must have enough cash on hand by June 1 to pay the bill. If you have not yet begun saving for this expense, divide the total needed by six.)

MONTH	TAXES—FEES	INSURANCE	SHOPPING	VACATION	OTHER	TOTAL EXPENSES
JANUARY						
FEBRUARY						
MARCH						
APRIL						
MAY						
JUNE						
JULY						
AUGUST						
SEPTEMBER						
OCTOBER						
NOVEMBER						
DECEMBER						
TOTALS						

Table D-6
Monthly Money Planner

INCOME

Salary and wages—(take-home pay) husband $_____

Salary and wages—(take-home pay) wife   _____

Interest (average month)   _____

Income from securities (average month)   _____

Received from income property (average month)   _____

Other monthly income   _____

TOTAL CASH INCOME FOR AVERAGE MONTH $_____

EXPENSES

Total monthly living expenses $_____

Total fixed monthly payments   _____

Total future expenses—monthly average   _____

TOTAL AVERAGE MONTHLY EXPENSES $_____

INCOME AVAILABLE FOR SAVINGS AND INVESTMENTS $_____
(Total expenses subtracted from total income)

Table D-7
Yearly Money Planner.

MONTH	INCOME	LIVING EXPENSES	FIXED PAYMENTS	FUTURE EXPENSES	SAVINGS AND INVESTMENTS	TOTAL ALLOCATIONS
JANUARY						
FEBRUARY						
MARCH						
APRIL						
MAY						
JUNE						
JULY						
AUGUST						
SEPTEMBER						
OCTOBER						
NOVEMBER						
DECEMBER						
TOTALS						

SAVINGS	NOW	END OF YEAR	INVESTMENTS	NOW	END OF YEAR
Emergency fund			Savings bonds		
Education fund			Mutual funds— securities		
Special purposes			Real estate		
Other			Other		
TOTAL			TOTAL		

EXHIBIT D-1 Sample Budget Report

Reprinted by permission of Budget Control Service, Inc. of Shelburne, Vermont.

```
                SAMPLE  MONTHLY  REPORT


        JOHN DOE
        100 MAIN STREET
        ANY TOWN, USA  99999
```

CATEGORY	JUN '75	YTD	DIFF	AVG	%
HOUSING	180.73	1084.38	0.00	180.73	15.0
IMPROVEMENTS	0.00	283.68	0.00	47.28	3.9
ELECTRICITY	64.68	554.65	1.35	92.44	7.7
PHONE	18.26	80.61	7.59	13.43	1.1
REFUSE	5.00	26.00	1.00	4.33	0.3
SEWER & WATER	0.00	70.00	-21.30	11.66	0.9
HOUSE MISC	0.00	75.60	-20.60	12.60	1.0
FOOD	333.06	1794.99	35.02	299.16	24.9
CLOTHING	22.72	400.55	-58.73	66.75	5.5
CLEANING SUPPLIES	17.00	81.50	0.50	13.58	1.1
HOUSEHOLD MISC	19.71	87.97	-23.09	14.66	1.2
CLEANING AND LAUNDRY	3.40	13.86	1.60	2.31	0.1
PERSONAL CARE	4.00	17.51	0.85	2.91	0.2
DOCTOR	2.50	38.50	2.50	6.41	0.5
DENTIST	30.00	84.00	24.00	14.00	1.1
MEDICINE	0.00	19.28	-6.22	3.21	0.2
MEDICAL MISC	48.50	48.50	48.50	8.08	0.6
AUTO REPAIRS & MAINT	13.56	298.85	-68.30	49.80	4.1
GAS & OIL	44.07	137.74	-3.49	22.95	1.9
AUTO INSURANCE	47.10	143.10	47.10	23.85	1.9
HOME INSURANCE	0.00	151.00	0.00	25.16	2.0
PROPERTY & SCHOOL TAX	0.00	345.60	0.00	57.60	4.8
OTHER TAX	22.72	22.72	22.72	3.78	0.3
LICENSES	0.00	71.50	0.00	11.91	0.9
FINANCE CHARGES	3.40	35.78	-1.31	5.96	0.4
CLUBS & ORGANIZATIONS	1.00	15.00	-9.00	2.50	0.2
GIFTS	31.84	98.26	-16.42	16.37	1.3
EDUCATION	18.00	158.00	3.00	26.33	2.1
PET CARE	31.21	64.21	28.21	10.70	0.8
BOOKS & SUBSCRIPTIONS	29.60	120.07	5.95	20.01	1.6
ENTERTAINMENT	51.60	149.41	51.60	24.90	2.0
CONTRIBUTIONS	0.00	32.00	0.00	5.33	0.4
CHILD CARE	27.50	43.50	27.50	7.25	0.6
HOBBIES	0.00	7.63	0.00	1.27	0.1
SPORTS & EQUIPMENT	0.00	89.87	0.00	14.97	1.2
SPECIAL NO. 1	45.00	286.95	0.00	47.82	3.9
SPECIAL NO. 2	53.87	203.90	53.87	33.98	2.8
TOTALS THIS MONTH	1170.03	7236.67	134.40	1206.11	

```
                SAMPLE  MONTHLY  REPORT


BUDGET CONTROL SERVICE, INC.
```

less in June for each category than he spent in May. The column AVG gives the average monthly amount spent for each category. Finally, the column marked % gives the percentage of total expenditures spent in each category.

You fill out the names of the categories that you want up to a maximum of 50. These are then entered into your account with Budget Control Service, Inc. Each month you enter the amounts you spent in these different categories (but you do not have to add them up yourself). The cost of such a budgeting system is usually only $2 to $4 per month after a one-time programming charge of $10 to $15 is paid.

SUMMARY

1. Budget making requires (a) keeping records, (b) determining fixed and flexible expenses, (c) balancing fixed plus flexible expenses with available income, and finally, (d) reorganizing and redetermining priorities if there is a budget surplus or deficit.

2. A cash forecast for each month can be estimated and then compared with what actually happened after the fact. Any difference must be made up and can signal excessive spending.

3. A college student's budget is slightly different from a general budget because of regular college expenses and because of gifts from parents and others that may occur irregularly.

4. Record keeping is essential to effective budgeting. Perhaps the easiest way to keep records is to use a checking account and save the canceled checks.

QUESTIONS FOR THOUGHT AND DISCUSSION

1. Do you feel that a budget is worthwhile for young people? When would it not be worthwhile?

2. Does making a cash forecast seem too time consuming for you?

3. What individuals would be most likely to benefit from making detailed budgets?

4. Is it possible to live your entire life without worrying about meeting your budget?

THINGS TO DO

By all means start making out your own budget.

SELECTED READINGS

Daly, M. "Family Money Management." See issues of *Better Homes & Gardens.*

"Family Budgets in Forty Big Cities." *U.S. News & World Report,* July 2, 1973, p. 80.

"Five-Year Plan for Managing Your Money." *Changing Times,* October 1973, pp. 43–46.

Holland, B. "How to Stop Scrubbing and Start Living." *McCall's,* June 1974.

Pellegrino, V. "Teaching Your Child about Dollars and Sense." *Today's Health,* October 1973, pp. 50–55.

"Spending and Saving: Readers Tell How They Do It." *Changing Times,* November 1976, pp. 21–23.

"To Save or Invest Successfully, Make a Money Plan." *Changing Times,* May 1974, pp. 15–18.

"When Your Budget Signals Danger." *Changing Times,* February 1977, pp. 33–35.

*

GLOSSARY OF TERMS

An inflation that has gotten out of hand. In the United States, we experienced hyperinflation in the South during the Civil War. Germany experienced hyperinflation after World War I when it took wheelbarrows full of German marks to buy a loaf of bread.

Nominal Dollars

Dollars measured by their face value and not by their purchasing power.

Relative Prices

The price of something relative to the price of other things. For example, if the price of apples goes up by 50 percent and the price of oranges goes up by 100 percent, then even though apples have a higher absolute price, they have a lower relative price with respect to oranges.

Cost-of-Living, or Escalator Clause

A clause, usually in a labor contract, giving automatic wage increases tied in some way to cost-of-living rises in the economy. Cost of living is usually measured by the Consumer Price Index.

An amount added to the cost of obtaining a loan to take account of the effects of inflation. If, for example, prices are rising at 5 percent a year, a dollar loaned out today will have a value of only 95¢ when it is received a year from now. The person who loaned that dollar will require an inflationary premium of 5 percent to take account of the decreased value of the dollar to be paid back.

The High Cost of Living

CHAPTER PREVIEW

☐ What has been the history of prices in the United States?
☐ How does inflation in the United States compare to that in the rest of the world?
☐ Does inflation hurt everybody equally?
☐ Why is it important to look at *relative* prices?
☐ What has happened to income as prices have risen?
☐ What is the effect of inflation on interest rates?
☐ How does inflation affect your income taxes?

8 The constant increase in the cost of living in the United States is a phenomenon none of us has been able to avoid noticing. Rising prices now seem as inevitable as death and taxes. We are continually reminded by newspaper and magazine articles that today's dollar is worth only 24 percent of 1939's dollar. Although prices have not always gone up at such rapid annual rates, they have been rising at a compounded rate of almost 1 percent per year from 1867 to the 1970s. The pace of inflation (defined as a *sustained* rise in prices), however, has not been even.

HISTORY OF PRICES

The erratic behavior of prices is shown in Figure 8-1. After shooting up at a rate of 25 percent per year during and after the Civil War, the price index *fell* at the rate of 5.4 percent from 1867 to 1879. That is equivalent to a halving of the price level in less than 15 years. During those years of falling prices, farmers and businessmen cried out, strangely enough, for higher prices—inflation and "greenbackism," as it was later called. Farmers thought that inflation would cause the prices of their products to rise faster than the prices of the products they bought. However, politicians apparently did not listen very well, for prices kept on falling, averaging a decline of 1 percent per year from 1879 to 1897. Prices then rose 6 percent per year continually until World War I. For several years after the war, prices fell drastically and then remained fairly stable until the Great Depression, which started in 1929. Wholesale prices dropped at an average rate of 8 percent a year from the

Figure 8-1
History of Prices in the United States, 1770–1978

Here we see the wholesale price index for the past two centuries. Prices have not always been rising, even though the experience of the past few years might lead us to that conclusion. Almost every war in our history has been associated with a rise in the wholesale price index. (The figure for 1978 is an estimate.)

Source: U.S. Department of Commerce.

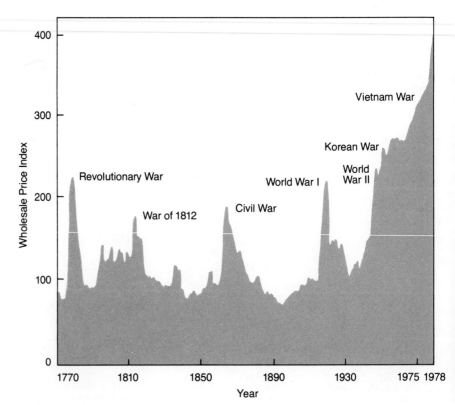

stock market crash until Roosevelt declared a "banking holiday" in March 1933. Roosevelt's attempts to raise prices were successful, and there was general inflation until 1937. Then prices leveled off until the beginning of World War II.

The rate of price rises during World War II was lower than those during both the Civil War and World War I. The wholesale price index rose 118 percent from August 1939 through August 1948—about 9 percent per year. From 1948 until the mid-1960s, prices remained quite stable except for a jump during the Korean War at the beginning of the 1950s. Since the Vietnam involvement around 1965, inflation has accelerated.

WHAT INFLATION MEANS TO YOU

Inflation is defined as a rise in prices year in and year out. It can also be defined as the reduction in the purchasing power of the dollars that you have and earn. To see where inflation will lead prices in the future, look at Exhibit 8-1. Here we show what the price of an average house will be approximately in ten years. If it is $50,000 in 1979 and the rate of inflation is 7 percent a year, by 1988 the average American family will have to come up with almost $92,000!

When comparing salaries in the past with salaries today, it is important to take account of inflation. In Exhibit 8-2 we show what the erosion by inflation does to a paycheck. If take-home pay in 1950 was $10,000, in 1977 it would have to be $25,381 just to stay even.

INFLATION IN OTHER COUNTRIES

The United States is not alone in its history of rising prices. Inflation seems to be a worldwide problem, as can be seen in Table 8-1. In fact, our rate of inflation is mild compared to those in many other countries. Some countries have had periods of **hyperinflation** that make our wartime episodes look like ripples in the monetary ocean. In 1939, Hungary had a price index set at 100; by January 1946, it was almost 5,500,000. A half year later, it was 20,000,000,000,000, or 2×10^{13}! This means that a commodity with a 1939 price tag of 100 forints would have cost 5,500,000 forints in January 1946, and by August of the same year it would have cost 20,000,000,000,000 forints. Imagine having to carry a wheelbarrow full of money to the store just to buy a loaf of dark bread!

WHO IS HURT BY INFLATION?

Do we necessarily suffer because of inflation, and, if so, is the suffering "equitably" distributed? Although we have observed that falling prices (deflation) generally bring misery, inflation certainly does not always mean prosperity. Even if it did, not everyone would benefit. When prices rise unexpectedly, those persons who have given credit to others are repaid in "cheaper" dollars—that is, dollars that cannot buy as much as before. When the price level goes up unexpectedly, any obligation fixed in terms of **nominal dollars** will cause creditors to lose and debtors to gain. The moral, of course, might be to borrow all you can if you expect an inflation that nobody else expects.

If everyone anticipates rising prices, the cost of borrowing (interest rate) will rise. People who lend money will demand higher interest rates as compensation. They know that if prices rise, the money they are repaid will buy less than when they lent it. If a person lends $8,000 (enough money to buy a Buick Riviera) when

EXHIBIT 8-1	**If 7 Percent Annual Inflation Continues for Ten Years, the Average House Will Cost:**			
	1979	$50,000	1984	70,128
	1980	53,500	1985	75,037
	1981	57,245	1986	80,289
	1982	61,252	1987	85,909
	1983	65,540	1988	91,923

prices are rising, by the time she or he is repaid, $8,000 may buy only a Dodge Dart. Debtors anticipating this decreased purchasing power will pay the higher interest rate. If you know that prices will rise 5 percent by the end of next year, you will not lend money unless you are compensated for the loss in purchasing power. You will charge 5 percent more than if you had expected no inflation: instead of 3 or 4 percent interest, you will demand 8 or 9 percent.

POCKET MONEY

All of us, in some sense, are bondholders because we carry cash with us. A dollar bill is basically a noninterest-bearing bond from the government. Its expiration date is infinity, and it pays zero cents a year in interest. Anyone holding cash during an inflation loses part of his or her real (as opposed to nominal) wealth when prices rise. The real value of your cash is what it can be traded for—what it can buy. When the price level goes up, the same amount of cash no longer buys as much. If you kept an average checking balance (which is considered to be like cash) of $100 in 1977, its purchasing power would have fallen by about 8 to 12 percent by the end of the year.

Inflation therefore causes people to lose purchasing power in proportion to the amount of cash they generally keep on hand. The only way to avoid this loss of purchasing power is to keep no cash balances. But, life without cash can be very inconvenient.

OTHERS WHO SUFFER
FROM INFLATION

In addition to the specific groups of people who can be hurt by inflation—creditors, bondholders, and those with cash balances—people with fixed incomes have suffered at least in the past. (Others, believe it or not, have actually benefited.) During the first part of the inflationary 1960s, there was price stability; during the

Table 8-1

World Rates of Inflation, 1976

Source: Federal Reserve Bank of St. Louis.

Belgium	8.6
Canada	7.2
France	9.9
West Germany	3.8
Italy	21.0
Japan	9.4
The Netherlands	8.4
Switzerland	1.0
United Kingdom	14.0
United States	5.0

EXHIBIT 8-2   **The Erosion by Inflation. What You Need to Stay Even.**

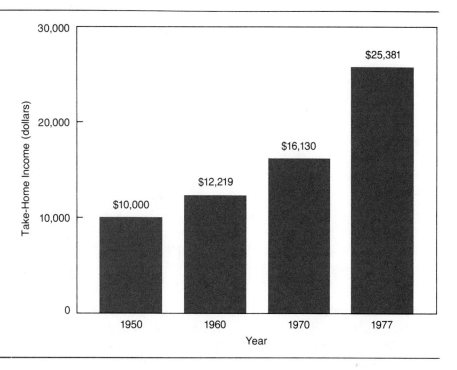

second part, prices started to increase at 1.3 percent a year, and then at as much as 6 percent a year.

The aged, who generally rely on fixed incomes, saw their real level of living fall during the period between 1964 and 1968. Social Security payments rose more than the price level, but the payoff from other retirement plans—bonds and fixed dollar-value financial assets such as savings and loan shares—did not. These payments actually fell.

Fixed Income People. Historically, all persons who have income that is fixed in nominal terms (that is, set at a dollar amount not altered to maintain a certain real level of living) will lose during unexpected inflation. Bonds and retirement payments usually pay a set amount of dollars a year. But if people were certain that prices would rise in the future, they would demand retirement plans that offered a constant real standard of living during their retirement years. Some are doing just that now.

Union Workers. Union workers also lost out during the many inflationary periods. Union workers are usually covered by long-term contracts; hence, when prices start to rise, many unions still have to wait to get wage increases. As an historical example, consider that for the three-year period between 1966 and 1969, union wage rates, after taxes, hardly rose at all in purchasing power. Since then, unions have attempted to make up for lost growth in real wages and have also tried to build into their contracts their expectations of a continuing inflation.

Ultimately, no general statement can be made that people are better or worse off during inflation. Individually, we must look at our wages and also at the value of all our assets such as a house and stocks. We must compare any changes in nominal quantities with changes in the purchasing power of the dollar in order to arrive at an idea of the real increase in our income and assets. If your house is worth 50 percent more but prices have risen 55 percent, your house has actually decreased in real value.

CONTRACTS
NEGOTIATED
IN REAL TERMS

It appears that *real* wages did not rise in many recent periods so that many workers did not actually improve their lot. We can easily see why this happened: no one expected prices to rise as rapidly as they did. If everyone feels that prices will keep rising at their current rate, workers will demand contracts that include purchasing power adjustments every year; bondholders will demand a yield (interest rate) that includes an inflationary adjustment; and retirement plan purchasers will demand variable, inflationary adjusted, future incomes. The only people who cannot completely avoid all negative effects of long-term, anticipated inflation are those who hold cash—which means all of us. We have to pay the tax imposed by inflation on the use of our currency and checking account balances as long as we continue using them.

RISING PRICES AND YOU

All of the general information about inflation may be interesting in and of itself, but, of course, what you want to know is how inflation affects you. First of all, you know that prices are rising, for that is the definition of inflation. How much prices have been rising in your area is, of course, more specifically applicable to decisions you make. Let us look at some of the average increases in prices of various consumer items over the period from 1960 to 1977. Table 8-2 shows the price rise of refrigerators, TVs, cars, and washing machines, as well as the price rise over the same period for the average of all prices, as represented by the Consumer Price Index. The Consumer Price Index is compiled by the U.S. Department of Labor, Bureau of Labor Statistics, which collects the prices of a market basket of goods and services every so often and finds out what the prices are; it then computes an index based on how these prices compare to those of some base period (1967 in Table 8-2).

CONSTRUCTING
THE CONSUMER
PRICE INDEX

The CPI is an index of the prices of some 400 goods and services obtained in 56 cities. The Bureau of Labor Statistics definition states that the Index covers:

> prices of everything people buy for living—food, clothing, automobiles, homes, house furnishings, household supplies, fuel, drugs, and recreational goods; fees to doctors, lawyers, beauty shops; rent, repair costs, transportation fares, public utility rates, etc. It deals with prices actually charged to consumers, including sales and excise taxes. It also includes real estate taxes in owned homes, but it does not include income or social security taxes.[1]

[1]U.S. Department of Labor, Bureau of Labor Statistics, *Supplement to Economic Indicators* (Washington, D.C.: U.S. Government Printing Office, 1967), p. 94.

Table 8-2

Price Changes for Certain Consumer Goods

The first column lists the Consumer Price Index for all items that consumers bought from 1960 to 1977. A price index for televisions, washing machines, electric refrigerators, and new and used cars is given for each year. Underneath each price index is what we call the relative price index, or the price of these consumer durables relative to the price of all other goods. Our base year is 1967 for both the relative price index and for the observed price index. So you see in the row after 1967 all the indices are 100. Obviously, the observed price index for many consumer durable goods has been rising at rates less rapid than the overall Consumer Price Index. In fact, the price index for television sets remained relatively constant after 1967, while the Consumer Price Index rose 25 percent. Thus, at the end of the period, the relative price of TVs had fallen around 25 percent. (1967=100; relative index is given in parentheses.)

Sources: U.S. Department of Labor, Bureau of Labor Statistics, *Handbook of Labor Statistics, 1972; Monthly Labor Review*, January 1978.

YEAR	CPI ALL ITEMS	TELEVISION SETS	ELECTRIC AUTOMATIC WASHING MACHINES	ELECTRIC REFRIGERATORS	AUTOS NEW	AUTOS USED
1960	88.7	127.1	110.7	116.8	90.6	104.5
		(143.3)	(124.8)	(131.7)	(102.1)	(117.8)
1961	89.6	123.8	107.4	115.2	91.3	104.5
		(138.2)	(119.9)	(128.6)	(101.9)	(116.6)
1962	90.6	117.7	104.5	112.5	98.0	104.1
		(129.9)	(115.3)	(124.2)	(102.6)	(114.6)
1963	91.7	114.7	103.0	109.6	93.4	103.5
		(129.9)	(115.3)	(124.2)	(102.6)	(114.9)
1964	92.9	112.1	101.6	107.4	94.7	103.2
		(120.7)	(109.4)	(115.6)	(101.9)	(111.1)
1965	94.5	107.3	100.2	104.2	96.3	100.9
		(113.5)	(106.3)	(110.3)	(101.0)	(106.8)
1966	97.2	102.1	99.7	100.2	97.5	99.1
		(105.0)	(102.5)	(103.1)	(100.3)	(103.2)
1967	100.0	100.0	100.0	100.0	100.0	100.0
		(100.0)	(100.0)	(100.0)	(100.0)	(100.0)
1968	104.2	99.8	102.5	101.3	102.8	—
		(95.8)	(98.4)	(97.2)	(98.7)	—
1969	109.8	99.6	104.6	103.1	104.4	103.1
		(90.7)	(95.3)	(93.9)	(95.1)	(93.9)
1970	116.3	99.8	107.3	105.8	107.6	104.3
		(85.8)	(92.3)	(91.0)	(92.5)	(89.6)
1971	121.3	100.1	104.1	108.1	112.0	110.2
		(82.5)	(85.8)	(89.1)	(92.3)	(90.8)
1972	125.3	99.5	110.5	108.7	111.0	110.5
		(79.4)	(88.2)	(86.7)	(88.5)	(88.2)
1977	183.0	137.1	148.0	141.0	146.0	188.0
		(74.9)	(80.8)	(77.0)	(79.8)	(102.7)

For a number of years the Consumer Price Index was based on a 1960-61 survey of a market basket of goods and services purchased by individuals. A new survey of spending patterns was done in 1972-73. The changes in individual spending patterns were taken into account in revising the CPI, which was newly issued in early 1978. The current Index measures the prices of a market basket of goods and services purchased by all urban workers.

Clearly, there are problems with the CPI. Even the newest one was five years out of date when it was put into effect. Officials at the Bureau of Labor Statistics would like to have a continuing survey of consumer spending patterns, thereby allowing them to update the Index regularly. However, that would require substantial increased government funding—something that is not likely to happen in the near future.

Do you notice something strange in Table 8-2? The prices of some goods have risen less than the Consumer Price Index. That tells you that the **relative prices** (given in parentheses below the observed price indexes) of certain goods are lower today than they were 20 years ago. This is an important distinction that you as a wise consumer should always make. It does not matter to you what the *absolute* (or observed) price level is; what matters to you in your purchases is the *relative* prices of those things you buy. If all other prices went up by 500 percent, but the price of washing machines went up only by 100 percent, then even though the *absolute* price of washing machines would be higher, washing machines would have become a very good deal because their *relative* price would have fallen dramatically.

AND INCOME, TOO

So far, our argument has been academic. If everything went up in price except your wages or income, you would really be in trouble. But Figure 8-2 shows the average income in the United States. It has been going up at 8.5 percent a year for the last five years. In other words, incomes generally go up not only as much as prices, but even a little more every year. Thus, even though prices have risen, most of us are actually better off at the end of the year because our wages or total incomes have risen even more. You may be convinced that rising prices are killing you, but you must take stock of what your real standard of living is: if your income went up by 7 percent and prices went up only by 5, your real standard of living went up by 2 percent, in spite of the inflation. Do not be taken in by arguments that we are all worse off because of inflation. Only those of us who do not have income increases that match or exceed the rate of inflation are truly worse off; and, historically, the incomes of few people have failed to keep up with inflation. Those who generally suffer are the ones mentioned above—people on fixed incomes and the like.

ANTICIPATING INFLATION

To avoid being hurt by inflation, you must anticipate it. And we generally anticipate inflation by looking at the behavior of past prices. If we think that inflation will continue, we will act accordingly. We will demand—if we have the power—higher salaries to take account of the inflation; we will realize that things are going to cost us more in the future; and we will not be satisfied, for example, with keeping constant levels of insurance or retirement benefits available for us, because we know that the real value of those items will be lowered by rising prices. Remember, the real value of anything is its implicit purchasing power. As prices rise, the real

**Figure 8-2
Per Capita Personal
Disposable Income**

Per capita personal
disposable income is
expressed in current
dollars. That is, it
is not corrected for
changes in the price
level. Notice that
it has been going up
steadily from 1919
until the present,
except for the Great
Depression when
it started going down.

Source: *Business Con-
ditions Digest*, U.S. De-
partment of Commerce and
Survey of Current Business,
various issues.

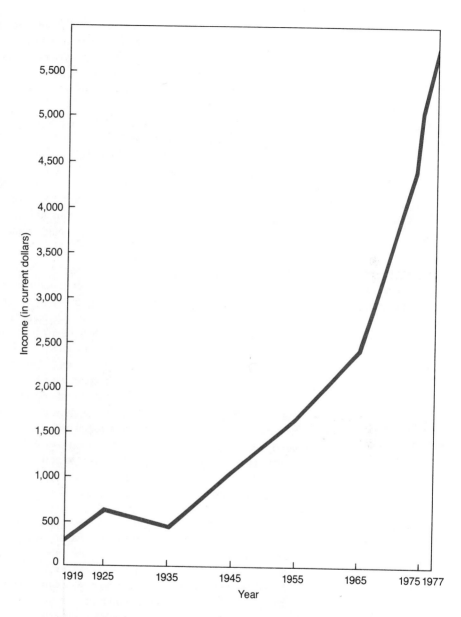

value of a $50,000 insurance policy falls because $50,000 buys less and less
every year.

**INTEREST RATES
AGAIN**

When we talk about interest rates, we must mention the relationship between
market interest rates—that is, the ones you have to pay—and the rate of inflation.
Every time you borrow money, you must pay a price for the use of that money.
Whenever inflation is anticipated, creditors wish to be compensated for the cheap-
ening of the dollars that they will be repaid. That is, creditors tack on an **inflationary premium** to take account of the depreciation in the dollars they will get back,
for those dollars will buy less. For example, if you borrow $1,000 and 1 year later
repay your creditor $1,000 plus interest and there has been no inflation at all, then

the purchasing power of the principal—$1,000—is exactly what it was a year before. However, if there has been a 10 percent inflation, your creditor will be able to purchase only $900 worth of goods and services because of that inflation: the purchasing power of that $1,000 will have fallen 10 percent. No one will want to loan out money unless there is an inflationary premium in addition to the normal interest rate.

Moreover, debtors are willing to pay that inflationary premium because they know that they are going to pay back their debt in depreciated dollars. If you subtract the anticipated rate of inflation from the interest rate charged you for a loan, you get the real rate of interest; that is, the real cost to you in terms of what you are giving up in purchasing power to have command over goods and services today instead of waiting. If the rate of inflation in the United States went to 100 percent a year, you would not be surprised, then, to see interest rates of 105 percent, if people thought that rate of inflation would remain in effect forever.

HOW TO TELL WHERE YOU STAND

How can you tell where you stand with respect to inflation? The easiest way is to try to figure out how many hours it takes you to earn enough income to buy your essentials. Compare the number of hours, for example, it might take you to work in order to pay for a good restaurant meal with how many hours of work it took to pay for that same meal five years ago. Do the same thing for other items you buy. In all probability, most of you will find that it takes fewer hours now to purchase essentials than it did five or ten years ago. What does that mean? It means that your real standard of living may have gone up, in spite of the inflation. Inflation per se is only bad to the extent that we do not anticipate it and/or cannot take account of it. Once it is fully anticipated, then everything adjusts with it: wages, interest rates, and investment plans. Witness what has happened in Israel, a country with a fairly steady rate of inflation for the last ten years: **cost-of-living clauses** are added on to just about all contracts. We are starting to see this in the United States also, where, in 1977, an estimated 6½ million workers were covered under contracts with cost-of-living clauses.

WHAT IS A COST-OF-LIVING CLAUSE?

A cost-of-living, or **escalator clause** in a wage contract is inserted to guarantee workers that they will not be hurt by unexpected inflation. A clause may read that workers' wages will go up 3 percent a year plus whatever percentage the Consumer Price Index went up. That way workers know that their real standard of living will go up by 3 percent a year no matter what happens to overall prices. As inflation becomes a more permanent part of American economic society, you will probably see more and more cost-of-living clauses inserted in contracts. Social Security benefits, as well as federal pension payments, are already tied to the cost of living. Food stamp allotments are another area where an escalator clause is in effect.

IF YOU KNOW PRICES ARE GOING UP, SHOULD YOU BUY NOW?

Many people think that in a period of inflation, all purchases for houses, stereos, cars, and the like should be made right away because prices will be higher in the future. This belief may or may not be true: if inflation is fully anticipated, then your basic decision about when to purchase a house or a car depends not in the least on inflation itself. Your timing of purchases should be based on your expected income, how much you want something, whether you are willing to wait, and so on. For example, say that you do not want to buy a car until next year, but you know

Table 8-3

The effect of Inflation on Take-home Pay

Because of graduated income tax rates, even families lucky enough to get raises matching the big increase in living costs wound up losing purchasing power. Here we show how a 9.4% inflation outruns a 9.4% pay raise.

	GROSS INCOME	FEDERAL INCOME TAX	EFFECTIVE RATE	AFTER-TAX INCOME IN YEAR 1 DOLLARS
Year 1	$14,000	$1,600	11.4%	$12,400
Year 2	15,316	1,890	12.3	12,164
Year 1	20,000	3,010	15.1	16,990
Year 2	21,880	3,506	16.0	16,646
Year 1	30,000	6,020	20.1	23,980
Year 2	32,820	7,035	21.4	23,361

the price is going up 4 percent because that has been the rate of inflation for a long time. If you buy the car this year, you will most likely borrow the money just as you would next year. Thus, for this year you will have to pay an interest rate on whatever you borrow. That interest rate will take account of the expected inflation of 4 percent, so you will be no better off by buying now than by waiting until next year and paying a higher price.

If you think inflation is more or less anticipated by everybody, you are not any better off buying now than waiting and paying a higher price in the future. And, as we have seen, as prices go up through inflation, income usually goes up also, and often even more so. In other words, the increased price of those potential purchases may be no greater relative to your income.

INFLATION AND INCOME TAXES

As we will see in Chapter 18, the United States has a progressive income tax system: as your income goes up, you have to pay a higher rate of taxation on the last several thousand dollars you earn. This has grave implications in a period of inflation. Suppose that all prices and wages went up every year by 20 percent. Your real income would not increase; that is, your level of living would be the same. Nonetheless, you *would* pay higher federal income taxes, because as your *nominal* dollar income rose due to inflation, you would jump into higher and higher income tax brackets. Hence, inflation can hurt you in that respect even if you anticipate it in all other respects. The only way out of this box is to persuade the government to express your personal exemption and the size of each tax bracket as a number of dollars times the price index: say that prices rose by 20 percent, and the personal exemption today is $750; when prices rose 20 percent, it should become $750 plus $150, or $900. The first tax bracket, taxes at 14 percent, should rise to 0 to $600 instead of the current 0 to $500, that is, an addition of 20 percent.

ARE YOU BETTER OFF OWNING A HOUSE DURING INFLATION?

Many people think that during inflation it is better to own a house because its value will go up. Although that sounds so obvious, so inevitably true, it is not true. Assume that you bought a $40,000 house. There is an inflation in home values of 10 percent a year. At the end of one year, you could sell that house for $44,000. Now, are you better off by owning it? Well, the cost to you of staying in the house is the same whether you own it or not. If someone else owned it and you were renting, you would be charged a higher rental fee. But since you own it, you in fact obtain an implicit rental value from having the house. You incur a higher opportunity cost for staying in it. The implicit rental value of that house will go up by 10 percent. You will implicitly be paying more to live in it. So on the one hand you gain, but on the other hand you lose in an equal amount. After all, you could sell the house for $44,000 and invest the money to get an explicit rate of return. The higher the value of the house, the higher the opportunity cost you are incurring by not selling it. It does not matter to you, actually, if you were given a house free. You are paying for the services rendered by that house whether you like it or not, because you always have the opportunity of selling it and investing the money. You are not made better off by the fact that inflation has caused the value of your house to go up, for it has caused the value of all housing services to go up. Hence, if you sold your house, you would have to pay a higher price for anything you moved into. (However, if the value of your house went up faster than the rate of inflation, you are obviously a wealthier person.)

But if the *relative* cost of housing has gone up, you may decide to purchase less of it: you may decide to sell your house, which has appreciated in value, and move into smaller, less expensive quarters, and do something with the money difference. That is a decision many of us rarely have to make because the *relative* price of housing generally does not change, although it has somewhat in the last few years. It may also change for you if you happen to live in an area that suddenly becomes a boom town, *whether or not you own the house and no matter what you paid for it.* An opportunity cost is not written in your checkbook ledger, but a rational consumer takes account of opportunities even if they are only implicit.

SUMMARY

1. Prices have not always risen in the United States; in fact, during some periods they have fallen. Falling prices over any period of time is called deflation.
2. Not everyone is hurt equally by inflation. However, everyone who holds cash is hurt by a rise in prices because that cash has a lower purchasing power. Inflation, in a sense, taxes the cash that you hold in the form of currency and checking accounts.
3. Whenever there is an unanticipated inflation, individuals on fixed incomes suffer because the purchasing power of those fixed incomes falls as inflation remains.
4. It is important to distinguish between a general rise in all prices and a specific or relative rise in the price of a commodity you are buying. Even though all goods have gone up in price recently, some have gone up at a slower rate than the average of all prices as expressed in the Consumer Price Index. Such things as televisions, cars, stereos, refrigerators, and washing machines now have a lower relative price than they had 20 years ago.
5. If incomes did not rise along with inflation, we would all be worse off. However, in the United States, incomes have consistently risen at a slightly faster rate than inflation, thus leading to a rising standard of living for Americans. The key to not getting hurt by inflation is to anticipate it.
6. Whenever inflation is anticipated, nominal interest rates will rise to take account of that inflation. In other words, an inflationary premium will be tacked on to interest rates to take account of the reduced purchasing power of the

dollars paid back. In order to figure out the real rate of interest, you must subtract what you expect will be the rate of inflation over the period of the loan.

7. More and more workers are being covered by cost-of-living, or escalator, clauses, which automatically increase nominal salaries whenever there is an increase in the Consumer Price Index. In addition, the workers' contracts usually are negotiated to include a real increase in wages of several percent a year or more.

8. With our progressive system of taxation, inflation can put individuals in higher income tax brackets even though their *real* income has not gone up. Thus, in real terms, the after-tax income falls and the individual is worse off.

9. In general, you are not any better off owning a home during a period of inflation as opposed to a period when there is no inflation. Only if the relative price of housing goes up is it better to own.

QUESTIONS FOR THOUGHT AND DISCUSSION

1. Why would anybody want inflation?
2. How can inflation be so terrible, since our paying a higher price for something yields somebody else that higher price as an increased income?
3. Do you have any idea of what a repressed inflation could be?
4. How many Americans do you think are covered by some form of cost-of-living clauses? (Hint: Social Security payments are now tied to the Consumer Price Index.)
5. Why would anybody sign a long-term contract if it had no cost-of-living clause?
6. Is it important to know the rise in absolute prices—that is, what has happened to the Consumer Price Index—or to find out what has happened to the relative prices of the things you buy?

THINGS TO DO

1. Go to the reference section of your library and look at *The Federal Reserve Bulletin*, *The Survey of Current Business*, *Business Conditions Digest*, or *The Monthly Labor Review*. Find out what inflation has been during the past year or so. These government documents contain several indicators that give different types of prices indexes. Does it matter which one you use?
2. Find out what has happened to the relative price of television sets, washing machines, refrigerators, and automobiles since 1977. (Hint: Find the Consumer Price Index for all items and divide it into the price index for the four items just listed.)

SELECTED READINGS

Bach, G. L. *The New Inflation: Causes, Effects and Cures.* Providence, R.I.: Brown University Press, 1973.

"Behind the Fears of Another Price Explosion." *U.S. News*, May 14, 1977, pp. 38-39.

"Can You Inflation-Proof Your Savings?" *Changing Times*, October 1974, pp.7-12.

Holt, Charles C., et al. *The Unemployment-Inflation Dilemma: A Manpower Solution.* Washington, D.C.: Urban Institute, 1971.

"How Government Itself Keeps Prices Rising." *U.S. News*, April 18, 1977, pp. 16-17.

Protecting Yourself Against Inflation

It is not easy for you to protect yourself against inflation, but there are some ways in which you can at least improve the protection you might have already.

MINIMIZING THE COSTS OF CASH

If you have an average checking account balance of $100 a year and there is a 10 percent inflation, the purchasing power of that checking account balance is going to fall by 10 percent. You will implicitly be paying an inflationary tax on holding cash. One way that you can reduce the size of this inflationary tax is to reduce the level of cash that you use. In other words, you can economize on the amount of cash you hold and put the difference in an interest-bearing asset. There are now several ways in which you can do this that were not available in the past. They are usually known as NOW, negotiable orders of withdrawal, or such things as transfunds or other similar arrangements whereby all or part of your excess cash earns interest while you are not using it. Obviously, the higher the rate of inflation, the more incentive you have to try these systems, for you are losing money every day on a checking account balance that earns no interest or on dollars you keep in your wallet or purse.

ADJUST YOUR LIFE INSURANCE

Once you have figured out your life insurance needs (a topic we discuss in Issue N), realize that they do not take account of inflation. Hence, adjust your life insurance policies every once in a while to take account of the decreased purchasing power implicit in the face value of those policies. Many insurance companies are now issuing "agreements for a cost-of-living benefit" by which every year you are charged a fee to have your existent life insurance policies increased in value to take account of inflation. Usually, the Consumer Price Index is used as a basis. For example, say that you have $10,000 worth of term life insurance a year which costs you $5 per $1,000. Your total payment at the end of the year would be $50. Now, say that in one year the Consumer Price Index went up by 10 percent. You would get a bill from the insurance company for $5. If you agreed to pay it, you would have a life insurance policy worth $11,000 in face value. You would still have the same real amount of protection and it would still cost you the same real amount, although the nominal, or dollar, payment would go up by 10 percent to take account of the inflation. Whenever possible, you might wish to purchase cost-of-living

benefit agreements for whatever insurance you have. Or every few years, make sure you take out more insurance to take account of inflation.

TAKING OUT LOANS

Whenever you take out a loan of any type, you obviously benefit if the future inflation rate is higher than that anticipated by the creditor. But do not bet on your being able to outsmart creditors; usually, the interest rate that you will pay reflects future rates of inflation. If, however, you are fairly confident that the rate of inflation today is higher than it will be in the future, you may attempt to get variable-interest-rate loan contracts, particularly if you happen to be taking out a home mortgage. At the very minimum, you would want your mortgage to have a no-penalty for prepayment clause put in so that you could pay it off and refinance it at a lower rate if interest rates in the future in fact fall. With variable interest rates, no one loses (and no one gains) from any changes in money-market interest rates that reflect changes in the rate of inflation.

RETIREMENT PLANS

Be certain that the retirement plan you take out is not of the fixed-sum type, unless that sum is so large that you will be able to live on it even if inflation continues until you retire. Variable annuities for retirement and life insurance policies are generally available. However, these are usually linked to the stock market, and the stock market, as we will see in Chapter 17, is an imperfect protection against inflation, although in the long run it does not do too badly. What you would really prefer is to have the face value of your retirement annuity plan automatically adjust for inflation; you would have to pay a higher premium each year to compensate for that adjustment. When you discuss your pension plan or your retirement plan with your employer or your insurance agent, be sure that all of these things are considered so that you can choose the plan that best enables you to avoid being surprised by a high rate of inflation in the future.

YOUR WAGES

One way to make sure that you do not get caught unprepared by an unexpected rise in prices is to have an escalator clause, which adjusts your wages automatically to changes in the cost of living. You may want to bargain for this individually with your employer or get your union representative (if you have one) to have an escalator clause put in the next contract.

TAXES

There is very little you can do to avoid the effects of inflation on raising your effective tax burden. The only thing you can do is always vote for candidates who ask for lower taxes.

MINIMIZING CASH HOLDINGS

Inflation can also be defined as the rate of reduction in the value or purchasing power of cash. Therefore, the faster the rate of inflation, the more costly it is for you to hold cash in the form of dollar bills and checking account balances. Hence, one way you can fight against a rising rate of inflation is by reducing your average cash holdings. You can do this by, for example, keeping excess cash in an interest-earning savings account (which still may not be a good deal, but certainly gives you a higher rate than zero). You can spend more time planning your expenditures so as to match the receipts of your income. In this way, you will not be required to carry as large an amount in your checking account or in your wallet. Of course, the larger your average checking account or currency balance, and the greater the rate of inflation, the more important this consideration is.

SOME WAYS TO COMBAT INFLATION THROUGH SMART BUYING

There are, of course, important buying techniques that one can apply at all times. During a period of inflation, these techniques become even more important. You may wish to use some or all of them every time you go out to shop.

1. **Compare values.** Take time to be sure you are comparing possible alternative ways to satisfy particular needs or desires, even within the same store.

2. **Buy for the intended use of the product.** Don't, for exam-

ple, use high quality wine for cooking purposes or fancy canned tomatoes for stew. Use dried milk solids for cooking rather than fresh milk.

3. **Buy basic styles in clothing.** To cut down on clothing budgets, stick to basic styles rather than high fashion.

4. **Buy store brand items.** Private brands can save you from 10 percent to 60 percent. This is true not only for food, but also for appliances. Some of Ward's ranges are actually made by Tappan. Many of their other appliances are made by Westinghouse. J. C. Penney's Penncrest appliances are mostly made by Hotpoint. Their power tools are made by Skil. Private brand liquor is usually the way some manufacturers move inventory while avoiding cutting prices on their advertised brand.

5. **Do not overpay for convenience.** The price is usually high per unit of quantity provided when you buy additional convenience in the form of pushbutton containers, aerosol cans, or buttered frozen vegetables; or when you buy at small convenience stores.

6. **Buy in larger quantities and store.**

7. **Take advantage of sales throughout the year.** Table E-1 gives you a bargain calendar indicating when stores usually have sales.

YOU CAN'T COMPLETELY PROTECT YOURSELF

The key to protecting yourself against inflation is to realize the decline in the purchasing power of money paid to you in the future. If you think through all of the exchanges you make

Table E-1

Know When to Shop

January
small electric appliances
drugs, toiletries
floor coverings, rugs
furniture

February
housewares, tableware

March
garden equipment and supplies

April
fabrics

May
tires

June
major appliances
lumber

July
floor coverings, rugs
furniture
garden equipment and supplies

August
floor coverings, rugs
furniture
paint, tools, hardware
patio furniture
tires

September
mufflers, batteries
paints, tools, hardware
housewares, tableware

October
major appliances

November
major appliances
silverware

December
toys (after Xmas)

or are going to make and include an inflationary factor, you will be ahead of the game. There is no way that you can completely protect yourself against inflation in a world where inflation has different rates that people cannot completely anticipate. If everything were written in real terms—that is, with purchasing power clauses or escalator clauses—then you would not have to worry. But not everything is, at least not yet. So you do have to worry. Do not lose sleep over it; just make sure you take advantage of every new inflation protector that you can buy, such as cost-of-living benefit additions to

your life insurance, cost-of-living escalator clauses on your wage contracts, and checking accounts in which you can earn interest on unused balances. You can learn to live with inflation. You may never like it. You may never be able to make it your friend. But you can make sure that it does not destroy your well-being, now or in the future.

SUMMARY

1. During inflation, it is important to minimize the cost of holding cash by reducing the cash you hold that does not bear

interest and the balance you have in your checking account.

2. It would be advisable to adjust your life insurance to take account of inflation (as well as all other insurance you have, such as on your home and on your personal effects).

3. Any retirement plans that you participate in, such as pensions, should be set up to take account of inflation. Therefore, at least part of your retirement income should be in the form of variable annuities that will reflect increases in the stock market. In the past, the stock market has reflected inflation, although it did not during most of the 1970s.

4. Whenever possible, a cost-of-living clause inserted into a labor contract will minimize any negative effect that inflation could have on your standard of living.

QUESTIONS FOR THOUGHT AND DISCUSSION

1. Inflation has been called a tax on cash. Why?

2. If your income goes up by 10 percent and prices do also, are you better or worse off?

3. Do all wages go up at least at the rate of inflation?

THINGS TO DO

Compute college tuition costs where you go to school for the last ten years. The Registrar's Office can probably provide the information or you can look through old catalogs. Find out the percentage increase over that period. Has it been greater or less than the change in the Consumer Price Index, which you can find in numerous government publications, such as the *Monthly Labor Review*, the *Annual Economic Report of the President*, or the *Survey of Current Business*?

SELECTED READINGS

Brimmer, A. "Why Inflation Hits Some People Less than Others." *Nations Business*, February 1977, pp. 38–40.

"Drive to Keep Prices from Soaring Higher." *U.S. News*, April 25, 1977, pp. 23–25.

"Galloping New Inflation of Fears." *Time*, March 14, 1977, p. 38.

"Plan for Fighting the Double Digits." *Time*, April 18, 1977, pp. 59–60.

Samuelson, P. A. "Hedging Against Inflation." *Newsweek*, May 27, 1974, p. 73.

Walinsky, L. J. "What Can We Do about Inflation?" *New Republic*, March 2, 1974, pp. 21–25.

*

GLOSSARY OF TERMS

Bankruptcy

The state of having come under the provisions of the law that entitles a person's creditors to have his or her estate administered for their benefit.

Consumer Durables

Goods that consumers buy that last more than a short period of time. Examples of consumer durables are stereos, television sets, cars, and houses.

Service Flow

The flow of benefits received from an item that has been purchased or made. Consumer durables generally give a service flow that lasts over a period of time. For example, the service flow from a stereo may be a certain amount of satisfaction received from it every year for five years.

Collateral

The backing that in many cases an individual puts up to obtain a loan. Whatever is placed as collateral for a loan can be sold in order to repay that loan if the debtor cannot pay it off as specified in the loan agreement. For example, the collateral for a new car loan is generally the new car itself. If the finance company does not get paid for its car loan, it can then repossess the car, sell it, and thereby attempt to pay itself.

Right of Rescission

The right to back down, or "bow out," on a contract or an agreement that has been signed. For example, before you sign an agreement to buy a set of encyclopedias, you might want to obtain a notice of cancellation that gives you the right of rescission during a three-day period.

Installment Contract

A loan made to be repaid in specified, usually equal, amounts over a certain number of months. The contract specifies amount and method of payment.

Holder-in-Due-Course Doctrine

A legal doctrine that allows a third party, such as a finance company that has purchased an installment contract, to continue to receive payments even if the product is defective.

Negotiable Orders of Withdrawal (NOW)

A type of check drawn on a special savings account offered in a couple of states in the United States; it is a request to withdraw funds from a savings account and transfer them to a third party, just as with a check on your checking account.

Transactions Costs

The costs associated with any economic activity. For example, the transactions costs of obtaining a loan might involve searching for the best deal, reading a lengthy contract, and so on.

The Overextended American

CHAPTER PREVIEW

☐ How much are Americans in debt, and what are the characteristics of that debt?

☐ What are the various sources of credit?

☐ Why do individuals borrow?

☐ What are interest rates all about, and what is their relationship to inflation?

☐ Can interest rate ceilings help consumers?

☐ How does the Truth-in-Lending Act affect you?

☐ How are banks regulated?

9 In 1786, the city of Concord, Massachusetts, the scene of one of the first battles of the Revolution, there were three times as many people in debtors prison as there were in prison for all other crimes combined. In Worcester County, the ratio was even higher—20 to 1. Most of the prisoners were small farmers who could not pay their debts. In August of 1786, mobs of musket-bearing farmers seized county courthouses to halt the trials of debtors. Led by Daniel Shays, a captain from the Continental Army, the rebels launched an attack on the Federal Arsenal at Springfield; although they were repulsed, their rebellion continued to grow into the winter. Finally George Washington wrote to a friend:

> For God's sake, tell me what is the cause of these commotions. Do they proceed from licentiousness, British influence disseminated by the Tories, or real grievances which admit to redress? If the latter, why were they delayed until the public mind had become so agitated? If the former, why are not the powers of government tried at once?

THE AMERICAN IN DEBT

Debt, as you can see, has been a problem in the United States from its colonial beginnings. In fact, The Society for the Amelioration of the Condition of Debtors was formed shortly before the American Revolution by a group of New York businessmen. Today, the overextended American is still with us. He or she is not the type of person you might think. Instead of a poor ghetto dweller in a disadvantaged situation (who has a hard time getting credit anyway), the overextended American is more accurately portrayed as a reasonably well-off blue-collar worker who makes $900 a month, typically with a spouse and two or more children. But his or her indebtedness (excluding the home mortgage) is in the neighborhood of $4,000 to $5,000. While these overextended Americans might be what people call "credit drunk" or compulsive buyers, they are more realistically described as simply average Americans who bit by bit got into debt deep over their heads. When they start to drown, they declare personal **bankruptcy**.

BANKRUPTCIES

Bankruptcies are on the rise. Every year almost a quarter million Americans use personal bankruptcy proceedings to seek refuge from what they consider excessive debts. The Constitution allows Congress "to establish an uniform Rule of Naturalization, and uniform Laws on the subject of Bankruptcies throughout the United States." So we have the Federal Bankruptcy Act to help us out. In 1960 there were fewer than 100,000 personal nonbusiness bankruptcies. By 1970 there were almost 180,000, and by 1978 the estimate is 220,000. Just because a person has filed for bankruptcy does not mean his or her life is ruined. In fact, many of those who have gone through bankruptcy proceedings eventually start using credit again; one estimate is that 80 percent of those who file for bankruptcy use credit and are in debt trouble again within five years.

In spite of people who continue to go into debt over their heads, and in spite of all the cries of the overextended American, the amount of debt outstanding in the United States keeps on rising.

THE INDEBTED SOCIETY

At least 50 percent of all Americans have outstanding installment debt at any given time. In 1976 the median debt for families with debt was almost $2,000. For families of adults under 45 years of age and no children, fully 25 percent had

$2,000 or more of outstanding debt. Figure 9-1 shows the total amount of aggregate debt in the United States over the past few decades. It has risen to a monumental $1¼ trillion and is expected to rise even more. Of course, part of this is due to inflation and another part is due to a rising population. For a better perspective, the bottom line in Figure 9-1 gives the inflation-corrected per capita debt in the United States.

We break down the total credit into categories in Table 9-1. Today, installment debt repayment now takes almost 15 percent of disposable personal income. People get credit from a variety of formal sources at which we will now look.

SOURCES OF CREDIT

There are numerous places where you can get credit when you want to buy something on time. Although not exhaustive, the following list indicates the range of possibilities.

COMMERCIAL BANKS

The most obvious place to obtain credit is a commercial bank. Today, the personal loan departments of commercial banks make almost 60 percent of the loans for automobile purchases, as well as almost 30 percent of all loans for other consumer goods.

SALES FINANCE COMPANIES

Sales finance companies buy installment credit from retail merchants; in this way, retailers sell the risk involved in loaning money. For example, a finance company may take over title to the car you bought. It collects a monthly or weekly payment from you and hands over the title to the car when you have finished the payments. Finance companies supply almost 30 percent of automobile credit and account for about 35 percent of all personal loans.

CONSUMER FINANCE COMPANIES

Consumer finance companies are small loan companies generally making small loans to consumers at relatively high rates of interest. These are the loan com-

**Figure 9-1
Total Private Debt in the United States.**

Total private individual noncorporate enterprise debt in the United States has been on the rise for many years, exceeding well over $1 trillion. We also indicate per capita total private and noncorporate enterprise debt expressed in 1967 dollars. That figure has more or less leveled off in the last few years.
Source: Federal Reserve Bank.

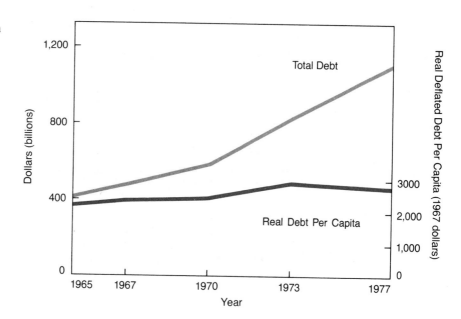

Table 9-1

Installment Credit

Source: *Survey of Current Business*, March 1977.

	DOLLARS (BILLIONS)
Total Installment Credit Outstanding	$178.0
By credit type:	
Automobiles	60.3
Revolving Bank Cards	14.0
Mobile Homes	11.4
Home Improvement	8.7
All Others	83.6
By holder:	
Commercial Banks	85.0
Finance Companies	39.7
Credit Unions	30.4
Retailers	18.7
All Others	4.2

panies you hear advertised on radio and TV and are the largest suppliers of installment cash loans—that is, loans that consumers usually obtain for buying things other than such durable consumer goods as cars, TVs, and stereos. There are perhaps 25,000 licensed consumer finance offices in America today. Such companies offer debt consolidation loans whereby a debtor pays off several small loans with the money from one big loan.

CREDIT UNIONS

Credit unions are special consumer cooperative agencies that are usually chartered by states and the federal government. You have to be a member of a credit union in order to use it. Teachers and workers in large unions or companies often have their own credit unions. Credit unions account for about 13 percent of all consumer installment credit.

CREDIT CARDS

Today, more than 50 percent of all families have at least one nongasoline credit card, and 25 percent have three or more. You are probably familiar with the most widely known of these—Master Charge, BankAmericard (VISA), and Chargex. There are about six thousand banks today that offer Master Charge, and four thousand that offer BankAmericard (VISA).

RETAIL STORES

An increasingly large number of retail outlets offer some form of credit to their customers. Virtually all major department stores such as Sears, Penneys, Marshall Fields, and Wards offer several types of credit arrangements to customers. These stores provide individual credit cards that are similar to Master Charge and BankAmericard.

NONCREDIT CARDS—PAY CASH AND PAY LESS

When you use a credit card, the merchant accepting it generally has to pay the credit card company a fee of up to 8 percent. Moreover, the merchant doesn't get his or her money until the credit slips are turned in and processed. Hence, if you pay cash, you save the merchant some money. Sometimes the savings get passed on to you.

The Fair Credit Billing Act that went into effect in October 1975 allows merchants to give customers up to a 5 percent discount for paying cash. However, these merchants are not obliged to grant such discounts. Before this legislation was enacted, merchants risked losing the right to accept a particular credit card if they offered such cash discounts. The new law says that a credit company cannot prohibit the granting of cash discounts by retail stores. In fact, Consumers Union brought suit against the American Express Company, which prohibited merchants using its charging facilities to openly offer cash discounts.

There are even "cash" cards that you can obtain now that, when shown to member merchants, allow you to obtain a "cash" discount. In the mid-1970s, there were at least three cash card companies—Equity Club International, Savers Clubs of America, and United International Club, Inc.—in existence with a total membership of about one-half million.

LOANS ON YOUR LIFE INSURANCE

If you have a life insurance policy with a cash value (whole or straight life, usually), then you may indeed be able to obtain a relatively low-cost loan on your life insurance policy. We discuss various life insurance policies in Chapter 16. Suffice it to say here that you usually pay something less than 10 percent for a loan on the value of your policy. You cannot be turned down for a loan from your insurance company, and no questions are asked about what the money will be used for. Your credit rating has nothing to do with whether or not you get the loan. You can take as long or as short a period you wish to repay. In fact, whenever the policy becomes payable—either because it matures or the owner of it dies—any outstanding loan is deducted from the amount of the insurance claim that the company must pay. Hence, any loan you take out reduces your insurance protection.

WHY BORROW?

Why should you ever borrow money? Some of you may be puritanical about it and answer, "There is no reason that you should ever borrow money. Pay cash for everything and never have debt hanging over your head." This is the attitude throughout much of traditional Europe today; there is a moral dislike of borrowing as a way to purchase goods and services.

The reason most of us borrow, however, is very simple. For example, you have decided that you want to buy an automobile. Now, you are not buying an automobile *per se*. What you are really buying are the *services* from that automobile for each day, week, month, and year that you will have it. In fact, what is really important to you is the cost per service flow per period. In other words, what does it cost you per month to operate that Ford, as compared to that VW or that Toyota? What will it cost you per month or per year to buy a new car instead of keeping your old one? Cars are sometimes called **consumer durables**, just as are houses, TVs, stereos, and other things that last a relatively long time. You do not consume them immediately; rather, you consume the services from them over a period of time: they are durable.

Now, when you go to the movies, you consume that movie during the hour and a half or two you are there, and you also pay for that movie when you consume it. When you go out to dinner, you eat the meal and that is the end of it. You pay for it on the spot, usually. What are you doing when you consume things and pay for them at the same time? You are synchronizing the payment for the good or service with the rate at which you are consuming it. Why not think of this as the reason for borrowing? You want to synchronize the payments for the services you are consuming from a consumer durable, such as an automobile, with the services themselves. Therefore, you do not feel obliged to pay for the car with cash because you are going to be using it over a certain number of years. What you decide to do usually is to purchase the automobile on time. You decide to borrow. *When you borrow, then, you are merely synchronizing your cash outlay to correspond more or less with the* **service flow** *from the good you purchased.* That is why you may wish to borrow.

There are, of course, other reasons why you may wish to borrow money. They include, but are not limited, to:

1. Taking advantage of advertised specials when you are short of cash.
2. Consolidating bills.
3. Having a safeguard in emergency situations.
4. Being able to shop or travel without having large amounts of cash.
5. Increasing *future* earning power.

DON'T BE FOOLED

A very astute savings and loan association once ran an ad in some national magazines. The ad pointed out that if you were to save for 36 months and buy a car with the savings, the car would cost you, say, $5,000 and you would have had to put in the bank only $4,600, the rest being made up by the interest you received over the three years. On the other hand, pointed out the ad, if you bought the car immediately and paid for it over 36 months, not only would you not receive interest on your savings, but you would have to pay a finance charge on the installment debt. The total price of the car might be $5,800. There is obviously a big difference between the two: $4,600 and $5,800. The conclusion, according to the savings and loan association: it is better to save now and buy later than to buy now and go into debt.

Is anything wrong with the reasoning in that ad? A crucial point was left out: during the three years in which you saved, you would not be enjoying the services of the car, or of the other things you could buy. You would be putting off your purchase for three years. Most people do not want to wait that long; they would prefer to have the services of the car immediately and pay the finance charge in order to do that. After all, the finance charge is merely a payment for using somebody else's money so that you can consume and that other person cannot, the other person being the saver who decided not to consume. You have decided that the implicit utility you get per service flow of whatever you buy is greater than the interest payments you have to pay your creditor in order to get the total amount of money to buy the goods right away. No moral judgment need be passed here: it is simply a question of comparing costs and benefits. The benefit of borrowing is having purchasing power today; the cost is whatever you have to pay in finance charges. Obviously, if the cost were zero, you would borrow as much as you could because you could buy everything you wanted today and pay back whatever you owed at some later date without any penalty. In fact, the ultimate consumer probably would like to die with an infinite debt. That way, he or she could consume all he or she wanted at everybody else's expense. You must remember, though, that creditors take a dim view of this type of behavior because it means financial losses for them. When you buy something on credit without the intention of paying back that loan, there is little difference between that action and stealing. You are taking something from somebody else without the intention of paying for it.

The benefits of borrowing are something that only you can decide. But the costs of borrowing are something of which we can be made aware.

WHAT IT COSTS TO BORROW

You are all well aware that borrowing costs. This should not surprise you: nothing is free. Why do you have to pay to borrow? Because somebody else is giving up something. What are they giving up? Purchasing power, or command over goods and services today. For other people to give up command over goods and services today, they have to be compensated, and they are usually compensated with what we call interest. Ask yourself if you would be willing to loan $100 to your friend with the loan to be paid back in 10 years, with *no* interest, just the $100 to be returned. Would you do it, even if you were sure of getting the money back? Probably not. You would have to sacrifice what the $100 would have bought, while your friend enjoyed it. Most people will not make this sacrifice for no reward.

ORIGINS OF INTEREST

The concept of interest dates back to the time of the Romans when the law stated that the defaulting party to a contract had to pay his or her creditors some sort of compensation. During medieval times lawyers used this legal tactic of *damna et interesse* to extract such compensation. Thus, *interesse* became a charge for the use of money under the guise of compensation for failure to perform a contract.

It is best to think of the interest rate you pay on a loan as the price you pay the lender for the use of his or her money. What determines that price is no different from what determines the price of anything else in our economy. The various demands and supplies for credit ultimately result in some sort of interest rate being charged for the various forms of credit.

But we cannot really talk about a single interest rate or a single charge for credit. Interest rates vary according to the length of a loan, the risk involved, whether or not the debtor has put up something as **collateral** for the loan (that is, secured it), and so on. One rule is fairly certain: the greater the perceived risk involved, the more the creditor will demand in interest payments from the debtor. Do not be surprised, then, that interest rates in the economy range all the way from relatively low to relatively high. Much of that difference in interest rates has to do with the riskiness of the loan involved.

Let us see why today interest rates are just about the highest they have been in the history of the United States.

INFLATION AND INTEREST RATES

You and I are well aware of what has become more or less expected of the economy—rising prices, or inflation. There is a very definite relationship between rising prices and high interest rates. But the relationship is not the simple one of causation that you may have been taught to expect. Contrary to popular belief, high interest rates do not and cannot *cause* inflation. When prices are rising, interest rates will have an inflationary premium tacked onto them. A simple example will show you why and reinforce our comments in Chapter 8.

Suppose that you are a banker who has been loaning out money at 5 percent a year for the last 20 years. Suppose also that for the last 20 years there has been no inflation. That 5 percent interest you have been charging is the *real* rate of interest you are receiving. It covers your costs and gives you a normal profit for your lending activities.

Now prices start rising at 5 percent a year, and you expect that they will rise at that rate forever. If someone comes in to borrow money, how much do you think you would want to lend at the 5 percent rate of interest that you have always charged?

Well, think about it. Say a person comes in to borrow $1,000 for a year. At the end of the year, with an inflation rate of 5 percent, the actual purchasing power of that $1,000 paid back to you will only be $950. If you ask for 5 percent, or $50 in interest payments, you will be compensated only for the erosive effect of inflation on the value of the money you lend out. What will you do? You will want to tack on an inflationary premium to the real interest rate that you had been charging when there was no inflation and none was anticipated. Hence, in periods of inflation, we find the inflationary premium tacked on everywhere. It is not surprising, then, that during an inflationary period when prices are rising at 5 percent a year, that interest rates would be 10 percent.

You, the demander of credit or the potential debtor, should not be put off at this higher interest rate. After all, you are going to be repaying the loan in cheapened dollars—that is, dollars that have lost part of their purchasing power through inflation. In fact, some interest rates did not react very rapidly to rising inflation in the early 1970s. Credit unions, for example, were giving out automobile loans at an effective interest rate of 8 percent per annum. If the rate of inflation is 6 or 7 percent, those loans cost people only a 1 or 2 percent real rate of interest. For example, I took out a National Defense Education Act student loan while I was in college in the 1960s. The rate of interest on those loans was 3 percent. Now that I have to pay them back, I am actually making money! That is right, I am making money on a loan, because the real rate of interest on a 3 percent loan with, say, a 5 percent rate of inflation is *minus* 2 percent. That is, there is a profit of 2 percent in holding off paying those loans back. This is not the kind of deal that most people get, because potential creditors generally tack on inflationary premiums whenever they think inflation is going to occur.

One thing that inflationary premiums have brought to a head is the problem with usury laws, to which we now turn.

THE WHY AND WHERE OF USURY LAWS

There have always been restrictions on interest rates, both for the lender and for the borrower. Everybody seems to think that moneylenders have some unique monopolistic power over others in the economy. Indeed, moneylenders have been so long condemned that dominant ethnic groups have historically shunned the profession, leaving it to minority groups. In the Western world the Catholic Church, in the Middle Ages, made laws against usury, the lending of money at "unreasonable" rates.

Today many states have laws against charging borrowers interest rates that exceed a specified limit. The persistence of legislation affecting the lending of money makes it clear that a widespread suspicion still lingers that the moneylender possesses some unique shady influence. Many individuals are in favor of limiting the amount of interest that can be charged on a consumer loan. However, since no action is cost-free, you should be aware of both the benefits and the costs of usury laws.

Remember, the selling of credit is no different from the selling of anything else. If usury laws are valid, then so, too, are government controls on every single price in the economy. While we really cannot fully go into the issue in this book, we can note some of the unpredicted effects of usury laws that went into effect in the state of Washington and of usury laws that are in effect in the state of Arkansas. Let us first take the case of Washington.

WASHINGTON STATE USURY LAWS— AN EXAMPLE

Prior to 1968, interest on consumer loans from the credit card companies—Bank-Americard, Master Charge, and so on—as well as on revolving credit loans from the big stores—Sears and others—was generally 18 percent per annum, or 1.5 percent per month in Washington. Many consumer advocates and concerned citizens felt that this rate of interest was much too high, that poor people were not able to afford credit. At that time, for example, commercial bank loans to some customers were going for as low as 9 percent. Poor people who obviously could

---

EXHIBIT 9-1   **The "Real" Rate of Interest**

The rate of interest you are paying on a $100 loan for one year	10%
The rate of inflation (loss in value of money) this year	5%

The difference between the rate of interest you are paying and the loss in the value of dollars you will pay back	5%

So 5 percent is the real rate of interest you pay when you are charged 10 percent on a loan and the rate of inflation is 5 percent.

---

not get bank loans at that low interest rate were supposedly being discriminated against, and they had to forego the benefits of being able to buy on time. A movement was begun to pass legislation against such usurious interest rates. In 1968, a motion was put on the ballot to set the maximum legal interest on consumer loans at 12 percent instead of 18 percent. It was felt that lowering the interest rate would benefit those who could not afford the higher rate. The measure passed quite easily and all the credit card companies and stores in the state were forced to lower their rates to 1 percent per month, or 12 percent per year.

What results would you predict? Obviously, lower cost credit. That is indeed true, but it turned out that the lower cost credit was not necessarily given to people whom the formulators of this new law had in mind. Two academics, John J. Weatley and Guy G. Gordon,[1] did a study of the effects of the law one year after it took force. Their conclusions were startling:

Low-income people who are marginal credit risks seem to have suffered the most from the enactment of the law because of the general tightening of credit.

What in fact did creditors do? They raised some prices, adjusted their credit practices and merchandise assortment, and raised charges or instituted new charges on other services, all in an effort to make up the lost revenues from their credit accounts. Both before and after the legal maximum limit was put on interest rates, there was a tremendous amount of competition for consumers' credit dollars. According to a study made of the profits of credit institutions, the price being charged did not lead to above normal profits. That is, the price being charged reflected only the costs of providing credit plus some normal rate of return or profit to the companies. (The results of the study by Weatley and Gordon confirm this supposition.) Creditors had to make up the lost revenues in one way or another. One way of doing it was by raising prices. Another way, of course, was by eliminating risky debtors.

In fact, a further study by Sauter and Walker[2] shows that "the largest proportion of retailers expect to react to interest ceilings by becoming more selective in

[1]"Regulating the Price of Consumer Credit," *Journal of Marketing* 35 (October 1971): 21–28.

[2]R. F. Sauter and O. C. Walker, Jr., "Retailers' Reactions to Interest Limitation Laws—Additional Evidence," *Journal of Marketing* 36 (April 1972): 58–61.

granting credit." This reaction would be in keeping with the retailers' desire to reduce costs and increase profits. Who is burdened by this reaction? Obviously, low-income and other "marginal" customers are forced to forego credit purchases and turn to more costly sources of funds, such as small loan companies, loan sharks, and pawnbrokers.

Another striking credit situation is found in Arkansas.

LOOKING AT ARKANSAS

For many years now, Arkansas has had a maximum interest limit of 10 percent. In the face of inflationary premiums that reflect expected inflation of 4, 5, 6, and sometimes 7 percent, a 10 percent rate of interest is insufficient to induce many retailers and credit companies to provide credit in Arkansas. The results are predictable, as evidenced by the city of Texarkana, on the border between Texas and Arkansas.

Interest rates in Texas are not looked at so carefully—that is, they are not really regulated. On the main street in this city, one side is Arkansas, the other side is Texas. On the Texas side, there are numerous finance companies, used car dealers, and TV and appliance stores. On the Arkansas side, there are many fewer, and in places none. The number of credit purchases in Arkansas is very small per capita compared to the credit purchases in Texas. Why is this so? Simply because the usury law is so restrictive in Arkansas that no suppliers of credit want to do business there. But there are suppliers of credit in Texas.

Are the people of Arkansas better off because of the 10 percent limitation in interest rates? To be sure, some of them are. But many of them are not. They must go to other states or forego credit purchases altogether. Or they may in fact end up working with loan sharks outside the law in order to borrow money when they think they need it desperately. Almost all economists agree that usury laws are generally detrimental to the general welfare of the people who are supposed to be helped.[3]

A number of banks have implicitly started charging higher interest rates without actually changing the stated interest rate. New York CitiBank, a major issuer of Master Charge cards, began charging cardholders a fee of 50¢ during those months in which the accounts were paid in full on time and for which no interest was charged. Some banks in West Virginia are charging an annual fee for the Bank-Americards (VISA) that they issue. New billing procedures have been instituted by other banks in which the finance charges begin on the day each purchase is posted to the account, rather than on the monthly billing date. And, finally, some banks have reduced the number of days they permit for credit card accounts to be paid in full without being charged interest. Seattle First National Bank, for example, reduced the time period from 25 to 21 days.

In any event, given the variety of lending institutions, all in competition, the Truth-in-Lending legislation passed by Congress in 1968 is a step in the right direction and an alternative to interest-ceiling regulation.

---

[3]The evidence continues to support this contention. A study by Donald F. Greer ("Rate Ceilings and Loan Turn-Downs,"*Journal of Finance*, December 1975, pp. 1376–1383), suggests that the impact of low rate ceilings falls heavily on marginal credit risks who rely on consumer finance companies for credit. Using a sample of 48 states, Greer found that a larger percentage of those who requested credit were rejected in those states that had low legal rate ceilings on interest rates.

TRUTH-IN-LENDING

The Truth-in-Lending Act, which is Title I of the Consumer Credit Protection Act of 1968, is essentially a disclosure law. Most kinds of installment debt now have to be properly labeled so that the consumer knows exactly what he or she is paying. The bill that finally passed in the Congress in 1968 had a long history. Former Senator Paul Douglas had introduced similar bills in the 86th, 87th, and 88th Congresses. He titled his bill "A Bill to Assist in the Promotion of Economic Stabilization by Requiring the Disclosure of Finance Charges in Connection with the Extension of Credit." The testimony and exhibits presented at the hearings before the Senate Committee on Banking and Currency, in 1960, 1961, and 1963, filled nearly 4,000 pages. Hearings in 1967 added another 1,200 pages. Lending institutions, retailers, and trade associations put up strong opposition to these bills; that is presumably why they were blocked for so many years. When President Johnson signed the Act, he stated succinctly, "As a matter of fair play to the consumer, the cost of credit should be disclosed fully, simply, and clearly."

How does a 5¾ percent discount rate compare to a 6 percent add-on rate? Is 1 percent per month on the unpaid balance a better deal than either of the two above? And what are finder's fees, points, and service charges? These kinds of questions, couched in difficult to understand terms which were typically used to describe credit plans prior to the enactment of Truth-in-Lending, provide an obvious reason for the legislation. Prior to 1969, the majority of consumers were unable to understand the variety of credit terminology or the many methods used for rate calculations. Consumers therefore found themselves poorly equipped to make intelligent comparisons among types of credit plans or among competitors.

The congressional purpose of the Act was "to insure a meaningful disclosure of credit terms so that the consumer will be able to compare more readily the various credit terms available to him and avoid the uninformed use of credit." The Act attempts to accomplish this purpose in several ways. It requires that all the various terms used to describe the dollar cost of credit, such as interest, points, etc., be described and disclosed under one common label, *finance charge*. Likewise, it abolishes all the various terms used to describe the cost of credit in percentage terms, such as discount rates, add-ons, and the like, and prescribes a uniform method of computation of a single rate known as the *annual percentage rate*. (We see below, however, that there are still problems with how this rate is computed.)

The Truth-in-Lending Act does not cover credit extended to corporations, trusts, government, and partnerships; it does not apply to private loans among friends and families, or to loans for business purposes or first mortgages; and the extension of credit must be for $25,000 or less, unless it is secured by real property such as in a typical home mortgage in which no limit applies.

The Truth-in-Lending Act also grants the consumer-borrower a **right of rescission** (cancellation) for certain credit contracts. (This is also called a cooling off period.) Section 125 of the Act gives the consumer three business days to rescind a credit transaction that results or may result in a lien on his or her home, or on any real property that is used or expected to be used as his or her principal residence. The right of rescission is designed to allow the person additional time to reconsider using his or her residence as security for credit. However, this right of rescission does not apply to first mortgages on homes.

The Truth-in-Lending Act also regulates the advertising of consumer credit. One of the primary purposes of the Act's advertising requirements is to eliminate "come-on" credit ads. For example, if any one important credit term is mentioned in an advertisement—down payment or monthly payment—all other important terms must also be defined. (The real effect of this provision has therefore been to eliminate the disclosure of *any* credit terms in most advertisements.)

A 1970 amendment to the Act provides federal regulations on the use of credit cards. This amendment prohibits the unsolicited distribution of new credit cards, and also establishes a maximum $50 limit on liability for the unauthorized use of each of such cards—that is, the owner of a lost or stolen card that has been used illegally by another person cannot be made liable to pay more than $50 on its illegal purchases.

ENFORCEMENT

A relatively novel scheme of administrative enforcement has been created whereby the Federal Reserve Board is given broad authority to write and administer regulations implementing the Truth-in-Lending Act. The Board's regulations are spread among nine federal agencies. Generally, those federal agencies with pre-existing supervisory authority over a particular group of creditors are also given Truth-in-Lending enforcement responsibility over them. For example, the National Credit Union Administration is responsible for federally chartered credit unions, and the Federal Home Loan Bank Board is responsible for federally chartered savings and loan institutions. Other enforcers include the Comptroller of the Currency, the Federal Deposit Insurance Corporation, the Department of Agriculture, the Civil Aeronautics Board, and the Interstate Commerce Commission. Enforcement of all remaining creditors not covered by the above agencies falls to the Federal Trade Commission. The FTC in essence puts out the bulk of federal enforcement effort. In fact, it estimates that its responsibility extends to nearly 1 million creditors, including all retail creditors and finance companies.

Obviously, the FTC would have great difficulty in attempting to enforce the Act against *all* local retailers throughout the nation. Hence, the Truth-in-Lending Act allows the provision that any state that enacts legislation similar to Truth-in-Lending and provides for "adequate" enforcement may apply to the Federal Reserve Board for an exemption from the federal Act and thereby obtain authority to enforce its own statutes instead. By 1975 Massachusetts, Maine, Connecticut, Oklahoma, and Wyoming had been granted such exemptions.

REVOLVING CREDIT

When the Truth-in-Lending Act was applied to revolving credit contracts, a battle was waged in Congress. Revolving credit, or open-ended credit as it is sometimes called, is a growing part of total consumer credit. Many department stores allow you to have revolving credit accounts. An open-ended credit account has three main characteristics:

1. The customer has a choice of paying the balance in full or in installments.
2. The creditor permits the customer to make purchases (or loans) at irregular intervals, usually by means of a credit card.
3. The creditor usually computes the finance charge on the *outstanding* unpaid balance.

The last aspect of an open-ended credit account has bothered consumers the most and has caused the Truth-in-Lending Act the most trouble. The fact is that many creditors used different techniques to compute finance charges on revolving credit accounts. The techniques are the following:

1. **Previous balance method:** The creditor computes a finance charge on the previous month's balance, even if it has been paid.
2. **Average daily balance:** The finance charge is applied to the sum of the actual amounts outstanding each day during the billing period divided by the number of days in that period. Payments are credited on the exact date of payment.
3. **Adjusted balance method:** Finance charges are assessed on the balance after deducting payments and credits.
4. **Past due balance:** No finance charge is assessed so long as full payment is received within a certain period, such as 25 days after the closing date of the last statement.

It is obviously important to know which method is used in assessing the finance charge that you must pay, for the different methods can result in widely varying finance charges. Table 9-2 shows the difference between the use of the previous balance method and of the adjusted balance method.

You see that the same monthly finance charge of 1 percent results in two different actual annual rates of finance charged, depending on which computational method is used by the creditor. The Truth-in-Lending Act requires that all revolving credit contracts and monthly bills must state the "nominal annual percentage rate." The nominal rate will equal 12 times the monthly rate. However, the nominal rate does not tell you the effective, or actual, annual rate. Retailers were given a further concession in one provision in the Truth-in-Lending Act whereby they are allowed to exclude from the disclosure of finance charges a certain minimum monthly charge on small unpaid revolving account balances.

The Truth-in-Lending Act does not actually give protection, only information. It is therefore a disclosure act. But information can be valuable; it can be the best protection around. It allows you, the consumer, who are looking for credit to shop around, to see exactly what you are paying and to know exactly what you are getting into. Figure 9-2 displays a typical disclosure statement. The Truth-in-Lending Act requires that an accurate assessment of the annual percentage rate be given; that is circled for you, and that is what you should look at when you

Table 9-2
Differing Resultant Finance Charges

METHOD	OPENING BALANCE	PAYMENTS	MONTHLY FINANCE CHARGE	ACTUAL FINANCE CHARGE	ACTUAL MONTHLY RATE	ANNUAL RATE
Previous Balance Method	$300	$100	1%	.01 × $300 = $3	1½%	18%
Adjusted Balance Method	$300	$100	1%	.01 × $200 = $2	1%	12%

ACCOUNT NUMBER				

SEARS, ROEBUCK AND CO.
DISCLOSURE STATEMENT

Sales Check No._____   Date _____ 19____

☐ Easy Payment Plan

☐ Modernizing Credit Plan

DESCRIPTION OF MERCHANDISE

OFFICE USE ONLY (Code 4 Sales)

NO. OF MONTHS	MONTHLY PAYMENT

CASH PRICE				
CASH DOWN PAYMENT				
UNPAID BALANCE OF CASH PRICE - AMOUNT FINANCED				
FINANCE CHARGE				
DEFERRED PAYMENT PRICE				
TOTAL OF PAYMENTS — THIS SALE				

This purchase is payable in installments pursuant to my Sears Easy Payment Plan—Modernizing Credit Plan Retail Installment Contract and Security Agreement.

Beginning _____, I will pay $_____per month for _____months and a final monthly payment of $_____until the amount financed and the finance charge for this purchase are fully paid.

If the **FINANCE CHARGE** exceeds **$5.00**, the **ANNUAL PERCENTAGE RATE** is | %

In accordance with my Sears Easy Payment Plan-Modernizing Credit Plan Retail Installment Contract and Security Agreement, a subsequent purchase may change the number and amount of my monthly payments, the amount of the Finance Charge and the Annual Percentage Rate of this purchase. Any such change will appear on my next monthly billing statement.

A copy of my sales check is attached hereto and incorporated by reference. Ownership of the merchandise described in such attached sales check remains in Sears until paid for in full.

If I pay in full in advance, any unearned finance charge will be rebated under the Rule of 78, after deducting a charge of $5.00.

11078-202 (F11363 WW) Rev. 12/72

Figure 9-2   A Typical Disclosure Statement

compare the various prices of credit from various dealers and companies. In addition, you may want to look at the finance charge, which is the total number of dollars you pay to borrow the money, whether directly or in the form of deferred payments on a purchase. These total finance charges include all of the so-called carrying charges that are sometimes tacked on to a retail installment contract, plus such things as "setup" charges and credit life insurance. These all contribute to your cost of having purchasing power today instead of waiting, of having command over goods and services right now, and of taking that command away from somebody else. Expressed as a percentage of the total price, it gives your annual percentage interest rate. In some cases, it may be very, very high indeed.

ELIMINATING CREDIT DISCRIMINATION

Since October 1975 it has been illegal to discriminate on the basis of sex and marital status in the granting of credit. The Equal Credit Opportunity Act went into effect that year. Regulations pursuant to the Act issued by the Federal Reserve Board prohibit:

1. Demanding information on the credit applicant's childbearing intentions or birth control practices.
2. Requiring cosignatures on loans when such requirements do not apply to all qualified applicants.
3. Discouraging applicant from applying for credit because of sex or marital status.
4. Terminating or changing the conditions of credit solely on the basis of a change in marital status.
5. Ignoring alimony and child support payments as regular income in assessing the credit worthiness of the applicant.

Basically, the Equal Credit Opportunity Act reaffirms a woman's right to get and keep credit in her own name rather than that of her husband, or of her former husband if she is divorced. Women who wish to establish their own lines of credit are advised by bankers to do the following:

1. Open a separate checking and savings account in your name.
2. Start an active separate credit history, assuming you can afford it.
3. Open a charge account at a retail store. When applying, list only your own salary, not that of your spouse.
4. Apply for a bank credit card.
5. Finally, take out a small loan and repay it on time. Even if you do not need it, this would speed up the establishment of your own credit reliability.

Increasingly, women will be able to obtain credit more easily because of the creation of women's banks. These banks are operated by women for women and the personnel take special care in providing credit to women who need it and who might have been discriminated against by other lending institutions.

PROBLEMS WITH INSTALLMENT CONTRACTS

Individuals who sign **installment contracts** when they purchase furniture, appliances, and the like have often found themselves in a bind. In many cases, the merchant who sells an item on an installment contract turns around and resells that contract to a finance company. Until recently, the **holder-in-due-course doctrine** applied. Under such a doctrine, even if you were sold a defective product, the holder in due course was entitled to continue to collect payments on that product, since he or she was not the original seller. When the holder-in-due-course doctrine applies, you cannot stop payment because of dissatisfaction over the product.

A new Federal Trade regulation rule on credit buying now gives private consumers (as opposed to commercial buyers) a defense against this practice. Installment contracts must prominently include a note that "the holder of this consumer-credit contract is subject to all claims and defenses that the debtor could assert against the seller." Consider the possibility of your buying a set of encyclopedias from a door-to-door salesperson. You agree to a specified monthly payment for a certain number of years. You sign on the dotted line. The encyclopedias are delivered and at first you are quite happy. Four months later, however, you discover that the binding is falling apart on 50 percent of them. You obviously have purchased a faulty product. According to the recent FTC rule, the finance company that is now in possession of the installment contract on which you are paying is just as responsible for the faulty encyclopedias as the original seller would have been.

Note that credit cards are not covered under the new FTC ruling. However, they are covered under the Fair Credit Billing Act, which eliminates the holder-in-due-course doctrine in credit card transactions of more than fifty dollars and within one hundred miles of the cardholder's home.

THE FAIR CREDIT BILLING ACT

Basically, under the rules set up pursuant to this Act, you can withhold payment until the dispute is resolved over a faulty product that you purchased and paid for by credit card. It is up to the credit card issuer, such as American Express or Master Charge, to intervene and attempt a settlement between you and the seller. You do not have unlimited rights to stop payment. You must exercise a good faith effort to get satisfaction from the seller before you do so. The rules seem to be, however, in the consumer's favor. You don't even have to notify the credit card company that you are cutting off payment (on that item). You just wait for the company to act. However, it is probably a good idea to let the company know what you are doing. Ultimately you can be sued by the credit card company if no agreement is reached. Other rules were also set up in the Fair Credit Billing Act. If you think there is an error in your bill, the card company must investigate and suspend payments until it does so. You simply write to the card company within 60 days of getting the bill, briefly explaining the circumstances and why you think there is an error. It is a good idea to include copies (not the originals) of the sales slips at issue. Under the law, the company must acknowledge your letter within 30 days and resolve the dispute within 90 days. During that period, you don't have to pay the amount in dispute or any minimum payments on the amount in dispute. And, further, your creditor cannot charge you finance charges during that period for unpaid balances in dispute. It cannot even close your account; however, if it turns out that there was no error, the creditor can then attempt to collect finance charges for the entire period for which payments were not made.

REGULATING BANKS

When you want to have a checking account so that you do not have to carry currency all the time and so that you can have a record of many important purchases, you go to a commercial bank. In the United States, commercial banks are extremely regulated. Much of the regulation is to prevent practices in which you, the consumer, would be hurt. But some of the regulations seem out of date.

Today there are about 14,000 commercial banks in the United States. Together they have total deposits of $225 billion. The average per capita amount of checking account plus currency is over $1,000. That is one large amount of money, right? When you go to a bank today and open a checking account, you have to make some decisions: what color folder to use for your checks, how personalized you want the checks to be (some banks even offer you pictures of sailing ships or pictures of yourself embossed on every check you buy). A lot of banks give you an option. If you keep a minimum balance, there is no charge for any check you write. You can write as many as you want. Other banks periodically offer you small appliances if you open an account with them for a specified

amount. Sometimes you see banks opening offices that are only blocks apart from each other and you cannot understand why.

The reason why is easy to see. The explicit interest rate that banks can pay on a checking account balance is fixed at a maximum of 0 percent per year—not very much, is it? But the deposits that you leave in the bank on average can be used by the bank to purchase interest-earning assets, like bonds or stocks or promissory notes in the form of loans to individuals and firms. Therefore, your unused checking account balances are used by the banks as an input in the sale of other services such as loans. (Your average checking account balance may also be used as a basis for deciding whether or not you are credit worthy and should be given a loan by that bank.)

They certainly would like to have all those inputs free of charge—that is, at a zero interest rate. But there is competition in the banking system. Banks find that it is beneficial—that is, profitable—to try to induce us to put our checking accounts in their particular one instead of another. How do they try to induce this? Well, the first thing they can do is offer us free checking services or pretty pictures on our checks; or, where legal, they can offer us convenience in the form of multitudinous branch offices. They can sometimes offer us small appliances to get us to put money in their particular bank. These are all ways of getting around the regulation that prevents banks from offering interest on checking account balances.

It is strange that the government maintains some bank regulations that seem not to be in the consumer's best interest. After all, we consumers would like to have the option of being paid a small interest rate on our checking account balances instead of having to receive a more or less hidden interest rate in the form of free services and many convenient bank locations. But the Federal Reserve instituted Regulation Q fixing the maximum interest rate on checking accounts at zero in order to prevent what it called cutthroat competition. That argument seems a little thin these days, does it not? Even proregulation Consumers Union came out against this restriction on interest rates in its June 1973 issue of *Consumer Reports* (pp. 420, 421).

Actually, in some cities you now have an option. A few savings and loan associations have gotten around Regulation Q and are offering a new type of account.

NOW IS THE TIME FOR *NOW*   Savings banks in several states have started **Negotiable Orders of Withdrawal (NOW)**. When you open a NOW account, you get a checkbook. It is not called that —it is called a negotiable order of withdrawal book. But it is a checkbook nonetheless, and in most cases merchants are not going to turn it down. The difference is that your balance in your NOW account earns the same interest as a regular savings account, 5 to 6 percent. For each withdrawal, however, the customer is charged something like 10 or 15¢. Obviously, if you write a lot of checks you would not find a NOW account very convenient as a substitute for a checking account, for the service charges would be more than the interest you would earn. But if you have normally high checking account balances and do not write very many checks, this is an obvious way to earn a little extra money.

As you can imagine, the commercial banks are fighting NOW accounts. The American Bankers Association is backing legislation, which may already have gone into effect, to prevent the spread of NOW accounts throughout the United

States. However, it is inevitable that sooner or later competition in the banking system will allow the consumer to earn money on those unused checking account balances. Just recently, in one major West Coast city, a "trans fund account" became available. You keep what you think is an adequate balance in your checking account to cover your expenses and the rest in a trans fund account, where you get the normal interest rate on your savings. Whenever you need money you call the bank. It immediately transfers the amount of your request to your checking account and mails you a transaction memo in verification. That way, as long as you do not need the money in your checking account, you earn interest in your trans fund account.

TOTAL BANKING SERVICES FOR ONE FEE

A number of banks have instituted a banking package for which they charge a single monthly fee, generally only $3. For that $3 fee you get a Blue Chip Account or a Gold Account or an Executive Account. Included in the fee are the following services:

1. Unlimited check writing.
2. Personalized checks, sometimes with your picture embossed on them or with a reproduction of a famous painting or landscape in your area.
3. Overdraft protection, whereby if you write checks for more money than you have in your account, you will automatically have funds transferred from either a credit card account or a personalized line of credit.
4. A safe deposit box.
5. No charge for travelers checks, cashiers checks, and money orders.
6. Preferred interest rates (sometimes) on personal loans.

And, in some cities, banking services have become so sophisticated that you no longer have to write checks.

THE CASHLESS SOCIETY

Some cities, like Lincoln, Nebraska, and Macon and Atlanta, Georgia, are trying a system of cashless, checkless spending, and it seems to be working. What is it all about? And does it mean that money will be useless? No, it does not. It means only that money will take another form. Money is in the form of cash—which consists of currency and checking account balances—that we use as a means of storing purchasing power. Since our receipts do not always match our expenditures, we generally keep some money in a checking account balance or in our wallets in order to make expenditures later on each month. In the cashless, checkless society, you would still need a checking account balance on which to draw even though you did not write a check and even though the transmission mechanism was semiautomatic at the beginning of each month. You would have to deposit your income checks into your account at the beginning of each month, just as you do now, although that, too, can be done automatically.

In those cities that allow cashless, checkless transactions, although you still keep part of your wealth in the form of a checking account balance, you are using it in a semiautomatic manner. When you make a purchase in a store, you merely give the merchant or salesperson a credit card which automatically transfers money from your checking account balance to the store's balance.

The cashless, checkless society is merely a means of reducing **transactions costs.** Instead of your having to write out checks every month for your mortgage, your phone, your milk, and your electricity, a computer does it automatically. The official banking term for computer money is electronic funds transfer system, or EFTS. There are basically three parts to an EFT system—teller machines, point-of-sale systems, and automated clearing houses.

Teller Machines. The recent EFTS development has involved teller machines. They are also called customer bank communication terminals or remote service units. They are located either on the bank's premises or in stores such as supermarkets or drug stores. Automated teller machines receive deposits, dispense funds from checking or savings accounts, make credit card advances, and receive payments. The device is connected on-line to the bank's computers.

Point-of-Sale Systems. Such systems allow the consumer to transfer funds to merchants in order to make purchases. On-line terminals are located at check-out counters in the merchant's store. When making a purchase, the customer's card is inserted into the terminal, which reads the data encoded on it. The computer at the customer's bank verifies that the card and identification code are valid and that there is enough money in the customer's account. After the purchase is made, the customer's account is debited for the amount of the purchase.

Automated Clearing Houses. Such clearing houses are similar to actual ones now in use in which checks are cleared between banks. The main difference is that the entries made are in the form of electronic signals—there are no checks used. Thus this is not a system for further automating the handling of paper checks. It is a replacement system. Such systems are especially useful to business persons for recurrent payments, like payroll, Social Security, or pension fund plans that come up every week or every month. The automated clearing house is really a glorified processing system.

This system saves you time and it saves the banks and companies money, also. After all, it is estimated that the banking system spends over $6½ billion annually just to process 30 billion checks. If this processing can somehow be reduced, you the consumer will benefit. This might cause some problems, but not serious ones. Since most of your fixed expenses for car payments, house payments, and the like are anticipated, anyway, their being paid automatically is not going to change your behavior. In the cashless, checkless society, you will get a statement at the end of every month just as you do now; in fact, you will probably always be able to phone in to find out where your finances stand. Since we are all faced with a budget constraint (we know that we cannot spend for long more than we make), checks and balances against overspending will have to be built into it. And, of course, that all goes back to formulating a budget and sticking to it.

Note that there are some serious consumer concerns over such a system. They are:

1. The inability to issue stop payment on a check when there is trouble with the seller of a good or service.
2. Fewer records are available.
3. The possibility of tampering and lack of privacy is increased.

4. There is a loss of "float," or the time between when you write a check and when the sum of the check is deducted from your account.

Electronic banking is, in effect, just an extension of the credit card society. A number of commentators on the American scene believe strongly that the introduction of the credit card has proved disastrous for our nation and our way of life. For example, Harvard sociologist and management consultant Daniel Bell believes that the Protestant ethic lingered on until the invention of the installment plan. According to Bell, "With credit cards, one could indulge in instant gratification." So, he reasons that when the Protestant ethic disappeared from our society, only hedonism remained.

Will electronic money even further the problems in our supposedly hedonistic society? Perhaps, but one basic fact remains unaltered: no matter what type of credit or money system we use, each family and each individual is faced with a budget constraint. If that individual or that family engages in more impulse buying because of credit cards or electronic money systems, then less funds will be available to purchase other items. This may mean more bankruptcies, but there is a limit to that: when one family goes bankrupt, someone else loses out. Those who lose out in bankruptcies are all of the creditors who will not be paid. In other words, there is a budget constraint or scarcity problem facing the entire nation at all times. If one person spends more than he or she actually has, then someone else is going to end up with less.

In any event, it appears that the overall consumer debt burden of families leveled off earlier in this decade. Perhaps families have reached a saturation point in their willingness to carry debt. Bankruptcy rates seem to have stabilized during the last decade and according to one researcher, "Personal bankruptcy rates appear to have peaked at a level which does not pose a significant threat to the stability of the American economy."[5]

You still may want to borrow money, even in this forthcoming society, so in the consumer issue that follows we will find out when and where and how you should go about getting credit.

SUMMARY

1. The largest nonhome consumer debt item in America is automobile loans.
2. At least 50 percent of all Americans have outstanding installment debt at any given time.
3. The sources of credit are many, including commercial banks, finance companies, consumer finance companies, credit unions, credit card companies, and retail stores.
4. Individuals borrow in order to obtain the services of large consumer items without paying for them at one time. The installment payments can be thought of as matching the service flow from whatever was purchased, such as a house or a car.
5. Interest is the payment for using somebody else's money today. As such, it is like any other price. During inflation, interest rates must rise to take account

[5]F. C. Yager, "Personal Bankruptcy and Economic Stability," *Southern Economic Journal*, no. 41, July 1974, pp. 96-104.

of the rate of inflation. Hence, interest rates are relatively high when the rate of inflation is high.

6. The real rate of interest you pay on a loan is the stated rate of interest minus the rate of inflation.

7. Usury laws set a legal maximum on the rate of interest that can be charged a consumer. Some studies of usury laws have shown that they hurt some consumers while helping others.

8. The Truth-in-Lending Act requires that both the total finance charge and the annual percentage rate be clearly stated on a loan agreement (except on first mortgages on homes).

9. You must be careful when computing the actual percentage interest rate you will pay on an open-ended credit account. Ask specifically whether one of the following four methods is used: previous balance, average daily balance, adjusted balance, or past due balance. As you saw in Table 9-2, the resultant finance charge can be much higher if, for example, the previous balance method is used instead of the adjusted balance method.

10. Banks in the United States are regulated so that they cannot pay interest to you on your checking account balances. Therefore, you should find a bank that gives you the most free services in exchange for your checking account. For example, some banks offer six to nine services for $3 a month.

11. Eventually, the United States may not use currency. Everything will be done electronically. This, however, will not change your budget-making plans or processes: you still cannot spend more than you earn.

QUESTIONS FOR THOUGHT AND DISCUSSION

1. Why do you think the aggregate amount of debt in the United States has been growing so much? Does it have anything to do with increased incomes? Increased population? Increased price level?

2. What is the difference between credit and debt?

3. The interest rate charged by different lenders varies tremendously. Does this mean that some of them have a monopoly? If not, how can you account for the differences?

4. Does it seem fair that those who pay cash pay the same price as those who use a credit card?

5. Can you think of some very specific reasons why you would ever want to borrow money? Or ever have?

6. Is it better to save and buy? Or to buy and go into debt?

7. Do you think it is appropriate that interest rates be regulated? If your answer is yes, how does the regulation of interest rates differ from the regulation of other prices in our economy?

8. During a number of years in this decade, the rate of inflation exceeded the rate of interest that some borrowers had to pay on their loans. What does that mean about the real rate of interest those borrowers were paying?

9. Do you think the Truth-in-Lending Act has been effective? Why?

10. Can consumers figure out how they are actually being charged for their credit? What information would be helpful in addition to that which now exists?

11. If you are charged a setup fee in addition to some annual percentage rate to borrow money from a credit card company, should that setup charge be included as part of the total finance charge? Would this raise or lower the annual percentage rate of interest?

12. Do you think banks should continue to be regulated so that they cannot offer interest on checking accounts? Is there a problem about possible cutthroat competition? What would be the result?

13. If you were the owner of a savings and loan association, how would you feel about the ability of commercial banks to offer interest on checking accounts?

14. Why have a number of banks started total banking services for a flat fee every month?

THINGS TO DO

1. See if you can find an adult, self-supporting person who has *never* gone into debt. (If you find one, ask how and/or why.)

2. Make a survey in your area of the various sources of credit. Find out what the various characteristics of those sources are and what the various charges on their loans might be.

3. Pick a consumer durable good, such as an automobile or an expensive stereo. Start calling around to find out where you could get the best loan. If there are big differences in annual interest rates charged for the loan, try to determine why.

4. Ask your neighborhood retailers who accept credit cards whether they give a discount for cash. If they do not, find out why not.

5. Ask someone who works in a savings and loan association what their feelings are about going into debt. See if that person thinks it is better to save and then buy, rather than to go into debt and have today.

6. Go to your reference library and find out from the *Monthly Labor Review*, the *Federal Reserve Bulletin*, the *Survey of Current Business*, or the *Business Conditions Digest* what the rate of inflation has been for the past five years. Then compare that rate of inflation with the interest rate you would have had to pay to borrow for the purchase of, say, a new car. Now calculate the real rate of interest that you would have been charged. Does that real rate of interest seem high or low? If it seems relatively low, can you figure out why it would have been so low?

7. Find out if there is a usury law in your state. Compare it to the so-called prime rate, or the rate of interest charged by banks to the lowest risk borrowers, that is, best borrowers. The prime rate can be found in the *Federal Reserve Bulletin* or in the local newspaper every once in a while. Or you can call up any local banker and ask him or her what the prime rate is. If your state usury law is close to the prime rate, ask the local banker whether that has caused any problems.

8. Obtain the disclosure statements from a number of local department stores and appliance stores that offer credit. Make a comparison of the annual percentage rates listed on the forms. Then call the credit departments and find out whether they use the previous balance, average daily balance, adjusted balance, or past due balance method of computing the finance charge. Now

see if that will make a difference in the annual percentage rate. If it does, find out from your local field office of the Federal Trade Commission why there are such discrepancies.

9. Make a survey of commercial banks in your area. Ask to speak with the assistant manager. Ask his or her opinion on the regulation from the Federal Reserve, called Regulation Q, which prohibits the payment of interest on checking accounts. Make the same survey again, but now call the assistant managers of savings and loan associations. Why do you think there will be a difference in your results?

SELECTED READINGS

Annual Report to Congress on Truth in Lending. Board of Governors of the Federal Reserve System (latest edition).

Bell, Daniel. *The Cultural Contradictions of Capitalism.* New York: Basic Books, 1976.

Buying on Time. New York State Banking Department, 2 World Trade Center, New York, New York 10047 (latest edition).

Chapman, J. "Women's Access to Credit." *Challenge*, January/February 1975.

"Family Spending: How Patterns Are Changing." *U.S. News*, December 6, 1976, pp. 79–81.

"Guide to Bank Services, A." *Consumer Reports*, January 1975, pp. 32-38.

Hendrickson, Robert A. *The Cashless Society.* New York: Dodd, Mead & Company, 1972.

Kaplan, Lawrence J., and Malteis, Salvatore. "The Economics of Loansharking." *American Journal of Economics and Sociology* 27 (1968).

"Merchants of Debt." *Time*, February 28, 1977, pp. 36–40.

Meyer, Martin J. *How to Turn Plastic into Gold.* Lynnbrook, N.Y.: Farnsworth Publishing, 1974.

"New Two-Tier Market for Consumer Goods." *Business Week*, April 11, 1977, p. 80.

Russell, Thomas. *Economics of Bank Credit Cards.* New York: Praeger, 1975.

"Shaking Up the Banks." *Consumer Reports*, May 1975, pp. 306–309.

"U.S. Families Start to Loosen the Purse Strings." *U.S.News*, December 27, 1976, pp. 79–81.

"When Your Budget Signals Danger." *Changing Times*, February 1977, pp. 33–35.

"Who's Going Bankrupt and Why." *U.S. News & World Report*, 71, (1971): 83.

"Women: To Your Credit." Baltimore, Md.: Commercial Credit Corporation, 1976.

"Workshop on Consumer Credit." *Journal of Home Economics*, January 1968.

Coping with the Credit Maze

GLOSSARY OF TERMS

Liabilities

Something for which one is liable or responsible according to law or equity, especially pecuniary debts or obligations.

Assets

The entire property of a person, association, corporation, or estate that is applicable or subject to the payment of his or her or its debts; or the items on a balance sheet showing the book value of property owned.

Net Worth

The difference between your assets and your liabilities, or what you are actually worth. If your liabilities exceed your assets, your net worth is negative.

Acceleration Clause

A clause contained in numerous credit agreements whereby if one payment is missed, the entire unpaid balance becomes due, or the due date is accelerated to the immediate future.

Add-on Clause

A clause in an installment contract that makes your earlier purchases with that firm security for the new purchase.

WHEN SHOULD YOU BORROW?

Some consumer economics books give you cut-and-dried formulas to tell you when you should borrow. It is not unusual to find a financial adviser telling consumers that they should borrow only for major purchases, such as automobiles. Just about everyone who buys a house automatically assumes that it is respectable to borrow; very few of us are in a position to chunk out $20,000, $30,000, $40,000, or $50,000 to pay the full cost of a house. Because we know that the housing services we consume per month represent a very small part of the total price (because houses last so long), it seems meaningless to spend all that cash; instead, we take out a mortgage. The same holds for cars, especially new ones. A car is such a large expense that very few of us consider that we should pay for it in cash; 71 percent of all new automobiles are purchased on credit. After houses and automobiles, though, the reasoning gets pretty fuzzy. Is it all right to buy a stereo on credit? Some financial advisers say yes, and some say no. Is it all right to buy furniture on credit? Some advisers say yes, some say no. Of course, for clothes and food, most financial advisers are adamant about the desirability of paying cash.

A Dollar Is a Dollar Is a Dollar

When you think about it, the reasoning behind such cut-and-dried rules is pretty shaky. Gertrude Stein once wrote that a rose is a rose is a rose; and so, too, a dollar is a dollar is a dollar. What does it matter what you say your dollar is going to buy? You cannot earmark it. If you make $100 a week and you spend $10 for clothes, $50 for food and lodging, and the rest on entertainment, how do you know which dollar you used for "essentials"—food and lodging and clothes—and which dollar you used for "nonessentials"—entertainment? You do not, because you cannot tell one dollar from another. What does it matter if you say you are going to use credit to buy your clothes and pay for your entertainment cash and carry? It does not matter. What is important for you is to decide what percentage of your anticipated income you are willing to set aside for fixed payments to repay loans. You should care about the total commitment you have made to creditors. You want to make sure you have not overcommitted yourself. By using Exhibit F-1 you can get an idea of what may be safe for you.

Values Enter In, Too

Value judgments enter in, too. Some will say that certain types of consumption activities are

EXHIBIT F-1   Determining a Safe Debt Load

ITEM	AMOUNT
Car payment	_____
Installment debt (department stores, etc.)	_____
1. _____	_____
2. _____	_____
3. _____	_____
4. _____	_____
Loan payments due	
1. _____	_____
2. _____	_____
3. _____	_____
4. _____	_____
Others	
1. _____	_____
2. _____	_____
Overdue accounts (e. g. phone, electricity, etc.)	_____
TOTAL OUTSTANDING	_____

Having thereby determined your short-term debt load, you are in a position to determine whether you want to extend it. Below are two methods by which you might decide:

A

10% of monthly income (after taxes) _____

multiply by 18 _____

SAFE DEBT LOAD RESULTS
(principal *plus* interest)

_____

B

Indicate your annual income after taxes _____

Subtract your annual expenditures on housing, food, and clothing

_____

Divide by 3

SAFE DEBT LOAD RESULTS

_____

frivolous and therefore you should never borrow money to engage in them. Be careful here, however. It is hard to determine which activities are frivolous and which are not, particularly somebody else's activities and not your own. You may deem it absolutely essential that you spend a large part of your income on entertainment to keep your sanity. I may say that you are wasting your money, that it is frivolous consumption and therefore you are not justified in borrowing for entertainment. Some people find it essential to get away from it all on their vacations; therefore, if they run out of money before their vacation, they may be willing to go into debt in order to fly away to Hawaii or Mexico or Florida. This is how they keep sane for the rest of the year's work. Hence, this activity may not be frivolous to them, although to an outsider it may look so.

Thus, when we judge each other's behavior, we can never tell whether the other's purchases are superfluous or not. Nor can we tell whether the other is borrowing for the "right" kinds of things or not. Again, what is important is that the total amount of indebtedness relative to a person's income not be excessive. In any event, you will be faced by a maximum amount of indebtedness that creditors will allow you to have. And they have some fairly simple rules for determining what your borrowing capacity is. Remember, however, that reliance on lending agencies to limit your borrowing is a mistake: you, the borrower, should be responsible for your own

needs. Creditors check your credit worthiness to protect themselves, not you.

WHAT IS THE MAXIMUM YOU CAN BORROW?

If you go to a bank or a credit company and ask for a loan, the loan officer will more than likely require you to fill out a form. On this form you list your **liabilities** and your **assets** so that the credit officer can come up with an estimate of your **net worth.** Figure F-1 shows a typical net worth statement. You have to put down all of your assets—whatever you own—and all of your liabilities—whatever you owe. The difference is your net worth. Obviously, if your net worth is negative, you will have a hard time getting a loan from anybody unless you can show that your expected income in the immediate future is extremely large.

You still do not know what your maximum credit limit is. That, of course, depends on the loan officer's assessment of your financial position. This will be a function of your net worth, your income, your relative indebtedness, and how regular your situation is. What does regularity mean? It can mean different things to different people, but in general it means the following:

1. You have been working regularly for a long period and therefore have been receiving regular income.

2. Your family situation is stable.

3. You have regularly paid off your debts on time.

Or your credit worthiness can be measured by the three C's that loan officers use as a guide to lending:

1. Capacity to pay back.

2. Character.

3. Capital or collateral that you own.

The behavior of loan officers may appear to some of you to discriminate against people with unstable living situations —that is, those who have unstable jobs, unstable family situations, and the like. That may or may not be true, depending on your definition of discrimination. But a loan officer is supposed to make decisions that maximize the profits for his company. At the going interest rate, he may decide to eliminate people who are high risks: loans will be refused to people who come in with records that indicate they will not pay off their debts as easily or as regularly as those people who seem more stable. If you are a credit buyer with an unstable living situation, one way that you can persuade loan officers not to refuse you is to candidly discuss your problems with him or her and produce a past record of loan repayments that was stable in spite of your unstable situation. Or, alternatively, you could offer to pay a higher interest rate.

You may sometimes nevertheless be refused credit because of a bad credit rating. Once, there was little you could do about this, but now under a new federal law, you have some recourse.

Figure F-1   A Typical Net Worth Statement

(Personal Financial Statement) .... OFFICE

Name ....   Address ....

Business ....   City...   Zip.................

Social Security Numbers:

Borrower: ....   Spouse: ....   Statement as of: ....

ASSETS				LIABILITIES			
Cash on hand and in banks...............				Notes payable banks:			
U. S. Government Securities—Schedule 1.........				Secured			
Stocks and Bonds—Schedule 1................				Unsecured			
Accounts receivable				Notes payable other...........			
Notes receivable				Accounts and bills payable...........			
Cash surrender value life insurance...........				Accrued taxes and interest...........			
Face Value $...............				Mortgages payable on real estate—Schedule 2........			
Real estate—Schedule 2...................							
Automobiles				Security Agreements			
Other assets—itemize				Other debts—itemize			
....				....			
....				....			
....				....			
....				....			
....				Total liabilities			
....				Net worth			
TOTAL ASSETS				TOTAL LIABILITIES AND NET WORTH...........			

SOURCE OF INCOME				GENERAL INFORMATION
Salary				Married (name of spouse) ....
Bonus and commissions................				Single ....
Dividends				Number of children...........
Real estate income..................				Other dependents ....
Other income				Are any assets pledged?...........
....				Defendant in any suits or legal actions?...........
....				Personal bank accounts carried at...........
....				Life Insurance - face amount, company, beneficiaries...........
....				....
TOTAL				....

DO YOU HAVE A WILL?   YES____   NO____

CONTINGENT LIABILITIES

Endorser or comaker...

Legal claims ....

Federal Income Taxes:

   1. Do you owe any Federal Tax for years prior to the current year?   Yes ☐   No ☐   Amount $................

   2. Are there any unpaid Federal Tax Assessments outstanding against you? Yes ☐   No ☐   Amount $................

Other ....

(see over)

EXHIBIT F-2   **Determining Your Net Worth**

Estimated amounts, end of this year

ASSETS

House (including furniture)—
   market value   _____

Car(s)—resale value   _____

Life insurance cash value   _____

Bonds, securities—
   market value   _____

Cash on hand   _____

Other (for example, stereo,
   cameras, savings accounts,
   land)   _____

TOTAL ASSETS   _____

LIABILITIES

Mortgage   _____

Loans   _____

Other   _____

TOTAL LIABILITIES   _____

NET WORTH
   December 31, 19__   _____

An annual net worth statement may help you and/or your family to keep track of financial progress from year to year. Essentially, your net worth is an indication of how much wealth you actually own. We generally find that young people have low net worths —or even negative net worths: that is, they owe more than they own—because they are anticipating having higher income in the future. As individuals and families get further down the road, their net worth increases steadily only to start falling again, usually when retirement age approaches and the income flow slows down or stops completely, thereby forcing the retired person or couple to draw on past accumulated savings. This very simplified statement of family net worth can be easily filled out. Just make sure that you include all of your assets and all of your liabilities. Assets are anything that you own, and liabilities are anything that you owe. It is all very simple.

WHAT TO DO WHEN YOU ARE REFUSED CREDIT

The Fair Credit Reporting Act (Title VI of the 1968 Consumer Credit Protection Act) was passed in 1970 and went into effect in 1971. Under this law, you have recourse when a credit investigating agency gives you a bad rating. Now, when you are turned down for credit because of a bad credit rating, the company that turned you down must give you the name and address of the credit investigating agency that was used. The same holds true for an insurance company.

The 1971 Act was meant to regulate the consumer credit reporting industry to ensure that credit reporting agencies supply information that is equitable and fair to the consumer. The problems that led to passage of the Act seem to have been the reporting of incorrect, misleading, or incomplete information, as well as one-sided versions of disputed claims. In addition, many people were concerned about the invasion of privacy involved in the distribution of such reports to those who did not really have a legitimate business need for them. These reports often contained material about a person's general reputation, personal characteristics or mode of living, and character.

The Act applies not only to the usual credit bureaus and investigating concerns, but also to finance companies and banks that routinely give out credit information other than that which is developed from their own transactions.

Under the rules of the new law, a credit bureau must disclose to you the "nature and substance of all information" that is included under your name in its files. You also have the right to be told the sources of just about all that information. If you discover that the credit bureau has incomplete, misleading, or false information, the Fair Credit Reporting Act requires that the bureau reinvestigate any disputed information "within a reasonable period of time." Of course, the credit bureau is not necessarily going to do it, but you do have the law on your side and you can go to court over the issue. In addition, at your request, the credit bureau must send to those companies that received a credit report in the last six months a notice of the elimination of any false information from your credit record.

Even if your have not been rejected for credit, you still have the right to go to a credit bureau and find out what your file contains. You also have the right to ask the credit bureau to delete, correct, or investigate items which you believe to be fallacious and inaccurate. The credit bureau then has the legal right to charge you for the time it spends correcting any mistakes. Also, the Fair Credit Reporting Act specifically forbids credit bureaus from sending out any adverse information that is more than seven years old. But there are important exceptions. Bankruptcy information can be sent out to your prospective cred-

itors for a full 14 years. And there is no time limit on any information for loans or life insurance policies of $50,000 or more, or for a job application with an annual salary of $20,000 or more. That means that adverse information may be kept in your file and used indefinitely for these purposes.

Problems with the Act

Critics of the 1971 Act have been numerous, and various proposals have been before Congress to amend the statute to increase its effectiveness. One of the main criticisms is that consumers cannot obtain a copy of the credit reports or have actual physical access to the files. Moreover, many critics contend that consumers who have asked for information from these agencies have been subjected to evasion, delaying tactics, or exorbitant charges. Many other consumers believe they are not receiving all of the information that is in their files. Of course, the credit reporting agencies have opposed any legislation that would give consumers direct access to the agency files. Their argument is that they would no longer have any sources of confidential information. And, moreover, there would be a substantial increase in the costs of providing accurate credit reports.

SHOPPING FOR CREDIT

Once you have decided that you want to buy some credit—that is, you want to get some goods now and pay for them later— then you should shop around. The Truth-in-Lending Act,

which requires a full statement of the annual interest rate charged, makes shopping much easier these days. This is certainly true if you are comparing revolving credit accounts: if the actual annual interest charge for one is 22½ percent, you know this is not as good a deal as another one at 18 percent.

But when looking at loan agreements, you have to be careful, because all have various contingency clauses written into them that may or may not affect you. For example, if you sign a credit agreement that has an **acceleration clause**—meaning that all of the debt becomes immediately due if you, the borrower, fail to meet any single payment on the debt—you could not likely pay that large a sum. Obviously, if you could not meet a payment on the debt because you lacked the money, you certainly would be unable to pay the whole loan off at once. The addition of an acceleration clause in a credit agreement increases the probability that whatever you bought on credit will be repossessed.[1]

You should also be aware of an **add-on clause** in installment contracts, particularly when you are shopping for furniture. An add-on clause essentially makes your earlier purchases security for the new purchase. Let's say that you buy furniture for your living room from a particular store on an installment

[1]Because loans with an acceleration clause usually can be obtained at relatively lower interest rates, they may still be a good deal for people who rarely or never default on loan payments.

EXHIBIT F-3   What You Can Do to Protect Yourself against Unfair Credit Reports

If you are trying to get insurance, credit, or a job, you may be subjected to a personal investigation. Under the Fair Credit Reporting Act of 1971:

☐The company asking for the investigation is supposed to let you know you are being investigated.

☐You can demand the name and address of the firm hired to do the investigating.

☐You can demand that the investigating company tell you what its report contains—except for medical information used to determine your eligibility for life insurance.

☐You cannot require the investigators to reveal the names of neighbors or friends who supplied information.

If the investigation turns up derogatory or inaccurate material, you can:

☐Demand a recheck.

☐Require the investigators to take out of your file anything that is inaccurate.

☐Require them to insert your version of the facts, if the facts remain in dispute.

☐Sue the investigating firm for damages if negligence on its part resulted in violation of the law which caused you some loss—failure to get a job, loss of credit or insurance, or even great personal embarrassment.

☐Require the company to cease reporting adverse information after it is 7 years old—with the exception of a bankruptcy, which can remain in the file for 14 years.

---

contract. Six months later, you decide that you want new furniture for a bedroom. You go back to the same store and buy the bedroom furniture on an installment contract also. If there is an add-on clause and you default in the installment contract for the bedroom furniture, you may lose both that furniture and the items you purchased for the living room, even if you have completely paid for that furniture.

It is also possible for a court order to allow a creditor to attach part of your property. Your bank account may be attached and used to discharge any debts. Or your wages may be garnished (attached)—that is, if a judgment has been made against you, your employer is required to withhold wages to pay a

creditor. (If this happens often, you may find it hard to keep or get another job.)

Figuring Out the Interest Rate You Are Paying

There is a relatively simple formula to give you the approximate interest rate you are actually paying on a consumer installment loan. The formula is:

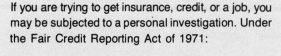

$$i = \frac{2 \cdot t \cdot C}{P(n+1)}$$

where the letters have the following meaning:

i = annual simple interest rate in decimal form

t = how many times a year you have to pay, for example, 52 if weekly, 12 if monthly

C = actual dollar cost of borrowing (finance charge)

P = the net amount borrowed

n = the number of payments in total

Let's take an example. Assume that you apply for a loan of $100. The finance company will give it to you for a service fee of $10 for a 1-year period, to be repaid in 12 monthly installments. You are told, therefore, that you are only paying 10 percent interest. But that is really not what you are paying. Let's put those numbers into our simple formula above. The net amount you are receiving is $100, so: P = $100; C = $10; t = 12; and n = 12. The formula becomes:

$$i = \frac{2 \times 12 \times \$10}{\$100 \ (12 + 1)} = 18.46\%$$

If it was a discount loan, you would only receive $90, and the formula would look like this:

$$i = \frac{2 \times 12 \times \$10}{\$90 \ (12 + 1)} = 20.5\%$$

If you wish to figure out what it would cost you to borrow $1,000 for any specified period of time, look at Table F-1. Here we show different specified annual percentage rates for different time periods.

Interest Rate and Taxes

To calculate the interest that you actually pay, you have to take account of inflation and of the taxes you save by borrowing. Interest payments and finance charges are usually tax deductible. Every dollar of interest payments you make is one dollar less of income on which you pay taxes. That means that your tax savings would be 20 cents on each dollar if you are in the 20 percent tax bracket; if you are paying an interest rate of 10 percent and your taxable income bracket is 20 percent, the after tax interest payment you are actually paying is only 8 percent. Obviously, the higher your tax bracket, the less it really costs you to borrow.

Where Should You Go for a Loan?

For some asset purchases you immediately know where to go for a loan. If you are buying a house, you obviously do not go to your local small loan company for a loan. Where do you go? You go to a savings and loan association, a commercial bank, or a mortgage trust company; or you sign a contract with the seller of the house. The real estate agent usually helps the buyer of a house secure a loan. If you want to shop around, the easiest thing to do is to call various savings and loan associations to see what interest rates they are charging or visit the ones that will not give out that information over the telephone. In Consumer Issue I, we discuss in more detail what you should look out for when you are borrowing money on a house.

To borrow for a car, again you probably will not go to a small loan company around the corner. Rather, you want to go to a

Table F-1

The Cost of Financing $1,000 on the Installment Plan

PERCENTAGE RATE (ANNUAL)	LENGTH OF LOAN (MONTHS)	MONTHLY PAYMENTS	FINANCE CHARGE	TOTAL COST OF LOAN
9.25%	6	$171.19	$ 27.14	$1,027.14
	12	87.57	50.84	1,050.84
	24	45.80	99.20	1,099.20
	36	31.92	149.12	1,149.12
10.5%	6	171.81	30.86	1,030.86
	12	88.15	57.80	1,057.80
	24	46.38	113.12	1,113.12
	36	32.50	170.00	1,170.00
12%	6	172.55	35.30	1,035.30
	12	88.85	66.20	1,066.20
	24	47.07	129.68	1,129.68
	36	33.21	195.56	1,195.56
13%	6	173.04	38.24	1,038.24
	12	89.32	71.84	1,071.84
	24	47.54	140.96	1,140.96
	36	33.69	212.84	1,212.84
15%	6	174.03	44.18	1,044.18
	12	90.26	83.12	1,083.12
	24	48.49	163.76	1,163.76
	36	34.67	248.12	1,248.12
18%	6	175.53	53.18	1,053.18
	12	91.68	100.16	1,100.16
	24	49.92	198.08	1,198.08
	36	36.15	301.40	1,301.40

EXHIBIT F-4   **Actual Interest Paid after Tax Deduction**

1. Assume your tax rate is 20 percent, that is, you must pay Uncle Sam 20¢ of the (last) dollars you earn.

2. Interest payments are tax deductible.

3. You borrow $100 at 10 percent, that is, you pay $10 interest.

4. But when calculating your taxes you get to deduct that $10 from your income *before* you compute your taxes owed.

5. Hence, what you do not have to pay Uncle Sam is $.20 \times \$10.00 = \$2.00$.

6. Your actual interest payment for that $100 loan is therefore $10 − $2 (in tax savings) = $8, or only 8 percent (instead of 10 percent) on a simple interest loan.

---

credit union or a commercial bank, where the loan for a car will cost less. Note that the interest rate for new cars is usually lower than for a used car. Why? Because the car is used as collateral, and the new car is generally easier to sell than a used car. You should note also that if you buy a car that is technically brand new—that is, you would be the first owner—but you purchase it after next year's models have entered the showroom, the lending agency may consider that to be a used car and charge you the higher rate of interest.

If you want to borrow money for purchases of smaller items, a credit union loan might be cheapest; the next best deal would be credit card companies, Master Charge and BankAmericard (VISA), for example.

The key to purchasing the best credit deal is to treat credit as a good or service just like anything else; use the same shopping techniques for purchasing credit that you would use to purchase anything else. Your having spent time to find the best deal for a car does not mean that your shopping should stop there. You may not be getting the best deal possible if you buy the credit for the car from the dealership or its affiliate. You may do better going to your local commercial bank. But you cannot predict: you have to compare and contrast.

NOTHING IS FREE

You often hear ads for companies that want to help you help yourself. They propose to consolidate all of your debts into one fixed monthly payment that will be lower than the total of what you are paying now to all of your creditors. But do not be taken in. It is impossible for the claim to be true; you cannot actually end up paying a smaller interest rate by consolidating your debts than by paying for them separately. Remember, you have already incurred any setup charges involved in taking out the various lines of credit that you want consolidated. Credit companies do

nothing for free. Like any other company, they will not render any service unless they make a profit on it. So if you let a credit company pay off all your existing debts and then lend you the total amount that they paid, you will have to incur the setup charge for that.

Sometimes debt consolidation *may* actually save you some money. If, for example, you consolidate all of your revolving credit accounts which charge you 18 percent into one 12 percent credit union loan, you will be better off (assuming that there are no early payment penalty charges on the revolving credit accounts).

It may be more *convenient* for you to have all your loans consolidated into one big one. Then you have to write only one check a month instead of many. But this service will not be handed to you without charge. You may in fact have a smaller monthly charge, but it will be for many more months, and you will ultimately end up paying higher finance charges for the whole consolidation package, and thus a higher total payment. If you detest keeping records and writing out lots of checks, you may want to incur this additional cost (and additional debt) by taking a loan consolidation. As long as you realize that nobody gives you anything for free, you can make a rational choice, knowing that there are always costs for any benefits you receive. Loan consolidation is certainly not going to pull you out of financial trouble if you really are in trouble. The only way out of such trouble is either by making a higher income or by cutting back on your current consumption so that you can pay off your debts more easily. (You could, of course, sell some of your assets to pay off your debts.)

DEBT COUNSELING

If you have gotten into financial trouble by overextending yourself, you may wish to consult some of the good nonprofit organizations working with people in debt troubles. Such work is generally called debt counseling. For example, there is a Financial Crisis Clinic run at Long Beach State University in California as a part of the program in financial counseling under the auspices of the Home Economics Department. You may wish to consult the home economics department of your local college or university to find out if a similar program is available in your area. There might be a local office of the Consumer Credit Counseling Service in your area. This is a nonprofit organization financed by the United Way and rebates from creditors. You are not

charged anything for using the service except for long distance telephone calls. These centers throughout the country have trained counselors who will sit down with you to analyze your situation. None of the offices will take over complete control of your finances, but they will help you deal with your creditors.

Talking over Dealings with Them

A counselor might draw up a budget, ask you to stick to it, and have you send them a certain amount of money each month to funnel out to creditors. If Consumer Credit Counseling Services does not think it can help you, you will be referred to another agency.

Other Steps You Can Take

If you only have one or two major bills that you cannot pay, you can talk to your creditors directly. Usually, they will be willing to set up an extension of an account. If you are a member of a credit union or have access to one, you might consider a consolidation loan at a lower interest rate than the average of what you are paying on a large number of installment contracts.

The most drastic step you can take is declaring personal bankruptcy, which we described in the beginning of the last chapter and in the appendix that follows. During a true bankruptcy proceeding, you do not need a lawyer; you do not have to pay $400 or $500 to hire an attorney. Not all of your assets will be taken, such as pensions, insurance proceeds, veteran's bene-

fits, and Social Security. You get to keep your home if you are head of the household and $1,000 of your personal property. On the other hand, debts that you must keep paying are back taxes, child support, and any secured claim debts, that is, ones for which you put up collateral. Basically, personal bankruptcy absolves you of unsecured debts, such as store charge accounts and finance company loans.

An alternative to personal bankruptcy is to apply for a Chapter XIII plan, which means that you propose to pay your creditors a certain percentage of the debts you owe them over a certain time period. If a majority of your creditors approve, the court can put the plan into effect. However, consumers are warned against attempting a Chapter XIII plan without the use of a lawyer because most consumers simply do not know how to put such a plan together, how to make a budget for themselves, or what arrangements to take care of. The Consumer Credit Counseling Service office can give assistance on this point.

Basically, many credit problems you run into result from the lack of a financial plan. Although such influences as credit advertising, credit selling, and other credit-oriented selling techniques tend to push families into the overuse of credit, you, the consumer, ultimately are the one who signs on the dotted line. If you have a sound financial plan, perhaps along the lines outlined in Chapter 7 and Issue D, no amount of advertising or fast talk will get you to overextend yourself financially.

SUMMARY

1. There is no definite way to decide which purchases should be bought on time and which should be bought with cash. Rather, one's total outstanding debt should not exceed what can be handled.

2. You determine your safe debt load by adding up all of your outstanding debt, which includes loan payments, department store payments, credit card payments, overdue accounts on telephone and electricity, and so on. One way of determining whether this is a safe debt load is by taking 10 percent of your monthly take-home pay (that is, after taxes), and multiplying it by 18. If your monthly debt is greater than what is safe, you must take steps to reduce it. These are outlined in the appendix to this consumer issue.

3. You should estimate your net worth regularly, perhaps once a year.

4. You determine your net worth by adding up all of your assets, which include the market value of your house, your car(s), your bonds, stocks, and other things. Subtract what you owe, such as your house mortgage and other loans. This gives you your net worth.

5. Keeping track of your net worth year by year gives you an idea of the financial progress you are making. If your net worth stays constant or goes down, you are spending annually more than you receive.

6. When applying for a loan, you must realize that the loan officer will look at your capacity to pay back, your character, and

what collateral you can put up to back the loan.

7. When applying for a loan, put your best foot forward—fill out the form either with a typewriter or print clearly. And when meeting the loan officer, dress appropriately: first impressions are important.

8. If you are refused credit, the Fair Credit Reporting Act allows you to demand that the firm hired to do the credit check tells you what its report contains, that it do a recheck, and that it insert your version of any facts in dispute.

9. When you shop for credit, shop as if you were buying any other good or service. Look for the best deal by (a) calling around to get the various offers of interest rates and monthly payments; (b) checking to see whether an acceleration clause is in your contract; (c) making sure all finance and setup charges are specifically stated in any contract; and (d) recomputing the finance charge yourself—do not take the loan company's word for it.

10. Be wary of debt consolidation schemes. They generally are expensive.

11. If you are in trouble, debt counseling may be required. Financial crisis clinics are run in many major cities in the United States. Check with your local college or university home economics department or in the white pages for Consumer Credit Counseling Service.

QUESTIONS FOR THOUGHT AND DISCUSSION

1. Is it important for you to determine why you are borrow-

ing money before you borrow? Would you feel safer borrowing money to buy a durable consumer good such as a refrigerator, TV, or stereo, rather than borrowing money for a vacation?

2. Do you think it is unfair for loan officers to delve into your character before they decide whether you are a good credit risk? Why or why not?

THINGS TO DO

1. Go to Exhibit F-1 and use either method A or method B to determine your safe debt load or the debt load of your parents. How much are you overextended or underextended? (Is it possible to be underextended in debt?)

2. Call several banks or credit departments of various stores in your area and ask them to send you a loan application. Fill out the net worth statement to see what your net worth is. Familiarize yourself with all of the various terms. If you do not know what they mean, ask your instructor or go to a dictionary. If it is appropriate, attempt to determine your net worth for the past five years. Has it gone up or down?

3. Call or write your local field office of the Federal Trade Commission. Ask about what activities the FTC performs in enforcing the Truth-in-Lending Act. See if they have changed over the last few years.

4. Calculate the actual interest paid after your tax deduction for a typical consumer loan. Try to calculate the actual interest paid by someone who is in the 70 percent tax bracket. Is there a big difference between the two corrected interest rates?

SELECTED READINGS

Before You Sign a Contract, HXT–95. Berkeley: Agricultural Extension Service, University of California.

Be Wise: Consumers' Quick Credit Guide. Washington, D.C.: U.S. Department of Agriculture, Government Printing Office, September 1972.

Buying on Time, HXT–93. Berkeley: Agricultural Extension Service, University of California.

"Hooked on Credit and Out of Control." *Changing Times*, February 1977, p. 34.

"The How and Why of Credit Buying." *Forecast*, November 1972.

"How Much Can You Afford to Owe?" *Good Housekeeping*, September 1974, p. 171.

"How Much Can You Borrow?" *Money*, October 1972.

"How to Shop for Credit." *Consumer Reports*, March 1975, pp. 171–178.

Main, J. "Who's a Good Credit Risk? Credit-Scoring Systems." *Reader's Digest*, May 1977, p. 197.

Main, Jeremy. "A New Way to Score with Lenders." *Money*, February 1977.

"Merchants of Debt." *Time*, February 28, 1977, pp. 36–40.

Nelson, P. "Giving Yourself Credit; Four Easy Steps to Establish Your Financial Identity." *McCalls*, March 1977, p. 106.

"New Generation of Credit Card Sleuths." *Business Week*, June 22, 1974.

"New Rights When You Buy on Time." *Consumer Reports*, May 1976, p. 302.

"Peeling Away Excess Credit Cards." *Money*, December 1976.

"Prospects Now for Borrowers and Lenders." *U.S. News & World Report*, January 20, 1975, pp. 58–60.

"Somebody Has a File on You." *Changing Times*, August 1975, pp. 41–44.

"When Credit Investigators Dig into Your Affairs. . . ." *U.S. News & World Report*, March 18, 1974, pp. 89–90.

"Why It's Good to Check Your Credit File." *Business Week*, December 7, 1974.

"Why You May Be Paying Too Much for Credit." *Changing Times*, August 1976.

APPENDIX: If You Have to Declare Personal Bankruptcy

Certain danger signals will tell you that you are not financially sound. If some of the following appear in your financial picture, you may have to take fast action to keep from "going under."

DANGER SIGNALS

1. You consistently postpone paying your bills.

2. You begin to hear from your creditors.

3. You have no savings, or not enough to tide you over a financial upset.

4. You have no idea what your living expenses are.

5. You use a lot of credit, having charge accounts all over town, several credit cards in your wallet, and paying only the minimum on each account every month.

6. You do not know how much your debts total.

HOW TO KEEP FROM GOING UNDER

You can do certain things to prevent yourself and your family from getting into deeper financial trouble. Some of the following common-sense actions will be of special help.

1. Itemize your debts in detail, making sure you note current balance, monthly payments, and when payments are due.

2. List the family's total monthly net income that can be counted on every month.

3. Subtract your monthly living expenses from your net income. Do not include the payments on debt you already have. The result will be the income you would be able to spend if you had no debts. Now subtract the monthly payments you are committed to making on all your debts. If you come out with a minus figure, you are obviously living beyond your means. If you come out with a very small positive figure, you still may be living beyond your means.

4. If you think you are in fact living beyond your means, what you have to do is clear: Notify everyone in your family that the money situation is tight. Tell them things are going to have to be cut back. You and every other spender in the family unit will have to start shaving expenses, such as those on recreation, food, and transportation.

IF THAT FAILS

If you are still in deep trouble and cannot pull out of it yourself, then you may have to devise a plan of action by yourself or with a debt counselor, as we discussed in the preceding consumer issue: Once you have made up that plan of action, go to your separate creditors and discuss it with them to see if you can work things out without going into personal bankruptcy.

GOING INTO PERSONAL BANKRUPTCY

You have the alternative of getting out of debt by going to court. But you may spend a great amount of money in doing so, and lose some of your property besides.

One law that allows you to declare bankruptcy is Chapter XIII of the National Bankruptcy Act—the Wage Earner Plan. It is a court-supervised plan for paying off your debt; it is not true bankruptcy. With the help of a

lawyer, you draw up a budget and a plan for repayment, usually over 36 months. You file your plan and your petition with the bankruptcy court in your area. Upon filing the plan and petition, you are immediately given relief from creditor harrassment and collection pressures.

The plan must be approved by both the court and creditors. Once it is approved, the court will appoint a trustee who receives your payments and distributes the money to the creditors. You must pay the trustee 5 percent of the amount he distributes; here is where the cost comes in. Court costs and lawyers' fees will add another several hundred dollars to filing a Chapter XIII.

Note that Chapter XIII is successful in only half the number of cases in which it is used. The other type is true bankruptcy, which is the only legal way you can cancel your debts without paying them. For you to file bankruptcy in a U.S. District Court, your debts do not have to exceed your assets by any particular amount, but you do have to be in deep financial trouble.

After filing, in effect you give

up all that you own. That is, the court has control over all your assets. A trustee is named to check on those assets available for distribution to creditors. The court will return to you tools and other items necessary for you to earn your living, as well as food, clothing, basic furniture, and perhaps, but not always, your home. Exactly what you can keep varies from state to state and should be looked into before you even consider declaring personal bankruptcy.

The benefit of declaring bankruptcy is that all your debts are wiped out except for taxes, alimony and support payments, and the debts that others have cosigned for you (which now become their debts), plus any secured debts.

The disadvantage has already been mentioned: you no longer have control over your property. But, in addition, bankruptcy puts a black mark on your credit record. What is more, you can get back into debt right away. After all, you have court and lawyers' costs (with Chapter XIII) which together might run to $500. And remember, you cannot file for bankruptcy again for another six years.

GLOSSARY OF TERMS

Engel's Law

A proposition, first made by Ernst Engel, that states that as a family's income rises, the proportion spent on food falls.

Marginal Buyers

Buyers who are just on the borderline between buying and not buying a product at the particular offering price. Marginal buyers for specific products are very concerned with price and quality of those products.

Basic Four

Four food categories needed for a nutritionally sound diet: (1) meat (or other protein source), (2) grains, (3) vegetables and fruits, and (4) dairy products.

RDAs

Recommended Dietary Allowances, usually specified in terms of a daily intake of a particular vitamin or nutrient.

Support Prices

A minimum price set by the government for a particular agricultural raw commodity. For example, the support price of wheat may be set at, say, $2 per bushel. That means that the farmer never has to sell his or her wheat below that support price.

Nonrecourse Loans

Loans made to farmers by a government organization in exchange for a particular commodity—say, wheat or corn. They are called nonrecourse because the government can never demand payment for the loan.

Target Prices

Prices set by the government for particular agricultural commodities such as wheat and corn. If the actual market price falls below the target price, farmers get a subsidy from the government for the difference.

The $300 Billion Stomach

CHAPTER PREVIEW

☐What are the characteristics of food consumption in the United States?

☐How do government inspection and labeling requirements affect the consumer?

☐Specifically, what does the Fair Packaging and Labeling Act do?

☐What are some of the attributes of good nutrition?

☐How do government agriculture programs affect consumer food prices?

☐What are the trends in food retailing and what is the future of convenience foods?

10 In one year, the average American consumes 170 pounds of red meat, 50 pounds of poultry, 14 pounds of fish, 41 pounds of eggs, 352 pounds of dairy products, 50 pounds of fats and oils, 80 pounds of fresh fruits, 140 pounds of fresh vegetables, 260 pounds of canned goods, 142 pounds of flour and cereal products, 120 pounds of sugar and other sweeteners, 15 pounds of coffee, tea, and cocoa. The total amount of money spent on food products is just as staggering: $250 billion estimated in 1978 alone. Americans consume more than 30 percent of the world's total agricultural output. We are feeding a very large and hungry stomach. We buy our food products at 300,000 retail stores that carry an average of 2,600 different products on their shelves at any one time. The number of brands of different types of foods—canned peas, carrots, soups, cereals—is probably many thousand when you include all of the regional specialties you can buy.

And since food bills take up between 20 and 35 percent of just about every American's budget, there is deep concern over rising food prices. Figure 10-1 shows the price index for foods over the last 50 years. When we talked about inflation in Chapter 8, we discussed some of the significance of this rise in food prices; and later in this chapter we will discover that at least one reason food prices are so high is that certain government programs are designed to keep them high.

FOOD AND INCOME

Even though we spend a total of $300 billion a year on food, that represents only 15 percent of income in the United States. Figure 10-2 shows that the percentage of American income spent on food consumption has actually been falling. Is this surprising? Well, it should not be. Ask yourself how much more food you could buy if you doubled your income. You could certainly buy better quality, and perhaps you

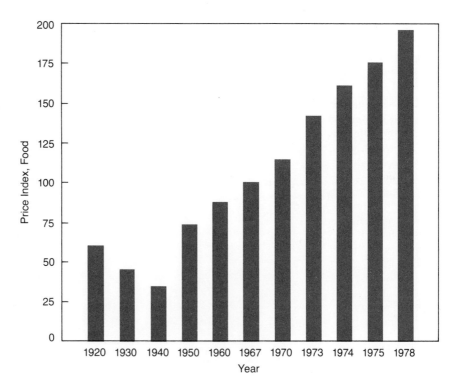

**Figure 10-1
Price Index, Food
(1967=100)**

An index of average food prices shows dramatic increases in the last half decade. In particular, since the so-called food crisis of 1973 up to the present, it has risen faster than almost every other component of the overall price index in the economy. (The 1978 figure is an estimate.)

Source: *Monthly Labor Reviews; Federal Reserve Bulletin.*

could eat in restaurants more often. But there is a limit, at least for most of you; and that limit is a physical one. Your stomach can hold only so much at any one sitting, and your body will maintain its weight only if you do not put in more calories than you use.

If people's expenditures for food had kept in line with their incomes over the past 150 years in the United States, we would be a nation of balloons, each running into each other and having trouble sitting in chairs, driving cars, and getting on buses. While there may be some tendency for the average American to be slightly overweight, we certainly are not a nation of corpulent slobs.

In 1856, a German statistician, Ernst Engel, made some budgetary studies of family expenditures and found that as family incomes increased, the *percentage* spent on food decreased—not the total amount spent on food, of course, but the percentage. A family making $25,000 a year certainly spends more on food than a family making $10,000 a year. However, even though the richer family has an income two and a half times larger than the other family's, the richer family does not spend two and a half times the amount that the other family spends on food.

Engel's Law has a fairly universal applicability, not only through time but across nations at any given moment. Remember our discussion of this in Chapter 7 in reference to the budgets of different families. Richer nations spend a smaller fraction of their total national income on food than do poorer nations. And we can predict that in the United States, if we become richer, our expenditures on food will become a smaller percentage of total expenditures.

Figure 10-2
Percentage of
Total Income in the
United States Going
for Food.

At the beginning of
the Great Depression
and for the following
20 or so years, the
percentage of dis-
posable personal
income going for food
remained at around
23 to 24 percent, but
in 1950 it started
dropping until it
reached about 15
percent in the 1970s.
It will probably
continue to drop as
our real income
goes up.

Source: USDA Agricultural
Economic Report No. 138;
supplement for 1971 and
National Food Situation
(USDA) November, 1976.

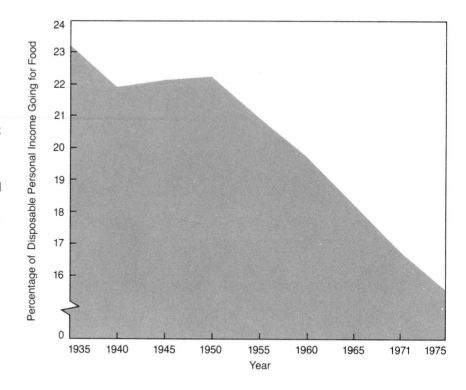

GOVERNMENT LABELING AND INSPECTION REQUIREMENTS

Because food is an essential part of every consumer's budget, the government has through the years established a system of inspection and labeling designed to aid consumers in making wiser choices about the food products we buy. You may not be aware of it, but the government is busy inspecting meatpacking houses and various food processing establishments in order to ensure that our food is processed in a clean, bacteria-free environment so that we will not suffer the harmful effects that sometimes result from improper food processing. The Food and Drug Administration goes so far as to determine periodically the quantities of rodent hair, mold, and insect residue in your peanut butter! The government is also attempting to enforce fair packaging and labeling, particularly in the form of the Fair Packaging and Labeling Act of 1966.

FAIR PACKAGING

The law came about through numerous criticisms directed at packagers. The quantity of contents were often inadequately or confusingly disclosed; there was no uniform designation of quantity by weight or fluid volume. For example, one producer would measure by ounces, while a competitor would measure by the quart or would measure by quarts and ounces combined. In addition, there was criticism of the use of presumably meaningless adjectives of exaggeration, such as "giant" or "jumbo," and the use of designations of servings, such as small, medium, and large, without any standard of reference.

The Act applies to such consumer commodities as foods and drugs, devices, or cosmetics that are subject to the Federal Food, Drug and Cosmetic Act, and to any other article customarily purchased for sale through retailers for consumption by individuals or for "use by individuals for purposes of personal care or in the performance of services ordinarily rendered within the household." The Federal Trade Commission at first proposed regulations that enlarged upon the term "consumer commodity" to include virtually everything. But when producers threatened substantial litigation if these enlarged regulations went through, the FTC instead listed 52 classes of products that it does not consider to be "consumer commodities" and therefore are not included under the Fair Packaging and Labeling Act of 1966.

The Act also authorized the secretary of commerce to attempt to limit "undue" proliferation of product package sizes. If the secretary determines that there is such an undue proliferation that consumers suffer an "unreasonably" impaired ability to make product comparison, then the secretary may request that manufacturers, packers, and distributors participate in the development of a *voluntary* product standard for that commodity. If no standard has been adopted within one year after such a request, or if the voluntary standard adopted is not observed, the secretary of commerce is supposed to report such determination to Congress.

The Act, which became effective in 1967, does not apply to tobacco, meat, poultry, and any other products covered by other federal laws. It requires, among other things, that the label of every consumer product covered must:

1. Give the net quantity per serving and number of servings in the package.
2. Not have "too much" air space or packaging material.
3. Identify the commodity and make clear the name and place of the business of the manufacturer, distributor, or packer.
4. Contain a statement in a standard location on the main display panel of the package of the net contents in units that seem appropriate for the product.

All of the federal efforts at fair packaging and labeling are aimed at providing consumers with a maximum amount of information so that we may make rational choices. And all such efforts may be gathered under the label "truth in packaging," or truth, plain and simple. But we have to be careful when we analyze the effects of truth in packaging acts passed by federal, state, or local governments. Take the case of air space in packages. If all consumers could be duped forever, the ultimate result of, say, cereal manufacturers putting their products in big boxes with quantities of air space would be that people would end up buying boxes of mostly air. Since that has not happened (at least not yet), we know that *some* consumers are informed.

Many of the informed consumers who keep producers in line are institutional buyers—government, hospitals, day camps, day care centers, summer camps— that buy great amounts of food and have nutritionists who make sure that the best food value is obtained. These large institutional buyers who take so much care in their food shopping are **marginal buyers**, because if they find out that a particular product they have purchased turns out to be a gyp, they switch immediately: they are right on the margin between buying it and buying the second-best choice. Fortunately, there are always a number of these buyers around. In fact, one study showed that fully one-third of all shoppers are marginal shoppers; they are very price conscious, and they take time and effort to establish the validity of the claims made by all ads and labels.

NET WEIGHT
SOMETIMES SPELLS
NONSENSE

Even though the Fair Packaging and Labeling Act requires that the net weight of canned foods be given, it is sometimes pretty hard to figure out what you are really buying. You have to find out, for example, what is the actual weight of the fruit in a can of pears because some brands will have more syrup than others. If you do not want the syrup, then you do not care how much *it* weighs.

The Food and Drug Administration has numerous requirements for the canning industry. The usual rule of thumb is that a container must be at least 90 percent full. However, since packing liquid, such as syrup for peach halves, can be legally added, the FDA requirement is obviously not very useful. The National Canners Association takes the position that part of the nutrients of the canned food end up in the liquids used for canning and so the liquid is part of the food product. Therefore, the NCA is against disclosing the drained weights on the outside of cans. But since it appears that the drained weight averages about the same percentage of labeled weight for all brands of a given product, it probably would not matter. We consumers would know that we are actually paying a higher price per average drained weight, but we would still have the same selection at about the same prices we have always been paying. In this example, it seems that the additional information is not going to make us much better off.

USDA GRADES—
ANOTHER LABELING
CONFUSION

In addition to FDA labeling requirements for canned or processed foods and meat inspection, the U.S. Department of Agriculture provides for grade marks on various meats and fresh produce. These grades are meant to guide the consumer as to the level of quality, but the labels are often misleading.

Meat. All fresh meats, with the exception of pork, are voluntarily labeled as to grade. Until several years ago, the top grade available in supermarkets was "prime" followed by "choice," but new government beef grading standards have taken effect after two years of controversy and court battles. Under these new standards, some beef will qualify for a higher grade than it did before.

Grading for quality should not be confused with inspection. All meat sold for human consumption is inspected for wholesomeness. Grading is voluntary and is supposed to predict the eating quality of the meat. It is usually a measure of fat content or marbling. Normally more than one-half the beef inspected by the USDA is also graded for quality. Of this, the USDA reports 5 percent graded prime, 78 percent graded choice, and 13 percent good. The rest was graded standard or utility and, along with most of the ungraded beef, will go into items like processed meats.

Poultry. Poultry, which was not under federal inspection standards until the Wholesome Poultry Products Act of 1968, is now subject to USDA grading. Poultry is graded solely on physically observable characteristics such as freezer burns, presence or absence of wing tips or other missing parts, or breaks in the skin. In other words, a grade of A on a turkey may mean that you get a tough old bird that just happens to have all its parts and suffers from no *observable* flaws. Similarly, a B bird, though technically a lesser grade, may be delicious but have a broken wing tip. Poultry grading does not guarantee quality; but you can be sure that a C rating means that the product is likely to appear physically unmarketable.

Table 10-1   Produce Grading

The U.S. Department of Agriculture has instituted a rather complex system of grading of products. For example, U.S. No. 1 is *not* the top grade for grapefruit but is for onions. For oranges from Florida, U.S. No. 1 is the third grade, the top grade being U.S. Fancy and the second grade being U.S. No. 1 Bright.

Source: U.S. Department of Agriculture.

COMMODITY	TOP GRADE	SECOND GRADE	THIRD GRADE	FOURTH GRADE
Apples (all states but Washington)	U.S. Extra Fancy	U.S. Fancy	U.S. No. 1	U.S. Utility
Apples (Washington)	Washington Extra Fancy	Washington Fancy		
Grapefruit (all states but Arizona, California, and Florida)	U.S. Fancy	U.S. No. 1	U.S. No. 1 Bright	U.S. No. 1 Bronze
Grapefruit (Arizona and California)	U.S. Fancy	U.S. No. 1	U.S. No. 1	U.S. Combination
Grapefruit (Florida)	U.S. Fancy	U.S. No. 1	U.S. No. 1 Bright	U.S. No. 1 Golden
Onions	U.S. No. 1	U.S. Combination or U.S. Commercial	U.S. No. 2	
Oranges (all states but Arizona, California, and Florida)	U.S. Fancy	U.S. No. 1	U.S. No. 1 Bright	U.S. No. 1 Bronze
Oranges (Arizona and California)	U.S. Fancy	U.S. No. 1	U.S. Combination	U.S. No. 2
Oranges (Florida)	U.S. Fancy	U.S. No. 1 Bright	U.S. No. 1 Bright	U.S. No. 1 Golden
Pears (Summer and Fall)	U.S. No. 1	U.S. Combination	U.S. No. 2	
Pears (Winter)	U.S. Extra No. 1	U.S. No. 1	U.S. Combination	U.S. No. 2
Potatoes (Note: Potatoes are also sold "unclassified," meaning ungraded)	U.S. Extra No. 1	U.S. No. 1	U.S. Commercial	U.S. No. 2
Tomatoes (Fresh)	U.S. No. 1	U.S. Combination	U.S. No. 2	U.S. No. 3

Other Food Products.   The USDA also provides for the grading of other food products such as eggs and milk and fresh fruits and vegetables, usually those that come prepackaged. In this area particularly, the grading is often misleading. Table 10-1 lists some of the grades applying to produce. As you can see, "U.S. No. 1" is not a sufficient guide to quality; in some cases it represents the third grade. Similarly, "U.S. No. 1 Bright" represents the second grade of oranges, but the third grade of apples.

Obviously, the best way to shop for groceries is to obtain the most palatable, most nutritious foods for the least amount of money. Some guidelines for doing this are presented in the following consumer issue. But in order to understand some of the recent legislation involving labeling requirements, we had best look at the question of nutrition here.

WHAT IS GOOD NUTRITION?

Many grade school students are taught about food in terms of the **basic four**: (1) meat (or other protein sources), (2) grains, (3) vegetables and fruits, and (4) dairy products. Sometimes the basic four are expanded to seven to include fruits, oil, and other food items.

The USDA developed the basic four food groups in 1956 to be used as an easy daily food guide to maintain a nutritionally sound diet. The basic four are represented in Table 10-2.

RECOMMENDED DIETARY ALLOWANCE

FDA guidelines on the nutrition labeling of processed foods are in **RDA's**— Recommended Dietary Allowances—and these are usually measured in daily intake. The RDA allowances, established by the National Academy of Sciences, state nutritional requirements for nutrients in metric measurement. On food labels vitamins, minerals, and protein are specified as percentages of daily RDAs; and protein, carbohydrate, and fat are listed in grams per serving. Calories per serving are also listed.

NUTRITIONAL LABELING

Nutrition labeling is voluntary for all foods except for foods that are enriched and fortified or those for which a nutritional or health claim is made. All nutrition information must follow this certain format:

1. Serving size.
2. Servings per container.
3. Caloric content or calories per serving.
4. Protein content or protein (grams and percentage of RDA).
5. Carbohydrate content or carbohydrate (grams).
6. Fat content or fat (grams).
7. Percentage of U.S. RDA of protein and selected vitamins and minerals.

What is a nutrient, anyway? It is a chemical substance in food that performs one or more of the following functions: furnishes body fuel needed for energy, provides materials needed for the building or maintenance of body tissues, and/or supplies substances that function in the regulation of body processes. Some important sources of nutrients are listed in Table 10-3.

Table 10-2   The Basic Four

Source: U.S. Department of Agriculture, *Your Money's Worth in Food*, Home and Garden Bulletin No. 183 (Washington, D.C.: U.S. Government Printing Office, 1974).

	DAILY RECOMMENDED SERVINGS	
	Number of Servings	Size of Each Serving
Meat (or other protein source)	2 or more	2–3 ozs. of cooked meat (lean), fish, or poultry. Alternatives: ½ cup cooked dry beans or peas, 1 egg, or 2 tbsps. peanut butter may replace one-half serving of meat.
Dairy Products	Child under 9: 2–3; Child 9–12, Pregnant Woman: 3 or more; Teenager, Nursing Woman: 4 or more; Adult: 2 or more.	8 ozs. milk—whole, skim, buttermilk, evaporated, or dry (reconstituted). Alternatives: one inch cube cheddar-type cheese, or ¾ cup of cottage cheese, ice milk, or ice cream may replace ½ cup of milk.
Vegetables and Fruits	4 or more, to include	A portion, for example, one medium apple, banana, or potato, half a medium grapefruit or cantaloupe (one portion should be equal to ½ cup).
	1 good or 2 fair sources of vitamin C	Good: grapefruit/grapefruit juice, orange/orange juice, cantaloupe, mango, raw strawberries, brussels sprouts, sweet red pepper, green pepper, broccoli. Fair: honey dew melon, lemon, tangerine/tangerine juice, watermelon, asparagus, cabbage, cauliflower, potato/sweet potato cooked in the skin, spinach, tomatoes/tomato juice.
	1 good source of vitamin A at least 3 times per week	Good: dark green and dark yellow vegetables and some fruits— apricots, cantaloupe, carrots, cress, mango, persimmon, pumpkin, spinach, yams, turnip greens and other dark green leaves, winter squash.
Grain Products	4 or more	Whole-grain or enriched only: 1 slice of bread or similar serving of baked goods, 1 oz. ready to eat cereal, ½ to ¾ cup of cooked cereal, corn meal, grits, spaghetti, macaroni, noodles, or rice.
Other Foods	If necessary, to round out meals and to meet the requirements for energy	Refined unenriched cereals and flours and products made from them, sugars, butter, margarine, and other fats (try to include some vegetable oil).

ON NOT BUYING OLD STUFF

We all like to buy fresh food. When we buy fruits and vegetables, we can see at a glance how old they are and whether or not they are worth the price. But when we buy canned items or processed meats and other such goods, we cannot really tell unless we open up the package or can. Few of us ever do that when we buy something wrapped in clear plastic. (It would be embarrassing if we were caught.) Because we do not know how old the processed food is that we buy, government truth-in-food-labeling activity has centered to some extent on food dating.

Table 10-3

Some Important Nutrient Sources

Protein	Thiamine
meat (lean)	pork (lean)
fish	enriched and whole grain bread and cereals
cheese	nuts
eggs	
poultry	**Riboflavin**
dried beans and peas	greens
peanut butter	milk
nuts	cheese
	enriched and whole grain bread
Vitamin A	and cereals
liver	
butter and margarine	**Calcium**
dark green vegetables	collard greens
dark yellow vegetables	kale
cantaloupe	turnip greens
apricots	mustard greens
peaches	milk
watermelon	cheese
	ice cream
Vitamin C	
brussels sprouts	**Iron**
broccoli	lean meat
cauliflower	liver, heart, and kidney
peppers	dried fruit
cantaloupe	dried beans and peas
strawberries	
greens	
citrus fruit	
citrus juice	

OPEN DATING

Food dating is not new; there is already food dating on the cans and many of the cartons you buy. For example, at the top of the carton of milk you bought you may see a date. This is usually the date by which the food should be sold to ensure its subsequent freshness for home use.

Photographers know about this already. Film has been dated for many years without government regulation, the date telling us would-be photographers when we should safely use the film. Outdated film often sells at a lower price than in-date film because the film is less likely to be good once out of date. The same is true, of course, with pastry items and bread. You know you can buy day-old bread and such things at certain bakeries at a lower price than fresh items. Why? Because generally the day-old stuff is not as good or as desired.

Presently, open dating is voluntary. No general regulations or standards have as yet been set to specify what types of dates and explanations should be used on products and how that date should be presented.

Many consumers are quite thankful for government help in requiring truth-in-labeling, truth-in-packaging, proper processing facilities, and the like. But consumers in general are increasingly dissatisfied with the government's consistent intervention in the food markets in order to keep the price of food high. You the consumer have been hurt by various agricultural programs designed not to help you but to help the farmer.

THE GOVERNMENT'S HELPING HAND IN AGRICULTURE

Farmers have always been considered an underprivileged group because, before government intervention, the price of their products suffered large swings from year to year. That meant that the variability in income for farmers was quite high. Some years it was feast; other years it was famine. To help out the farmer, the government entered into numerous arrangements of which you probably are not aware.

THE DEPRESSION AND THE AAA

During "the First Hundred Days" of the Franklin D. Roosevelt administration, when the nation was suffering the greatest depression in its history, a variety of legislative acts were passed to bring the economy back to its feet again. Whether or not these acts were effective in that respect is not our concern here. Our concern is the Agricultural Adjustment Act of 1933 (and its later version of 1938), which was the legal foundation of the AAA, the Agricultural Adjustment Administration. As well as establishing a system of conservation of agricultural lands, acreage restrictions, and so on, the act established **support prices** for a number of agricultural products.

What is a support price? Well, it is just what the term suggests. When the government supports the price of a product—say, wheat—at a certain fixed amount per bushel, any farmer who cannot sell wheat on the open market at the stated support price can always sell it to the government. That means, in effect, that the price will not go below the fixed supported price. For many years, the support price was below the market price, so the government was not called upon to buy many agricultural products. However, after World War II, the situation changed.

The government found itself with larger and larger "surpluses" of agricultural products, because the unrestricted price was lower than the support price, and farmers were therefore selling much of their wheat and corn and other produce to the government.[1] To cut back on these surpluses, the government instituted more and more acreage restrictions. That is, farmers who wanted to take part in the price support efforts of the government had to agree not to cultivate a certain amount of their lands. But farmers are not stupid; they put into fallow (disuse) their worst lands and added more fertilizer, seed, and hands to the lands that they could cultivate. As a result, over a seven-year period total acreage cultivated fell by 30 percent but total output increased by 17 percent!

THE RESULTS

What did these programs mean to consumers over all of these years? Obviously, one thing and one thing only—higher food prices. Had the government not attempted to keep the price of agricultural products high so as to help farmers, we would have been paying lower food prices all along, at least during the period from about 1948 to 1972. In 1973, the government scrapped some major aspects of its agricultural program. All of the acreage restrictions were to be lifted for 1974 and **target prices** were substituted for support prices. But because the world price of agricultural products was quite high in 1973, target prices were set at a relatively high level in comparison with past supported prices or past unrestricted market prices. Therefore, while in the future we may not be subjected to the higher food prices that once came from government supports, we *will* be subsidizing farmers whenever the market price falls below the target price.

During quite a few years in the 1960s and 1970s, we food consumers paid a total cost of $5 billion a year in higher food prices because of government programs. In addition to that, we made $5 billion a year in direct payments to farmers to bring their incomes up.[2] Many of us would probably not be so upset about that transfer to farmers if it were indeed the poor farmers who were getting the money. But that was not the case. In 1973, for example, 45 percent of all payments to farmers went to the top 7 percent of the income-earning farmers. That does not sound like a redistribution of income to the poor.

AND MILK, TOO

The Agricultural Adjustment Act of 1933 and of 1938 (the first one was declared unconstitutional by the Supreme Court) established another government program that makes the milk you drink higher priced than it would be otherwise. It is perhaps instructive to see why the government had to step into the picture.

---

[1]The transaction was not called a sale. The farmers got a **nonrecourse loan** from the Commodity Credit Corporation. But the effect is the same as a sale; in a nonrecourse loan, although he may one day choose to buy back the produce on which the loan was issued, the farmer does not have to do so.

[2]Charles L. Schultze, *The Distribution of Farm Subsidies: Who Gets the Benefits* (Washington, D.C.: The Brookings Institution, 1971).

Earlier in the century, before government participation in the market for agricultural products, farmers, through their cooperatives, attempted to bargain with dealers for a two-price system in which milk that was to be resold for fresh milk would fetch a higher price for the farmer than milk that would be resold for manufacturing cheese, butter, yogurt, and cottage cheese. However, in the absence of monopoly power, it is extremely difficult if not impossible to maintain price differentials that do not reflect production cost differences. Milk dealers who are going to resell what they buy as fresh milk could inevitably find milk producers who would sell their milk at about the same price as the cost to those manufacturing milk products. There was occasional violence and there were milk strikes in order to maintain the two-price system that farmers wanted for their own benefit. But in the absence of any government support, such two-price systems are unstable and lead to instability in milk prices both for producers and for dairies and bottlers (usually called handlers).

Because farmers could not maintain a monopoly pricing situation, they decried the market for milk as being extremely "unorderly." Milk price instability, caused by the efforts of farmers to maintain discriminatory pricing for their output, was deemed socially undesirable and therefore the competition causing this was to be eliminated. Because such a large number of producers were involved, it was impossible for competition to be eliminated without government support.

Because milk producers therefore increased their efforts to obtain support for their monopoly pricing efforts, the AAA has a provision for federal control over the marketing of fluid milk. The AAA still allows producers of milk sold to the public as fresh milk to force marketing controls upon dairies and handlers. The federal government controls over 60 percent of today's milk markets and the states control the majority of the rest. It is quite obvious to any disinterested bystander, and particularly to you and me as consumers of fresh milk, that federal milk marketing controls have been established for the benefit of milk producers, not for the public.

The effect of federal tinkering in the milk market has been to help out the fluid milk market producers and hurt manufacturing milk market producers. If you happen to like cottage cheese, yogurt, butter, and the other products made from milk, you are perhaps better off, because the supply of those products is larger now than it would have been without federal controls. But if you happen to like fresh milk, you are worse off, because you are paying a higher price than you would have paid in the absence of controls. A few years ago the U.S. Justice Department brought suit against 13 milk associations because they were violating antitrust statutes. They had banded together to keep the price of fresh milk artificially high.

THE PUBLIC INTEREST   In general, the types of government programs designed to help special-interest groups must be looked at with a cautious, skeptical eye. Many advocates of regulation and government programs realize that in the past producer or business interests have been served much more than consumer interest or public interest. However, that does not necessarily mean that such government regulation and programs should be scrapped. Rather, according to some, all interests should be involved in making many of the decisions that are now made by government regulators. That is, producer interests, labor interests, and consumer interests would be represented on the boards of many of these regulatory agencies. Then perhaps the public interest, which may be a compromise of producer, labor, and consumer interest, would be best served. This interesting idea is receiving growing support in Congress.

TRENDS IN FOOD RETAILING

If you wanted to buy something to eat for dinner in a small village in Africa or India or some other less-developed country, you would not drive down to your local supermarket and pick out meat in clean plastic-wrapped packages and vegetables in cans or freezer packages. Rather, you would go to small stalls in an open air market and buy what you wanted from a local merchant, who might even be the person who had raised the steers or the corn, peas, or carrots. In fact, that is how much food shopping used to be done even in the United States; and we still see some remnants of it like roadside fruit stands on well-traveled highways in agricultural areas. But in general, as consumers of food products, you and I do not go to open air markets; we go to a supermarket or, at the very least, to a small mom-and-pop store on the corner. Today, as we mentioned in the opening paragraph of this chapter, there are 300,000 retail markets in the United States. In some areas, the trend is toward closed circuit TV shopping.

BUYING FOOD BY TV

In Stockholm, Sweden, the Home Shop is one to which you never have to go to buy your food. You merely dial in whatever you want to buy from the store's bi-weekly catalog. Ordering is done quickly, and your order is filled by a conveyor belt system and delivered to your door. Stockholm food customers give this store almost 3½ percent of the city's total food business.

Certain self-contained living units around our country also have closed circuit TV food shopping. In some apartments, there is a closed circuit TV. You dial the grocer in your building. If he or she is not busy, your call is accepted and through your TV you get to watch your choices being picked for you. You specify what size piece of meat you want to buy, what size head of lettuce, and so on. We have come a long way from the one-to-one food buying experienced by our ancestors in open air markets.

Some of us may get a tinge of nostalgia when we think about how exciting and pleasurable buying food in those big markets must have been. In fact, some of us can do it in the few open air markets that still exist in the United States. Remember, though, the reason we now have impersonal supermarkets and may someday have closed circuit TV or telephone food shopping is that many of us do not like to spend, or cannot afford to spend, much time getting food to eat. Americans appear unwilling to pay the time price, and so we see trends toward faster and faster retailing methods that save us more and more time. Many observers feel that our entire life style emphasizes speed, "efficiency," and machine effort; and our social values, perhaps reinforced by marketing techniques, push us to these choices.

Basically, then, the so-called work ethic has come to mean work for money income only, and time spent on other activities is considered wasted. Hence, it is not surprising that we see such a big trend not only toward faster shopping techniques, but also toward the use of more and more convenience foods.

THE GROWING
TREND TOWARD
CONVENIENCE FOOD

The food industry is now providing us with buttered peas, frozen corn on the cob, stuffed baked potatoes, cheese in a spray can, complete frozen dinners, frozen tacos—you name it and you can buy it already prepared. Just pop it into the oven and wait.

Why Convenience Foods.   Why are Americans buying so many convenience foods? The answer is quite easy: because our high incomes lead us to place a high value on our time. Americans are no lazier than other people. We are merely willing to pay more than others in both money and lower food quality to save time. We prefer to use our time otherwise.

One of the reasons people like to buy convenience food is that it equals built-in maid service. You need none of the pots and pans and cutting utensils of old for something that is already prepared and frozen, buttered and made ready to eat after only heating. This eliminates a good part of kitchen chores. Certain convenience foods give you less nutrient value than if you spent the time making the dish yourself. Again, that is just part of the price you pay for convenience, and you should be aware of it. People who are more concerned about nutritional value and dislike consuming large quantities of food additives shy away from convenience food, but they pay a price for that: the people who always cook meals from scratch spend more time in the kitchen than the people who always cook TV dinners or canned dinners.

We can make no ultimate judgment about whether convenience foods are good or bad for the American consumer. As long as you know exactly what you are getting, then you can make the choice. We will point out in the following consumer issue on food buying that, looked at realistically, the cost of convenience is sometimes astronomical. If you decide that the cost is sometimes too high, you will choose foods that are not so convenient.

Not All Convenience Foods Are the Same.   But perhaps it is incorrect to lump all convenience foods together. While some increase sugar in the diet, such as Tang in place of frozen orange juice, and others provide nonfood, such as frozen cream pies, others provide real convenience, such as frozen fresh-cut string beans. The latter gives you a reasonably fresh vegetable out of season with the time-consuming preparation job (that is, cutting and cleaning) already done.

The trend toward packaged foods is definitely on the upswing; restaurants, even some of the best ones, now have prefrozen convenience foods on their menus without your knowledge. It might surprise you to find that some parts of a $35 meal in an expensive French restaurant are actually frozen foods. Well, you should not be surprised, because the cost of food-preparing labor in restaurants has risen so much that to stay in business, even the best restaurants have to cut corners. And one way of cutting corners is to buy convenience foods.

The cost of convenience is often an important factor in consumer decision making. A year-long study of 162 convenience foods was recently completed by the Economic Research Service and the Agricultural Research Service (USDA). Of the 162 convenience foods studied, only 36 percent had a cost per serving

Figure 10-3   Universal Product Code (UPC)

This rectangular array of numbers and bars is appearing on more and more food packages. Called the UPC, it will be used in the automated checkout systems that supermarkets will be installing. In this example, the 24000 numerals specify a Del Monte product; the 01391 indicates that it is a can of green beans, and the zero indicates that it is a grocery product. There is a character on the extreme right side of the numbers that cannot be identified with the human eye; this character provides a signal if the code marking has been tampered with. The laser cannot read the numbers; it reads vertical bars. Two dark and two light bars of varying width have been assigned to each number.

lower than their home-prepared or fresh counterpart. However, consumers of these convenience foods paid a lower time "cost" in preparing them for eating.[3]

UNIVERSAL PRODUCT CODING (UPC)

The Universal Product Coding label as shown in Figure 10-3 provides a system of registering purchases by means of an optical scanning device—a laser. The laser beam scans the symbol and sends information to a computer, which looks up the price.

What will happen at the checkout counter in the supermarket then? The checkout clerk will pass each item over a small window with a laser beam beneath it. The computer is sent a signal, looks up the price, and sends it to the cash register. In addition to displaying the price, the cash register will be able to print a receipt listing the price of each item by its name.

This system may speed up the checkout process (if the same number of checkouts is maintained) and perhaps reduce the chance of human error at the checkout point and at the price labeling point.

Needless to say, there are many good points. But are there any bad points? Consider what would happen if the computer, hooked up to each cash register in the supermarket, were to malfunction in the midst of a peak shopping hour! Another point is the controversy about whether or not prices will appear on individual items or appear simply on the shelf with the unit price. This makes comparison shopping very difficult indeed. For instance, if you have bought a can of corn in one

[3]Larry G. Traub and Dianne Odland, "Convenience Foods—1975 Cost Update," *Family Economics Review*, Winter 1976.

aisle, you will probably have forgotten its price by the time you reach the frozen foods section; you cannot make a comparison of prices, therefore, unless you return to find the price of the can of corn.

DISCOUNT STORES

The nation's discount stores are growing at a rate of at least 15 percent a year. In 1977 they accounted for 20.8 percent of the nation's nonfood retail stores. In 1960 there was one discount store for every 39,600 households; by 1980 it is estimated that there will be one store for every 8,000 households. Numerous discount stores are now selling food at prices that are sometimes distinctly lower than their non-discount counterparts. Back in the 1960s, the National Commission on Food Marketing saw that food discounting in general merchandise discount houses had increased from practically nothing to over 10 percent of all food business by the end of the 1960s. Also, increasing numbers of supermarkets are becoming discounters.

How does a discount store operate? It cuts its costs in servicing you, the food consumer, and hence is able to cut its prices to induce more of you to buy from the discount store instead of from a regular market or department store. How does it cut costs? It reduces the variety and number of brands it sells, and in some cases entirely eliminates nationally advertised brands in favor of local, usually cheaper, versions. Thus, the store has lower inventory costs, lower ordering costs, and lower stocking costs. These costs can be significant and may account for a large part of the price reduction in discount establishments. A discount store can also cut costs by having less checkout help, no one to take your groceries to your car, and so on. You pay for discount prices by getting less service.

Fortunately, there is a wide range of choice for the food consumer. Those of you who want to pay high prices and have many services can go to high-priced food stores, and those of you who do not want to pay the price can go to discount stores. How much choice you actually have is, of course, dependent on the size of the city you shop in—the larger the city, the larger the choice.

The following consumer issue should enable you to stretch your food dollars further and to get the best deal for your monthly food budget.

SUMMARY

1. The percentage of total United States income spent on food has been declining steadily since the beginning of this nation. This is characteristic of goods that are necessities as opposed to luxuries. As income rises, the percentage spent on necessities falls.
2. A German statistician named Ernst Engel made this statistical discovery back in 1856, and it is now called Engel's Law.
3. The Fair Packaging and Labeling Act became effective in 1967; it requires that the labels of most consumer products give the net quantity per serving; identify the commodity; and make clear who manufactured, distributed, or packed it and where. The Act authorizes the Secretary of Commerce to limit undue proliferation of product package sizes.
4. There are a number of so-called marginal buyers who shop carefully for many food items. They have an important effect on the price and quality of what we buy. The most obvious marginal buyers are institutions that must feed a large number of individuals.

5. The U.S. Department of Agriculture provides grades for meats, fresh produce, poultry, and other items. However, these grades can be confusing. Produce grading is even more confusing. The top grade of grapefruit is U.S. Fancy, but the top grade of pears is U.S. No. 1. In order to understand which are the top grades, you must learn Table 10-2.

6. Nutrition can be thought of in terms of the basic four—meat, dairy products, vegetables and fruits, and grain products. Daily recommended servings are given in Table 10-3.

7. Open dating of food products can be helpful not only in determining whether the product is out of date, but also in determining which product should be used first.

8. Since the Great Depression, an agricultural program has been in effect in the United States. For many years, the government set minimum prices for various products such as wheat and corn, guaranteeing that consumers would end up paying higher prices for food products in order to benefit the incomes of farmers. The current agricultural program now has three sets of prices: the market price is what is paid for, say, wheat and corn on the market. The target price is the price that the government thinks the farmers should receive; if they receive less, the government makes up the difference. The support price is the minimum price that farmers can receive on the open market for their goods.

9. In most instances, milk prices are "stabilized" by government regulation or government-supported private regulation.

10. There is a growing trend toward frozen convenience foods because as Americans become richer, they are willing to pay more to save time. That is, their higher incomes lead Americans to place a higher value on their time, and they therefore prefer the built-in maid service of a convenience food even though it costs them considerably more than putting the food together themselves.

QUESTIONS FOR THOUGHT AND DISCUSSION

1. Why would you expect the citizens of less-developed countries to spend a larger percentage of their income on food than the citizens of the United States?

2. Is it useful to look at the price index of food to figure out whether food is a "good" or "bad" deal? (Hint: How many hours does it take today to obtain enough income to buy a week's food compared to the number of hours it took 50 years ago?)

3. Is there a limit to the reduction in the percentage of disposable personal income going for food? Could it ever reach zero?

4. When you go to the supermarket to buy meat, do you look for a particular grade of meat? Does USDA grade labeling help you make wiser consumer choices?

5. Is it possible to get two identically graded cuts of meat from two different markets and have one be much better than the other?

6. Food manufacturers are adamant in their distaste for fair packaging laws. Why should they care?

7. Do you think it would ever be possible to get food manufacturers to reverse the proliferation of product package sizes voluntarily?

8. Do you think that the net weight of canned items should exclude any liquids?

9. Why do you think food grading came into being?

10. Do you engage in food planning to make sure that you get the proper amounts of different types of nutrients? Why or why not? If you do so, how much time does it involve?

11. Open dating for film has been around for many, many years, yet it has only recently been used in food packaging. Why do you think it has taken so long to be used for food?

12. What are the pros and cons of government agricultural price support programs? Is there any way that these programs could reduce the price to consumers of critical food products?

13. Do you prefer to have a constant price for milk throughout the year or a fluctuating price whose average is lower than the constant price?

14. Are there government controls that can benefit both producers and consumers simultaneously? Or is it merely a trade-off?

15. How much of your diet consists of convenience foods? Is that good or bad?

THINGS TO DO

1. Add up how much food you eat every week. Now add that up for the entire year. Do you eat more or less than the average for the nation?

2. Look at the latest issue of the *Monthly Labor Review* or the *Federal Reserve Bulletin*. See what the index of food prices has done in the last few years. Is there a continued upward trend?

3. At your local meat market, try to determine the differences among the various grades of meat. Ask the butcher if there is a distinct difference between the top two grades of meat, and if the top grade is worth the extra money.

4. Go to the produce section of your local market. Try to figure out the U.S. Department of Agriculture labeling on the various types of apples, grapefruit, onions, oranges, and pears. Can you tell the difference between U.S. No. 1, U.S.Fancy, and U.S. Extra No. 1? Ask the grocer what he or she thinks the differences are between the various grades.

5. Write down what you have eaten in the last seven days. How closely did you stick to the recommended minimum servings of the basic four on an average daily basis?

6. The next time you go grocery shopping, find out which products use open dating. If some of the cans you purchase have numbers on them, ask the grocer what those code numbers mean. Often they refer to canning dates and other dates that might be important in your purchase decision (although they might merely identify the packing plant).

7. Call up your local dairy. Find out the difference between the price of fluid milk —that is, milk that will be resold only as a fluid—and the price of manufacturing milk—that is, milk that will be used for ice cream, butter, yogurt, cottage cheese, etc. Ask the dairyperson to explain why there is such a big difference.

8. Look at some of the convenience foods you buy. Try to estimate the price you are paying for convenience. Then try to figure out whether that price is rel-

atively high or low in terms of the time you save by buying and eating the convenience food.

SELECTED READINGS

"Bitter Reaction to an FDA Ban; Saccharin." *Time*, March 21, 1977, pp. 60-61.

Boyd, Jacque. "Food Labeling and the Marketing of Nutrition." *Journal of Home Economics*, May 1973.

Cascioli, D. M. "Checking Out the UPC." *What's New in Home Economics?*, March 1974.

"Coming Soon: Computerized Checkout Counters." *Changing Times*, February 1975.

"Drastic Changes in Diet Urged by Senate Committee Report." *Consumer Newsweekly* 6 (January 17, 1977).

Fleck, Henrietta. *Introduction to Nutrition.* New York: The Macmillan Company, 1971.

"Food Prices: What the Winter Wrought." *Forbes*, April 1977, p. 14.

"Food—The Global Crisis that Won't Go Away." *Changing Times*, November 1975, pp. 33–36.

"Fresh Foods." *Better Homes and Gardens*, April 1975.

"How to Use USDA Grades in Food Buying." *Home and Garden Bulletin*, no. 196, Washington, D.C.: U.S. Department of Agriculture, Government Printing Office.

Key Nutrients, 2d ed. Washington, D.C.: Government Printing Office, 1971.

Martin, Ethel Austin. *Nutrition in Action.* New York: Holt, Rinehart and Winston, 1971.

"Much Higher Food Prices Coming?" *U.S. News*, February 14, 1977, p. 20.

Myerson, B. "Food We Eat: Enough Is Not Enough." *Redbook*, April 1977, p. 96.

"Peachy Idea Is Finally Ripening; Weight Labels on Canned Food." *Consumer Reports*, February 1977, p. 65.

Starr, J. "The Psychology and Physiology of Eating." *Today's Health*, February 1973.

Western, Joe. "How the Public Got Milked." *The National Observer*, April 2, 1977.

How to Get the Most for Your Food Dollar

GLOSSARY OF TERMS

Unit Pricing
Pricing of food products expressed in a well-known unit such as ounces or pounds.

Complementary Resources
Resources that are used when purchasing or using other resources. For example, the complementary resources used in shopping are your time and often your automobile.

Health Foods
Foods that may include vegetarian, dietetic, and other products not necessarily free of chemical additives.

Natural Foods
Foods that do not contain artificial ingredients, preservatives, or emulsifiers.

Organic Foods
Foods that are grown without the use of chemically formulated fertilizers or pesticides.

The high cost of food may make you want to economize in food shopping. Some general ideas on how to get the best dollar value in relation to some very specific food attributes, the most important being nutrition, are given in this consumer issue. But you will want still more food information, because no one shops for nutritional value alone, no matter on how limited a budget. You can probably satisfy all your nutritional requirements for a mere fraction of your present food spending by living on soybeans and raisins. But you are not likely to take that kind of a nutritional diet to heart. If you want to see why, read on.

Unit Pricing

In several U.S. cities, **unit pricing** of all food items is now required by law. What is unit pricing? Instead of a label on the shelf under the product indicating only the price, there must now be a label also specifying the price per convenient unit of measurement (that is, weight or liquid measure). Whereas before you needed a calculator to determine if 7½ ounces of tuna fish at 65¢ is cheaper than 6½ ounces at 59¢, the store has now calculated this for you and posted the results for you to see. This makes it much easier to determine the "best buy" of any particular item. In effect, for canned goods and other prepackaged foods, you are now being told what you have always been told for meats and produce—that is, that pork chops are $1.89 per pound, but pork blades (which look nearly the same, but are slightly tougher and fattier) are $1.39. Of course, unit pricing does not account for differences in quality or personal preferences. It merely translates into comparable figures the price differences you observe in the market. In so doing, it usually makes it possible for you to capitalize on what "specials" are available. Formerly, when certain brands of canned goods were on special, they still might cost more than the usual price of other brands not being featured. While some price differences reflect differences in quality, other differences might be due to advertising. In some cases, neither may matter to you—you may feel that canned tomatoes are canned tomatoes, and whether one brand is firmer than another does not matter since you are just going to mash them into spaghetti sauce anyway. It is especially when you do not prefer one particular brand over another that unit pricing is valuable. And in all cases, it allows you to see just what you are paying for your favorites.

Shopping for Specials

Many shoppers know that one way to save money on food is to shop for specials, and that the way to find specials is to look in the local newspaper. Some consumers attempting to get the best possible deals will spend time combing through supermarket ads. They will cut out the ads and go to the various supermarkets to get whatever they need that is on special. Although this method is fine for some individuals, the time you spend looking for specials is valuable, both the time spent looking in the ads and that spent shopping. Also valuable is the money you spend shopping for specials, the money spent as wear and tear on your car and on the gasoline that you have to consume when you go to several stores instead of one.

Unfortunately, there can be no hard and fast rules about how long you should spend looking through newspaper ads and to how many stores you should go. Against the potential savings from buying specials at various supermarkets, you must compare the anticipated costs of driving your car to those supermarkets, plus the value you place on the time that would be involved. Hence, you know it would not be worthwhile to drive five miles to a more distant supermarket merely for its special on mustard and black peppercorns. However, if that same market had a special on meat that you could purchase for the rest of the week's meals, then it might be worth your while to go to it.

Substituting One Thing for Another

From our discussion about shopping for specials, you should realize that you can substitute various resources to do a particular task. If you decide that you want to spend fewer dollars for food, you can spend more time looking for specials. In other words, you substitute your time for the food dollars that you would have spent had you not looked for specials. When you take a car to shop at several different markets, you use a **complementary resource** in your attempt to reduce your food budget. Whenever you use a complementary resource, you have to realize that you incur a cost, even if you did not pay for it directly or immediately.

Once you understand substitution and complementarity in resource use, then you are well on your way to being a rational, and indeed thrifty, shopper. Some consumers become fanatical about buying food on specials only. They have lost track of means and ends. The original end in mind, of course, is getting the most value for your food dollar, taking into account all of the combined resource costs that go into food shopping. While fanaticism for specials can lead to an uneconomical overuse of time, only you can decide whether that has happened to you, because only you know the value you place on your own time.

The optional use of time leads us to a discussion of when it is rational for you to purchase convenience foods that you know will cost more at the supermarket.

TO BUY OR NOT TO BUY THAT TV DINNER

Convenience foods are just that —foods made for your convenience to save you time and energy. Whether or not you like their taste is, of course, up to you, but you should be aware of the cost of convenience. For example, perhaps you have seen breaded veal steaks on the shelves these days. A close look shows that there is an average of about 30 percent breading, and 20 percent beef (which may be more nutritious than veal in amount of usable protein, but nonetheless usually costs less) added to the veal, for this is the limit permitted by the U.S. Department of Agriculture's regulations. So, all in all, those breaded veal steaks are only about 50 percent veal. If the price per pound package is, say, $2.50, then you are paying $5.00 per pound for ground veal steaks with some hamburger and bread thrown in. However, if you can find the same ground veal in the market, you will find that it costs $3.00 a pound, ground beef is $1.00 a pound, and readymade bread crumbs are $.40 a pound. That means that homemade veal steaks made just the same way as you buy them in the package would cost you $1.82 per pound.

In addition, for example, you will find that the sugar in pre-sweentened breakfast cereals is costing you $1.50 a pound. You will find also that you pay about twice as much per ounce for peas that are frozen in butter sauce as for peas for which you have to add your own butter during cooking. (And the frozen butter sauce includes not only butter, but water, too.)

What are you paying for convenience? In some cases, you are paying as much as 100 percent or more (as above) for convenience. Is it worth the price? That, of course, depends on how highly you value your time, and on how highly you value the taste differences between what you prepare and what the producer prepares.

American families seem to be placing more value on their time: the percentage of total food budgets spent on frozen convenience foods is rising from about 27 percent in 1955 to 35 percent in 1965 to an estimated 46 percent in 1978.

What's in Convenience Foods?

In deciding about convenience foods, you ought to keep in mind several other considerations. If we have no real reason for staying out of the kitchen, why pay the price of convenience? And further, it sometimes seems that the only way to make any sense out of the labeling and fancy packaging of some convenience foods is by trusting to providence that what you are buying is wholesome. In other words, if you want to figure out just what nutritive value many convenience foods actually have, you must spend at least part of the time that such foods are meant to save.

NUTRITION

According to some nutritionists, many convenience foods do not give a high amount of nutrition for their cost. We buy food for two reasons: the pleasures of eating and nutrition to keep our bodies healthy. The nutritional aspect of food is often ignored by on-the-go, busy consumers who have "better" things to worry about. But after a little time deciphering the nutritional

value of different types of food, the wise food consumer can purchase more nutrients per food dollar. One of the basic nutrients needed to maintain a healthy body is protein, and there are various inexpensive ways of obtaining it.

A major source of quite inexpensive protein is peanut butter. The average protein content in most peanut butter brands is about 25 to 30 percent, and the total protein supplied by two peanut butter sandwiches and an 8 ounce glass of milk would be almost 85 percent of the daily protein allowance recommended for a ten-year-old by the National Academy of Sciences–National Research Council. Peanut butter is also a great source of niacin, phosphorus, and magnesium. At the same time, this above-mentioned meal would provide one-third the daily calorie need of a ten-year-old. Knowing the nutrient values of different foods is important for obtaining a good diet.

AMERICANS ON THE MOVE

Most Americans do not always consume a good proportion of the different types of foods that a good diet requires. In fact, the percentage of Americans who have poor diets—that is, who have less than two-thirds of the allowances indicated by the RDAs—appears to be increasing. According to the U.S. Department of Agriculture surveys, 15 percent of the American population had poor diets in 1955, 21 percent in 1965, and 24 percent is estimated for 1975. (Using a broader definition of

nutrition, a 1974 Agriculture Department study indicated that more than half the people of the United States do not eat nutritionally correct meals.)

The same U.S. Department of Agriculture surveys show that the percentage of poor diets decreases as the income level of the family unit increases, since real incomes are rising in the United States. No one has yet explained this anomaly. It may in part be due to the increasing availability of "empty calories," that is, calories with little or no nutritive content (which are heavily advertised). It is often easiest, particularly if you value your time highly, to eat a huge amount of sugars and starches; they are readily available and are often the easiest things to grab "on the run." But there are other reasons as well why an estimated 24 percent of families had poor diets in 1975. First and foremost, of course, is ignorance of what good nutrition means. But many of us who should, and often do, know better simply do not take time to have a good diet. Either we are in too much of a hurry, are on miracle diets to become slim and attractive, or our lives are simply too disrupted.

To counter this growing trend toward poor diets, the government and representatives of the food industry have cooperated to produce an informative 32-page booklet on nutrition. The booklet, "Food Is More than Just Something to Eat," explains how diet at any age can affect the length and quality of your life. For example, experts say what a young girl eats now is likely to affect the kind of preg-

nancy she could have years later. The booklet tells what foods are the best sources of various nutrients and how to combine them into a helpful diet. (To get a free copy, write Nutrition, Pueblo, Colorado 81009.)

In addition, the commonly held idea that a good diet is economically costly turns out to be a myth. A study done by George Stigler in 1945[1] used a technique called linear programming to figure out what a good diet would actually cost for a year. Can you guess the figure he came up with in that year for a good diet? He came up with the grand total of $59.88. In today's dollars, that would still be less than $325. How did he do it? Well, you have to eat quantities of soybeans and cabbage to remain on Stigler's diet, but you would get all the known nutrients your body requires.

That means, of course, that all

Americans except the very, very poor could have a nutritional diet if they were willing to sacrifice variety in their food intake; but most of us are not willing to make such a sacrifice. And in fact we pay quite a bit for variety. We do not merely eat to live, some of us live to eat (at least a little bit). We enjoy eating and we like it to be an occasion to look forward to. How many of us would look forward to two meals a day of soybeans?

Of course, there are many alternatives between the low-cost, high-nutrient soybean and cabbage subsistence diet and the high-cost, low-nutrient diet of junk foods and empty calories. Nutritionists have insisted for years that a healthy, balanced food intake need not be unpleasant or dull. Why do Americans shun the healthful diets they can afford better than anyone else in the world? The ultimate answers are beyond the scope of this book. They have to do, among other things, with people's values.

Are Fast Food Meals Nutritious?

In a 1975 study made by *Consumer Reports* testing Burger Chef, McDonald's, Burger King, Pizza Hut, Kentucky Fried Chicken, Hardee's, Arby's, and Arthur Treacher's, it was found that there are six nutrients most often in short supply in fast food meals. They are biotin, folacin, pantothenic acid, total vitamin A, iron, and copper.

They concluded that if you include such nutritious foods as beans, dark green leafy vegetables, yellow vegetables, and a variety of fresh fruits in your other meals, you should be able to overcome the nutritional deficiencies incurred by regularly eating fast food meals.[2] For the summarized evaluation of *Consumer Reports*, see Exhibit G-1.

HEALTH, NATURAL, AND ORGANIC FOODS

Most of us are aware that so-called health, natural, and or-

[1] "The Cost of Subsistence," *Journal of Farm Economics*, 1945.

[2] "How Nutritious Are Fast-Food Meals? " *Consumer Reports*, May 1975, pp. 278-281.

EXHIBIT G-1   **Fast-Food Chains, One Bite at a Time**

Here, in summary, is the evaluation of the nutritional quality of each meal measured in the study made by *Consumer Reports.*

Our Burger Chef meal consisted of a "Super Shef" hamburger, french fries, and a chocolate shake. It would load children with half their total daily need for calories and come close to supplying half the calorie needs of an adult, too. The greatest nutritional drawback of the Burger Chef meal was its high carbohydrate content—higher in weight than that of any of the other meals. Most of those carbohydrates were empty calories of sweetness in the shake. (The same criticism can be made of the other shakes we tested; see facing page.) The meal was low in biotin, folacin, and pantothenic acid for adult and child; vitamin A for adult.

We ordered a "Big Mac" hamburger, french fries, and a chocolate shake. The McDonald's meal provided less meat than the other burger meals and less total food. So perhaps the familiar advertising theme, "You deserve a break today at McDonald's," refers to the dietary break of slightly fewer calories than you get at the other hamburger chains. The protein content was more than adequate. The meal was low in biotin, pantothenic acid, and total vitamin A for both age groups.

We bought the "Whopper" hamburger, french fries, and a chocolate shake. That meal contained more meat and less potatoes than the other two burger meals—and more fat, which probably came from the meat. As with the Burger Chef meal, calories came to half of a child's daily needs and nearly half of an adult's. The meal was low in biotin, folacin, pantothenic acid, and copper.

PIZZA HUT

Here we bought a 10-inch "Supreme" pizza —a pie appliquéd with tomato sauce, cheese, ground sausage, mushrooms, pepperoni, onions, and green pepper—and a cola drink. It provided the most protein of any of the meals, far exceeding a whole day's RDA for any age. Yet the total calories weren't unusually high, and the fat content was the lowest of all. This was clearly the best food buy, considering that the pizza alone would provide a single meal's worth of protein for two persons. But it's by no means perfect. Surprisingly, considering its constituents, this meal was the only one that failed to have one-third the RDA for vitamin C for both adult and child. (The high baking heat probably destroyed the vitamin C.) The meal was also low in biotin and pantothenic acid for both age groups, and it contained more sodium than anyone on a sodium-restricted diet should have at one meal (see facing page).

Kentucky Fried Chicken

Colonel Sanders' meal contained three pieces of fried chicken, french fries, a roll, and a chocolate shake. That added up to half the daily calorie need of the adult and to more than half of the child's needs. (But it's probably unlikely that many 7-year-olds could chew their way through all that food.) This meal contained considerably more meat than the hamburger meals and, as a direct consequence, a lot more protein—more than a whole day's RDA for adult and child. An excess of protein does no harm other than the harm done by the excess of calories likely to follow too much of any food component. (Note: we weighed the meat without the bone but with the breading—we just couldn't successfully separate the breading from the chicken. However, we believe the weight of the breading was not so high as to affect the general outlines of our findings.) With all that meat came more fat than in any of the other meals tested: The Colonel's frying process results in a greasy bird in hand; not only do your fingers need lickin', they need washin'. All in all, the Kentucky Fried Chicken meal represents a lot of food for the money, perhaps even a surfeit of food. The meal was low in biotin, folacin, and vitamin A for adult and child.

Hardee's

This meal consisted of a flaked and formed steak, a bun, french fries, and a chocolate shake. Calories, protein, carbohydrates, and fat were fairly comparable to that of the burger meals. And the steak was comparable to a hamburger (a "flaked and formed steak" is just shredded meat tenderized and formed into the shape of a steak). The meal was low in biotin, pantothenic acid, and total vitamin A for both age groups.

Arby's

Arby's serves up sliced beef on a bun, two potato patties, and cole slaw (the roast beef plate). We also bought a chocolate shake. Arby's main contribution to fast-food technology appears to be its mastery of the art of paper-thin slicing. We counted an average of 28 slices of beef per sandwich, each slice *nine-thousandths* of an inch thick. But all those slices weighed only 2.7 ounces. That's an adequate portion of meat, but not a generous one. Thus the meal contained less protein than any of the other meat meals, although enough for one of three daily meals. Arby's meal also contained the second highest measure of carbohydrates, and, again, a lot of that was empty calories from the shake. It also fell short in biotin, folacin, pantothenic acid, total vitamin A, and copper for both age groups.

Arthur Treacher's

This meal contained two pieces of breaded fried fish, french fries, and a cola drink. That added up to the fewest total calories and the least amount of protein. We don't mourn the low calorie count, and there was still enough protein to provide one-third the daily needs of man and child. But this meal contained too little biotin, pantothenic acid, niacin, thiamine, total vitamin A, calcium, magnesium, iron, copper, and zinc for both adult and child.

ganic foods are more expensive than their counterparts in regular supermarkets. Anything grown "organically" seems to cost more. Anything with that special health food look and label seems to be a bit more expensive than its regular counterpart on the grocery shelf. Of course, you must decide wheth-er you want to pay the extra price. Many people are concerned about the chemical natures of their diets and are therefore willing to go to great lengths to have organic foods— even sometimes growing their own without the use of chemical fertilizers and pesticides. You should be aware of the possibil-ity of being defrauded in your health food purchases. At this point, you're probably wondering what the difference is among health, natural, and organic foods. Here are some broad, although widely accepted definitions:

1. **Health foods** may include vegetarian, dietetic, and other products not necessarily free of chemical additives.

2. **Natural foods** do not contain artificial ingredients, preservatives, or emulsifiers.

3. **Organic foods** are grown without the use of chemically formulated fertilizers or pesticides.

There is a question as to the effectiveness of these foods. Most people in medical science indicate that you cannot expect miracles just by eating so-called natural foods and taking large quantities of vitamins. In fact, taking too many vitamins can do you harm. According to the FDA, this is particularly true for vitamins A and D. Most doctors now believe that if you eat a well-balanced diet, you are likely to get all of the vitamins you need to stay healthy. Any supplements are generally superfluous. If they make you feel better psychologically, however, you may still wish to take them.

WAYS THAT YOU CAN BE CHEATED BY FOOD STORES AND WHAT TO DO ABOUT IT

Probably, the bulk of food stores attempt in no way to cheat you. But because some do, you should be aware of the methods that they can use and how you can guard against these unsavory practices. A few of the better-known techniques for robbing you of value for your food dollar are:

1. Adding water to the cereals used in making processed meats, thereby adding the weight of the water. You end up paying meat prices for water.

2. Soaking turkeys, oysters, chickens, and hams in water or juice overnight, thus adding several ounces to their weight.

3. Placing rolled up chicken-neck skins in the breast cavities of the birds. Hence, you pay chicken prices for neck skins.

What you can do. Call your local weights and measures inspectors, who will be listed in your telephone directory yellow pages, and tell them you think you may have been cheated. Save your purchase so that it can be used as evidence. After your accusation has been confirmed by an inspector's purchase in the same store, the offending merchant will be warned or prosecuted if he or she is a repeat violator.

4. Boring holes in counter-poised weights, reducing them by anywhere from 10 to 20 percent. This short-weighting technique has been found in several states.

5. Hooking lead sinkers to the underside of the weighing pan.

6. Attaching one or more one-ounce magnets under the scale pan.

What you can do. The easiest thing to do is to purchase a good household scale and use it to check the weight of all purchases that you suspect have been short-weighted. If you find the items short-weighted, you may try taking them back to the store manager. In this way, the manager is given a chance to correct an honest error, if it is one, or a warning signal that you are a smart shopper who cannot be easily cheated.

7. There are probably an infinite number of other ways in which you can be short-weighted. It is up to you to figure out if in fact this trick is being played on you. If you think this is consistently happening, you have the choice of either shopping at a different store or reporting the dishonest operator to the proper agency, such as the weights and measures inspectors in your area.

ACTUALLY DOING IT

Before we leave this topic, we should consider your actual trip to the supermarket. There are several things to consider.

First of all, what kind of preparation for the trip have you made? Many shoppers prefer planning menus for the week (at least the suppers), often taking into account the meat specials that week. Generally, once the meats are decided upon, the rest of the supper menus follow rather naturally. Usually, such advance meal planning would encompass a week at a time, although some shoppers prefer to do it just once every ten days.

If you have decided not to pay much attention to advertised specials, and therefore not to read the supermarket ads in your newspapers, meal plan-

ning can often take place in the store itself in much the same way. You go first to the meat counter and decide what your meals will center on by looking at the specials (or even just the prices). Some times, especially with relatively high meat prices, you may also wish to check the prices of canned or fresh fish, eggs, or cheese, and feature these or other meat substitutes in your meals.

Other consumers prefer to engage in a kind of "reasoned" impulse buying. In other words, they know roughly what they consume in any given week, and vary only a few items on any given trip to the supermarket.

In any case, whether you do your food planning at home beforehand or in the supermarket, there are a few ways you might be able to save.

1. Try different brands of the same product; they can be similar in quality and nutritional value and yet may vary widely in price.

2. Large quantities are often bargains, but only if they can be kept safely until they can be used up completely.

3. Try not to shop when you are hungry. Research has shown that when you are hungry, you are more likely to indulge in impulse buying.

4. Check all shelves, as lower-priced items are often placed above or below eye level. Also check the value of the items placed in the center aisle or at the front of the store with care as they may be marked as sale items, but in fact are being sold at the regular price.

SUMMARY

1. Unit pricing is required by law in many cities. When you go shopping for food, you should compare unit prices instead of trying to determine whether a 7½ ounce can of tuna fish is cheaper than a 6½ ounce can when the former sells for 72¢ and the latter sells for 64¢.

2. Shopping for specials is one way to save consumer dollars for food. Specials are generally listed in throwaway newspapers or ads in regular newspapers, as well as in the markets where you shop. Be careful though: do not drive 15 miles just to go to a market that has salt on special. The savings you will realize on the salt will be less than the cost in extra gas (unless, of course, you are buying a ton).

3. Generally you should compare the potential gains from shopping for specials with the potential costs, particularly in terms of your time and other complementary resources.

4. You end up paying about twice as much per ounce for peas, string beans, and carrots that are frozen in butter sauce. Ask yourself if this price is too high for the extra convenience.

5. One of the basic nutrients needed to maintain a healthy body is protein, and there are various inexpensive ways of obtaining it such as peanut butter, dried beans and peas, and nuts.

6. Even though American incomes are growing, the percentage of families estimated to have poor diets is rising.

7. One way to avoid being cheated by food retailers is to measure what you buy with your own scales. Once you find a store that does not cheat you, you can continue to shop there with some assurance of honesty on the part of the retailer. In fact, repeat buying will usually yield high returns because the retailer's income is mostly from customers who continually come back.

8. Advanced meal planning can be helpful as a guide to careful shopping in the supermarket.

QUESTIONS FOR THOUGHT AND DISCUSSION

1. Why did it take so long for unit pricing to become more or less common in retail food markets?

2. Is it ever advisable to comb through all supermarket ads? If so, when?

3. Some nutritionists contend that TV dinners lack many basic nutrients. Others contend that they taste awful. Nonetheless, TV dinners sell very well. Why?

4. Do you think the amount of basic nutrients should be clearly labeled on the front of every item sold in a market?

5. Why do you think meat is such an expensive food item?

6. How can you explain the fact that Americans have increasingly poor diets even though they are getting richer as a nation?

7. What is the most important aspect of your diet? Nutrition? Variety? Cost? Convenience?

THINGS TO DO

1. Check the markets in your area to see which ones engage in unit pricing if it is not required by law in your area. If some do not, ask the managers why. Do you think unit pricing adds to the cost of selling food products?

2. Look at all of the local newspapers for one day and compare specials on national brand food items. What is the percentage difference from the normal price and the special price? Can you compute the extra time it would require to obtain the specials? If so, what would have to be the value of your time to make it worthwhile for you to go especially to the one store with the special?

3. What other resources are complementary to food shopping besides your automobile or other form of transportation? List them and estimate their yearly cost just for food shopping.

4. Sit down and write a list of all of the foods you eat that could be labeled as convenience foods.

5. Query your local restaurateur's food buying habits. Ask him or her how many of the items sold on the menu are prefrozen. When you go into a seafood restaurant, ask which items are fresh, fresh frozen, or just frozen. Try to get an honest answer. Can you tell the difference between fresh and fresh frozen seafood?

6. As an experiment, find out how much you spend on food without any advanced planning, and then compare it with what you will spend on food if you carefully plan your meals ahead of time for a week period. Is the difference worth the effort? (Usually it is.)

7. As a class, make a list of commonly used foods. Specify brands and amounts. Each class member should price items in three different markets and make a comparison in class.

SELECTED READINGS

Anderson, W. Thomas, Jr. *The Convenience-Oriented Consumer.* Austin: University of Texas, Graduate School of Business, Bureau of Business Research, 1971.

"Buy the Product, Not the Package." *Changing Times*, April 1977, pp. 21–23.

"Combating Nutrition Misinformation." *Forecast*, May–June 1972.

"Competitiom and the Price of Food." *Consumer Reports*, May 1974, pp. 412–414.

Cross, Jennifer. *The Supermarket Trap.* Bloomington: Indiana University Press, 1970.

Kramer, Mary, and Spader, Margaret. *Contemporary Meal Management.* New York: John Wiley & Sons, 1972.

Erhard, D. "Nutritive Education for the Now Generation." *Journal of Nutritive Education*, Spring 1971.

"Food and Nutrition." *Consumers' Research Magazine*, October 1974, pp. 60–67.

"Food and Nutrition." *Consumers' Research Magazine*, October 1976, pp. 54–62.

"Fresh Foods." *Better Homes and Gardens*, April 1974.

Holden, G. "Food and Nutrition: Is America Due for a National Policy?" *Science*, May 3, 1974, pp. 548–550.

"How to Use USDA Grades in Buying." *Home and Garden Bulletin*, No. 196, Washington, D.C.: U.S. Department of Agriculture, Government Printing Office.

"Labels that Tell You Something." *Journal of Home Economics*, April 1972.

Lauda, Frani. "Playing the Supermarket." *Sphere*, April–May 1972.

"Name Brands vs. House Brands." *Changing Times*, August 1973.

"New Beef Grades: What Do They Mean?" *Better Homes and Gardens*, April 1977, p. 101.

"Size-Up of Today's Shoppers." *U.S. News*, November 22, 1976, p. 53.

Taylor, E. T. "Unit Pricing and Open Dating." *Family Economics Review* June 1972.

Trager, James. *The Food Book.* New York: Grossman Publishers, 1972.

Your Money's Worth in Foods, G-183. Washington, D.C.: U.S. Department of Agriculture, Government Printing Office.

APPENDIX: All You Need to Know about Metric (for Your Everyday Life)

Today over 90 percent of the world's population is committed to the metric weight and measurement system. The United States is the only major industrialized country that has not yet converted to the metric system.

ARGUMENTS AGAINST CONVERSION

Who will pay for the conversion? Will the costs lie where they fall or will there be federal assistance to individuals and companies? No one is sure about this point and it has become one of the stronger arguments against conversion.

People will also have to be retrained if we change to the metric system. This will be both costly and time consuming. This not only leads to a temporary loss of productivity, but increases the element of human error because of the unfamiliar units of measurement.

ARGUMENTS FOR CONVERSION

One of the more important arguments for conversion is to eliminate our competitive disadvantage when dealing with other countries using the metric system. We must trade or sell either using our present system of measurement or their current metric system. Many American companies have been forced to have both systems in use, necessitating the production of a double inventory. This is costly indeed and would no longer be necessary if the United States converted to the metric system.

The metric system has a decimal base and logical relationships between the basic units as can be seen below. It is easier to learn and easier to use than our present system.

The experiences of other countries who have gone metric, for example, Great Britain, indicate that conversion was easier and less expensive than anticipated.

METRIC IS BASED ON DECIMAL SYSTEM

The metric system is simple to learn. For use in your everyday life you will need to know only ten units. You will also need to get used to a few new temperatures. Of course, there are other units that most persons will not need to learn. There are even some metric units with which you are already familiar: those for time and electricity are the same as you use now.

There are separate units of metric measurement for each physical quality, such as weight, volume, length, and temperature. Gram, liter, meter, and Celsius (this term is used today in place of centigrade) are the basic units, with standard prefixes used for decimal fractions and multiples of the basic units. Though this is true for the basic units of gram, liter, and meter, standard prefixes are not commonly used for temperature.

BASIC UNITS

Meter: a little longer than a yard (about 1.1 yards).

Liter: a little larger than a quart (about 1.06 quarts).
Gram: about the weight of a paper clip.

COMMON PREFIXES (TO BE USED WITH BASIC UNITS)

Milli: one-thousandth (0.001).
Centi: one-hundredth (0.01).
Kilo: one-thousand times (1,000).

For example:
1,000 milimeters = 1 meter
100 centimeters = 1 meter
1,000 meters = 1 kilometer

Let's work through an example using both our current system of measurement and the metric system of measurement.

Current System

You recently bought some property 1,500 yards long and 1,200 yards wide. How many square miles of property do you own?

```
    1,500 yards
  ×  1,200 yards
    300,000
    1,500
    1,800,000 square yards in
property
```

In order to find the number of square yards in a square mile, it is necessary to multiply 1,760 times 1,760 because 1,760 yards = 1 mile.

```
    1,760
  ×  1,760
    105,600
    12,320
    1,760
    3,097,600 square yards in mile
```

Divide the number of square yards in a mile into the number of square yards you bought.

```
            .58
  30,976 ⟌ 18,000.00
           15,488.0
            2,512.00
            2,478.08
              33.92
```

You own 0.58 square miles of property.

Metric System

You recently bought some property 1,400 meters long and 1,100 meters wide. How many square kilometers of property do you own?

```
    1.4 kilometers
  ×  1.1 kilometers
    1.4
    1.4
    1.54 square kilometers
```

You own 1.54 square kilometers of property.

You can see from this example that the use of the metric system is by far easier than our current system. Not just easier, but it will cut down on the time needed to complete calculations.

There is no doubt that the metric system is coming; the question is when.

OTHER COMMONLY USED UNITS

Millimeter: 0.001 meter = diameter of paper clip wire.
Centimeter: 0.01 meter = width of a paper clip (about 0.4 inch).
Kilometer: 1,000 meters = somewhat further than ½ mile (about 0.6 mile).

Kilogram: 1,000 grams = a little more than 2 pounds (about 2.2 pounds).
Milliliter: 0.001 liter = five of them make a teaspoonful.

Other Useful Hints

Hectare: about 2½ acres.
Tonne: about one ton.

For more information, you can write to the Metric Information Office, National Bureau of Standards, Washington, D.C. 20234. Also, you can send away for a metric converter to Metric Converter, P.O. Box 4994, Des Moines, Iowa 50306 ($1 plus a large, self-addressed, stamped envelope). This is a slide converter that will change any of our present units of measurement into metric units.

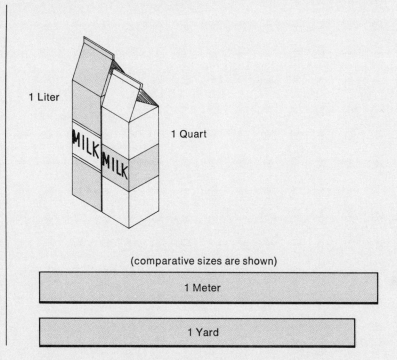

(comparative sizes are shown)

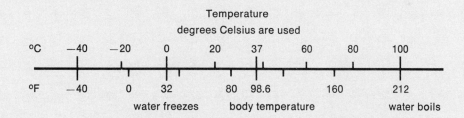

Temperature
degrees Celsius are used

°C	−40	−20	0	20	37	60	80	100
°F	−40	0	32	80	98.6	160		212

water freezes   body temperature   water boils

GLOSSARY OF TERMS

Free Good

A good that has a supply greater than what people demand at a zero price; for example, air to burn in an auto engine.

Cease and Desist Orders

Legal orders from a federal agency or a judge requiring that a certain activity stop immediately. For example, the Federal Trade Commission can issue a cease and desist order against a fur manufacturer's deceptive labeling practice.

Generic Name

The general or nontrademark name of a product. For example, the trade names of a particular type of fiber may be Antron, Cantrece, Qiana; but the generic name of that fiber is nylon.

More than Just Keeping Warm

CHAPTER PREVIEW

☐ What are the characteristics of the clothing industry?

☐ What determines the types of clothes we buy?

☐ How do clothes fit into family budget formation?

☐How does durability affect the price of clothing?

☐ How has the Flammable Fabrics Act affected the production and sale of clothes?

☐ What are the federal statutes relating to the labeling of clothing products?

11 It is estimated that American families spent $80 billion on clothing in 1977. Together, all of us purchased $80 billion worth of shoes, pants, hats, jockey shorts, brassieres, panties, hose, suits, ties, shirts, skirts, and socks. Clothing expenditures account for between 6 and 11 percent of the typical American's total budget.[1] Clothing is a major industry, now employing over a million workers in any one year. The fashion business, of course, occupies large amounts of advertising and media space, and probably for many people a significant amount of mental space.

There are approximately 7,000 wholesale clothing outlets, more than 90,000 retail clothing outlets, and 25,000 or more manufacturers. It is hard to tell how many manufacturers of clothing there are because so many small ones go into and out of business in any one year (or month, for that matter). In addition to all these market outlets for clothing, countless men and women make at least some of their own or their family's clothes, accounting for approximately $3 billion of sales in fabrics, yarns, notions, and other sewing needs.

Recent years have seen the upsurge of discount clothing stores; these stores usually have fewer salespersons and charge for services such as alterations and hemming that are "free" in nondiscount stores. In general, discount stores that offer true bargains have a smaller variety of sizes, styles, colors, qualities, and perhaps brand names. This is how they reduce their costs so that they can in fact sell you clothes at a lower price than nondiscount stores.

Shopping for clothing can be time consuming. By one estimate, the typical homemaker spends 100 hours a year shopping for clothes for the family. We are indeed a clothes conscious society; that cannot be denied.

WHY SO MANY CLOTHES?

Everybody must be aware that the typical American has more clothes than actually needed in order to provide physical protection from the cold, sun, wind, and rain. Obviously, then, most clothing is no longer within the realm of a so-called necessity. Rather, it is a consumer good that gives pleasure and serves more than the basic necessities. In the last consumer issue, you were shown that a food budget of only $325 a year, if wisely spent, would allow you to have all the nutritional and caloric values you needed to stay healthy. Unfortunately, that food budget required you to eat soybeans for every other meal, or almost.

The same analysis can be made with respect to clothing. You could purchase very durable, sturdy, and even fairly attractive clothing that would last you far longer than you may want to keep it. In this manner, you could reduce your clothing budget considerably. You could also buy secondhand clothes from Goodwill Industries and other secondhand establishments. These clothes would protect you from the elements, but they would not serve another purpose—variety. Variety, as has often been said, is the spice of life. Variety in clothing is no different.

CUSTOMS

The types of clothes we buy are often determined by customs in the community, although in the United States this is less true than it was. It is certainly only by custom that men wear trousers and women wear skirts. After all, in Scotland men

[1]*The 1973 Yearbook of Agriculture* (Washington, D.C.: Government Printing Office), p. 8.

wear skirts also; and in the United States, more and more women are wearing pants or pants suits whenever and wherever they wish without being exposed to ridicule or discrimination. Why do men wear ties and collars while women usually do not? Again, the only explanation is custom. These customs change slowly. It took many years before fancy restaurants admitted tieless men in turtleneck sweaters.

Have you ever asked yourself why men's clothing has buttons on the opposite side from women's clothing? Custom must be the answer. But customs are not created in a vacuum; most are created to appease or satisfy a large segment of the population. Once customs are well established, they are hard to break, simply because the majority of the society accepts them or even enjoys them. Only when a significant and aggressive minority find the customs disturbing, are they changed. Later in this chapter, we will talk about the changing attitudes toward dress in the United States.

MENTAL ATTITUDE

Clothing that pleases us as wearers, and that we think pleases those who see us, often contributes greatly to our attitude toward our fellow humans. One of the strongest motivations of dress is preservation of the self-concept or self-image of the wearer through the enhancement of the body. This is an aesthetic consideration, that is, one having to do solely with beauty. Even among primitive tribes, self-adornment is a stronger motivation than protection from the elements, or thrift, or durability. And this motivation in clothing selection has nothing to do with snobbery. It merely indicates a positive self-concept, which is healthy and beneficial.

WHERE WE BUY OUR CLOTHES

Some of you may balk at such a value system because it places high importance on a material good. Nonetheless, it cannot be denied that many, many people feel better when they are dressed in a manner they think is attractive. In addition, many people feel better when they think they are dressing in a manner that identifies them to the rest of society as belonging to a particular socioeconomic class. This is an important problem in self-awareness and self-identification well known to psychologists.

CLOTHES, FAMILY HAPPINESS, AND BUDGET FORMATION

How a family dresses can sometimes be important for adding to family satisfaction. Again, some of you may find this idea reprehensible because it puts too much weight on a material aspect of life instead of a spiritual aspect. But just as variety in diet contributes to more than physical well-being, so, too, can clothing be one of the material aspects of life that contribute to self-image and self-esteem. The fact remains, for example, that parents who approve of how their children dress are often more satisfied and proud to be the heads of the family. Similarly, children as well as their parents may take great pleasure in being part of the family unit that "dresses up" to go to church on Sunday or to visit friends. But each member of the family has his or her own idea about what fashions are appropriate for himself or herself and for the others in the family. This may cause conflicts within the family or spending unit for two reasons: (1) the family's budget will, by necessity, curtail some of the clothing spending desired by each member; and (2) members of the family who have clothing habits significantly different from those of other members may feel pressure to conform.

INDIVIDUALITY AND CONFORMITY

To avoid the problem of family conflicts about individual dressing styles, it is important that each member's individuality or "living space" not be violated. This is something that can be discussed during family councils or between individual members of the spending unit. Because clothing habits reflect each person's values and aesthetics, no set rules about dressing can be made absolute for any person at any time. If one member of the spending unit wishes to rebel and buy clothes that are indeed different from everyone else's, this attempt at individuality must not only be understood but also accepted (at least in part). As with everything else, compromises will have to be made about dressing habits within a spending unit, as well as about the size of each member's clothing expenditures.

THE BUDGET AGAIN

Clothing enters into the budget-making decisions of every spending unit. Such decisions cannot be avoided because clothes are so important. One way to decrease the friction within the family or spending unit is to discuss each individual's desires or needs for clothes at a family council when the budget is being formed. The problems of democratic money management and the agreed upon rules of democratic decision making within any spending unit will apply to clothing decisions also. It is best that the head or heads of the spending unit not attempt to impose his, her, or their value judgments on the other members by dictating clothing tastes and rules of fashion.

THE FASHION INDUSTRY AND WHO DECIDES

The fashion industry is fascinating enough to merit an entire study in its own right. In the United States alone, it is the fourth largest industry in annual sales. How fashions are decided and how they affect you, the consumer, is important information for your clothing decision making. We are all aware of "high" fashion, but most of us are not direct consumers of it. However, whatever happens in the salons of Christian Dior, St. Laurent, or Chanel, or whatever is designed by Bill Blass, Geoffrey Beene, or Sonja Rykel eventually filters down to less expensive ready-to-wear clothes. Indeed, the respected designers in France, the United States, and elsewhere have themselves entered the ready-to-wear market in the past decade.

WHO DICTATES FASHION?

The immense size of the fashion industry and its supposed modes of deciding our fashion leads us back to the eternal question of consumer versus producer sovereignty. Are fashions dictated by you, the consumer, or are they dictated by the whims of producers? Nobody will ever know who truly dictates fashion, but we can consider a few salient facts. Not all fashions dictated by designers actually take hold. The midiskirt failed through the resistance of women. Fashions in cars can also fail to take hold: the Edsel cost the Ford Motor Company a quarter of a billion dollars in losses.

Although changes in fashions cause earlier "obsolescence" than some consumers would prefer, we do have the choice of either wearing classic fashions that seldom change or of wearing old-fashioned clothes. We do not have to give in to the whims of the fashion industry. But if so many companies are able to make at least a normal profit by continually coming out with new fashions, there must be quite a few consumers who do want variety in their clothing styles, and who do want fashions to change so that they can buy different styles of clothes every year. You and I might find such changes a disagreeable waste of scarce resources. But who is to say what is important for making people happy? On the other hand, even if you have decided that your clothing needs consist of replacing your one pair of jeans every six months or so, you might find that in order to get the same style that you wore last year would mean a lot of hunting. So the success of the fashion industry might merely reflect changing availabilities of replacement articles: the fact that you now buy your jeans with flared pants legs may have nothing to do with your eagerness to adopt changing styles.

If, however, people are made happy by the availability of new fashions, then it would be a value judgment to say their happiness is false. As long as we consumers are aware of the cost of purchasing fashion happiness, we certainly must have the right to decide whether we want to give up other things in order to buy fashionable clothes at a higher price than that for merely utilitarian clothes. We consumers may not be king, particularly with respect to fashions, but because nothing is being forced on us either, the consumer always has the choice of not being drawn into the passing fashion parade.

CHANGING ATTITUDES TOWARD CLOTHING

The attitudes of people, particularly young people, toward clothing are changing. Whether we are witnessing a trend or merely a random cycle is not clear, nevertheless a large number of young people prefer to dress in what might be termed a less than impeccable manner. Styles of the day, not only in the United States but also in such countries as France, often dictate blue jeans, T-shirts, sweat shirts, army fatigues, coveralls, and boots. Adults sometimes cringe at this particular fad or trend, but nonetheless we must recognize one important aspect: casual dress is often less expensive than more formal dress, mainly because it is cheaper to construct less impeccable garments. And less impeccability costs less than more impeccability; it is at least likely that it costs less in maintenance time. The changing trends among young people's dressing habits might also reflect their lower valuation of material things as compared to intellectual and spiritual ones.

Many changes in clothing styles, even among adults, have come about apparently because of the increase in recreational and, in particular, sporting activities.[2] The influence of recreational clothing styles on everyday dressing habits has been quite noticeable in the last few years. Fashions that have become popular for hiking, backpacking, skiing, sailing, and tennis have crept into day-to-day wearing apparel. In its share of total clothing expenditures, recreational clothing has itself been growing by leaps and bounds.

Are we going to ultimately end up in casual dress all the time? No one really knows, but in the last few years it has become quite obvious that many Americans are no longer happy in more formal attire even when they go to what are usually considered formal occasions.

No matter how informal you decide to become, you are still going to be faced with choices, and you still have to decide how to spend your clothing dollar. In the next consumer issue we will see how your dollars can best be spent, and how to tell what you are actually buying.

DURABILITY VERSUS PRICE

Many people accuse the clothing industry of creating obsolescence. That may or may not be true. But it is certain that to have more durable goods we generally have to pay more; to buy a dress or a suit that should last five years, you might have to pay more than for a similar item of less durable material and workmanship that should last only three years.

All of us must decide how much durability we want to pay for. Some manufacturers, such as Monsanto, are now "wear dating" their clothing items: a tag is attached to the garment indicating the guaranteed wear period, usually a year. Thus, the consumer can sometimes determine how much durability is being purchased.

In some cases, we have tried to come full circle by producing paper underwear, paper dresses, and other items made out of paper products that are thrown away after they are used several times. This would be the ultimate in planned obsolescence. But at least in this case, the obsolescence is planned by the consumer, because those of us who buy such articles do so knowing that they will soon be thrown away. Nobody is being fooled, for the manufacturers tell you explicitly how many times you can plan on wearing such a piece of clothing. Information is not a problem.

WHY PURCHASE
CLOTHES THAT
WEAR OUT SO FAST?

Now, why would any of us in our right minds purchase such a highly nondurable piece of clothing? The answer is pretty obvious: you need not worry about upkeep or cleaning when you know the item will be thrown away; and you can change fashions often this way, even as frequently as every three days. For you fashion conscious consumers, this may seem ideal, if you are willing to pay the very high implicit price.

[2]The increased percentage of women who work outside the home, as well as higher valuation of time, may also be factors.

DURABILITY NOT FREE   If durability were a **free good**, we could be fairly certain that producers were creating obsolescence. But durability is not a free good. You usually have to pay more for materials that last longer; and that price may be more than you wish to pay. Depending on your tastes and your budget, you may be better off buying less durable clothes and replacing them more often—especially if the cost of cleaning rises relative to other costs. Whenever the maintenance costs of an item go up relative to other costs, you have more incentive to replace the item rather than to maintain it and repair it.

Once you know that durability is *itself* a good, you can make more rational choices when buying clothing items. You are purchasing a suit or a dress, for example, because of the service flow it yields per unit time period. Thus, if you buy a jacket that you think will last five years, you should figure out what the cost per year is; if it costs $100, but another jacket that will last only one year costs $75, the first jacket is obviously not more expensive in cost per service flow per year. You should know, also, that many durable clothes are actually cheaper than the same type retailed as a "fad." For example, there is little durability difference between a $5.99 men's polyester and cotton shirt and one for $10.99. However, the fit, stitching, and finishing may be far superior in the $10.99 shirt. That may be the only difference, but one that you may be willing to pay the extra $5 for.

In your own shopping forays, remember that you should figure out the cost per year of owning a piece of clothing. It would also be important for you to understand the maintenance costs of particular materials. A clothing label that says "dry clean only" may indicate that the item will cost you more to maintain than another item in the same line labeled "may be machine washed." This kind of information is important in figuring out the relative costs of different pieces of clothing (and also a good reason for labeling requirements).

THE TREND TOWARD LESS FLAMMABLE PRODUCTS

The U.S. government has increasingly required that children's clothing be non-flammable. In 1953, Congress passed the Flammable Fabrics Act. It was passed in response to public indignation at the deaths and injuries caused by highly flammable wearing apparel. Congress enacted this particular piece of protective consumer legislation in order to create a federal regulatory scheme that would uniformly prohibit "the introduction or movement in interstate commerce of articles of wearing apparel and fabrics which are so highly flammable as to be dangerous when worn by individuals. . . ." In its original form, the Act was applicable only to the manufacturing and sale of a narrow range of articles susceptible to flammability—wearing apparel and fabrics to be incorporated into wearing apparel. Also, the Act explicitly excluded from its control certain items of wearing apparel such as hats, gloves, and footwear. The original version of the Act, although helpful, seemed to fall short of the protection it was expected to give the consuming public. Congress had failed to include many articles that created significant hazards and had failed to permit establishment of more stringent standards of flammability.

The 1967 amendment specifically prohibits the manufacture and sale of any product, fabric, or related material that fails to conform to an applicable standard or regulation. More specifically, manufacture or sale of such a flammable product was to be considered an unfair method of competition under the Federal Trade

Commission Act. In addition, the 1967 amendment repealed the specific wearing apparel exclusions of the 1953 Act. While the original Act gave the Department of Commerce power only to recommend new standards and left Congress itself with the power to change the standard, the amendment gave the department the authority to determine the need for new enforceable standards of flammability. The Department of Health, Education, and Welfare was made responsible for providing statistical data on test injuries and analyses.

As can be imagined, this divergent responsibility for administering the Act created substantial problems of coordination. In 1972, the entire responsibility for administration and enforcement of the Flammable Fabrics Act was taken from the three agencies—FTC, Department of Commerce, and HEW—and given to the newly created Consumer Product Safety Commission.[3]

THE COSTS INVOLVED

We all agree that we would prefer our products to be totally nonflammable, everything else being equal, because whenever they catch fire, there is a potential high cost to the person wearing them. The Flammable Fabrics Act was originally aimed at children's clothing that "burst into flames" when near a lighted match, causing serious injuries to many children. Such accidents as a result of the properties of some of the newer synthetic fibers have been greatly reduced. But the trend seems to be toward even greater flame retardant capabilities. Many of the families who are unwilling to spend part of their budgets to reduce this probability even more think it is already low enough. But they will have less and less of a choice because products, especially children's pajamas, will be sold only if they are extremely flame retardant (the criterion often being that they never burst into flame, and ideally will smolder and self-extinguish when the source of flame is removed).

Parental unwillingness to purchase flame retardant clothing may be due to a lack of awareness of how flammable some items and many new synthetics have been or still are. But new synthetic fabrics appear on the market all the time and seldom are labeled as to flammability. Parents, whether motivated by reasoned concern for costs or by partial or total ignorance of product hazards, will still have the option of making their own children's clothes and using cheaper and more flammable materials. Even if the government requires that all children's clothing be totally flame retardant to be sold in the marketplace, it will be impossible to entirely prevent such behavior. (This is going to be even more prevalent since it was discovered that an important flame retardant chemical called Tris could cause cancer.)

THE TREND TOWARD BETTER LABELING

The government has been active in improving the labeling standards for furs, wool, and textiles. The Federal Trade Commission has, since its beginning, been responsible for enforcing federal statutes relating to wool, fur products, and household textile articles. For example, the Wool Products Labeling Act of 1939 protects producers, manufacturers, distributors, and consumers by requiring that manufactured wool products be uniformly labeled to indicate the percentages of wool and

[3]See pages 32—33.

any other fibers in them. The FTC is authorized to issue rules and regulations, to make inspections, and to issue **cease and desist orders**. The Fur Products Labeling Act was designed to protect consumers and competitors by making it unlawful to misbrand, falsely advertise, and falsely invoice fur products. The statute was originally passed in part because of the widespread use of exotic-sounding euphemisms such as "Baltic Lion" and "Isabella Fox" for such unexotic furs as rabbit, dogskin, skunk, or alley cat. As the Wool Act does for wool, the Fur Act makes it unlawful to distribute or advertise and sell a fur product that is misbranded or falsely invoiced. The Fur Act goes one significant step beyond the Wool Act in that it requires *informative advertising* as well as labeling of fur products.

In 1958 the Textile Labeling Act was passed. Basically, it requires that all wearing apparel, floor coverings, draperies, beddings, and other textile goods used in the household be informatively and truthfully labeled and advertised. A product is considered misbranded if it is not correctly labeled with the percentage of each fiber present that makes up 5 percent or more of the product's weight. Additional information must be stated, such as identification of the **generic (nontrademark) name** of the fiber, the country of origin, and the manufacturer.

Critics of the Textile Labeling Act point out that the information provided is only helpful to those consumers who understand the qualities of various clothing materials used. However, the type of fiber alone is often not sufficient indication of the wearing qualities of the garment in question. For example, yarn size in nylon products can yield one of the strongest fabrics (such as "rip-stop" nylon used in tents and sleeping bags) and one of the most fragile, such as in hosiery, with many variations in between. Finishes can also cancel out fiber characteristics, or provide beneficial characteristics not available in the fiber. For example, cotton is one of the most absorbent fibers, but it can be made water-resistant, as is polished cotton. In sum, most labels containing fiber content (as provided for by the Textile Fiber Products Identification Act) are useful on clothes only to the extent that consumers have knowledge of fibers, fabrication methods, and finishes.

SYNTHETIC FABRICS

Because of the many synthetic fibers used today, it is becoming more and more important for consumers to increase their knowledge in order to be able to make intelligent purchases. Table 11-1 is a partial guide to synthetic fibers used in apparel.

If you wish to have more information, you might want to order one or both of the following booklets:

1. A current fiber chart from:
    Man-Made Fiber Producers Association, Inc.
    1150 17th St., N.W.,
    Washington, D.C. 20036

2. Fibers and Fabrics, NBS Consumer Information, Series 1, from:
    The National Bureau of Standards
    U.S. Dept. of Commerce
    Washington, D.C. 20230

Table 11-1

A Partial Guide to Synthetic Fibers Used in Apparel

GENERIC NAME	SELECTED BRAND NAMES	CHARACTERISTICS
Acetate and Triacetate	Acete Estron (FR = Flame resistant) Arnel	Dries rapidly. Heat sensitive; press with cool iron on wrong side. May be dry cleaned. Dissolved by organic solvents, such as nail polish remover. Abrasion resistance is poor. May be used in blends to increase flame resistance. Triacetate is more abrasion resistant and may be ironed with a moderate iron. Do not *twist* or stretch when wet, as both have lower strength when wet.
Rayon	Fontison (FR = Flame resistent) Zantrel	High absorbency, soft, economical. May be similar to cotton in appearance. Some finishes used on rayon may be sensitive to chlorine bleach. May be machine washable (gentle cycle) and dried at low temperatures, or hand washed and hung to dry. Avoid wringing or twisting when wet. Iron at low temperature. Follow manufacturer's directions.
Nylon	Antron Cantrece Qiana	Lightweight; exceptionally strong, durable. May be machine washed and dried. White nylon may tend to pick up other colors and soil in laundering. Wash whites separately.
Polyester	Dacron Fortrel Trevira Kodel	Lightweight, durable, colorfast. Excellent wash and wear characteristics. Oily soil and oil-born stains may be difficult to remove.
Acrylic	Acrilan Creslan Orlon	Soft, lightweight, bulky (low weight with high warmth). In appearance, may be similar to wool. Good colorfast qualities. Moderate abrasion resistance. May be machine washed and dried or dry cleaned. Be sure to follow manufacturer's directions for cleaning.
Modacrylic	Dynel Elura Verel	Similar to acrylics; very sensitive to heat. Uses: for deep pile coats, as simulated fur, and for wigs. Flame resistant. May be dry cleaned or machine washed and dried at low temperatures. Follow manufacturer's directions carefully.
Spandex	Lycra	Used in elastic construction, foundation garments, swimwear, suspenders. Resists deterioration from grease, oil, and perspiration and is more powerful and durable than rubber. Machine or hand wash at low temperatures.
Metallic	Lurex	Metallic fibers usually coated with plastic. Will not tarnish. Used ornamentally in apparel and home furnishing fabrics. May be laundered or dry cleaned. Coating may melt if it becomes too hot.
Olefin	Herculon Marvess Vectra	Lightweight and durable. Heat sensitive. Primarily used for carpets, but increasing usage for purses, belts, and men's knitted sportswear. Machine wash and dry at low temperature. Use a fabric softener in the final rinse. Avoid laundromat dryers and do not iron 100% olefin fabrics.
Rubber	Lastex	Used in elastic constructions, such as foundation garments, waistbands, suspenders. High stretch and recovery properties. Easily damaged by grease and oil, including body oil.

CARE LABELING

More informative for your clothes buying excursions are the care instructions required as of July 1973 by the FTC trade rule of 1971. This ruling specifies that all fabrics be labeled as to the laundering or dry cleaning that will be required to maintain the garment's original character. In other words, when you go to a store, you can now assess how much time or money will be entailed in maintaining the garment you purchase. For instance, labels vary from "Dry Clean Only" to "Leather Clean Only" to "Machine Wash, Warm, Tumble Dry"—nine different classifications in all. Some manufacturers have even added further care categories.

As confusing as this might sound, it is an acknowledgment by the FTC and textile manufacturers that fabric content is not sufficient to tell you anything about what you are buying. Although durability information is still not explicitly available, permanent labeling as to care instructions is certainly a great aid in purchasing clothing. No longer will you find that that skirt or pants you just threw in the machine was supposed to be dry cleaned or that another item should not have been put in the dryer. What these labels represent is a more sophisticated version of the "drip-dry" or "wash and wear" categories we previously had. It is now possible to determine just what you are getting yourself into when purchasing clothing—that is, you will have to iron this stuff, or wait for it to hand dry, or incur the sometimes higher expense of dry cleaning. And the regulation does not apply solely to prefabricated garments; persons who choose to sew for their families are also being given care labels to sew into the garments with each piece of fabric,

Fortunately, the Federal Trade Commission has proposed to revise its care labeling rule, which has been in effect since 1972. This proposal will call for more explicit labeling instructions and, if adopted, will have to specify washing and drying methods and temperatures, use and type of bleach, and temperatures for ironing, if needed. If an item can be washed or dry cleaned, the manufacturer will have to include that information on the label. Dry cleaning instructions will have to specify the type of solvent to be used if not all commercially available solvents are appropriate.

```
Machine wash warm,
gentle cycle
Wash dark colors and
prints separately
Tumble dry low setting
Remove promptly and
hang
Do not use bleach on
colors or prints
If touch-up is desired,
use cool iron
100% NYLON
                    302
```

Now that you know what to look for on the labels and have presumably decided what kind of styling and durability you are in the market for, let us see how to economize on your clothing purchases.

SUMMARY

1. Clothes are purchased for other than mere physical protection. They are purchased because of custom and also because of the improvement in mental attitude that appropriate clothes give the wearer.

2. Different socioeconomic classes typically dress differently as a matter of class identification to impart information to other members of society.

3. Family conflicts about individual dressing styles and clothing budgets can be resolved through democratic family decision making. Generally, it is important to compromise in terms of the individual's desire to either conform or not conform with family dressing habits.

4. It has been said that fashions are dictated by the fashion industry. However, the flop of the midiskirt a few years ago is at least one instance of the consumer's rebellion.

5. Generally, more durable clothes are higher priced. When you are deciding which clothes to buy, it is important to take account of how long they will last. Then you can compare clothes on the basis of the price per year rather than on the basis of the total purchase price.

6. In 1953 Congress passed the Flammable Fabrics Act, which was amended in 1967. The Act requires that the manufacture and sale of fabric or fabric products conform to an applicable standard or regulation. This is particularly important for children's bedtime clothing.

7. Numerous acts apply to correct labeling of fabrics and fur. The Fur Act, for example, requires informative advertising as to the actual content of the products in question.

8. Labels indicating the appropriate care of the garment are now available to customers.

9. Current information on fibers can be obtained from the National Bureau of Standards or from the Man-Made Fiber Producers Association.

QUESTIONS FOR THOUGHT AND DISCUSSION

1. What determines how many clothes you buy each year? How much extra do you spend on clothing for variety and style?

2. How many of your decisions about clothing are based on custom?

3. What are the prevalent clothing customs in your community?

4. Do you agree that clothing imparts information to the onlooker? Or do you think "you can't judge a book by its cover"?

5. Do you think that every member of a spending unit should be allowed to dress in his or her own way without regard to the general ideas held by the spending unit?

6. Do you think that fashion designers dictate what fashions will be or that they cater to what the public wants? What evidence do you have?

7. Have you noticed a changing attitude toward clothing in your lifetime?

8. Do you think it is fair that more durable clothes cost more than less durable clothes? Do you care about durability in your own clothing purchases?

9. Why do you think it has taken so long for Congress to act on flammable fabrics?

10. Why are some parents unwilling to buy flame retardant clothing for their children? Do you think that they should be required to do so by law?

THINGS TO DO

1. Write a list of all of the clothes you have bought in the last year. Also list all of the clothes you no longer wear. From the first list, decide what were actual necessities and what were "frills." From the second list, decide which clothes

were still serviceable. Now ask yourself how much you have spent for clothing in excess of what was actually necessary.

2. Make as long a list as you can of all of our clothing habits that are based purely on custom. Why are customs different in different parts of the United States and in different countries?

3. Contact a fashion designer or a fashion designer's assistant. Try to find out how decisions are made on which fashions will be selected for any particular year or season. Why do you think spring fashions are shown long before spring occurs?

4. Examine the labels on all of the clothes you have. How helpful are they in telling you what the fabric is made of, how durable it is, how it should be washed, and so on? Can you think of better labeling that would be more helpful to you the consumer?

SELECTED READINGS

Buck, George S. *Flammability Report.* Textile Industries, November 1971.

"Care Labeling of Wearing Apparel." *Family Economics Review*, March 1972.

"Clothing, Textiles, Shoes." *Consumers' Research Magazine*, October 1976, pp. 127–130.

"Fabrics and Fire: What You Don't Know *Can* Hurt You." *What's New in Home Economics*, April 1971.

"Flame-Retardant Ban Dishevels an Industry; Children's Sleepwear Chemical Tris-BP." *Business Week*, April 18, 1977, pp. 45–46.

Halloway, I. N., and Houston, B. J. "Flammable Fabric Issues." *Journal of Home Economics*, May 1974.

"How Much Other People Spend on Clothes." *Changing Times*, August 1972.

"Institute Report: Garment Care—Facts You Should Know When the Label Is Incomplete." *Good Housekeeping*, February 1975.

Look for that Label. Washington, D.C.: Federal Trade Commission.

Getting the Most for Your Clothes Shopping Dollar

WHERE TO BUY AND HOW MUCH TO SHOP

Where you buy clothing will be dictated by your preferences in styles. Some stores differentiate themselves by catering to different tastes, or by offering different qualities of goods, or by presenting a store atmosphere—in the kinds of salespersons and the help they offer—different from that of other stores. Also involved, of course, is a certain amount of status: shopping at Saks Fifth Avenue implies a different self-image than does shopping at J. C. Penney.

In some stores you will find very modish, young looking clothes, and in other stores traditional styles or even old-fashioned, older looking clothes. (With the revival of 1950s fashions, it is sometimes difficult to tell the difference.) In any case, the style you prefer is the first consideration. The next consideration is whether or not you should go to a discount store (if there is one in your area). Whether or not you do depends on how much you value the variety and the services that may be offered by nondiscount stores (and, of course, whether or not you feel your self-image is consistent with discount shopping). One of the services that is often foregone in discount stores is the continuous help that may sometimes be received from a salesperson. Many consumers do not prefer to have assistance from salespersonnel, while others require constant attention. If you find a store where a salesperson is extremely knowledgeable about the durability and other characteristics of the clothes that are sold in that store, you might be willing to pay a slightly higher price than you would in a discount establishment. The difference in price, you predict, will more than be made up for by the information that you are given by the salesperson. Again, this is a choice that cannot be made for you, and it is one that you cannot figure out perfectly. You may make a mistake; but this is one method by which you become an informed shopper. You acquire information ("experience") as you make mistakes so that the next time you will make the right decision about the purchase.

SHOULD YOU SHOP AROUND FOR VALUES?

Whether to shop around for values is another matter of personal choice. Obviously, if you can buy the identical piece of clothing for a lower price in one store than in another, and both stores give the same amount of service in hemming, alterations, allowing returns, and so on, you

should buy the cheaper item. But finding the best deal involves using your time, and you must decide how valuable your time is. Also, you must decide whether you actually enjoy shopping. Some consumers detest going to store after store in search of the best deal on a particular piece of clothing. In such a situation, you might even end up ordering clothes through the mail. You are less likely to get exactly what you had in mind, but you are spared the time of walking, taking the bus or subway, or driving your car around to different stores. Many clothing outlets, particularly those for shoes and recreational equipment, offer service by mail with take-back provisions. You can also order through catalogs from Wards, Sears, Penneys, Spiegels, or other stores, and again take-back provisions are usually very liberal. Here you save your time, but you do not get to see the article in question until it is delivered to your door. (Remember, however, that service to your door means that you pay a higher price for the product; in many cases, you can arrange to pick up the items at a catalog desk in the store nearest you.)

Look at Exhibit H-1 for some hints on the best time of the year to buy certain articles of clothing at sale prices.

Characteristics of Stores

There are certain characteristics of each retail clothing store that you may want to check into before you choose the one in which to shop. How good a reputation does a store have? Can

EXHIBIT H-1 When to Shop for Clothing Price Savings

January
costume jewelry
furs
handbags
lingerie
sportswear
winter clothing—all groups

February
sportswear
millinery

March
infant's wear
ski equipment, skates

April
dresses
millinery
suits (men's and boy's)
infant's wear

May
handbags
lingerie
sportswear

June
summer clothing

July
bathing suits
handbags
lingerie
millinery
summer clothing—all groups

August
bathing suits
furs

September
children's clothing

October
back-to-school clothing

November
children's clothing
dresses
suits (men's and boy's)

December
children's clothing
suits (men's and boy's)

you be certain about the quality of its products? One way to find this out is to ask your neighbors or your friends. Another way is to see what percentage of its sales is to repeat customers. If you find friends and neighbors going back often to the same store, it may give good service and sell a fairly reputable product. If you have your own predetermined evaluations of particular brands, then you pick the store according to the brands it carries. How you then decide which store to go to depends on:

1. What kind of service do you get?

2. How do you get along with the salespeople?

3. What are the take-back or exchange provisions?

4. What kind of sales does it have, etc.?

5. What is the refund policy for faulty merchandise or merchandise not wanted?

6. What is their policy on billing, past due bills, etc.?

Most of your common sense notions about shopping will apply here as they will whenever you spend money.

USING THE MAILS

As we mentioned earlier, if you want to save shopping time, you can use the services of some mail order firm—that is, one that sends you catalogs from which you can choose those products you intend to buy. Most catalogs also provide you with useful information, such specifications as type of fabric, the warranties applying, and so on. This often allows for less hurried comparative shopping in the home. Moreover, if you decide to shop on credit, credit terms are usually spelled out. Note also that you may want to read the catalog first and then go to your usual clothing store to compare with what the catalog firm has to offer. This is comparison shopping the easy way. The key, of course, is to find a reliable mail order house; there are literally hundreds of them.

CASH OR CHARGE?

Most consumer consultants generally recommend that all clothing be purchased with cash because buying on credit costs more money. That is true for the reasons we discussed in Chapter 9. If you buy on credit, you will have to pay a service charge (interest) for borrowing that money. But remember our earlier discussion on the flow of services from any item. If you buy a nightgown and charge it, you can expect that it will last at least as long as the time pe-

riod you might take to pay off the balance. In a sense, you are then spreading out the payments for the item so that they correspond with the use of that item.

Your considering the purchase of clothing does not give you any built-in reason to pay cash or to charge. Your decision will be based on how much overall debt you want to carry, and this depends on what income you expect to make in the future, how much you value present consumption over future consumption, and what the charges will be for purchasing things on time.

Remember, though, that you are better off financially if you are allowed to charge goods for 30, 60, or 90 days without paying any interest. This way, you get the use of that money for that particular period and you also get the use of the clothes you buy, with no charge for that simultaneous use. But be careful to make sure that in fact there are no hidden charges for paying 30 or 60 days later. Also, see if there is a discount for paying cash. In this case, you may decide that you would rather get the cash discount because you were going to pay the bill fairly soon anyway.

BUYING PRINCIPLES

Many buying principles can be applied to shopping for clothes to guarantee that you get the best deal for your money. We treat them briefly below.

Comparative Shopping

We know that you should compare values—that you should look at the price of a product in

one store and compare it with a similar product in another.

Durability: Remember the discussion about durability in the previous chapter. That two pieces of clothing look the same does not necessarily mean they are the same: one may last longer than the other. You would not be truly comparing values if you automatically bought the cheaper item. You should find the most favorable relative cost per unit of service offered by each clothing item. And this service includes the ability to exchange easily with the store, to get a refund if the clothing is defective, and so on.

Styles: Quite obviously, if you choose basic or classic styles, you will have less of an incentive to change those styles and, hence, your desired clothing budget may be smaller. But, of course, you give up some things —the joy of wearing highly fashionable clothes and of wearing new clothes more often.

Needs: You should be careful to buy clothes that, as some consumer economists say, "fit your needs." Only you can come close to knowing what your true needs are. And you should avoid one pitfall in shopping for clothes: do not become a bargain fanatic. That is, do not buy everything on sale just because it is on sale. Instead, take an inventory of the items you have and decide where you really have a deficiency in your clothing stock. (See Exhibit H-2.)

In general, you should remember that you can save up to 25 percent on many clothing items if you buy store brands

EXHIBIT H-2   Figuring Out Your Clothing Needs

1. What do you have already?

2. What clothes are required by:
    a. your job or school?
    b. your social life?
    c. your recreational activities?

3. How many changes of clothes do you require to meet your minimum standards of:
    a. cleanliness?
    b. variety?
    c. social status?

4. How do your answers to questions one through three square with the income that you can spend?

---

instead of national brands. If you are not enamored with brand names per se, you can make quite a few savings (depending, of course, on the quality of the house brand).

Care: You should decide in advance of purchase how much time and money you are able to give to clothing care. Be sure to check labels for care instructions; dry cleaning can be an expensive alternative to hand or machine washing, but it is sometimes mandatory in the proper care of certain fabrics.

SUMMARY

1. Clothing shopping begins with a decision about what type of clothes to buy and in what price range. These two attributes will considerably narrow down the range of possible retail stores in which to go.

2. When shopping for clothes you should take into account the time and use of other complementary resources involved.

3. When making a decision about where to shop, check into the reputation of a store. You can find this out from friends who have shopped there before, as well as by seeing which brand names are carried in that store (if in fact you know which brand names are reliable).

4. Check out the kind of service you will get before you make a purchase. What are the take-back guarantees and exchange provisions?

5. You can use the mail to save shopping time. Get catalogs from Sears, Wards, Spiegels, and other companies to find out the exact attributes of some of the clothes you wish to buy. Then you can use that information as a comparison when you go shopping in the retail stores in your area.

6. Whether to pay cash or to charge your clothing purchases should be decided by the total amount of debt you are already handling, not on the particular purchase made. Go back to Exhibit F-1 on page 189, to find out if in fact you have a safe debt load. Make sure you do not exceed it just because you are enamored of a particular article of clothing.

7. Durability is an important quality of any piece of clothing you purchase. Try to compare clothing articles by their cost per year. That means you have to know the durability and also the cost of maintaining the particular piece of clothing.

8. If you buy highly stylish clothes, remember that styles will change more often for you than if you buy more classical styles. You pay for stylishness.

9. Purchasing store names instead of national brand names may save you up to 25 percent. Consider it as a possibility.

QUESTIONS FOR THOUGHT AND DISCUSSION

1. How often do you shop for durability?

2. Do you want salespersons to offer help in a clothing store? Or would you rather pay a lower price and shop at a discount store?

3. How much time do you spend shopping for clothes? Do you spend more or less time trying to find good buys than you do for food? If you do, is this rational? Why?

4. Is it just being lazy to actually order articles of clothing through the mail? For whom would this be the most appropriate consumer behavior?

5. What determines your clothing needs? Do you think about them often?

6. Do you think that males looking for clothes spend more, less, or the same amount of time than do females?

THINGS TO DO

1. Make a list of your clothing inventory. Write down how

often each item has to be replaced. Try to determine whether you replace the item more often than is absolutely necessary and, if so, why you do that.

2. Order some of the major mail order catalogs. After you've gotten several of them, compare the clothing in each with the prices in each. If there are significant differences, can you determine why? Now try to establish whether your local retailers sell the same items at the same price. If there is a significant difference, ask your local retailers why.

3. Order the two guides to fibers mentioned in the last chapter. Compare them with our partial guide to synthetic fibers. See how up-to-date this guide is compared to what you received in the mail. Why do you think that the characteristics of certain fabrics may change over time?

SELECTED READINGS

Buying Clothes for Your Family, HXT-N. Berkeley: Agricultural Extension Service, University of California, 1970.

"Home Water Repellent Treatment for Fabrics." *Consumers' Research Magazine*, February 1977, pp. 34–36.

"How to Shop and Care for a Suit." *Consumers' Research Magazine*, February 1977, p. 41.

Messinesi, D. "Tips on Packing and Planning; Clothes for Traveling." *Vogue*, December 1976, p. 142.

Removing Stains from Fabrics, HG-62. Washington, D.C.: U.S. Department of Agriculture, Superintendent of Documents, 1972.

Shopping Care to Fabric Care, HXT-55 Berkeley: Agricultural Extension Service, University of California, October 1970.

"Textiles of the 70's: Maze or Miracle?" *What's New in Home Economics*, September 1970.

"Ways to Make Clothes Last Longer." *Changing Times*, October 1970.

Your Clothing Dollar. Money Management Institute, Household Finance Corporation, Prudential Plaza, Chicago, Ill. 60601, 1972.

GLOSSARY OF TERMS

Townhouses

Houses that share common sidewalls with other houses.

Modular Homes

Factory manufactured living unit sections put together at the home site.

Pro Rata

Proportionately according to some exactly calculable factor.

Lease

A contract by which one conveys real estate for a specified period of time and usually for a specified rent; and the act of such conveyance or the term for which it is made.

Marginal Tax Rate

The last tax bracket that a taxpayer finds himself or herself in after figuring out how much is owed the government. In our progressive tax system, tax rates go up as income goes up, but only on the last or marginal amount of income. Your marginal tax bracket could range anywhere from 0 to 70 percent.

Capital Gain

An increase in the value of something you own. Generally you experience a capital gain at the time you sell something you own, such as a house or a stock. You compute your capital gain by subtracting the price you paid for whatever you are selling from the price you receive when you sell it.

Housing Voucher

An alternative method of providing those in need with housing services. A housing voucher would be for a specified amount of money that could be used only in the purchase of housing services. It would be used as an alternative to providing public housing.

Site Value

The value of the land on which a house or other building sits. The site value is determined by many characteristics of the site, such as the view, the shrubbery, and the proximity to a city.

Mortgage

A loan for a house, co-op, or condominium apartment.

Discount Points

Additional charges added to a mortgage that effectively raise the rate of interest you pay.

Putting a Roof Over Your Head

CHAPTER PREVIEW

☐ What is the nature of the housing industry?

☐ What are the different types of dwellings we live in?

☐ What is more advantageous: renting or buying?

☐ What has the federal government done to cope with the housing problem?

☐ What is the nature of crimes against property, and what is being done about them?

☐ Why is housing so expensive?

☐ What are some of the problems with the moving industry?

12 If you happen to be an Eskimo living in the Yukon Territory, putting a roof over your head is complicated but not impossible: you make an igloo. If you happen to live in the bush country of Tanzania, putting a roof over your head takes some time, but eventually your thatch hut will be just what you need. If you were a pioneer settling down on some cleared land in the Old West, putting a roof over your head would have meant making a log cabin.

Today, by way of contrast, if you are Mr. and Mrs. Superwealthy, deciding on a new roof over your head may involve $30,000 in architect's fees, $100,000 for a plot of land (not too small, of course), and perhaps another $100,000 for quite a nice house. And then again, if you are the average new home buyer, you have a three-bedroom house with 1,300 square feet of floor space that, with its land, had a market value of $51,000 in 1978.

Housing is a necessity, even for the poorest of humans, but we know that the various types of housing services that people seem to "need" vary drastically from region to region, from suburb to suburb, and from person to person. The variety of houses that one can purchase seems almost infinite. And the price range that one has to look at is also large. Housing is just like clothes or food: once we pass a certain minimum level, the rest depends on our tastes and preferences. And our tastes and preferences must be put into line with the reality of our limited budgets.

Early Americans must have had just as many fanciful ideas about how they would like to live as we have. But today, some of us—in fact, most of us—live like kings compared to earlier Americans. Why is that? Simply because we are all richer. Each year for the last 150 years, our real incomes have gone up at about 1½ percent per capita. And we have spent an increasing proportion of our budgets on housing services, mainly because most of us really do like to cater to our fancies. We like the good life, and that includes a spacious house with many special features that make it seem like our own.

THE HOUSING INDUSTRY

There are now more than 50 million single-family dwelling units in the United States. There are at least 20 million apartments and another 7½ million mobile homes. In almost any one year, more than 1 million new houses are being built, and between 3½ and 5 million families buy homes.

Americans also like to add on to existing houses, as evidenced by the $8½ billion we spend every year for add-ons, improvements, and maintenance. The number of houses in the U.S., as depicted in Figure 12-1, has been rising at the rate of about 2½ percent a year for the last 25 years.

However, these figures can sometimes be deceiving. A truer picture of our circumstances might emerge from measuring how much additional services we are getting from the rising housing stock. It is one thing for 1 million one-bedroom apartments to be built, and it is quite another to have 1 million four-bedroom houses. After all, why do we buy houses or mobile homes, or buy or rent apartments? We buy or rent them for the services they yield, just as we buy clothes or cars or anything else that lasts. When we buy a house, we expect to reap an implicit rate of return in the form of housing services over a number of years; thus, it is important not to get confused between the existing stock of housing and the *flow* of services from that stock.

Figure 12-1
Growth in Housing in the United States

The number of housing units has risen from a little more than 8 million in 1890 to 80 million in 1976.

Source: U.S. Department of Commerce.

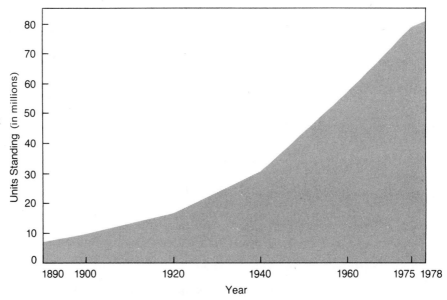

What we are buying is not the house itself, but how much pleasure we get out of living in it month in and month out. And that pleasure is a function of its size, the conveniences it has, how pretty the view is, what the neighborhood is like, and everything else that can contribute to our happiness when we are home. Generally, the reason there is "no place like home" is because all of us try to make our homes as special as possible so that we get the greatest amount of utility or services from them. That is why, also, it is important to realize that when we buy a $75,000 house, we are getting a larger flow of services per month than if we had bought a $30,000 house.

People who have their own houses built incur tremendous money and time costs, worry, and stress. Why do they do it? Many of them incur all those costs so that they can specify the exact house that will maximize the utility and pleasure from the roof over their heads.

DIFFERENT TYPES OF ROOFS

We mentioned before that it is important to distinguish between the different levels of housing services that are being added to our housing stock. Everybody is familiar with single-family dwellings, but fewer people are as familiar with multiple-family dwellings, such as duplexes, high-rise apartments, and so-called tenements. Additionally, in the United States we have seen a rise in condominiums, cooperatives, **townhouses**, **modular homes**, and mobile homes.

Further below we will talk about why so many mobile homes are being built. Basically, the cost per service flow from mobile homes is considerably lower than from regular dwellings because mobile homes can be built by different rules and construction techniques than are required for regular houses. Many consumers know what a mobile home is, but few are totally clear about what a co-op or condominium is. So let us look at these two new types of ownership arrangements.

In a building of cooperative apartments, each dweller owns a **pro rata** (proportionate) share of a nonprofit corporation that holds a legal right to that building. In addition, a member of a cooperative:

1. Leases the individual unit he or she occupies.
2. Accepts financial responsibility for his or her own payments; additionally, accepts responsibility for increases in assessments if one or more members fail to make their payments.
3. Pays a monthly assessment to cover maintenance, service, taxes, and mortgage for the entire building.
4. Votes to elect a board of directors.
5. Must obtain approval from the corporation before remodeling, selling, renting, or changing his or her unit.

Much cooperative housing has been produced for middle-income families, although recently it has become more popular with higher-income families in such places as New York City. In 1978 it is estimated that there is well over $3 billion worth of cooperative housing in the United States, serving more than 290,000 families.

Cooperative housing grew only slowly until 1950, when legislation was passed that allowed the Federal Housing Administration (FHA) to insure the mortgages of cooperative housing units. Today, numerous business organizations design, finance, contract for construction, and then sell cooperative housing projects to prospective member-residents. In many cases, after the cooperative unit is sold, another profit-making organization can be hired to manage the entire unit.

Since the new ruling in 1950, the FHA has insured over $3½ billion in cooperative housing mortgages for 1¾ million middle-income families. In certain states there are state mortgage plans, which have worked out quite well. For example, the United Housing Foundation, in New York, built Co-op City in the Bronx. That "city" accommodates 15,000 families of moderate to middle income.

Co-ops themselves are nonprofit organizations and are therefore owned and operated solely for the benefit of the members. The FHA estimates that the costs of living in cooperative apartments are about 20 percent less than renting comparable apartments from a private landlord. It is interesting to speculate how this 20 percent differential could continue to exist. Perhaps it does because, for one thing, maintenance costs would be lower in the co-op since the owner-members take better care of their apartments than renters would. The fact that co-ops are nonprofit organizations and other apartments are profit-making ventures definitely will contribute to the 20 percent price differential. Also, fuller occupancy and lower turnover would contribute to lower operating costs. And, as we mention below, owner-members can claim income tax deductions that are not available to renters.

Members in cooperative units have a right to sell their particular unit when they decide to move. They recoup any difference between what they owe on their mortgage and what the resale price of their unit is. In general, the co-op itself has the first option to buy the apartment that is put up for sale. In most cases, if the apartment is to be sold to someone else, the members of the cooperative must approve the sale.

Condominiums.   In condominiums, which are a newer type of ownership than the cooperative, the apartment dweller has the legal title to the apartment that he or she owns. A condominium owner, however:

1. Does have joint ownership interest in the common areas and facilities in the building, such as swimming pools and tennis courts.
2. Must arrange his or her own mortgage and pay taxes individually on his or her unit.
3. Must make separate payments for building maintenance and services.
4. Does not accept financial responsibility for other people's units or their share of the overall operating expenses.
5. Votes to elect a board of managers who supervise the property.
6. Has the right to refinance, sell, or remodel his or her own unit.

   Condominiums have become especially popular in resort areas where the owners do not live year-round. In 1972, 25 percent of all new housing units constructed were condominiums, and that percentage by 1978 was estimated to be up to 27 percent.

Some housing experts contend that condominiums have certain advantages over cooperative units, and therefore we should see a continued growth in condominiums relative to co-ops. In many situations, owners who want to sell their condominium apartments are under fewer restrictions than are the owners of a co-op unit. The condominium can be sold without the approval of a board of directors. With a condominium, if the owner of a unit defaults on a payment, it only affects the mortgage. In the case of a cooperative unit, any owner who defaults causes the other co-op members to chip in an amount to cover what has been defaulted. Condominium owners are usually free to rent or lease their units to anyone. Finally, condominium owners can own up to three units but are not required to live in more than one of them.

TAX ADVANTAGES

We will see below the various tax advantages of owning a home. All of them apply to condominiums and cooperatives. Basically, all local taxes and interest on the mortgage for the prorated share in the cooperative and the entire share for the condominium unit are deductible from income before taxes are paid. Because this benefit is not directly available to renters, it is one of the reasons a number of people prefer to own condominiums or join a cooperative instead of renting an apartment, even though an apartment in a cooperative or condominium looks the same and gives the same types of housing services.

TWO OTHER TYPES OF HOUSES

Two other types of individually owned housing units are townhouses (sometimes called row houses) and modular homes. The former is a regular house with a front and backyard but with common sidewalls. The obvious advantage of a townhouse is economy, for its construction permits savings on the cost of land, insulation, windows, foundation, roofs, and walls. Some townhouses are sold as condominiums. One main problem with such housing units may be lack of adequate soundproofing through the shared walls and the proximity of neighbors.

Modular homes consist of factory manufactured living unit sections that can be arranged in various ways. The two types of modular units are "wet" and "dry." The former include plumbing, baths, heating, and kitchen equipment; the latter consists of living, dining, and sleeping rooms. The sections are transported from the factory to the building site, where they are assembled on a permanent foundation.

Because of the increase in housing costs, many consumers are finding it necessary to find alternate housing arrangements. Currently there is an increase in demand for a smaller, more affordable home. To reduce housing costs, buyers are giving up the separate living and dining rooms in favor of a family room, extra bathrooms, paved driveways, finished basements, and landscaped lots, just to name a few.

MOBILE HOMES

Figure 12-2 shows the increase in mobile home construction since 1963. Mobile homes are one of the most popular forms of low-income housing in the United States today. Why? One reason is favorable tax treatment in those states that tax them as vehicles instead of as homes. Another reason is that with mobile homes you may get more housing service per dollar spent, because mobile homes are often built on an assembly line with nonunion labor and without very restrictive building codes. That means that alternative, less costly building techniques can be utilized. Evidently, because so many Americans are buying mobile homes, those circumstances detract little or nothing from the quality or safety of the dwelling unit. However, we should note that not all has been perfect in the mobile home industry: California, for one, felt the need to regulate the way mobile homes could be built.

The Department of Housing and Urban Development (HUD) finally passed nationwide standards that mobile home manufacturers have to meet. These standards relate to thickness of insulation, airtightness of structure, and so on. It has been estimated that the new standards will raise mobile home costs from $500 to $1,500 per unit. Not everyone necessarily desired these new standards. In particular, individuals buying mobile homes in areas where the climate is very temperate are not too interested in paying the extra money to make sure that the home is airtight. This is just another example of how difficult it is to satisfy everyone when nationwide rules are made.

RENTING A PLACE IN WHICH TO LIVE

Until recently, it was common for renters to be looked down upon as people who were unable to manage their money correctly. The proof, of course, was a lack of home ownership. But this attitude has been changing, and today many people rent apartments or houses by choice even though they could easily buy their own home.

There are several reasons individuals wish to rent instead of buy:

1. Renters have greater mobility than those who own homes.
2. No down payment is involved; nor credit checks for securing a mortgage. (But there may be a breakage or cleaning deposit.)
3. Renters are freed from the maintenance tasks and depreciation that home owners must face.
4. The exact cost of purchasing housing services can be easily figured for the period of the lease.

Figure 12-2 Mobile Homes Built Each Year

The growth of mobile homes over the last decade and a half has indeed been startling. This rapid growth rate is obviously caused by home buyers finding mobile homes a better buy than conventional housing.

Source: Federal Reserve Board of Governors, and Mobile Home Manufacturers Association.

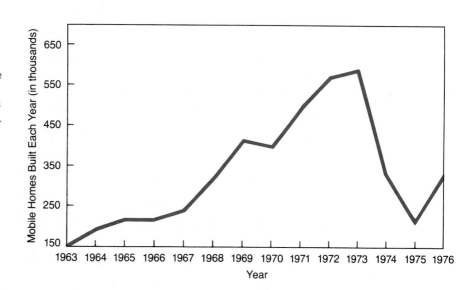

5. Renters don't have to worry about property values because they do not own the property.
6. It is easier to resist excessive spending on home improvements.
7. Your future housing needs in terms of the size of your family do not have to be estimated carefully.
8. Renters can take the necessary time to become familiar with a new community before investing in a house.
9. Common recreation facilities may be insured.
10. There is no loss of interest on investment of savings.
11. There is no liability of ownership.

Some apartments are rented on a month-to-month basis with the rent paid in advance. The renter or tenant automatically gets the right to live in the apartment for the next month. In this type of tenant/landlord relationship, the contract may be terminated on 30 days' written notice. Given the proper 30-day notice, the rent can be raised at any time, or the tenant can be asked to leave. There are advantages and disadvantages to this short-term contract. On one hand, renters can move when they wish without giving a long advance notice. But on the other hand, there is the uncertainty of possibly being asked to leave on short notice, or of finding the rent raised sooner than had been anticipated.

Alternatively, renters may obtain a **lease**. This is simply a long-term contract that binds both landlord and tenant to specified terms. The lease, which is usually for one year, generally requires one month's rent in advance, and perhaps one month's rent as a cleaning, breakage, or security deposit.

As with any contract, you would want to be aware of all provisions of the lease. Most leases tend to protect landlords more than the tenants. We go into this important topic in Issue J on how to rent a place to live.

THE ADVANTAGES OF BUYING RATHER THAN RENTING

We have pointed out some of the advantages of renting as opposed to buying a place to live. Here we can briefly list the advantages of buying a housing unit.

1. Freedom of use: you can remodel it or make it into anything you want.
2. Offers an investment option that historically has been a good hedge against inflation.
3. Causes you to save because part of your monthly payments create equity interest in the housing unit.
4. Allows the tax benefits of being able to deduct interest payments from income before paying taxes.
5. Allows you to save taxes by "doing it yourself."

The last point is sufficiently misunderstood to spend some time explaining it. The best way to understand it is to consider a numerical example. Suppose that your house needs repainting. You get a number of bids for the labor, averaging $2,000. How much do you have to earn to get $2,000 *after taxes*? That, of course, depends on what your **marginal tax rate** is. If your marginal tax rate is 50 percent, then you would have to earn $4,000 in order to have $2,000 to pay someone to paint your house. If you decided to "do it yourself," you in effect would be working for yourself but not declaring the income that you earned, that is, the $2,000 worth of services that you performed, rather than paying someone else. So, instead of spending your time working to earn $4,000 of which $2,000 goes to Uncle Sam and $2,000 to the house painter, you spend time painting the house yourself and avoid any taxes at all because, as of yet, the Internal Revenue Services does not require you to estimate the market value of do-it-yourself services performed around the house.

INVESTING IN A HOUSE

It is fairly certain that the population will continue to grow for some time to come, and hence there will be pressures on land prices in spite of everything else. Does this mean that you should invest in a house with land around it because you are certain that it will go up in value?

If you consider your housing purchase an investment, you are not *guaranteed* making any more than if you had invested in something else. The reason is fairly simple. Because it is well known that the value of land has risen over time as population increased, many people take that into account when they try to purchase land or houses, and the price of land is consequently bid higher. If something is so obvious that you and I know about it, how can we expect to make a killing on it? If we think we can, we are fooling ourselves. Buying a house may or may not be a good investment, but do not expect to get rich simply because you bought a big house with plenty of land. The price you paid for that house probably reflected everybody else's anticipation of rising land values. What you will usually get is a normal rate of return on your investment, which will be equivalent, in essence, to the rate of return you could have gotten had you invested the money elsewhere and rented a house. Many people nevertheless want to buy instead of rent, and many of their compelling reasons have to do with the special tax advantages that we briefly mentioned earlier.

THE TAX GAME

Did you know that if you buy a house and borrow the money to pay for it, all of the interest payments that you pay to the bank can be deducted from your income before you pay taxes? This may not mean much to you if you are not in a very high tax bracket, but when you get up into a higher one, it will make a big difference.

For example, suppose you buy a $30,000 house and were somehow able to borrow the entire $30,000. Let's say that the interest you paid every year on that $30,000 came to $3,000. You would be able to deduct that $3,000 from your income before you paid taxes on it. If you were in the 70 percent tax bracket, you would get a tax savings of $2,100; the interest on your loan would in effect only be costing you $900, which is pretty inexpensive. Now you know why, as people get into higher income tax brackets, it generally pays to buy a house instead of renting.

This tax policy is an implicit subsidy to the housing industry and to all of you who own houses and have any taxable income. The Joint Economic Committee figured out that the implicit subsidy was costing the U.S. Treasury $2.6 billion a year.[1] Unfortunately, the benefit from this implicit subsidy is directly proportional to your marginal tax bracket, which, of course, is directly proportional to how much

[1]Joint Economic Committee, *The Economics of Federal Subsidy Programs* (Washington, D.C.: U.S. Government Printing Office, 1972).

you make. Since poor people are poor because they make little money, they are not in a high marginal tax bracket. Thus, even if they deduct all of their interest payments for their house, the implicit tax savings will be little, or sometimes zero. This interest rate subsidy to homeowners has not been very useful in helping out lower-income people.

Taxes and housing are related in another way that you may want to know about. If you buy or build a house for $20,000 and sell it ten years later for $30,000, you have made $10,000. And generally, you would be taxed on that sum, for it is a **capital gain**.[2] However, if you buy another house of equal or higher price within 18 months, you pay no capital gains taxes at all until much later.

HOUSING AND EDUCATION

Most education from kindergarten through twelfth grade is provided by public school systems. Because these public school systems are at least in part financed by property taxes, it is not unusual to find more agreeable school systems in areas where property values are high and where the total property taxes collected are usually large. Of course, between property tax revenues and quality of education there need not be this relationship, but it is sufficiently common to consider it when buying a house (or even when deciding where to rent). In other words, when you buy a house, you are buying a complementary good that goes with it—education for any younger children you happen to have. In areas that have better elementary (or "primary"), junior, and senior high schools than other areas, the housing prices may be correspondingly higher. Note that this is true so long as children are not bused out of their neighborhood to another part of town. Also note that if you have no school age children, you are still required to pay property taxes.

As parents we have some choice in the quality of our children's schooling even without sending them to private schools, but only if we are willing to move to where we feel there are better schools. The quality of schools is obviously a strong selling point for some suburban areas. One need only drive around with a real estate agent in Scarsdale, New York, or in Beverly Hills or Palo Alto, California, where the public schools are considered above average. The real estate agent will certainly let you know.

HOUSES DO NOT LAST FOREVER

Remember that when you buy a house, you are not buying the house for itself but for the services that it yields. And the way you get a constant level of services from a given house is by maintaining it. Houses have a tendency to fall apart just like anything else you own. And repairing them can sometimes be expensive. We will see below that the average increases in craftsmen's wages are among the highest in the nation. The same is true for the wages of persons who come to fix your sprinkler system, your clogged drain, your leaking roof, or your broken furnace. Because the maintenance expenses on a house can be extremely important, you should figure out how much it will cost to keep up. If you have one with a large front or back lawn and much shrubbery, you know that you will have high

[2]Capital gains tax rates are generally lower than normal personal income tax rates.

maintenance expenses for the grounds. You or someone else in your family must do the work or you must hire a gardener. In either case, you pay more for your housing services—but, of course, you get more in aesthetic pleasure. You have to plan to repaint most houses every few years. If it has carpets, they have to be cleaned professionally every once in a while.

All maintenance costs should be included in the costs per year of having any particular house. After all, you are buying a service flow for, let us say, a year at a time, and you should not be fooled into ignoring some of the very important costs of obtaining those services.

RENTING VERSUS BUYING AS INVESTMENTS

Consider the argument that rent money is wasted by the tenant, whereas payments on a home are not wasted because you are building up equity. This is clearly ridiculous. In either case, you are paying for a housing service. For example, even if you buy a $25,000 house and pay for it with cash, you still have costs, even though you have no house payments. You have the costs of maintenance and taxes. But more important, there is an implicit opportunity cost, because you have $25,000 tied up in that house. After all, that $25,000 could earn a return if you invested it in the stock market or got interest in a savings and loan association. Realistically speaking, the implicit opportunity cost of the $25,000 you paid for the house might be as high as 10 percent, or $2,500: you are paying $2,500 a year; plus taxes of possibly $500; plus maintenance and depreciation, which might add

another $1,000. That means that even if you pay cash, the implicit cost of owning a $25,000 house will be around $4,000 a year.

Against this cost you must weigh the value of the services you receive plus any appreciation in the land value. Say the land itself is worth $10,000. It might appreciate at 7 percent a year. That would mean you would deduct $700 from the total cost to get a net cost per year of a little over $3,000. Do you still think that to buy is cheaper than to rent? What equivalent value in services could you get in a rented house or apartment for $250 a month? There is no other way to make the decision.

Buying a house rather than renting one presupposes that you have made a fundamental value judgment. Owning your own home involves many hidden costs. You are the one who must worry about upkeep, maintenance, and changes in zoning laws. If you rent, you have no such worries. The question is: can you get what you want in a rented apartment or house? If your tastes are similar to the average, perhaps that is possible. If you have special preferences, you will have a difficult time renting exactly what you want. When you rent you are usually not allowed (or do not necessarily want) to make changes in the dwelling, at least not permanent changes. In a home that you own, you are free to make such changes.

COPING WITH THE HOUSING PROBLEM

The federal government has been concerned with the problems of slum housing since the initiation of public housing programs in the 1930s. The goal of the Housing Act of 1949 was "realization as soon as feasible . . . of a decent home and suitable living environment for every American family." Twenty years later, the problem was still with us, and in passing the Housing and Urban Development (HUD) Act of 1968, Congress reaffirmed the 1949 goal and specified the construction or rehabilitation over the next ten years of 26 million housing units, at least 6 million of which were to be for low- and moderate-income families.

After four decades of government attention, the problem still persists, and federal policies have been at best a mixed blessing. Between 1950 and 1960, for example, the fraction of U.S. dwellings deemed "substandard" fell from 36.9 percent to 18.2 percent. However, a substantial contribution to this reduction during this decade was made by the private housing market, which upgraded more than 2 million substandard dwelling units to standard quality. In the next decade, the National Commission on Urban Problems found that 1 million dwellings, most of them inhabited by low-income families, had been demolished under one government program or another. Through 1967, only 700,000 public housing units had been constructed in their place.

URBAN RENEWAL

Of the various government efforts, the urban renewal program alone was responsible for the plowing under of 400,000 dwelling units. This program, which was the federal government's major attack on the decay of the central city, has failed to eradicate slums, as we are all painfully aware. Urban renewal is a cooperative program between the federal government and local authorities. Local authorities develop a comprehensive, detailed plan for urban renewal—including the area to be rehabilitated, the area to be leveled, and the complex of housing and other facilities to be erected in place of the existing buildings. The new facilities typically

include low-income public housing to replace that destroyed; they also generally include middle- and high-income apartments, hotels, and commercial enterprises that will be financed by private capital.

Once approved by the federal government, the program gets underway with the leveling of the area to be reconstructed. Typically, a long period of five to ten years follows before construction begins. During this period, the area remains a wasteland. The delay has been the result not only of bureaucratic red tape, but also of the reluctance of private capital to construct enterprises of doubtful profitability in such circumstances. The consequences—according to many impartial observers and even those in government itself—have been quite simply that the poor have become worse off; for during the five- to ten-year interval, the supply of low-income housing has been reduced. Forced out of the areas to be leveled, the poor have had to find other homes, thereby increasing the demand for existing low-income housing and raising the price of those dwellings further.[3] As the price of low-quality housing rises, the owners of better-quality housing on the fringes of slum areas have had an incentive to break up their dwellings into smaller ones and to allow them to deteriorate to be consistent with the quantity or quality demanded by the poorer potential residents. Hence, urban renewal has not eliminated slums but—according to some—has actually caused them to spread to other parts of the city. Demolition of slums serves mainly to relocate them, not to eliminate them.

LACK OF
COORDINATION

Another major problem facing us is a lack of coordination between governmental programs. For example, in some large cities, there might be an urban renewal agency *and* a public housing authority. These two could be working against each

[3]Some observers contend that there currently is plenty of low-income housing in places like San Francisco, but that the middle-class won't move out of it!

other with the housing authority getting public funds to build housing right where the urban renewal agency wants to have a highway built. That is just one example. An examination of governmental housing policies among various agencies in any major city will yield many more.

ARE THERE ANY SOLUTIONS?

Obviously, the past solutions to the lack of "adequate" low- and middle-income housing have not been overwhelmingly successful, although a number of people have benefited from the government programs. One solution has been suggested by a number of home economists, consumer advocates, and government economists. Since we have had such bad luck in the past with trying to have the government build housing units or subsidize them, why not merely give poor people **housing vouchers** (or more income, for that matter)? In this way, they themselves could choose whether they wanted to spend more for housing or buy a minimum amount with the housing vouchers. The problems that arise when the government itself gets into the housing market would occur no more. Instead, as the demand for certain types of housing increased because people with the housing vouchers desired it, private industry would start to provide it. In the long run, the supply of housing would grow—which is, in fact, what we really want. Not only do we want the supply of housing to grow as fast as the population, but we want the quality of housing to improve for less wealthy Americans. Although housing or rent vouchers would be no cure-all, it is clear to most observers that our past efforts to solve our housing problems have not worked out perfectly either.

WHY DOES IT COST SO MUCH TO BUY A HOUSE?

In 1955 the average single-family house cost $14,500. In 1978 the estimate is over $50,000 as we see in Figure 12-3. Not only have the costs of houses themselves gone up, but so, too, have property insurance rates, the costs of maintenance repairs, mortgage interest, and property taxes. Why do houses cost so much today? And what determines their costs in different areas of a city—or, for that matter, of the world?

One reason that the price of housing units has been going up so much is because the value of their sites, the land they are on, has also been going up. Let us find out what determines site values.

DETERMINING THE VALUE OF LAND

Land is generally thought of as being in fixed supply. Of course, we can fill in areas of a bay and do other such things, but not much of an increase in the total supply of land results. The value of a piece of land is determined by the same things that determine the value of anything else: the forces of supply and demand interact. Why does a piece of land with a view over a bay cost more than the same piece with no view? Obviously because the demanders—that is, you the consumers—place a value on having a view and you are willing to pay for it. Demanders like you will bid up the price of the view lot so that it reflects the utility received from having the view.

But many other things besides the view determine the **site value** of land. One of the most important determinants is property taxes. If you own an acre in one section of town and you have to pay $5,000 a year in taxes, that same acre in

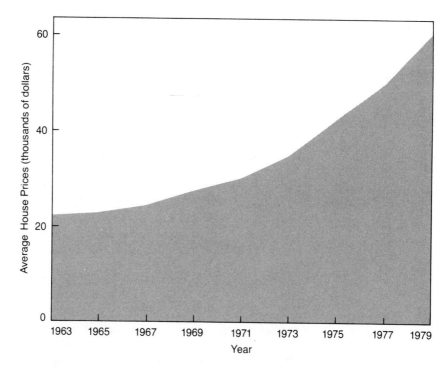

**Figure 12-3
How House Prices
Went Up.**

(Figures for 1978 and
1979 are projections.)

Source: U.S. Census Bureau.

another section of town where you would only have to pay $2,000 in taxes will be worth a lot more. Why? Simply because the cost of owning it would be smaller and therefore people like you and me might bid up the price of the lower-taxed land to reflect the tax savings.

POLLUTION EFFECTS

The amount of pollution in an area also affects the price of the land, because pollution is a source of disutility. The same piece of land with the same house on it will have a lower value in a highly polluted area than in a less-polluted area. Why? Simply because consumers like you and me bid up the price of the land where there is less pollution. You have an indication of what might happen if suddenly all of the smog was eliminated from the Los Angeles Basin: property values in the hitherto smoggy areas would immediately rise; and the relative value of land in the outlying, less smoggy areas would fall, because those pieces of land would now be less special. If you are a property owner in a polluted area of a city, you obviously will benefit from any unanticipated reduction in pollution in your area. Your benefit is in the form of an increase in the value of your property, which means that when you sell it, you can get more for it.

There are a host of other aspects of land that determine its value. Noise pollution caused by automobile and air traffic is an important factor. If a freeway that takes you downtown in ten minutes is near your land but out of ear shot, the value of your land is going to be higher than if the freeway did not exist. Land close to stores, shopping centers, schools, and other such facilities will also be more valuable.

In other words, all the amenities of living are somehow figured into the site value of land. Whenever any of them changes, the site value changes also. If you live in a pollution-free area but a factory suddenly moves in, the value of your land will fall. If a bridge is built across a lake, thus shortening the trip between your land and the city from 1 hour to 20 minutes, your land will increase in value. If the crime rate increases in your area, the value of your land will fall; if the crime rate decreases, the value will rise.

BUILDING COSTS, BUILDING CODES, AND YOU

To build a house, you cannot just buy the lumber, bricks, and pipes and build it. Why not? Because many elements of that house must be checked out by a city building inspector. Unless you live in an otherwise uninhabited area, there are city, state, or federal building codes to be met.

What are building codes? They are codes by which builders must abide if they are to get certification for their work. Building codes are generally thought of as a means by which consumers are protected from unscrupulous methods of putting together a dwelling. A building code that gives a certain thickness of wire for electricity presumably protects you against short circuits and fires from them. A building code that gives a certain thickness plasterboard protects you from having a poorly insulated house, or one that will crack easily.

However, not everybody who has studied housing codes thinks they are all for the good of the consumer. Considering how unbelievably rigid local building codes can be, many observers are amazed that we have as much housing as we actually do. If you look at an identical house in different cities, you will find that the price of building it varies greatly because of variations in the codes. Some codes require, for example, that roof trusses be spaced 24 inches apart; others say that 16 is the necessary minimum. There are at least 13,000 code authorities in the United States; and in each city or state there may be hundreds of inspectors making sure the codes are carried out. A house need not be safer in Boise, Idaho, than in Mesa, New Mexico, but the codes, when looked at in this way, certainly will tell you differently. Why is there all this variation? Much of it is due to custom and habit, but much else is due to the lobbying of very powerful special interest groups when the codes were drawn up.

UNIONS AND BUILDING SUPPLIERS

If you are a member of a plumbers' union and someone invents inexpensive plastic pipe that does not require a sophisticated plumber, you would realize that in the future there will be less demand for your services if houses could be built with this plastic pipe. It would be in your best interests to make sure that the housing code was not changed to allow the less expensive plastic pipe to be used. This is exactly what happens, as the hearings for plastic pipe in Seattle, Washington, exemplify. The people against plastic pipe contended it was unsafe. How did they demonstrate it was unsafe? They took a brick and dropped it from ten feet over the pipe and showed that the pipe would break. They poured gasoline on the pipe, lit it, and showed that it would melt, therefore "proving" that it was unsafe. What was actually being done? People—that is, plumbing union members—were fighting against a new innovation that would bring the cost of housing and the income of plumbers down.

Not only the building tradesmen have a special interest in making sure building codes favor them; so, too, do local suppliers and many manufacturers. Local suppliers may persuade the drafters of building codes to require very specific materials, sometimes even by brand names. In this way, the supplier will benefit from the building code, while you, the consumer, will often lose out.

Basically, building codes are materials-oriented instead of function-oriented. They specify, for example, the number of studs instead of the strength of the wall. They specify the thickness of the wallboard instead of its insulation properties. Consumers would be much better off if building codes were altered to specify functional characteristics that were deemed adequate to protect the consumer, rather than specifying the types of materials used and the ways houses must be built. Whether a union or nonunion tradesman works on a housing unit does not necessarily determine its quality. And if you were aware of how much more expensive union workers are than nonunion workers, you would understand the trend toward using assembly line methods that do not require anybody from the plumbers' union, the construction workers' union, or the electricians' union. Figure 12-4 shows the average wages of building union members over the last 25 years. They have risen faster than just about any other wages in the economy. It is not surprising that, for example, most of the time a large percentage of union construction workers do not have union work, because their wages in 1977 averaged over $8 an hour. Many of them prefer to take nonunion wages on the side (and presumably against union rules) rather than remain unemployed for so many months out of the year.

**Figure 12-4
Growth in Wages
of Union Con-
struction Workers**

Average hourly
earnings of union
construction workers
has been on the rise
for many years. In
1975 it was some-
where in excess of $7
to $8 an hour.

Source: U.S. Department of
Labor, Bureau of Labor
Statistics, *Handbook of
Labor Statistics*; and *Survey
of Current Business*.

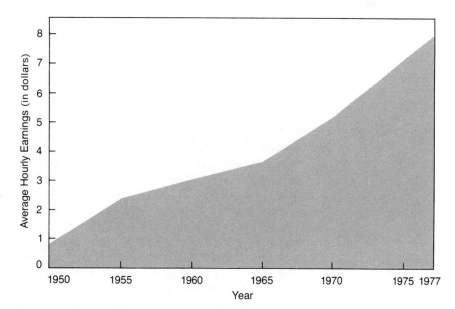

GETTING A MORTGAGE AND WHAT IT IS ALL ABOUT

Unless you are really cash rich, you will have to pay for a good part of your house by a **mortgage**. What is a mortgage? A mortgage is merely a loan that a bank or trust company makes on a house. In some states you hold the title to the house; in others, the mortgagee does. In nine states plus the District of Columbia, a special arrangement is made whereby the borrower (mortgagor) deeds the property to a trustee—a third party—on behalf of the lender (mortgagee). The trustee then deeds the property back to the borrower when the loan is repaid. If the payments are not made, the trustee can deed the property to the lender or dispose of it by auction depending on the individual state's law. As the mortgagor, you make payments on the mortgage until it is paid. More than 90 percent of all people who buy homes do so with a mortgage loan.

SOURCES OF MORTGAGES

There are basically four sources of mortgage money, the most important being savings and loan associations, which account for almost 50 percent of all home loans made. The second most important are mortgage companies, which account for somewhere around 20 percent. Commercial banks then follow. Mutual savings banks make some mortgage loans, particularly in the East. There is a whole category we'll call "other," which includes pension funds, mortgage pools, insurance companies, mortgage investment trusts, and state and local credit agencies. Only under special circumstances can you get a mortgage loan from one of these institutions.

THE KINDS OF MORTGAGES

There are basically three kinds of mortgages. Although you may not be eligible for two of them, all three are available from the same sources: commercial banks, savings banks, mortgage bankers, savings and loan associations, and insurance companies.

1. Conventional mortgages. Most conventional mortgages run for 20 to 30 years. However, in recent years savings and loan associations have been reluctant to write mortgages for 30 years; and, in fact, some of them are charging higher interest rates for mortgages that last so long. Naturally, the rate of interest charged is determined by conditions in the money market (but also subject to state usury laws, which we discussed in Chapter 9). Interest rates in the past few years have been at record highs or close to them. This should not, however, be a surprise when you consider the high inflation rates of recent years. The mortgagee's interest rate has to take account of any expected loss in the purchasing power of the dollars that will be paid back to it in the future.

With a conventional mortgage loan, the money that the lender risks is secured only by the value of the mortgaged property and the financial integrity of the borrower. To protect the investment from the start, the conventional lender, such as a savings and loan association, ordinarily requires the down payment of anywhere from 5 to 25 percent of the value of the property. Some private insurers will protect lenders against loss on at least a certain portion of the loan. When such extra security is provided, the lender may go to a higher loan figure. The borrower, of course, pays the cost of the insurance.

If you make a very large down payment, lowering the risk of lending, the lender may be willing to grant you a slightly lower interest rate, perhaps a fraction of a percent below the prevailing local rate.

Conventional loans can be arranged on just about any terms satisfactory to both parties. Different lenders favor different arrangements, which means it will pay you to shop around. And because most borrowers pay off their mortgages well before maturity, it is wise to look around for liberal conditions on prepayment; you will not want to pay a penalty if you wish to prepay.

2. Veterans Administration mortgages: These loans can be obtained only by qualified veterans or their widows. The interest rate charged is administered rather than determined strictly by the forces of supply and demand in the money market. The VA loan is guaranteed rather than insured. That is, the government simply promises that on an approved loan it will repay up to a certain amount or a certain percent, say, 60 percent. The borrower has no insurance premium to pay.

Loans with nothing down are possible under the VA program, often for amounts of up to $70,000 or more and for up to 30 years. However, you cannot get a loan on a VA-financed house for more than the VA appraisal of its current market value, nor mortgage it for longer than the VA estimate of its remaining economic life. All VA loans can be prepaid without penalty. Recently, VA loans have become available for second mortgages and for mobile homes.

Although the Veterans Administration makes some mortgage loans directly to veterans—usually in rural areas where lenders are not making guaranteed loans—in all other circumstances a would-be borrower should go to the usual funds of mortgage money, such as a savings and loan association, a mutual savings bank in states where they exist, commercial banks, and mortgage companies. It is particularly useful to check with the bank, savings and loan, or mutual savings bank where you happen to be a saver or depositor. If they have a history of your past records, they probably will be more accommodating to you.

3. FHA mortgages: The Federal Housing Administration issues insurance covering the entire amount of an FHA loan. This added security enables qualified borrowers to obtain a much more generous loan in relation to the value of the property than they could obtain with an uninsured loan. Of course, to the borrower, a bigger loan means a smaller down payment.

Generally, it is possible to borrow 97 percent of the first $15,000 of the appraised value of an approved house that you intend to live in yourself, plus 90 percent of the next $10,000, and 80 percent of the rest up to $35,000. The maximum interest rate that can be charged has usually been below market interest rates. But, you also have to pay a ½ percent premium for the insurance, and a 1 percent origination fee (a fee for the work of drawing up the papers) is also permitted. The loan can be for as long as 35 years, not to exceed three-fourths of what the FHA estimates is the remaining economic life of the dwelling. There are no penalties for prepayment.

You can apply for an FHA insured mortgage loan just as you would apply for any other loan. The lender—be it a savings and loan association, mortgage company, or commercial bank—will supply you with the necessary forms and help you complete them. If that lender is willing to make the loan, the application to the FHA insuring office will be submitted for you. When your application reaches the FHA office, the staff will process it, and this may be a time-consuming endeavor. The FHA staff will analyze the transaction, including your qualifications as a mortgagor, the estimated value of the property, and so on.

Although the FHA has no arbitrary rules with respect to age or income, these factors are considered for their possible effect on your ability to repay the loan over the period of the mortgage.

The FHA also sponsors a subsidy program for low- and moderate-income families. In this program, down payments can be as low as several hundred dollars and interest as low as a couple of percentage points.

The big difference between FHA loans and so-called conventional loans is that the FHA interest is not determined strictly by market conditions, but is set at an arbitrary rate by the Secretary of Housing and Urban Development. Usually, the secretary tries to fix a rate well below the lowest prevailing market rate. However, this practice has been associated with a curious "point" system.

WHAT ABOUT POINTS?   Sometimes you may be asked to pay **discount points**. This is merely a device to raise the effective interest rate you pay on a mortgage. This will occur whenever there are restrictions on the legal interst rate that can be charged you for your mortgage loan. You may think this unfair, but if you are faced with the possibility of either paying the discount points or not getting the loan at all, you may decide to pay the implicitly higher interest rate.

A point is a charge of 1 percent of a loan. This charge may be assessed against the buyer, or the seller, or both. To see how a discount point system works, say you have to pay four discount points on a $25,000 loan: that means that you get a loan of $25,000 minus 4 percent of $25,000, or only $24,000. However, you pay interest on the full $25,000. Obviously, the interest rate you pay on $25,000 understates the actual interest you pay because you get only $24,000. Some states have laws against discount points, and FHA and VA have restrictions on buyers paying points (so they are charged to the seller, but ultimately passed on to the borrower in the form of a higher price).

MORE FLEXIBLE PAYMENT ARRANGEMENTS

Many young people who have been saving for a home may be able to buy one sooner than anticipated because of government rules that became effective in 1974. The aim of the new rules is to permit savings and loan associations to arrange schedules of flexible mortgage payments with borrowers.

In effect, young people may now be able to tailor their monthly mortgage payments to both their present budget and to any anticipated increases in income later on. The rules permit home buyers to contract to make lower monthly payments during the first few years of their mortgage, and increase the payments later on when presumably their income would be greater. However, the lower payments must at least cover the current interest on the mortgage and can continue for no more than five years.

As an example of how this new system works, below is a 30-year mortgage of $30,000 at 8 percent interest (an interest rate that is relatively high by historical standards but probably lower than the one prevailing when you read this book). Monthly payments are given for both a conventional and a flexible plan.

Years	MONTHLY PAYMENTS	
	Standard Plan	Flexible Plan
1st through the 5th	$ 220	$ 200
6th through the 30th	$ 220	$ 230
Payments on principal	$30,000	$30,000
Payments on interest	$49,200	$51,000
Total cost	$79,200	$81,000

Notice that the interest charges under a flexible plan are somewhat higher than under a conventional plan. That is because you do not begin to pay back the principal until six years after you take out the mortgage loan. Essentially, then, you have the loan for a longer period.

LIMITATIONS ON
FLEXIBLE PAYMENT
SCHEDULES

Flexible payments are limited to mortgages on single-family, owner-occupied homes. The down payment for any home subject to flexible payments may be as low as 5 percent of its price. Older people, perhaps those nearing retirement, can also take advantage of flexible mortgages given through savings and loan associations. A flexible mortgage here, however, would be the reverse of the example above—higher monthly payments during the first few years decreasing with time when the home buyer might be living on a fixed retirement income that is lower than his or her actual income when the mortgage was taken out.

VARIABLE RATE
MORTGAGES

One of the newest concepts in mortgage lending is the variable rate mortgage (VRM), which links required interest payments to the lender's (mortgagee's) cost of money. Essentially it allows sharing the impact of inflation between the lender and the borrower, thus encouraging lenders to make long-term mortgage loans, which they otherwise would not want to do. As of 1977, California, Massachusetts, Illinois, Ohio, Virginia, and Wisconsin had approved the concept. Basically the lender is allowed to raise the interest rate when interest rates in the economy go up due to inflation. There is a maximum amount that the rate can be raised in any time period. Moreover, the lender has to lower the interest rate if interest rates in the economy go down. In times of widely varying rates of inflation, VRMs are destined to become a common mortgage instrument.

**MAKING
THE MOVE**

Ours is a mobile society. One in five U.S. families moves once every year; among people 25 to 34 years old who have gone to college, almost 38 percent move every year. The average American moves twelve times in his or her lifetime. The decision to move often comes from a desire to change location, to go to a place with a better school system, or to be in a different climate. Sometimes a move is forced on a family by a job commitment. Whatever the reason, when moving comes around (unless you are lucky) you have too many personal possessions to be moved in your Chevy or Volkswagen. Either you rent a truck or you must call in a professional mover. Even in the best of circumstances and with the best movers to help you, you are not in for a picnic. Moving at its worst can be a total disaster causing an incredible amount of stress. In the next consumer issue some pointers are given about how to choose a moving company, what to prepare for, and how to make things generally easier for yourself. Do not expect too much, however. Moving is never easy.

One must also include in the cost of a move the time and energy that must be expended. All costs taken together must be considered before a final decision concerning relocation is made. Professional moves are expensive but the "U-Haul" price isn't exactly peanuts, especially if you have rented a truck that only gets five to eight miles per gallon of gasoline. If the move is a long one and if another vehicle must also be driven, the expenses mount quickly.

There are many problems in the moving industry, some of which can never be worked out. Many of them, however, are the result of government-business rela- tionships that do not seem to benefit the consumer at all. Moving is an industry regulated by the Interstate Commerce Commisssion, an agency set up in 1887 to regulate some of the abusive practices of railroads. Since then, the ICC has increasingly taken over regulation of all forms of transportation, including, as we mentioned, moving. As a result, at one and the same time you have a friend and a foe. You have a friend because many ICC regulations are designed to benefit you; in addition, if something goes wrong and you think you have been cheated, you can complain to the ICC and you will often get a redress of your grievances. On the other hand, you have a very definite foe, because the ICC frequently does things at the behest of the industry to help the industry and not the consumer.

The stifling of competition, with the help of the regulatory agencies involved, is not unknown in this industry. For example, if a large moving company wants to service a state in which it does not yet have a license to service, hearings are held to find out whether the company should be allowed to service that state. There are generally no reasons to prevent such competition because we, the consumers, will benefit from it ultimately through better service and/or lower prices. However, because the movers already servicing that state will lose some of their business to the new competition, they fight to prevent the competition.

How they do it is rather interesting. A hearing is held in which the competitors find people who have been moved by the company wishing to gain entrance into the state. These people have to be special: they have to have had problems in their moves. The competitors pay the travel expenses for them to come to the hearings to complain. But the company that wants to move into the new state fights back. It pays the travel expenses for individuals whom it has moved and who are content to come testify in its favor. What a comedy! The battle of sob stories versus glowing reports! Somehow it seems no better than a hearing at which gasoline is poured over a plastic pipe and set on fire to demonstrate the unsafe- ness of the pipe. But consumers should expect such behavior, because special producer interest groups always look out for their own special interests and not for general interests. If it happens otherwise we are lucky. Here perhaps is where organized consumer groups could help out.

No matter what kind of housing services you intend to purchase, you should have some idea of the best way to buy and sell a house, how to evaluate a rental, what to do when you make the move, and how to insure it all. These topics will be discussed in the following consumer issues.

SUMMARY

1. Americans purchase many different types of housing services—those from residential houses, apartments, condominiums or cooperatives, mobile homes, townhouses, and modular homes.

2. Individuals purchase or rent a house or apartment in order to obtain the flow of services from that particular asset. The flow of services from an expensive house is obviously more than from a less expensive house.

3. Cooperatives and condominiums are becoming increasingly popular types of ownership arrangements. In a cooperative situation, the co-op is a nonprofit corporation that is owned and operated solely for the benefit of its members —that is, the individuals who own residences in the building. Members of a co-op can sell their particular unit when they decide to move, but the members of the co-op must approve the sale.

4. The owner of a condiminium has title to the unit he or she occupies. The condominium owner has fewer restrictions than the co-op owner. For example, the condominium owner can rent or lease the unit to anyone and can own up to three units although living in only one of them.

5. An alternative to the traditional house is a mobile home, which is less expensive because it is generally not constructed by union workers, nor as extensively regulated by construction codes.

6. Renting is an attractive alternative to buying because there is greater freedom of mobility, there is no down payment, there are no maintenance tasks, and the exact cost can be easily figured out.

7. Urban renewal involves destruction of dilapidated housing and construction of better housing in its place. However, urban renewal has been judged less than a total success because during the time that leveling and construction of new units are underway, the supply of low-cost housing to the poor is greatly reduced.

8. An investment in a house does not guarantee you a higher than normal rate of return on your investment. In fact, in our system, any investment that is well known cannot guarantee you ahead of time a higher than normal rate of return.

9. A sometimes recommended alternative to urban renewal and public housing is the institution of housing vouchers: needy families would be given certificates with a specified amount of money on them that could be used only to purchase housing services.

10. Housing is so expensive for two reasons: the cost of construction and the cost of the land or site on which the house is put.

11. The more attractive the site, the more expensive it will be. A site can be attractive for any number of reasons, such as the absence of air and noise pollution, a beautiful view, closeness to shopping, and a nice neighborhood. Construction costs are high because of restrictive building codes that require expensive construction materials and techniques, and because of relatively high construction industry wages.

12. If at all possible, you may wish to obtain a Veterans Administration mortgage or a Federal Housing Administration insured mortgage. Ask your real estate agent or the banks you have contacted about these possibilities.

13. You may also wish to take part in a flexible mortgage payment plan whereby you pay a lower amount during the first five years and a higher amount from

then on. You may have to pay a higher interest rate on a flexible payment schedule, however.

14. All real estate taxes and interest payments on mortgages for houses are deductible from your federal income taxes.

15. Your choice of housing may determine the education for your children because public school systems are financed in part by property taxes that depend on the value of the property in the area around the school.

16. The moving industry is regulated by the Interstate Commerce Commission. That regulatory agency has set regulations that benefit you when you make a move, but it has also allowed the elimination of much competition in the moving industry.

QUESTIONS FOR THOUGHT AND DISCUSSION

1. Why do you think housing is such a special commodity?
2. When somebody tells you that they are going to buy a $40,000 house, does that sound like a lot of money? (What is the average price of a new house today?)
3. Is it better to buy or rent a house?
4. If you had to live in either a co-op or a condominium, which would you choose? Why?
5. Do the tax advantages of owning a home benefit everyone equally? (Hint: What about our progressive tax system?)
6. Why has there been a change in the attitude toward renting versus home owning?
7. Why do you think urban renewal has often been deemed a failure?
8. If you were in charge of solving the housing problem, what would your solution be?
9. Do you think housing vouchers would be a good alternative to current government attempts at helping poor people have adequate housing? Why or why not?
10. Can you make a list of other determinants of the value of land than those given in the text?
11. If you buy a house for $40,000 in 1978 and sell it for $50,000 in 1985, are you better off? (Be careful: What about inflation?)
12. What are the costs of having building codes? What are the benefits?
13. Why has there been such a rapid growth in the construction of mobile homes in the last ten years?
14. Which is the best kind of mortgage: conventional, VA, or FHA?
15. Do discount points seem "unfair"?
16. If you are certain that a cleaning deposit for a rented apartment or a house will actually end up being a cleaning fee, has your effective rent been raised or lowered?
17. "Since the amount of land available is fixed and the population is growing, land has to be a good investment." Evaluate.

THINGS TO DO

1. If you are living in a house, or you know someone who is, try to determine the exact cost per month of living in it. Make sure you include the maintenance costs, the opportunity cost of the difference between the value of the house and the mortgage (sometimes called the equity in the house), the interest on

the mortgage, and so on. When you have come up with a monthly figure, search around your neighborhood to find out what sort of apartment or house you could rent for that amount. Is buying obviously a better deal than renting?

2. Send away for literature on the numerous condominiums that are advertised in the travel section of newspapers and also in the housing section of the Sunday editions. See what advantages there are to buying a condominium rather than a co-op or other dwelling unit. Do you find advantages that were not listed in the text? What are they?

3. See if there is a local office of HUD (Housing and Urban Development). Ask them to send you all of their literature on what they are doing to help out the housing problem. Evaluate it for its impact on the poor, the middle class, and the upper class. Find out if there have been any objective standards set by which to judge the success or failure of various housing programs.

4. Discuss the concept of housing vouchers with anybody who is convinced there is a housing problem. Find out what the pros and cons are from other individuals' point of view. Could the concept of vouchers be applied to other specific necessities, such as education, food, or entertainment?

5. Call up a real estate agent and ask where the best housing investments should be. If the agent tells you that land on the water or land with a view is always a good investment, ask why.

6. Call City Hall. Try to get a copy of the building codes for your area, or at least find out how you can read parts of them. Find a specific feature, such as wiring or plumbing, and ask when those codes were set up. Find out if there have been any technological advances since then, and try to determine whether the building code should be changed.

7. Make a comparison between the cost per square foot of buying a new mobile home and the cost per square foot of buying a regular home.

8. Get a copy of the pamphlet issued by the U.S. Congress Joint Economic Committee entitled The Economics of Federal Subsidy Programs (Washington, D.C.: Government Printing Office, 1972). Read the section on housing and draw your own conclusions.

9. Can you see how decisions about what kind of car to buy resemble decisions about what kind of house to buy when you consider maintenance problems?

10. Find out how property taxes are figured in your area and how the money is spent.

11. Call up the local office of HUD or FHA. Ask what special government help can be provided you if you decide to buy a house. Find out what the income limitations are. In other words, does the special help apply only to poor people, or to middle-income people also?

SELECTED READINGS

Aaron, Henry J. Shelter and Subsidies: Who Benefits from Federal Housing Policies? Washington, D.C.: The Brookings Institution, 1972.

"Age of Automation Arrives for Housing Industry." What's New in Home Economics, April 1972.

"Annual Housing Surveys." Family Economics Review, Fall 1976, pp. 22-23.

"Buy or Rent a Home?" U.S. News, April 25, 1977, p. 86.

Fredlind, Daniel R. *Residential Mobility and Home Purchases*. Lexington, Mass.: Lexington Books, 1974.

"Gaining Momentum: A Drive to Stop Suburban Sprawl; Farmland." *U.S. News*, March 21, 1977, pp. 82-84.

Gross, P. "How to Home In on a Place to Live." *House & Garden*, January 1977, p. 54.

"Land Boom in the Farm Belt." *Forbes*, April 15, 1977, pp. 25-26.

"Modular and Mobile Homes; Recreational Vehicles." *Consumer Bulletin Annual*, 1973.

Moore, C. "You Can Fix Up an Old House, But Is It Worth It?" *Money*, November 1974.

Perl, Lila. *The House You Want*. New York: David McKay Co., 1965.

Rowen, C. T., and Mazie, D. M. "America's Housing Problem: The Great Shortage." *Reader's Digest*, January 1975, pp. 63-66.

"VRMs Go Vroom in California." *Forbes*, April 15, 1977, pp. 110-114.

"What's Happening to the Cost of Building a House?" *Changing Times*, June 1973.

Buying, Selling, and Insuring a Place to Live

GLOSSARY OF TERMS

Earnest Money

Sometimes called a deposit on a contract or an offer to purchase a house. It is the amount of money that you put up to show that you are serious about the offer you are making to buy a house. Generally you sign an earnest agreement or a contract that specifies the purchase price you are willing to pay for the house in question. If the owner selling the house signs, then generally you are committed to purchase the house; and if you back down, you can lose the entire earnest money or deposit.

Title

The physical representation of your legal ownership to a house. The title is sometimes called the deed.

Real Property

Property in physical structures and in land.

Title Insurance

Insurance that you pay for when you buy a house so that you can be assured that the title or legal ownership to the house is free and clear when you buy the house. If, for example, you purchase a house and pay for title insurance and six months later the builder who put on a new bathroom sues you because the former owners did not pay for the work, the title insurance

company may be forced to come up with the money.

Basic Form Policy

Homeowner insurance policy that covers 11 risks.

Broad Form Policy

Homeowner policy that covers 18 risks.

Comprehensive Form Policy

Homeowner policy that covers all risks except usually flood, war, and nuclear attack.

The American dream seems to be that each of us will own his or her own home. Let us assume that you share that dream. When you decide to buy a house, you should figure out how much you can safely spend.

HOW MUCH CAN YOU AFFORD?

It is very easy to get carried away with buying housing services. A nice house is something that makes you and your family feel good and probably proud. But a nice house may also mean many unanticipated financial headaches. To make a sound decision, you should first calculate the level of your *dependable* monthly income for, say, the first third of all the mortgage payments due on a house. In other words, if you happen to be making a quantity of extra money this year, to count that

as permanent may get you into trouble. Be conservative.

Next, you must figure out respective monthly housing expenses. This includes your payments on a mortgage, insurance premiums, taxes, costs of maintenance repair, heating, air conditioning, electricity, telephone, water, sewage, and things like that. Your mortgage payments may be higher than you think. Table I-1 can be used to estimate monthly payments on different sized mortgages. That table gives how much per month you would have to pay on a mortgage per $1,000 borrowed. Remember that this is just the amount you would have to pay on the loan. In addition, you would be paying on insurance and taxes. In Table I-2 we present a chart you can use to calculate the monthly costs of owning your home.

Remember, you can rarely finance 100 percent of the cost of the house. You may have to pay one-fifth of the purchase price as a down payment. In addition, there are closing costs, which we discuss below. Table I-3 gives rules for estimating how much housing you can afford. It tells you, for example, that the purchase price divided by your annual income should come to 2.0 or less. Another helpful rule of thumb is that you should not spend more than

Table I-1

Monthly Mortgage Costs per Thousand Dollars

If you borrow $35,000 for 30 years at 9½ percent, it will cost you 35 × $8.41, or $294.35 per month for 30 years for principal and interest on the loan.

INTEREST RATE	LENGTH OF MORTGAGE		
	20 years	25 years	30 years
7.5 %	$ 8.06	$7.39	$7.00
7.75	8.21	7.56	7.17
8.0	8.37	7.72	7.34
8.25	8.53	7.89	7.52
8.5	8.68	8.06	7.69
8.75	8.84	8.23	7.87
9.0	9.00	8.40	8.05
9.25	9.16	8.57	8.23
9.5	9.33	8.74	8.41
9.75	9.49	8.92	8.60
10.0	9.66	9.09	8.78
10.25	9.82	9.27	8.97
10.5	9.99	9.45	9.15
10.75	10.16	9.63	9.34
11.0	10.33	9.81	9.53

Table I-2

HOUSING EXPENSES PER MONTH	CURRENT	FUTURE
Mortgage payments		
Property taxes		
Insurance		
Heating oil		
Gas, electricity, water and phone, sewage		
Yard care, trash pickup, etc.		
Savings fund for repairs, remodeling, and maintenance		
Other		
Total		

one-fourth of your take-home pay for housing payments. These are only rough rules, but they do serve as a guide: if you buy a $40,000 house on a yearly income of $8,000, you are asking for trouble. After housing expenses, food, and transportation, you will have no money left over for desired recreation, medical bills, clothing, or saving.

New versus Used

As with the purchase of almost any goods that last a long time, you can choose between an older house and a new house. The new ones are advertised in the

Table I-3

A Guide to How Much Housing You Can Afford

Most savings and loan association loan officers will use the rules alongside to determine how much housing you can afford. Rule 1 states that the purchase price of the house should not exceed 2 times your yearly gross income. Rule 2 states that your monthly mortgage payment should be no more than 25 percent of your total monthly income. Rule 3 states that all of your debt payments combined, including your mortgage payment, should not exceed one-third of your monthly income. And rule 4 indicates that most savings and loan associations will not loan you more than 95 percent of the purchase price of your house. And generally, the maximum is closer to 80 percent, and in some cases, even as low as 65 percent.

Source: The United States Saving and Loan League.

1. $\dfrac{\text{Price}}{\text{Income}} \leq 2.0$ (1.5 might be safer)

2. $\dfrac{\text{Mortgage payment}}{\text{Monthly income}} < 25\%$

3. $\dfrac{\text{All debt service}}{\text{Monthly income}} < 33\%$

4. $\dfrac{\text{Loan amount}}{\text{Value}} < 95\%$ (usually around 80%)

---

home section of your Sunday newspaper every week. In some years, as many as 2 million new housing units are built in the United States. On the other hand, an "older" or second-hand house might make as much sense or more for you than a new one. Of course, you must be more careful about future maintenance problems with an older home, but using an inspection service ahead of time can avoid that problem, as we will discuss later. Older houses have the advantage of already having the property landscaped. Often they provide more space for the same money than a new house.

DECIDING WHERE YOU WANT TO LIVE

Even before you start looking for the kind of house you want to buy, you must first decide where you want to live. Below is a list of the most important kinds of variables you have to take into account.

1. Relationship to work. Is the area you are looking at near your work or distant from it? If distant, is there good transportation by bus, train, or a freeway that is not congested at the time you have to go to work? If you happen to work in an area where most people in your city work, you will find that the farther away from the work center, the cheaper land will be, all other things remaining constant. But you make up the difference in this price of land by having to spend more time, which has a value, and more money for transportation to and from work.

2. Property taxes. Find out what the average assessment is in the area in which you are thinking of living. This is an important out-of-pocket cost that you have to take account of in calculating your housing needs relative to your means. Property taxes often seem to have a direct relationship to the school system.

3. Schools for your children. Make sure you check out the schools in the area you are considering. If you think they are not going to be suitable, then you will probably come to feel unhappy about your children's education, and you may wind up spending money for private education. Go to the schools to which you think you might have to send your children. Talk with the teachers and the principal. See what kind of philosophy is behind the teaching experience there. If it differs from yours, be careful; you may not want to live in that area. (Busing will alter this consideration greatly.)

4. Shopping. How close will your house be to the kind of stores that have free parking? Or will you have to pay for parking every time? Generally, the farther away a house is from shopping, the lower will be the value of the land, all other things being constant. But you will make up the difference in extra time and expense transporting yourself to the shopping centers.

5. Air quality. Is the area polluted or clean? Is it close to factories or is it close to the mountains? The site value of the land will take into account the different levels of pollution, but you may place a much higher value on clean air than do the rest of the consumers in the housing market. If you have special respiratory problems, you definitely will be willing to pay for an unpolluted air environment in the form of higher housing costs.

6. Noise pollution. How close is an airport? Is one in the planning stage? Can you hear an expressway or freeway during rush hour? Can you hear traffic from a second story bedroom but not from a livingroom?

7. Crime. If you are worried about crime rates in your prospective area, you can check with real estate agents in different sections of town, the police department, neighbors, and statistics from the police department annual reports. Usually, the police are obligated by law to give you those statistics. You can also check the deductible clause in homeowner's insurance for an indication of theft in the area.

8. The neighborhood. What kind of neighbors will be around you? Are they people who have the same life style as yours? Will you feel uncomfortable at home? If you have children, do other people in the area have any the same age? If not, that can present problems.

9. Zoning and development. Are nearby undeveloped areas zoned for industry, housing, apartments? Is there going to be further development in the area? All these things should be checked out, either with a responsible real estate agent or by doing it yourself.

10. Traffic. How easy is it to get in and out of your driveway? Will your children face a dangerous experience crossing the street?

WHEN TO USE A REAL ESTATE BROKER

You can start a housing search by first looking in the classified section of a newspaper. This will require much time, many telephone calls, and actually going out to see houses that might interest you. If you are casually looking for a house, this may be the best way to do it. Generally you will save a real estate broker's commission if the people advertising are selling the house themselves. However, the majority of ads are placed by real estate companies, so you end up paying the brokerage fee even if you find the house through the newspaper. If you decide to use a broker, it is wise not to take the first one who comes along without checking. To check out brokers, call several of them, tell them what you want, and have them show you a few houses. You will find out very soon how serious each broker is about servicing you. You will also find out whether he or she understands your tastes and preferences and can therefore act as you would act in searching for a house. If you know individuals in the area who have used brokers, find out which of the brokers have given satisfactory service. It will be helpful if you have a good idea of what your housing needs are and what you specifically do and do not want.

What Does a Broker Do?

Essentially, brokers provide buyers and sellers of houses with information. Information, remember, is a costly resource. This is particularly true with such a nonstandard product as a house. Every house is different from every other, and it is difficult to get buyers and sellers together for such nonstandard products. Generally, for standard products, or even for nonstandard products that do not cost very much, there are no brokers. But in the housing market, the reverse is true: a house is the largest purchase any family will make, and it involves something that is, so far, completely nonstandardized. The broker, then, saves you information costs by engaging in the search procedure for you and for the seller. He or she becomes a specialist in matching up the wants of buyers with the supplies of sellers.

How Much Will You Pay?

For selling a house, most brokers charge a fixed fee that is paid, at least nominally, by the seller. But do not be fooled about how fixed this fee is. In times of bad housing markets, you can bargain with a broker over a house you think you want to buy. You can stipulate, for example, that you will buy the house if a refrigerator, a stove, or some such thing is supplied. Or in a good market, the seller can do the same thing; the seller will agree to pay the fixed commission, but over a seven-year period. This means that, in effect, the commission will be worth less to the broker and cost less to the seller of the house. Such arrangements are against

the rules of brokerage societies, but that should not worry you. The very fact that brokers have fixed commissions is against present antitrust laws. If brokers can break the Sherman Antitrust Act, then, in your own best interests, you can try to persuade them to break their own rules governing fixed commission rates.

Brokers can do many things besides helping you find the house you want. They can also help you arrange for the financing, make sure that the papers are in order, and even do the bargaining for you.

HOW TO BARGAIN

Most Americans are unaccustomed to bargaining. Goods and services are sold in a marketplace at set prices that you can rarely get lowered. But buying a house is a different situation. The asking price is generally not the final sale price. If you are unaccustomed to bargaining for a house, or you feel uncomfortable doing it, you can let a real estate broker do it for you.

You might get a general idea of how much profit the seller is trying to make by finding out what was paid for the house before. You can look at the deed to the house, which is a public document. It can be examined at the office of the County Clerk or County Registrar of Deeds. You can find out what the house costs by looking at the federal tax stamps affixed to the deed when the ownership was transferred. The stamps cost $1.10 for every $1,000; thus, if a deed

has $33 worth of stamps, the owner paid $30,000. (Don't forget the impact of inflation on the price during the years since the person purchased the house.)

Many times, sellers do not expect to get the price they are asking on their houses. They set a price that they think may be, say, 5 or 10 percent more than the price they will finally receive. It is up to you to find out how far they will go in discounting that list price. You can start out by asking the real estate broker whether he or she thinks the price is "firm." Because the broker's commission is a percentage of the sale price, the higher that price, the more the broker benefits, but not if it means waiting months or years for a sale. The broker's desire to get that commission as soon as possible is an incentive to arrange a mutually agreeable price so that a deal will be made. Note, though, that it is probably best to assume that the broker works for the seller and represents the seller's interests rather than the buyer's. You may want to bargain, for example, on a $45,000 list price for, say, $42,000 plus the refrigerator, freezer, washer, and dryer that are already in the house. This sort of bargaining happens all the time. You should not accept the list price just because you think you want the house. Although that price may be the lowest you can get it for, it may not be. You only know if you bargain; and if you are unwilling to do it yourself, ask the broker to do it. The broker may ultimately decide to take a low-

---

EXHIBIT I-1   Homebuyer's (or Renter's) Guide, or How to Decipher What the Ads Say

---

Convenient to shopping:	bathroom window overlooks the local A&P parking lot
Family room:	unfinished basement with a 60-watt bulb
$200 to heat:	$640 to heat
Desirable corner:	corner
Entrance foyer:	door
Only 10 minutes from . . .	only 45 minutes from . . .
Many extras:	recent owners have left behind half-used bar of soap, numerous rags and coat hangers, and three switches that are connected to nothing
Immaculate:	the walls in the kitchen are not quite as greasy as the grease rack at Sam's Standard Station
Piazza:	porch
Gleaming bathroom:	bathroom
Comfortable:	very small
Cozy:	even smaller
Cute:	itsy bitsy
Victorian:	many drafts
Colonial:	built prior to the first Eisenhower Administration
Gracious colonial:	forget it—too expensive
Leisure home:	enter only during July and August
Make an offer:	say something funny

---

er (implicit) commission rate in order to seal the deal. The first stage of sealing the deal is signing a written earnest or binder agreement.[1] But before this is done, certain basic, common-sense precautions must be taken.

BEFORE YOU SIGN ANYTHING

Before you sign anything, make sure you are getting a house that

[1]The earnest or binder agreement may also be called a sales or purchase contract.

is structurally sound. Pay an expert to go over everything in the house that could cause problems—wiring, frame, signs of termites, plumbing, sewage, and so on. Often, you can get this done for $25 or $50, but for more expensive houses you will have to pay $100 to $200. It is money well invested unless you are an expert at figuring out what can go wrong with the house just by looking at it. Look at the listings under "building inspection service" or "home inspection service" in your telephone directory yellow

pages. Again, these companies are selling the same thing that a broker is selling—information. Such information can save you hundreds, if not thousands, of dollars in repairs you would later discover had to be made. Often, if structural faults in a house can be shown up by a building inspector, you can have the seller of the house agree to pay for the repairs even after you take over the house itself. Or this can be a point in bargaining: the price that you agreed on can be reduced by the amount of the repair costs.

WHAT HAPPENS WHEN YOU DECIDE TO BUY?

Generally, when you have decided to buy a house, you make an offer and put it in writing. You must also put up **earnest money** or deposit binder money. The earnest agreement or binder, which is usually good for 24 hours, states in some detail your exact offering price for the house and lists any other things that are not normally included with a house but are to be included in this deal, such as washers and dryers. Within 24 hours the seller of the house either accepts or rejects the earnest agreement or binder. If the seller accepts and you try to back down, the earnest money you put up, which may be several thousand dollars, is legally no longer yours. But sometimes you can get it back even when you decide against the house after signing the agreement. In any earnest agreement, it is often wise to add an escape clause if you are unsure about getting financing. Put in a statement like, "This earnest agreement is contingent upon the buyer's obtaining financing from a bank for X thousand dollars." Remember, the earnest agreement (called an "offer" in California) is your proposal. Put in what you want. Let the seller change it—then you review it.

If the earnest or binder agreement has been accepted, then a contract of sale is drawn up. This is sometimes called the sales contract, conditional sales contract, or a purchase contract. Usually the signing of a contract of sale is accompanied by a deposit, which may be 10 percent of the purchase price paid to the seller. Often the buyer merely adds to the existing earnest money to bring it up to the desired amount.

The deposit may be put into an escrow account or a trusteed savings account that earns interest from the time it is paid to the seller to the time the buyer takes possession of the house. When any substantial sum is involved, it is, of course, advantageous to the buyer to have the deposit put into a trusteed savings account with the interest accruing to the buyer rather than the seller. This is particularly advantageous if there is a large time difference between the signing of the conditional sales contract and the actual date of possession of the house.

CLOSING COSTS

Table I-4 indicates the typical closing costs on a $40,000 house. Quite a bit of money, isn't it? You didn't realize that it would cost so much. Closing costs can end up being 3 to 4 percent of the total purchase price, and that is money that you have to come up with in

---

Table I-4

Typical Closing Costs on a $40,000 Home

The service or setup charge on a mortgage usually varies from 1½ to 2½ percent, the lower figure being applied to a loan that is 75 to 80 percent of the purchase price of a house. If, for example, on a $40,000 house, you put a down payment of 20 percent, or $8,000, you would have to pay a setup or service charge of 1½ percent of $32,000, or $480. Title insurance would range from $13 to $90. A recording fee would be another $6, and various other things added in would make the total closing costs 3 to 4 percent of the value of the house, or, for a $40,000 house, about $1,200 to $1,600.

Service charge:	on 75 or 80% loan = 1½%
	on 90 or 95% loan = 2 to 2½%
Title insurance:	on 75 or 80% = $13.15
	on 90 or 95% = $60 to $90
Recording fee:	about $6
Insurance on home in case of fire	about ¼% of sale price
The bank also collects the taxes on the house	
Credit report:	$10 to $15
Appraisal fee:	$75 to $100 (on VA and FHA $50)
TOTAL CLOSING COSTS:	3 to 4% of house value

EXHIBIT I-2   **An Estimate of Cost and Cash Requirements for Purchasing a House**

Loan Amount $_____   Purchase Price $_____

ESTIMATED COSTS

Service Charge $_____

Title Insurance   _____

Recording Fee   _____

Due Seller for _____ Taxes   _____

Fire Insurance Premium   _____

Interest from _____ to _____   _____

Tax Registration   _____

Allowed Toward _____ Taxes   _____

Assessments   _____

Credit Report   _____

Escrow Fee   _____

Appraisal Fee   _____

    TOTAL $_____ *

ESTIMATED CASH REQUIREMENTS

Down Payment $_____

Estimated Costs $_____

Subtotal $_____

Less Earnest Money $_____

    TOTAL $_____

ESTIMATED MONTHLY PAYMENT AT ___% FOR ___ YEARS

Principal & Interest $_____

Taxes   _____

Insurance   _____

Mortgage Life Insurance   _____

Mortgage Disability Insurance   _____

    TOTAL $_____

* Plus Reimbursement to Seller for Unused Fuel Oil

front, in addition to your down payment. That means that you have to have cash for closing costs. Exhibit I-2 shows a form that you can use to figure costs when you plan to buy a house.

Something mentioned in Table I-4 that you should know about is **title insurance.**

TITLE SEARCH AND INSURANCE

Often when you purchase something as large as a house, you must be sure that you really own it, that no one with a prior claim can dispute your **title** to the land and structure. Any one of the following four methods of search can inform you if you do in fact have title, free and clear, to the property:

1. An abstract. Usually a lawyer or title guarantee company will trace the history of the ownership of the property. The resulting document is called an abstract, and it will indicate whether any claims are still outstanding. Note, however, that the abstract, no matter how lengthy it might be, does not guarantee that you have the title. Nonetheless, if the search has been careful, it provides reassurance.

2. Certificate of title. In some areas of the country, this is used in place of an abstract. An attorney merely certifies that all the records affecting the property have been looked at and, in the opinion of the attorney, there are no claims on it. Note, however, that the attorney is not guaranteeing his or her opinion, and cannot be liable if some

obscure claim does arise in the future.

3. Torrens certificate. This is a certificate issued by a governmental unit giving evidence of title to real property. It is used mainly in large cities. You can get it faster and it is usually safer than an abstract or certificate of title. An official recorder or registrar issues a certificate stating ownership and allowing anyone who has prior claim on the **real property** to sue. If no suit develops, then a court will order the registrar to record the title in your name; a certificate to this effect will be issued.

4. Title insurance. A title guarantee company will search extensively through the records pertaining to the property you wish to buy. When it is satisfied that there are no prior claims to that property, it will write an insurance policy for you, the new owner. The insurance policy guarantees that if any defects arise in the title, the title company itself will defend for the owner and pay all legal expenses involved. Note that this may sound better than it actually is. Title insurance generally does not cover governmental actions that could restrict use or ownership of the property you just bought. Often title insurance excludes mechanics liens not recorded with the proper official agency when the policy was issued. In other words, if work was done on the house and not paid by the former owner, it is possible, even with title insurance, that you end up paying for that work.

You should always ask the seller for a copy of paid bills for any obviously recent repairs or additions to the home.

THE REAL ESTATE SETTLEMENT PROCEDURES ACT

A recent law requires that all closing costs be specifically outlined to you before you buy a home. Under the 1976 revisions of the Real Estate Settlement Procedures Act, when you go to buy a house and borrow money to pay for it:

1. The lender must send you, within three business days after you apply for a mortgage loan, a booklet prepared by the U.S. Department of Housing and Urban Development outlining your rights and explaining settlement procedures and costs.

2. The lender must give you, the applicant, within that three-day period, an estimate of most of the settlement costs.

3. The lender must clearly identify individuals or firms that he or she may require you to use for legal or other services, including title insurance and search.

4. If your loan is approved, the lender must provide you with a truth-in-lending statement showing the annual interest rate on the mortgage loan.

5. Lenders, title insurers, and others involved in the real estate transaction cannot pay kickbacks for referrals.

For further details about RESPA regulations, you may write the Assistant Secretary for

Consumer Affairs and Regulatory Functions, Real Estate Practices Division, Department of Housing and Urban Development, Room 4100, Washington, D.C. 20410.

Reducing Title Insurance Costs

If the property you are purchasing is already covered by a title policy, you might be eligible to get a reduced rate on the one you want to take. You ask for a reissue. The lower reissue rate will only apply to the original face value of the old policy. The regular rate will apply to the difference between what you are paying for the house and the original value.

REDUCING MORTGAGE COSTS

Careful shopping for a mortgage is, of course, of utmost importance. Note that for every one-half of 1 percent that you reduce the interest rate on your mortgage, you will save $4.08 a year per $1,000 of mortgage. Hence, on a 30-year, $30,000 mortgage, that would be a total savings of $3,672 over the 32-year period.

The larger your down payment, the better your chances of getting a lower rate. Therefore, you can reduce mortgage costs by making as large a down payment as possible. (But then you can't earn explicit interest on all the money tied up in your house.)

The shorter the term that you make your mortgage, the lower will be your overall interest payments and generally the

greater will be your ability to receive a preferred interest rate; thus, attempt to make the payment period as short as possible while keeping your monthly mortgage payments manageable.

When you go shopping for a mortgage, you should know the language of the mortgage trade:

1. Prepayment privilege. You can prepay the mortgage before the maturity date without penalty. This is something you might do later on if interest rates in the economy fell below what you were actually paying. You would pay the mortgage off by refinancing it at a lower interest charge.

2. Package mortgage. This mortgage covers the cost of all household equipment as well as the house itself. This is something you might try to get if you do not have the cash to buy furniture and you think you can get a lower interest charge through a mortgage company than through other credit sources. (Some finance experts advise against this because you pay interest on the money for the equipment long after you have used it up.)

3. Open end mortgage. This mortgage allows you to borrow more money in the future without rewriting the mortgage. With an open end mortgage you can add on to the house or repair it and have the mortgage company pay these new bills. The mortgage company then charges you a larger monthly payment or increases the life span of your loan.

INSURING YOUR HOME

Types of Insurance Policies

There are basically two types of insurance policies you might buy for a home.

1. Standard fire insurance policy which protects the homeowner against fire and lightning, plus damage from water and smoke caused by the fire and fire department. If you pay a little bit more, the coverage can be "extended" to protect you against damages caused by hail, windstorms, and explosions.

2. Homeowner's policy which provides protection against a number of risks under a single policy, allowing you to save over what you would pay if you bought each policy separately. It covers both the house and its contents. In addition to standard fire policy coverage, liability coverage can also be obtained.

Different Types of Policy Coverage

1. Property coverage includes garage, house, and other private buildings on your lot; personal possessions and property whether at home or while you are traveling or at work; and additional living expenses that would be paid to you if you could not live in your home because of a fire or flood.

2. Liability coverage—there are basically three types: (a) personal liability in case someone is injured on your property or you damage someone else's property and are at fault; (b) medical payments for injury to others who are on your property; and (c) coverage for the property of others that you or a member of your family damages.

Forms of Homeowners' Policies

There are a number of forms of homeowners' policies, each covering more risks than the other. In Exhibit I-3, we show what each is like. As you can see, the **basic form** covers 11 risks, the **broad form** covers 18 risks, and the **comprehensive form** covers those 18 risks and

all other perils except those listed at the bottom of the chart.

Adding a Personal Articles Floater Policy

You may wish to pay a slightly higher premium to insure specific personal articles. This would be done under a personal articles floater addition to your homeowner's policy. You might want to insure specific cameras, musical instruments, works of art, and jewelry in this manner. You will be asked to submit a

list of those things that you wish covered and some affadavit giving their current market value. Note that when you insure under a floater, you have provided all risk insurance and therefore can omit the covered property from your fire and theft policies.

Personal Effects Floater Policy

There is also a personal effects floater policy that you can take out to cover personal items when you are traveling. In most

EXHIBIT I-3   Forms of Homeowners' Policies
Source: Reprinted by permission of Insurance Information Institute

FORMS   **RISKS**

COMPREHENSIVE / BROAD / BASIC

1. Fire or lightning
2. Loss of property removed from premises endangered by fire or other perils
3. Windstorm or hail
4. Explosion
5. Riot or civil commotion

6. Aircraft
7. Vehicles
8. Smoke
9. Vandalism and malicious mischief
10. Theft
11. Breakage of glass constituting a part of the building

12. Falling objects
13. Weight of ice, snow, sleet
14. Collapse of building(s) or any part thereof
15. Sudden and accidental tearing asunder, cracking, burning, or bulging of a steam or hot water heating system or of appliances for heating water
16. Accidental discharge, leakage, or overflow of water or steam from within a

plumbing, heating, or air-conditioning system or domestic appliance

17. Freezing of plumbing, heating, and air-conditioning systems and domestic appliances
18. Sudden accidental injury from artificially generated currents to electrical appliances, devices, fixtures, and wiring (TV and radio tubes not included)

All risks except: flood, earthquake, war, nuclear attack, and others specified in your policy. Check your policy for a complete listing of risks excluded.

cases, a personal effects floater is not called for because your regular homeowner's insurance covers you. Note that a personal effects floater covers only the articles when they are taken off your property; therefore, you need insurance for them when they are on your property. The policy does not cover theft from an unattended automobile unless there is evidence of a forced entry. In general, even when there is evidence of forced entry, the company's liability is limited to 10 percent of the amount of insurance and to not more than $250 for all property in any one loss. You can have this restriction removed from the policy upon payment of an additional premium.

Flood Insurance

You will notice that even a comprehensive homeowner's insurance policy does not cover floods. If you live in an area that may have flooding due to hurricanes and the like, it is advisable to purchase federally subsidized (that is, by all federal taxpayers) flood insurance. You must live in an area designated eligible by the Federal Insurance Administrator of the U.S. Department of Housing and Urban Development. Your insurance agent will be able to tell you if you are.

HOW MUCH INSURANCE SHOULD YOU HAVE?

Suffice it to say here that you should have 80 percent of the total value of the house insured —that is, 80 percent of its replacement value. If you have at least that much coverage, you can collect the full replacement cost, not the depreciated value, of any damaged property (up to the limits of the policy). For example, say your ten-year-old roof is damaged in a fire. It costs you $2,500 to replace it. If you have at least 80 percent coverage on your house, your insurance company must pay you the full amount of the roof damage, whereas if your house is covered for less than 80 percent of replacement, you will get less. Specifically, you will be paid only that portion of the loss equal to the amount of insurance in force divided by 80 percent of replacement cost of the entire house times the loss on the roof. If your house would cost $40,000 to replace and you have only $20,000 of insurance, then on your roof damage of $2,500, you will be paid:

$$\frac{\$20,000}{\$32,000} \times \$2,500 = \$1,563$$

You need not insure your house for the full replacement value for two reasons: (1) the land has a value that would not be destroyed in a fire or flood, and (2) even if the house were totally burned down, the foundation, sidewalks, driveway, and such things would be still standing. Be careful, though: if you are living in a house you bought many years ago, the cost of replacement may be much more than you think. Remember that in the last chapter we discussed the phenomenal increase in construction costs. Take that into account now and make sure that your insurance keeps pace with it. You may want to have an arrangement with your insurance company whereby the value of your insurance is increased 10 percent every year or two to keep pace with construction increases. Avoid being left in the cold if your house burns down.

Accurate Appraisal of Replacement Cost

You may wish, or be required by the lender, to use the services of a professional appraiser in order to get an accurate replacement value of your house. You will have to pay from $50 to $200 to do so if you have someone come out to look it over. You can find appraisers in your yellow pages. You can also fill out a form and pay a lot less if you use the services of companies such as GAB Business Services, Inc., 1101 State Road, Princeton, New Jersey 08540 (telephone 800-621-2306). Write or call for a GAB valurate and return it with a check for $9.95. You will get back an appraisal based on your local labor materials cost. American Appraisal Associates, Inc., of Milwaukee, Wisconsin, provides a similar service but only through certain insurance agents. You can ask your local insurance agent to evaluate the house; or, if you know a local home builder, he or she may be able to help you out. Your banker might also be of help.

PREPAYING INSURANCE AND TAXES

Most mortgage sellers require the mortgagor—that is, you the homeowner—to prepay taxes and insurance as part of your monthly payments. If a savings and loan association is the mortgagee, a special reserve account is set up within the savings and loan association, and home insurance and taxes are paid from it every year. This way the mortgagee does not have to worry about foreclosure on the house because of unpaid taxes or problems if the house burns down and is not insured.[2]

COPING WITH REPAIRS

One way to avoid having to make many repairs is to keep things well maintained, but this, of course, takes your time and money. It is often useful to keep a list of repair people you know to have been honest and to have given you high quality service. Also, if you continuously use the same repair people, they establish a working relationship with you. There may be organizations in your city that, once you have joined one, can simplify your repair problems by reducing information costs. The American Home Owners Association, which was organized in Milwaukee, Wisconsin, in 1969, has spread to at least six other states. If you become a member, you pay between $10 and $20 a year to cover emergency calls for which the first half hour is given without charge. Every-

[2]The special reserve account that you must pay into monthly may not earn interest for you. Rather, the holder of that account uses it in a way that will earn interest for the mortgaging institution.

thing else is paid for at straight time rates—that is, with no overtime pay. The AHA locates what it thinks would be competent repair people in your area. Problems have occurred with similar services in some areas, so you may wish to investigate the services to which you are thinking of subscribing. Information on the American Home Owners Association can be obtained from 5301 West Burleigh Street, Milwaukee, Wisconsin 53210.

Also available is a prepaid repair and maintenance program called Palace Guard, which is a service of the American Home Owners Association. It is similar to a life or casualty protection policy, except that instead of covering you it covers major equipment in your house. It may cover central heating and cooling systems; sheet metal duct work; electrical and plumbing systems; plumbing fixtures; hot water heaters, water softeners; and built-in appliances including oven, range, dishwasher, and garbage disposal. Local divisions of the American Home Owners Association administer the Palace Guard program and can give you full details. Basically, you pay a set fee once a year for this service.

Buying Repair Insurance

An increasing number of used-home buyers purchase warranties or insurance against defects in the home. These contracts protect new owners against such things as defective plumbing and wiring, and sometimes appliance, roofing, and struc-

tural defects. Such warranties have been available to buyers of new homes for quite a number of years; these warranties are issued through builders affiliated with the National Association of Home Builders. Some plans give protection against major structural defects for up to ten years.

For $150 to $300 per year, buyers of used homes can obtain similar coverage. One of the largest warranty providers is American Home Shield Corporation based in Dublin, California. It offers its program through over two thousand agents in California, New Jersey, Florida, and perhaps by the time you read this, in Arizona and Texas. The basic yearly fee is around $200; however, homeowners must pay a $20 fee for each service call. Certified Homes Corporation, based in Columbia, Maryland, offers warranties in 16 major areas, mainly in the northeast. It gives an 18 month contract, but only to homes found in good condition after the inspection. It is estimated that 2 million used homes will be covered by such warranties by the end of this decade. It might be worthwhile for you to check out the availability of such insurance policies in your area.

MAKING THE MOVE

If you are moving from one part of the country to another, you can employ the services of moving consultants. But this will generally be useful only if you are in an upper-income bracket. Otherwise, your time may be worth less than a moving consultant's time.

Although the government regulates movers, you cannot necessarily be certain of a guaranteed move. Some regulations apply to the moving industry, and you should be aware of the most important of them to take advantage of any benefits they might bestow on you:

1. The moving van must come on the promised day. The company can be fined up to $500 if it fails to do so.

2. The price estimates must be based on the moving company's actual physical inspection of whatever you ask it to move.

3. Well in advance of the actual moving day, a mover must give you, the customer, an *Order for Service*, which states the estimated price of the move and the mutually agreed-upon pickup and delivery dates.

4. The shipment must be delivered and all services performed on payment of the estimated amount plus no more than 10 percent additional in the case of an underestimate. Anything you owe them above 110 percent of what they estimated in writing you have 15 working days to pay.

How to Pick a Mover

Picking a mover is a very tricky problem because surveys of people's reactions to different movers show that even within one moving company there is extreme variability in quality of service. The level of complaints seems to be about the same for each of the largest firms: North

American Van, United, Bekins, Allied, and Arrow Mayflower. If you get two or three estimates made of your moving costs, do not be fooled into giving the job to the lowest estimate, because the ICC has made sure that the industry charges about the same price for weight and mileage.

Don't Cut Time Corners

Do not try to postpone your move to the very last minute. Make sure that you have the movers come a few days before you have to vacate your house. Sometimes movers do not come to your old house on time, and that may spell disaster if you are supposed to leave the day the mover has been scheduled to come. You can get by without your furniture for a day or two, but what will you do if you have to stay around after you were supposed to vacate the premises?

Appliances

You must pay extra to have appliances prepared for moving.

It's probably better to call your regular repair services and have them do it. Also have them explain what must be done to put things back into service later on.

Watch Out!

When the movers are loading your belongings, make sure you see a copy of the inventory form and look at what they mark to describe the condition of your furniture. A series of code letters indicate scratched, marred, gouged, cracked, soiled, and so on. If you think the movers' description is exaggerated, make sure it is changed or threaten to call the whole thing off. If the description of damage to your furniture is exaggerated before it leaves, then you will have no recourse for a damage payment if your furniture is damaged in transit. Because a full 25 percent of all moves end in some dispute over damages, this is an important point. The ICC suggests that you personally observe the weighing of the empty truck, its loading, its reweigh-

ing, and its unloading. When your furniture is finally delivered, be there. You should also personally check off the items on your inventory sheet as they are unloaded. Do not sign an inventory sheet, no matter what the driver says, until you've had the time to notice all damage and all loss.

Having your goods moved by a firm that is fully insured and/or bonded does not mean anything. Unless otherwise arranged, any carrier's liability for your goods damaged in transit is limited to 60¢ a pound, thus if a $400 portable color TV weighs 60 pounds and it is completely destroyed, the carrier is only liable up to 60¢ × 60 pounds or $36.00. There are two ways to get extra protection:

1. Do not set a specific value on your goods. The mover's maximum liability becomes $1.25 per pound; thus, a 4,000 pound shipment would have a $5,000 maximum liability. You get full value up to the maximum for anything damaged or lost minus depreciation.

2. Insure the actual dollar value of your goods. This protection costs 50¢ per $100 of value.

Making a Claim

There's a good chance you will want to make a claim for lost, broken, or damaged items. There is generally a claims bureau in most cities, and somebody will be sent out to estimate damage or to take things to be repaired. Note that under a 1972 ICC rule the van line on an interstate move is "absolutely responsible for all acts or omissions" of its agents. If you fail to get satisfaction, call the nearest Interstate Commerce Commission office. If that also fails, write to the Director of the Bureau of Operations, Interstate Commerce Commission, Washington, D.C. 20423. If you think you have been badly abused, you may want to go to small claims court, which we described after Consumer Issue B.

An Alternative

If you have some extra time and some friends to help, and you want to save some money and avoid fights with movers, you can always rent a truck from U-Haul, U-Drive, or various other companies. Remember, though, you must count the time and fatigue costs of this particular moving method. Because the cost of moving yourself is directly related to the income you forego, or the implicit value you put on the leisure time lost in doing the moving, you may find moving yourself the most economical way. People who are students during the school year and do not have summer jobs, for example, have a very low opportunity cost and, therefore, may wish to take advantage of this low opportunity cost by renting a U-Haul. On the other hand, if you were a high-income executive, it would not make sense for you to spend two weeks driving a truck across the United States in order to save moving expenses, for you would give up much more in lost income.

Problems with Self-Moving

If you decide to move yourself, be aware of a number of problems that may occur:

1. You may not have any experience loading a trailer. The weight must be distributed evenly in the vehicle to prevent trailer jackknifing.

2. Be sure to place large, heavy items on the bottom and fill open spaces with small items. If you can, strap down your items.

3. Be careful of back strain. This is a frequent result of self-moving.

4. Be wary of inexperienced helpers, both their abilities and strength.

5. Realize that unless you make sure it's in effect, you will not be insured during the move.

6. Be wary of the emotional and physical stress involved in being your own mover—take it easy.

7. Be sure that you have someone to help you unload at your destination. Paying for casual labor can be expensive—in money and damaged goods.

SUMMARY

1. A general rule of thumb in determining how much housing you can afford is no more than about two times your annual income. Recently, however, financial experts have begun to counsel consumers to be more conservative and not to pay more than 1.5 times the consumer's annual income for a house.

2. In deciding where you want to live, you must look at: (a) the relationship to work, (b) property taxes, (c) schools in the neighborhood, (d) proximity and completeness of shopping, (e) air quality, (f) noise pollution, (g) crime, (h) the general neighborhood, (i) how the area is zoned, and (j) traffic.

3. If you are buying or selling a house, you will probably find the services of a real estate broker helpful. However, remember that those services will cost you.

4. A real estate broker essentially brings together buyers and sellers. He or she is therefore a provider of information.

5. If you are selling a house, try to bargain with potential brokers on the commission they will charge you. You can bargain about when you will pay the commission (because a commission paid over a five-year period is less costly to you than a commission paid immediately upon the sale of the house) and certain other details of the sale. Shop around for a broker, just as you would shop around for anything else.

6. When you are buying a house, shop around for a broker, also. Find one who understands your needs and does not attempt to get you into a house that you do not want or will not be happy with. You can also bargain with brokers when you are buying a house. If, for example, you are ready to make a purchase, you may ask the broker to do such things as buy you a refrigerator and stove if he or she wants you to purchase the house, actually split the commission with you (where that is legal), put a new carpet in, or have the house painted at the expense of the broker.

7. You can let the broker do the bargaining for you if you are unused to that activity.

8. When bargaining on a house, never let the seller know that you are excited about the purchase. In fact, the seller should not learn anything about you at all. That is why it is best to have a broker do your bargaining so that your emotions cannot get involved in the activity and so that you do not "show your hand."

9. It is usually advisable for you to have a building inspection service come out to the home you wish to buy before you make any offer whatsoever. Look in your yellow pages for such services. If you are truly concerned, have more than one inspection service look at the house.

10. When figuring out the cost of a house, remember that you must take into account the closing costs, which can run as high as 3 or 4 percent of the purchase price of the house. This money must be in cash, as must the down payment on that house. Generally, you must purchase some form of title insurance in order to obtain a mortgage. However, if you are in doubt, hire your own lawyer to do the title search.

11. Shop for a mortgage just as you shop for anything else. Seek out the best deal in terms of the down payment required, the annual percentage interest rate charged, and whether or not there is a penalty for early prepayment in case you decide to sell the house after a few years.

12. Make sure that you obtain sufficient insurance on your house so that at least 80 percent of its value is covered. Shop around for housing insurance, making sure you check out each company's policies with respect to how much they will pay you for personal furnishings lost in a fire, what they will pay you for alternative housing if you are forced to leave your home because of a fire, and so on.

13. Moving can be a traumatic experience. You can avoid some of the traumas by taking several steps: plan well in advance, work all of the details out with the potential mover, set your actual moving day for several days before you must leave your house or apartment, take a complete inventory of what you are shipping, check the mover's log to make sure that more defects in your furniture are not recorded than actually exist, and do not expect perfection. You may wish to try some of the smaller movers. Many consumers indicate that they receive better service from other than the top five large moving firms.

QUESTIONS FOR THOUGHT AND DISCUSSION

1. Do you think that a mortgage rate of 8½ percent is high? Why?

2. Why would you want to borrow on a mortgage for 30 years instead of 15 years?

3. Would you prefer to buy a new or a used house? Why?

4. Can you think of any other features of a house you should look at in addition to the ten listed in the text?

5. Do you think real estate brokers charge too much?

6. Would you ever pay more than the asking price for a house?

7. Which type of title insurance do you think is best?

8. Why do you think mortgage companies require you to pre-pay insurance and taxes?

9. Is it always best to repair everything that goes wrong in a house?

THINGS TO DO

1. Call a number of savings and loan associations and find out what their interest rate is on a 20-year, $30,000 mortgage on a $50,000 house. If you find significant differences, ask why.

2. Drive around your town into different residential areas. Try to figure out why one area is more expensive than another.

3. Look in the yellow pages under Real Estate Brokers and see what some of the large ads say. Try to figure out whether it is possible for one broker to do a better job than another.

4. Obtain a typical contract or earnest agreement from a broker in your area. Go over the details with the broker. Find out whether the agreement is more beneficial to the buyer or to the seller. (Actually, it should be most beneficial to the broker.)

5. Get a copy of a typical mortgage agreement from a savings and loan association. Try to read the small print.

SELECTED READINGS

"Filing a Home Insurance Claim? You May Be in for a Shock." *U.S. News*, February 21, 1977, pp. 77–78.

Financing for Home Purchases and Home Improvements: A Guide to Financing Costs and Home Buying Ability. Washington, D.C.: Federal Housing Administration (latest edition).

Harris, Marlys. "Buy Now, Sell Now: The Old-House-to-New-House Game." *Money* 6 (April 1977).

Home-Buyer's Checklist. National Homebuyers and Homeowners Association, 1225 19th Street, N.W., Washington, D.C. 20036 (latest edition).

"Homeowners vs. Lenders: A Question of Interest." *Consumer Reports*, March 1973.

"How's HOW Now?" *Consumer News*, March 1, 1976, p. 2.

"How to Avoid the Ten Biggest Home-Buying Traps." *Consumer Bulletin*, August 1969.

"How to Keep Down the Cost of Buying a Home." *U.S. News*, March 21, 1977, pp. 39-42.

"Learn to Spot What's Wrong with a House." *Changing Times*, February 1970.

"The Legal Side of Owning a House." *Changing Times*, July 1973.

Mager, Bryon J. *How to Buy a House.* New York: Lyle Stuart, 1965.

Questions and Answers on Guaranteed and Direct Loans for Veterans. Washington, D.C.: Veterans Administration, 19.

"Warranties Playing Increasing Role in House Sales." *Consumer Newsweek* 5 (May 10, 1976).

Watkins, Arthur M. *How Much House Can You Afford?* New York Life Insurance Company, Box 10, Madison Square Station, New York, New York 10010.

"Yes, You Can Sell Your House Yourself." *Changing Times*, March 1977, pp. 19-22.

Renting a Place to Live

GLOSSARY OF TERMS

Residence Contents Broad Form

This is a renter's insurance policy that covers possessions against 18 risks. It includes additional living expenses and liability coverage in case someone is injured in your apartment or house that you are renting.

If you have decided that you wish to rent, you are faced with at least four problems:

1. Obtaining information on rental units available.

2. Making sure you get the right rental unit for you.

3. Making sure the contract or lease is appropriate.

4. Knowing what to do when you have valid complaints after you have rented the housing unit.

INFORMATION ABOUT RENTAL UNITS

There are basically four ways that you can obtain information about potential rental units. They are:

1. Ads in the local newspapers.

2. Listing agencies.

3. "For Rent" signs in front of apartment buildings and homes.

4. Friends and acquaintances.

The only source of information that people are not always familiar with concerns rental information agencies that go by the name of Rentex, Apartment Hunt, and so on. Basically, you pay a fee—$20, $30, or $50—which usually gives you the right to an unlimited number of searches through the files of the agency. In principle, these files are updated and give you information that will save you time and keep you from fruitless inspections of apartments that are not suitable for you. For example, if you definitely want to keep a pet in your apartment, many vacant rental units can be eliminated without even going there because they do not allow pets on the premises. If you have small children, this also may be a factor to consider; many apartments do not allow children at all.

Consumers' experiences with rental listing agencies are mixed. Some report that the listings are up-to-date and accurate. Others contend that the listings were so inaccurate that they wasted more time than they would have had they merely called ads in the newspaper.

A number of rental listing agencies practice a form of "bait and switch." They put a listing in the classified ad sections of local newspapers for an extremely advantageous rental unit. When you call the agency, you are told that you must pay an advance fee for an "exclusive" list of available houses and apartments. When you ask for the address of the "too good to be true" rental unit listed in the newspaper, you are told that that one has been rented "but we have lots of other listings." Unlike real estate brokers who receive a commission *after* they have found you a place to live, rental listing agencies do not refund their fees if you do not find a place to rent through their listings. It is not surprising that the New York Better Business Bureau issued a press release a few years ago indicating that "all advance fee rental agencies [are] not in the public interest." Some states have outlawed them.

MAKING THE RIGHT CHOICE

When looking for a rental unit, it is often helpful to carry a checklist with you to make comparisons. In that way, you will not sign a lease on an apartment or house only to discover that you had forgotten to inquire about a very essential attribute of the rental unit that now you find out doesn't exist. Exhibit J-1 is just a partial checklist. You can make up your own and add important factors that you desire.

EXHIBIT J-1	Apartment A	Apartment B	Apartment C	Apartment D
Monthly rent (including all expenses that you have to pay directly, such as utilities, recreational fees, parking fees, etc.)				
Size of security or cleaning deposit				
Are pets allowed?				
Is there a manager or superintendent on the premises at all times?				
Garbage disposal facilities?				
Laundry equipment available on the premises?				
Is the laundry room safe?				
When can the laundry room be used?				
Is there a lobby?				
Is there a doorman?				
Will you have direct access to your unit?				
If there is an elevator, what is its condition?				
Is the apartment close to public transportation if you need it?				
Is it close to food stores?				
Entertainment?				
Other shopping?				
Are there sufficient electrical outlets?				
Are carpets and drapes included?				
Is there enough closet space?				
Are there safe and clearly marked fire exits?				
Are the tenants around you the ones you want to live near (children, singles, retired, etc.)?				

THE THORNY PROBLEM OF SECURITY DEPOSITS

It is virtually impossible these days to rent any type of housing unit without leaving a "refundable" security (cleaning or breakage) deposit, usually equal to one month's rent. The deposit is supposed to be returned to you if you leave the apartment in an "appropriate" condition. Landlords argue that they need security deposits because they find damage by carelessness in many cases.

Not even the majority of states have laws regulating security deposits. You can look at deposits in either of two ways: (1) you are never going to get it back; thus divide the number of months you are going to live in the rental unit into the security deposit to come up with the "surcharge" you are actually paying per month. Or, (2) you can attempt from the beginning to have a strong case in favor of getting the money back. To do that, consider the following:

1. Go through the apartment with the manager or owner the day you move in, marking down every single indication of wear and tear or damage that already exists. Make sure you have a copy of that set of notations; sign it yourself and have the landlord who is with you sign it. Better yet, have it notarized. In some cases, it might be better to live in the apartment a few days to find out in more detail what doesn't work. This is particularly true if you have rented a furnished apartment or house.

2. Retain copies of all bills for improvements, repairs, or cleaning that you had done in order to have evidence that you carefully maintained the unit.

3. Take fairly detailed snapshots showing the condition of the apartment when you moved in and when you leave. Have them developed and provided by a company that puts the date on the picture.

4. If the building you live in is sold, obtain a letter from the former owner explaining who is keeping the security deposit money.

5. Find out what your local regulations are. If they require that the apartment be left "broom cleaned," you sweep up the apartment and then show the job to the superintendent or the manager.

6. If you do all of the above, you will be ready to go to court if your deposit is not refunded. When you are clearly prepared, most landlords tend to return your security deposit.

MAKING SURE THE LEASE IS OKAY

Most standard form leases seem to put everything in favor of the landlord (who usually provides it!). There are a number of clauses that you may want to attempt to cross out.

Clauses to Avoid

Confession of judgment. If your lease has this provision, your landlord's lawyer has the legal right to go to court and plead guilty for you in the event that the landlord or landlady thinks his or her rights have been violated—that is, that the property has been damaged or the terms of the lease have not been lived up to. If you sign a lease that has a confession of judgment provision, you are admitting guilt before committing any act. Such a clause is, in fact, illegal in some states.

Waiver of tort liability. If this provision is in your lease, you have given up in advance the right to sue the landlord if in fact you suffer injury or damage because of your landlord's negligence.

Arbitrary clauses. These are any arbitrary clauses such as those that give the landlord the ability to cancel the lease because he is "dissatisfied" with your behavior. Some leases include clauses that

1. Forbid immoral behavior.

2. Forbid hanging pictures on the wall.

3. Forbid you to have overnight guests (this is usually done by way of requiring that the apartment can be occupied only by the tenant and members of the tenant's immediate family).

4. Forbid you to assign or sublease.

5. Allow the landlord to cancel the lease and hold you liable for rent for the balance of the lease if you are one day late.

6. Allow the landlord to enter your apartment when you are not there (except in case of emergency, of course).

7. Make you liable for all repairs.

8. Make you obey rules that have not yet been written.

9. State that you agree that the premises are "fine" as they are.

Clauses to Add to Your Lease

1. If the person renting the unit to you says that it comes with dishwasher, disposal unit, and air conditioner, make the lease specifically list them.

2. If you have been promised the use of a recreation room, a gymnasium, a parking lot, or a swimming pool, make sure that the lease says so specifically. Also, have it indicate whether or not you must pay extra for the use of those facilities.

3. If the landlord has promised to have the apartment painted, have this indicated in the lease. If you wish to be able to choose the color, also have that in the lease.

4. In certain cases, you may be able to negotiate a right to premature cancellation if you are transferred to another job. Usually, however, you must negotiate the amount you pay the landlord for exercising this privilege. Hopefully, it will be less than the security deposit.

5. If you wish to have any fixtures, shelves, furnishings, etc., installed by you become your property when you leave the premises, specify this in the lease.

What to Do When You Have Trouble with Your Landlord

If you believe that you have been unfairly treated by your landlord or landlady, there are sev-eral steps that you can take. If you are acting alone in your complaint, you can do the following:

1. Explicity indicate what your grievance is, such as the day-time temperature in your apartment falling to 55°, a stopped-up sewage system, a continuously leaking toilet, a refrigerator whose freezing compartment doesn't work, and so on.

2. Make a number of copies of the complaint list. Mail one to the manager or owner, one to the housing inspector (if one comes to your complex), and one for yourself. If there is an organized tenants group in your area, send one to it. You can find out if there is by writing the National Tenants Organization, 425 Thirteenth Street N.W., Washington, D.C. 20005.

3. Whenever you contact the agency that administers the housing code in your area, request a visit from a housing inspector who will certify the validity of your complaint.

Withholding Rent

If the complaints you have are serious enough, you may in some states have the legal right to withhold part or all of your rent. Approximately half the states allow the tenant to deduct repairs from the rent; they also provide for not paying any rent when the dwelling is "unlivable." Many states also have procedures for rent strikes that can be done legally. Note that if you repair and deduct from your rent the cost of repairs, there may be a limit to how much money can be used. In many states, the limit is one-half a month's rent or $100, whichever is greater. In Massachusetts, the limit is two month's rent; in New Jersey, there is no fixed maximum.

A Final Alternative

Even before considering withholding rent, you might consider a more meaningful alternative—looking for another apartment where you won't have similar problems. It is a rare situation indeed where there are virtually no other rental units available in your area for you to choose among. When one manufacturer's product does not satisfy you, you often turn to a competitor. The same principle could be applied to rental units.

MAKING SURE YOU HAVE INSURANCE

Homeowners are not the only ones who can get an insurance policy to cover loss through fire, theft, and the like. While it is true that your landlord or owner of your building is liable for damage to the building and for injuries occurring in common areas such as the lobby or hallway, you are responsible for protecting the inside of your dwelling, as well as being liable for accidents that occur there. Renters' insurance is called **residence contents broad form**. It is a homeowner's policy that covers personal possessions against the 18 risks described in the previous consumer issue. It includes additional living expenses and liability coverage.

Before you look for a rental

policy, make a detailed inventory of your possessions. Decide on the coverage you want, and then do some comparison shopping.

Note that household possessions are usually insured for half their value. Everything, including linens and plants, should be listed in your inventory. The inventory list must be kept in a safe place away from the dwelling, and a copy can be given to your insurance agent.

A general policy for, say, $5,000 of property insurance and $50,000 of liability coverage will probably run less than $100 a year, depending on where you live.

If you are in a high crime area and cannot find commercially available insurance, then you can apply through the Federal Crime Insurance Program and the Fair Access to Insurance Requirements (FAIR) Plan. The former covers loss by burglary; the latter covers fire, vandalism, and windstorms. Neither plan gives you liability coverage. Ask a commercial insurance agent in your area where you can obtain information on policies available through these programs or write HUD, Washington, D.C., for an informative booklet.

SUMMARY

1. Information about rental units can be obtained from newspaper ads, listing agencies, "for rent" signs on apartment buildings, and friends and acquaintances.

2. When comparing apartments, a fairly sophisticated checklist can be used to make a more objective survey.

3. If you desire to obtain your security (cleaning or breakage) deposit back when you vacate a rented unit, you must take certain precautions such as going through the unit with a manager or landlord the day you move in and checking off all damage that has already occurred. You may also want to retain copies of bills for improvement repairs and cleaning and take snapshots of the condition of the apartment when you moved into it.

4. When signing a standard form lease, avoid confession of judgment and waiver of tort liability and all arbitrary clauses.

5. Grievances with managers or owners can be handled through a housing agency in your city or an organized tenants' association.

6. Insurance can be purchased through a residence contents broad form policy.

QUESTIONS FOR THOUGHT AND DISCUSSION

1. Do you think that rental listing agencies should be made illegal?

2. When would it be appropriate to completely ignore using a checklist to make comparisons among potential rental units that you are looking at?

3. Why do you think certain apartment owners consistently get away with keeping security deposits?

4. Do you think a confession of judgment clause should always be made illegal?

THINGS TO DO

1. Obtain a standard form lease contract. Find out how many arbitrary clauses are inserted. Is there a confession of judgment and a waiver of tort liability?

2. Find out if there is a tenants' organization in your neighborhood by writing the National Tenants' Organization, 425 Thirteen Street N.W., Washington, D.C. 20005.

3. Obtain literature from your local organization (if it exists). Is that organization attacking some of the problems mentioned in this consumer Issue?

SELECTED READINGS

"How to Read a Lease." Consumer Reports, October 1974, pp. 707–711.
"Moving to an Apartment: What to Look for; What to Avoid." Bibliography in Retirement Living, November 1976, pp. 29–32.
"Problem with Noise in an Apartment." Excerpt from Quieting: A Practical Guide to Noise Control. Consumers' Research Magazine, February 1977, p. 25.
"Tenant Protection: Paths to Reform." Consumer Reports, January 1975, pp. 56–59.

GLOSSARY OF TERMS

Consumer Durable Goods

Goods used by consumers that have a lifetime that exceeds one year, for example, washers, dryers, refrigerators, stereos.

Full Warranty

A warranty under which the consumer merely informs the warrantor that the product is defective or doesn't work right. Then the warrantor must fix the product within a reasonable amount of time without charge.

Limited Warranty

Other than full warranty.

The Appliance Society

CHAPTER PREVIEW

☐ What is a consumer durable?
☐ How does one decide when to buy an appliance?
☐ Should appliances be bought on credit?
☐ What types of warranties are there?

13 Buying a house is only one aspect of providing for services in the home. The other aspect is the equipment that must be purchased, used, taken care of, and replaced. We are talking about an investment in **consumer durable goods**, where such goods are defined as items that have a lifetime of several years or more. These include washers, dryers, television sets, stereos, freezers, refrigerators, stoves, vacuum cleaners, sewing machines, dishwashers, trash compactors, water softening equipment, water heaters, and floor polishers. The list goes on and on. In the following chapter, we will treat another consumer durable—the automobile—and in Chapter 19 we will look at recreational equipment, such as campers, trailers, and boats. All such consumer durable goods have these characteristics:

1. They yield a service flow over their useful lifetime.
2. The purchase price does not represent the price that is actually paid for one year's service flow. The purchase price is greater.
3. Their purchase is often financed on credit.
4. They wear out or depreciate.
5. They must be cared for and repaired.
6. They are often replaced when no longer usable.
7. They may be covered by some form of property insurance.

THE SAVING ASPECT OF BUYING EQUIPMENT

We pointed out above that the purchase price of a consumer durable good, such as a washing machine, exceeds the actual price that the consumer pays for one year's service flow, or one year's amount of services yielded from that item. For example, if the washing machine costs $400, but is expected to last ten years, then in the most simplified case the service flow per year costs approximately $40. What if the individual paid cash for the washing machine? That would mean that in fact the individual was consuming only $40 out of the original $400 and saving the rest. It may sound funny to think in terms of a purchase of a washing machine being part consumption and part saving but, in fact, it is. Consider that there is an implicit income stream equal to the flow of services to be received from the washing machine during each of the following nine years. We value it at approximately $40 a year, so after the expenditure of $400 on the machine, there is $360 left over as saving that will be consumed at the rate of $40 per year for nine more years.

Another way of looking at it is by comparing what it would cost to have clothes laundered outside the home or what it would cost in change every time the homemaker went to a laundromat and essentially rented the services of the laundromat's washing machine. If it would cost approximately $40 a year in both extra time and expenses to take the laundry to a laundromat throughout the year, then, in fact, owning a washing machine is actually "saving" $40 a year (disregarding repair costs, etc.).

Thus, when making spending decisions on consumer durable goods, it is important to keep straight how much of that spending is actual consumption for that year and how much is actual saving for future years. This is true for houses, washing machines, cars, and any other consumer durable good. An expenditure of

$5,000 on new furniture is not all pure consumption. A large percentage of that is saving in the sense that a flow of services from that new furniture will be available for use by the family for many years to come.

DECIDING ON BUYING EQUIPMENT

A consumer durable good is in many senses just like a machine that a business buys. Businesses are able to reach decisions on the advisability, that is, the profitability of investing in different types of business equipment. We can use some similar analysis in attempting to determine whether or not a new piece of consumer equipment should be purchased. That is, when and how much should you invest in new furniture, a new washing machine, a new refrigerator, or a new dryer?

The way we do this is by looking at the costs and the benefits of the purchase of a consumer durable item. We must, therefore, look at first the cost side and then the benefit side. Let's think in terms of all costs and all benefits being expressed in dollars per year. Consider a hypothetical example in which a couple is debating the advisability of purchasing a freezer in order to store food purchased on sale in larger quantities for a longer period of time.

THE COSTS SIDE OF THE PICTURE

The costs side of any durable good will, at a minimum, include: depreciation, operating costs, repairs, and interest.

1. **Depreciation.** Let's take a simple example in which the freezer has a ten-year life period, at the end of which it has a zero value and must be scrapped. Its full purchase price is $500. The average annual depreciation will be $50 a year. Actually, this is an understatement of the amount of depreciation in the first year and an overstatement of what it is in the latter years of the useful life of the freezer. It would be virtually impossible to sell it at the end of one year for $460. Just as with automobiles (discussed in Chapter 14), equipment in the home depreciates more the first year than in any other year during its ownership. We'll ignore that fact for the moment.

2. **Operating costs.** Most durable goods, and particularly a freezer, will use some form of energy. In this case it will be electricity. Many appliances indicate the amount of electricity they use, and you can estimate what that will cost you per year. For simplicity, let's assume that this will be $30 per year.

3. **Repairs.** Although a freezer is relatively free from repairs, it will have to be serviced occasionally over the ten-year period. You might even buy a service contract that would explicitly require a payment of so much per year in exchange for complete coverage of all replacement of parts and labor. Let's say that that would cost on average $20 per year (either for directly paid repairs or a service contract).

4. **Interest.** If the $500 for the freezer has to be borrowed, then an explicit interest payment must be made. On the other hand, if the consumer has $500 in his or her savings account and withdraws it, he or she is paying an *implicit* interest rate equal to the interest foregone on that $500. For simplicity, let's say that the $500 is in a bank account yielding 6 percent per year. Interest of 6 percent times $500 equals $30 a year in lost interest (ignoring compounding).

5. **Total costs.** We find then the total cost on average per year of service from the freezer.

Depreciation	$ 50
Operating costs	30
Repairs	20
Interest	30
TOTAL	$130

Now we must turn to the benefit side.

BENEFITS

The benefits from having a freezer will include, but are not limited to, reduction in food bills, convenience, reduced food spoilage, and less time and gas spent on shopping trips.

1. **Reduction in food bills.** Depending on the size of the freezer, the family who owns it can take advantage of sales of meat, frozen fruit juices, frozen vegetables, ice cream, fish and poultry, and a few other items that can be frozen and stored. Also, the freezer allows the family to grow large quantities of food at home and put it "under wraps" for a long time. Finally, some foods can be bought in bulk at reduced per unit prices, for example, a side of beef. Let's assume that over a one-year period, this saves the family $95.

2. **Convenience.** It is certainly more convenient to be able to pop into the laundry room or to the garage and remove a few steaks for dinner rather than having to go to the market. It is difficult to put a dollar figure on the value of this convenience, but if a person values such convenience very highly, then this will be an important benefit factor.

3. **Less time and gas spent on shopping trips.** If a person can spend less time going shopping by doing it less often because of the freezer, then we can place a value on that person's saved time.[1] This is the opportunity cost that we talked about in consumer Issue C. Again, it is difficult to talk in terms of what this opportunity cost is without knowing specifically the person's alternatives and the value that that person places on them. However, we can get a monetary handle on the reduction in gas costs and automobile expenses in general from going shopping by looking at the price of an average trip to the grocery store. Let's assume that the total savings in opportunity costs and reduced automobile expenses is $30 a year.

4. **Other benefits.** These benefits will include, as mentioned above, less spoilage of food and the like.

5. **Total benefits.** We can add up the total benefits as follows.

Reduced food bill	$ 95
Convenience	?
Reduced time and automobile expenses	30
Other	?
TOTAL	$125 + ? = ?

---

[1]We call this complementary resource saving, a topic we discussed on page 222.

If those items for which we entered a question mark had a combined value of more than $5, we would have to say that the benefits outweighed the costs for this particular durable good.

THE QUESTION OF BUYING ON CREDIT

When we considered one of the costs of buying a consumer durable good, we mentioned that many are purchased on time through the credit market. What should the wise consumer do when deciding upon how to finance the purchase of a new washer or dryer or freezer? That is basically a question that we answered in Chapter 9 and consumer Issue F. The *reason* you are borrowing money has little to do with whether or not you *should* borrow it. What is important is that you maintain a safe debt load. Just because you are able to obtain relatively easy financing for a new washer or a new dryer does not automatically mean that you should buy it on credit. If doing so will put you over your estimated safe debt load, then you should definitely not buy on credit. If that means that at that particular time you cannot afford a new washer or new dryer, then you will have to make do with what you have. That may mean going to a laundromat, but it will also mean staying out of financial difficulties and having greater peace of mind.

It is really not correct to say that paying cash is the least expensive method of payment because you pay no finance charges. When you purchase a consumer durable good on credit, you are buying two separate items. One is the durable good, such as the washer or dryer; the other is the use of someone else's money for a specified period of time. In both cases a cost is involved. In the latter, it is interest; and in the former, it is the purchase price or the annual average price per year of useful life of the equipment. As in all cases when purchasing credit, you must use the same shopping techniques as you would use to buy anything. We have covered these techniques already in Chapter 9 and consumer Issue F.

COPING WITH FAULTY EQUIPMENT

One major aspect of owning consumer durables is that some times they may be defective, needing repair or replacement. Of course, we are all used to buying products for which there is a statement attached attesting to a "money back guarantee" or "full satisfaction guaranteed." Such guarantees are often not worth much more than the paper on which they were printed. Warranties on equipment have traditionally been varied in scope and applicability. Consumers often have not known what was really being guaranteed and what was not. According to the President's Task Force report on appliance warranties and service:

> The majority of the major appliance warranties currently in use contain exceptions and exclusions which are unfair to the purchaser and which are unnecessary from the standpoint of protecting the manufacturer from unjustified claims or excessive liability.

The Federal Trade Commission early in this decade observed that automobile warranties given by car manufacturers and dealers were not "adequate." Even a survey by an appliance-industry organization, the *Major Appliance Consumer Action Panel* (MACAP), revealed that many warranties did not state the name and address of the warrantor, did not mention the product or part covered, did not indicate how long the warranty was good for, did not indicate what the warrantor would actually do and who would pay for it, and did present the coverage in "legalese" that would be difficult for the average consumer to understand.

THE NEW WARRANTY ACT

Much of this has been changed by recent legislation. The Magnuson–Moss Warranty–Federal Trade Commission Improvement Act of 1975 closes many of the loopholes that manufacturers had included in their warranties. The Act does not require that a manufacturer provide a written warranty or a guarantee, but if a warranty is offered, it has to comply with certain legal provisions. They are as follows:

1. Any warranty on a product that costs $15 or more must include a simple, complete, and conspicuous statement of the following: name and address of warrantor, what is covered and for how much, a step-by-step procedure for placing warranty claims, how disputes between the parties will be settled, and the warranty's duration. This must be available to the consumer as pre-purchase information.
2. The new law also insists that manufacturers cannot require as a condition of warranty that the buyer of the product use it only in connection with other products or services that are identified by brand or corporate name. In other words, the maker of a flashlight cannot require that the purchaser use only Duracell batteries in that flashlight for the warranty to be effective.

FULL VERSUS LIMITED WARRANTIES

If a warranty meets minimum federal standards, it can be designated a **full warranty.** If it doesn't, it must be designated explicitly as a **limited warranty.** Under a full warranty, the consumer merely informs the warrantor that the product is defective, does not work properly, or doesn't conform to the written warranty. The warrantor must then fix the product within a reasonable amount of time and without any charge whatsoever. In fact, in order to obtain the designation "full warranty," the warrantor must pay the consumer for all incidental expenses if there are unreasonable delays or other problems in getting the warranty honored.

Further, the Federal Trade Commission now has the power to set a limit to the number of unsuccessful repair attempts possible under a full warranty. If after a reasonable number of repairs the product is still defective, the customer can choose between a refund or a replacement. The replacement must be made free of charge. If the refund option is chosen, the warrantor can deduct an amount for "reasonable depreciation based on actual use."

Full warranties apply to both initial purchasers and those who buy the product secondhand during the warranty period.

SETTLING DISPUTES

Under the new law, consumers who are unsatisfied with what the warrantor has done for them must try an informal settlement procedure first. Then, if still dissatisfied, the consumer may sue and is entitled to recovery of purchase costs, damages, and attorney's fees if the suit is won.

If there are a large number of consumers who all feel that they have been victimized by fraudulent warranty, they may engage in a federal class action suit.

The requirements for such a suit are that at least one hundred consumers with a minimum claim of $25 each be involved. The total amount in controversy must be at least $50,000.

THE COST SIDE OF IMPROVED WARRANTIES

Usually, something good doesn't come about free of charge. The beneficial aspects of improved warranties and expanded product liability mean that aggrieved consumers will be better off. However, at least part of these benefits will be paid for by consumers as a group. Consider just the product liability side of the question.

Manufacturers are now liable for many injuries that consumers suffer when using products that they were not liable for a number of years ago. Injured consumers can now collect for pain and suffering and the like, if it is due to a faulty product; this is true even in some cases where the consumer was using the product in an inappropriate manner. Manufacturers now are faced with an increasing number of liability suits. From 1970 to 1977 the number of product liability claims jumped almost 45 percent, according to Insurance Services Office, a national insurance rating and advisory organization. The average loss per claim in the United States has jumped 250 percent in that same time period.

Manufacturers have attempted to protect themselves from such increased claims by increasing the amount of liability insurance that they purchase. Such insurance policies protect manufacturers from damage claims filed by users of the manufacturer's product. But, as liability claims have increased in both number and size, so, too, have the insurance costs paid for by such manufacturers. The average member of the National Machine Tool Builders Association paid $71,000 for product liability in 1976, as opposed to $10,000 in 1970. It is clear that these increased costs that manufacturers must sustain are and will continue to be passed on to the consuming public. That means that the prices of the equipment that you buy will be higher because of your ability to get larger awards if you are injured when using the product. Moreover, manufacturers will be more inclined to provide safer and higher quality products in order to avoid more costly lawsuits because of someone being injured by a defective product. But, that means that equipment will, therefore, have a higher price tag because of the expenses involved in making that equipment safer and of higher quality. We can surmise that the consumer will be faced with a smaller array of qualities to choose from in the equipment market. Lower quality, less safe products will gradually disappear. For many consumers, such a change is beneficial. They prefer to pay a higher price for a safer product and not have to worry about avoiding less safe products. Low-income persons, however, may not feel they can afford the more expensive item.

TWO SYSTEMS OF PRODUCT LIABILITY —A PROPOSAL

There are consumers who do not think that they are getting a fair deal because of increased product liability. They say that they do not want to pay the higher price for the higher quality product, but would prefer to have the lower quality product and have more income to spend on other items. One possible way to satisfy both those who want safer products and those who do not is to allow manufacturers to set up two types of product liability systems. The first type would basically be a no-fault system in which no matter what happened, the consumer who purchased the product would be fully reimbursed for pain, suffering, lost income, inconvenience, and the like due to the use of the manufacturer's product. This would be similar to a full warranty. The consumer would have to pay extra for this full liability aspect of the product. The product would also be offered with no liability or very little. In other words, it would be extremely difficult for the consumer to sue the manufacturer if that consumer opted for this liability system. However, those consumers would not have to pay the higher price. They could buy the product at a "bargain" knowing full well that they could not sue very easily if they suffered injury using the product.

Is such a system workable? That we do not know. What we can say is that in such a system consumers could be given the choice of either paying or not paying for full product liability. Today, if current trends continue in the courts, all consumers will be required to pay the higher price of full product liability even if they don't want to.

SUMMARY

1. Consumers purchase consumer durables that yield a service flow over a lifetime, are often financed on credit, wear out, and must be cared for and replaced.
2. The purchase of a consumer durable involves part consumption and part saving because the durable by definition does not wear out immediately. In order to make rational decisions on buying equipment, cost-benefit analysis must be undertaken.
3. Costs of a durable good include, at a minimum, depreciation, operating costs, repairs, and interest.
4. Whether or not credit should be used to purchase a durable good is basically a question of whether a safe debt load has been reached.
5. Legislation passed in 1975 tightened the definition of warranty that manufacturers can use. Improved warranties, however, will lead to higher priced goods and perhaps a reduced quality array.

QUESTIONS FOR THOUGHT AND DISCUSSION

1. Why is the purchase of a stereo a form of saving?
2. Is there any special reason that individuals associate buying consumer durable goods with buying on credit?
3. Why must we consider interest if we purchase a consumer durable with cash?
4. Do you think it is possible for manufacturers to offer better warranties without raising the price of the product?

THINGS TO DO

1. Look at the warranties of any consumer products that you have recently purchased or are about to purchase. Do any of them give full warranties? If they are limited warranties, under what conditions can you have the product repaired or replaced? Calculate the amount of saving that went into the purchase of a durable good that you now own. (Hint: Figure out how many years it will last.)

SELECTED READINGS

"Automatic Washers and Dryers." Changing Times, April 1977, pp. 16–18.

Nader, R. "Ralph Nader Reports: Magnuson–Moss Warranty Act." Ladies Home Journal, October 1976, p. 66.

Perham, J. C. "Dilemma in Product Liability." Duns Review, January 1977, pp. 48–50.

"Warranty Regulations Give Consumer Rights. . . ." Consumer News, January 15, 1976, pp. 2–3.

Buying and Servicing Your Consumer Durables

Every household must constantly make decisions about buying, repairing, and replacing consumer durable items. A college student may merely rent most items, along with an apartment or a dormitory room. That is to say, basic household furnishings are paid for in the monthly or school year payment for rent. A single person just out of college or a young couple starting a household together will have a large number of purchase decisions to make, particularly when they move into their first house.

PLANNING IS IMPORTANT

Different consumer durables last for different periods of time. They must therefore be replaced at different periods of time. For example, the average replacement age of a washing machine is 10 years; a dryer, 14 years; ranges, freezers, and refrigerators, 15 years. These figures will change depending roughly on how well the item is taken care of, its initial quality, and the frequency of use. For example, a washing machine will last longer in a family where there are no children because it will not be used as often.

Given that major appliances have a limited life, one must plan for potential future use, not just what is needed for the next year or so. For example, a couple setting up a household who plan to have more children than they currently have may consider purchasing larger capacity refrigerators and ranges in anticipation of having more mouths to feed in a few years. The same would be true for a washing machine. It may be more expensive to buy a small clothes washer now and have to replace it with a larger capacity one three years from now when there is another child in the family.

Operating Costs

When making plans for the purchase and use of major equipment items, operating costs must also be considered. Such costs can be estimated for the near future, but not for the distant future because of the rapidly changing energy scene. At the end of this issue, we give some tips on how to save energy costs. Right now, let us consider whether you should choose to have gas or electric appliances. This problem will not be faced by those individuals who do not have the choice—many areas in the United States do not offer natural gas to area residents. Liquid propane that is stored in large cylinders can be used as a substitute. (It is delivered directly to the house.) To make a rational calculation in choosing between gas and electric major appliances, one must consider the following factors:

1. Relative cost of gas and electricity in your specific area.

2. The difference in the initial cost of the appliance, depending on whether it is for gas or electric energy sources.

3. The availability of the alternative energy sources in your area in the future.

4. Comparative costs of installing either type of equipment.

5. Your preferences.

Servicing Costs

In making a spending plan for durable goods, you must also consider what servicing costs will be. This can be easily done in the case of major appliances that have specific full warranties for one, two, or three years. It can also be easily calculated if you decide to purchase a service contract each year after the full warranty has terminated.

Filling out the spending plan. Table K-1 presents a possible spending plan sheet for you to fill out. Some people like to plan one year ahead; others, two; and others, three. The planning period really is a function of how rapidly you believe your economic situation is going to

Table K-1   Consumer Durable Spending Plan for the Period _____ to _____

PURCHASES OF CONSUMER DURABLES	ESTIMATED COSTS	DATE OF ANTICIPATED PURCHASES	AMOUNT OF MONEY TO ACCUMULATE EACH PLANNING PERIOD
Washer			
Dryer			
Refrigerator			
Freezer			
Range			
Oven			
Dishwasher			
Trash Compactor			
Vacuum Cleaner			
Carpets (list each room separately)			
Furniture (list each room separately)			
Blender			
Toaster			
TV			
Stereo			
Other Consumer Durables			

COST OF OPERATION AND SERVICING	ESTIMATED COST	ESTIMATED FREQUENCY	AMOUNT OF MONEY TO ACCUMULATE EACH PLANNING PERIOD
Washer			
Dryer			
Other			

Total amount of money available to spend for purchase and servicing of consumer durables during planning period: _____

change. The faster you think it will change, the shorter your planning period should be.

If the total cost of the household equipment that you plan to buy or replace during the planning period exceeds the amount of money that you anticipate you will have available, then obviously you must change your plans. You can postpone or eliminate purchases; you can also look for substitutes. If you cannot "afford" a new washing machine or buy one when you start a new household, then you can seek the services of laundromats. If you desire a larger capacity refrigerator, but cannot "afford" one, the substitute you will use will be your time, effort, and the use of your car in going to the store more often.

BUYING TIPS

Although it would be difficult in a few pages to present all of the different buying principles that relate specifically to each major and minor appliance that you might buy—as well as giving characteristics of different types of rugs, furniture, and bedding—we can present a few general principles that might help you in making decisions on consumer durables.

1. Before you begin checking various stores, check consumer information publications, such as *Consumer Reports* or *Consumers' Research Magazine*. Also ask your friends about their experiences with various dealers and appliance brands.

2. Do comparison shopping at all times.

3. Attempt to compare prices based on a constant quality unit of the consumer durable. In other words, take into account the service offered by different dealers, the convenience of their locations and so on when comparing prices.

4. Read and understand all contracts before signing. Know what your obligations are.

5. Do not "overspend" your time in comparison shopping. Checking two or three reliable dealers may be sufficient; any more time spent may not yield a sufficient enough potential saving.

6. Check guarantees and warranties before purchasing the item. Make sure you understand what they mean. Any points that are not clear should be clarified by the seller (in writing preferably).

7. Use a shopping list and keep it practical. Include all relevant information that is necessary when making a choice on the consumer durable you are buying. For example, if you are going to look for a carpet, bring along room size and a sample of the paint and fabrics in the room to coordinate the carpet color. Or, ask the store owner if you can take some samples with you to see how they look in your home.

8. Consider how the item will be used before you make your choice. Don't spend money, for example, on a highly durable carpet that will be in a room used only occasionally.

9. Consider which features of the durable good are most im-

portant to you. If you truly dislike cleaning an oven, then a self-cleaning one is important, even though its operating costs may be quite high.

10. Remember that quality and price often, but not always, go hand in hand. Thus, you may seek out lower quality durable goods if the item is necessary and you do not think you can afford the higher quality, or if the item is for temporary or limited use.

SHOPPING FOR SAFETY

Safety may be one of the most important aspects of any product you buy; thus, it is important for you to consider the safety features of any possible consumer durables on your shopping list. In Table K-2 you can check off the safety features that are available for the items you wish to buy.

SERVICING YOUR CONSUMER DURABLES

Virtually all consumer durable goods require some type of servicing and care throughout their useful life. In fact, homeowners can attest that the more appliances there are in the household, the more time and money must be spent in having repairs done.

The Pros and Cons of a Service Contract

Whenever a new appliance is purchased—particularly a washer, dryer, freezer, refrigerator, and, to a lesser extent, stereo equipment—it is possible to purchase a service contract that

Table K-2

A Safety Checklist for New and Used Appliances

☑ **1.** When door or cover is open, washer, dryer, dishwasher, or microwave range automatically stops.

☑ **2.** The "off" controls are indicated plainly and clearly.

☑ **3.** Both stationary and portable appliances have three-pronged grounding electric plugs, particularly those to be used outdoors or in damp places (not, however, on toasters and open coil heating units).

☑ **4.** Trash compactors and self-cleaning ovens have safety locks so that they cannot be opened during operation.

☑ **5.** Refrigerators, dryers, and freezers have doors that can be pushed open from inside so that children cannot be trapped.

☑ **6.** Control knobs are beyond the reach of small children.

---

covers all parts and labor for a specified period after the full or limited warranty runs out. For example, if you purchase a refrigerator from J. C. Penney or from Sears, they will offer you a full service contract for a specified amount. In a sense, a service contract is really a purchase of insurance. You pay a predetermined amount of money each year in order to avoid the possibility of having to pay a larger amount on costly repairs. You are betting that you would have paid a larger amount in repairs than the service contract actually costs. The seller of the service contract is betting that on average for all of the individuals who have purchased such contracts, the repairs will cost less than the total amount collected. Clearly, on the average, the seller of service contracts must be right because the seller must make a profit on that venture. Does that mean that

you always lose out by purchasing such a contract? No, you do not. That would be equivalent to saying that you lose out on a life insurance policy unless you die prematurely. If a service contract is looked at as the purchase of insurance, then buying it makes sense for individuals who do not want to face the prospect of unusually large repair bills at any time during the year.

There is another positive aspect to purchasing a service contract. You may have a tendency to have smaller, less important repairs carried out more frequently under a service contract than you would if you had to pay each time you called the serviceperson. In so doing, you may extend the useful life of the appliance, thereby delaying the need to replace that appliance.

Money magazine does not believe that service contracts on

many appliances are warranted.[1] The suggestion is that you base your decision on whether to buy a service contract on the first year's performance of the appliance. Refrigerators, freezers, and clothes dryers have very low repair frequency rates during the second through fifth years. Unless you bought a lemon, which should be obvious during the first year, the money on a service contract for any of these appliances is probably unwarranted. The same holds for a central furnace until it is several years old.

Before you call a serviceperson. Because service calls are costly, you should go through a checklist before you actually make a commitment to pay someone to repair your appliance. That checklist might be as follows:

1. Make sure that you have read carefully and followed all of the manufacturer's instructions. In many instruction booklets for durable goods there is a troubleshooter's checklist that may help you solve your problem very simply. Many wasted dollars are spent on service calls just to have the serviceperson unplug the drain in a self-defrosting refrigerator even though the owner could have done it very easily with the help of the instruction booklet hints.

2. Check fuses or circuit breakers.

[1]"Unwarranted Appliance Service Contracts." Money, February 1977, p. 62.

3. Make sure gas, water, or electric connections have been turned on correctly.

If all of that fails, call the serviceperson and make sure you give the model number of your appliance (taken from the nameplate). This often avoids paying for two service calls: one to see what was wrong and the second to bring a part that could have been in the serviceperson's truck to begin with.

WHAT TO DO WHEN YOU HAVE A COMPLAINT

If you have a complaint about a consumer durable that has not been satisfied by the seller of that good, you may wish to contact the company that manufactured or distributed the product. A polite letter telling what has taken place and what you want the company to do about it may usually bring some action. Address your letter to the customer relations department; be sure that you make a copy of

your letter; and be sure that you enclose a copy of sales slips, guarantees, agreements, cancelled checks, receipts, or contracts. Never mail the originals! Send your complaint by either certified or registered mail, return receipt requested.

If you still do not receive satisfaction, you may wish to contact one of the following private organizations:

1. Appliances: Major Appliance Consumer Action Panel (MACAP). See Exhibit K-1.

2. Carpets and rugs: Carpet and Rug Industry Consumer Action Panel (CRICAP), Box 1568, Dalton, Georgia 30720.

3. Furniture: Furniture Industry Consumer Action Panel (FICAP), Box 951, High Point, North Carolina 27261.

If you still do not receive satisfaction, you may wish to contact your state's Consumer Protection Agency, which we listed in consumer Issue A.

CUTTING DOWN ON ENERGY USE

The operating cost of appliances is higher today than it has been for the past 25 years. Therefore, you might wish to try to reduce your energy bills associated with the use of appliances in your household. Although the following list of energy saving tips is by no means complete, it may help you save many dollars a year if you carefully apply it to your daily activities in the household.

WAYS TO SAVE ON ENERGY

1. Bake several items at once when possible. Also, baking is less expensive in the long run than cooking on the top of the range because ovens shut off for part of the baking period.

2. Defrost freezer or freezing compartments when frost is one-quarter inch thick. This will increase the efficiency of your freezer.

EXHIBIT K-1 **The Right Way to Complain**

If you have a problem that you haven't been able to get satisfactory action on locally, write or call the manufacturer, giving all details. If that doesn't solve the difficulty, write or call collect, MACAP, 20 N. Wacker Dr., Chicago, Illinois 60606. Telephone: 312-236-3175.

Include the folowing information:
☐ Your name, address, and telephone number.
☐ Type of appliance, brand, model, serial number.
☐ Date of purchase.

☐ Dealer's name and address and service agent's name and address if different from dealer.
☐ Clear, concise description of problem and service performed to date.

MACAP cautions that it is important to keep receipts of repairs even when a service call is under warranty. The receipts may be required to prove an appliance needed excessive repairs and should be replaced.

10. Use smaller electric appliances for specialized jobs to save on electricity, for example, toast bread in a toaster, not in the oven.

11. Buy an air conditioner that has a very high energy efficiency rating (EER) and keep the thermostat up. Make sure the filter is clean on the air conditioner, and do not use it as an air circulator.

12. Don't leave an electric coffee maker plugged in.

13. Turn your thermostat down in the winter and install a timer, which cuts the heat off during your sleeping hours.

14. Where possible, reduce wattage of lights or switch to fluorescent lamps.

You can probably think of other ways to save on energy; however, note that reducing energy expenses often means a reduction in some convenience that you might enjoy. As an example, what you have to do is realistically compare the value you place on the benefits of a warmer household in winter with the cost of a higher fuel bill.

SUMMARY

1. Because major appliances have a limited life, it is useful to set up a household plan to determine needed purchases and replacement.

2. When making plans for purchases, operating costs must be considered. These are a function of the relative costs of gas and electricity, initial cost of appliance, and installation costs.

3. Service contracts are available on most appliances. Experts

3. Check the seals on your freezing compartment and refrigerator doors for cracks and wearing.

4. Increase the temperature setting on your refrigerator freezer: 39° is usually adequate in the food compartment; 5° in the freezer will allow food to be stored there for about four months.

5. Minimize hot water use. Only run full loads in your washing machine, dishwasher, and dryer. This will save on both water and energy.

6. Use cold water and cold water detergent in your washing machine for articles that are not severely soiled.

7. Use the lowest temperature possible when drying your laundry.

8. Eliminate the heating cycle in your dishwasher. Simply open the door and let the air, which is free, dry your dishes.

9. Turn the thermostat on your water heater down: set the upper temperature at 140°, the lower at 120°.

recommend, however, that they are not necessarily a good deal for refrigerators, freezers, and clothes dryers, which have low frequency of repair records.

4. Complaints on appliances may be lodged with the Major Appliance Consumer Action Panel, the Carpet and Rug Industry Consumer Action Panel, and the Furniture Industry Consumer Action Panel.

QUESTIONS FOR THOUGHT AND DISCUSSION

1. Should you be concerned about a potential energy "crisis"?

2. When would it be advisable to purchase a service contract on a major or minor appliance?

3. Most items listed in the safety checklist in Table K-2 are required by law. When would you therefore want to use such a checklist?

THINGS TO DO

1. Write MACAP to obtain information on how successful that organization has been.

2. Take the safety checklist, Table K-2, with you to an appliance store. Are there any particular brands of appliances that do not conform to that checklist? Ask the salesperson if he or she knows why.

SELECTED READINGS

Edgerton, Jerry. "A Cool Look at Air Conditioning." *Money* 6 (April 1977).

Handbook of Buying Issue. Consumers' Research Magazine, October 1977.

Redstrom, R. A. "Practices in the Use of Home Freezers." Paper presented at the *45th Annual Agricultural Outlook Conference*, 1967, Consumer and Food Economics Institute, Agricultural Research Service, U.S. Department of Agriculture.

Ruffin, M. D., and Tippett, K. S. "Service-Life Expectancy of Household Appliances: New Estimates from U.S.D.A." *Home Economics Resource Journal* 3 (1975): 159–170.

"Shopping Tips: Automatic Washers and Dryers." *Changing Times* 31 (April 1977).

Tippett, K. S., and Ruffin, M. D. "Service-Life Expectancy of Household Appliances." *Family Economics Review*, Summer 1975, pp. 3–6.

GLOSSARY OF TERMS

The costs that are incurred by an individual and no one else. The private costs of driving a car, for example, include depreciation, gas, insurance, and so on.

No-Fault Auto Insurance
A system of auto insurance whereby, no matter who is at fault, the individual is paid by his or her insurance company for a certain amount of medical costs and the damage to the car.

Social Costs
The costs of an action that society bears. Social costs include both private costs and costs that the individual does not bear. For example, the social cost of driving a car includes the private costs plus any pollution or congestion caused by that automobile.

Getting There by Car Is Half the Worry

CHAPTER PREVIEW

☐ How much do we spend on transportation?

☐ What are the safety aspects of automobiles?

☐ How do safety standards affect the cost of a car?

☐ What are the characteristics of the automobile repair industry?

☐ What are the characteristics of the automobile insurance industry?

☐ Is no-fault insurance a good deal?

☐ Why don't we have more mass transit in the United States?

14 Someone who wanted to name the twentieth century would not be wrong to call it the Age of the Automobile. From a modest beginning at the turn of the century, when a few courageous souls drove around in Stutz Bearcats, Hupmobiles, and Model Ts, but especially from the moment Henry Ford developed low-cost mass-production techniques to put out a $870 "Tin Lizzie," until the end of the 1970s, when fully 88 percent of all American families owned cars, we have seen the automobile become a pervasive part of American life. There is no way to escape it, or at least it seems so. The trend toward multiple car families is also continuing, as Figure 14-1 shows. Today, fully one-third of American families have two four-wheeled vehicles in their driveways.

WE SPEND A LOT ON CARS

In the United States today there are close to 110 million cars. The number of new cars turned out by the factories every year sometimes exceeds 11 million. Money spent on purchasing automobiles, on automobile repairs, and on other related expenses accounts for 12 percent of total income in the United States. The automobile industry itself is also huge. One out of every six people in the United States

Figure 14-1 Trend in Multiple Car Ownership

The trend in multiple car ownership is continuing upward. In 1957, only 13 percent of families in the United States had two or more cars; in 1971, the figure reached almost 30 percent. (Later years are estimates.)

Source: *1971-72 Survey of Consumers*, Lewis Mandell, George Katona, James N. Morgan, Jay Schmiedeskamp, Contributions to Behavioral Economics (Institute for Social Research, The University of Michigan: Ann Arbor) 1973.

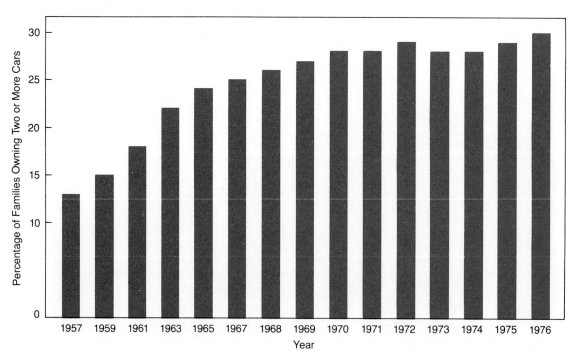

is in some way concerned with automobiles, whether it be as a factory worker in Detroit or as an employee of a company making spare parts or servicing cars. The notion behind the famous statement, "Whatever is good for General Motors is good for America," could derive from the sheer numbers involved in automobile-related employment.

However, the total amount of money spent in the private transportation industry does not give a true indication of the total cost to society. We will talk later about the *social* cost of driving, but first we will discuss that painful aspect of driving your car—accidents.

FOUR-WHEELED COFFINS

Some have depicted the automobile as a four-wheeled rolling coffin. Why? Because approximately 50,000 Americans are killed every year in vehicle accidents, and two million others are injured. The economic costs of the injuries, deaths, and property damage exceeds $38 billion annually. Then there is the cost of pain and suffering, both for those involved in the accidents and for their loved ones. We can put no dollar figure on this tragic aspect of private transportation.

Many highway deaths could have been avoided had the drivers been more careful. But, according to many observers, many others could have been avoided if additional safety features were required on automobiles. In 1958, the Ford Motor Company tried to sell additional safety to the American car-buying public, but nobody bought and Ford lost money. Finally, after the exposés by Ralph Nader in his book *Unsafe at Any Speed*, Congress started moving; and the result was the Motor Vehicle Safety Act of 1966, the basis of most current safety requirements on automobiles.

Some of the requirements imposed on car manufacturers by the National Highway Traffic Safety Administration are:

1. Dual braking systems
2. Nonprotruding interior appliances
3. Over-the-shoulder safety belts in the front seat
4. Head restraints on all front seats
5. Seat belt warning system and ignition interlock
6. Collapsible, impact-absorbing arm rests
7. Impact-absorbing instrument panel

THE COST OF SAFETY

All of the safety devices that must be put on cars these days constitute additions to the supply of safety for automobile transportation. Unfortunately, as we have continuously pointed out in this book, nothing is free. Automobile safety devices raise the costs of automobiles. You the consumer pay for that safety directly out of your pocket. But, of course, you get a benefit—a safer mode of transportation.

It is not known, however, whether the total amount of automobile safety on the highway has dramatically risen because of the safety standards. After all, some people react to the higher relative cost of automobiles by not buying new cars as frequently as before. And the older the car, the higher the probability is of a mechanical failure that could cause an accident. The average age of cars being driven on the highway today has risen as the costs of new cars have increased because of the required safety devices.

Alternatives are available that might reduce the numbers of accidents and injuries on the highway. Although their availability does not necessarily make these alternatives *preferable*, they are still worth thinking about.

At least half of all U.S. highway deaths are in one way or another related to drinking. Perhaps 50 percent of the 10,000 or so pedestrians killed every year are drunk, and 50 percent of the drivers involved in fatal highway accidents are legally drunk. To be legally drunk, a driver must have had the equivalent of three martinis on an empty stomach. Thus, many instances of poor driver judgment may be related to alcohol-induced slowness of mind and reflexes, which is not actually legal drunkenness.

If so many accidents are caused by drunk drivers, one alternative to the solutions already tried for increasing highway safety involves reducing the number of drunks on the road. This would mean, for example, much higher fines and stiffer jail sentences. In Sweden, for example, where there is an alcoholism problem, accidents caused by drunk driving are relatively few. Why? Simply because the costs of being caught driving drunk are tremendous—jail and huge fines. Any time people get drunk in Sweden, they either stay where they are, they let somebody else drive, or they call a taxi or take a bus. With stiff enough fines in the United States, the same thing could be true here. Generally, though, we have been extremely lenient with drunk drivers no matter what they do on the road. You can find people with four and five drunk-driving arrests on their records still driving. Generally, only when they kill or maim somebody do they realize their mistake. And even then they may eventually be drunk on the road again.

There is a reversal in that trend, however. We are now seeing stiffer penalties for drunk driving and more stringent classifications as to when a person may be considered "legally drunk."

Another way of preventing fatalities and injuries resulting from accidents is to cut down on the number of road hazards and increase the ease with which people can drive safely. This would require break-away signs, energy absorbing materials at off ramps and around bridge abutments, and so on. Some experts have estimated that we could save more lives by investing in better roads than by paying the billions of dollars a year in additional costs for safer cars. Also, sturdier cars that withstand accidents use up more resources and take more gas to drive—further costs of safety.

Another way of reducing highway accidents is to lower speed limits. There was a consensus among highway experts in early 1974 that the energy crisis-induced reduction in highway speed limits significantly reduced traffic fatalities. For some reason, advocates of safer cars did not, at least until then, strongly suggest lower speed limits as an alternative.

THE PRIVATE COST OF DRIVING

The cost of driving a car involves more than making a monthly payment, although that is part of it. The **private costs** of driving include such things as wear and tear, repairs, gas and oil, insurance, and taxes, in addition to whatever payments are made and whatever the implicit cost is if you paid cash. (Remember the discussion in Chapter 12 when we talked about whether to buy or rent.) Table 14-1 shows the estimated cost of operating an automobile as given by the American Automobile

Table 14-1

Cost of Operating an Automobile

Source: *Your Driving Costs*, American Automobile Association, 8111 Gatehouse Road, Falls Church, Virginia 22042, 1977 ed.

	LOW COST AREA (Small towns, rural locations)	HIGH COST AREA (Large metroplitan areas)
Subcompact	14.6¢/mile	22.8¢/mile
Compact	15.6¢/mile	24.1¢/mile
Intermediate	16.8¢/mile	25.5¢/mile
Standard size	18.5¢/mile	28.2¢/mile

Association. It ultimately costs about 15¢ to 28¢ a mile to run a car. The repairs on cars can be quite expensive. And, in addition, you have an information problem about whether or not you are being asked to pay for more than you need when your car breaks down.

THE REPAIR INDUSTRY

The automobile repair industry is immense. There are at least 100,000 mechanic's garages in the United States, as well as 200,000 gas stations that also give repair service. In total, we probably spend $10 billion a year on automobile repairs. The labor costs for auto repairs have increased rapidly in the last few years. Obviously, it is important that you find a reputable repair shop for your car. If you know of none, ask your friends and acquaintances where they have gotten good repair work. Because repeat customers are generally going to be treated better, it is also advisable to take your car back to the same garage if you are satisfied.

Some consumer economists believe that preventive maintenance avoids large repair bills. This is true, but you must take account of the maintenance costs themselves. In the long run, it may be cheaper not to keep your car in perfect condition, but rather to let some things (other than brakes, tires, and safety-related parts) wear out and replace them only when they do, or trade in your car every few years. Some state governments buy fleets of cars that they do no servicing on at all for a year and then trade in. This seems to be cheaper than trying to maintain the cars and, as the price of repair services rises, will become still cheaper by comparison. You will thus have two choices: buy a car that you expect to keep only for a short period of time, or buy a car that has a reputation of very low service requirements. Each year, the April issue of *Consumer Reports* relays its readers' experiences with the repair needs of different makes and years of cars. This is an important aid when you try to assess the annual cost of operating an automobile. A Mercedes, for example, may be extremely expensive at the outset; but according to owners' reports, repairs are fewer and further between. Also, as you would expect, the actual physical depreciation of that car is much less than that of cars costing half the price. Hence, when checking out an automobile, look not at its list price, but rather at the implicit price you will have to pay per year. When viewed in this manner, a Mercedes may not be twice as expensive as a Ford.

THE AUTOMOBILE INSURANCE INDUSTRY

When you buy a car, one of the first things you must think about is insuring yourself against theft, fire, liability, medical expenses, and damage. Very few people drive without automobile insurance. Whether most people have adequate insurance is another matter, and we will discuss what is adequate in the following consumer issue.

The insurance industry is a regulated one: every state has its insurance commissioner who passes judgment on the rates charged by various insurance companies. Although there is a tendency for any regulated industry to have quite a few regulations that stifle competition, the automobile insurance industry still remains competitive in many situations. It is not unusual for different prices to be charged for the same amount of insurance. But prices can be misleading, because different insurance companies offer different qualities of service: one company may be less willing to pay off claims than another; one may have an insurance adjuster at your house immediately if you have a small accident: another may never send one out, leaving you to do the adjusting yourself. Although insurance costs are not consistently related to quality of service, they do consistently differentiate among different classes of drivers.

Why? Simply because the probability that an accident will occur is different for these different classes. Competition among the various insurance companies has forced each one of them to find out which classes of drivers are safer than others and offer those classes lower rates. For example, because statistics tell us that single males from 16 to 25 have the highest accident record of all drivers, these drivers pay a much higher price for auto insurance. And because statistics tell us that female drivers have fewer accidents overall than male drivers, women in a family often pay lower insurance rates for cars that they use exclusively.

NO-FAULT INSURANCE, PROS AND CONS

No-fault auto insurance is "an idea whose time has come." Some policy-makers believe, however, that the place for no-fault action is at the state level, not at the federal level. Labor and consumer groups, however, were dissatisfied with the pace of state action and the lobbying tactics of no-fault opponents. Therefore, pressure was brought upon the Senate and the House to institute a federal plan. Supporters of such plans indicate that over a period of time it will save motorists a billion dollars a year in auto insurance premiums. Under a no-fault insurance system, your insurance company does not first have to decide whose fault the accident was before payments are made to you for medical expenses due to injuries sustained in the accident. In a traditional liability-based fault system, a determination must be made as to who caused an accident. The insuror of the party deemed "at fault" then pays the bills of the other party—medical, automobile repairs, lost earnings, and in some cases pain and suffering.

No-fault insurance is not a new idea. Almost all insurance is already no-fault. For example, when you purchase life insurance (unless you die by suicide shortly thereafter), the life insurance company pays without asking about fault. The same is true of fire and homeowner's insurance, as well as health and accident insurance. If you break an ankle and are covered under a medical plan, the insuror does not ask you whose fault it was before your medical bills are paid.

Original proponents of no-fault auto insurance believed that the system would soon be adopted by all states in the union; however, as of 1977, only 16 states had converted to "pure" no-fault. They were Colorado, Connecticut, Florida, Georgia, Hawaii, Kansas, Kentucky, Massachusetts, Michigan, Minnesota, Nevada, New Jersey, New York, North Dakota, Pennsylvania, and Utah. Another 8 states had passed some modified form of no-fault automobile insurance. In most no-fault states, the no-fault laws apply only to bodily injuries. Property damage claims are settled by standard liability and collision sections of automobile insurance policies as they have been in the past.

If you live in a no-fault state, that does not mean you cannot sue the other party in the case of an automobile accident. Generally, you have to satisfy certain "threshold" criteria before you are allowed to sue for pain and suffering, inconvenience, lost wages, and deprivation of the company of a spouse. The medical threshold level ranges from a few hundred dollars up to a couple thousand dollars in the 16 no-fault states. In other states all that is required is that you suffer serious injury or permanent disfigurement before being allowed to sue.

REDUCING LEGAL
FEES

Originators of the no-fault system pointed out that only 44¢ of each premium dollar in fault-based insurance went toward paying the injured parties in an automobile accident. Much of the remaining 56¢ of each premium dollar went to the cost of litigation—to lawyers. Proponents of no-fault reasoned and still do that such a system would reduce dramatically the amount of needless expenditures on legal fees, particularly when minor injuries were involved.

WHAT HAS ACTUALLY
HAPPENED?

Has the reduction in legal expenses after the introduction of no-fault led to lower premiums in no-fault states? The data are not all in, but a preliminary survey among the 24 states that have some form of no-fault insurance does not lead us to any definite conclusion. From 1970 to 1976 premiums rose less in 15 of those 24 states than in all the remaining states without no-fault; thus, no-fault seems to have a slight edge in terms of keeping premiums down. This, of course, is not sufficient evidence to claim total success for the new type of auto insurance.

No doubt there will continue to be attempts at introducing federal legislation that will require some form of no-fault in all states. For the last several years, bills have been reintroduced to do just that. One of the early proponents of no-fault, University of Illinois law professor Jeffrey O'Connell, would like to see just that, for he still believes that "no-fault is simply a better use of the money. It assures you a prompt payment for real bills, rather than just the chance at a jackpot."

SHOULD YOU BUY AND HOLD?

Frequently the question comes up as to whether it is better to buy a new car every year or so, or to buy and hold a car for ten years until it essentially has no resale value. A few years ago, the U.S. Department of Transportation conducted a study designed to come up with some exact answers to this question.

The Department of Transportation looked at the actual costs of depreciation, insurance, repair bills, maintenance, and so on for a 1970 full-sized, "big-three" (Ford, GM, Chrysler) four-door sedan equipped with V8 engine, automatic transmission, etc. They compared buying a car and keeping it for ten years against buying a new car every year, or every two or three years. After a certain number of years, the car that is held for ten years became a second car in a two-car family and was driven fewer miles. The study showed that to buy a new car every other year would cost you $4,000 more over a ten-year period than keeping one for ten years. In this case it was cheaper to buy and hold. Unfortunately, this conclusion is only a starting point for you in making your own decision about whether to buy a new car or not.

If you hold a car for ten years and even keep it in very good condition, you have not purchased the same kind of transportation services as you would if you buy a new car every other year. If cars become safer every year, you do not have the benefit of new safety features. This is probably less important now because most basic safety features have been required for some time. But what if you had bought a car before dual brakes and safety laminated glass were required? You would be driving a much different piece of machinery than if you traded in your car every two years and got the benefits of the new safety features.

You lose the psychic benefits of styling changes and of that new-car feeling or smell when you get into one. These are all very nebulous and hard to quantify; they might mean much to you or very little.

However, now with the pollution equipment required on new cars, the decision whether or not to buy one is even more complicated. Some automotive engineers maintain that 1971 or 1972 was the last good year to buy a car, because after that the pollution equipment has made the engine so bad and so expensive to run that you are better off not buying a new car. The trend seems to have reversed itself recently.

Gas mileage for newer cars is better than it was a few years ago. In deciding whether or not to keep an older car, one must therefore also take into account the reduced gas mileage of some older cars compared to their newer counterparts. A new VW might be getting 30 miles a gallon while one 10 years old might be getting only 17 miles a gallon. Depending on how much you drive, this difference in gas consumption could add up to a considerable sum over a year period.

THE SOCIAL COSTS OF DRIVING

When you get into your car and fire it up, you incur, in addition to the private costs, the **social costs** of driving. You are all aware of them, particularly if you live in Los Angeles, New York, or Washington, D.C. One of the biggest social costs of driving has been air pollution. That engine does not just pull your car around. It also emits by-products that, when added together, do little good for your lungs or mine. In some places, they can do so much harm that many people refuse to live there. Pollution from automobile exhaust contributes 60 percent to total pollution in the major U.S. cities today. This is, of course, why the federal government as well as individual states have started regulating the pollution output of automobile engines. And this is also why standard automobile engines with pollution abatement equipment do not run like the ones you were familiar with five years ago. It just has not been easy to eliminate the harmful by-products of internal combustion.

Thus, now you, the individual driver, are being forced to take account of the social cost you impose on the rest of society in the form of pollution: you are forced to purchase automobile engines that have pollution abatement equipment, for which you pay directly in a higher purchase price and indirectly in the form of reduced power and higher gas consumption.

Private automobile transportation involves other social costs that are equally obvious: one of them is congestion. Congestion on bridges, highways, and in inner cities is a problem of social concern, even though private individuals, at least until now, were not forced to pay the full price of driving their cars. That price includes making other people late for work or making them spend more time in their own cars. In other words, by the mere fact that you get on a crowded bridge, you slow down everybody else a wee bit. When you add up the value of everybody else's time, you see that you impose a pretty high cost. And the same is true of every other person on that bridge.

The obvious solution is to make people pay the full cost of their driving by charging them more. Many will decide to cross the brdige at other than rush hours, or to go to work in car pools. Someday we may get to such a full costing solution. In the meantime, we build highways, freeways, expressways, bridges, underpasses, overpasses, parking lots—ad nauseam—until, if we keep on this way, eventually the landscape will be one massive automobile metropolis. Many people are clamoring for a change in this trend; they want mass transit. Unfortunately, mass transit on a large scale seems to be far in the future.

MASS TRANSIT

The proposed solutions to the automobile problem are many and varied. In the San Francisco Bay Area, BART (Bay Area Rapid Transit) has developed an integrated rapid transit network. In Flint, Michigan, passengers have been enticed by a fleet of luxury buses, complete with air conditioning, stereophonic music, and in some cases even a "bus bunny" to handle complaints. There are at least 40 major cities throughout the world that are building new subways or are adding to existing systems. Planners throughout the world estimate that when all of their systems are finished, 12.5 billion passengers a year will be riding subways. Through its Urban Mass Transportation Assistance Act of 1970, the U.S. Congress provided $3 billion in federal funds for constructing subways. Congress stated that it intended to appropriate an additional $7 billion later.

Subways are not cheap to build. They typically cost about $8 million a mile to install, and many are even more expensive because soil conditions are so bad that pilings have to be driven, water has to be drained, and so on. In Washington, D.C., the subway system will have 98 miles of service and will cost at least $3 billion, making it one of the most expensive single public works projects ever undertaken in the United States.

However expensive subways seem to be, many engineers are convinced that they are the long-run solution to the urban congestion problem. In London, for example, a group of engineers concluded that it would take an 11-lane highway to transport the 25,000 commuters who could be served hourly by a new subway line.

Some economists are not so optimistic about the future of mass transportation. In fact, some studies have shown that mass transportation will never effectively replace the auto and stop congestion if some current conditions continue to exist. Among those conditions is the fantastic amount of subsidization that private automobile drivers receive.

SUBSIDIZING
THE AUTOMOBILE

Highway travel that is most immediately competitive with mass transit—rush hour commuting in automobiles by private citizens—is subsidized to such an extent that mass transit may never be able to pay even its own operating costs, much less repay its construction costs. Urban motorists pay very little, perhaps only one-third, of the true cost of driving their cars to the city. For example, they do not pay for urban street maintenance and repairs, street cleaning, snow removal, traffic signals, or traffic police.

Most of these costs are incurred by all taxpayers because they are generally paid for out of city revenues. In addition, urban motorists who park in the streets use valuable land for which they pay no rent or property taxes, as must other people who occupy scarce land. Only a small parking meter fee is charged. Motorists use all of the capital invested in city streets but pay no tax comparable to the property or corporation income taxes imposed on users of these other forms of capital. When cities decide to improve streets and highways, the money is often borrowed and the interest costs are subsidized by the federal government.

THE FAILURE OF BART

The embarrassed proponents of San Francisco's BART must now agree with the above analysis. The system was originally budgeted at $1 billion, and it ended up costing at least $600 million more than that. In September 1975, the system opened with a series of equipment breakdowns, millions of dollars of lawsuits, and massive operating deficits. The number of people riding on BART is at least 25 percent less than predicted.

BART's major objective was a lessening of traffic congestion on major arteries into the city. In fact, when a bond issue was attempted in 1962, a report stated that BART would divert thousands of travelers from their automobiles and alleviate highway congestion in order to allow the city to grow.

What has happened? Almost 60 percent of BART riders have simply switched from commuter bus lines. The remainder of BART's passengers were new riders. Many of them were individuals who lived on the other side of the bay in Oakland and Berkeley, who formerly did their shopping there. With the advent of BART, they moved their business over to San Francisco. There has been virtually no impact on traffic congestion. The same number of cars are using the Bay Bridge into the city; the same number of cars seem to be parking in the city's municipal parking lots.

Of course, one of the reasons that BART was not the smashing success that it was supposed to be had to do with the price of a ticket. It turns out that it is actually cheaper in some cases to drive a car into the city rather than to take BART. That certainly is not a good way to get people to switch to mass transit. But more important, BART suffers from the same problem that all other mass transit schemes suffer from—a fixed route, proximity of other passengers, and fixed time schedules.

PARA-TRANSIT

There must be alternatives to a fixed route mass transit system. We can list several of them here.

Bring Back the Jitneys. The dictionary defines a jitney as a "bus or car, especially when traveling a regular route, that carries passengers for a small fare, originally five cents." Basically, then, jitneys are either private cars or small mini-buses that drive along the street picking up passengers who wave them down and dropping them off where they want. Jitney systems operated and even flourished in the United States prior to World War I. They were effectively forced off the roads by the lobbying efforts of municipal bus and street car systems. Today there is an illegal jitney system flourishing in Pittsburgh. It operates between downtown Pittsburgh and neighborhoods to the east. Jitneys are legal along Chicago's King Street, San Francisco's Mission Street, and Atlanta's Boardwalk. The value in jitneys is that they can be provided by individuals with their own private automobiles whenever they are needed and they do not suffer the fixed route restrictions of a standard mass transit system.

Reform Taxi Regulations. Many, if not all, taxi systems in the United States are severely regulated by municipal governments. Virtually all studies have shown that this regulation restricts the number of taxis available, thus limiting the availability of a convenient form of public transportation.

Attempt to Find New Ways to Organize and Encourage Car Pools. One possibility to encourage car pools is for the employer to provide a mini-bus vehicle to an employee to drive back and forth to work. The employee can use the van as a personal car provided that he or she agrees to carry at least, say, eight passengers to and from work every day. Another way to encourage car pools is to give priority on special lanes in the highway for those cars that have three or more passengers. This has been done in a number of cities and on a number of toll bridges where cars with a certain number of passengers pay a lower fee or none at all. A few years ago a Federal Highway Commission study showed the savings that are possible by car pooling, as shown in Table 14-2.

The list can go on and on about ways in which we can find alternatives to mass transit. What does seem to be clear is that alternatives should be looked at now more than ever before because the standard method of setting up transit systems in many major cities in the country does not look so enticing after the failure of so many of them.

Table 14-2		ANNUAL ROUND TRIP COST AND SAVINGS		
Car Pool Savings: 1977	HOME TO WORK	SUBCOMPACT (Pinto, Datsun, Vega, VW, Colt)	COMPACT (Nova, Dart, Maverick, Pacer)	STANDARD (Matador, Cutlass, LTD, Caprice)
Source: For a complete report on the car pool study, write to the Department of Transportation, Federal Highway Administration, Washington, D.C. 20590.		**Cost of Driving to Work Alone**			
		$982	$1,177	$1,561
	20 Miles (40 miles Round Trip)	Savings per Person in:		
		2-person carpool $449	$ 545	$ 734
		3-person carpool 585	712	963
		4-person carpool 645	796	1,077
		5-person carpool 693	845	1,145

Meanwhile, many of us still must buy and use cars in the absence of adequate mass transit, or of sufficiently forceful inducement to use mass transit. If you must buy a car, whether to meet your needs or satisfy your desires, the following consumer issue should give you some guidance as to how to go about it.

SUMMARY

1. Fully 88 percent of all American families own cars.
2. Multiple car ownership has increased to over 30 percent.
3. Highway deaths number around 50,000 a year, and property damage caused by the automobile exceeds $28 billion.
4. The National Highway Safety Administration sets standards for production of new cars. The cost of increased safety, however, is not insignificant.
5. An alternative to making a car safer is to make the highway safer by eliminating drunk drivers.
6. The automobile repair industry is indeed huge in the United States, accounting for perhaps $20 billion of consumer expenditures a year. Preventive maintenance is important in eliminating large repair bills; however, some preventive maintenance may be more costly than it is worth, particularly if you do not plan to keep your car very long.
7. The automobile insurance industry is regulated, but there is enough competition for you to benefit from shopping around.
8. No-fault insurance eliminates the liability-based system that has been in effect for so long. Essentially, if you have no-fault insurance, your insurance company pays you in case of an accident no matter who was at fault.
9. Buying and holding a car for many years may seem to be the least expensive way of obtaining transportation. However, you lose out on the benefits of any improved product safety and quality found in newer model cars.
10. The social costs of driving include the pollution, noise, and congestion caused by automobiles.
11. As long as the automobile continues to be subsidized so heavily, it is doubtful that mass transit will ever become a reality throughout the United States as a substitute for the private automobile.

QUESTIONS FOR THOUGHT AND DISCUSSION

1. Why do you think Americans spend so much for automobiles?
2. Automobiles in America are much larger than in Europe. Why?
3. Even though they are told that speed kills, American drivers continue to drive as fast or faster than the speed limit on highways. Why?
4. Can you distinguish between those safety features in a car that benefit only the occupants of a car and those that benefit so-called third parties?
5. Why does safety cost? Why has the automobile industry not provided a perfectly safe car?
6. Do you think it would be difficult to eliminate drunk drivers?
7. What cost do you, or would you, take into account when purchasing a car?
8. Do you think there is a monopoly in the automobile insurance industry?
9. Do you think no-fault insurance is "fair"?
10. What has Congress been doing to reduce the social costs of driving?
11. What are some ways mass transit could be furthered in the United States?

THINGS TO DO

1. Write to the Federal Highway Safety Administration for a listing of safety requirements on cars. Which ones do you think are appropriate or inappropriate?

2. A few years ago a safety requirement was suggested that would oblige automobile manufacturers to relocate gasoline tanks and protect them from crashes in order to avoid fire. The Ford Motor Company asserted that the requirement would raise the price of each car by $11.20, and estimated that there were only six to seven hundred auto fire deaths annually. Ford concluded that the new safety standard would not be worth the price. Assume that 12 million cars are produced a year. What is the total cost of this new safety feature? If the Ford Motor Company is right about the number of auto fire deaths annually, what is the implicit value placed on human life? Is it too high or too low?

3. Find out what the growth rate of bicycle and motorcycle sales has been in the past decade. Has this growth rate exceeded the growth rate of automobile sales? Can you think of reasons?

4. Write to your state's insurance commissioner for information on how the commissioner protects you from insurance companies.

5. Contact an independent insurance adjuster and talk to him or her about his or her work. How are claims handled? What are the most prevalent types of accidents in your area? How should you file a claim?

6. Write to the Federal Highway Administration in Washington, D.C., asking for their estimate of the current cost per mile for operating a subcompact, compact, and standard size car. Compare it with the figures in Table 14-1. Now, in percentages, figure out the relative costs. Is it now more or less expensive in operating cost per mile to have a standard size car compared to a compact?

7. Find out from the National Highway Traffic Safety Administration what safety equipment this year's cars had to have. With this knowledge, would you feel safer in a newer car? How much would you be willing to pay for this additional safety?

SELECTED READINGS

"BART Beleaguered." *Time*, (September 30, 1974), p. 82.

Forbes, M. S., Jr. "Rails Are Not the Solution." *Forbes*, April 15, 1977, p. 23.

Gregory, M. H. "No Fault, Antitrust and Cars that Crash." *Motor Trend*, (June 1974), p. 8.

Nader, Ralph. *Unsafe at Any Speed: The Designed-in Dangers of the American Automobile*. New York: Grossman Publishers, 1972.

National Observer Staff. "Group Auto Insurance and Cutting into Insurance Costs." *The Consumer's Handbook II*. Princeton, N.J.: Dow Jones Books, 1970.

O'Connell, Jeffrey. *The Injury Industry and the Remedy of No-Fault Auto Insurance*. Consumers Union, Commerce Clearing House, 1971.

"San Francisco: A Brainy System with Big Headaches; Bay Area Rapid Transit System." *Business Week*, February 16, 1974.

"Subcompact Cars Still the Most Costly to Repair." *Consumer Newsweekly*, January 24, 1977.

"Where No-Fault Auto Insurance Stands Today." *Changing Times*, November 1976, p. 13.

Buying Transportation

GLOSSARY OF TERMS

Liability Insurance

Insurance that covers suits against the insured for such damages as injury or death to other drivers or passengers, property damage, and the like. It is insurance for those damages for which the driver can be held liable.

Umbrella Policy

A type of supplemental insurance policy that can extend normal automobile liability limits to $1 million or more for a relatively small premium.

Zero Deductible

In the collision part of an automobile insurance policy, the provision that the insured pays nothing for any repair to damage on the car due to an accident that is the fault of the insured. Zero deductible is, of course, more expensive than a $50 or $100 deductible policy.

Assigned Risk

A person who is seeking automobile insurance and has been refused coverage. That person is assigned to an insurance company that is a member of the assigned risk pool in that person's state.

SHOULD YOU BUY A NEW OR A USED CAR?

When most of us go out to purchase transportation, we face a problem: we are tempted to buy something new. There are certainly good reasons for buying a new car instead of a used one. A new car has never been owned by someone else; therefore, you have to worry only about how you will treat it during its first few years, not about how it was treated beforehand. A new car may be safer, it may run smoother, it may be more stylish—although today these various aspects are not as subject to annual changes as they were in the past. On the other hand, new cars do not always run as well as used cars; to some buyers, they do not always look as nice; and they may not always be as comfortable. Nonetheless, you may choose a new car simply because you like to have things that are new. Be aware, however, of the price you are paying for that new car: a full-sized domestic car may automatically depreciate about $1,000 when you take it off the dealer's showroom floor.

Nevertheless, in some cases, when you buy a new car you get the benefit of an extremely desirable warranty. American Motors, for example, had the following warranty for its 1977 automobiles: 12 months or 12,000 miles on the complete car, from windshield wiper blades to complete engine overhaul if needed. (See Exhibit L-1.) Volkswagen has a warranty which gives you 12,000 miles (or one year) of servicing on any parts that might need replacement, plus a total of 2 years or 24,000 miles on the internal parts of the engine and transmission; and Volkswagen will tow you to the nearest dealer or give you a rental car if yours has to be kept overnight for any warranty repair.

THE FINANCIAL BENEFITS OF LEASING A NEW CAR

Many individuals no longer buy a new car. Rather, they lease one from a new car dealer for a 2- to 4-year period. In some cases, leasing for 3 years is cheaper than buying and selling or trading in the average car. Hertz Corporation Car Leasing Division contends that over 60 percent of all new cars are leased or rented in California. Nationally, 1 in every 4 cars is now leased, as compared to 1 in 25 some 15 years ago. In the typical 36-month (closed-end) lease, you pay a specified monthly figure for the use of the car. You take care of it as if it were personally owned. At the end of 3 years, you walk away from it. In many

EXHIBIT L-1   Sample New Car Warranty

AMC Buyer Protection Plan II:
1977 AMC Full 12-Month/12,000 Mile New Car Warranty
Full 24-Month/24,000-Mile Engine
and Drive Train Warranty

When you buy a new 1977 AMC car from an AMC dealer, American Motors Corporation* guarantees to you that for 12 months or 12,000 miles from the date of delivery or first use, whichever comes first, it will, except for tires, pay for the repair or replacement of any part it supplies which proves defective in material or workmanship. American further guarantees that for 24 months or 24,000 miles from the date of delivery or first use, whichever comes first, it will pay for the repair or replacement of the following parts which it supplies if they prove to be defective in material or workmanship: cylinder block, heads and valve train; internal engine parts; intake and exhaust manifolds; water pump; flywheel; crankshaft pulley; transmission; torque converter; clutch assembly; drive shaft and U-Joints; rear axle housing and its internal parts.

Normal service adjustments are not covered by this guarantee beyond the first 4 months or 4,000 miles of use, whichever comes first. Normal service adjustments include, but are not limited to: wheel alignment and balancing; headlight alignment; adjustments to carburetor, distributor timing, clutch, brake, transmission linkage and bands, belts, doors, windows, hood, rear deck lid, and tailgate.

All we require is that the car be properly maintained and cared for under normal use and service in the fifty United States or Canada and that guaranteed repairs or replacements be made by an AMC dealer.

No other express warranty is given or authorized by American. American shall not be liable for loss of use of vehicle, loss of time, inconvenience or other incidental or consequential damages. Some states and provinces do not allow limitation or exclusion of consequential damages so the above exclusion and limitation may not apply to you. This warranty gives you specific legal rights and you may also have other rights which vary from state to state or province to province.

*In Canada: American Motors (Canada) Limited

Reprinted with permission of American Motors Corporation.

larger cities, the auto insurance that is included in your leasing agreement is sold to you at a lower rate than if you had bought it on your own for a privately owned car.

For many individuals, an important advantage of leasing a car is the convenience of accounting for the business use of a car. If you use your car 50 percent of the time for business, you simply figure that 50 percent of your annual lease cost is deductible from your income before you pay taxes.

IF YOU DECIDE
TO BUY A NEW CAR

If you decide to buy a new car, the questions are: where to buy it, which one to buy, and what accessories to purchase.

The Dealer

1. **Location:** Where to buy depends on a number of factors, the most important being how far the dealer is from your job or home. After all, you must take the car in for servicing, and a new car, no matter how good it is, is going to have at least a few problems in the beginning. If you value time and convenience

highly, and you can conveniently leave your car off at the dealer and walk to work or walk back home, you will be ahead of the game.

2. Dealer service facilities and personnel: To find out about the dealer's service facilities and personnel, ask specific questions about them, such as: what does the dealer do to make service easier for customers? What is the size and reputation of the service department? How long is service work guaranteed —0 days, 30 days, or 90 days? How much electronic diagnostic equipment does the shop have? Are there provisions for replacement transportation while your car is in for service? When is the service department open? All of these questions are important and should not be glossed over because, as we all know, cars, whether they be new or used, require servicing.

3. Dealer reputation: Talk to customers who have bought from the dealer and have used his service department to find out how satisfied they are. Or, better yet, take your present car in for servicing and see how satisfied you are with their service department. (This is important for both new and used car purchases.)

4. The deal offered: Obviously the deal offered is of utmost importance in all of the above considerations. You may be willing to pay a slightly higher price at a specific dealer who you like very much and who has a good reputation for service, but *only* a slightly higher price. Shopping around

is, of course, a necessary step for most people when they buy a car.

GETTING THE BEST DEAL ON A NEW CAR

There are differences in prices for the same car with the same accessories depending on the dealer you buy from and depending on your bargaining skills. However, remember at the onset that the differences in prices for the same car will never be great, particularly for the lower priced subcompacts and compacts. Thus, it will not be worth your while to go to 25 dealers to bargain on a particular car. In fact, one study showed that after 3 dealers, the probability of getting a better deal was very small.

You can obtain dealer cost and a list price on all cars and options from auto guides sold at newsstands such as in the December issue of *Changing Times*, and in some paperback books, such as Edmund's and Car/Puter's *Autofacts*, or you can fill out a form on which you list the car and all the options you want to buy and send it to Car/Puter International, Inc., 1603 Bushwick Avenue, Brooklyn, New York 11207. For $10 you will receive a computer printout showing dealer cost and list price for that car with all its options. Dealer markups vary from 17 percent to 25 percent depending on whether the car is a subcompact, compact, intermediate, or full size model. Luxury cars, such as Cadillacs and Lincoln Continentals, have a markup of 25 percent. When we speak of markup here, we

are referring to the difference between what the dealer pays for a car and what is shown on the sticker pasted to the car window.

Shopping by Phone

Although many dealers refuse to give out prices over the telephone and others will only give you the sticker price, there are some, especially foreign car dealers, who will tell you exactly what your final cost will be. In fact, if you are assertive enough over the telephone, sometimes you can negotiate a deal without ever visiting the showroom. Consider the following tactic. Call the dealer and ask to speak to a salesperson. Immediately indicate that you were just disappointed by a competing dealer who had "low balled" you. That is, you had been quoted one price and then the salesperson upped that figure when you were just about to close the deal. Telling the salesperson this over the phone right away alerts him or her that you have shopped around, are serious, and won't cave in for a higher than stated price. When the salesperson on the phone suggests a particular figure for the car you want with the options you want, ask him or her if that is the best that can be done. In many cases, the salesperson will be forced to be honest with you and will probably offer you a lower price just in order to get you to come into the showroom.

Things to Watch Out For

Once you have reached an agreement with the salesperson, make sure that the exact car and optional equipment that you want are listed plainly on the order and that that order is countersigned by someone in authority, such as the sales manager of the dealership. Also, have at least the following four things listed on the order:

1. There will be no increase in price—the price shown at the bottom of the order is the total price to be paid on delivery.

2. There will be no reappraisal of your trade-in.

3. There will be no substitutions of nonfactory equipment for anything that you order on the car.

4. The car will be delivered within a reasonably specific time period.

Finally, make sure that you don't fall for the "switch" that a salesperson might try to get you to agree to. For example, several days after you place your order, a salesperson might call you back telling you that the factory is jammed up with orders and that it will take you longer to get your car. The salesperson then might say that the identical car has been located at another dealership but has a few extra options you didn't want for about $320 more. It is possible that in such cases the salesperson may just be getting you to buy a more expensive car. Another possibility is for your car to come in and for the dealer to install several options, stating that they were on the car when the dealer received it, and that you will have to pay an extra $200 or $300 if you want to accept that car. You can check

this by comparing the options on the car with the list posted on the car window.

Using a Buying Service

If you want to skip all of the haggling and frustrations associated with bargaining for a new car, you may wish to use a buying service. Such a service is simply an intermediary that offers the car from $125 to $500 above factory cost, depending on the basic price and the size of the car. You buy the car from a regular dealer but at a guaranteed price. Warranties, rebates, and service are the same. Those who do not favor car buying services contend that the buyer does not usually select the dealer and that the service after the sale may be less dependable, more inconvenient, and more costly than had the car buyer chosen the dealer.

One such car buying service is United Auto Brokers, which is a subsidiary of Car/Puter

International, Inc. Most cars can be ordered for $125 over dealer's cost.

What Type of Car to Buy?

Deciding on what new car to buy depends at least in part on how much money you want to spend. You should figure out the exact yearly out-of-pocket costs you will incur for different price ranges and then decide which one you are willing to pay for. Remember, many times when you go up the ladder of car prices you are not buying any more safety or speed, but only styling, prestige, and so on. Be aware of the price you are paying for these qualities.

You should also be aware of the various operating costs of the new cars you look at. Compacts are cheaper to run than full sized cars; but they hold fewer people comfortably and less baggage, and they give you less protection in a big crash.

What options you should buy

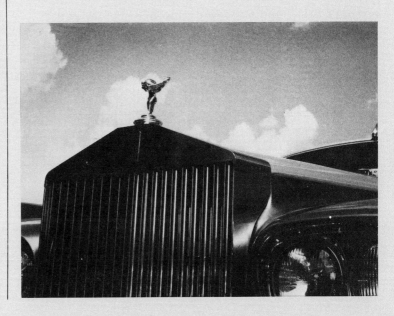

EXHIBIT L-2	What Are the Advantages, Disadvantages, and Seating Accommodations of the Sizes?		
SIZE	**ADVANTAGES**	**DISADVANTAGES**	**SEATS**
SUBCOMPACT	Lowest-cost available in U.S. Extremely easy to handle, park, garage. Excellent fuel mileage. Low operating, maintenance costs. Uncomplicated engines, usually 4-cylinder. Good second, or son-and-daughter car.	Slightly stiffer ride, usually because of short wheelbase and light weight. Limited space for passengers, cargo. Luxury interiors and some optional equipment not available on all models.	Two front, somewhat crowded. Two rear, crowded.
COMPACT	Low initial cost. Low operating, maintenance cost. Good fuel mileage. Easy to handle, park, garage. Fair cross-country car. Excellent for commuting. Good size for family of two adults, two small children.	Less-smooth ride than next sizes up. Less comfortable than larger cars for frequent long trips. Passenger and cargo space somewhat limited. Instruments, option choices somewhat limited.	Two to three, front. Two, rear.
INTERMEDIATE	Good room and comfort at low cost. Not as bulky as full-size cars. Easy to handle in traffic, to park, to garage. Relatively low-cost operation and maintenance. Well balanced for long-trip road car; gives good ride. Adequate passenger and cargo space. Good choice of engines, options, etc. Fairly good on fuel mileage.	Not as spacious for big families or those with lots of luggage. Not as well suited for heavy loads or heavy-duty trailer towing. May need V–8 engine for hill-country operation.	For normal trips: Three, front. Three, rear. For long trips: Two, front. Two, rear (or three children).

(continued on next page)

EXHIBIT L-2 Continued

SIZE	ADVANTAGES	DISADVANTAGES	SEATS
FULL SIZE	Most stability and riding comfort. Widest choice of options and equipment. Best long-trip car. Hauls heavy loads. Tows trailers easiest. Excellent for bigger families. Provides most space for passengers, cargo.	Costs more to buy, operate, maintain. Lower fuel mileage. A bigger size to handle, park, garage. More complicated and heavier.	Three, front (bench seats). Three, rear in comfort.

also depends upon your taste relative to your income. Some options are wise to take, even if you don't want them. It would be ridiculous to try to get a stick shift on a Cadillac because when you want to sell it, fewer people would want to buy it. You should also consider things like power steering and power brakes on the larger cars, because without these features they are again very hard to sell (and very hard to drive and park while you own them).

Tires are an important feature on any car and something that you probably will not want to compromise on. Radial tires seem to offer the most protection, to be the safest handling, and are sometimes the longest lasting. Today, many new cars come with radials; if the car of your choice comes without them, you should consider immediately trading in the standard tires for radials.

Another accessory that you may definitely want to consider is a rear window defogger. Most rear windows now have them as a standard equipment, but some do not. If you live in a cold climate, the extra $30 or $60 is well worth it on those cold mornings when you would not otherwise be able to see out the rear-view mirror. Of course, the assumption is that you are willing to pay for safety; only you can decide whether you are.

In Table L-1 we give you a chart that you can fill in to compare the actual cost of four different types of cars you may want to buy with different options.

TRADING IN YOUR WHEELS

When you trade in your old car, you can be fairly certain you will get no more than the standard trade-in price listed by the National Automobile Dealers Association in its Official Used Car Guide, or "blue book." It might be a good idea for you to look up this information your-

self. Your local bank will usually have a copy.

Here is an area where private sellers are just as guilty of irresponsibility as dealers. How often have you heard of friends trying to trade in an old clunker with many things wrong with it? Usually, they assure the dealer that the old clunker is running perfectly and nothing is wrong with it.

It is generally a good idea to bargain on your trade-in after you have finalized the new car sale with the dealer. Then you won't have to deal with what is called "high ball" gimmick. The salesperson will quote you a price for your used car as a trade-in that exceeds by $200, $300, or even $500 its blue book value. Presumably, you might be deluded into thinking that you are getting a bargain; however, the additional price you receive for your trade-in will merely be included somewhere else in the price of the new car. What you can assume is that

Table L-1   Price Comparison Chart

	CAR #1	CAR #2	CAR #3	CAR #4
LIST PRICE				
OPTIONS				
Power Steering, Brakes				
Automatic Transmission				
Nonstandard Engine				
Air Conditioning				
Rear Window Defogger				
Special Radio/Tape Deck				
Limited Slip Differential				
White Wall Tires				
Tinted Glass				
Vinyl Roof				
Tires—Radial, Oversized, or Snow				
Speed Control				
Fuel Economy Indicator				
Other				
Freight Charges				
Federal Excise Tax				
Dealer Service Charge				
State Sales Tax				
State Registration and Licensing Fees				
TOTAL COST				
Subtract Trade-in or Down Payment				
TOTAL AMOUNT TO BE PAID TO DEALER				

you will get the wholesale price of the car as a trade-in if it is in good condition. You can attempt to sell the used car yourself, but, remember, then you must incur the time and hassle costs of doing so (for example, changing the title, taking care of sales taxes, etc.).

IF YOU BUY A USED CAR

If you decide to buy a used car, there are a number of things you must think about. Because you do not know how any given car was treated before you buy it, you must be especially careful about its condition. One way of making certain that no major things will go wrong is by having an independent mechanic check the car over before you commit yourself to buying it. You may be charged for this, just as you will be charged by a building inspector who checks out a house you want to buy.

You are buying information from the mechanic. This information may save you hundreds of dollars in the future; the mechanic may point out that the transmission is about to go, that the gaskets leak, and so on. You may wish to take the car to an electronic diagnostic center that will charge from $15 to $50 to electronically analyze all major aspects of the car you intend to buy. Generally these centers do not do repair work themselves. They can usually give you an indication of what it will cost to have the used car repaired if anything shows up in their diagnosis.

Another way of insuring yourself against major repair expenses is by working with used car dealers who have 90-day written warranties on their products. Sometimes you have to pay for such a warranty and sometimes its price is merely included in the price of the used car. You are buying a type of insurance that costs you a little in the beginning but reduces the probability that you will pay out a lot in the future. Very rarely, a used car may still be covered by the manufacturer's 1-year, 12,000-mile, or 2-year, 24,000-mile warranty. Because such a used car is worth more to you than those without warranties, you will be willing to pay more.

One thing you can check out by yourself on a used car is whether it has been in a major accident. Look for mismatched colors in the paint and for ripples, bumps, and grainy surfaces on the bodywork. These will indicate extensive repainting

and therefore extensive repairs. Such discoveries may not dissuade you from wanting to buy the car, but they should persuade you to have some shop testing done by an independent mechanic.

There are numerous methods of examining a prospective used car purchase. These can be found in the section on buying a used car in any annual *Consumer Reports Buying Guide.* It gives you more than a dozen on-the-lot tests, and eight to ten driving tests that you can do yourself. It also tells you approximately what each repair job will cost if you notice something wrong. However, because nothing can duplicate a shop test by a good mechanic, this step is highly recommended unless you have an extremely good warranty with the deal. You might also be able to get a helpful brochure from your local consumer affairs office. If you are purchasing a used car from a dealer, ask the dealer if he or she will give you the name and address of the car's previous owner. Then query this person on possible problems, defects, or advantages of the car.

GETTING GOOD REPAIRS

Every car owner is faced with the problem of having his or her car repaired. Finding a good repair shop or an honest mechanic may be a difficult job in your area. There are currently two private programs being developed to certify reliable workmanship on cars, one for mechanics and one for garages.

CERTIFYING MECHANICS

The National Institute for Automotive Service Excellence began certifying mechanics in 1972. In order to be certified by the Institute, a mechanic must pass a written examination and have at least two years of experience in the area being tested. There are now over 94,000 certified automotive mechanics in one or more of eight categories, including automatic transmission, manual transmission and rear axle, front end brakes, electrical system, engine repair, heating and air conditioning, and engine tune-up. Additionally, there are about 17,200 mechanics who have mastered all eight tests and have been certified as "general mechanics" by the Institute. If you are interested in seeking the services of a certified mechanic, you can send away to the National Institute for Automotive Service Excellence, 1825 K Street N.W., Washington, D.C. 20006. For $1.95 they will send you a list of certified mechanics and their locations.

CERTIFYING GARAGES

The American Automobile Association has begun a program to certify reliable garages and service stations. So far the program is relatively small, but it may eventually become as big as the program for certifying mechanics. The garages must meet American Automobile Association requirements for covering scope of service, customer service, equipment, number of persons on the premises, and so on. Once a garage is certified, it must offer members of the American Automobile Association who request it a written estimate of work to be performed. The garage must also make available any replaced parts after repairs are completed and guarantee its work for 90 days, or 4,000 miles, whichever comes first. Perhaps more important, each participating garage has agreed in writing to accept AAA's decision on any complaint turned in by a member of that organization.

MAKING SURE YOU DON'T GET GYPPED

There are a number of auto repair ruses that are used by some unscrupulous repair shops to gyp customers. One is replacement of ball joints in the front suspension. These parts do wear out, but they are fairly sturdy, and some movement is acceptable, anywhere from ⅛th to 3/16 of an inch. An unscrupulous mechanic may put your car on a hoist, turn your wheel to the side and wiggle it to make it appear that the ball joint is about to jump from the socket. Before you have the ball joints replaced, get the opinion of another mechanic; you may not need that repair job. The same test is true for the idler arm, which is a short piece of metal in the lower steering mechanism of the car. Another favorite trick is to convince you that you need new piston rings because you have a smoking exhaust; that may not be the case. Get a second opinion. And finally, if you keep needing to add automatic transmission fluid, that does not necessarily mean that

you need a new transmission or a complete overhaul. Rather, it may mean that you need a new modulator valve in the transmission, which can be replaced for less than $25.

WHEN THOSE NEW CAR REPAIRS GO WRONG

The former Director of the Office of Consumer Affairs, Virginia Knauer, told a meeting of automobile dealers that: "Every month complaints about automobiles head the list of problems that consumers write to me about." In order to counter the problems that customers have with dealers and with repairpeople, an organization named AUTOCAP was formed.

How Does It Work?

Say you are dissatisfied with the car that you just bought from a dealer. You call a toll free number in your state and register your complaint. You are immediately mailed a form on which to detail your problem. When you return the form to AUTO-CAP headquarters, the dealer involved is notified by mail and urged to work out the problem with you, the customer. If this fails, the matter goes before AUTOCAP for arbitration. The arbitrating panel consists of four dealers and three public members.

It is a painless job to arrive at a "just" settlement when a dealer and a customer can agree. Obviously, the panel is not a court of last resort; it has no enforcement powers and relies on dealer cooperation to handle complaints satisfactorily. But,

according to the Connecticut dealer and panel head, Richard D. Wagoner, dealer cooperation has been excellent: only two dealers had balked in the first year of operation.

When Things Get Sticky

When the going gets sticky on a matter of warranty or car performance, AUTOCAP goes directly to factory representatives. So far the results have been satisfying; manufacturers have cooperated in all respects.

And if you, the customer, feel that you did not get fair treatment at AUTOCAP's hands, you can still go to the state motor vehicle agency or take private legal action. The following automobile dealer organizations are operating AUTOCAP under sponsorship of the National Automobile Dealers Association as this book goes to press:

Kentucky Automobile Dealers Association, P.O. Box 498, Frankfort, Kentucky 40601.

Metropolitan Denver Automobile Dealers Association, 70 West 6th Ave., Denver, Colorado 80122.

Automotive Trade Association of National Capital Area, 8401 Connecticut Ave., Chevy Chase, Maryland 20015.

Central Florida Dealer Association, 1350 Orange Ave., Winter Park, Florida 32789.

Idaho Automobile Dealers Association, 2230 Main St., Boise, Idaho 83706.

Greater Louisville Automobile Dealers Association, 332 W. Broadway, Louisville, Kentucky 40202.

Cleveland Automobile Dealers Association, 310 Lakeside Ave., West, Cleveland, Ohio 44113.

Oklahoma Automobile Dealers Association, 1601 City National Bank Tower, Oklahoma City, Oklahoma 73102.

Oregon Automobile Dealers Association, P.O. Box 14460, Portland, Oregon 97214.

Utah Automobile Dealers Association, Newhouse Hotel, Salt Lake City, Utah 84101.

Louisiana Automobile Dealers Association, 201 Lafayette St., Baton Rouge, Louisiana 70821.

Indianapolis Automobile Trade Association, 822 North Illinois, Indianapolis, Indiana 46204.

Connecticut Automotive Trade Association, 18 N. Main St., West Hartford, Connecticut 06103.

The four largest domestic automobile producers have offices to handle customer complaints when dealers are unable or unwilling to clear up troubles with your new car. You can write to these offices directly. They are: American Motors Corporation, Owner Relations Manager, 14250 Plymouth Road, Detroit, Michigan 48232; Chrysler Corporation, Your Man in Detroit, Box 1086, Detroit, Michigan 48231; Ford Customer Service Division, Owner Relations Department, Park Lane Tower West, 1 Park Lane Boulevard, Dearborn, Michigan 48126; General Motors Corporation, Owner Relations Manager, 3044 West Grand Boulevard, Detroit, Michigan 48202.

If you wish to find out about an older car having a possible safety defect, you can call the Auto Safety Hotline at the National Highway Traffic Administration in Washington, D.C. The Hotline serves to exchange information about auto safety defects between the public and the government. You can report problems that you have had with cars in order to help others, as well as finding out about defects in a car you might own or wish to own. The Hotline operator can tell you if a used car you are attempting to purchase has ever been included in a recall campaign by the manufacturer. The number to call is 800-424-9393. You can also check to see if the used car you bought was fixed if it was recalled by the manufacturer for a defect. This would save you the possibility of driving a car with a known safety problem that wasn't fixed when it should have been.

FINANCING THAT PURCHASE

A new or used car is usually such a major purchase that at least part of it has to be financed by credit. Do not automatically accept the credit that the dealer offers you when you decide to buy a car. Shop around for credit just as you shop around for anything else. Fortunately for you, the Truth-in-Lending Act of 1968 requires every lender to disclose the total finance charge you will pay and the actual annual interest rate to be paid. Thus, the credit offered you by the dealer can be compared to the credit offered you by competing sources such as banks

and finance companies. Remember that in many cases if you default on your car payment, that car can be repossessed. This is a real possibility, because in some states finance companies can take your car away from you without a judicial hearing. Do not buy a car that is more expensive than you know you can afford. If the car is repossessed, you are bound to lose out.

Where to Borrow for a Car

You can go to insurance companies, loan companies, banks and savings institutions, credit unions, and auto dealers themselves. Generally, credit unions offer the most beneficial rates on automobile loans, so if you are a member of one or can become a member without too much trouble, find out what you will be charged there.

Banks are the second most commonly used source of financing automobiles, after the auto dealers themselves. What your local banker will charge you depends on your credit rating, the amount of down payment or trade-in value on the car you are buying, and the general state of the economy.

You may wish to look to auto insurance companies that sometimes issue car loans. They may do this through a bank or through their own subsidiaries. To find out if this is possible, give your auto insurance agent a call.

You will find that if you go to a small loan company or to a dealer, you will pay the highest annual percentage fee for an auto loan.

EXHIBIT L-3   **What Your Car Loan Will Cost per $1,000 Borrowed**

Annual Percentage Interest	ONE YEAR		TWO YEARS		THREE YEARS		FOUR YEARS	
	Monthly Payment	Total Finance Charge	Monthly Payment	Total Finance Charge	Monthly Payment	Total Finance Charge	Monthly Payment	Total Finance Charge
9	$87	$50	$46	$ 97	$32	$145	$25	$195
10	88	55	46	107	32	162	25	218
11	88	61	47	119	33	179	26	241
12	89	66	47	130	33	196	26	264
13	89	72	48	141	34	213	27	288
14	90	78	48	152	34	231	27	312

Note: Figures have been rounded to nearest dollar.

What Length of Loan to Take Out

Most consumer experts recommend that automobile loans be taken out for the shortest time period possible. They point out that you end up paying a relatively high interest charge when you take out a three- or four-year car loan. On a typical $4,100 loan, you end up paying, on average, $8.37 a month in additional interest in order to get your payments reduced by $52.00 a month. Additionally, you end up having a hefty balance to pay when you are ready to trade in your car before the end of four years.

Does that necessarily mean that you should not take out a four-year auto loan? No, it does not. You are really asking the question about how much you should be in debt. The fact that it is associated with an automobile is irrelevant. If you think you would be uncomfortable having a debt outstanding for four years then that may be a reason to opt for a shorter time period. However, the benefit you lose by doing so is that you must use more of your discretionary fund to pay off the automobile loan's monthly payment and will therefore have less to spend on other items during that period. The fact that it costs you in additional charges to keep an auto loan outstanding longer should not be surprising. You are asking to use someone else's money for a longer period. If you think that you can borrow at a lower rate using something rather than an automobile as collateral, then it would be more costly to take out a four-year auto loan. As with all borrowing decisions, you must balance the benefits of having more cash available for other purchases against the increased cost for borrowing more or for borrowing for a longer period of time.

GETTING AN ADEQUATE AMOUNT OF INSURANCE

An important step when buying an automobile is making sure you have adequate automobile insurance. Many kinds of insurance coverage can be offered to you. The most important is liability insurance.

Liability: This insurance covers bodily injury **liability** and property damage. Liability limits are usually described by a series of three numbers such as 25/50/5, which means that the policy will pay a maximum of $25,000 for bodily injury to one person, a maximum of $50,000 for bodily injury to more than one person, and a maximum of $5,000 for property damage in one occurrence. Most insurance companies offer liability up to $300,000 and sometimes $500,000. The cost of additional liability coverage is relatively small. It is wise to consider taking out a much larger limit than you would ordinarily expect to need, because today personal injury suits against automobile drivers who are proven negligent are sometimes astronomical. Some dependents of automobile accident victims have been successful in suing for $1 million.

Some people are not even happy with the maximum liability limits offered by regular automobile insurance coverage. These people can purchase a separate amount of coverage under a policy usually known as an **umbrella**. Umbrella limits sometimes go as high as $5 million.

Medical payments: Medical payments on an auto insurance policy will cover hospital and medical bills, and sometimes funeral expenses. Usually you can buy $2,000 to $5,000 for around $10 or $15 a year. This insurance protects all the passengers in your car.

Collision: Insurance of this type covers damage to your own car in any type of collision not covered by another insured driver at fault. It is usually not advisable to purchase full coverage (otherwise known as **zero deductible**) on collision. The price per year is quite high because the probability is so high that in any one year small repair jobs will be required and will be costly. Most people take out $50 or $100 deductible coverage, which costs about one-quarter the price of zero deductible.

Comprehensive: Comprehensive auto insurance covers for loss, damage, or anything destroyed by fire, hurricane, hail, or just about all other causes, including vandalism. It is separate from collision insurance. Full comprehensive insurance

is quite expensive. Again, $50 or $100 deductible is usually preferable.

Uninsured motorists: This type of coverage insures the driver and passengers against injury by any driver who has no insurance at all, or by a hit-and-run driver. Many states require that it be in all insurance policies sold to drivers. The risk is small, so the premium is relatively small.

Accidental death benefits: Sometimes called double indemnity, this coverage provides a lump sum to named beneficiaries if you happen to die in an automobile accident. It generally costs very little, but even so, it may not be desired if you feel that you have already purchased a sufficient amount of life insurance.

How to Shop for Insurance

Shopping for automobile insurance is usually easier than shopping for a car. You may want to look first to your local credit union or some special insurance source available to you if you are a member of certain organizations. Sometimes companies get special rates for their employees. If you are a government employee, you can often get special types of automobile insurance from a government employees' insurance company. However, when comparing insurance companies, remember that you should also look at the service they give. You can shop for insurance by figuring out the exact policy you want, including liability,

uninsured motorist, medical, collision, comprehensive, and perhaps towing, with the specific limits you want; then get a written statement from several insurance companies' agents. Insurance premiums can vary by 90 percent or more depending on what company you select.

The insurance agent you work with is also important. If one in your area has the reputation of being fair and knowledgeable, you may want to take suggestions from that person. Again, you are being sold information as part of the package. (You may also be buying "clout" if you are dealing with a company agent rather than a broker for many different companies.)

There are basically two types of policies, family and special. Generally, when you ask for an insurance quote, you will be quoted for a family automobile policy. It includes liability, comprehensive collision, uninsured motorist, and medical in the amount you specify. A cheaper, but more restricted type of policy is deemed special. It is restricted to better than average drivers and combines bodily injury and property damage liability, accidental death, and uninsured motorist protection. So instead of offering you separate amounts on those items, a lump sum maximum is given per accident. If that maximum is, say, $100,000, then compensation of any one person, to a group of people or for property damage, will not exceed $100,000. In most cases under a special policy, medical payment insurance only pays the difference between what the medical bill is and what your health insurance pays. In other words, you cannot collect the full amount from both policies. Finally, under a special policy, you purchase collision and comprehensive insurance separately. Also, you may be able to get safe driver policies, reductions if you have taken driver training, and so on. All of these possibilities should be discussed with prospective insurance agents.

To help you compare insurance policies, we present Table L-2. When calling around to get insurance, you can fill in the chart and compare policies.

Problems of Insuring Young Drivers

Parents do not have to be told how expensive it is to insure a young driver in a family, particularly if that driver is a male. There are ways of reducing such auto insurance expenses, however. One way is to limit the son or daughter's driving to an occasional use of the family car. Occasional use is defined by most insurance companies as using the car less than 50 percent of the time. That means that if the car is used for going out on weekends or occasionally to school, then the young driver qualifies for the lower rate. However, if the car is used every day for driving to school, then the lower rate does not apply. There are some companies that give discounts if the driver has a B or better average in school, and there are discounts for compact and subcompact cars. A drivers education course will also qualify some students for an auto insurance discount.

Tips on lowering automobile insurance rates:

1. Don't buy coverage that you don't need, such as collision insurance on an older car. For example, if you have a five-year-

Table L-2 Comparing Auto Insurance Companies

KIND OF COVERAGE	LIMITS DESIRED	COMPANY		
		A	B	C
1. Liability:				
Bodily injury	$_____/person, $_____/accident	_____	_____	_____
Property damage	$_____/accident	_____	_____	_____
2. Physical damage:		_____	_____	_____
Compensation for total lost	blue book wholesale price	_____	_____	_____
Collision	$_____/deductible	_____	_____	_____
3. Medical payments	$_____/person	_____	_____	_____
4. Uninsured motorists	$_____/person, $_____/accident	_____	_____	_____
5. Accidental death benefits		_____	_____	_____
6. Towing		_____	_____	_____
7. Comprehensive	$_____/deductible	_____	_____	_____
8. Other		_____	_____	_____
ANNUAL TOTAL		_____	_____	_____

old car whose blue book value is relatively low, you may not want to bother with collision insurance because you never collect more than blue book value (and damage may be more than the car is worth).

2. See if a special policy is suitable for your needs, rather than a more expensive family automobile insurance policy.

3. Avoid high-performance or expensive cars for which auto insurance is much higher than on other cars.

4. Take a higher deductible on collision and comprehensive insurance. Remember, the higher the deductible, the lower the premium.

5. See if you qualify for a discount for not smoking, not drinking, belonging to a car pool, having an accident-free record for the past three years or more, having a car with heavy bumpers or a passive restraint system, driving a compact car, or keeping your mileage low each year.

6. Don't use your car for work if other transportation can be obtained.

7. Don't duplicate insurance. If you have a comprehensive health and accident insurance policy, then you don't need medical payments in your automobile insurance plan.

8. Pay your insurance premium for the full period rather than in installments. (Note, however, that you lose the use of that money during the time period.)

9. Any time your situation changes, notify your company.

Do this when your estimated yearly mileage drops, when you join a car pool, when a driver of your car moves away from home, and so on.

WHEN YOU ARE REFUSED INSURANCE

Sometimes because of a bad driving record, you will be refused liability coverage by an automobile insurance company. When this happens, you become an **assigned risk**. You must first certify that you have attempted within the past 60 days to obtain insurance in the state in which you reside. A pool of insurance companies (or sometimes the state) will then assign you to a specific company in the pool for a period of three years. At the end of three years, you can apply for reassignment, provided you are still unable to purchase insurance outside the pool.

If you are an assigned risk, you can only purchase the legal minimum amount of insurance in your state. In most cases, you will pay a much higher premium for the same amount of coverage than someone who is not an assigned risk.

TIPS ON SAVING FUEL

1. Don't buy gasoline that has an octane rating higher than is recommended by the car manufacturer.

2. Avoid stop-and-go driving.

3. Reduce your use of your air conditioner if you have one.

4. Turn the engine off whenever it is going to be idling for more than a minute.

5. Consolidate errands in order to keep short trips to a minimum.

6. Use radial tires.

7. Do not underinflate tires.

8. Reduce car weight by keeping the trunk clear of unnecessary items.

9. Drive smoothly and steadily, maintaining as constant a speed as possible.

10. Avoid jack-rabbit starts and sudden stops at intersections.

SUMMARY

1. When looking for a new car dealer, consider location, dealer service facilities and personnel, dealer reputation, and the deal offered.

2. Generally, new cars have problems that you will want the dealer to take care of. Hence, the fact that the dealer is nearby and willing to handle such warranty problems is an important consideration when choosing a dealer.

3. Deciding on the size of a car should involve not only purchase cost, but running costs, as well as ride smoothness, acceleration, availability of options, and handling.

4. The purchase of a used car requires as much shopping as for a new car, or more, for the mechanical condition of the car is now in question. If you wish to have a warranty, purchase a used car from a dealer offering a 1-month or 300-mile warranty. However, you will have to pay a higher price for that benefit.

5. Shop for automobile financing just as you shop for any other product. Shop on the basis of down payment required, setup charges, actual finance charge, and actual annual interest, as well as the number of months required to pay. Remember, the sooner you pay off the loan, the smaller the interest paid. On the other hand, the less money you will have for other purchases.

6. There is a minimum insurance required to drive an automobile in all states. However, it is generally quite cheap to purchase additional coverage. For example, it may cost you only $3 more a year to increase your liability from $50,000 to $150,000.

7. Shop for automobile insurance systematically, asking each potential company its price for a standard policy, such as $25,000 for bodily injury to one person, a maximum of $50,000 bodily injury to more than one person, and a maximum of $5,000 for property, plus $10,000 medical payments, plus $100 deductible collision, full comprehensive and uninsured motorist. After you have received the different bids on such a policy, find out the pay-off procedures in case of an accident. Is there a claims department? How well is it set up? How fast will it operate? How soon can you get a loaner car in case of an accident?

QUESTIONS FOR THOUGHT AND DISCUSSION

1. For a few years, one car company had a 50,000 mile or 5-year warranty on the drive train of its new automobiles. This warranty is no longer avail-able. Why do you think it was discontinued?

2. Why do you think some automobile companies have longer warranty periods than others?

3. Many automobiles are obviously less safe than others. Why do you think people knowingly drive such unsafe cars?

4. Do you think that the most important factor in deciding which car to buy is the amount of gasoline it consumes?

5. In 1973 and 1974, large American cars stopped selling well. Do you know why?

6. Why is the interest rate you pay for an automobile loan higher than what you would pay for a home mortgage?

7. Would you prefer to take out an automobile loan for 24 months or 48 months?

8. What is the most important safety feature a car can have?

9. Would it ever be considered rational to not carry automobile insurance?

THINGS TO DO

1. Even if you are not in the market for a new car, try shopping for one over the phone. Pick a particular make, body style, and set of accessories. Call five different new car dealers in your area. See if you can get an actual quote on the phone. See if there are any big differences among the quotes you get. You will be surprised at how little they vary.

2. Make a list of the various new car warranties available for cars such as Ford, Chevrolet, Oldsmobile, Volkswagen, Volvo, and Mercedes. See if the more expensive cars have a better warranty.

3. Go to the library and get the latest December Annual Buying Guide of Consumer Reports. Look at the section on buying a used car. Could you perform the eight to ten on-the-lot tests given in that section? Have you ever tried the driving tests given in that section when you were out looking for a used car?

4. Find out whether your area has a local office of AUTOCAP, which is under National Automobile Dealer Association sponsorship. See what AUTOCAP in your area has done.

SELECTED READINGS

Aerospace Education Foundation. The Safe Driving Handbook. New York: Grossett & Dunlap, 1970.

"Auto Insurance Companies Offer Cost-Cutting Advice to Motorists." Consumer Newsweek 6 (November 15, 1976).

"Buying a Used Car." Changing Times, January 1975.

"Changes in Auto Insurance that May Affect You." Changing Times 31 (April 1977), pp. 37–38.

Consumer Action Auto Insurance Guide. San Francisco Consumer Action, 26 Seventh Street, San Francisco, CA 94103.

Every Ten Minutes. New York: Insurance Information Institute, 1974.

"Good Bets in Used Cars; Some Used Car Models to Avoid." Consumer Reports, April 1977, p. 240.

GLOSSARY OF TERMS

Outpatient Services

The services of doctors and/or hospitals that do not involve the individual remaining as a registered patient in the hospital.

Inpatient Services

Services rendered to an individual by doctors and/or a hospital while the patient remains in the hospital at least for one night.

Naturopath

A practitioner of a system for treating disease that emphasizes assistance to nature and includes the use of natural medicinal substances and physical means (such as manipulation and electrical treatment).

Ethical Drug Industry

The industry that produces the drugs that are sold by prescription only. To be contrasted with patent drugs, which are sold over-the-counter without prescriptions.

Price Discrimination

Charging different people different prices for the same item.

The Health Care Dilemma

CHAPTER PREVIEW

☐ What has Medicare to do with the high cost of medical services?

☐ Why have there been so few medical doctors in the United States?

☐ What are the restrictions on entry into the medical care industry?

☐ How does the American Medical Association fit into all of this?

☐ What has the Food and Drug Administration done to protect the consumer from injurious drugs?

☐ What has the restriction on advertising drug prices done to the cost of drugs to consumers?

☐ What is group health all about?

☐ What are HMOs?

15 The woeful lack of adequate health care for large segments of the American population has been long decried by Congresspersons, Presidents, laypersons, and even doctors. There have been many suggested solutions to our health care crisis, some of which have already been enacted in the form of Medicare and Medicaid. But even before those programs went into full effect, Senators and Congresspersons started demanding more comprehensive medical care insurance.

In addition to the problems of inadequate supplies of medical care, concerned legislators and citizens could not help noticing the spiraling costs of obtaining what medical care is available. Figure 15-1 shows the Consumer Price Index and the price indexes of various health care services, the latter having risen considerably faster than the overall CPI. Thus, not only is health care more expensive than it was, but its *relative* price is rising; it is more expensive in relation to other services than it once was.

MEDICAL CARE EXPENDITURES

The expenditures for medical care in the United States have increased dramatically in the last four or five decades. We spent only $4 billion on medical care in 1929. We increased our spending to $40 billion by 1965. It is well over $166 billion today. In 1929 expenditures on medical care represented 4 percent of total national spending, but today's expenditures represent nearly 10 percent. We can say, therefore, that as real incomes rise, Americans demand not just more medical care, but more than is in proportion to the rise in incomes.

WHY DOES MEDICAL CARE COST SO MUCH?

Nobody expects medical care to be free. After all, it uses resources, and resources themselves are never free. But many people have wondered why medical care costs have been going up so much faster than all other costs. This has happened for several reasons. The first has to do with the increases in demand brought about by government programs.

WHEN MEDICARE STARTED

Prior to Medicare—"free" medical care for the aged—Congressional estimates of what that program would cost were many times less than the actual cost turned out to be. This can be easily explained, for the demand for medical services is responsive to the price charged. When Medicare was instituted, the actual price of health care services to many people was drastically lowered. In some cases, the price was reduced to zero. As the price fell, the quantity demanded rose—and rose so much that the available supply of medical care services was taxed beyond capacity. The only thing that could give was the price, and it gave. Hospital room charges have skyrocked since the imposition of Medicare. But Medicare is not alone in causing drastic increases in medical prices.

INSURANCE FRAMEWORK

Approximately 80 million Americans are covered by some form of private medical insurance. Most of this medical insurance pays a certain part of hospital expenses. Herein lies the problem: insurance rarely covers **outpatient service**. Rather, it covers only **inpatient service**. Individuals covered by insurance therefore have an incentive to go to the hospital to be taken care of by their private doctors. And their

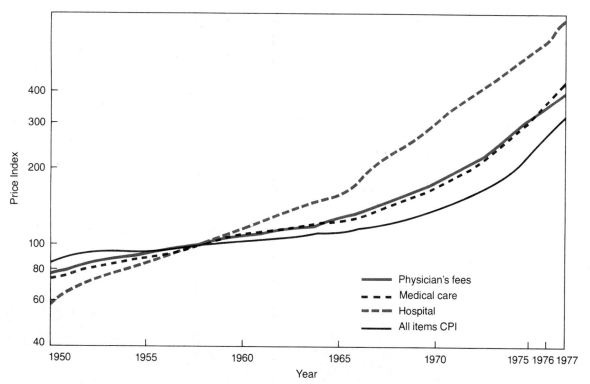

Figure 15-1
Consumer Price Index vs. Medical Price Index (1957–1959=100)

Here we show what has happened to the indexes of various prices in our economy. Hospital prices have risen the most rapidly, and physician's fees, as well as the overall index of medical care prices, have risen faster than the Consumer Price Index.

Source: U.S. Department of Labor, Bureau of Labor Statistics.

private doctors have an incentive to send them to the hospital in order to collect the insurance payments, knowing full well that fewer patients would be able to pay for the services performed in their doctors' offices because they would not then be covered by insurance. Additionally, insurance plans generally have very little control over the number of tests and examinations that are performed on patients. Hospitals have an incentive, therefore, to use the most exotic techniques possible and doctors to order them, knowing full well that patients will have a large percentage of the costs reimbursed by insurance companies. The problem is that patients covered under insurance do not pay the *direct* costs of the medical care they receive in a hospital. Hence, they demand much more than they otherwise would. This increase in quantity demanded causes hospital expenses to go up, all other things held constant.

OTHER REASONS

There is an increased sophistication in the medical field, having developed into many new areas of diagnosis, surgery, drug treatment, and physical therapy. With all the specializations, Americans are demanding better health care that, in turn, costs more. Along with the increased specialization has come the need to visit two or more specialized doctors, rather than one as in the past. This, of course, raises the cost of medical care. Additionally, you are getting better services than before. Many hospitals now have complete staffing around the clock and use much more sophisticated equipment. All of this costs more. Recently an even more important phenomena, malpractice insurance expenses, has caused medical costs to rise even more.

MALPRACTICE

Individuals are suing their doctors and hospitals more than ever before. Juries are awarding larger amounts more often than ever before. The result? Skyrocketing malpractice insurance costs. Just look at a few examples. In 1972 Baylor University Medical Center in Dallas, Texas, paid $11,000 for malpractice insurance; in 1976, the bill was $1.5 million! In 1974, Mt. Sinai Hospital Medical Center in Chicago paid $281,000 for $6 million in malpractice insurance; in 1976, the same insurance companies wanted $3 million to provide the $6 million in coverage. Had

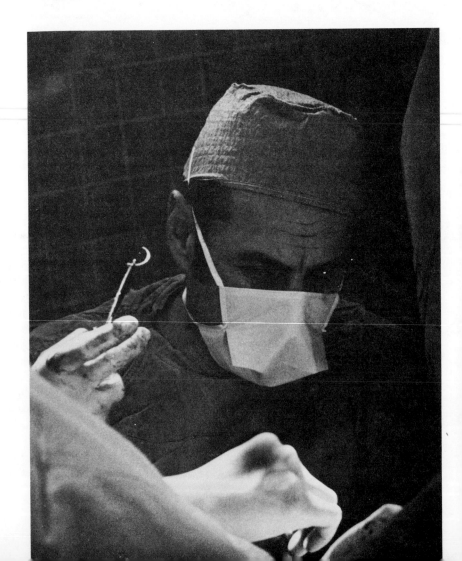

the hospital paid the premium sought by the insurance companies, the daily cost of malpractice insurance to the patient would have gone up from $7 to $22 per day. A number of hospitals have stopped paying regular insurance companies for such coverage. Instead, they are self-insuring; that is, they set aside a certain sum of money each month into a reserve account to cover any claims against them in malpractice lawsuits. Unfortunately, this means that some hospitals could conceivably go out of business if an extraordinarily large malpractice suit was won by a former patient.

We also find that hospitals may protect themselves from additional malpractice suits by engaging in excessive testing and prolonged stays in intensive care units after surgery. This adds to medical care costs.

Some concerned individuals have suggested that the government step in to offer malpractice insurance to hospitals that do not feel they can "afford" the now higher rates. However, this would mean that hospitals could then force the general taxpayer to cover any of their mistakes. In the future, there may be other solutions to the malpractice insurance problem, but today it remains a problem indeed.

THE SHORT SUPPLY OF MEDICAL CARE

Medical care consists of a number of items, including but not limited to the services of physicians, nurses and hospital staff, hospital facilities, maintenance of the facilities, and medications and drugs. What determines the supply of the most important item (at least up until now) in the total medical care package—physicians' services?

THE PRODUCTION OF MEDICAL DOCTORS

In 1975, 72,000 people took the Standard Medical School Admissions Test; only 13,500 were accepted in medical schools. Applicants to the Harvard Medical School run almost 3,500, but the class size remains at fewer than 150. Some students apply to as many as ten different medical schools, and when turned down reapply two or three times. Moreover, probably two or three times as many students do not bother to apply because they know the odds are so much against them. Why is there such a large discrepancy between those who want to go to medical school and those who are accepted? If you compare the number of students who wish to attend law school with the number of students who actually go, the discrepancy is much smaller than that for medical school. The reason for this greater discrepancy is not hard to find: the number of medical schools in the United States is severely restricted, as is the number of entrants into those schools.

RESTRICTIONS

The question is: restricted by whom? In principle, restriction on the number of medical schools is due to state licensing requirements that universally prohibit proprietary medical schools (schools run for profit). Also, it is difficult for a university that does not have a medical school to suddenly start one. A university can start a graduate department of romance languages without asking permission of any agencies or boards, just as it can start a law school without asking anybody. However, unless the medical school is accredited by the state, the graduates are not even allowed to take the licensing exam required for practicing medicine.[1]

[1]Licensing of doctors is now done under the requirements of the National Board of Medical Examiners. Among the national requirements are two years of college, four years of medical school with a final examination, and an internship.

THE PAST

In the first decade in this century, there were 192 medical schools in the United States. By 1944, that number had declined to 69. The number of physicians per 100,000 people dropped from 157 in 1900 to 132 in 1957. It appears that the American Medical Association and the so-called Flexner Report (discussed below) were responsible for the reduced growth rate in the supply of physicians.

THE AMA WINS OUT

The American Medical Association was started in 1847. As it still does today, it represented practitioners in the field of medicine. From the period of 1870 to 1910, there was a struggle between the AMA and medical educators over who should control the number of doctors allowed to practice. This became a battle over who should control medical schools themselves. The American Medical Association won the battle; it essentially has complete control over medical education in the United States. To become licensed in any particular state, a medical school graduate must have obtained a degree from a "certified" medical school. The certification is nominally done by the states themselves; however, in all cases the states follow exactly the certification lists of the American Medical Association. If the AMA were to decertify a particular medical school, you can be sure the state involved would also decertify that same school. Graduates coming out of that decertified school would find themselves barred from legal medical practice.

THE FLEXNER REPORT

In all probability, the regulation and certification of medical schools was based on the outcome of the famous Flexner Report. In 1910, the prestigious Carnegie Foundation commissioned Abraham Flexner to inspect the existing medical education facilities in the United States. Flexner's recommendations resulted in the demise of half of the existing medical schools of the day. He asserted that they were unqualified to teach medical education. It is interesting to note that Flexner had absolutely no qualifications himself for deciding which medical schools were to be rated class A. Flexner was not a physician; he was not a scientist; and he had never been a medical educator. He had an undergraduate degree in arts and was the owner and operator of a for-profit prep school in Louisville, Kentucky. Moreover, his evaluation of existing medical schools consisted of a grand inspection tour—nothing more, nothing less. Sometimes Flexner evaluated an entire school in one afternoon. He decided whether a medical school was qualified by estimating how well it compared with the medical school at Johns Hopkins University.

It is also interesting to note that Flexner was examining the *inputs* and not the *outputs* of these particular schools. Instead of finding out how well or how qualified the doctors were who *graduated* from the different schools, he looked at how doctors were taught. This would be equivalent to your instructor giving you a grade on the basis of how many hours you spent studying rather than on how well you did on the final exam (even though you might find that preferable).

WHY DID THE AMA SEEK CONTROL?

It is not hard to find the motive behind the AMA's desire to control medical schools. We merely need quote from an earlier head of AMA's Council on Medical Education, Dr. Beven, who said in 1928:

> In this rapid elevation of the standard of medical education . . . the reduction of the number of medical schools from 160 to 80, there occurred a marked

reduction in the number of medical students and medical graduates. We had anticipated this and felt that this was a desirable thing. We had . . . a great oversupply of poor mediocre practitioners.

Dr. Beven's statement can be analyzed to mean that, if the supply falls, the price will therefore rise. On the other hand, if the supply increases, the price will fall.

AMA'S MOTIVES NOT SATISFIED

If we look at the American Medical Association's avowed motives, we realize that even those were not satisfied. The AMA maintained that the qualifications of many doctors were deficient—that is, the public was being disserved by doctors who were doing damage to unsuspecting patients. Medical school licensing was intended to weed out the most unqualified students and to eliminate the possibility that an unsuspecting sick person could be treated by an inadequately trained, yet licensed doctor. It is strange, therefore, that in 1910 the AMA did not seek to analyze the qualifications of the current crop of physicians. Closing one-half of the medical schools eliminated a *future* supply of supposedly unqualified doctors. But the current supply of supposedly unqualified doctors was allowed to continue practicing until retirement or death—as were those generations of unsuspecting citizens allowed to seek the aid of anyone who happened to have an M.D. degree, qualified or not. Somehow, this type of behavior does not seem consistent with the AMA's desire to raise the quality of medical services in the United States.

Moreover, it is difficult to understand why doctors are not reexamined periodically if they wish to continue practicing. Even a brilliant medical student from an excellent medical school could become lax in his or her medical practice and after a period of years become unqualified. Because there is no recertification procedure, the public can still be subjected to the malpractices of unqualified doctors.

SELF-TREATMENT

In addition, it is not obvious that the quality of medical care improved as much as the AMA professed. After all, there are two ways of obtaining medical services: one is self-diagnosis and self-treatment; the other is reliance on the medical care industry. If the price of a physician's diagnosis and treatment goes up, then one might expect that the quantity demanded would fall. Reliance on self-diagnosis and self-treatment would increase. People would decide to go to doctors only after their symptoms became alarming. It may be that the increase in quality and, therefore, price of doctors' services resulted in a decrease in the *total* quantity of medical care utilized because physicians were consulted less often. Moreover, we must presume that some people might forego the services of a licensed physician in favor of some alternative method that may be of "inferior" quality, such as **naturopaths** or faith healers. When the service of licensed physicians becomes more costly, there is an increase in the demand for substitute healing services from chiropractors, midwives, naturopaths, and so on.

And, of course, a real danger is present when consumers engage in extensive self-treatment. There are considerable numbers of over-the-counter medicines available to us all, many of which are quite powerful. And the tendency has been to become quite glib about self-prescription, even to the point of overuse of those medicines. It is one thing for a doctor to tell you to take three aspirin every four hours, and something else altogether for you to make that decision; you are often unaware of the possible side-effects and consequences of determining your own dosage. This problem becomes particularly acute with what children learn from their parents about taking medicines. If they see their parents taking a pill for almost everything, a certain appeal develops; and the result is usually dangerous and often fatal. You might have noticed that all recent advertisements for over-the-counter medications have been accompanied by the warning, "Use only as directed." This is an attempt to counter the serious health hazard presented by self-prescription. When in doubt, it is usually best to see a doctor.

THE FUTURE SUPPLY

The current shortage of physicians has been figured at something like 50,000. However, recent rates of medical school graduation and the addition of foreign-trained physicians who are immigrating to the United States will eliminate this shortage. In addition, Congress has enacted a number of programs to increase the supply of medical personnel. For example, in 1971 the Comprehensive Manpower Training Act and the Nurse Training Act were passed; $3 billion was provided for this purpose. Actually, some researchers believed that "there [was] a distinct possibility of excess capacity in medical schools and a surplus of physicians by the late 1970s."[2]

DRUG REGULATION

The **ethical drug industry** has always presented a problem to regulators and consumers. The information problems are sometimes insurmountable. Even the drug companies often do not know the effectiveness or the side effects of a drug. Doctors rarely take the time to get exact information on all the drugs they use, and in the past drug companies have not always carefully screened the drugs they sold. The largest regulator of drugs in the United States is the federal Food and Drug Administration.

Drug regulation is a difficult task. Consumers spend more than $12 billion for drugs a year, of which about $5 billion are sold only by prescription. Drugs save many lives and reduce the suffering for many illnesses. More than 90 percent of the prescriptions written today are for drugs that 30 years ago did not even exist.

WHAT THE FDA DOES

Since the Kefauver-Harris Amendment to the 1938 Food, Drug and Cosmetic Act passed in 1962, the FDA has had quite detailed, extremely lengthy procedures that a company must go through before approval can be given for a new drug. The steps may take years for a drug company to complete before it can get approval for a new drug.

THE BENEFITS
AND COSTS OF FDA
REQUIREMENTS

Did you realize that if aspirin had to go through the current FDA requirements for drug certification, it would fail to pass muster? Do you know why? Because it is not known why it works, and it is known to have side effects if too many are taken. Certainly aspirin would at least require a prescription if it were under current rulings. Now ask yourself this: Do you think it should be dispensed only by prescription? Do you think it should be taken off the market because nobody knows

---

[2]Charles T. Stewart, Jr., and Corazon M. Siddayao, *Increasing the Supply of Medical Personnel: Needs and Alternatives.* Washington, D.C.: American Enterprise Institute for Public Policy Research, 1972, p. 66. This seems to be what is happening in certain urban areas. However, a shortage of doctors is still apparent in most rural areas in the United States.

how it works? Yet we are certain that taking too much of it can give you duodenal ulcers and kidney dysfunction. If you believe it should be taken off the market, then you will agree with the spirit of the 1962 Kefauver-Harris Amendment. If you have doubts, then read on.

A study was done by Dr. Sam Peltzman a few years ago. Among the costs of the 1962 FDA amendment, he found that the entry rate of new drugs into the market had slowed considerably. His conclusions were the following:

> The 1962 Drug Amendment sought to reduce consumer waste on ineffective drugs. This goal appears to have been attained, but the costs in the process seem clearly to have outweighed the benefits. It was shown [in the study] that the amendments have produced a substantial decline in drug innovation since 1962.
>
> The net effect of the amendment on consumers, then, is comparable to their being taxed something between 5 and 10 percent on their . . . drug purchases. [3]

As with all legislation, consumers have to weigh the costs against the benefits in deciding where they stand. The benefits of preventing certain drugs from entering the market are that no one suffers the side effects. The costs are those mentioned above. Dr. Peltzman believes the costs outweigh the benefits, but you may interpret his data differently. One thing is certain: we all have the same interpretation of the data about drug prices.

RESTRICTIONS IN PHARMACEUTICAL SALES

Did you know that only 5 percent of prescriptions are compounded by the pharmacist? The other 95 percent the druggist fills by dropping pills into bottles and/or merely typing the patient's and doctor's names and dosage instructions on the local druggist's label, which is then pasted on a bottle supplied by the manufacturer. Why, then, does it cost so much to get drugs? One reason has been restriction of price competition among druggists: it is not considered "ethical" to advertise prescription drug prices. Thirty-seven states had expressly prohibited drug price advertising for many years. In many cases you could not even get druggists to discuss on the phone what they charge for filling a prescription or what their prescriptions cost. They mentioned professional ethics.

Pharmacy practices came to light back in 1972 when the federal Price Commission then in existence was going to require that retailers display base prices of their best-selling drugs. The American Pharmaceutical Association claimed that this would be a police state method of holding down prices. Unfortunately for us the consumers, the Price Commission backed down; it did not require the posting of prices. Instead, pharmacies were told they could provide consumers with the standard list of wholesale drug prices and the store's professional fee or mark-up for filling a prescription.

Because most druggists did not post prescription prices, it was (and still may be) more difficult for us to shop around for bargains, as we can for other goods. It was not surprising, then, that a 1967 AMA study in Chicago showed price differentials of 1200 percent for exactly the same drug! The U.S. Justice Department drew the obvious, logical conclusion:

[3]Sam Peltzman, "An Evaluation of Consumer Protection Legislation: The 1962 Drug Amendments," *Journal of Political Economy*, 81 (September/October 1973): 1089–1090.

Differentials such as these can only exist when they are unknown to potential customers; for a given choice, most consumers would refuse to pay 10 or 12 times the going price for a drug available elsewhere. The cost to the public of the lack of price competition is enormous.

In 1976, the magazine *Money* priced three of the ten most prescribed drugs in four stores in five cities. *Money* found as much as 406 percent difference in the price for a given drug. The results were as follows (price on a per pill basis):

Drug	Lowest Price	Highest Price	Spread
Valium (5 mg.)	8.9¢	23.2¢	161%
Darvon Compound-65	7.6¢	19.8¢	161%
Tetracycline (250 mg.)	4.9¢	24.8¢	406%

THE SUPREME COURT INTERVENES

In 1976 a landmark case for consumers was handed down by the U.S. Supreme Court. A consumer activist, Lynn Jordan in Virginia, decided she had had enough of not being able to shop around for the lowest priced prescription drugs because a Virginia law banned prescription drug price advertising. She, along with the consumer council that she headed in the Virginia State AFL-CIO, sued and won.[4] It has been ruled unconstitutional for states to forbid pharmacies to advertise prices for prescription drugs, even though statute or pharmacy board regulations prohibit it. According to Justice Harry A. Blackmun, "Advertising, however tasteless and excessive it sometimes may seem, is nonetheless dissemination of information as to who is producing and selling what product for what reason and at what price." If consumers are to make more intelligent marketplace decisions, they need the "free flow of commercial information," according to Blackmun and the Court.

Even before the Supreme Court decision, some states had gone further and actually required the posting of drug prices. Since January 1, 1974, New York State pharmacists must post the price and name of the 150 most frequently prescribed drugs. Boston, since 1971, has required the posting of 100 most frequently prescribed drugs and their prices. California, Minnesota, New Hampshire, and Texas have followed suit. The Food and Drug Administration, toward the end of 1973, decided to help standardize pricing information to be given to consumers. It said that it would prescribe the format to be used for the posting and advertising of prescription drug prices.

GENERIC VS. BRAND NAME DRUGS

Prescriptions for drugs can either be written in terms of the drug's generic name or its brand or trademark name. The price of the drug that is not trademarked is much less. Only about 10 percent of all new drug prescriptions are written with the generic name of the drug. What does this do? It raises the consumer's drug bills. We might ask why doctors often prescribe expensive brand name drugs. It may be that physicians become accustomed to certain proven drugs and automatically prescribe them. It may even be because physicians are courted by drug companies that give them free golf balls, free dinners, and the like. A druggist is

[4]*Virginia State Board of Pharmacies* vs. *The Virginia Citizens Consumer Council*—74-895.

required to make no substitution when filling out a prescription that mentions a brand name. However, one study of a penicillin drug called Ampicillin, its generic name, showed that even though 53 percent of the prescriptions had that name on them, 98 percent of the sales were for major brand names. When you consider that the brand name price is usually two to four times more expensive than the lowest generic price, you can see what this does to health care costs.[5]

The Food and Drug Administration believes strongly that there is no significant difference in quality between the generic and brand name products tested. Nonetheless, there are strong proponents of brand name drugs. They believe that generic drugs are not as effective as brand name drugs. They measure effectiveness by the amount of active medication that is absorbed from the intestine into the bloodstream.

A number of consumer groups and consumer advocates strongly supported a bill introduced in the Senate by Senator Gaylord Nelson of Wisconsin in 1973. Had that bill passed, pharmacists would have been required to use the generic drug if the generic name was put on the prescription. Some advocates, such as Consumers Union, want to go even further—completely eliminate the use of brand names for drugs. And so, the generic versus brand name controversy continues.

ALTERNATIVE HEALTH CARE SYSTEMS

The traditional health care system has been the standard "fee for service" between doctor and private patient; but in recent decades alternatives to this system have become numerous. Although we lack the space to go into all of them, we will discuss group health and HMOs (Health Maintenance Organizations).

GROUP HEALTH

Group health service is basically a hospital made up of all different aspects of health care services in which doctors work for a salary, not for a fee. You become a member of a group health care plan by paying a specific fee determined by the number of members in your family. All group health services are then provided without charge, except for certain drugs. In some plans you can pick your own doctors from among those on staff, in others you cannot. Group health plans stress preventive medicine in their practice. The AMA has fought against prepaid medical plans such as Kaiser, Group Health Cooperative of Puget Sound, Health Insurance Plan (HIP) of New York, and Ross Loos. With these medical plans, everybody is charged the same price for the same service. All plans are prepaid, and the charges are not a function of subscribers' incomes. There is no way to **price discriminate** as there is with the typical "fee for service" method of payment that most physicians use.

The AMA has used various tactics to discourage doctors from participating in group medical plans. Many doctors have been expelled from their county medical associations and therefore can practice specialties only with the group medical plan hospital. But the AMA has not always succeeded in squelching budding medical establishments that promote competition with private physicians and do not price discriminate. For its efforts, the AMA has been prosecuted under the Sherman Antitrust Act in Washington, D.C., and under other state antitrust acts. Nonetheless, about one-third of the states have declared group health plans illegal.

[5]Brand name prescription drugs may cost thirty times more than their generic counterparts.

HMOs

Toward the end of 1974, many Americans were asked by their employers whether they wanted to drop group health insurance in favor of prepaid medical care. Those employees who chose that particular option became members of an HMO, or Health Maintenance Organization.

HMOs range from group practice setups like clinics with such extras as specialists, affiliated hospitals, and dentists to individual practice foundations in which doctors continue to practice in their own offices but take HMO patients in exchange for a share of the premium.

Employees were given this opportunity to switch from group health to prepaid medical care by a provision in the Health Maintenance Organization Act of 1973. Under the law, any company of 25 or more workers that has some sort of group health insurance plan must negotiate a group HMO contract and offer it to employees, provided that there is a qualified HMO in the area and only if the employer is first contacted by an HMO organizer. The legislation requires HMOs to accept individual members as well as groups of employees. (Note that this HMO concept is separate from national health insurance, which is discussed below.)

The list of basic services that must be covered by the monthly premium includes: hospital and physical care, including maternity; x rays and laboratory tests; psychiatric treatment emergency care; preventive health services, including regular checkups; birth control services; alcoholism and drug abuse treatment; and, for children only, dental checkups and eyeglass examinations.

Obviously, this coverage is more extensive than the typical health insurance program outlined early in this chapter. Thus, HMO premiums are anywhere from at least $5 a month more than a very good health insurance program up to $30 more than some group health plans.

Proponents of HMO legislation, however, point out that the higher premium cost is more than made up in savings in out-of-pocket medical expenses. Why? Simply because HMOs save considerable money on hospitalization, largely by treating people in the doctor's office instead of sending them to the hospital.

PROBLEMS WITH HMOs

The 1973 law proved to be unrealistic, however. By 1976, only 12 of the 181 prepaid health groups in the United States qualified as HMOs. The huge Kaiser Foundation health plan, which was the model of the law, didn't even qualify and it has three million subscribers. Critics of the 1973 law point out that in writing it, Congress required HMOs to offer so many medical services that the cost would be too high, thus not allowing the HMOs to compete with traditional health insurance plans. Moreover, the law requires that HMOs open membership rolls to all comers for 30 days a year. That would, according to critics, leave HMOs with a disportionate number of chronically ill and elderly patients.

NATIONAL HEALTH INSURANCE

National health insurance is not a different way to provide medical services, but it pays for them in a different way. Note that insurance for everyone will do nothing for the supply problem in medical care. Its chief benefit will be to make sure that whatever medical services an individual obtains will be paid for by a national insurance plan. However, that plan has to be paid for somehow, and you know how it will be paid—by taxes. A national health insurance plan essentially benefits those people who are sick more often than those people who are not, unless it is organized around preventive health care.

At the writing of this book, national health insurance had not yet become a reality for all Americans. Numerous bills had been proposed in Congress, and no doubt one of them will be in effect during the second edition of this text. While Nixon was President, he proposed a Comprehensive Health Insurance Plan (CHIP). The leading alternative to Nixon's plan was identified with Senator Edward M. Kennedy. The contrast of the two plans was quite obvious. Nixon wanted to build on the existing system with private insurance companies maintaining their current role. Employees were to be offered private health insurance by their employers who would pay 75 percent of the premium. On the other hand, the Kennedy "National Security Act" would have been, in its first form, a completely public program financed by employer and employee payments to a trust fund and modeled on the Social Security system. The Kennedy plan offered much broader coverage than the Nixon plan.

There have been so many plans proposed in the last few years that it would take many pages to describe all of them. They include the Long-Ribicoff Plan, the AMA Plan, the Ford Administration Plan, and others.

A few years ago, Consumers Union presented what it considered to be five minimum goals that any national health plan must meet.[6] They are as follows:

1. *Everyone's health care needs should be covered, and the entire population should be included within the system.*
2. *There should be no connection between the patient's income and the extent or quality of care dispensed by doctors, hospital, and others.*
3. *The plan should be financed progressively and in a manner open to public scrutiny.*
4. *The plan should provide incentives for efficiency, control over the cost and quality of services, and encouragement of alternative or innovative systems of delivering health care.*
5. *The administrators of the program should be accountable to the public, and consumers should have a voice in the administration.*

One aspect of national health insurance that many of its proponents often ignore involves how consumers would respond to the different insurance plans. Economists have pointed out that Medicare caused the quantity of medical care demanded to increase dramatically, thus driving up costs. Studies have shown that private insurance causes medical care costs to increase because of increased demand for more sophisticated treatment and increased demand for treatment more often. If such studies are correct, then we can predict that any national health insurance plan that does not require individuals to pay any direct expenses for medical care actually used will lead to more individuals demanding more medical care more often. We cannot say whether this is good or this is bad, but point it out as a possible result of a truly comprehensive national health insurance scheme.

[6]*Consumer Reports*, February 1975, pp. 119–122.

HEALTH EDUCATION

Critics of our current health care delivery system point out that less than one-half of one percent of the billions of dollars that we spend each year are spent on health education. Thus, it might be possible to improve the health of Americans without driving up costs if more individuals were taught what they have to do to maintain their health. This would mean more time, effort, and money allotted to health education from preschool all the way through college. It would mean offering more health maintenance courses throughout the country. It would mean having hospitals spend time with patients who are recuperating, teaching them the do's and don'ts of proper health care.

SUMMARY

1. The relative price of health care services has been rising. In particular, hospital costs have gone up dramatically in the last few years.
2. Medicare, which drastically lowered the price of health care services to many aged people, as well as insurance schemes that do not show the consumer the direct costs of medical care, have caused the demand for medical care services to rise dramatically.
3. One of the reasons that medical care services have always been so costly is because the number of medical doctors in the United States is restricted.
4. The relatively high cost of medical care has caused many consumers to perform self-diagnosis and self-treatment.
5. The federal Food and Drug Administration regulates the ethical drug industry in the United States. A 1962 amendment to the Food, Drug, and Cosmetic Act has significantly lengthened the time that it takes for a drug company to get a new drug certified as safe.
6. Until recently, in almost all states prescription drug prices were not posted and, in fact, could not be posted according to the rules of pharmaceutical associations. This had the effect of reducing competition among pharmacies and increasing prices to consumers for prescription drugs.
7. Alternative health care delivery systems are now in use in the United States, such as group health and health maintenance organizations.

QUESTIONS FOR THOUGHT AND DISCUSSION

1. Do you think it is fair that health care services can rise in price?
2. Should health care services be a right and not a privilege?
3. What is the difference between health care services and other services performed in our economy?
4. Why would insurance schemes increase the demand for hospital services?
5. What is the argument for restricting the number of medical school graduates?
6. The AMA has been called this nation's strongest union. Why?
7. Do you think more patent drugs should be sold by prescription only? Or do you think more prescription drugs should be sold without a prescription?
8. What is the argument in favor of restricting advertising of prescription drug prices?
9. What is the argument against that restriction?
10. Do you think the future will see more group health care facilities or fewer?
11. Why would the AMA try to stop group health care from proliferating?

THINGS TO DO

1. Discuss the arguments concerning medical costs or short supply of medical care in this chapter with someone in the medical care profession. Are the opinions of the textbook author and the person you spoke to the same? If so, elaborate. If not, how do they differ? What would account for these differences?
2. Obtain a copy of a code of ethics for medical doctors, or for dentists. Is there any mention of the patient in such a code of ethics?
3. Ask a medical doctor you know why practicing physicians are not recertified periodically.
4. Call up several pharmacies in your area to find out the price of 50 capsules of 250 mgs. of tetracycline. If they will not give you the price on the phone, ask them why not. See if there is much difference among the prices quoted. If there is, ask why.

SELECTED READINGS

"America's Health: Fallacies, Beliefs, Practices." *FDA Consumer*, October 1972.

"As Health Costs Soar . . . Needed: A New Direction for Our Medical System." Interview with Walter J. McNerney, President, Blue Cross Association in *U.S. News & World Report*, March 28, 1977.

First Facts About Drugs, FDA Fact Sheet 1712-0122. Washington, D.C.: Consumer Product Information, 1970.

Fuchs, Victor R. *Health, Economics, and Social Choice*. New York: Basic Books, 1975.

Gwinup, Grant. *Energetics*. New York: Bantam Books, 1972.

"Hidden Costs of Drug Safety; FDA's Regulations Effect on Drug Industry Re-
First Facts about Drugs, FDA Fact Sheet 1712-0122. Washington, D.C.: Consearch Projects." *Business Week*, February 21, 1977, p. 80.

Kennedy, Edward M. *In Critical Condition: The Crisis in America's Health Care*. New York: Simon & Schuster, 1973.

Krizay, John, and Wilson, A. *The Patient as Consumer–Health Care Financing in the United States*. Lexington, Mass.: Lexington Books, 1974.

Lamberg, L. "Your Doctor's Prescription: Is It Greek to You?" *U.S. News*, February 14, 1977, pp. 47-48.

Margolis, R. J. "National Health Insurance—The Dream Whose Time Has Come?" *New York Times Magazine*, January 9, 1977, pp. 12-13.

Medicines: Participation and Over-the-Counter, FDA Fact Sheet 7700-024. Washington, D.C.: Consumer Product Information, 1970.

"National Health Insurance: Which Way to Go?" *Consumer Reports*, February 1975.

The Rising Cost of Hospital Care, 1955-1971. Washington D.C.: Bureau of Labor Statistics, U.S. Department of Labor, 1973.

"Safety Muddle at FDA." *Business Week*, April 4, 1977, pp. 73-74.

"Uproar Over Medical Bills." *U.S. News & World Report*, March 28, 1977.

Your Medicare Handbook. Washington, D.C.: U.S. Department of Health, Education, and Welfare, Government Printing Office, 1977.

How to Keep Your Medical Costs Down

GLOSSARY OF TERMS

Limitation
Upper limit on payment of a health insurance policy; for example, it covers 120 days and then you begin to pay.

Major Medical
The type of medical insurance that covers only major medical costs. A major medical policy might, for example, pay 80 percent of all bills in excess of $500 a year.

Deductible
The minimum amount that you have to pay in medical bills before your insurance policy takes effect.

Coinsurance
A joint assumption of the financial risk, usually between you, the insured, and your insurance company. You are a coinsuror with the insurance company if you are required to pay a certain portion of your medical bills.

Waiting Period
The period during which an insurance policy is not in effect or for which you will be paid nothing on the policy. For example, if there is a waiting period of 30 days under a particular policy, you may have to be disabled for 30 days before a payment is made to you for loss of earnings.

Paramedic
A paraprofessional medical practitioner; a person with limited medical training who performs prescribed medical services, generally of a minor nature, under supervision.

Preexisting Ailment
A health defect or disease that afflicted you before you took out insurance. Generally, preexisting ailments are not covered by insurance policies.

HOW TO KEEP YOUR MEDICAL COSTS DOWN

There is no way that you can eliminate completely the costs of medical care for you and your dependents. However, you can insure yourself against at least extraordinary costs and, if you see fit, against all normal medical care expenditures throughout the year. In this consumer issue, we will give the pros and cons of different types of medical insurance coverage, including an explanation of how Medicare and Medicaid affect you.

KEEPING HEALTHY

One of the best insurance policies you can take out against excessive medical costs is a consistent, comprehensive program of keeping fit. All of us know what we *should* do, but many of us have a tendency to let ourselves become run down, hypertensive, overweight, and so on. This is not the place to go into detail about particular ideas on preventive care of the human body. Suffice it to say that the following are generally agreed to be important in keeping you out of the doctor's office for other than periodic health examinations:

1. **Good diet.** This means getting all the minimum amounts of vitamins and nutrients in a regular manner and in the right quantity. The right quantity is usually such that you do not become overweight or, for some persons, too much underweight. Good diet does not require a high income; as we pointed out in Chapter 10, even people with low incomes can obtain a nutritious diet if they are willing to sacrifice variety.

2. **Adequate exercise.** Medical people are fairly well convinced that if you exercise, you feel better, you sleep better, and you are less prone to serious cardiovascular illnesses. Again, this does not require money: for example, jogging is free.

3. **Moderation of foreign substances.** There is much less agreement on this point than on the others, but many experts believe that if you want to play it safe, you should not abuse

your mind and body with such drugs as nicotine, alcohol, hallucinogens, uppers, downers, and the like. They also counsel not becoming a patent medicine freak; hypochondria can lead to an overuse of medicines that may eventually cause serious bodily damage.

But how do you take care of the expenses when they come?

TYPES OF MEDICAL INSURANCE

Below you will find five basic categories of medical service for which health insurance can be purchased. No doubt you can find other categories for special problems.

Hospital expenses. Experts believe that over 90 percent of persons in the United States are now protected under some voluntary programs that will cover at least part of medical care costs arising from illness or accident. Hospital expense protection provides benefits toward full or partial payment of room, board, and services any time you are in a hospital. Usually it includes use of operating room, lab, x rays, medicines, and incidental care. Table M-1 shows a typical payment pattern for hospital expenses under the policy. Almost all insurance companies that issue any sort of total health insurance package will issue hospital expense insurance.

Surgical insurance. Almost all Americans who have some sort of hospital insurance also have surgical insurance, which pays for the services of a surgeon. Generally, there is a fee schedule that fixes the maximum amount **limitation**. Table M-2 gives an example. Any excess over the stipulated maximum must be paid either by another type of insurance policy or out of your own pocket. Since the higher the maximum limits

Table M-1

Typical Hospital Payments under a Typical Insurance Plan

HOSPITAL SERVICES	TOTAL HOSPITAL CHARGES	AMOUNT PAID BY INSURANCE COMPANY
Room and board 31 days at $85 per day	$2,635	$2,025
X rays, laboratory work, medicines, etc.	800	400
Use of operating room, recovery room, cast, dressings, etc.	150	150
Physicians' fees	600	220
TOTALS	$4,185	$2,795

for surgery, the higher the cost of the insurance, you must decide what risk you want to take.

Regular medical protection. This type of protection pays for visits to the doctor's office as well as all x ray, diagnostic, and laboratory expenses related to such visits. There is generally a maximum number of calls allowable for each sickness, and also a one-call deductible. In many cases, when you have your family covered under your medical insurance policy, only you, the subscriber, are covered

under regular medical insurance provisions. Your spouse and your children are covered only in case of accidents. This type may cost you more on annual premiums than you would pay to the doctor in an average year.

Major medical. What happens when a very serious or prolonged illness comes along, or a terrible automobile accident requiring $50,000 worth of medical expenses? If you do not have **major medical** insurance, you are faced with a financial disaster,

which may take years to pull out of. Major medical insurance takes over where all basic health plans discussed above stop. Over 85 million Americans are now covered under these policies. The maximum coverage ranges from $5,000 to $50,000, and in some cases to a quarter of a million dollars. This maximum may apply to one illness or to the total of many illnesses during a policy year.

Major medical is cheaper if you have a basic policy, but you can often buy it alone. Under a major medical plan, after a specific **deductible**, say, $100 to $1,000, the insurance company will reimburse you for 80 percent of all your medical expenses for a single illness up to the maximum amount that you have contracted for. This is a feature called a **coinsurance** clause, requiring you, the policy holder, to pay 20 percent of the total bill. Note that even though you end up paying part of your bill when there is a coinsurance clause, you might be better off with such insurance in times of rapidly rising medical costs. If

Table M-2

Surgical Insurance Benefits

Appendectomy	$ 375
Gall bladder removal	580
Hernia repair	340
Tonsillectomy	200
Thyroid removal	600
Benign tumor	210
Prostate gland removal	380
Fracture, closed reduction of femur	390
Fracture, closed reduction of rib	75
Brain tumor	2,900
Intervertebral disc removal	924
Kidney removal	628
Eardrum incision	36
Boil, incision	19

you are covered by a fixed schedule of rates, you end up paying a larger and larger difference if those rates do not go up as medical costs rise. Coinsurance, on the other hand, means that you only pay a certain percentage, say, 20 percent of the rising medical rates; the insurance company pays the rest. Most major medical coverage is sold under group plans as part of a comprehensive medical insurance scheme.

Disability insurance. Almost 80 million persons are covered by this form of insurance that guarantees you benefits if you can no longer work because of accident or illness. Such insurance compensates you for your wages lost. Sometimes this is called salary continuation insurance. Under many policies, you can expect to get 50 to 65 percent of your normal earnings if you are making average wages. Because the probability that illness will prevent you from working increases with your age, it is a good idea to get a noncancellable policy that offers you protection through your entire working life. Such a policy will be more expensive, of course. Many policies have a **waiting period**—that is, a period following your disability during which you receive no payments. The longer the waiting period, the less you have to pay for this type of insurance, obviously. Be careful when you buy health and disability insurance: find out how long the waiting period is. A one-year waiting period may render the policy useless to you except for permanent injuries. That may not be what

you want; you may want the policy to go into effect 30 days after an accident or the onset of an illness.

One of the most recent additions to disability insurance is its availability for homemakers who spend full time tending to household and family affairs. Their value to the family can be measured in terms of what it would cost to replace their services—housekeeping, babysitting, cooking, etc. As of 1976, there were at least four companies selling homemaker's disability insurance: Aid Association for Lutherans' form ADA (available to Lutherans only), Mutual of Omaha's form 3760M, Ohio State Life Insurance Company's form A-1650, and World Insurance Company's form A6503. Ohio State's coverage is available only as a rider to a husband's disability policy with the same company. Annual premiums depend on the age of the homemaker and the length of the waiting period. For a typical policy on a 35-year-old homemaker that would pay $200 a month for 2 years, the premium would cost approximately $100 annually.

OTHER TYPES OF INSURANCE

Dental Insurance

Although few insurance policies cover dental work, such coverage is becoming an increasingly important part of all health insurance policies. Because it is generally provided only on a group basis, if you are not part of a group—such as a large company, government agency, labor union, and so on

—you may be unable to buy dental insurance.

There has been quite a dramatic rise in the number of persons with dental expense protection. In 1967, 2.3 million people were covered under dental insurance plans. By 1977, 25 million people were protected by some form of dental insurance. The largest providers of that protection were private insurance companies that insured 18 million persons under regular dental plans. Blue Cross–Blue Shield covered 2.6 million individuals; the remainder were covered by Dental Service Corporation and union welfare funds.

Most dental insurance is a standard prepayment plan that covers 80 percent of the cost of treatment after some sort of deductible, such as $50 or $100. There is a fairly low maximum that can be paid in any one year, usually $600 to $1,000. Table M-3 shows hypothetical fixed allowances for different dental treatments.

Mental Health Insurance

Although most health insurance does not cover the increasingly

---

Table M-3

Typical Dental Insurance Benefits

Cleaning	$ 14
X ray	22
Extraction	13
Silicate filling	17
Removable space maintainer	69
Anesthesia	24
Crowns, porcelain	126
Maxillary dentures	243

grave problem of the cost for mental health, some plans are starting to be considered. Several unions already have coverage for psychiatric services as well as treatment for alcoholism.

WHERE SHOULD YOU GO FOR HEALTH INSURANCE?

A variety of organizations will sell you health insurance. The largest are Blue Cross and Blue Shield; the next largest are the commercial insurance companies. In addition, there are labor union plans, community organization plans, and consumer cooperatives, as well as group health plans, one of which may be available in your locality.

Blue Cross and Blue Shield

Formed in 1929 by a group of Dallas schoolteachers, Blue Cross had a membership of over 500,000 by 1938. Today it has about 80,000,000 members with almost 80 Blue Cross plans throughout the nation.

Blue Shield, on the other hand, was established in 1946 by the coordinators of the Associated Medical Care Plans. Blue Shield, originally sponsored by the AMA, is sometimes known as the Doctors Plan because Blue Shield subscribers can choose the doctor of their choice. While Blue Cross is concerned primarily with hospital insurance, Blue Shield is concerned with surgical and general medical.

Of all those who have any kind of insurance for hospital care, over 40 percent participate in one of the 74 autonomous Blue Cross plans. Many Blue Cross group policies offer a 120-day Blue Cross plan that gives you full hospital protection for 120 days in a semiprivate room. Obviously, you save money if you can participate in a group Blue Cross plan. If you are not already aware of the possibility of joining a group plan, ask your employer, your fraternal organization, or any other organization that you may be a part of. Somewhere you ought to be able to get group coverage.

Many people take out Blue Shield as well as Blue Cross because Blue Shield covers the cost of physicians' services. Blue Shield plans contract with participating physicians to accept payment according to a preplanned fee schedule. If you select a physician who does not participate in the plan, Blue Shield gives you a cash refund up to a set amount on a given fee schedule; you make your own financial arrangements with that doctor. You can plan on paying a monthly rate of between $30 and $50 for family coverage, particularly if you are involved in a combination Blue Cross–Blue Shield arrangement.

In addition to Blue Cross–Blue Shield, there are almost one thousand nonaffiliated health insurance plans to choose from. All are independent of both Blue Cross–Blue Shield and insurance companies. However, these thousand plans cover only 5 percent of all persons receiving health care insurance. Among the most significant independent organizations are the various group health plans that you and your family can participate in for a fixed fee irrespective of your income.

Group Health

As a member of a group health plan, you receive health care from a group health hospital where doctors are paid a salary (that is, their income is not based on the number of operations they do or the number of patients they see). Today there are about 30 to 35 community group practice plans. However, almost 95 percent of the total subscribers to group health plans belong to the largest nine. One of the largest is Kaiser Permanente Medical Care Program. It has over 2½ million members and operates in California, Oregon, Hawaii, Washington, Colorado, and Ohio. The cost varies. In 1974, for example, it cost $51.55 a month for a family of four in Washington State. This covers surgical and hospital care, but each visit to a doctor costs more; and if a baby is born in the hospital, an extra charge of $150 is made. (Some group contracts may allow complete maternity coverage and free visits to the doctor.) Drugs are sold at below retail cost.

The pros and cons of group health. According to a 1967 report of the National Advisory Commission on Health Manpower, the quality of many group health plans was equal to the medical care available in most communities; and members' medical care costs were at least 20 to 30 percent less than those obtained elsewhere. Cost is controlled mainly by eliminating unnecessary health care, particularly hospitalization. One reason for this is that partner doctors generally get a year-end bonus, depending on the difference between total revenues and total costs. Doctors, therefore, have an incentive to prevent illnesses before they become serious enough to require hospitalization. It is not unusual to find highly computerized testing services that check for 50 to 100 possible medical ills and make a medical history that can be kept.

Detractors of group health care maintain that because the doctors are essentially profit sharers, they will stint on needed hospitalization. Moreover, many patients complain about the impossibility of seeing the same doctor every time. There are also may be long waits for certain medical procedures.

Group Health Cooperative of Puget Sound–Seattle. Group Health in Washington State is slightly different from many of the other group health plans. For example, it is a cooperative health care plan; all members have voting status and therefore set policy at the annual meetings. The program serves more than 150,000 people, both members and those obtaining similar medical coverage through various group insurance plans, usually through their place of employment. The only difference between membership status and group membership status is being able to vote on policy.

Group Health Cooperative also covers all medications, including patent medicines if they are prescribed by a physician. The plan generally allows

for an annual physical examination and unlimited office visits, including specialists. There is an additional maternity charge ($250) for delivery at the hospital, but the membership voted in 1973 to eliminate any extra charge for contraceptive services (at a cost of about 28¢ to all members). Unusual medical needs, such as dialysis, are often covered, but most apparatus (such as respirators, artificial limbs, or eyeglasses—though the latter are available at less than retail cost) that are not used in the hospital involve an extra charge. Much of the routine care is provided by nurse practitioners and **paramedics**, but each patient is encouraged to select and regularly visit a family doctor.

WHEN YOU GET OLDER

When you get older, you may not have to bother about a private medical care insurance plan. You may be satisfied with Medicare benefits, although you might want supplemental health insurance as well to cover some of the aspects of medical care that those public plans do not provide for.

The Medicare program became effective July 1, 1966. It was an addition to the Social Security Act and has been amended a number of times. Twenty-five million persons are eligible for the hospital insurance provided under the Medicare program. Insurance companies and Blue Cross–Blue Shield participate in the Medicare program as fiscal intermediaries for the government. Medicaid is slightly different

than Medicare. Under Title 19 of the Social Security Act, the states may expand with federal matching funds their public assistance to persons regardless of age whose income is insufficient to pay for health care. The Medicaid program became effective January 1, 1966.

Medicare consists of two parts. The first is a compulsory hospitalization insurance, Part A, and is financed by contributions from employees and employers. The second, Part B, is a voluntary medical insurance program designed to help pay for physician's services and some medical services and supplies not covered by the hospital part of Medicare. Part B is financed by monthly premiums shared equally by those who choose this protection and the federal government.

Medicare Part A

The hospital insurance plan pays most of the cost of service in a hospital or extended care facility for covered people 65 years or older.[1] You get the cost

[1] Under the 1972 amendments to the Social Security Act, individuals under the age of 65 are extended Medicare coverage if they require hemodialysis or renal transplantation for chronic renal disease and if they are currently fully insured or entitled to monthly Social Security benefits or are the spouses or dependent children of such insured or entitled individuals. Medicare protection is also extended to people 18 years old and over who are receiving Social Security or Railroad Retirement monthly benefits based on disability and who have been entitled to such benefits for at least 24 consecutive months.

of nursing services, semiprivate room, meals, inpatient drugs and supplies, laboratory tests, x ray and other radiology services, use of appliances and equipment, and medical social services. There is, however, a hospital deductible amount that is "intended to make the Medicare beneficiary responsible for expenses equivalent to the average costs of one hospital day." As of 1977 this deductible was $125 per hospital benefit period (defined as a period of illness not interrupted for more than 90 days). In other words, if a particular period of illness lasts for 18 days, and then the person is well for 45 days, and then ill again (that is, requiring hospitalization or confinement to a nursing home or other extended-care facility), the first and second illness would have occurred in the same benefit period. If the person were well for 75 days, then the new hospitalization would constitute another benefit period and again be subject to the $124 hospital deductible amount.

Under this program, any illness must commence with a hospital stay of at least three days if extended-care facilities are to be covered. After the hospital stay, any referral to an extended-care facility must commence within 14 days (except where a problem arises regarding space availability, etc.). If nursing care does not begin within 14 days, it is not covered under Medicare. And Medicare recipients are subject to later deductible amounts depending on the length of illness:

1. First 60 days: all specified benefits are covered except the $124 deductible.

2. Days 61 to 90: the same items are covered, but the deductible becomes $31 per day.

3. After 90 days: recipients are entitled to what Social Security calls their "lifetime reserve" of 60 days additional coverage, with a $62 per day deductible.

This "lifetime reserve" is just that—it can only be used once during the recipient's lifetime. If one illness requires 105 days of confinement in a hospital or extended-care facility, a subsequent illness would only have a remaining 45 days under that lifetime reserve; it does not "renew" itself, as do the other periods of coverage, with subsequent benefit periods.

Hospital insurance pays for all covered services in an extended-care facility for the first 20 days of such services in each benefit period, and all but $10.50 per day for up to 80 more days in the same benefit period provided that all of the following apply: you are in medical need of such care; a doctor has ordered such care; you have met the requirements indicated above (at least three days' hospital stay and admittance to an extended-care facility within 14 days of hospital discharge); and you are admitted for further treatment of the same condition for which you were treated in the hospital.

Subsequent to either a hospital stay or a covered nursing facility stay, you may be eligible for home health benefits, including occupational therapy, part-time services of home health aides, medical social services, and medical supplies and appliances for as many as one hundred home health visits.

All the benefits of Part A require treatment in participating health care facilities (most facilities do participate). And the law further specifies that the various dollar amounts charged to recipients, such as the $124 deductible and daily amounts, are subject to annual review, so that by the time you read this, the figures may have changed substantially. In no case does Part A cover doctor's services. But Part B does.

Medicare Part B

This supplementary medical insurance plan will help you pay for the cost of doctors' services, as well as other medical costs, if you are over 65 and a participant. There is a charge, however, which was $7.70 per month in 1977. You have to sign up as soon as you become eligible. Otherwise, when you sign up later (as you can once any year between January 1 and March 31), you pay a penalty fee of 10 percent for each year you were eligible but not enrolled.

Essentially, the federal government pays half of the cost of this medical insurance, and you as beneficiary pay the other half. The amount you pay is reviewed annually to ensure that it is in keeping with current medical costs. Recently, however, changes in the law provided that your monthly payments cannot increase beyond the percentage increase in general Social Security benefits, so in the future the government may end up paying more than half of the coverage.

The medical insurance program helps pay for the following:

1. Doctors' fees in a hospital, office, or home for surgery and other services.

2. Home visits

3. X rays, surgical dressing, diagnostic services.

4. Drugs administered by a doctor or nurse as part of treatment.

5. Doctors' services for lab, x rays, and other services (covered 100 percent if you are a bed patient in a hospital; covered as other benefits if you are not).

6. Limited services of chiropractors, ambulances, some physical therapist coverage (with a payment limitation), services of certain practitioners, such as Christian Scientists and naturopaths.

Under no circumstances should you be led to believe that the supplementary medical insurance under Medicare pays for the full costs of any of the above listed services (with the single exception of doctors' lab, x-ray services). First, there is a $60 deductible every year. After that, you pay 20 percent, and the insurance plan pays 80 percent, just as with major medical insurance. And the medical insurance does not cover routine checkups, eye examinations, hearing examinations, glasses or hearing aids, immunizations, routine dental care,

self-administered prescription drugs, nor the first three pints of blood received in any given year.

Medicaid

As mentioned before, Medicaid is an addition to Medicare. It is health care for the needy regardless of age. Because it is state administered, the particulars vary from state to state and, therefore, we will not go into them here. Those in need under the age of 65 will find that Medicaid in some states is very generous and in others, practically nonexistent.

COVERING THE GAPS IN MEDICARE INSURANCE

Medicare is paying less and less of total medical bills for older people. There are a number of alternative supplements that older persons can rely upon to fill in these gaps. In fact, there is a group of insurance policies called Medigap that is designed as supplemental insurance to fill some, but never all, of the gaps in Medicare's coverage. Annual premiums range from about $75 a year to over $300, depending on the extent of benefits. Blue Cross–Blue Shield sell Medigap policies; other sellers of Medigap policies are insurance companies and associations for retired persons, such as the National Council of Senior Citizens and the American Association of Retired Persons, in conjunction with the National Retired Teachers Association. When comparing Medigap policies, one should look at at least three salient aspects:

1. Does the policy provide for payment of all or only a percentage of actual charges unmet by Medicare? If not, then the policy is a fixed one and is more likely to not cover the bills unmet by Medicare.

2. How many of Medicare's gaps does the policy fill in? For example, does it fill in the Medicare deductibles for hospital stay and medical bills? Does it fill in the coinsurance that the recipient must pay? Does it fill in long-term care in nursing homes and outpatient prescription drugs?

3. What is the exclusion for preexisting illnesses? If it is six months, the policy is obviously more advantageous than if it is a year.

WHAT ABOUT MAIL ORDER HEALTH INSURANCE?

You have probably seen many ads with pictures of famous people recommending different types of mail order medical insurance. Although some of them are not a very good deal, others are just as good a deal as any other type of medical insurance. Right now there are about 180 companies in the mail order insurance business, covering only about 2½ percent of the total health insurance industry, but that percentage is growing. National Liberty Corporation, for example—the leader in mail order health insurance—increased its sales about 20 to 30 percent a year for the past eight years. If you decide to buy, you must be careful about what you are getting. You should be aware that the IRS ruled that premiums for mail order supplemental disability insurance policies are not tax deductible, whereas premiums for major medical and basic hospitalization policies such as Blue Cross are. (No reason has been given for this discrimination against mail order companies.)

Reading the Ads

If you read an ad that touts coverage up to $1,000 a month for hospital expenses, divide 30 into $1,000 and you get the rate of $33.33 a day. Hence, you have to spend the entire month in the hospital to get that $1,000. If you stayed in the hospital for only 10 days, you would get only $333.33. That is why you would never want to be caught with only mail order supplemental insurance. It is meant to be just that—a supplement.

The premiums are low, but so, too, is the coverage. As an example, if you are 55 years old, you would be charged $120 for that $1,000 a month supplemental coverage. But if you also wanted it for your spouse who was about the same age, it would cost you about $240–$250.

Even if you buy the supplemental coverage, you may have difficulty in getting paid off because various companies have strict definitions of **preexisting ailments**, by which they can reject your policy claims. Table M-4 shows the ten leading mail order health insurance companies and what percentage of premium dollars are returned in benefits. This table obviously tells you that the best deal around is group health insurance if you have no objections

to its disadvantages and can qualify for coverage.

If you pick one of the companies for mail order insurance that gives you a pretty good payback on average—say, 60 percent or so—then you can expect to be paying for an insurance deal that is as good as any other nongroup policy. Mail order insurance usually provides about one-fourth the benefits of regular insurance. But then again, it also costs about one-fourth what regular medical insurance costs. It is obviously not a superior "deal," but what many companies offer is not a gyp either. To make sure of what you are getting into, get the Argus Chart of Health Insurance from the National Underwriters Company, 420 East

Fourth Street, Cincinnati, Ohio 45202. Or send away to the Research Institute for Quality Health Plans, Inc., 1611 Foster Street, Lake Charles, Louisiana 71601 for a reformulation of the Argus chart. These two sources can serve as useful guides in choosing a health insurance company.

Is mail order health insurance a good idea for older individuals? According to a 1974 study conducted for the Senate Special Committee on Aging, it appears that mail order coverage usually doesn't fit the needs of older people, and companies tend to promise more than they ultimately deliver. According to that study, "The pattern of mail order deception is well known by now to the [state]

Table M-4

How Leading Mail Order Health Insurance Companies Pay Off

(Percentage of premium dollar returned in benefits). Included for comparison are industry-wide average on group health insurance (not including Blue Cross) and individual policies of all types—mail order and non-mail order. Mail order insurance is always an individual policy, not group. Policy type is guaranteed renewable unless otherwise noted. Figures represent 1976 business.

Sources: 1977 Argus Chart of Health Insurance, published by the National Underwriter Co.

89.1	Group health insurance, average for all commercial companies
67.2	Physicians Mutual Insurance (Omaha, Neb.), all individual policies
64.4	Commercial Travelers Mutual Insurance (Utica, N.Y.)
66.9	Bankers Life and Casualty (Chicago)
65.2	Colonial Penn Life (Philadelphia)
58.7	Individual policies of all types, industry average
52.2	National Liberty Group (National Home Life Asssurance of Missouri, National Liberty Life of Pennsylvania, National Home Assurance of New York)
46.8	Union Fidelity Life (Philadelphia)
44.3	J. C. Penney (Buena Park, Calif.)
39.3	American Family Life (Columbus, Ga.)

departments of insurance throughout the nation."

CUTTING MEDICAL COSTS— SOME POINTERS

1. Find out more information on staying healthy. Develop rules and follow them.

2. Have a family physician diagnose your complaints and refer you to a specialist only when one is necessary.

3. When looking for a doctor, get several names from a local hospital or medical society. Telephone the doctor and ask for a list of fees and methods of practice.

4. Pick your doctor before you get sick. (Also, get a physical!)

5. If you have a choice, pick your hospital. Avoid being admitted on a Friday if your problem won't be dealt with until Monday and there's no real reason for you to be there.

6. See if hospital tests before surgery can be done on an outpatient basis to avoid unnecessary room and board charges.

7. Explore the alternative of walk-in surgery.

8. Cut prescription costs by asking your doctor to specify the generic name of the drug.

9. Shop around for prescription drug prices. Many pharmacists will now give prices over the telephone. If you are going to be using a medicine over a long period of time, buy the pills in larger quantities.

10. Make sure that your insurance coverage is adequate and that all members of your family are covered.

11. If possible, opt for a policy with a larger deductible, particularly if you and your family are not involved in numerous small illnesses.

12. Obtain group protection as opposed to individual or family policies if you can.

13. If you pay your own premiums (as opposed to your employer), pay quarterly or annually, rather than monthly.

14. Occasionally compare your health insurance policy with alternatives to see if you are still getting the best deal.

15. If your doctor or specialist tells you that you need elective surgery, always consult at least one other specialist for an opinion.

16. Read some of the more recent books on medical care, such as *The Medicine Show*, put out by the editors of *Consumer Reports*; and *The Consumer's Guide to Successful Surgery* by Dr. Seymour Isenberg and Dr. L. M. Elting (New York: St. Martins Press).

17. You might want to take a look at a publication put out by the Washington Center for the Study of Services, *Washington Consumers' Checkbook Health*, available from Suite 303, 1910 K Street N.W., Washington, D.C. 20006.

PROVIDING FOR THE ULTIMATE EXPENSE

We all know the cliché that nothing is certain except death and taxes. We will discuss taxes in a later chapter; here, let us briefly examine alternatives to the typical expensive American funeral.

The funeral business is indeed big business. The National Funeral Directors Association represents some 14,000 of the 27,000 funeral directors in the nation. The funeral industry as a whole is probably in for some economic difficulties in the future. The death rate is going down, and obviously the funeral market is limited by the death rate. Nonetheless, the over 25,000 funeral homes must share the less than 20 million deaths annually, and therefore the average number of funerals for each funeral home is not very large—around 80 a year. Over 60 percent of funeral homes average only one funeral a week. On the other end of the scale, there are some very famous ones—such as Forest Lawn Memorial Park in Los Angeles, which averages more than 5,000 funerals a year.

The funeral industry of late has been facing increasing costs, not only for the kinds of equipment they need, such as coffins and hearses, but also for their labor needs. It is not surprising that the estimated price of a typical burial has been rising, nor that the funeral industry has become more competitive.

Prefinanced Plans

The Federal Trade Commission has accused a number of funeral directors of using high-pressure promotion to get people to sign up for prefinanced burial and funeral plans. Of course, there is nothing wrong with planning ahead, but you must be careful that the commission paid to a salesman who signs you up for a burial ahead of time is not excessive.

In 1978, the estimated total cost for a typical funeral service was approximately $1,750. If you wish to provide for much less expensive funeral outlays for yourself or your family, a good investment would be purchasing *A Manual of Simple Burial* by Ernest Morgan.[2] This manual gives you the choices that are open to you. You will find out about memorial societies, organ banks, etc.

For example, the Continental Association of Funeral and Memorial Societies, of which there are over one hundred members in operation, will arrange for a dignified but economical burial service for a member of your family. The Societies may arrange with a local firm for a cremation without embalming, which can cost less than $200.

[2]Burnsville, N.C.: The Celo Press, 5th ed., 1971, $1.50.

What One Must Do When a Funeral Is Necessary

1. Take care of the immediate needs of the bereaved.

2. Contact the funeral director and the clergyperson preferred by the family.

3. Notify the attorney who cared for the affairs of the deceased.

4. Secure personal data and any special requests or instructions of the deceased affecting the funeral services; contact the local newspaper for the obituary.

5. Make necessary arrangements with a cemetery.

6. Cooperate with the funeral director and attorney in securing forms for filing claims with insurance companies, banks, fraternal groups, veteran or military organizations, governmental offices, and others.

Making Sure the Funeral Costs Do Not Skyrocket

Once you have decided on a funeral director, obtain a written statement of the charges at the time that the funeral arrangements are to be made. The statement should contain the following:

1. Services, including merchandise selected, and the total price.

2. The supplemental items of service or merchandise requested and the price of each item.

3. The terms of payment.

4. The items for which the funeral director will advance his or her cash, such as flowers, long distance calls, etc.

Funeral directors often quote a single amount for "standard" services. These include the casket and the use of the funeral home facilities and a hearse. However, they do not include the cemetery plot (which could have been chosen earlier), the burial or crematory fees, and such items as flowers, obituary notices, and the clergyperson's honorarium.

In addition to the type of funeral service, you will have to decide on at least the following four items: casket, cemetery space, grave, and cremation.

After the funeral, a number of legal items have to be dealt with. They are covered in more detail in the appendix on Estate Planning given after Chapter 20.

SUMMARY

1. One of the best ways to reduce health care costs is to remain healthy by good diet, adequate exercise, and moderating use of foreign substances.

2. Medical insurance can provide payment for hospital expenses, disability, surgery, and regular medical protection such as routine office calls.

3. In addition, major medical insurance will cover up to 80 percent of large medical expenses, sometimes up to $250,000.

4. Medical insurance can be purchased through your job; through various group plans; and individually from such companies as Blue Cross, Blue Shield, or commercial insurance agencies. If you are in doubt about the possibilities, call several insurance brokers to find out what policies are available.

5. The largest health insurer today is Blue Cross–Blue Shield.

6. As an alternative, a group health care plan may be appropriate. Generally it is cheaper than buying insurance either individually or through your place of employment. Group health services often pay for just about all medical expenses incurred except dental expenses. To find out about group health care in your area, you might check with any large employer that offers a variety of health options to its employees. Or write any of the large group health plans, such as Group Health Cooperative of Puget Sound or H.I.P. in New York City; most major group health plans have a policy of easy transfer among each other, so they are likely to maintain a listing of other similar programs.

7. Medicare is a hospital insurance plan that pays most of the cost of service in a hospital or extended-care facility for covered individuals 65 years of age and older. If this is something you are concerned about, it is best to call your Social Security Office to get the exact coverage that would be available for you. There are Social Security Offices in just about every major city in the United States. Or you can write the Social Security Administration, Washington, D.C., for this information.

8. If you are older, you may wish to partake in supplementary medical care insurance provided by Medicare Part B.

9. Mail order health insurance is certainly not as good a deal as the advertisements indicate. However, it may be a useful supplement and should be looked into carefully for those who do not carry large amounts of medical insurance to begin with. Generally, though, mail order insurance should be used as a supplement, not as a substitute for another insurance policy.

10. *A Manual for Simple Burial*, by Ernest Morgan, will give you information on simple, low-cost burials that can be provided for ahead of time.

QUESTIONS FOR THOUGHT AND DISCUSSION

1. Teenagers are notorious for their poor diets. However, the teen years are generally the years when most individuals have the least amount of illness. Why?

2. Do you think that the medical insurance industry should be more strictly regulated in the premiums it charges individual members?

3. Why is it cheaper to be a member of a group insurance plan than subscribe individually?

4. When would it be worthwhile to purchase a major medical policy with a large limit, say, $250,000?

5. Do you think group health is a workable concept?

6. Do you prefer to have a doctor whom you see all the time, or would you like to see a variety of doctors? Would this influence your answer to question 5?

7. Medicare costs much more than individual recipients put in. Who pays for the difference?

8. When would you want to have a mail order insurance policy?

THINGS TO DO

1. Obtain the payment schedules for at least two medical insurance plans. Make comparisons between the two. If they are vastly different in coverage and payment, does this difference correspond to a distinct difference in the premiums that must be paid? If not, what do you think is the reason for the difference?

2. Find out about dental insurance in your area. Can you figure out why it has taken so long for dental insurance to catch on?

3. Order some of the free booklets from Blue Cross–Blue

Shield. Read through them to see if the information there can give you an indication of why medical costs have been rising so rapidly.

4. Compare the coverage and payment schedule for a private insurance plan such as Blue Cross–Blue Shield with what would be covered under Medicare Part A and Medicare Part B. Which is a better deal?

5. Find the state statutes governing cremation. Check with various funeral homes regarding their cremation practices and costs. When is cremation a less expensive form of interment than burial?

SELECTED READINGS

"Adding Insult to Injury." *Forbes*, March 1, 1977.

Boroson, W. "Diagnosing Your Health Insurance." *Money*, September 1975.

Effect of Co-Insurance on Use of Physicians Services. Social Security Bulletin, June 1972.

"Group Therapy for Runaway Medical Bills." *Money*, May 1973.

"How to Judge a Dentist." *Consumer Reports*, July 1975.

"How to Pay Less for Prescription Drugs." *Consumer Reports*, January 1975.

Main, Jeremy. "Curbing Funeral Costs." *Money* 6 (March 1977).

Simmons, Henry E. "Brand vs. General Drugs: It's Only a Matter of Name." *FDA Consumer*, March 1973.

"Those Picky Car and Health Insurers." *Money* 6 (April 1977).

GLOSSARY OF TERMS

Whole Life Insurance

Insurance that has both death and living benefits. That is, there is a savings aspect to the policy by which part of your premium is put into a type of savings account.

Term Insurance

Life insurance that is for a specified term (period of time) and has only a death benefit: it is a form of pure insurance with no savings aspect.

Decreasing Term Insurance

A term insurance policy where the premiums are uniform throughout its life, but the face value of the policy declines. Sometimes called a home protection plan because the face value declines much in the same way a mortgage due on a house declines.

Annuity

An amount payable yearly or at other regular intervals. Also, the right to receive or the obligation to pay such an amount.

Living Benefits

Benefits paid on a whole life insurance policy while the person is living. Living benefits include fixed and variable annuities.

Underwriter

The company that stands behind the face value of any insurance policy. The underwriter signs its name to an insurance policy, thereby becoming answerable for a designated loss or damage on consideration of receiving a premium payment.

Income Transfer

A transfer of income from some individuals in the economy to other individuals. This is generally done by way of the government. It is a transfer in the sense that no services are rendered by the recipients. Unemployment insurance, for example, is an income transfer to unemployed individuals.

Other Forms of Protection: Life Insurance and Social Security

CHAPTER PREVIEW

☐ What are the principles behind life insurance?
☐ What are the different types of life insurance?
☐ How does whole life compare with term insurance?
☐ What are the different types of living and death benefits and how can they be received?
☐ What are annuities and why would you want them?
☐ What is Social Security all about and what are its defects?

16 We have discussed home insurance, liability, automobile insurance, and medical insurance at some length. These are basically forms of protection or income security. Two additional forms of protection not yet discussed are life insurance and Social Security, to which we now turn.

SECURITY

A sense of security is important for most families. In fact, psychologists contend that the average American wants a sense of security more than just about anything else in his or her life. Some of the major hazards to *financial* security are listed below with the ways that Americans provide for these hazards:

1. Illness: health and medical insurance, a savings account for emergency, Medicare and Medicaid.
2. Accident: accident insurance, a savings account, state workmen's compensation, Social Security, aid to disabled, veterans benefits.
3. Unemployment: a savings fund for such an emergency, unemployment compensation.
4. Old age: private retirement pension plans, savings account, annuities, Social Security old age insurance.
5. Premature death: survivors' insurance under the Social Security Act, life insurance, workmen's compensation, savings, and investments.
6. Desertion, divorce: savings, investments, aid to families with dependent children.
7. Unexpected, catastrophic expenses: health insurance, property insurance, liability insurance.

The responsibility for providing family economic security may be assumed by the family, relatives of the family, charitable institutions, employers, or the government. Until recently, financial security was provided primarily by the first three, but now employers and the government are being looked to for this kind of protection.

PREMATURE DEATHS

The mortality rate in the United States has been on the decline for many years, as it has in the rest of the world. People are suffering from fewer fatal diseases than they used to and are living longer, as can be seen in Figure 16-1. Nonetheless, every year there are at least 300,000 premature deaths. For example, in 1975, 259,074 males and females from the ages of 25 to 55 died. In many cases, a premature death can lead to financial hardship for dependents. Consider that when a person who is responsible for a household and children dies, those responsibilities must be made up after the premature death. This can bring financial hardship to a family unit. The same is true when the major wage earner dies, but in a more obvious manner. Both cases call for financial protection against the burden imposed by such a premature death. Just about everybody will agree with that, and therefore it is not unusual to find an extremely large life insurance industry in the United States.

Figure 16-1
Life Expectancy

At the start of the twentieth century the average American at birth could expect to live a little more than 47 years. By the middle of the century this number had jumped to almost 70.

Source: *Historical Statistics of the United States*, U.S. Bureau of the Census, p. 25, and U.S. Department of Commerce.

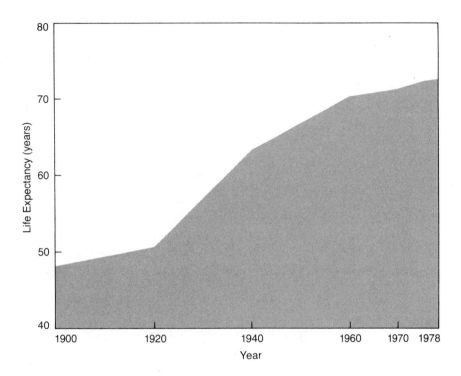

SELLING LIFE INSURANCE

The life insurance industry in the United States has grown rapidly. In 1900, there were a mere 84 life insurance companies selling some 14 million policies with a total face value of only $7.5 billion. By the beginning of the 1960s, there were some 1,441 companies selling 282 million policies, with a face value of $10,200 of life insurance per family. By the beginning of the 1970s, there were 1,800 companies. In 1976 the average American family had $29,100 in life insurance or a total of $12 trillion. Over 90 percent of all wife-husband families have life insurance. It represents 85 percent of the assets that males leave at their deaths. The average U.S. household spends over $1,000 a year to insure its family members and their possessions. Employment in the insurance industry has also been growing. In the last 30 years, it has increased from 600,000 to 1.53 million. We can expect that the industry will continue to grow as the American economy grows.

HISTORY OF INSURANCE

The first recorded life insurance policy was written in June 1536 in London's Old Drury Ale House. A group of marine **underwriters** agreed to insure the life of William Gybbons to the grand sum of $2,000. This coverage was obtained for an $80 premium (unfortunately for the underwriters, he died a few days before the policy was to run out). And so it was that life insurance became a sideline for marine underwriters. Then, in 1692, the Society for the Equitable Assurance of Lives and Survivorship began issuing policies covering a person for his or her lifetime. Old Equitable, as it became known, continues in existence today. In North

America the first corporation to insure lives was the Presbyterian Minister's Fund, which was started in Philadelphia in 1759. By 1800 there were only 160 life insurance policies in force in the United States. The industry had to wait until after the Civil War before it flourished.

PRINCIPLES BEHIND LIFE INSURANCE

Life insurance is just like any other type of insurance: if the risk is spread among a large enough number of people, the premiums that have to be paid will be small compared to the coverage offered. In any particular age group, only a very small number will die in any one year. If a large percentage of this age group pays premiums to a life insurance company in exchange for a benefit payment in case of premature death, there will be a sufficient amount of money to pay off the survivors of those few who die.

Given a long enough time for collection of data about the group and about the particular disaster—in this case, premature death—insurance companies can predict with great accuracy the total number of premature deaths in any one year. They therefore can estimate the total payout they will incur if they insure the group; hence they can predict the rates for each member of the group in order to meet this payout, plus a profit for the company.

THE DIFFERENT TYPES OF LIFE INSURANCE

Although the insurance principles outlined above are simple to grasp, the variety of insurance programs that you can purchase are indeed many and complex. In this chapter we outline the basic types of life insurance policies. In the consumer issue following this chapter are some ideas to help you determine your own life insurance needs,, and some recommendations about what is the appropriate type of insurance for you.

Life insurance falls basically into two types—term and whole life—but there is also a variety of others that we will discuss.

THE TWO BASIC TYPES OF INSURANCE

Whole life insurance combines protection with a savings plan, whereas **term insurance** offers pure protection. Whole life is also called straight life, ordinary life, or cash-value insurance; these are merely different names for the same life insurance.

TERM INSURANCE

Premiums for term insurance, unlike those for whole life, commonly go up at the end of each term, such as every five years, if you wish to keep the same face value on your insurance policy. The increased premium reflects the rising probability of death as age increases. Thus, it will cost you relatively little to buy term when you are 25 years old, but by the time you are 60, your premiums will have risen dramatically. However, by that time you probably will not want as much term insurance because your children will be well on the way to financial independence, and you will have built up other forms of financial resources for any dependents you still have. That means that you can reduce the premium burden by reducing the amount of insurance carried to protect your family. Families often choose term insurance that has a level premium, but a decreasing face value. Such a policy is called **decreasing term insurance**. Because the face value of the policy decreases much in the same way the amount owed on a mortgage, such policies are often called home protection plans. If one is taken out that has a face value equal to the amount of a mortgage on a home, then if at any point during the life of the mortgage the breadwinner dies, the home can be paid off with the insurance.

Standard term insurance is often labeled one-year term, or five-year term, because those are the intervals, or terms, between premium increases. Other periods are also available. A term policy is called renewable if the coverage can be continued at the end of each period merely by payment of the increased premium without the need of a medical examination. The renewability feature must of necessity add to the cost of the policy, but if you wish to preserve your insurability despite any changes in your health, you certainly would want to pay the extra costs for this feature. Term policies are commonly renewable until the policyholder reaches some age of retirement, such as 65 or 70. All coverage then stops.

In one sense, the premiums for any term policy are constant for the life of the policy, but since most term policies are written with a one-year or five-year "life," the constancy of premium is not too meaningful. The premium is truly constant throughout a long period of time only with decreasing term insurance, in which the face value falls every year.

CONVERTIBILITY

Often, riders can be attached to term policies that give you the privilege of converting them into other than pure insurance without the necessity of a medical examination. You pay for this additional feature, however. If you have a convertible term policy, you can convert it into whole life without any problems. The main reason you might want to convert is to continue your coverage after you pass 65 or 70. After converting the policy, you would pay whole life premiums based on your age at the time of conversion. Most insurance experts believe that the two features mentioned above, convertibility and renewability, should be purchased. They give you much flexibility at a not inappropriate additional cost.

Table 16-1 shows the costs of $50,000 of one-year renewable term insurance

Table 16-1

A Typical $50,000 Yearly Renewable Term Policy, Male, Age 35

YEAR	ANNUAL PREMIUM	YEAR	ANNUAL PREMIUM
1	$ 165.50	11	312.50
2	172.50	12	339.00
3	181.00	13	368.00
4	192.00	14	400.00
5	204.50	15	435.00
6	219.00	16	473.50
7	235.00	17	515.50
8	252.00	18	560.50
9	270.50	19	609.50
10	290.50	20	642.50
20th Year Total	$ 6,838.50	Total at Age 65	$17,893.00

for a male aged 35. If this man keeps $50,000 of term insurance until age 65, he will pay in a total of $17,893. He will have no cash value in the policy, as he would in a whole life policy.

WHOLE LIFE INSURANCE

Whole life insurance accounts for perhaps half of the total value of all life insurance in force in the United States. The average payoff value of such policies is around $15,000. Life insurance salespersons will almost always try to sell you a whole life policy because it is more profitable for them and their companies.

PREMIUMS

Whole life premiums generally remain the same throughout the life of a policy. As a result, the policyholder pays more than is necessary to cover the company's risk in later years. Table 16-2 gives an example of a $10,000 ordinary life insurance policy with an annual level premium of $222.70 for a male aged 35. In the first year, of the $222.70, $205.50 goes to the insurance company to cover insurance costs, and $17.20 goes to the savings fund for the purchaser of the policy. By the sixth year, the deposit to savings is greater than the level annual premium, and stays greater throughout the life of this particular policy. You can see in the summary of this policy that by the twentieth year—that is, when our policyholder is 55 years old—there is a total amount of cash value, or savings, in that policy of $5,608.97, after having paid in $4,454. The savings aspect of this policy, then, is $1,154.97. That is, at the end of 20 years, the policy represents a type of savings account.

Owners of whole life policies often take comfort in the fact that their premiums are level and therefore represent one of the few costs that do not go up with inflation. (However, the real value of the policy, as well as the premiums, declines as the buying power of a dollar falls.) True, the cost is relatively high to begin with, but it gets no higher. The exact level of premiums that you would pay for a $10,000 ordinary life insurance policy as represented in Table 16-2 depends on your age when you buy the policy; the younger you are the less it will be because the company expects to collect many years of premiums from you. The older you are, the greater it is.

As we will see when we compare whole life with term insurance (already discussed), whole life is relatively expensive because it is a form of financial investment as well as an insurance protection. The investment feature is known as its "cash value." In Table 16-2 the cash value at the end of 20 years was in excess of $5,000; and at age 65, it was actually in excess of the face value of the policy. You can, of course, cancel a whole life policy at any time you choose to and be paid the amount of cash value it has built in. Individuals sometimes "cash in" a whole life policy at the time of their retirement when the cash value can be taken out either as a lump sum, or in installments called **annuities**, which are discussed later in this chapter. These are the so-called living benefits of a whole life policy.

LIVING BENEFITS

Living benefits are the opposite of death benefits. The death benefit of a life insurance policy is obviously the insurance that you have purchased. The living benefit, on the other hand, includes the possibility of converting an ordinary policy to some sort of lump sum payment or retirement income. In any one year, up to 60 percent of all insurance company payments are in the form of these so-called "living" benefits.

Table 16-2

Composition of Savings and Operating Charges in 20-year Ordinary Life Premiums

$10,000 ORDINARY LIFE

Dividends* to Purchase Paid-up Additions

Annual Premium: $222.70   Male Age: 35

YEAR	DEPOSIT TO SAVINGS	DEPOSIT TO INSURANCE	TOTAL SAVINGS
1	$ 17.20	$205.50 –	$ 17.20
2	179.71	42.99	196.91
3	190.43	32.27	387.34
4	201.97	20.73	589.31
5	213.47	9.23	802.78
6	225.43	2.73 –	1,028.21
7	237.14	14.44 –	1,265.35
8	250.35	27.65 –	1,515.70
9	262.61	39.91 –	1,778.31
10	275.17	52.47 –	2,053.48
11	270.17	47.47 –	2,323.65
12	282.60	59.90 –	2,606.25
13	294.64	71.94 –	2,900.89
14	306.82	84.12 –	3,207.71
15	320.64	97.94 –	3,528.35
16	333.21	110.51 –	3,861.56
17	346.11	123.41 –	4,207.67
18	360.95	138.25 –	4,568.62
19	376.12	153.42 –	4,944.74
20	391.60	168.90 –	5,336.34

SUMMARY

	20TH YEAR	AT AGE 65
Total Savings	$5,608.97*	$10,566.83†
Total Deposits	$4,454.00	$ 6,681.00
Net Gain	$1,154.97 –	$ 3,885.83 –

*Dividends are neither estimates nor guarantees, but are based on the current dividend scale.
†Includes Terminal Dividend.

Note that the level premium for a whole life policy is paid throughout the life of the policyholder—unless you reach the ripe old age of, say, 95 or 100.

BORROWING ON YOUR CASH VALUE

One of the features of a whole life insurance policy is that you can borrow on its cash value any time you want. The interest rate on such loans is relatively favorable. For example, it is 5 percent in New York State. However, if you should die while the loan is outstanding, the sum paid to your beneficiary is reduced by the amount of the loan. In any event, the borrowing power given you in the cash value of a whole life insurance policy can be considered a type of cushion against financial emergencies. However, if you ever have to drop a whole life insurance policy because you are unable to pay the premiums or because you are in need of its cash value, you most certainly will take a loss. And, of course, you will give up the insurance protection.

WHEN YOU REACH RETIREMENT AGE

When you reach retirement age, you can discontinue premium payments on a whole life policy and choose one of the following:

1. Get protection for the rest of your life, but at a lower value.
2. Get full protection, but for a definite number of years in the future.
3. Get a cash settlement that gives back whatever savings and dividends that have not been used to pay off the insurance company for excessive costs it has incurred for your particular age group.
4. Convert the whole life policy into an annuity where a specified amount of income is given each year for a certain number of years.

DEATH BENEFITS

In most life insurance policies, you specify a beneficiary who receives the death benefits of that policy. If you bought a $10,000 ordinary life policy and have not borrowed any money on it, when you die your beneficiary will receive $10,000. However, there are certain options that can be used for settling a life insurance policy. Before you purchase any insurance policy, the particular settlement terms that are available should be discussed with the underwriter of that insurance. There are generally four option settlement plans that can be decided upon:

Plan 1:   Lump sum payment.

Plan 2:   The face value of the insurance policy is retained by the insurance company, but a small interest payment is made to the beneficiary for a certain number of years or for life. At the end of a period, the principal is then paid to the children or according to the terms in the contract.

Plan 3:   The face value is paid to the beneficiary in the form of installments, either annually, semiannually, quarterly, or monthly. The company makes regular payments of equal amounts until the fund is used up. In the meantime, the company adds interest on the money remaining to be paid out. There are two types of options here. Each payment is for a specific amount where the payments are spread out over a specific time period. If each payment is made for a specific amount, then the length of time during which the payments will be made depends on the amount of income payment, the face value of the policy, and the rate of interest guaranteed on the policy. If payments are spread out over a given time period, then the amount of each payment depends on the number of years the income is to be paid, the face value of your policy, and the rate of interest guaranteed on the policy.

Plan 4:   Regular life income is paid to the beneficiary. The insurance company guarantees a specified number of payments or payments that will total to the face value of the policy. If the beneficiary dies before the guaranteed payments have been made, the remainder goes to the estate of the beneficiary or as directed in the contract. This is sometimes called an annuity plan.

In sum, whole, straight, or ordinary life insurance gives you pure insurance plus forced savings and, hence, the possibility of retirement income as can be seen in Figure 16-2. You can instead buy pure insurance, that is, term insurance, at a lower cost than whole life. You can invest the difference in your own saving and retirement plans and perhaps be better off (or at least no worse off) if you can get a higher rate of return on your savings than the insurance company offers. The latest research suggests that whole life can be a sensible long-term investment for those who could otherwise expect their own investments to earn only about 4 percent *after taxes*. But if, on your investments, you can make 5 percent or more after taxes, whole life may not be the type of policy for you.

Figure 16-2   How Whole Life Insurance Works to Provide both Savings and Protection

Here you see a typical whole life insurance policy for a 35-year-old male with a face value of $50,000. It's "cash value" is represented by the bold line; cash value and dividends accumulate throughout the life of the policy. The annual level premium is $1,073.50.

Source: New England Mutual Life Insurance Company.

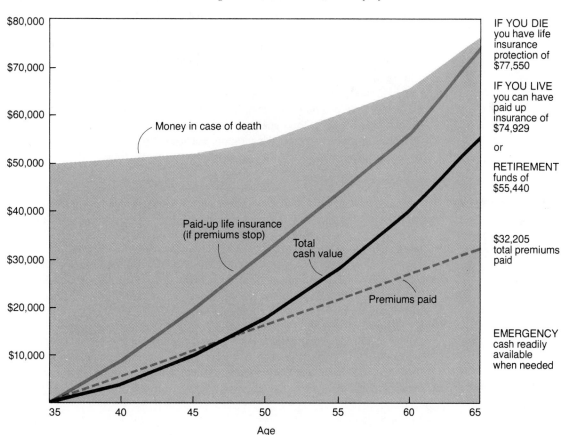

LIMITED PAYMENT WHOLE LIFE

Limited payment is whole life insurance with a slight twist: it is payable only at the death of the insured, and the premiums are payable only for a stated number of years or until the insured reaches a certain age, such as 60 or 65. The insurance is called limited because payments are limited to 10, 20, 25, or 30 years: if you took out a 20-year limited payment whole life policy, you would have to pay premiums for 20 years after which the entire policy would be paid up (regular whole life premiums are paid until you, the insured, dies). Obviously, the premium rate must be considerably higher for this type of policy than for an ordinary life policy, because it is fully paid up at a much earlier date. The distinguishing feature between limited life and whole life is that while the premiums are level in both cases, they end after a specific time period with a limited policy, but continue until the death of the insured in a standard whole life policy.

Generally, for any fixed amount of money that you want to spend on insurance, limited payment life policies give you less protection when you are young than either whole life or term insurance does. Limited payment life insurance might be appropriate if you expect to have a very short career at a high income level, such as a professional athlete or a rock star does. For the rest of us mere mortals, it is not usually a good idea, although there are some exceptions.

Endowment Insurance.   This type of insurance policy is a combination of a temporary life insurance policy and periodic saving. While the policy is in force, the beneficiary will be paid the full face value if the policyholder dies. However, if the policyholder lives after the endowment policy ends (at age 65 or after a specific period of 10, 20, or 30 years), you, the policyholder, get the face value paid to you or to someone you designate. It can be paid to you or your designate in the form of a lump sum or an an annuity—that is, a payment either over a specified period or until you or your designate's death. Because an endowment policy guarantees to pay the policyholder or the beneficiaries the face value, you are sure to be paying the highest price for this type of insurance. But you will also get the highest amount of savings out of it that you can get with an insurance policy.

TYPES OF INSURANCE COMPANIES AND THEIR POLICIES

There are basically two types of insurance companies—stock and mutual. These companies generally issue two types of policies—participating and nonparticipating.

Stock Insurance Companies.   A stock insurance company has stockholders who own it. They take the risk and loss and are entitled to any profit. Stock companies sell life insurance at guaranteed rates, which are kept as low as possible because of competition. If they are set too low, the stockholders take a loss; if they are more than sufficient, the stockholders obtain a profit.

Mutual Insurance Companies.   A mutual insurance company is a cooperative association that persons establish for the purpose of insuring their own lives. There are no stockholders. General mutual company rates are set high enough to cover all contingencies.

Participating Policies.   Because a mutual company has to take account of all cost increases during the year, it generally sets rates that will cover all costs plus any extraordinary ones. At the end of the year, it will figure what its costs actually were and refund its participating members—those who are insured—a pro rata share of the difference. This refund is generally called a dividend. In other words, it is a partial return of your insurance premium; hence, the premium charged you by a mutual company offering a participating policy generally (although not always) is an overstatement of your actual net cost per year because you get a refund or dividend at the end of the year.

Nonparticipating Policies. Stock companies generally issue nonparticipating policies. You receive no refund or dividend at the end of the year; thus, the premiums you pay represent the actual cost of your policy.

COMPARING NONPARTICIPATING WHOLE LIFE AND TERM POLICIES

It is interesting to see a numerical comparison of two nonparticipating policies, one whole life and the other term, when we invest the difference between the premiums of the lower priced term policy in a 5 percent savings account that yields 5 percent compound interest before taxes. This was done by the editors of U.S. News & World Report Books. The individual is assumed to be a 35-year-old man. He can purchase $10,000 of whole life for an annual premium of $191.10 or 5 year renewable term for an annual premium of $64.50; that is, $126.60 less. The difference is put annually into a savings account that compounds at 5 percent a year. Table 16-3 shows the results of these hypothetical calculations. As can be seen, the term insurance policy plus a savings account yielding 5 percent will always provide more cash "value" than a whole life policy.

Note, however, that nothing has been said about federal and state income taxes that must be paid. Cash value increments in whole life insurance policies are relatively tax-free; thus, at the end of 20 years when this individual surrenders his whole life policy, there would be virtually no income tax to pay. On the other hand, the interest earned on the savings would have been taxed each year. The amount

Table 16-3

Cash in Whole Life Policy versus Cash in Savings Account

The following table compares cash values in a $10,000 nonparticipating whole life policy with deposits in a bank at 5 percent compounded interest before taxes, which are made with savings derived from buying $10,000 of 5-year nonparticipating term insurance instead of whole life and decreasing it as the savings fund grows so that the total of decreasing term and increasing savings always is $10,000. Both insured persons begin at age 35.

Source: Reprinted from the book, *How to Buy Insurance and Save Money.* Copyright 1975, U.S. News & World Report, Inc., Washington, D.C. 20037. By permission.

END OF YEAR	IN $10,000 WHOLE LIFE POLICY	IN SAVINGS FUND WHILE CARRYING TERM INSURANCE
1	none	$ 133
2	none	272
3	$ 160	420
5	480	740
10	1,370	1,633
15	2,350	2,703
20	3,420	4,027

Note: All figures to nearest dollar.

of the reduction and the available savings would, of course, depend on the individual's marginal tax bracket. The higher the marginal tax bracket, the less beneficial it is to buy term insurance and put the difference into a savings account.

OTHER WAYS
TO PURCHASE
LIFE INSURANCE
POLICIES

In addition to life insurance that you buy as an individual, you may also be eligible for certain other types of life insurance policies that are generally offered to you at more attractive rates.

Group Insurance.   Group insurance is usually term insurance written under a master policy that is issued to either a sponsoring association or an employer. Some types of group insurance are currently offered to employees of universities and large businesses, to members of ski associations and professional associations, and the like. Per $1,000 of protection, the cost of group insurance is generally lower than individually obtained insurance for many reasons, but the two main ones seem to be the lower selling costs and the lower bookkeeping costs. The selling costs are lower because the employer or sponsoring group does all the selling; there is no commission to be paid to a selling agent. And the bookkeeping costs are lower because, again, the employer or the association may do all the bookkeeping. Generally, no medical examination is required for members of the group unless they want to take out an abnormally large amount of group insurance. Today there are perhaps 400,000 master group life insurance policies outstanding in the United States.

Industrial Insurance.   This type of insurance involves weekly premiums—usually costing 10¢, 20¢, or 50¢—which are collected at the home by an insurance agent. The insurance agent visits the home and writes a receipt for these very small sums. Industrial policies are written for very small face values, usually $500, or no more than $1,000. Believe it or not, there are 85 million industrial policies in force today. The average death payment is, of course, small and so the percentage of the total amount of life insurance in force is small.

Savings Bank Insurance.   As of the late 1970s, only three states offered savings bank insurance: New York, Connecticut, and Massachusetts. You must either live or work in those states in order to purchase the insurance. The rates are quite low because, again, there are no selling costs. You go directly to the savings bank to buy the insurance. Generally, savings bank life insurance gives you a better deal than other forms of life insurance, but, of course, you do not get the benefits of any information that salespersons from other commercial companies might be able to give you.

Credit Life Insurance.   If you take out a loan, in many cases you may be forced to buy insurance, in the amount of the loan, on your life. The reason is simple: without such insurance, if you die with part of the loan outstanding, the creditor may have trouble collecting it. But if the creditor is named the beneficiary in the life insurance policy you are required to take out as part of the loan, then the creditor is assured payment of any remaining amounts due. Today there are almost 100 million credit life insurance policies outstanding. The average amount per policy is small, being perhaps $1,300. Because most credit life insurance is written on a group basis, it is relatively inexpensive. However, be careful, because a creditor may in fact be abusing the right to force you to take out insurance. Check to see that the rate you are actually paying is commensurate with other group policy rates. If it is not, then the difference you pay should be added to the total finance charge in order for you to figure out the true percentage rate of interest that you are paying on the loan.

SOME SPECIALIZED INSURANCE POLICIES

There are a number of special life insurance policies that are offered by a variety of companies. They include combination plans and variable life insurance policies. Every year, new ones are added, and old ones are modified. Only a lengthy talk with an insurance agent could get you all the latest, most complete descriptions.

COMBINATION PLANS

A number of companies are offering combination plans that give you a combination of different types of insurance.

Family Plan. This is an insurance plan that is a combination of some term insurance and some whole life insurance. Under the family plan, every member of the family has some insurance; newborns are automatically covered so many days after birth.

Family Income Plan. This is also a combination term insurance and whole life insurance policy. It is designed to provide supplemental income to the family should the breadwinner prematurely die. In a typical 20-year family income policy plan, if the policyholder dies, his or her beneficiary might receive $10 per month for each $1,000 of the term portion of the policy during the balance of the 20 years. Then, at the end of the twentieth year, the beneficiary would receive the face value of the whole life portion of the policy, either in a lump sum or in monthly installments. There is a variation on this policy called the family maintenance plan. With such a plan, the monthly payments continue for a full 20-year period *after* the insured dies.

Extra Protection Policy. This policy also combines term and whole life insurance in double, triple, and even quadruple amounts. A triple protection policy, for example, gives, for each $1,000 of whole life insurance, $2,000 of term insurance. The term insurance usually continues until age 60 or 65 and then expires; however, the whole life portion of the policy remains in force. Insurance experts point out that these policies give less protection for the extra premium dollar than the family policies mentioned above. However, the extra protection continues for a longer time period.

VARIABLE LIFE INSURANCE

A number of companies are now offering variable life policies in which the death benefit is based on the performance of the stock market, that is, on the performance of the stocks in the insurance company's portfolio. Thus, the better the market performs over the life of the policy, the more cash the beneficiary will receive. If the stock market performs as it has historically, then variable life insurance seems like a pretty safe bet. However, if it does less well, like it has in the past decade, it is not as good as a regular whole life policy. Usually such policies have a minimum face value. Alternatively, one can have the minimum benefit increased by at least 3 percent each year for, say, 15 years. One, of course, has to pay higher premiums for such an expanded policy.

MODIFIED LIFE POLICIES

Modified life plans are generally sold to newly married couples or a young professional person just starting out. For the first three to five years, the policy is term insurance. It then converts automatically to whole life protection at a higher premium. In the trade, it is called Mod 3 and Mod 5.

OPTIONS AND CLAUSES

There is a virtual cornucopia of clauses and options that can be added to whole life and term insurance policies. We talk about only a few here:

1. **Guaranteed insurability option.** This option is sold with whole life policies; it allows the policyholder to purchase additional insurance at specified ages and amounts without having to meet medical qualifications.
2. **Automatic premium loan option.** With this provision, the insuror will automatically pay any premium that is not paid when due. The premium then becomes a loan against the cash value of the policy. This option will continue until a total of the automatic loans is equal to the cash value; then the policy is terminated.
3. **Convertibility.** A clause or option applied to term insurance policies that allows you to switch the policy to whole life or endowment at standard premium rates regardless of any change in your health.
4. **Accidental death or double indemnity.** An additional sum that is paid to your beneficiary if you die as the result of an accident. It usually doubles the face amount of the policy and therefore is called double indemnity.
5. **Incontestability.** Most policies have a clause that denies the company the ability to challenge statements made in your application after two years if you should die; thus, even if you made false statements, they cannot nullify the policy after a stated period.

ANNUITIES

Unlike life insurance, an annuity is issued on a bet that you will not live. An annuity pays the policyholder for living; it generally provides for periodic payment of a fixed sum, either yearly, monthly, or weekly. Certain kinds of annuities provide for partial retirement income and therefore eliminate the need to pay, for example, large life insurance premiums as in a level payment plan discussed above. Annuities can provide safe retirement income in a relatively easy manner (you cannot readily spend your savings) and can also provide tax advantages by deferring income tax payments until a later date, when most individuals are in a lower marginal tax bracket. There are several types of annuities, among them the relatively new variable annuities.

VARIABLE ANNUITIES

Under this type of annuity, you can either pay small sums into a plan over a period of years, or pay a large sum shortly before retirement to provide retirement income. This is the only type of annuity that may be "inflation-proofed," as the sum you receive on a fixed regular basis is not in itself fixed; it varies with the stock market return, for the money you pay in is invested in the stock market. Your payments depend on the market value of the common stocks in your account.

Variable annuities often yield a greater return than fixed annuities. Of course, this is in part due to the greater risk involved, because if the stock market declines during the period you are collecting against your variable annuity, so, too, does the amount you receive in payments.

FIXED ANNUITIES

The most common type of annuity is a fixed annuity. The advantages of a fixed dollar annuity generally given by insurance experts are that they provide you with freedom from investment worry and protection against a depression. Fixed annuities are of two general kinds, named according to the time at which the income is to start:

1. **Deferred life annuity:**   This type of fixed annuity is most often purchased a number of years before retirement age. It can be purchased either by making annual premium payments over a number of years, or by paying a lump sum some years before the annuity income would begin. Either way, payment is made some years before the date on which you desire income to begin.
2. **Immediate annuity:**   This type of fixed annuity is usually purchased just before retirement, often in place of or in exchange for a level payment whole life policy. Its premium must be paid in a single lump sum.

Whether you choose a deferred or an immediate annuity, there are several options, at different prices, as to the kinds of payments you will receive:

1. **Straight life:**   You are guaranteed a fixed income for life, but all payments cease at your death (in this case, the company providing the annuity is clearly betting on your death);
2. **Temporary:**   You are guaranteed a specified income for a certain length of time only.
3. **Installments certain:**   You are guaranteed income for the remainder of your life; in addition, you are guaranteed payments for a certain period—say, 10 or 20 years—even if you do not live that long, and your beneficiary collects. If you die before the end of the guaranteed period, your beneficiary collects. If you live longer than the guaranteed period, you still receive income, because this payment plan guarantees that period in addition to income for the length of your life.
4. **Installment refund:**   In this case, you are again guaranteed payments for life. In addition, rather than a guarantee for a specific period, your heirs are guaranteed installment payments until such time as the balance on what you paid is returned.
5. **Cash refund:**   This plan is similar to the installment refund, except that at your death the balance is paid to your heirs in a lump sum.

6. **Joint and survivorship:** Two or more persons (usually husband and wife) are guaranteed an income for life as long as either is living. This type of payment plan most clearly eliminates the need for life insurance.

It should be noted that annuities are a relatively expensive investment; that is, they yield a relatively low rate of return. Table 16-4 shows some average costs of annuities. And Table 16-5 indicates how annuities compare with other types of investment. As with whole life insurance, an important factor to consider when thinking about annuities is how well you could invest in alternative income-producing assets, and this includes considering the forced savings nature of annuities. In most cases, younger persons should invest in some form of life insurance before considering annuities. And it is perhaps best to diversify your investments anyway; there is no ideal investment designed to meet every individual's needs.[1]

[1]There is, however, a tax advantage to annuities that is important to high income individuals who have high marginal tax brackets. The interest credited to annuity cash values is not taxable as income until you begin to receive your annuity income. Generally this income annuity is obtained during the retirement years when you will be in a lower tax bracket.

Table 16-4   Comparison of Costs of Two Kinds of Annuity

IMMEDIATE SINGLE PREMIUM ANNUITY (Income to Begin at Once)

Age		Monthly Income per $1,000			Cost of $10 of Monthly Income		
Male	Female	Straight Life	10 Years Certain	Installment Refund	Straight Life	10 Years Certain	Installment Refund
50	55	$4.93	$4.88	$4.73	$2,030	$2,050	$2,110
55	60	5.51	5.41	5.20	1,838	1,847	1,920
60	65	6.30	6.08	5.81	1,605	1,644	1,721
65	70	7.36	6.87	6.56	1,375	1,455	1,524
70	75	8.80	7.73	7.50	1,145	1,293	1,331

DEFERRED ANNUAL PREMIUM ANNUITY (For Men Age 65 When It Starts*)

Age at Issue	Monthly Income per $100 a Year Purchase			Cost per Year of $10 of Monthly Income		
	Straight Life	10 Years Certain	Installment Refund	Straight Life	10 Years Certain	Installment Refund
30	$33.17	$31.33	$30.38	$ 30.15	$ 31.92	$ 32.92
35	26.49	25.01	24.50	37.75	39.98	40.82
40	20.57	19.42	19.03	48.61	51.49	52.55
45	15.34	14.49	14.20	65.19	69.01	70.42
50	10.71	10.12	9.92	93.37	98.81	100.81
55	6.62	6.26	6.13	151.06	159.74	163.13

*A woman would receive 15 to 20 percent less in annuity income per $100 of annual premium than a man of comparable age at issue.

Table 16-5   Comparison of Annuity Against Savings or Investment

COST OF AN ANNUITY			RETURNS ON INVESTING OR SAVING THE SAME AMOUNT TO YIELD $100 A MONTH TO LIVE ON		
Purchaser:	Life expectancy:	$100 a month guaranteed for life costs:	You can live on dividends or interest only if your money earns:	With lower earnings, you can tap both interest and principal and your money will last:	And if still living, your life expectancy will then be:
A woman age 62	19½ years (49% live at least 20 years)	$17,300	7%	At 3%, 19 years At 4%, 22 years	At 81, 9 years At 84, 7½ years
A man age 65	14½ years (27% live at least 20 years)	$13,750	8¾%	At 3%, 14 years At 4%, 16 years	At 79, 7½ years At 81, 7 years

INVOLUNTARY BENEFIT PROGRAMS— THE CASE OF SOCIAL SECURITY

During the depths of the Depression, the nation realized that numerous people had not provided for themselves in case of emergencies. It was also realized that a large percentage of the elderly population, which could not rely on its children for support, became destitute. In an effort to prevent a recurrence of so much pain and suffering by elderly people, the Congress passed the Social Security Act of 1935. By January 1940, when the first monthly benefit started, only 22,000 people received payments. Today, however, well over 90 percent of people 65 or older are receiving Social Security benefits, or *could* receive them if they were not still working. Today, over 14 percent of the population is receiving all or part of its income from the Social Security Administration. If U.S. population growth continues to slow down, the average age of the population will continue to rise. Hence, the total number of people eligible and on Social Security will increase as a percentage of the total population. Figure 16-3 shows the past and projected percentage of the population 65 and over.

We entitle this section "Involuntary Benefit Programs" because you and I, with few exceptions, have no choice. If we work, we must participate in the Social Security program. Self-employed people had been able to avoid it, but today they must pay self-employment Social Security taxes if they do not work for someone else. If you work for someone else, your employer must file Social Security taxes for you if you earn over $50 in any quarter. Of the people earning money in the United States, those who contribute to Social Security make up fully 95 percent. There is no way to escape it. Why Social Security has been made obligatory is sometimes difficult to decipher. Basically, according to supporters of the program, it is to insure that all older Americans have at least a basic living income and hence will not need welfare payments.

THE PROVISIONS OF THE SOCIAL SECURITY ACT

The Social Security Act provides benefits for old-age retirement, survivors, disability, and health insurance. It is therefore sometimes called the OASDHI. It is essentially an **income transfer** program, financed out of compulsory payroll taxes

Figure 16-3
U.S. Population
over Age 65

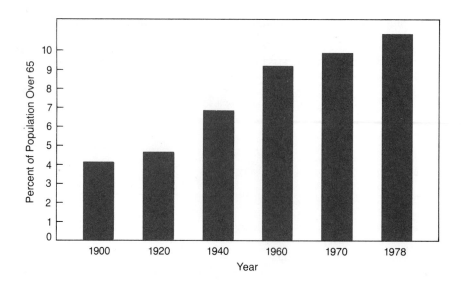

levied on both employers and employees, whereby those who are employed transfer income to those who are unemployed. One pays for Social Security while working and receives the old-age benefits after retirement. The benefit payments are usually made to those reaching retirement age. Also, when the insured worker dies, benefits accrue to his or her survivors. There are special benefits that provide for disabled workers. Additionally, Social Security now provides for Medicare, which we outlined in the last chapter.

The Social Security Act of 1935 also provided for the establishment of an unemployment insurance system. Unemployment insurance is not really a federally operated program. Rather, it is left to the states to establish and operate such programs. Although all 50 states have these programs, they vary widely in the extent and the amount of payments made. Programs are basically financed by taxes on employers. These taxes average about 2 percent of total payroll. A worker who finds himself or herself unemployed may become eligible for benefit payments. The size of these payments and the number of weeks they can be received vary from state to state. Currently, about 73 million workers are covered by unemployment compensation.

BASIC BENEFITS OF SOCIAL SECURITY

In the following consumer issue you will learn where to get information with which tentatively to figure the benefits that you are allowed under Social Security. (The predictions must be tentative because Congress frequently changes the benefits.) But right now, to discuss the basic benefits you can count on, Social Security in essence is a form of life insurance. Every time you have a child, the maximum life insurance benefit of Social Security is automatically restored, and its term is automatically increased to a potential 21 years. Here is what you can expect from Social Security:

1. Medicare payments in the future.
2. If you should die, payments to your beneficiary.

3. If you should die, payments to your children until they have gone through college.
4. Payments to you or your dependents if you are totally disabled and unable to work.
5. A retirement annuity—that is, a payment of a certain amount of money every month after you retire until you die. This payment, however, is legislated by Congress and can be changed by Congress.
6. If you die, a modest lump sum payment, presumably to take care of burial expenses.

Whenever you figure out your insurance needs, you must first consult the basic coverage that you have on your Social Security. You will learn how to do that in the following consumer issue.

PROBLEMS WITH SOCIAL SECURITY

A number of respected researchers have looked into Social Security and come to some pretty depressing conclusions. In the first place, you have to remember that Social Security is not really an insurance policy in the sense that you are guaranteed a certain amount of money. Your beneficiaries get that amount of money only if you die, just as with a regular insurance policy; but if you live, you get retirement payments that are a function not of how much money you have put in, but rather of what Congress legislates. Future Congresses may not be as kind as past Congresses. You may find yourself with a very small retirement income if you rely only on Social Security.

HOW SOCIAL SECURITY IS PAID

Social Security in theory is supported by a tax on the employee's income that is matched by the employer. However, you must realize that generally you, the employee, pay for much of the whole thing because your wages could be all that much higher if the employer did not have to contribute. The combined Social Security and Medicare tax for 1978 was set at 6.05 percent on the worker's income with an equal amount paid by the employer. This tax was applied only to the first $17,700 earned a year.[2] After that, it was no longer applicable. Hence, the Social Security contribution, otherwise known as a payroll tax, is highly regressive. (It is indicated on your payroll receipt as FICA—Federal Insurance Contributions Act.) Note, though, that benefits are proportionally greater for low-income earners than high-income earners, partially compensating for the regressive nature of the tax. The tax rates, moreover, have been increasing rapidly, more than doubling since 1967. Nonetheless, few seem to have seen the regressive nature of this particular income tax and the fact that for the majority of taxpayers it is greater than the income taxes they pay. In Table 16-6 we show the legislated increases in Social Security and Medicare (hospital insurance) tax rates for 1977–1986 and after. (Congress can change these at any time.)

[2]By law this tax base automatically rises whenever the rate of inflation reaches specified levels.

Table 16-6	PERCENT OF COVERED EARNINGS	
Federal Insurance Tax Rates		
Years		Social Security and Medicare Total
1977		5.85
1978		6.05
1979		6.13
1981		6.65
1982		6.70
1985		7.05
1986		7.15

Source: U.S. Department of Health, Education, and Welfare, *Your Social Security*, August 1973.

IF YOU WORK AFTER 65, YOU MAY NOT GET PAID

The Social Security Act, as it currently stands, penalizes you tremendously if you decide to remain working past the retirement age (65), for you can earn only $3,000, after which you get reductions in your Social Security check. If your earned income exceeds that figure, Social Security benefits are reduced $1 for every $2 earned. "Earned" has a very strict meaning here. It means income that is made as a wage-earner, not as dividends, interest, or pensions. If you decide to invest a lot of money, you can be making millions of dollars and still get full Social Security. But if you decide to be a hard worker and continue getting wages, you may lose all of your Social Security payments if you earn, for example, $5,000 a year. It is conceivable that you could work till the age of 70 and never get one penny of benefits from Social Security, even though you were forced to pay in your entire working life. Your decision to work after age 65 certainly will be influenced by this highly regressive taxation system. I say "taxation system" because you are obviously taxed if for every dollar you earn, you get to lose 50¢ in Social Security benefits. That sounds like a tax rate of 50 percent, does it not? (That is in addition to taxes that you pay already, such as Social Security and income.) This seems a bit steep since under the federal personal income tax system, the 50 percent marginal tax rate does not apply to individuals unless they make incomes of well over $30,000. But for people over 65, this 50 percent rate starts at $3,000 and continues until the worker reaches age 72. After that, you can earn any amount without loss of benefits.

This is one aspect of the Social Security program that many observers feel is quite unfair. It penalizes work for older people. Professor Carolyn Shaw Bell of Wellesley College also points out that the Social Security system is not insurance, but rather a transfer. People who are working pay Social Security taxes. People who get Social Security benefits receive the income that is taxed away. Essentially, it is a subsidy from younger workers to older, retired people. There is also a transfer from those who continue to work after 65 to their peers who do not work. At the beginning of this decade, for example, there were three million people over 65 in the labor force, a full 22 percent of older men and 10 percent of older women.

These three million people, according to Professor Shaw Bell, are "unjustly hemmed in between bleak job market prospects on the one hand, and the necessity, on the other, of paying out of their meager earnings to support not only themselves but others of their own age." That is to say, of course, that these three million people who are working are continuing to pay Social Security taxes.[3]

Supporters of the way Social Security is currently handled point out that Social Security benefits are meant to replace lost earnings. Hence, if a person continues to earn above the "magic" amount after age 65, his or her earnings have not been lost. The insurance, that is, Social Security, therefore doesn't pay the benefits, just as a fire insurance policy doesn't pay if a fire has not occurred.

OTHER FACTS ABOUT SOCIAL SECURITY

As Carolyn Shaw Bell points out, Social Security is not truly an insurance program: "contributions" do not go into a trust fund that is used to pay you an annuity when you retire.

Those who view the payroll tax as a contribution to a trust fund would have trouble understanding how Social Security actually works. The trust fund in 1974 was approximately $50 billion, enough to cover perhaps one year of benefits. A private insurance program or pension fund must, by law, have a trust fund that at any moment could finance all of the benefits promised to its members. But the benefits owed members of Social Security are valued at more than $2.5 trillion! Those who have suggested that individuals be allowed to voluntarily withdraw from the system have been lambasted by such supporters of Social Security as Nelson Rockefeller and the late President Johnson. Rockefeller predicted that such withdrawal would lead to the collapse of the Social Security system.

If this is so, then we must conclude the system is not actuarially sound, as trust funds are legally required to be. Rockefeller's prediction is unquestionably correct. Note, however, that at the system's inception in 1935 it was hoped that by around 1960 it would be actuarially sound. This hope was not realized.

FICA collections started in 1937, but benefits were delayed until 1940. The starting tax was 2 percent—1 percent each on employer and employee on the first $3,000 of income. Since no one received any benefits for three years, the trust fund became sizable. Thus, although in 1940 the Social Security tax was to go up, it did not. The increase was delayed for a long time. In fact, it was not until 1950 that it did rise to 3 percent (1.5 percent on each party). Additionally, coverage has been greatly expanded.

One can surmise that the politics of Social Security are the cause of increased coverage and greater benefits, for these two campaign promises win votes. Social, economic, and political pressures combined have escalated benefits to levels undreamed of in 1940. Checks were as little as $10 per month, $41.20 at most. By the mid-1970s, the minimum was $100 and the maximum was close to $400 per month for a man retiring at age 65. On the other side, taxes paid have skyrocketed. When the system started, collections were $30; by 1965, the maximum any worker could pay was only $174; by 1977, the maximum had jumped to $965.25.

[3]Carolyn Shaw Bell, *Challenge* (July/August 1973), p. 22.

What is actually taking place is that those who are working today are paying taxes to finance retirement payments to those who are no longer working. Each year there has been a slight surplus, which has been put into the relatively small trust. But what does the trust really do with those "surplus" Social Security contributions? It purchases U.S. Government bonds, thus helping to finance such things as military expenditures. If you and I were contributing to a quasi-private trust fund, such use of our contributions would be deemed inappropriate, at the least.

If you contribute to a private insurance or pension plan, what you ultimately receive is based on how much you put in, and income taxes would be paid on the benefits, which is not the case with Social Security.

There is, to be sure, a relationship between how much you put into Social Security and how much you get out, but it is a tenuous relationship at best. In 1975 the maximum wage-related benefit was about 3 times the minimum, whereas the maximum so-called average monthly wage on which benefits were based was 80 times the minimum sufficient to qualify. But the range would be even greater if account were taken of the total number of years the worker has paid into Social Security. The fact is that the benefits received are much more closely related to your marital status or the number of children in your family than to how much money you have paid into it.

There are other anomalies in the benefit payment system that could not be justified if Social Security were truly an insurance system. For example, the later you enter the system, the better off you are, because as long as you worked the minimum number of quarters, you will receive the same benefits as someone else who has worked many, many more. Who profits by this? Generally, the wealthier in our society benefit because they start work later. But this is not the only benefit to the high-income class. People with higher incomes generally have longer life expectancies and will therefore tend to receive payments for a longer period. Blacks are discriminated against doubly because they go to work sooner and die much earlier. And because of the regressive nature of the tax, the higher your income, the higher is the ratio of benefits received to taxes paid. It is not surprising that Social Security has been called the poor's welfare payment to the middle class.

Clearly, then, Social Security pays very different benefits to individuals who have paid in "contributions" of exactly the same amount; and, on the other hand, Social Security will pay exactly the same benefits to individuals who have paid in vastly different "contributions."

The government has on occasion contradicted itself when referring to the insurance principle of Social Security; more precisely, it has been selective in its invocation of that principle. For example, in a court test of the constitutionality of the rule prohibiting benefit payments to persons deported for subversive activities, the Social Security Administration rejected entirely the insurance concept: "The OASI [Old Age, Survivors Insurance] is in no sense a federally administered 'insurance program' under which each worker pays 'premiums' over the years and acquires at retirement an indefeasible right to receive for life a fixed monthly benefit, irrespective of the conditions which Congress has chosen to impose from time to time." There we have it. The insurance principle is officially endorsed in support of all Social Security *taxes* and rejected when benefits are denied.

SUMMARY

1. The major hazards to financial security are illness, accident, unemployment, old age, premature death of the person giving financial support, desertion, divorce, and unexpected catastrophic expenses.

2. Life insurance can take many forms, the most popular being term and whole life.

3. Term insurance is generally for a five-year period, after which time a higher premium must be paid to obtain the same face value in insurance because the probability of death has increased as the individual becomes older.

4. Whole, straight, or ordinary life insurance involves pure protection in addition to a savings plan whereby part of your premiums are put into investments that return interest to the policyholder. At any time, a whole life policyholder has a cash value in his or her policy.

5. Whole life insurance has living benefits: you can, for example, borrow on your cash value; you can get protection for the rest of your life at retirement; you can get a cash settlement; and you can convert your whole life policy to a stream of income—called an annuity—over a certain period of time.

6. There are two types of insurance companies: stock and mutual.

7. Mutual insurance companies generally issue participating policies whereas stock insurance companies issue nonparticipating policies.

8. Death benefits can be paid to your beneficiaries in a lump sum equal to the face value, or as interest on the face value of the insurance policy plus principal at the end of a specific period, or in installments until the face value has been paid.

9. There are a number of specialized life insurance policies, such as a family plan and a family income plan, as well as extra protection policies and variable life policies where death benefits are based on the performance of the stock market.

10. An annuity can be obtained from an insurance company to provide income for retirement or for some other purpose. There are fixed annuities and variable annuities, the latter making a payout depending on the rate of return in the stock market; the former has a fixed payout because only fixed income investments, such as bonds, are purchased by the company issuing the annuity.

11. Social Security is a form of social insurance in the United States. It provides for living and death benefits.

12. However, Social Security is not an insurance policy in the normal sense of the word. Basically, contributions to Social Security are merely transfers from those who work to those who do not work.

13. Social Security taxes are paid both by the employer and by the employee. However, in the economy as a whole, employees receive salaries that are lower by the amount that employers must pay to Social Security. After all, that payment is a cost of hiring employees.

14. Under current law, individuals from age 65 to 72 who work often lose benefits from Social Security because their incomes are too high. In addition, they continue to pay Social Security taxes.

QUESTIONS FOR THOUGHT AND DISCUSSION

1. Who do you think should have life insurance?
2. Why would an insurance salesperson try to sell you a whole life policy?
3. Why is a life insurance premium cheaper for college students than for older adults?
4. When would it be worthwhile to borrow on the cash value of a whole life insurance policy?
5. Do you know anybody who would be a good candidate for limited payment whole life insurance? Would you ever be a good candidate?
6. Why would someone choose decreasing term insurance with a constant premium rather than level term insurance with an increasing premium?
7. When do you think it would be appropriate to have a convertibility feature in your term insurance policy? That is, when do you think it would be advantageous to pay the extra price to have the option of changing your term insurance into whole life insurance?
8. Why do you think group insurance is cheaper than individually written insurance?
9. If you had the choice, would you choose a variable or a fixed annuity?
10. Do you think Social Security is a good deal?

THINGS TO DO

1. Try to determine whether life insurance companies make a higher profit than other companies in the United States.
2. Phone several life insurance agents in your area and ask what the premium cost is of a $10,000 straight or whole life insurance policy. Is there great variation?
3. Check newspaper ads for mail order life insurance policies. In light of the analysis presented in this chapter, how do you interpret the claims made?
4. Select two nationally prominent politicians and compare their stands on Social Security measures. Credit sources of information.

SELECTED READINGS

Annuities from the Buyer's Point of View. American Institute for Economic Research, Economic Education Bulletin 10.7, August 1970.

Brittain, J. A. "The Social Security System Is Not Perfect, But It's Not Bankrupt." *Challenge*, January/February 1975.

"Campus Life Insurance at Best a Delusion, At Worst a Snare." *Consumer Reports*, March 1977, pp. 168–171.

Denenberg, Herbert S. "Insurance in the Age of the Consumer." *Best's Review*, April 1970.

Chen, Yung-Ping, and Chu Kwang-wen. "Future Funding of Social Security and the Total Dependency Ratio." *Monthly Labor Review* 100 (February 1977).

Greene, Mark R., and Swadener, Paul. *Insurance Insights*, Cincinnati, Ohio: Southwestern Publishing Company, 1974.

Henle, P. "Social Security Reform: A Look at the Problems." *Monthly Labor Review*, February 1977, pp. 55–58.

Hopp, M. A., and Sommerstad, C. R. "Social Security Reform: A Look at the Problems." *Monthly Labor Review* 100 (February 1977).

Lampman, Robert J. "Generational Equity and Social Security." *Monthly Labor Review* 100 (February 1977).

"Life Insurance: How It Can Help You Build a Nest Egg." *Better Homes and Gardens*, March 1975.

"Life Insurance: What You'd Better Know Before You Buy." *Changing Times*, March 1977, pp. 36–40.

Pechman, Joseph A., Aaron, Henry J., and Taussig, Michael K. *Social Security: Perspectives for Reform*. Washington, D.C.: The Brookings Institution, 1968.

"Profile of a World Overflowing with People." *U.S. News & World Report*, March 28, 1977, pp. 54–55.

"Social Security Promising Too Much to Too Many?" *U.S. News & World Report*, July 15, 1974, p. 26.

Steinhell, Charles M. "Variable Life Insurance." *Best's Review*, October 1970.

"Will Social Security Be There When You Need It?" *Changing Times* 31 (February 1977).

How to Meet Your Insurance Needs

Before you go on in this consumer issue to figure out how much insurance you should buy, what type it should be, and where you should get it, first sit back and think about who should be insured in your family. You have to take into account the Social Security benefits you have coming, and that sometimes is not easy. You then have to look at the actual economic (or financial) dependency that anybody has on a particular member of a spending unit. If you are a single college student, for example, it is usually not recommended that you have any insurance at all (unless you want to use it as a forced savings mechanism, or as insurance against becoming medically uninsurable later on in life). By the same token, it is usually absurd for a family to insure its children unless the children contribute a substantial amount to the family income. If the unfortunate day occurs when one of them dies, the family's earning power generally will not fall. This is not necessarily true for a homemaker, however, who frequently contributes explicitly to the family earnings stream by employment outside the home as well as implicitly through the implicit value of services rendered to the family. In this case, the family unit may want to take

out an insurance policy on the homemaker's life. The basic wage earner should, of course, be the one with the most insurance because if he or she dies prematurely, the *spending* unit will suffer the greatest loss.

SOME INSURANCE BUYING RULES

Insurance is another item competing for your consumer dollar, just as is a new bicycle, a new car, or new house. When you make an expenditure on life insurance, you obtain a certain amount of satisfaction in knowing that your dependents will be financially secure in the event of your premature death. Note, however, that there are other possible uses of these same funds that also yield satisfaction; thus, there is no pat answer or formula that will tell you exactly how much insurance is best for you.

1. Identify the major risks that you and your family reasonably face; insure them according to the *potential* loss that they can produce.

2. Insure big losses, not small ones.

3. Never buy an insurance policy until you have compared at least two, and perhaps more, companies, not only on the costs but on the terms of coverage.

4. Limit your losses and control your risk through preventive measures.

ARE YOU UNDERINSURED?

There is a good chance that you are underinsured if anybody depends on you for even part of their livelihood. If, however, you live alone or are young and unmarried, or even are married but your spouse also contributes to the family kitty, then you may not need much (if any) life insurance. If, however, you are married and have children, or a spouse who depends on you for at least part of his or her income, then you probably should have some form of life insurance. You should first realize that Social Security is the basis of all your protection needs, assuming you are covered by Social Security. You will have to find out from your local Social Security office exactly what kind of benefits your dependents have coming in case of your death.

An assumption will be made in this consumer issue that you yourself should make when trying to figure out your insurance needs: assume that you drop dead tomorrow. How much would be left for your dependents, in what form, and over what period? This is not an easy thing to figure out, so plan on spending some time. You may want to work it out with an insurance agent, but you can probably do it on your own.

GETTING YOUR SOCIAL SECURITY FIGURED OUT

The first thing you should do is write the Social Security Administration, giving them your Social Security number and the name on your Social Security card and asking for a current report of your account. You can request a statement of your earnings every year. It is best to do it at least once every three years because there is a time limit on when errors can be corrected. You can obtain a "Request for Statement of Earnings" card like the one pictured in Exhibit N-1. After you have received this, take it to your local Social Security office and request the following facts:

1. Survivors' benefit for a spouse and one child under 18.

2. Survivor's benefit for a child 18 through 21 as a full-time unmarried student.

3. Survivor's benefit for a spouse and two or more children under 18.

4. Maximum family payment allowed.

5. Widow's or widower's pension benefits starting at 62; widow's pension benefits starting at 60.

6. Total disability benefits for the wage earner, spouse, and two or more children.

7. Total disability benefits for wage earner, spouse, and one child.

EXHIBIT N-1 Request for Statement of Earnings Card

| | REQUEST FOR STATEMENT OF EARNINGS | SOCIAL SECURITY → NUMBER | |
| DATE OF BIRTH → | MONTH | DAY | YEAR |

Please send a statement of my Social Security earnings to:

NAME { MISS MRS. MR. _____

STREET & NUMBER _____

CITY & STATE _____ ZIP CODE _____

Print Name and Address In Ink Or Use Type-writer

SIGN YOUR NAME HERE
(DO NOT PRINT) _____

Sign your own name only. Under the law, information in your social security record is confidential and anyone who signs another person's name can be prosecuted. If you have changed your name from that shown on your social security card, please copy your name below exactly as it appears on your card.

The Social Security Administration will also gladly send you a booklet that will help you figure this all out yourself. Or you can write directly to Superintendent of Documents, Washington, D.C., requesting a copy of U.S. Department of Health, Education, and Welfare publication, *Estimating Your Social Security Retirement Check* (SSA) 73-10047, December 1972. In Table N-1 we give a schedule of benefits that were currently available in 1976.

One thing to be wary of are books claiming to give you information on how to obtain Social Security benefits that you thought were unavailable. You might see an ad that proclaims "Ten million people whose average age is thirty are collecting Social Security benefits today." That statement is true, but it refers to young blind people, disabled workers, and dependent survivors who get Social Security checks. You can get all the information you need

to know from your nearest Social Security office. Don't waste your money on a book claiming to make you rich off the system.

Now that you have this information, you can figure out the financial condition of your family. Go back to page 191 and see how a net worth statement was done when you applied for a loan. Figure out your net worth, for that gives you a starting point. The average net worth of American families in the United States is estimated at $25,000.

You now have two major details of your financial situation in case you have dependents and die tomorrow: Social Security payments to your dependents and a net worth that is left to them. Now you must figure out a monthly income goal for spouse and children under 18, a lump sum education-fund goal for each child, a monthly retirement income goal for a widow or widower starting at age 62, and a monthly income goal, if any, for a widow or widower

Table N-1   Current Social Security Benefits

Source: Social Security Administration

MONTHLY RETIREMENT BENEFITS (PAYABLE STARTING JULY 1977)

| Average Yearly Earnings | FOR WORKERS | | | | FOR DEPENDENTS[1] | | | | |
	Retirement at 65	at 64	at 63	at 62	Spouse at 65 or child	at 64	at 63	at 62	Family[2] Benefits
$923 or less	$114.30	$106.70	$ 99.10	$ 91.50	$ 57.20	$ 52.50	$ 47.70	$ 42.90	$171.50
$1,200	147.10	137.30	127.50	117.70	73.60	67.50	61.40	55.20	220.70
2,600	216.00	201.60	187.20	172.80	108.00	99.00	90.00	81.00	324.00
3,000	236.40	220.70	204.90	189.20	118.20	108.40	98.50	88.70	361.40
3,400	253.50	236.60	219.70	202.80	126.80	116.30	105.70	95.10	408.30
4,000	278.10	259.60	241.10	222.50	139.10	127.60	116.00	104.40	475.30
4,400	297.90	278.10	258.20	238.40	149.00	136.60	124.20	111.80	528.10
4,800	315.40	294.40	273.40	252.40	157.70	144.60	131.50	118.30	575.30
5,200	331.60	309.50	287.40	265.30	165.80	152.00	138.20	124.40	622.20
5,600	347.90	324.80	301.60	278.40	174.00	159.50	145.00	130.50	645.10
6,000	364.50	340.20	315.90	291.60	182.30	167.20	152.00	136.80	668.60
6,400	380.80	355.50	330.10	304.70	190.40	174.60	158.70	142.80	692.10
6,800	398.20	371.70	345.20	318.60	199.10	182.60	166.00	149.40	715.70
7,200	418.70	390.80	362.90	335.00	209.40	192.00	174.50	157.10	740.70
7,600	437.10	408.00	378.90	349.70	218.60	200.40	182.20	164.00	764.90
8,000[3]	453.10	422.90	392.70	362.50	226.60	207.80	188.90	170.00	792.90
8,400	462.80	432.00	401.10	370.30	231.40	212.20	192.90	173.60	809.90
8,800	474.20	442.60	411.00	379.40	237.10	217.40	197.60	177.90	829.80
9,200	484.50	452.20	419.90	387.60	242.30	222.20	202.00	181.80	847.80
9,400	488.60	456.10	423.50	390.90	244.30	224.00	203.60	183.60	854.80
9,600	492.50	459.70	426.90	394.00	246.30	225.80	205.30	184.80	861.90
9,800	498.00	464.80	431.60	398.40	249.00	228.30	207.50	186.80	871.30
10,000	502.00	468.60	435.10	401.60	251.00	230.10	209.20	188.30	878.50

[1] If a person is eligible for both a worker's benefit and a spouse's benefit, the check actually payable is limited to the larger of the two.
[2] The maximum amount payable to a family is generally reached when a worker and two family members are eligible.
[3] Benefits shown from this point on can be paid to workers who retire at 65 in years after 1977.

between child rearing and retirement. This latter is optional depending on whether or not you want the widow or widower to have to work.

FIGURING OUT HOW MUCH INSURANCE TO BUY

Neither you nor anyone else can estimate *exactly* how much life insurance you should buy. That depends not only on all of the factors mentioned above, but also on how "safe" you want to be. After all, buying insurance means that part of your income can no longer be used for other purchases. You have to decide how much you want to give up in order to be "fully" insured. Nonetheless, you can get a general idea of how much life insurance you need by roughly estimating the income you would require to maintain the level of consumption you are used to. This means figuring out basic monthly expenditures for the entire family (minus expenditures that would have been made solely for the deceased), including such things as mortgage payments. In Table N-2, we give a list that you might want to fill in to estimate your family's monthly expenses. Next you must estimate the monthly income (independent of any insurance benefits, of course) that would be available after the death of one of the income earners in the family. These include all of the items listed in Table N-3.

Putting It All Together

Next, put together your estimated monthly income and your estimated monthly expenses to find out the deficit that must be made up by life insurance proceeds. In Table N-4 are computed, as an example, the annual needs that must be made up by life insurance for a typical family with expenditures of $1,040 per month. Table N-4 is almost self-explanatory; all we have done is make predictions for a number of years into the future. These predictions include expenditures, benefits, and so on. We have left

Table N-2 Family Monthly Expenses

Housing	$_____
Utilities and household operation	$_____
Clothing	$_____
Food	$_____
Medical care	$_____
Automobile expenses	_____
Recreation	$_____
Incidentals	$_____
Total needed per month	$_____

Table N-3 Monthly Available Income

Social Security	$_____
Income from any investments	$_____
Earnings of living members of the family	$_____
Job-connected survivor benefits	$_____
Trusts and other income	$_____
Total income per month	$_____

Table N-4 Annual Needs that Must Be Made Up by Life Insurance (for a Typical Family with Expenditures of $1,040 per Month)

	YEARS IN FUTURE				
	1-3	4-10	11-13	14-30	Retirement
Basic monthly expenditures including house payments	$1,040	$1,240	$1,100	$ 900	$ 700
Deduction of deceased's expenses	150	150	150	150	100
Expenditures without the deceased	$ 890	$1,090	$ 950	$ 750	$ 600
Income not work related Social Security	$ 400	$ 360	$ 300		$ 300
Job connected survivor benefits	200	200	200	200	200
Inheritance			280		
Total benefits not work related	$ 600	$ 560	$ 780	$ 200	$ 500
Monthly needs (expenditures minus benefits not work related)	$ 200	$ 530	$ 170	$ 550	$ 100
Annual needs (monthly needs × 12)	$3,480	$6,360	$2,040	$6,600	$1,200
Earnings of living family members per year	?	?	?	?	?
Life insurance needs	?	?	?	?	?

out the earnings that living members of the family can contribute to making up annual needs. That's why we have put in question marks. We have also put in a question mark about how much the proceeds from life insurance must be to make up the difference between annual needs and earnings of the living family members.

Tomorrow Is Not the Same as Today

We all realize that tomorrow will not be the same as today. This is particularly true when we think about what our basic monthly expenditures will be. After all, in our current period of rising prices, it becomes difficult to predict from today's prices what the future cost of living will be. If this isn't complicated enough, you must realize that an insurance policy, if paid off in one lump sum payment, can be invested to yield a flow of income. That means that if you require proceeds of $10,000 a year for ten years, you need not buy an insurance policy with a face value of $100,000. Instead, you can buy one with a lower face value; if premature death occurs, a less than $100,000 lump sum payment could be invested so that $10,000 a year would be forthcoming and at the end of ten years nothing would be left of the lump sum payment. But the problem of trying to evaluate future dollars by today's dollars is a rather complicated problem, particularly when we don't know how well investments will do in the future. Table N-5 presents one example of the monthly income(s) provided per $1,000 of life insurance proceeds paid out by an insurance company as an optional alternative to the lump sum payment. You can get a rough idea of how much life insurance you need by taking an average of the monthly needs from Table N-4 and using Table N-5 to decide how much insurance to buy. If, for example, you required $596 a month for the next 18 years, you would want to buy a $100,000 life insurance policy. Of course, that's probably too high a face value, given that you can receive higher than 3 percent even from insurance companies. Note, though, that as the cost of living rises every year, you will need more than you planned. Even though the interest rate you can earn on the insurance proceeds will go up, the increase may just cover the increase in the cost of living, so

Table N-5
Monthly Proceeds per $1,000 of Life Insurance

The monthly income provided per $1,000 of face value on a life insurance policy, based on an interest rate of 3 percent. This interest rate is obviously very low by today's standards, because a savings and loan account will yield much more than that. This table thus gives a very conservative idea of how much income would come from $1,000 of insurance. If you had $100,000 of insurance, you would simply move the decimal point two places to the right: for example, $100,000 worth of life insurance would provide $596 a month in income at an interest rate of 3 percent, if this particular option were chosen from an insurance company for 18 years.

NUMBER OF YEARS	MONTHLY PROCEEDS
2	$42.86
3	28.99
4	22.06
5	17.91
6	15.14
7	13.16
8	11.68
9	10.53
10	9.61
11	8.86
12	8.24
13	7.71
14	7.26
15	6.87
16	6.53
17	6.23
18	5.96

using Table N-4 may not actually be that conservative an approach to deciding how much insurance you need.

AN ALTERNATIVE WAY TO FIGURE OUT HOW MUCH LIFE INSURANCE YOUR FAMILY NEEDS

You may wish to compare the calculations that you have just made with a new method to figure out your insurance needs developed by financial counselors at the First National City Bank in New York (Citibank).

Citibank's economists, personnel, and insurance specialists have calculated that a family can maintain its standard of living with an after-tax income of 75 percent of its after-tax income before the death of the breadwinner. Citibank believes that if a family winds up with less than 60 percent of the pre-death level of after-tax income, its living standard will be seriously lowered. Thus, in Table N-6 there are net income replacement columns labeled 75 percent and 60 percent, which are target net after-tax income replacement levels that insur-

ance should provide. The chart is titled "The Multiples of Salary." Basically, it tells you how many times your current gross salary you should own in life insurance to provide either 75 or 60 percent of your current after-tax income to your family if you should die. The chart assumes that your family will also receive Social Security benefits. In figuring out the chart, Citibank's staff assumed that insurance proceeds would be invested to produce, after inflation, a rate of return of 5 percent a year. Moreover, it is assumed that the principal from

Table N-6   The Multiples of Salary Chart (for Net Income Replacement)

To calculate the amount of life insurance needed for either net replacement level, multiply your present gross salary by the number under that level.

If your gross income or spouse's age fall between the figures shown, take an average between the multiples for nearest salaries and ages.

Social Security benefits will be part of both levels.

If personal liquid assets (savings, predictable inheritance, retirement plan, investment, etc.) equal one year of gross salary or less, use them as part of the fund for the small-emergency reserve and final expenses. If they equal more than one year, subtract that extra amount from the insurance needed to replace income.

People with no personal assets who can't afford the 75 percent level might try for at least 60 percent. The average family would then face some lowering in level of living but wouldn't be financially devastated.

Your Present Gross Earnings	PRESENT AGE OF SPOUSE							
	25 Years*		35 Years*		45 Years*		55 Years†	
	75%	60%	75%	60%	75%	60%	75%	60%
$ 7,500	4.0	3.0	5.5	4.0	7.5	5.5	6.5	4.5
9,000	4.0	3.0	5.5	4.0	7.5	5.5	6.5	4.5
15,000	4.5	3.0	6.5	4.5	8.0	6.0	7.0	5.5
23,500	6.5	4.5	8.0	5.5	8.5	6.5	7.5	5.5
30,000	7.5	5.0	8.0	6.0	8.5	6.5	7.0	5.5
40,000	7.5	5.0	8.0	6.0	8.0	6.0	7.0	5.5
65,000	7.5	5.5	7.5	6.0	7.5	6.0	6.5	5.0

*Assuming federal income taxes for a family of four (two children). there are four exemptions and the standard—or 15 percent itemized—deductions. State and local taxes are disregarded.
†Assuming you have only two exemptions. (Any children are now grown.)
Reprinted by permission of First National City Bank, New York.

the insurance policy would be gradually eaten up, so that it would disappear by the time of the surviving spouse's death.

Take an example. If your spouse is 25 years old, your gross earnings are $9,000 a year, and you wish to provide him or her with 60 percent of your after-tax income if you were to die, you need to have in force three times your gross earnings, or $27,000 worth of life insurance. This figure may seem low, but it takes into account a higher Social Security benefit that a younger spouse would obtain.

NOW THAT YOU HAVE FIGURED OUT HOW MUCH, WHAT SHOULD YOU BUY?

Say that you calculate that you need $50,000 worth of life insurance. What should you do? A number of life insurance plans were presented in the previous chapter, the most important being term, whole life, limited payment whole life, and endowment. All but term insurance include some element of saving. Thus, you are not only buying pure insurance, you are also investing and getting a rate of return. Your decision whether to buy pure insurance or to buy savings will determine the payments you must make to the insurance company. The cheapest way to buy insurance is, of course, to buy term: you buy only protection. If you already have a satisfactory savings program, you may not wish to save additional sums with an insur-

ance company. Many insurance experts agree that the cheapest insurance you can buy is term, and if you want additional saving features, you will get a higher rate of return by going elsewhere than insurance companies.

Consumers Union points out, as do several other research organizations, that if purchasing whole life insurance is compared with buying term and investing the difference—that is, the difference between the whole life premium and the lower term premium—the combination of term and other investments will yield a larger sum of money at the end of any period. A critic of this conclusion, Mr. Herbert S. Denenberg, contends that this comparison is true only if you manage to get somewhere around a 6 percent rate of return on your savings (over a long period of time) if you invest them yourself. He contends that if you expect to get only 4 percent, you are better off buying whole life.[1] We will see in the following chapter on savings and investment that it is quite difficult not to get 6 percent on savings in a variety of ways. Therefore, we will stick to the conclusion that your best bet is buying term insurance and making your savings plan without involving an insurance company.

However, insurance salespersons have numerous arguments

[1]Herbert S. Denenberg, "Consumers Union: No Help for Insurance Shoppers," *Business and Society Review*, No. 6 (Summer 1973), pp. 107–108.

as to why you should not buy term insurance but should buy whole life. They will say that whole life is a bargain, or even "free," because you eventually get back much or all of your money. Note, however, that if you die, your beneficiary will get only the face value on the policy and not the additional cash value. Salespersons use the cash value aspect of whole life to tout its desirability over term insurance. Because term has no cash value, salespeople will tell you that it is "just throwing money down the drain." This "down the drain" argument ignores the fact that the term premiums are lower than whole life premiums in the early years. For a man 25 years old, whole life premiums in the early years may cost three to four times more than term premiums.

Life Insurance Sold on Campus

There are a large number of insurance agents who have become familiar figures on many campuses. Many college students are contacted four to six times a year by insurance agents. The way the insurance agent approaches a premium-paying problem of the poor student is by offering to finance on credit the first annual premium and even the second, with a loan to be paid off perhaps five years later. This student policyholder typically signs a policy assignment form, which makes the insurance company the first beneficiary if the student dies. Thus, the insurance company will make sure that it can collect the unpaid premium and interest. Generally, buying insurance as a college student is not advisable because most college students do not have dependents.

What If You Need Someone to Force You to Save?

If you like the idea of having forced savings, then buying whole life insurance may be the way to do it. The insurance premiums are something you feel you have to pay and you know that part of the premium goes to a savings plan. The lower rate of return on savings left with an insurance company is compensated for by the fact that you have any savings at all, savings that you would not have had otherwise because you have no will power. This is something only you can decide.

If Your Income Is High

As another argument for favoring whole life over term, some insurance agents point out that for individuals in extremely high income brackets, it may be better to buy whole life insurance, borrow on that insurance to pay the premiums, and be able to deduct the interest payments on the borrowing from ordinary income so that taxes do not have to be paid.

SOME ADDITIONAL CONSIDERATIONS

A fact that we have not yet mentioned about a permanent or whole life insurance policy contract is that it is essentially a piece of property and has certain characteristics that are perhaps unique. Under current law, provided that the permanent insurance plan is set up properly, it can accumulate income, tax free: dividends as well as interest on cash value are not taxable as current income. Essentially, then, you get a higher return than is actually shown in your life insurance saving plan because you are not paying a tax on the savings you are accumulating. Remember that if you have a regular savings account, you have to pay federal and sometimes state income tax on the interest earnings of that account.

Another fact that may or may not be important for most individuals is that death benefits on ordinary or straight life insurance policies usually go to age one hundred, so that except in very rare cases there is always going to be a death benefit.

TAKE ADVANTAGE OF GROUP PLANS

Whenever you can take advantage of group term insurance plans, you probably should do so to take care of at least part of your life insurance needs. For reasons mentioned in the previous chapter, group insurance is generally cheaper than individually issued insurance.

SHOPPING AROUND FOR INSURANCE

One thing is certain: it generally is unwise to buy insurance from the first insurance salesperson who knocks on your door. Because large sums of money may be involved, it is usually advisable to look over several plans. Be warned, however: life insurance policies are incredibly complex. If you can find a knowledgeable insurance salesperson who represents a large number of companies and who can explain the benefits of each program and give you in simple language the average annual costs per $1,000 of five-year renewable term insurance, you are well on your way to being able to pick a company to insure you. A good source of information on comparative life insurance costs can be found in a series of studies presented in *Consumer Reports* (see the January, February, and March issues of 1974). Consumers Union presents the basic facts on the types of policies available and compares different companies on the basis of a sophisticated index that takes account of dividends, interest, and earnings on the policies. Not everyone can buy insurance from some of the companies listed. For example, only teachers and staff members in schools, universities, and educational or scientific institutions can buy insurance from Teachers Insurance and Annuity Association of America, one of the lowest cost insurance policies available. If you work or live in Massachusetts, New York, or Connecticut, you can take advantage of extremely low cost five year renewable term insurance available from the mutual savings banks.

SOME WAYS TO CUT INSURANCE COSTS

1. Don't carry insurance on children. Either save the premiums or use them to buy additional term insurance for yourself.

2. Consider term as opposed to whole life insurance.

3. If you don't smoke or don't drink, try to find insurance companies that give discounts to nonsmokers or nondrinkers. See if you fit into a preferred risk category.

4. Attempt to buy insurance on group plans through your employer or any organization of which you are a member.

5. Pay your premiums annually instead of quarterly or monthly.

6. If you have a participating policy, don't let your dividends or refunds accumulate on deposit with the insurance company at a lower rate than the money could earn at a savings institution.

SUMMARY

1. In deciding whom to insure, make your decision basically on who is dependent on whom and what financial stress would be undergone when an individual prematurely dies.

2. Information about the basic benefits that you are allowed under Social Security can be obtained from the Social Security Administration, Washington, D.C., or your local office.

3. Basic insurance buying rules are: (a) identify and insure major risks according to potential loss, (b) insure big rather than small losses, (c) always compare at least two companies on costs and terms of coverage.

4. If you want a forced saving plan, then you may wish to purchase whole life insurance. However, if you can save on your own, you generally will do better by purchasing lower cost term insurance and putting the difference in high (long-run) income-yielding assets such as long-term savings certificates, the stock market, and so on.

5. Shopping for insurance requires the same skills as shopping for any other consumer product: information is the key. You may wish to consult *Consumer Reports'* special issues in 1974, which rate life insurance companies by their respective costs.

QUESTIONS FOR THOUGHT AND DISCUSSION

1. Can you think of any reason why children should have life insurance?

2. Can you think of any reason why a college student should purchase life insurance?

3. Are you underinsured?

4. Are you overinsured?

5. If you are relatively young, is it possible for you to figure out what Social Security will pay you on retirement?

6. Who should buy term insurance as opposed to whole life?

THINGS TO DO

1. Try to determine whether you are overinsured or underinsured. If you are underinsured, go to the next project.

2. Call at least two, preferably three or four, insurance agents. Take the time to sit down with each of them to discuss your insurance needs. Find out what their recommendations are for an adequate amount of insurance. Ask why they are not suggesting you purchase term or decreasing term insurance.

3. Take a look at the special reports in the 1974 issues of *Consumer Reports.* If you already have insurance, see where your insurance company rates relative to other ones. Would it be worthwhile for you to change policies?

SELECTED READINGS

Denenberg, Herbert S. "The Decline and Fall of Cash Value Life Insurance." *Best's Review*, October 1970.

Denenberg, Herbert S. *The Insurance Trap: Unfair at Any Rate.* Racine, Wis.: Western Publishing Company, 1972.

Denenberg, Herbert S. *A Shopper's Guide to Life Insurance.* Harrisburg, Penn.: Pennsylvania Insurance Department. April 1972.

"A Guide to Life Insurance." *Consumer Reports*, Part 1, January 1974; Part 2, February 1974; Part 3, March 1974.

"How Much Life Insurance Do You Need?" *Changing Times*, January 1972.

"Insurance Salesmen Admit Unethical Practices on Campuses." *Consumer Newsweekly*, March 21, 1977.

"Life Insurance Rip-Off of College Students Totals $5 Billion a Year." *Consumer Newsweek* 5 (October 20, 1975).

Main, J. "How Much Life Is Enough?" *Money*, January 1974.

"Six Fine Points to Check in Your Life Insurance Policy." *Changing Times*, July 1973.

"They're Selling College Kids Bad Buys in Insurance." *Changing Times*, March 1974.

"What's Happening to Life Insurance Dividends?" *Consumer Reports*, November 1976, pp. 659–662.

"Will Social Security Be There When You Need It?" *Changing Times*, February 1977, pp. 24–28.

GLOSSARY OF TERMS

Saving

The act of not consuming or not spending your money to obtain current satisfaction.

Stock Market

An organized market where shares in businesses are traded. These shares are generally called stocks. The largest stock market in the United States is the New York Stock Exchange. The second largest is the American Stock Exchange.

Bonds

A type of debt that a business or a government issues to investors. A bond represents a promise to pay a certain amount of money (called interest) each year. At the end of a specified amount of time, the principal on the bond is repaid to the bondholder.

Compound Interest

Interest that earns interest. For example, if you put a dollar in a savings account that earns 5 percent each year and you leave the interest in, it is compounded. At the end of the first year you would get 5 cents interest; at the end of the second year you would get interest of 5 percent times $1.05, or a compound interest of 5.25 cents.

Time Deposits

Another term for a savings account in a commercial bank. It is so called because in theory you must wait a certain amount of time after you have given notice of your desire to withdraw part or all of your savings. However, this requirement is generally not exercised by the bank.

Common Stocks

Another name for an equity. A common stock is a legal claim to the profits of a company. For each share owned, the common stock owner generally has the right to one vote on such questions as merging with another company and electing a new board of directors.

Equities

A legal claim to the profits of a company. This is another name for stocks, generally called common stocks.

Preferred Stocks

Actually a type of debt obligation like a bond that a company sells to investors. Preferred stocks pay a specified dividend every year (or at some other interval). If the company goes bankrupt, preferred stockholders have the right to collect on their investment before common stockholders obtain any of the liquidated assets of the bankrupt company.

Capital Gain

The difference between the buying and the selling price of something you own when the selling price is higher than the buying price.

Capital Loss

The difference between the buying and the selling price of something you own when the selling price is lower than the buying price so that in fact you take a loss.

Option

A contract conveying a right to buy or sell designated securities at a specified price during a stipulated period.

Call

An option to buy a specified amount of a security at a fixed price at or within a specified time.

Put

An option to sell a specified amount of a security at a fixed price at or within a specified time.

Inside Information

Information about a company's financial situation that is obtained before the public obtains it. True inside information is usually only known by corporate officials or other "insiders."

Mutual Fund

A fund that purchases the stocks of other companies. If you buy a share in a mutual fund, you are in essence buying shares in all of the companies that the mutual fund invests in. The only business of a mutual fund is buying other companies' stocks.

No-Loan Mutual Fund

A mutual fund that has no service charge for buying its shares.

Saving and Investing

CHAPTER PREVIEW

☐ How much do Americans save every year?

☐ Why do people save, and what determines how much they save?

☐ What is the nature of compound interest?

☐ What are the various types of savings institutions?

☐ What are some of the general facts about investing and the yields on investments?

☐ What is the stock market all about?

☐ Is it ever possible to "get rich quick" in the stock market?

17 Almost two-thirds of all American families have savings accounts, and over 30 million Americans have stocks or bonds. The total amount of **saving** in the United States in any one year may exceed $100 billion for the rest of the 1980s. We see in Figure 17-1 the amount of saving over time in the United States.

THE TENDENCY TO SAVE

The tendency to save in the United States has existed ever since the country started. The relationship between consumption and personal disposable income over the last three-fourths of this century has been almost constant. This implies that what Americans do *not* consume, that is, save, is about 12 percent of their income year in and year out. What they do with their savings will be discussed below. Why people save is a question many of you may be asking. The common answer is that we save for a rainy day.

WHY SAVE AT ALL?

If you think that saving is for a rainy day, you are right. The reason you may want to save is either to leave a large estate to your heirs, or to provide for yourself and your family during periods when your income is abnormally low. When are those periods? Obviously, at times when you are disabled or after you retire. We can look at saving, then, as a way to spread out your consumption over your lifetime so that it remains smooth even when your income fluctuates or sometimes falls to zero, especially after you retire. Even if you are very, very poor and just barely making a living, you know that some time in the future you will no longer be able to work. You will either reach mandatory retirement or you will become so unproductive that nobody will be willing to hire you. Your income stream will be cut off. Unless there are children, a benevolent government, or private charities that will take care of you, you will face starvation unless you have accumulated savings.

Therefore, you must decide today how much of your current meager income (assuming you are very poor) you want to set aside for those retirement years when you can no longer work. Unless you will literally starve if you reduce your current level of consumption even by a very small amount, you probably will attempt to save a little bit, however small, out of your meager income. Most people would rather reduce current consumption by a small amount to at least be able to exist after they can no longer work. Were they not to reduce their current consumption at all, they might face certain starvation as soon as their income stream stopped.

Thus, saving is a method by which individuals can achieve an optimal consumption stream throughout their expected lifetime—"optimal" not meaning adequate or necessary, but rather the most desirable from the individual's point of view. If you face the constraint of a very low income for all of your life, in most cases you would still want to provide some savings to live on when you can no longer work.

SAVING AMONG THE POOR

There is a common notion that in many countries people are so poor they cannot save at all because they are barely subsisting. This belief is not true. Many anthropological studies of villages in India, for example, have revealed that saving

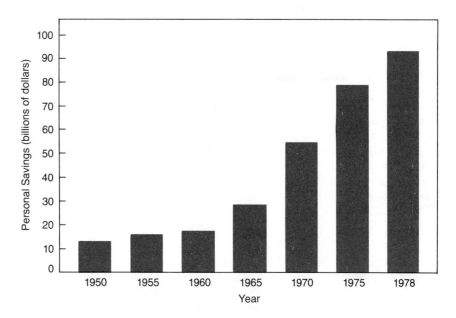

Figure 17-1 Personal Savings in the United States for the Last 25 Years

Personal savings have been going up at fairly steady rates for the last quarter of a century. Note, however, that part of this increase in savings is due to inflation, because we have not corrected for it in this chart.

Source: U.S. Department of Commerce.

is in fact going on; but it takes forms that we do not recognize in our money economy. In some places, for example, saving involves storing dried onions. In Table 17-1, which shows the saving rates for different countries of the world, even the poorest countries have a saving rate that is positive.

WHAT DETERMINES HOW MUCH YOU SAVE?

If you want to save something for that rainy day, what determines the amount you save? We can offer a few ideas here. Obviously, the more money you can make on your savings, the more you will want to save (if nothing else changes). In other words, if a savings and loan association offered to give you 50 percent interest a year on anything you put in it, you probably would want to save more than you do now when a savings and loan association gives you an interest rate of less than 10 percent, and actually not much more than 5 or 6 percent.

Look at it this way: the only reason you save is so that you will have money later on to buy things. If you were to put $100 in a savings account today and get $150 back next year, the price of buying something next year would be pretty low (assuming that the rate of inflation is relatively low). If, on the other hand, you put $100 in the savings account today and you got only $101 back next year because the interest rate is 1 percent, then the implicit price of goods one year from now is not so cheap.

Table 17-1

Saving Rates for Different Countries in the World

Amazingly, the saving rates for different countries in the world vary within a small range. A relatively poor country like Korea saves at about the same rate as a relatively rich country like the United Kingdom.

Source: United Nations Statistical Year Books.

COUNTRY	TOTAL AMOUNT OF SAVINGS AS A PERCENT OF GROSS DOMESTIC PRODUCT
Finland	20.1
Switzerland	18.9
Netherlands	18.8
Australia	18.3
France	17.9
West German Federal Republic	17.5
Belgium	16.7
Norway	16.4
Fiji	16.0
Venezuela	15.7
Spain	15.2
Italy	15.1
Sweden	14.9
Luxembourg	13.4
South Africa	13.4
Korea	12.5
Ireland	12.3
Canada	12.0
Portugal	11.8
United Kingdom	11.5
Denmark	10.3
Philippines	10.2
Honduras	10.1
Jamaica	9.8
Panama	9.2
Malaysia	8.4

Of course, to decide whether to save, or how much to save, you look at more than the interest rate on your savings; you also look at how you value consumption today as opposed to consumption tomorrow. Obviously, when you put off spending $100, you do not get the pleasure from whatever you might have spent it on: you have to wait. If you are impatient, even a high interest rate on savings may not induce you to save much at all. Those of you who are not so impatient about consuming may save more.

Another major determinant of how much of your current income you think you should save is how variable your income is. For example, people who have stable incomes from secure government employment generally save a smaller percentage of their income than do people who are in business for themselves. Obviously, the more variable your income, the more likely you are to have years when your income is lower than usual. Hence, during the years when it is higher than usual you will generally save more.

Moreover, how much you will save depends on how much future retirement income you decide that you should have and on how much you earn. To fully understand how much you will have in the future, you must understand compound interest. Obviously, if you earned no interest at all, your total savings at the end of a specified saving period—say, 30 years—would be exactly what you put in. But that is not what usually happens: you should earn interest on whatever you save.

THE NATURE OF COMPOUND INTEREST

If you decide to save by not consuming all of your income, you can take what you save and, loosely speaking, invest it. You can put it in the **stock market** or you can buy **bonds**—that is, lend money to businesses. You could also put it in your own business. In any event, you might expect to make a profit or interest every year in the future for a certain period of time. To figure out how much you will have at the end of any specified time period, you have to compound your savings. To do so, you have to use a specified interest rate. Say you put $100 in a savings and loan association that yields 5 percent per year. At the end of one year, you have $105. At the end of two years, you have $105 plus 5 percent of $105, or $5.25. Thus, at the end of two years, you have $110.25. This same compounding occurs the third year, the fourth year, and so on.

THE POWER OF COMPOUNDING

The power of **compound interest** is truly amazing. Table 17-2 shows one dollar compounded every year for 50 years at different interest rates. At an interest rate of 8 percent, one dollar will return $46.90 at the end of 50 years. Thus, if you inherited a modest $20,000 when you were 20 years old and put it in an investment that paid 8 percent compounded annually, at 70 years of age you would have $938,000. Now it is not so hard to understand how some people become million-aires. It usually does not take much in brains or business acumen to get an 8

Table 17-2
One Dollar Compounded at Different Interest Rates

Here we show the value of the dollar at the end of a specified period after it has been compounded at a specified interest rate. For example, if you took $1 today and invested it at 5 percent, it would yield $1.05 at the end of the year. At the end of 10 years, it would be equal to $1.63, and at the end of 50 years, it will be equal to $11.50.

In this table, interest is compounded once a year at the end of every year. There are other ways of compounding interest, such as semiannually (once every six months), daily, and continuously. The actual compound factor in this table would have to be altered for each compounding scheme. Clearly, the more frequently a given interest percentage is compounded, the larger the return after a given period of time.

YEAR	3%	4%	5%	6%	8%	10%	20%	YEAR
1	1.03	1.04	1.05	1.06	1.08	1.10	1.20	1
2	1.06	1.08	1.10	1.12	1.17	1.21	1.44	2
3	1.09	1.12	1.16	1.19	1.26	1.33	1.73	3
4	1.13	1.17	1.22	1.26	1.36	1.46	2.07	4
5	1.16	1.22	1.28	1.34	1.47	1.61	2.49	5
6	1.19	1.27	1.34	1.41	1.59	1.77	2.99	6
7	1.23	1.32	1.41	1.50	1.71	1.94	3.58	7
8	1.27	1.37	1.48	1.59	1.85	2.14	4.30	8
9	1.30	1.42	1.55	1.68	2.00	2.35	5.16	9
10	1.34	1.48	1.63	1.79	2.16	2.59	6.19	10
11	1.38	1.54	1.71	1.89	2.33	2.85	7.43	11
12	1.43	1.60	1.80	2.01	2.52	3.13	8.92	12
13	1.47	1.67	1.89	2.13	2.72	3.45	10.70	13
14	1.51	1.73	1.98	2.26	2.94	3.79	12.80	14
15	1.56	1.80	2.08	2.39	3.17	4.17	15.40	15
16	1.60	1.87	2.18	2.54	3.43	4.59	18.50	16
17	1.65	1.95	2.29	2.69	3.70	5.05	22.20	17
18	1.70	2.03	2.41	2.85	4.00	5.55	26.60	18
19	1.75	2.11	2.53	3.02	4.32	6.11	31.90	19
20	1.81	2.19	2.65	3.20	4.66	6.72	38.30	20
25	2.09	2.67	3.39	4.29	6.85	10.80	95.40	25
30	2.43	3.24	4.32	5.74	10.00	17.40	237.00	30
40	3.26	4.80	7.04	10.30	21.70	45.30	1,470.00	40
50	4.38	7.11	11.50	18.40	46.90	117.00	9,100.00	50

percent rate of return in the long run. Somebody who had invested in the stock market 50 years ago would have received much more than 8 percent. There are a number of people around who inherit moderate amounts of money when they are quite young. If this money is put in the stock market and left there to compound itself, it grows to quite unbelievable amounts after 30 or 40 years. Hence, we should be careful about assuming the astuteness of elderly millionaires; they could have been very conservative, done nothing with the money they inherited except

EXHIBIT 17-1   How Compound Interest Helps You Build a Nest Egg

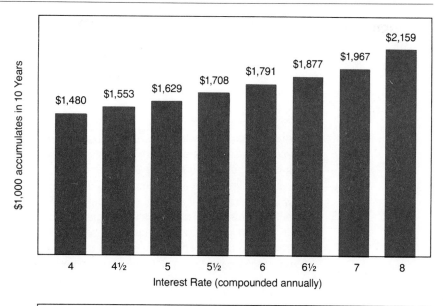

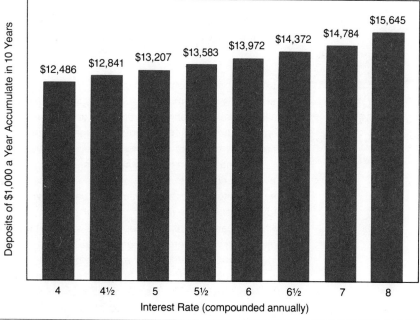

put it in the stock market and leave it there. No business sense would be needed at all and the person could easily become a millionaire by the age of 65.

In Exhibit 17-1 you can see what $1,000 will compound to in ten years at different interest rates and also what would happen if you deposited $1,000 a year, each year, for ten years.

EXHIBIT 17-2   **The Difference Between Compound and Simple Interest**

At 5 percent simple interest, 1¢ becomes approximately $1 if it is invested at the birth of Christ at 5 percent simple interest.

On the other hand, 1,978 years later, the 1¢ invested at 5 percent compounded annual interest grows to about $8,174 followed by 36 zeros!

The power of compound interest should also tip you off as to the true worth of many investment schemes. Take high-priced paintings. Often art dealers will tell you that paintings are good investments. They will cite, for example, a Picasso that a couple purchased for only $5,000 and then sold for $15,000. You have to find out, however, when it was purchased. Usually, if you look at the length of time for which the painting was held, the actual gain in value might be very modest, say, only 3 percent a year. After all, if the painting cost $1,000 in 1953, at a 3 percent compound interest, it would be worth over $2,000 in 1978. The couple who sold it in 1978 could boast that they doubled their investment, while they probably could have done better if in 1953 they had put their $1,000 into a savings account that yielded 4 or 5 percent; they would have done even better if they had put that money into the stock market, because then their rate of return would have been 8 to 12 percent. Usually, because people get some consumption pleasure out of having paintings in their homes, they are willing to receive a lower rate of return than they expect from money in some other type of investment.

TYPES OF SAVINGS INSTITUTIONS

The most common savings institution, and the one familiar to people for the longest time, is the commercial bank. Commercial banks offer **time deposits**—so called because in principle you must allow time between the day you announce your intention to withdraw your savings and the day you withdraw them. Time deposits in commercial banks generally offer the lowest interest yields around.

The main purpose of some banks is to only accept deposits and lend these out for a long term to reliable borrowers at higher rates of interest than the banks pay depositors. These institutions are called *savings banks*. They are intended to provide a safe place in which the small investor can invest his or her savings. As with commercial bank time deposits, a savings bank deposit often requires that a notice be given before the money is allowed to be withdrawn. There are various types of savings banks, the main two being stock and mutual.

The *stock savings bank* is organized and conducted for profit by the owners of its capital stock. The greater number of stock savings banks are located in the midwestern United States. These banks are under the regulation of the state in which they are chartered.

The *mutual savings bank*, on the other hand, is owned by its depositors. In effect, the depositors simply pool their savings, which are invested by a board of trustees and a hired manager. Depositors are not paid a fixed rate of interest on their deposits; whatever earnings are made from the investment belong to the depositors and are divided among them in proportion to their deposits.

The object of *savings and loan associations* is to encourage thrift, but at the same time to assist present and future homeowners. The names by which these associations are known vary in different parts of the country; they can be called savings and loan associations, cooperative banks, or building and loan associations.

Generally, when you put money into a savings and loan association, you get a passbook that indicates you are a shareholder in that organization. As a member, you are entitled to receive interest on your deposits. Savings and loan associations are not generally authorized to handle checking accounts. Currently, the savings in these associations are insured up to a maximum of $40,000 per account.

Credit unions are one of the fastest growing savings institutions in the nation. Credit unions are owned by their membership. They have three purposes:

1. To help their members save.
2. To enable their members to borrow money for "good" purposes at lower than market interest rates.
3. To educate members in money management.

As a member in a credit union, you usually buy shares that are marked on your share booklet. In effect, credit unions are really cooperative small-loan banks that lend amounts to their members at reasonable rates of interest. Federal and state laws vary as to the maximum amount that may be loaned by the credit union.

Not just anybody can join a credit union. Generally, you must be a member of some organization because the credit union is usually for a particular group.

HOW INTEREST IS
COMPUTED ON YOUR
SAVINGS ACCOUNT

The American Banker's Association estimates that there are at least 54 ways of computing interest on passbook deposits. A public interest group called San Francisco Consumer Action estimates that there are almost 200 ways to compute interest.[1]

There are basically four interest calculation methods currently used.

1. **Day of deposit to day of withdrawal.**   This is the easiest to understand and the most advantageous to the saver. You obtain interest for the exact amount of time period your money stays in the savings account. Sixty percent of savings and loan associations use this method, as do 50 percent of commercial banks.
2. **Last in, first out.**   Withdrawals are deducted from the most recent deposits in the quarter and then from the next most recent ones; used by about 5 percent of commercial banks.
3. **First in, first out.**   Withdrawals are deducted first from the starting balance of the interest period and then from later deposits. You automatically lose interest on withdrawals from the start of the interest period, rather from the dates on which the withdrawals were actually made. About 15 percent of commercial banks use this method.
4. **Low balance.**   Using this method, you are paid interest on the lowest balance in an account during the quarter or other accounting period. Thirty percent of commercial banks use this method.

[1]*It's in Your Interest—The Consumer Guide to Savings Accounts*, Consumer Action, 26 Seventh Street, San Francisco, California 94103 ($4.00). Also, *Colorado Consumer Guide to Banks*, available from the Colorado State Treasurer's Office, 140 State Capitol, Denver, Colorado 80203 ($1.25).

To see how these different methods can affect the amount of interest you earn on a savings account, consider how much a hypothetical account would earn where the balance is between $1,000 and $4,000 over six months. There are two deposits totaling $3,000 and three withdrawals, adding up to $2,000. The interest figure used is 6 percent. For the six-month period, the following interest is earned:

1. Day of deposit: $75.30.
2. Last in, first out: $58.44.
3. First in, first out: $52.44.
4. Low balance: $44.93.

The difference is obviously quite important when attempting to find the highest rate of return on a savings account. The method used in computing interest on your passbook account is most important when you have an active account with frequent deposits and withdrawals. The method used becomes less crucial as your account becomes more stable.

THE SIMPLE FACTS ABOUT INVESTING

There are many things that you can do with your accumulated savings: you can keep all or part of them in cash, which earns no interest at all and in fact loses value at the rate of inflation. You can put them into a savings and loan account that gives a relatively low rate of interest but is extremely secure. You can invest your money in shares of stocks of various corporations. You can invest your money in U.S. Savings Bonds, which yield a relatively low rate of interest and in fact are only a slightly better deal than just keeping your savings in a passbook account with a savings and loan association or a commercial bank. You can purchase land. You can purchase consumer durable goods, such as cars, houses, and stereos, which yield a stream of services over their lifetime. You can do an infinite number of things with your savings. The question is what should you do? Well, to start with, that depends on your goals; what your goals are will tell you how much risk you want to take.

There is an unfortunate fact that we have alluded to time and again: you cannot get anything free. If you go into an investment deal in which you expect to make a killing, you may be sure that the risk you are undertaking is relatively high.

RISK AND RATE OF RETURN

There is no way out of the dilemma that the higher the prospective rate of return you expect to get on any investment, the higher the risk you take. That is why if you are offered a "deal" that you are told will make you 50 percent a year, you may be certain that the risk of losing everything is pretty high. On the other hand, if you take your savings and invest them in a savings and loan association you may make only 6 percent a year, but you do not risk losing your entire savings.

A better way to understand why you cannot get a high rate of return without a high risk is to understand why no particular investment "deal" is necessarily any better than any other, at least unless you have some pretty specialized information. Let us explain this by taking a specific example—making money on the stock market. But first, we need a few facts.

SOME FACTS ON
THE STOCK MARKET

The stock market is the general term used for all transactions that involve the buying and selling of shares of stock issued by companies. These stocks are pieces of paper giving the owner the right to a certain portion of the assets of the company issuing the security. Most stocks are **common stocks**, called **equities**. Say a company wishes to expand its operation. It can obtain the money capital for expansion by putting up part of the ownership of the company for sale. It does this by offering stocks, usually common stocks, for sale. If a company worth $1 million wants $200,000, it may sell stocks. Suppose one person, you, owns the company and you arbitrarily state that there are 100,000 shares of stock that you own completely; you would then have to put out on the market about 20,000 shares of your stock, which you would sell at $10 a share. You would get the $200,000 for expansion and the people who paid the money would receive 20,000 shares of your stock. They would have claim to one-fifth of whatever the company earned as profits.

There are many different submarkets within the stock market. At the top of the ladder are the big ones: the New York Stock Exchange and the American Stock Exchange. Measured by dollar value, about 65 percent of all stock transactions are carried out at the New York and the American. There are also regional stock exchanges throughout the country as well as the national over-the-counter market and regional over-the-counter markets. These markets are somewhat less organized than the New York, American, and regional exchanges. The stocks are usually not traded as often in the over-the-counter market as those on the big exchanges. Stocks in companies that are small and less well known than bigger companies are usually traded in the over-the-counter market. There are more than 50,000 different stocks that are bought and sold in the over-the-counter market. Over-the-market dealer brokers regularly quote about 9,500 issues. In the financial pages of large daily newspapers, you will find some of the 2,000 of the most active issues for which daily or weekly quotes are given.

PREFERRED STOCKS
AND BONDS

Preferred stock is a fancy name for what is simply the debt of a company. It is called "preferred" because, in the event of distributable earnings, or in the event of liquidation or bankruptcy, the holders of that stock have a preferred claim against the company prior to that of the common stockholders. That is, whatever assets can be retrieved are distributed first among preferred stockholders, after bond-holders have been paid. A preferred stock is actually a type of bond that can be defined very simply. A bond is basically an I.O.U. or promissory note of a corporation, usually issued in multiples of $1,000. A bond is evidence of a debt in which the issuing company usually promises to pay the bondholders a specified amount of interest for a specified length of time and then to repay the loan on the expiration date. In every case, a bond represents debt: its holder is a creditor of the corporation and not a part owner, as is the shareholder or stockholder. So you can see that preferred stock is merely a bond, except that failure to pay the interest or dividend on preferred stock does not legally allow the preferred stockholder to sue the company. The preferred stockholder simply has preference to the earnings, if any, for payment of interest before any dividends can be paid to the common stockholders. Sometimes the preferred stock is "cumulative": if any arrears of unpaid dividends (or interest) accumulate, the common stockholders cannot take any dividends until the preferred stockholders have been paid.

CAPITAL GAINS
AND LOSSES

Preferred stock may also be convertible, which means that the preferred stockholder has the option to exchange—that is, convert—it into common stock at a preset exchange rate. There are also such things as convertible bonds, which can also be exchanged for common stock at some preset exchange rate.

Stocks can go up and down in price. If you buy a stock at $10 and sell it at $15, you make a **capital gain** equal to $5 for every share you bought and then sold at the higher price. That is called an appreciation in the price of your stock, which you realized as a capital gain when you sold it. If the value of your stock falls and you sell it at a loss, you have suffered a **capital loss** because of the depreciation in the market value of your stock. Some stocks pay dividends, but not all do. (Dividends are paid by checks mailed to the stockholders.) Normally, when you buy a stock that has never paid a dividend, you expect to make money on your investment by an increase in the value of the stock. That is, if the company is making profits but not giving out dividends, it must be reinvesting those profits. A reinvestment in itself could pay off in the future by higher profits. The value of the stock would then be bid up in the market. Your profit would be in the form of a capital gain rather than by dividend payments.

THE OPTION MARKET

Since 1973, when the Chicago Board Options Exchange opened for business, the trading in **options** has grown rapidly. The estimate for 1978 is 33 million options contracts traded. The listed options are basically **calls**—contracts giving their owners the right to buy 100 shares of the stock at a predetermined price (called the striking price) at any time up to a predetermined maturity date. The Securities and Exchange Commission also permits the trading in listed **puts**—the right to sell

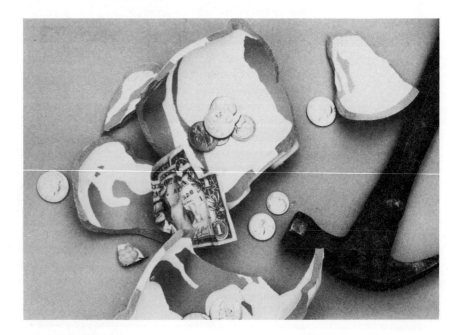

EXHIBIT 17-3   **Comparison of Stocks and Bonds**

Stocks	Bonds
1. Represent ownership (except preferred stocks).	**1.** Represent owed debt.
2. Have no fixed dividend rate (including preferred stocks).	**2.** Require interest be paid whether or not any profit is earned.
3. Allow holders to elect board of directors, who in turn control the corporation (except holders of preferred stock).	**3.** Usually entail no voice in or control over management.
4. Have no maturity date; the corporation does not usually repay the stockholder.	**4.** Have a maturity date when the holder is to be repaid the face value.
5. Are issued by all business corporations (and are purchased by stockholders).	**5.** Need not be issued by corporations.
6. Allow holders to have a claim against the property and income of the corporation after all creditors' claims have been met.	**6.** Give to bondholders a prior claim against the property and income of the corporation, which must be met before the claims of stockholders.

---

stocks at predetermined prices. The options on any particular stock mature at three-month intervals. The longest mature in nine months.

The buyer of a call captures any rise in the price of the stock above the so-called striking price. That is a valuable right and, hence, buyers have to pay for it. Calls seem attractive to buyers because they get all the action in the stock while putting in only a fraction of its value. The maximum amount they can lose is the cost of the call. On average, options sell for about 5 to 15 percent of the price of the underlying stock.

WHAT AFFECTS THE PRICE OF A STOCK?

Some observers believe that individual psychological or subjective feelings are all that affect the price of a stock. If people think a stock will be worth more in the future, they will bid the price up. If they think it will be worth less in the future, the price will fall. However, that is not a very satisfactory theory. What are psychological feelings based upon? Usually, such feelings are based upon the expected stream of profits that the company will make in the future. Past profits may be important in formulating a prediction of future profits. However, past profits are bygones, and bygones are forever bygones. A company could lose money for 10 years and then make profits for the next 15.

If a company gets a new management team that has a reputation for turning losing companies into winning ones, people in the stock market might expect profits to turn around and rise. If a company has a record number of sales orders for future months, one might expect profits to go up. Whenever profits are expected to rise, we typically find a rise in the value of the stock. That is, people bid up the price of the stock. Any information about future profits should be valuable in assessing how a stock's price will react.

MAKING MONEY IN THE STOCK MARKET

You have probably heard of the infamous J. P. Morgan: he was supposed to have made his fortune by manipulating the stock market. You have also probably heard of persons becoming millionaires overnight by making astute investments in securities. You may even have a parent who talks much about the stock market, follows the *Wall Street Journal*, reads the financial page of the local newspaper, talks about the prices of various stocks going up or down. Making money in the stock market seems as easy as calling up your stockbroker for the latest "hot" tips.

GETTING ADVICE ON THE MARKET

Try an experiment: look in your yellow pages under "Stock and Bond Brokers" and pick a phone number at random; call it; ask to speak with a registered representative or an account executive (in the old days, called "customers' men"). Talk to this broker as if you had, say, $10,000 to invest. Ask him or her for advice. You will probably be asked what your goals are. Do you want income from your investment? Do you want growth in your investment? Do you want to take a chance? Do you want to be safe? After you tell the broker the strategy you wish to pursue, you will be told what are the best stocks to buy. If you ask the broker what he or she thinks the market in general will be doing over the next few months, you are bound to hear an opinion, and an authoritative one at that. After all, if you want to know what to do with your garden, ask the person who runs the local nursery. If you want to know about your car, ask your local mechanic. That is, you generally seek out specialists in whatever is your interest. Why not seek out a specialist, then, when you are interested in making money?

A broker is a specialist, one from whom you can get much useful information. A broker can tell you all about the stock market and can give you quotes on all the different stocks—that is, what their prices are and how many of them were sold in the last few days and what the history of the prices was. You can be told about the various types of securities you can buy—stocks listed on the big exchanges like the New York and the American, over-the-counter stocks that are sold only in very restricted sections of the country, preferred stocks, bonds, convertible debentures, puts, calls, warrants, and so on and so on. A stockbroker is the person you should ask concerning all these different avenues of investment.

But the broker is *not* the one you should ask about which particular stock to buy. *The broker is no more likely to be right than are you.* You might even select the stocks to purchase by throwing a dart at a list of stocks in the New York Stock Exchange. If you are shocked by this revelation, consider that the stock market is the most highly competitive market in the world, and information costs there are perhaps the lowest of any market in existence.

PUBLIC INFORMATION

Information flows rapidly in the stock market. If you read in the *Wall Street Journal* that International Chemical and Nuclear (ICN) has just discovered a cure for cancer, do you think you should rush out and buy ICN stock? You might, but you will be no better off than if you had bought any other stock. By the time you read about ICN's discovery (which will mean increased profits in the future for the company), thousands and thousands of other people will have already read it. A rule that you should apply, and one that will be explained several times in this chapter, is that *public information does not yield an above-normal profit or rate of return.* Once information about a company's profitability is generally known, that information has a zero value for predicting the future price of the stock. The only information that is useful is what we call **inside information**.

CAPITALIZATION

True inside information is just that: it is information that is not generally known. Information that becomes public is capitalized upon almost immediately; people consider what it means for future profits and bid up the price of the stock to a level that reflects the expected future increase in profits. Information is used almost immediately in the stock market because it flows so rapidly. There have been studies on the value of information contained in the *Wall Street Journal* or the *New York Times*, and it turns out that this information is useless for assessing which stocks to buy. Even information about national or world events cannot tell you whether the market in general will go up or down.

Studies have also been done on the profitability of information acquired by insiders in companies—that is, by corporate officers. Officers in a company are required to file statements of their transactions in their own company's stocks with the Securities and Exchange Commission, the regulator of the stock market industry. Statistical studies have shown that when insiders (corporate officers) sell their stocks in their company, the price of the stock usually falls within 30 days; when insiders buy their own company's stocks, the price of the stock usually rises within 30 days. Obviously, there is a value to having inside information. (Note that it is illegal for officers to tell outsiders any inside information that can then be used to make money on the company's stock.)

HOT TIPS

What about the hot tips your broker might have? It is highly dubious that it will be true inside information. After all, if it were really inside information, why would it be given to you? Why would the broker not take advantage of it himself or herself, get rich quick, and quit being a stockbroker? The broker's information might have come from the brokerage's research department. Almost all stock brokerage companies have large research staffs that investigate different industries, different companies, and the future of the general economy. These research departments issue research statements on different companies and industries in the economy. There are recommendations as to which stocks are underpriced and, therefore, should be bought. *The value of this research information to you as an investor is zero.* You will do no better by following the advice of research branches of your stock brokerage company than you will by randomly selecting stocks—particularly stocks listed on the New York and American stock exchanges. Nevertheless, the amount of research on those companies that is completed by firms, individuals, organizations, governments, and so on is indeed staggering. Because information flows so freely, by the time you receive the results of research on a particular company, you can be sure that thousands and thousands of other people have already found out. And because so many brokerage firms employ research analysts, you can be sure that there are numerous analysts investigating every single company that has shares for sale in the open stock market.

THE RANDOM WALK

Recall, from your high school physics course, your study of Brownian motion of molecules. They jumped around randomly; there was simply no way to predict where a molecule would jump next. This is exactly what happens when something follows a random walk; it goes in directions that are totally unrelated to past directions. If something follows a random walk, no amount of information of the past is useful for predicting what will happen in the future. The stock market would be expected to exhibit a random walk merely because it is so highly competitive and because information flows so freely. Examining past prices on the market as a whole or on individual stocks would not be expected to yield any useful information as to prices in the future. Years and years of academic research on the stock market have left little doubt that the stock market is, indeed, a random walk. (If you find out otherwise, you may be able to get rich very quickly.)

A stock is not like a dog—which is to say, it will not eventually come home to its former price. Indeed, because a stock does not know where its home is and does not have a mind or a purpose, what has happened to that stock in the past does not matter. You can find no usable information by examining past stock prices. Or, according to Nobel Prize winning economist Paul Samuelson:

> Even the best investors seem to find it hard to do better than the comprehensive common-stock averages, or better on the average than random selection among stocks of comparable variability.[2]

WHAT ABOUT
INVESTMENT PLANS?

Investment plans and sophisticated investment counselors are numerous. In their advertising, they guarantee you a higher rate of return on your stock dollars than any place else. A typical piece of advertising might show, for example, the average rate of return for investing in all of the stocks on the New York Stock Exchange. An investment counselor would show you that his stock portfolio makes 15 percent a year, rather than the average 8 percent by buying all stocks together. However, these investment counselors usually neglect to point out that the 15 percent rate of return does not take account of the investment counseling fees nor the trading costs—that is, brokers' commissions—for buying and selling stocks. Investment services usually do much trading: they go in and out of the market—buying today, selling tomorrow. Each time someone buys a stock or sells a stock, that person pays a commission to the broker. Thus, the more trading your investment counselor does for your account, the more trading costs you incur. In fact, in almost all cases that have been thoroughly examined, investments made through counselors do no better than the general market averages because any special profits they make are eaten up by brokerage fees and their own counseling fees. Thus, you would be better off just paying brokerage fees and not using the services of an investment counselor.

MUTUAL FUNDS

This fact was confirmed in a study of **mutual funds**. Mutual funds take the money of many investors and buy and sell large blocks of stocks; the investors get dividends or appreciation in their shares of the mutual fund. The mutual fund, then,

[2]Paul Samuelson, *The Bell Journal of Economics and Management Science*, 4 (Autumn 1973): pp. 369–374.

is a company that invests in other companies but does not sell any physical product of its own. You can buy shares in mutual funds just as you can buy shares in General Motors. The study of mutual funds mentioned above concluded that mutuals that did the least amount of trading made the highest profits, an expected result if one understands the competitive nature of the stock market.

THE TWO TYPES
OF MUTUAL FUNDS

A mutual fund or investment trust is principally either of two types: the *closed end* and the *open end*. Shares in closed end investment trusts (mutual funds), some of which are listed on the New York Stock Exchange, are readily transferable in the open market and are bought and sold like other shares. These companies are called closed end because their capitalization remains the same unless action is taken to change, which is seldom. Open end funds sell their own new shares to investors, stand ready to buy back their old shares, and are not listed on the stock exchange. Open end funds are so called because their capitalization is not fixed; they issue more shares as people want them.

The only commission you pay to buy closed end mutual funds is the standard commission you would pay on the purchase of any stock. On the other hand, there are two types of open end mutual funds, a no-load and a load. The **no-load mutual fund** charges no setup or loading charge for you to get into the fund, while the load mutual fund charges you about 8 percent to get into the fund. Both may charge a yearly management fee. The salesperson or stockbroker who sells you an open end mutual fund with a loading charge usually keeps most of that charge as commission. Mutual fund experts divide open and closed end funds into the following categories:

1. **Income funds.** This fund attempts to achieve high yields by concentrating on high dividend common stocks or bonds or a combination.
2. **Balance funds.** To minimize risk, these funds hold common stocks and a certain proportion of bonds and preferred stocks.
3. **Maximum capital gains funds—dividend income incidental.** These are often aggressively managed and take higher than average risks by buying little-known companies.
4. **Long-term growth funds—income secondary.** Fund managers go after larger, more seasoned, higher quality growth stocks that do not generate dividends.
5. **Specialized funds.** A fund that restricts itself to certain types of securities, such as gold mining stocks.
6. **Money market funds.** Fund managers buy only certificate of deposits and bills sold by the U.S. Treasury (see page 436 for more information).

In addition, there are the following types of closed end funds:

1. **Real estate funds.** Otherwise known as REITs, or real estate investment trusts. These are of two types, a mortgage trust, which borrows money from banks and relends it at a higher rate to builders and developers; and equity trusts, which own income-producing property.
2. **Dual purpose funds.** A type of closed end fund that sells two classes of stock—income shares and capital shares. The first group of purchasers receive all the fund's net income; the second group participate only in capital gains.

UNIT TRUSTS

Since 1961 investors have been able to receive tax-free interest income on unit trusts. The sponsors of these trusts buy a large number of tax exempt bonds sold by municipalities. There is no management and no addition to the original portfolio. The trust is held until maturity. All unit trusts have sales charges, typically 3.5 to 4.5 percent of the total value of the trust. This is a once-and-for-all payment, however. There is no annual management fee because there is no management. There may be a slight annual expense to take account of bookkeeping, however. New unit trusts are available every few weeks. One example is a municipal investment trust fund series offered jointly by Merrill Lynch, Bache, and Reynolds Securities—all reputable brokerage firms.

IS THERE NO WAY
TO GET RICH QUICK?

The general conclusion to be reached from our analysis of the stock market is that all of the investing schemes everybody talks about are really quite useless for getting rich quickly. That does not mean, of course, that some people will not get rich by using them. Luck has much to do with making money in the stock market— just as it does with winning at poker or craps. If you do make money with your particular scheme, it does not mean you are extra smart, a better investor, or a prophet. You may just be lucky. You may, however, make more than a normal rate of return on your invested capital if you spend a tremendous amount of time searching out areas of unknown profit potential. But then you are spending resources—your own time. Your fantastic profits can be considered as payment for the time you spent—the value of your opportunity cost—analyzing the stock market and different companies.

The question still remains: How can you make money? You know that you can make a normal rate of return by merely throwing a dart at the listing of stocks in the New York Stock Exchange. Pick eight stocks, for example, and just keep buying them with your investment dollars. Never sell until you need money for retirement. Over the long run, you will probably make around an 8 to 15 percent rate of return. On the other hand, you might want to pick particular stocks if you have inside information or information that is better than the tips anybody else has. In such a case, you stand to gain more than by randomly picking stocks. Also, if you think you can somehow evaluate public information better than anybody else can, you may want to do more than select random stocks. But before you decide whether you can evaluate better than others, you had better think seriously about how many others there are in the world. The stock industry is huge. Why do you think that you can do better than everybody else at evaluating public information?

**OTHER SUREFIRE
SCHEMES**

By now, you ought to be quite suspicious about any special investment deals that become available. Because there is so much competition in the investment markets, and because you, as a single consumer, are not likely to be smarter than any of the experts around, you should consider every single investment as a trade-off between risk and rate of return. The higher the potential rate of return, the higher the risk. There is no reason why you should expect you can do better than average unless you have some special information. Real estate is a good example.

REAL ESTATE

Will Rogers once said, "It's easy to make money, just figure out where people are going and then buy the land before they get there." Now, how does that fit in with our discussion? Obviously, if Will Rogers knew this astute proposition, all of the experts know it, too. What do you think happens when it is known where people will be going? That information will be used by others, who will thereby bid up the price of land in the places where people are going. Only if you think you have such information ahead of everyone else can you expect to make a higher than normal rate of return in any type of land investment.

Do not be taken in by such statements as "land is always a safe investment." The value of land can fall like the value of anything else. The fact that the overall price of land has been going up for a long time does not mean that you will make more than what you could make, say, investing money in a savings and loan association. Although on average you might make more in land, on average you also take a greater risk because many times land deals fall through completely.

You can think of a thousand and one other investment opportunities to which the same logic applies. Just remember that you do not get something for nothing: any time you do something with your savings, you are going to be subjected to the rigors of a competitive marketplace. Only special information is valuable. Otherwise, you will get no more, on average, than a normal rate of return.

PENSIONS AND RETIREMENT PLANS

If you are involuntarily or voluntarily covered by a retirement or a pension plan, you are saving: that retirement or pension plan is in fact a savings plan. Moreover, if you have anything other than term insurance, you are also saving, because the cash value of whole or ordinary insurance can be turned into retirement annuity.

SETTING UP YOUR OWN PENSION PLAN

For many people, one of the smartest ways to save is by setting up a personal pension plan. The reason that it is beneficial to save via an individual retirement plan is because you do not pay taxes on the allowed amount of savings put into the plan nor on the interest and dividends that the plan generates until you take the money out, usually at retirement. In effect, you are being given an interest free loan from the government that earns interest itself on which you can defer taxes for many years and pay them usually when you are in a lower tax bracket. The benefit of putting away, say, $1,500 a year in a tax free retirement plan is directly proportional to your marginal tax rate. If you were in the 50 percent tax bracket, for example, you would have, had you not put the money in the plan, paid Uncle Sam $750 in taxes; instead you put the $1,500 in the approved plan, earn interest on the total amount for however many years it is in effect, and then pay taxes only as you take money out of the plan on a retirement basis. There are basically two plans available to individuals who are self-employed or whose employers do not provide pension plans.

KEOGH PLANS

The Keogh Act of 1972 was passed in order to help self-employed individuals set up their own pension plans. Modified by the Employment Retirement Income

Security Act of 1974, a Keogh Plan retirement program allows you to set aside a maximum of 15 percent of your earned income up to a maximum of $7,500 a year into your private pension plan. You are penalized if you take the money out of the plan before you are 59½ years old, unless you are totally disabled. You must take money out of the plan when you reach 70½, even if you have not retired and still have current income. Many insurance companies, mutual funds, and banks have developed master plans that simplify the setting up of a Keogh fund.

INDIVIDUAL RETIREMENT ACCOUNT

A relatively newer retirement system is the IRA. You may contribute to an IRA account and deduct on your tax return $1,500 or 15 percent of your earnings each year, whichever is less. Each year's contributions can be made in one lump sum or installments. In principle, no contributions can be made to an IRA account in any year in which money currently is being put in another pension program that qualifies for tax advantages; however, your existing IRA can continue and earn further taxes or dividends and interest. Like the Keogh plan, you must withdraw from the plan in the year you reach 70½ and you pay a penalty on funds withdrawn before age 59½ (you pay regular income taxes plus a 10 percent penalty). An IRA account can be managed by you. You can decide which investments to make and which not to make; however, a number of banks have already set up IRA accounts to ease the management problem in recordkeeping.

SETTING UP A SPOUSE'S PENSION PLAN

A spouse may now have a pension plan of his or her own. Under the 1976 Tax Reform Act, an employed husband or wife can set up either a jointly owned IRA and contribute 15 percent of income up to $1,750, or two separate IRAs with up to $875 going to each. Previously, a nonemployed partner in a marriage was not eligible for an IRA. In the case of a divorce, the nonsalaried spouse will own his or her IRA.

DEFERRED ANNUITIES

If you do not have the qualification to start your own Keogh or IRA plan, then a deferred annuity may be one way to invest and save. Using a deferred annuity, you take income that has already been taxed and invest it in the annuity, deferring annual payments until you, the owner, decide you want them; you can also get the money in a lump sum. Essentially, you are sheltering the interest on your investment during the time period you do not take out any money. There is no tax on withdrawals, up to the original amount invested. These annuities are sold mainly by stockbrokerage firms. Some plans allow for additions to monthly payments after the initial purchase.

How to be a wise investor is outlined in the following consumer issue. But remember that spending much time researching investment possibilities does not necessarily mean that you are wise. Only if you think you have acquired special information can you, on average, expect to get a higher than normal rate of return. You also must consider all the time spent in researching that information. If your time is worth something, it may not be worth your while to spend it in that manner. You may want to pay somebody else to do it, or you may want to play it safe, as you will see in the following consumer issue.

SUMMARY

1. Individuals save in order to provide for income during periods when their earning capacity falls, such as during sickness or after retirement. Hence, even in poor countries individuals save a positive amount of income every year. In addition to the rate of return or interest you obtain from your savings, the variability of your income will also determine how much you save. The higher the interest paid and the higher the variability of your income, the more you will save.

2. In our competitive society, very few things come free of charge. Hence, any investment deal you go into with your savings cannot guarantee you a higher than normal rate of return unless a large amount of risk—that is, a high chance of losing everything—is involved.

3. When trying to figure out how much savings you will have accumulated after a certain amount of saving, you should consult a compound interest table such as we have presented in Table 17-2. If, for example, your savings were invested at an average yield of 8 percent, at the end of 20 years every dollar invested will have grown to $4.66.

4. In addition to commercial banks, there are numerous types of savings institutions, such as savings banks (stock and mutual), savings and loan associations, and credit unions.

5. In the stock market, shares of American businesses are bought and sold just about every weekday throughout the year. When you buy and sell stocks, you may either sell them for more than you paid and experience a capital gain, or sell them for less than you paid and experience a capital loss.

6. When you buy a share in a company, there is no guarantee that you will receive dividends or that you will make any particular rate of interest on your investment. However, if you loan money to the company—that is, buy one of their bonds—you are guaranteed, as long as the company does not go bankrupt, a specified dollar interest payment every year and a specified principal payment when the bond matures or when the bond's life runs out. It is important to purchase bonds only if the interest rate paid at least compensates you for inflation that you anticipate.

7. It is generally a waste of time to consult stock market analysts in deciding which stocks to buy for your investment portfolio. This is because the stock market is one of the most highly competitive markets in the world and any useful information is immediately used by those who perceive it. Thus, the price of a stock represents all of the information (properly discounted) that exists about the company, the industry, or the economy as a whole.

8. Stockbrokers can be useful to explain how the stock market works, the different types of securities you can buy, and so on.

9. Do not be taken in by so-called investment plans that purport to guarantee you a higher than normal rate of return in the stock market. Generally, these investment plans consume any above-normal rates of return in the fees they charge you or the commissions you must pay to buy and sell stocks often.

10. Mutual funds may be an easy answer to your investing problems, for they purchase a wide variety of stocks. It is generally advisable to buy into a no-load mutual fund, which has no sales charges. Also, it may be possible to buy into mutual funds that purchase a nearly random selection of stocks and

therefore do not have any management expenses. These mutual funds will eventually be offered to you at a lower management fee than those currently in existence.

11. All schemes to make you richer should be investigated thoroughly, for, on average, they very rarely guarantee you a higher than normal rate of return unless you accept a higher amount of risk. For example, even though the amount of land is fixed and the population is growing, real estate is not always a good investment. That is an example of public information that has zero value as a guide to where to invest your accumulated savings. The same would be true for any arguments telling you that the best investments are antiques, oil and gas wells, old paintings, cans of food, and so on.

QUESTIONS FOR THOUGHT AND DISCUSSION

1. "Poor people barely have enough to survive on and therefore cannot save anything for a rainy day." Do you agree or disagree?
2. What determines how much you save?
3. Would it make a difference whether the interest on your savings were compounded daily, weekly, semiannually, or every year? If so, what difference?
4. Why do you have to worry about the rate of inflation when you invest your savings?
5. What is the maximum yield you can obtain from putting your money in a savings and loan association today? Is that yield greater than the rate of inflation? Are you taxed on the interest you receive?
6. "Risk and rate of return are positively related." Do you agree with that statement? Why or why not?
7. Which do you think are a better investment—stocks or bonds?
8. Do you think stockbrokers have more information about which stocks to buy than you have?
9. What is the value of public information?
10. Do you think the small investor should be given special treatment by the stock exchanges and brokerage houses?
11. "The stock market is the backbone of American capitalism." Comment.
12. Do you believe the so-called random walk theory of stock prices?
13. Why do you think there were no mutual funds in existence 50 years ago?
14. The value of land has always gone up. If that is true, why do investors not put all their money in land?

THINGS TO DO

1. Try to figure out what percentage of your income you save. Remember that the purchase of a so-called consumer durable, such as a television set, a stereo, a house, or a car, is a form of saving because you receive income from that consumer durable for a long period of time. The income you receive is the satisfaction you obtain from the durable.
2. Assume that by the time you retire at age 65, you want to have $100,000 saved up. Also assume that you can earn 10 percent per year on your savings. Determine from Table 17-1 how much you have to put in the bank today to have $100,000 at age 65 at a 10 percent rate of return.

3. Call up an antique dealer and ask that person about the investment opportunities in antiques. Find out what the rate of return is on investing in antiques. Is this rate of return higher or lower than what you could expect if you put your money in a savings and loan association?

4. Find out the different rates of return offered by the various savings institutions. Why do you think there is a difference?

5. Visit a local credit union—say, one for labor union employees or schoolteachers. Get a copy of the credit union's requirements. Try to find out why there is a restriction on who can use the credit union. Compare the rates on a car loan or a personal loan from that credit union with what you would have to pay at a commercial bank. Why do you think the difference exists, if it does? (It usually does.)

6. If you live in one of the large cities that has a stock exchange, go visit it. You will be able to see a competitive market in action. Also, you can usually pick up information on stock markets and how they work. Call up a brokerage firm in your area to ask if there is a national or regional exchange near your place of residence.

7. Look at the financial page of any newspaper. Find out what all of the various financial quotations actually mean, either from your instructor or from a stockbroker.

SELECTED READINGS

Baruch, Hurd. *Wall Street: Security Risk*. London: Acropolis Books, 1972.

Credit Union Statistics. National Credit Union Administration, 2025 M Street, N.W., Washington, D.C. 20456 (latest edition).

Credit Union Yearbook. Credit Union National Association, 1616 Sherman Avenue, Madison, Wisconsin 53701 (latest edition).

"Credit Unions Move Deeper into Banking." *Business Week*, April 11, 1977, p. 52.

Friend, Irwin; Blume, Marshall; and Crockett, Jean. *Mutual Funds and Other Institutional Investors: A New Perspective*. New York: McGraw-Hill, 1970.

Lorie, James H., and Hamilton, Mary T. *The Stock Market*. Homewood, Ill.: Richard D. Irwin, 1973.

"Markets and Investments." See issues of *Business Week*.

"Once-Meek Credit Unions Take on the Banking Industry." *U.S. News*, February 21, 1977, pp. 85–86.

"The Need for Truth-in-Savings." *Everybody's Money*, Summer 1972.

Saving and Loan Fact Book. U.S. Saving and Loan League, 221 North LaSalle Street, Chicago, Illinois 60601 (latest edition).

Understanding Bonds and Preferred Stocks. New York Stock Exchange, 11 Wall Street, New York, New York 10005.

"Why So Many Lawsuits Against Mutual Funds?" *Changing Times*, November 1972.

Wiesenberger, Arthur. *Investment Companies*. New York: Arthur Wiesenberger & Company (published annually).

Your Insured Deposit. Federal Deposit Insurance Corporation, 550 17th Street, N.W., Washington, D.C. 20429, 1972.

How to Be a Rational Investor

GLOSSARY OF TERMS

Real Rate of Return

The rate of return received on any investment after the effect of inflation has been taken into account. For example, if you receive a 10 percent rate of return on an investment and the rate of inflation is 5 percent, your real rate of return is only 5 percent.

Dow Jones Industrial Average

A stock market performance indicator that consists of the price movements in the top 30 industrial companies in the United States.

Third Market

A network of traders who bypass the major stock exchanges.

Tax Exempts

Investments that yield income that is tax exempt. Generally, tax exempts are municipal bonds with an interest rate that is not taxed by the federal government.

Treasury Bills

Short-term obligations of the federal government. Treasury Bills are for specified terms of three, six, and twelve months. If the term on government debt is from one to seven years, the certificates are called Treasury Notes; for periods greater than seven years, Treasury bonds are issued, such as U.S. Savings Bonds.

Bankers Acceptance

A bill of exchange draft payable at maturity that is drawn by a creditor against his or her debtor. Bankers acceptances are short-term credit instruments most commonly used by persons or firms engaged in international trade. They are comparable to short-term government securities (for example, Treasury Bills) and may be sold on the open market at a discount.

Liquidity

The "moneyness" that an investment has. The most liquid asset you can own is, of course, cash; it trades dollar for dollar. The next most liquid asset you could own might be a savings account. A house would be an illiquid asset.

As you saw in the last chapter, the various schemes you could follow to get rich quickly in the stock market are useless because the stock market is so highly competitive. That is true for just about every investment opportunity you could partake in with your savings. Nonetheless, you must do something with your savings if you want to insure yourself against inflation. In Consumer Issue E you received some specific tips on how to deal with inflation, but some of them bear repeating here.

INFLATION AND THE INTEREST RATE

You should make sure that the **real rate of return** on your investments is at least positive. For example, you should not be content with buying a Series E Savings Bond from the U.S. government at 5½ or 6 percent interest if the rate of inflation is 5½ or 6 percent. If you do such a thing, your real rate of return will be *negative*, because you have to pay taxes on those earnings. In a period of uncertainty about the future rate of inflation, you should probably invest at least some of your savings in mutual funds that buy only short-term debt, which we discuss in more detail toward the end of this consumer issue. You get essentially the same interest rate that the big money market people get. Right now, if you have very small amounts of savings to invest, there is little else that you can do to protect yourself against inflation. If, however, your goals are long range, the stock market has been shown to be (at least until recently) a relatively safe investment.

EVIDENCE ON THE STOCK MARKET

Numerous studies on the stock market have shown that on the average you can expect to make 8 to 15 percent per year if you

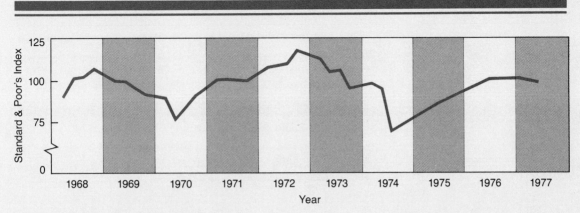

Figure O-1 Common Stocks Stand Still

reinvest all dividends and refrain from trading for a long period of time. As long as you assume that what has happened in the past will keep on happening, then a stock market investment can be reassuring. Columbia University economist Phillip Cagan, under the auspices of the National Bureau of Economic Research, conducted one of the most recent studies of the stock market and found that in the United States and in most other countries of the world the rate of return on common stocks over long periods has been positive, even allowing for inflation. Only during periods of very rapid inflation have stock prices lagged considerably behind consumer prices. Of all the world's stock markets, according to Professor Cagan, the U.S. market has done especially well in outpacing inflation.[1]

What does this mean for the buyer of stocks? If you decide to buy common stocks, the easiest

[1]Phillip Cagan, "Common Stock Values and Inflation—The Historical Record of Many Countries," *Supplement* No. 13 (New York: National Bureau of Economic Research), 1974.

thing you can do is randomly pick and then hold them until you want to retire. Do not look at the newspaper every day to see what the price of the stock is doing. Do not call a broker for advice on what to do. Just pick at random; do not worry about your choices; and in the long run you will get 8 to 15 percent, which is hard to beat.

However, if you ever have a desperate need of those savings for something like a medical emergency, you may be in trouble. Figure O-1 shows what the stock market did from 1968 to 1977. Its performance was not very impressive. Figure O-2 shows the **Dow Jones Industrial Average**, which is a composite indication of the value of the top 30 industrial shares in the New York Stock Exchange. But in this figure *the averages have been corrected for inflation and the amount of profits the companies pour back into the company*. This, then, is the Dow Jones average in *real* terms. It has not been very impressive over the last five or six years. In fact, it has been lower in the 1970s than it was in the 1950s. Nonetheless, those of you who are looking 20 or 30 years into

the future will find it hard to go wrong by just putting your money into the stock market randomly. Of course, you may want to use the services of a mutual fund or an investment service, which we discussed in the previous chapter. But remember that mutual funds or investment counselors are not going to help you much if high service charges are involved in buying their shares or using their services, particularly if they have a philosophy of "churning"—that is, buying and selling frequently on special tips.

Buying an Index Fund

If you really believe strongly in the random walk theory of the stock market, then your best bet is to purchase shares of a so-called index fund. A large number of pension plan managers have put much, if not all, of their available money into index funds, which basically try to simulate what the average of the stock market does. The fund will buy, for example, 250 to 475 of Standard & Poor's 500 stocks, with the holding weighted to match the industry weightings in the inde:.. For

Figure O-2   The Dow Jones Industrial Average Corrected for Inflation and Retained Earnings

In this figure the Dow Jones depicted in Figure O-1 has been corrected for inflation since 1930, using 1967 as the base. The averages also show correction for the 3 percent retained earnings that is the average for the economy. The figures given are the closing highs for each year. The corrected Dow Jones hit its peak back in 1965 and 1966, and has done little since then.

Source: *The Dow Jones Averages, 1885–1970*. Annual High Closing quotation. Dow Jones & Company, 1972; and Bureau of Labor Statistics.

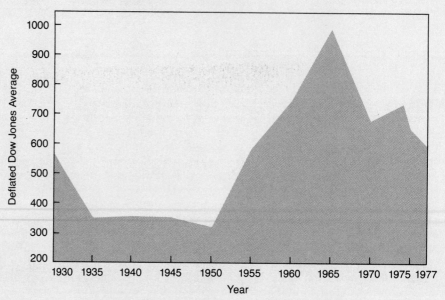

example, IBM accounts for 6.5 percent of the market value of the Standard & Poor's 500 and so it usually is weighted at 6.5 percent in index fund portfolios. The first index fund was offered by Wells Fargo Bank in San Francisco. It was soon followed by Bankers Trust Company of New York; the Vanguard Group in Valley Forge, Pennsylvania; American National Bank & Trust Company of Chicago; and Batterymarch Financial Management in Boston. As of 1977, no index funds were directly available to the small investor. Because index funds involve no trading and no research, their service charge or

management fee runs about .01 percent versus traditional advisory fees of 0.5 percent. It is conceivable that by the time you read this, a large number of brokerage houses will be offering index funds to the small investor.

In general, it is best to look for a no-load fund, that is, one that does not have a sales charge when you buy into it. If you decide to purchase mutual funds, you may decide also to buy insurance against loss. Certain funds underwritten by Harleysville Mutual Insurance Company of Pennsylvania will offer insurance for some of your losses over a long-run period, if

in fact the value of the fund drops. An account can be insured for 10, 12½, or 15 years.

The insurance costs 6 percent of the amount invested. The premium is paid in monthly installments over the guaranteed period from the dividends in the fund. If the shares in the mutual that you own do not earn enough to cover the premiums on the insurance, the fund cashes in shares to make up the difference. In addition, your account is charged an administrative fee of one-fifth of 1 percent of the investment, up to an annual maximum of $12.

The insurance covers the amount invested, including the

fund's sales charge, the insurance premium, and the administrative fee. For example, if over a ten-year period you put in $11,400 in purchase price of shares, sales charge, insurance premium, and administrative fees, and at the end of ten years, you could only get $10,000 for your shares, you would be entitled to a $1,400 reimbursement from Harleysville Mutual. As of 1977, the following funds offered insured accounts: Alpha Research Corporation, Atlanta; Colonial Management Associates, Boston; Delaware Management Company, Philadelphia; National Securities and Research Corporation, New York; Oppenheimer Management Company, New York; Waddell & Reed, Kansas City; and Wellington Management Company, Valley Forge, Pennsylvania.

Picking a Broker

If you decide to buy stocks, you usually can do so only through a broker. But if you use the random walk theory, you will need the broker only to execute your orders; that is, to buy and sell stocks. You won't want him or her to give you any advice at all about which stocks to buy and which stocks to sell, when to leave and when to enter the market. You may, therefore, wish to use the services of a discount brokerage firm. In Exhibit O-1, you see one ad for a cut-rate brokerage firm. To do business with a discount broker, you telephone your order in to a trading desk, which buys or sells the stocks you want and later confirms the trade, usually by mail. Most discount brokers have a toll-free 800 number.

Within five business days after the transaction, you must either send a check for the securities you bought, or deliver the stock certificates of the securities you sold. New customers to discount brokerage firms are usually required to put down part or all of the cash to make their first buy order or to furnish stock certificates before their first sell order. Most discounters have a minimum fee per transaction, which tends to discourage orders of under $1,000. Minimum fees range from $15 to $35. Most discounters figure their commission based on the old fixed rate New York Stock Exchange schedule.

Most discounters have a two-tier pricing plan. There is a higher commission rate for trades on major stock exchanges; a lower one for trades on the **third market**. The third market is a network of traders who by-pass the major stock exchanges.

In any event, you should pick a broker who meets your needs. If, as many people do, you like the psychological benefit of having a broker to call you often with hot tips, then you want to get an outgoing one who will be calling you all the time. But if you value your time and get few kicks out of the stock market per se, then just call any broker in the book, let it be known that you never want to be called, and that all you want is for your orders to be executed. Because there is a penalty in the form of a higher service charge for smaller orders, wait until you have enough saved to order your shares of stocks in blocks of one hundred or more.

If you want to know more about the ins and outs of the stock market, there are hundreds of books to consult. Most will give you different schemes, but if you believe what you read in the previous chapter, you will ignore them. Probably, the

EXHIBIT O-1   **Cut-rate Brokerage Fees**

Commissions

Ours   ## Theirs

$22 maximum per 100 shares   **$50 average per 100 shares**

Applies to the Top 500 Exchange Listed Stocks and all over-the-counter stocks. Commission per 100 shares is pro-rata portion of a prepaid fee covering commissions for round-lot transactions.

An average Stock Exchange Commission for orders above $2000 in value for stocks selling for $15 and up. Commission per 100 shares is charged on each transaction.

Let's say you want to buy 200 shares of U.S. Steel.

You can either go to a conventional Exchange Member broker to buy it or you can come to us.

If you go to them, it will cost you about $130 in commissions. If you come to us it will cost you $44, maximum.

You pay the same price for the stock and get the same account services, either way.

That kind of difference, more than $\frac{3}{8}$ths of a point per 100 shares, can make trading in the market worthwhile again.

And over the long run, it can materially increase your overall returns.

Here's how we do it.

First, we save you from paying for stock analysts you don't use. We simply give no advice.

Second, we use the tried and true account practices and services of an Exchange Member firm to safeguard and maintain your accounts.

And, third, we add a new dimension to save you time as well as money, the Third Market.

When you place your order for any one of the Top 500 Listed stocks in the Third Market it is executed at the Exchange price and confirmed to you in minutes, and in one phone call. Plus all the shares in your market order are executed at the single market price you have agreed to before execution.

When we use the Third Market, you don't wait to find out if you bought something or wait to find out what you paid for it.

That's the gist of what you save at Source and how we do it.

For all the details read our brochure, "Saving Money on Commissions."

Send for it by mailing the coupon below. Or call us and we'll put one in the mail today.

Call toll free: (800) 221-2251   (212) 425-3420 (N.Y. State residents)

Please send me your free brochure: SEND TO:
"Saving Money On Commissions"   Source Securities Corporation
                                        70 Pine Street, New York, N.Y. 10005

NAME _____
ADDRESS _____
CITY _____ STATE _____ ZIP CODE _____

Members Securities Investor   Members National Association
Protection Corporation   of Securities Dealers

SOURCE SECURITIES CORPORATION
70 PINE STREET, NEW YORK, NEW YORK 10005 (212) 425-3420

most widely read and most informative book on the stock market is *How to Buy Stocks*, by Louis Engel, available (sometimes free) from Merrill Lynch, Pierce, Fenner and Smith Inc. and also (for about $1.50 in paperback) from Bantam Books.

What about Bonds?

As you learned in the previous chapter, bonds are an alternative to stocks, and many people have them as a form of savings. However, for the reasons mentioned above, you must be careful. Unanticipated inflation can make bonds a bad deal. This is particularly true, of course, for low-interest U.S. Savings Bonds, but it may also be true for any other type of bond—federal, state, and municipal government, plus corporate—that is long term and has an interest rate that fails to fully reflect the decreasing purchasing power of the dollars you loaned the people who gave you the bond. Remember, if you expect the inflation rate to be 5 percent a year and you buy a long-term bond that yields only 6 percent, you will make only 1 percent rate of return in real terms. That is not very much, is it? (But, of course, it is better than not buying any asset at all.)

In effect, bonds are fixed income-bearing types of investments. You buy a bond and it yields you a specific annual interest rate or return in dollars. In other words, if you buy a bond that yields you $50 a year and it cost you $1,000, you receive a 5 percent rate of return; if it cost you only $500, you get a 10 percent rate of return. Gen-

erally, as with all investments, the higher the rate of return, the higher is the risk. What is the risk? The risk is that the issuer of the bond will not be able to pay interest—or will not be able to pay at all.

If you decide to buy any bonds at all, make sure you go through a broker who knows what he or she is doing in the bond market. Tell the broker how much risk you are willing to take and when you want the bonds to mature. You can buy bonds that mature in 1990, 2000, 2010, or in six months if you want. Bonds are issued by the U.S. government, by state and local governments, and by corporations. For some people, there is an advantage to buying local municipal bonds.

Tax Exempt Bonds

Municipal bonds generally are **tax exempt**—that is, the interest you earn on those bonds is not taxed by the federal government, and in some cases it is not

taxed by state governments, either. Nevertheless, these bonds are not always a special deal. Unless you are in a higher income tax bracket—in fact, unless you are in about the 32 percent or above income tax bracket—tax exempt bonds offer you no advantages over nonexempt bonds. Because the bond market is highly competitive, and everybody knows of the savings in not having to pay taxes on interest from these municipal bonds, their price is therefore bid up so that only people in the higher tax brackets get any special benefit. In fact, if you were in the 14 percent tax bracket and you bought a tax exempt bond, you would be worse off than if you bought nonexempt bonds, because the effective yield would be so low.

To decide whether a tax exempt bond is worth buying, you first determine how the yield compares with the rate you can earn on another investment that is not tax exempt. Table O-1 shows the yield in your particu-

Table O-1 The After-Tax Return on Tax Exempt Municipal Bonds

	AFTER-TAX YIELD*				
	Taxable Income				
Market Yield	$16,000-20,000	$24,000-28,000	$32,000-36,000	$44,000-52,000	$64,000-76,000
4.50%	6.25%	7.03%	7.76%	9.00%	10.00%
5.00	6.94	7.81	8.62	10.00	11.11
5.50	7.64	8.59	9.48	11.00	12.22
6.00	8.33	9.37	10.34	12.00	13.33
6.50	9.03	10.16	11.21	13.00	14.44
7.00	9.72	10.94	12.07	14.00	15.56
7.50	10.42	11.72	12.93	15.00	16.67
8.00	11.11	12.50	13.79	16.00	17.78

*Based on Joint Return.

lar tax bracket. Say that you are in the $16,000 to $20,000 bracket and the tax exempt yield was 6.0 percent. That would be equivalent to a 8.33 percent rate of return from some other investment that did not have this special tax advantage. On the other hand, if you were in the $32,000 to $36,000 bracket, the 6.0 percent would be equivalent to 10.34 percent of taxable interest. (State taxes are not figured in the table because the rates and rules governing taxability of municipal bonds vary widely.)

Tax exempt bonds are usually available in both $1,000 and $5,000 denominations. Unfortunately, most of the newer bonds are being issued in $5,000 denominations, so small investors cannot directly purchase them. However, you can buy shares in tax exempt bond mutual funds instead of buying the bonds themselves.

Financial Backing Differs

Note that tax exempt bonds are classified not only according to the organizations that issue them—states, territories, cities, towns, villages, counties, local public housing authorities, port authorities, water districts, school districts—but also according to the sources of funds that the issuing organizations can utilize to pay interest and principal. As an example, *general obligation* tax exempt bonds are backed by the full credit, and ordinarily by the full taxing power, of the state or municipality. On the other hand, *revenue* tax exempt bonds are backed only by revenues from a specific activity,

such as a water supply system or a toll road. In addition, bonds are rated according to their riskiness, all the way from very risky to not risky at all. Owners of bonds issued by New York City found out all too painfully that tax exempt municipals may not be such a good deal. You have to be wary with them just as with all other investments.

Tax Exempt Mutuals

Perhaps the hottest item to be offered a small investor in decades are tax exempt mutual funds, that is, funds that buy tax exempt bonds. The Tax Reform Act of 1976 authorized the formation of these funds. Any legally constituted investment company, after receiving clearance from the Securities and Exchange Commission, can sell shares to the public and use the proceeds to acquire a diversified portfolio of municipals. The interest is passed back to shareholders and is tax free. If you are in a sufficiently high income tax bracket, these municipal funds may be for you. As of 1977, the six biggest, in order of present size, were: Fidelity Mutual Fund Limited of Boston ($2,500 minimum order); Kemper Municipal Bond Fund Limited, of Chicago ($1000 minimum and 4.75 percent commission); Dreyfus Tax Exempt Bond Fund, Inc., of New York ($2,500 minimum); MFS Manage Municipal Bond Fund of Boston ($1,000 minimum, 4.75 percent commission); Scudder Manage Municipal Bonds of Boston ($1,000 minimum); and Federated Tax Free Income Fund of Pittsburgh ($1,000 minimum).

Tax exempt bond funds are

not a "perfect" investment. They carry risks, too. Bond prices can drop and even agencies with good credit ratings can quickly get into trouble, such as New York City. Moreover, management fees that are assessed on a yearly basis may eat away at that tax free income. Nonetheless, tax exempt funds are something that probably should go into many individuals' portfolio of investments.

FUNDS FOR INVESTING IN SHORT-TERM SECURITIES

Starting a few years ago, interest rates on short-term bonds such as 90-day U.S. **Treasury Bills** began rising. The rates quoted on other short-term financial instruments like commercial bank certificates of deposit were even higher. The stock market was at that time (and may still be) languishing, with rates of return that were either barely positive or, in fact, negative. It was not surprising, then, that mutual funds got into the action to provide small investors with the opportunity to partake in the relatively high interest rates on certain short-term securities such as those mentioned above. The reason that small investors have always been unable to partake in these short-term financial securities is because the minimum amount required is usually too large. For example, certificates of deposit are usually in denominations of $100,000 or more. **Bankers acceptances** are sold only in denominations of $5,000 or more. And more recently, Treasury Bills are only sold in denominations of $10,000 or more, although for a number of years they were sold in $1,000 units. In any event, mutual funds that invest their assets—that is, the mutual fund shareholders' dollars—into short-term securities have been flourishing. We will describe a few of them below, but basically they are all the same. They will buy such things as certificates of deposit, bankers acceptances, commercial paper, U.S. Treasury Bills, notes, and bonds, and so on. They buy no common stocks or anything that is very long term; at least they did not when the funds first started in business.

Hedge Against Inflation

These funds, at least in 1974 and 1975, seemed to be one of the best hedges against inflation that was available for a small investor. Why? Simply because the interest rates on the short-term bonds that these funds bought seemed to reflect better than other investments the relatively high rates of inflation that were experienced at that time, and which are probably being experienced now. The rates of return on these funds varied from 8 to 9½ percent in 1974. And some of them enabled investors to invest as little as $50 a time after an initial larger investment was given to the fund. This is certainly preferable to the alternative of putting your money into a savings and loan association where the interest rates are regulated by the Federal Reserve System at unreasonably low levels that do not compensate at all for the inflation rates of the 1970s.

In the latter part of the 1970s, interest rates in the economy fell and thus the rates of return

on these money market funds were not very attractive. If, however, interest rates fell because of the public's correct anticipation of less inflation in the future, then the rate of return on these funds will in the long run be sufficient to compensate for what little inflation there is.

Some Representative Funds

Listed below are some representative funds that specialize in short-term securities. This list is not exhaustive and should not be taken in any way as a recommendation for those listed.

1. Fund for Investing in Government Securities, Inc., American Express Investment Management Company Advisor and Distributor.

Minimum initial purchase is $1,000.

2. Dreyfus Liquid Assets, Inc. 600 Madison Avenue New York, New York 10022

Minimum initial investment is $1,000 if forwarded by a securities dealer (stockbroker), or $5,000 if done individually. Subsequent investments must be in the amount of at least $1,000.

3. Fund for Federal Securities A Wellington Management Company Mutual Fund P.O. Box 823 Valley Forge, Pennsylvania 19482

A minimum initial investment of $1,000 is required, but additional investments of $50 or more may be made at any time.

4. Oppenheimer Monetary Bridge, Inc. 1 New York Plaza New York, New York 10004

The minimum initial investment is $1,000 with minimum subsequent investment of $25.

If you are interested in any of these funds, you can contact them directly or talk to your stockbroker. In many cases, your stockbroker receives 90 percent of the sales charge and, therefore, would be interested in informing you about the various attributes of each of the funds. A stockbroker, however, apparently does not get any commission on selling the Dreyfus Liquid Assets, Inc., mutual fund shares. Also, while that fund appears to have essentially a lower sales charge, it is not completely certain, for its management fee has a maximum of 1 percent a year that you pay year in and year out, whereas the other funds have management fees that may be only one-half percent a year and sometimes lower. So for those other funds, you may pay an initial higher sales charge, but the management fee each year is presumably smaller. Your decision as to which fund to invest in would then have to depend on how long you thought you were going to keep your investment dollars in these specialized types of mutual funds.

REAL ESTATE DEALS

Of course, by now you will be suspicious of any "special" high-yield real estate deals. But you should not necessarily rule out real estate as a possible

Table O-2   Various Savings Outlets

Here we show the various saving outlets, ranging from cash to unimproved real estate. Column 1 lists how well your principal is protected. Column 2 lists how good these particular investments have been as an inflationary hedge. Column 3 lists average rates of return in the late 1970s. Column 4 indicates how well you can expect that return to continue year in and year out. Column 5 indicates what kind of transactions costs are involved in getting in and out of the particular types of investments. Column 6 indicates whether or not you have a liquid asset. And column 7 gives you your chances for long-term growth.

Source: Adapted from "What to Do With Your Savings," *Changing Times.*

	(1)	(2)	(3)	(4)	(5)	(6)	(7)
SAVINGS INVESTMENT	PRINCIPAL	INFLATION	RATE OF RETURN %	CERTAINTY OF CONTINUED RETURN	LOW CHARGES OR FEES	LIQUIDITY UNDER ALL CONDITIONS	CHANCE FOR LONG-TERM GROWTH
Cash	Exc.	Poor	0	—	—	Exc.	None
Life insurance	Exc.	Poor	3–5(a)	Exc.	Fair	Exc.	Poor
United States savings bonds	Exc.	Poor	6	Exc.	Exc.	Exc.	Poor
Savings account in commercial bank*	Exc.	Poor	4½	Exc.	Exc.	Exc.	Poor
Bank savings certificates	Exc.	Poor	(b)	Exc.	Exc.	Exc.	Poor
Mutual savings bank*	Exc.	Poor	5	Exc.	Exc.	Exc.	Poor
Federal savings & loan assoc.*	Exc.	Poor	(c)	Exc.	Exc.	Good	Poor
Credit union	Exc.	Poor	5½(d)	Good	Good	Good	Poor
Corporate bonds	Good	Poor	4–7, 7½, 9	Exc.	Good	Good	Poor
Corporate stock	Fair	Exc.	3½–8	Good	Good	Good	Good
High-grade preferred stocks	Good	Poor	7½–9	Good	Good	Good	Poor
High-grade convertible preferreds	Good	Good	4–4½, 5–9	Good	Good	Good	Good
Convertible bonds	Good	Good	3–4½, 5–9	Good	Good	Good	Good
Investment companies (mutual funds)	Fair	Exc.	3½–5½	Good	Poor	Good	Good
Common trust funds	Fair	Fair	4–6	Good	Fair	Good	Fair
Real estate mortgages (as investments)	Fair	Poor	6½–7¼, 7–9	Fair	Poor	Poor	Poor
Unimproved real estate	Fair	Good	—	Poor	Poor	Poor	Good

*Insured up to $40,000 FDIC or FHLIC.
(a) Depends on your tax bracket.
(b) Under $1,000: 5% @ 20–89 days, 5½% @ 90–364 days, 6% @ 1–2½ years, 6½% @ 2½–4 years, 7¼% @ 4 years or more.
(c) Pass book 5¼%; 90 day notice 5¾%, minimum: $1,000, 5¾ @ 90 day–year, 6½% @ 1 year–2½ years, 6¾% @ 2½ years–4 years, 7½% @ 4 years–6 years, 7¾% @ 6 years or more.
(d) Industry average.

investment for your savings, as long as you avoid being taken in by any real estate scheme—particularly those introduced by door-to-door salespersons or mail ads. If you have any interest in land in the middle of Arizona or Texas or Florida, investigate before you invest. Generally, you are locked into those deals for many, many years before you can get any money out at all—that is, they are extremely illiquid. Moreover, the selling charges may be incredibly high, and many of them border on being frauds. If you do decide to go into real estate, remember that rate of return is positively related to risk: the higher the potential rate of return that someone offers you on a real estate deal, the higher the risk you are going to take. Just as long as you are aware of that, you will not be duped.

VARIETY IS THE SPICE OF INVESTMENT

It is generally advisable to seek variety in your savings plans, for several reasons. First, not all of your savings should be in illiquid assets. If you have a disaster that requires money quickly, you would like to have some cash or savings account reserve that you can take out immediately without losing anything. Remember, however, that for keeping cash you pay a cost—the cost of the rate of inflation that shrinks the purchasing power of those dollars.

The second reason is that you can reduce your overall risk by having a large variety of different investment assets. There are

no fixed rules to follow, although many investment counselors have their own. They might say to have a certain fraction of your assets in cash, a certain fraction in a savings account, and so on. But there is no scientific rule or reason behind any advice like this. You must decide yourself how much **liquidity** you want, how much risk you want to take, how many long-term investments you want, how many short-term investments you want.

Remember, as you increase the variety of risks that you have in your investment portfolio, you lower the overall risk involved in that whole portfolio, but you also lower the overall rate of return you will receive. You may want to gamble as part of your investment program. You may want to buy, for example, penny stocks that sometimes jump tremendously in value. You may want to buy stocks on local over-the-counter markets that have a high variability and sometimes really hit. But you certainly should not put all your eggs in this basket because if you lose you will have nothing. On the other end of the spectrum, you could be absolutely safe by keeping everything in the savings account; but because you would be unable to make a higher rate of return, you probably do not want to do that, either. Remember, successful investment does not mean making a killing. It means preventing yourself from suffering losses that deprive you of retirement savings and, at the same time, being reasonably certain that you will get a

normal rate of return on those savings. Any other goals that you choose may cost you.

SUMMARY

1. Whenever you try to ascertain the rate of return from any investment, subtracting the rate of inflation from the interest rate you receive on your investment will give you some notion of the real rate of return.

2. Even though the American stock market did not perform very well during most of the 1970s, historically it has been an excellent hedge against inflation. Anybody putting savings into the stock market and leaving them there and reinvesting all dividends obtained would have received an 8 to 15 percent rate of return from the 1920s through the 1960s.

3. It is advisable to diversify your investments: have some in cash, some in a savings account, some in the stock market, some in bonds, and some in mutual funds that buy only short-term government securities or certificates of deposit and bankers acceptances.

4. It pays to shop around for the best deal in the commission you must pay to purchase stocks because different brokerage firms have different rates.

5. Unless you are making enough income to be in a relatively high income tax bracket, it is not worthwhile for you to purchase tax exempt municipal bonds. Leave them to the wealthier Americans.

6. Be wary of real estate deals, particularly those touted by door-to-door salespersons or mail advertising announcements. You never get something for nothing. No investment deal can truly offer you a higher than normal or competitive rate of return unless you are willing to take a higher amount of risk.

QUESTIONS FOR THOUGHT AND DISCUSSION

1. Why do you think so many people have bought U.S. Savings Bonds?

2. Why do you think the stock market did so poorly in the early part of the 1970s (and perhaps may still be doing poorly)?

3. The rate of return on the stock market is basically the rate of return to American business. So long as American business continues to make a rate of return of around 10 percent, so, too, should investors in the stock market. Do you agree or disagree?

4. Why do you think you can obtain so much free research from various brokerage houses?

5. What do you think determines the price of a stock?

6. What is the difference between a corporate bond and a government bond?

7. Why do you think the interest earned on municipal bonds is not taxed by the federal government?

8. Why is there so much diversity of opinion about what are appropriate investments?

THINGS TO DO

1. Write a list of any investments you have (or would like to have). Figure out which one of them has any hedge against inflation. Figure out what your average yearly rate of return is (or would be) on those investments.

2. Find the Consumer Price Index increase for last year; that is, find out what the rate of inflation was. Then compute the real rates of return on Series E Savings Bonds, savings accounts, and any other investment you have information on. Can you explain how some real rates of return are actually negative? Why would any investor leave money in such an investment?

3. Call a stockbroker and have information sent to you on mutual funds in the United States. Find out the characteristics of growth funds versus income funds versus high-risk funds versus low-risk funds. How would you decide which mutual fund to buy? Find out the difference between load and no-load mutual funds. Why would anybody want to pay the sales commission to buy a load fund as opposed to a no-load fund?

4. Look at the next to the last page of the *Wall Street Journal*, which shows the Dow Jones Industrial Average. Can you see any pattern in what has happened to the average price of stocks?

5. Find out the latest rates for purchasing less than $2,000 worth of stock. Try to determine why some investment brokerage houses charge less than others.

6. Read a book on the stock market, such as *How to Buy Stocks* by Louis Engel. Now read a book on how to get rich quickly in the stock market. What is the difference in the information obtained from these two books? How valuable is the information from the second book?

7. Find out from a stockbroker or a local financial service what the interest rate is for tax-exempt municipal bonds. Does that interest rate exceed the rate of inflation?

SELECTED READINGS

American Research Council. *Your Investments*, (latest edition). New York: McGraw-Hill.

Amling, Frederick. *Investments: An Introduction to Analysis and Management*, 2d ed. Englewood Cliffs, N.J.: Prentice-Hall, 1970.

Chestnutt, George A., Jr. *Stock Market Analysis: Facts and Principles*. Greenwich, Conn.: Chestnutt Corporation (latest edition).

Doane, C. Russell, and Hurll, Charles W., Jr. *Investment Trusts and Funds from the Investor's Point of View*. Economic Education Bulletin XI.2, American Institute for Economic Research, March 1971.

Dyson, E. "They Can Get It for You Wholesale; Discount Brokers." *Forbes*, February 15, 1977, p. 42.

Ehrbar, A. F. "Some Kinds of Mutual Funds Make Sense." *Fortune*, July 1975, p. 57.

Encyclopedia of Stock Market Techniques. Larchmont, New York: Investors Intelligence, Inc. (latest edition).

Engel, Louis. *How to Buy Stocks —A Guide to Successful Investing.* New York: Bantam Books, 1975. A free copy may be obtained upon request to Merrill Lynch, Inc., 1 Liberty Plaza, New York, New York 10006.

Farrell, R. J. "Weep Not for the Individual Investor." *Forbes*, January 15, 1977, pp. 102–103.

Feinberg, Phyllis. "Those Bouncing New Tax-Exempt Funds." *Money* 6 (January 1977).

"Forbes Mutual Fund Survey." Issued annually in the August 15 issue of *Forbes*.

"Good News for the Geese," *Forbes*, April 15, 1977.

"How to Cut Costs When you Buy or Sell Stock." *Changing Times*, February 1977, pp. 21–23.

"How to Pick the Best Savings Account." *Consumer Reports*, February 1975, p. 90.

"Mutual Funds—A Cold, Hard Look." *Changing Times*, September 1975, pp. 24–28.

Reilly, F. K.; Johnson, G. L.; and Smith, R. E. "Inflation, Inflation Hedges, and Common Stocks." *Financial Analysts Journal*, January/February 1970.

Rukeyser, Louis. *How to Make Money in Wall Street.* Garden City, New York: Doubleday, 1974.

Sosnoff, M. T. "Market Trends." See issues of *Forbes*.

Woy, James B., ed. *Investment Information: A Detailed Guide to Selected Sources*, Management Guides Series, No. 19. Detroit, Mich.: Gale Research Company (latest edition).

GLOSSARY OF TERMS

Free Rider Problem

The problem that, with certain types of goods and services, individuals attempt to get a "free ride" by not paying for what they use. For example, many persons, if asked how much they were willing to pay for national defense, would say "nothing," hoping that others would pay for national defense. Those who don't want to pay want a free ride.

Proportional Taxation

A system of taxation in which the rate of taxation is uniform no matter what the size of income. For example, proportional taxation of 20 percent would take 20 percent of an income of $100, and also 20 percent of an income of $1 million.

Progressive Taxation

A taxing system in which the higher one's income, the higher the tax bracket one is put in. In a progressive system, you pay a higher rate on the last dollar you earn than on the first dollar you earn.

Average Tax Rate

Simply the total amount of taxes you pay divided by your income.

Regressive Taxation

A system in which, unlike progressive taxation, as you earn more and more income, your tax rate falls.

Loopholes

Legal methods by which your tax liabilities can be reduced.

Special Interest Groups

Groups in society that have a special interest in common. Special interest groups generally attempt to influence government legislation to benefit their own particular groups.

Paying for Government

CHAPTER PREVIEW

☐ What are the different theories that justify taxation?

☐ What type of tax system do we have in the United States?

☐ How important is the federal personal income tax as a source of government revenues?

☐ What is the history of our progressive tax system?

☐ What are tax "loopholes" all about?

☐ How do special interest groups affect what the government does with our tax dollars?

18 The government provides you with numerous goods and services. It generally provides you with a court system, police, firefighters, public schools, public libraries, and myriad other programs to help specific groups in the nation. Governments do not run on thin air, however; they have to be financed. And in the end the only way a government can be financed is by having you, the consumer, give up part of your income to it. You have to do it now to the tune of about 40 percent of every dollar you make. Much of that, of course, is returned to you in the form of transfers such as Social Security, unemployment compensation, and the like; but at least 25 percent is direct expenditures by governments as can be seen in Figure 18-1. That ammounted to fully $480 billion in 1978. Government is big business. We will give you a few ideas on how you can expect governments to behave based on some simple economic principles that you apply to your own day-to-day decision making. Before we do that, however, let us look at various methods of taxation and some of the principles behind them.

THE WHYS AND WHERES OF TAXATION

Governments—federal, state, and local—have various methods of taxation at their disposal. The best known, of course, is the federal personal income tax, which generates almost 45 percent of all taxes collected by Uncle Sam. At the state and local levels, personal income taxes are not as popular; property taxes make up the bulk of the taxes collected. In addition to these taxes, there are corporate income taxes, sales taxes, excise taxes, inheritance taxes, and gift taxes. We will not attempt to investigate all of these taxes in detail.

FIRST, A LITTLE THEORY

Naturally, everybody would prefer a tax that someone else pays. Because we all think that way, no tax could be invented that everyone would favor. Economists and philosophers have come up with alternative justifications for different ways of taxing. The three most often discussed principles of taxation are: benefits, ability-to-pay, and sacrifice.

THE BENEFIT PRINCIPLE

One doctrine of taxation that has been widely accepted is the *benefit principle.* According to this principle, people should be taxed in proportion to the benefits they receive from government services. The more they benefit, the more they should pay; if they benefit little, they should pay little. This principle of taxation has problems in application, however. First of all, how do we determine the value people place on the goods and services the government provides? Can we ask them? If people think that others will pay their way, they will claim, upon being asked, that they receive no value from government services. For example, they will tell the interviewer they are unwilling to pay for national defense because they do not want any of it—it is of no value to them. Here is the **free rider problem**. We all want to be free riders if we think we can get away with it. If you think everybody else will pay for what you want, then most likely you will gladly let them do so. The problem is schematized in Figure 18-2. How much national defense will you benefit from if you agree to pay and everyone else also pays? $90,000,000,100. How much will there be if you do not pay but everyone else does pay? $90,000,000,000. If you think everyone else will pay, would you not be tempted to get a free ride?

444

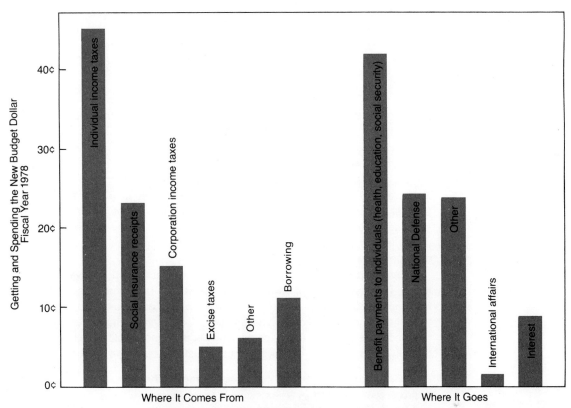

Figure 18-1 Where $1 in Federal Government Revenue Comes from and Where It Goes, Fiscal Year 1978
Source: Office of Management and Budget.

One way out of this dilemma is to assure that the higher a person's income, the more services he or she receives, and therefore, the more value he or she gets from goods and services provided by the government. If we assume that people receive increases in government services that are *proportional* to their incomes, then we can use this benefit doctrine to justify proportional taxation.

Figure 18-2 Scoreboard for National Defense

The free rider is the one who will gladly let everyone else pay for him or her. If you don't pay your share of national defense but everyone else does pay, there will still be $90,000,000,000 available for the country's defense. Whether you pay or not seems to make very little difference.

	If you pay	If you do not pay
If everyone else pays	$90,000,000,100	$90,000,000,000
If no one else pays	$100	$0.00

Proportional Taxation.   **Proportional taxation** is merely a system by which tax-payers pay a fixed percentage of every dollar of income. When their income goes up, the taxes they pay go up. If the proportional tax rate is 20 percent, you pay 20¢ in taxes out of every dollar you earn. If you earn $1,000, you pay $200 in taxes; if you earn $1 million, you pay $200,000 in taxes.

Progressive Taxation.   At this point, we should contrast proportional taxes with **progressive taxation**. If a tax is progressive, the more you earn, the more you pay in taxes, as with the proportional system; but, in addition, the *percentage* taken out of each additional dollar earned rises. In the terminology of marginal and average, we can describe progressiveness as a system by which the marginal tax rate goes up.[1] (So does the **average tax rate**, but not as much.) In the example illustrated in Table 18-1, the first $100 of income is taxed at 10 percent, the next $100 at 20 percent, and the third $100 at 30 percent. The average rate is always equal to or less than the marginal rate with a progressive tax system. With a proportional system, the marginal tax rate is always the same, and it equals the average tax rate.

Can the benefit principle of taxation be used to justify progressiveness? Yes, it can. The only additional assumptions needed are: (a) the *value* people obtain from increased goods and services provided by the government goes up faster than their income, and/or (b) the *amount* of government goods and services received goes up faster than income. The benefit principle alone, without one of these two assumptions, cannot be used to justify progressive taxation.

Regressive Taxation.   As you can imagine, **regressive taxation** is the opposite of progressive taxation. Any tax system that is regressive takes away a smaller and smaller additional percentage as income rises. The marginal rate falls and is usually below the average rate. As an example, imagine that all revenues of the government were obtained from a 99 percent tax on food. Because we know that the percentage of Income spent on food falls as the total income rises, we also know that the percentage of total income that would be paid in taxes under such a system would likewise fall as income rises. It would be a regressive system.

Social Security taxes are a good example of a regressive system. The individual contributor pays 6.05 percent on income up to a maximum level. In 1978, for example, that maximum was $17,700. A person making twice that amount, $35,400, pays exactly the same Social Security taxes; thus, that person's average tax rate for Social Security falls to one-half of 6.05 percent, or only 3.025 percent. As income goes up past the maximum level, the average Social Security tax falls.

THE ABILITY-TO-PAY DOCTRINE

The second principle of taxation considers people's ability to pay. It states that those who are able to pay more taxes *should* pay more taxes. Obviously, people who make more money should generally be able to pay higher taxes. But do we make them pay taxes that go hand in hand with income (a proportional system)? Or do we make them pay taxes that go up, but at a rate that is not in proportion to their income (a regressive system)? To answer the questions, we must decide

[1]We first looked at marginal tax rates when discussing the tax benefits of home ownership in Chapter 12.

Table 18-1

A Progressive Tax System

The percentage of tax taken out of each additional dollar earned goes up; that is, the marginal tax rate increases progressively.

INCOME	MARGINAL RATE	TAX	AVERAGE RATE
100	10%	$10	$\dfrac{\$10}{\$100} = 10\%$
200	20%	$10 + $20 = $30	$\dfrac{\$30}{\$200} = 15\%$
300	30%	$10 + $20 + $30 = $60	$\dfrac{\$60}{\$300} = 20\%$

whether their ability to pay rises faster than, in proportion to, or slower than their income. Whatever assumption we make determines whether we use a progressive, proportional, or regressive tax system. The ability-to-pay doctrine would lead us to recommend progressiveness only if we assume that ability-to-pay rises more rapidly than income.

THE SACRIFICE DOCTRINE

The third principle of taxation holds that the sacrifice people make to pay their taxes should be equitable. It is generally assumed that the sacrifices people make when paying taxes to the government become smaller as their incomes become larger. When a $100 tax is paid, a millionaire is surely sacrificing less than a person who only earns $1,000 a year. The pleasure that the millionaire gives up for that last $100 is less than the pleasure that the other person gives up for that last $100. Again, we are faced with the problem of determining how fast satisfaction from income rises as income itself rises, and this involves a value judgment. If the satisfaction from income rises at a rate that is more than, equal to, or less than in proportion to income, we will end up justifying a system of progressive, proportional, or regressive taxes, respectively.

THE PERSONAL FEDERAL INCOME TAX

You are probably all aware that the personal income tax system in the United States is of the progressive kind. In Table 18-2 we see part of the 1978 tax schedule. Notice that as income rises, the marginal tax rate rises. The rate applicable to the previous lumps of income stays the same, however. Many students think that if you are in the 50 percent tax bracket you pay 50 percent of all your income to the federal government. That is not the case. You may pay 50 percent of your income to the government on your last (marginal) $15,000 earned. However, income made before that last bracket is taxed at progressively lower and lower rates. Even in the 50 percent bracket, you will pay only 32.6 percent of your taxable income to the government. As we see in Table 18-3, personal income taxes account for almost 45 percent of all federal revenues. They should not be taken lightly.

Table 18-2
Federal Personal Income Tax for a Childless Couple, 1978

Here we show the different income brackets and the marginal tax rates along with the average tax rates. As you can see, the marginal tax rates go up to a maximum of 70 percent. However, if income qualifies as being "earned," the maximum is 50 percent. All wages are considered earned income, but interest on bonds or dividends from stocks is not.

NET INCOME BEFORE EXEMPTIONS (BUT AFTER DEDUCTIONS)	PERSONAL INCOME TAX	AVERAGE TAX RATE, PERCENT	MARGINAL TAX RATE, PERCENT
Below $ 1,500	$ 0	0	0
2,000	70	3.5	14
3,000	215	7.2	15
4,000	370	9.2	16
5,000	535	10.7	17
10,000	1,490	14.9	22
20,000	3,960	19.8	28
50,000	16,310	32.6	50
100,000	44,280	44.3	60
200,000	109,945	55.0	69
400,000	249,930	62.5	70
1,000,000	669,930	67.0	70
10,000,000	6,969,930	69.7	70

HOW OUR PROGRESSIVE SYSTEM CAME INTO BEING

The Constitution gives Congress the authority "to lay and collect taxes, duties, imports and excises. . . ." No reference was made to an income tax at the time the Constitution was drafted. But in 1894 the Wilson-Gorman Tariff Act provided for individual income taxes of 2 percent on incomes above $4,000. The country knew about income taxes from the period during the Civil War, when $4.4 million of such taxes were collected. Nonetheless, the concept of income taxation set forth by the Wilson-Gorman Tariff Act was violently challenged and had to be settled by a

Table 18-3
Federal Revenues Accounted for by Personal Income Taxes

During the Depression, individual income taxes accounted for less than 20 percent of federal revenues. Now, however, individual income taxes account for almost 45 percent of federal revenues. The importance of the personal income tax has increased.

Source: U.S. Department of Treasury.

FISCAL YEAR	PERCENT OF FEDERAL REVENUES ACCOUNTED FOR BY PERSONAL INCOME TAXES
1927	25.7%
1932	19.0
1936	16.7
1940	15.5
1944	39.5
1950	40.7
1955	45.1
1960	45.6
1965	43.8
1969	44.9
1971	43.0
1974	42.3
1976	44.6

Supreme Court decision in 1895. Finally, in 1913, the Sixteenth Amendment was passed. The Amendment reads as follows:

> AUTHORIZING INCOME TAXES. *The Congress shall have power to lay and collect taxes on incomes, from whatever source derived, without apportionment among the several states, and without regard to any census or enumeration.*

Section 2 of the Underwood-Simmons Tariff Act of 1913 provided for a 1 percent rate on taxable income with an exemption of $3,000 plus $1,000 more to a married head of household. Notice the concept of exempting the first several thousand dollars of income from taxes. Today we have personal exemptions equal to $750 for every member of the family. A single person is allowed a $750 exemption, whereas the head of a family with a spouse and three children is allowed a $3,750 exemption.

The Underwood-Simmons Tariff Act also provided for a surtax that was levied progressively on income over $20,000 with a maximum total tax rate of 7 percent on income over $500,000. These taxes may seem paltry in comparison with today's rates, but they were considered quite large in those times. The concept of progressiveness was first introduced and met with considerable debate in 1913; the debate raged for several years thereafter. Today, there is no doubt that progressiveness is here to stay, at least in principle. However, the apparently progressive nature of our personal income tax system has declined somewhat in recent years. Up to 1961, the maximum tax rate was a whopping 91 percent. Today it is only 70 percent, and if you receive all your money by the sweat of your brow, you face a 50 percent maximum rate.

LOOPHOLES

Our progressive tax schedule does not bear a very close relationship with what actually happens in the United States. Everybody knows that there are a tremendous number of **loopholes** in our tax laws. Attempts at closing these loopholes have been resisted by those most strongly affected. When the 1969 Tax Reform Act was finally put into law, it had been altered with so many amendments that even attorneys and accountants could not figure out how to use it. Wise persons renamed the 1969 legislation the "Lawyers' and Accountants' Relief Act"; it was certain that these professionals would see a great increase in the business of helping mere mortals figure out how to complete their tax forms.

Tax shelters or loopholes are devices that allow individuals in high-income brackets to take advantage on their personal income tax return of various business incentives such as accelerated depreciation, the deduction of intangible oil-drilling expenses, capital gains preferential rates (discussed below), and so on. Prior to the 1976 Tax Reform Act, it was relatively easy for a group of, say, dentists to form a partnership to drill an oil well. From that moment on, they were able to pay for part or even all of their investment by deducting a combination of these special incentives just mentioned against their dental income. By merely giving up dollars that otherwise would go in taxes, or at least so it seems, they had a chance to bring in a well and strike it rich.

Using similar reasoning, many, many people have invested in tax shelters or loopholes. In 1965, partnerships in the major tax shelter industries of livestock, real estate, petroleum, and natural gas reported $900 million in net losses and $1.4 billion in net profits. By 1971, losses were $4.2 billion and profits were only $2.4 billion. The reason for this growth is quite obvious: the once sparsely populated upper-income brackets, where people start to look seriously for tax shelters (say, 40 percent or 50 percent and up), have become increasingly crowded as inflationary forces and rising real incomes have begun to move much larger numbers of people into such high levels of taxable income.

The Tax Reform Act of 1976 sharply curtailed the number of loopholes that high-income individuals could enjoy. It eliminated the possibility of writing off a larger sum than one had actually invested in some project, such as cattle raising or oil drilling. It also increased taxes that had to be paid on any income that was previously sheltered from income taxes. It is fairly certain that the impact of the 1976 Act will be to reduce the size of the tax shelter industry.

CAPITAL GAINS

One of the biggest loopholes in personal income taxation has concerned capital gains rates. A capital gain is defined as the difference between the buying and selling price of a capital asset, such as a stock, a bond, or a house. If you buy a share of Silver Syndicate Mining stock for $13 and, being a financial wizard, are able to sell it for $67, your capital gains are $54. In the past, capital gains have been taxed at one-half a person's marginal tax rate, up to a maximum of only 25 percent. Recently, however, there have been changes in the tax laws so that capital gains are not treated so favorably. In order to qualify for the lower capital gains rate, assets must be owned for at least 12 months. Over the years, special interest groups have succeeded in getting more and more of their income classified as capital gains. Today the following types of income, for example, are eligible for preferential capital gains tax treatment: patent royalties, oil exploration, and cattle raising.

If we look at taxes as a percent of income, without including capital gains as part of income, we come up with a set of tax payments similar to those given in Figure 18-3. When we include capital gains, the figures change quite drastically.

**Figure 18-3
Effective Rates
of Taxation**

Source: J. A. Pechman and B. A. Okner, *Who Bears the Tax Burden?*, Washington, D.C., The Brookings Institution.

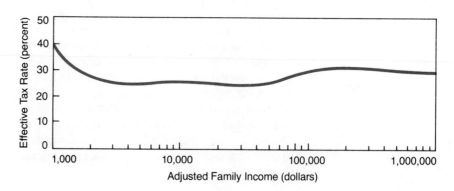

Table 18-4

The Burden of Federal, State, and Local Taxes by Income Class

Here we see that taking account of capital gains, taxes on $15,000 and over fall from 38.1 percent to only 26 percent.

Source: M. B. McElroy, "Capital Gains and the Concept in Measurement of Purchasing Power," *Business and Economic Statistics Section Proceedings of the American Statistical Association*, 1970, p. 138.

1968 INCOME	TAXES AS A PERCENT OF TOTAL INCOME	TAXES AS A PERCENT OF TOTAL INCOME AND CAPITAL GAINS
Less than $4,000	17.5%	26.6%
4,000–5,999	26.0	25.4
6,000–7,999	25.8	24.5
8,000–14,999	24.2	21.9
15,000 and over	38.1	26.0

All the progressiveness of our tax system disappears. Look, for example, at Table 18-4, which was taken from total income data and from the Tax Foundation Incorporation studies on 1968 incomes. Included are state and local taxes as a percentage of income.

THE IMPACT OF HIGHER TAX RATES ON THE WAY PEOPLE WORK AND PLAY

As inflation pushes more and more people into higher and higher tax brackets, they find themselves faced with a difficult dilemma—the more they make, the more the government takes from them. It is not surprising then that individuals have responded by altering some of their behavior patterns and also by seeking ways to avoid higher and higher taxes. We will look briefly at four such relatively new phenomena. They have to do with (1) barter, (2) do-it-yourself activities, (3) buying consumer durables, and (4) leisure.

THE NEW BARTER SOCIETY

Barter has existed in America at least since Peter Minuit got the Indians to trade Manhattan Island for some blankets and beads in 1626. However, barter is an expensive way of making exchanges. It is much more rational to use money as a medium of exchange. Nonetheless, barter has been coming back in recent years and not for the reasons that you might think. It has little to do with the higher cost of living or inflation in general. Rather, it can basically be treated as a way to avoid paying income taxes.

Take a simple example. A dentist needs approximately $1,000 worth of legal services to set up a new pension plan; a lawyer needs approximately $1,000 worth of gold inlays to replace silver fillings. Assume that both are in the 50 percent tax bracket; thus, if they individually went out and purchased the needed services, each would have to earn $2,000 in order to have $1,000 after taxes to pay for those services. If, on the other hand, they make a trade—bartering lawyering services for dental care—no taxes will be paid if the deal is kept from the IRS. They each will be saving $1,000 in taxes but will end up with exactly the same amount of services they wish to buy in the first place.

The IRS is aware of the new barter society and looks at it with a wary eye. Of course, barter arrangements are difficult for the IRS to track down when people don't declare them. The law on this matter is clear, however. You are supposed to declare income realized in any form.

There are a growing number of barter groups throughout the nation. Useful Services Exchange is a nonprofit clearinghouse in Reston, Virginia. Learning Exchange in Evanston, Illinois, probably has 50,000 participants by now. Vacation Exchange Club (which we look at in Consumer Issue Q) allows people to barter houses for their vacation time, as does Holiday Home Bureau. The Business Owners' Exchange in Minneapolis has about 500 members, including lawyers, dentists, and CPAs. Each must pay a $150 membership fee. They can trade their professional services, as well as cars, boats, etc. The Business Owners' Exchange issues checks that look like commercial bank checks and sends members monthly statements listing sales and purchases, although no real money is exchanged. United Trade Club in San Jose, California, has almost 2,000 members, including doctors and lawyers.

Barter is back.

DO-IT-YOURSELF
ACTIVITIES

We have already explained the tax advantages of do-it-yourself activities to the homeowner back in Chapter 12. To repeat, rather than earning income that is taxable to hire someone to repair or maintain your home, you can provide the services yourself, not declare those do-it-yourself services as income, and avoid paying taxes. The do-it-yourself society has increased dramatically in the United States, in part because of rising repair and construction costs, but also because of individuals being put into higher tax brackets, thus making it more beneficial for them to avoid taxes in this manner.

BUYING CONSUMER
DURABLES

The less well known effect of the high tax rate is the increased incentive for individuals to buy more consumer durable goods, such as boats, tennis courts, bigger homes, and quadrophonic music systems, as opposed to their saving and investing more money in normal outlets. Consider a numerical example. A family has $10,000 that it wishes to save. It has a large number of normal options for those savings: savings and loan association account, a mutual fund, and so on. Let's assume that it can obtain a return before taxes of 10 percent per annum. Let's also assume that that family is in a 50 percent tax bracket; thus, its after-tax rate of return on that $10,000 saving will be only 5 percent, or $500 a year. Now consider that it has the option of having a tennis court installed that will also cost $10,000. A tennis court is a consumer durable item. It is a form of investment because it yields a stream of (implicit) income in the future in the form of the pleasure derived from playing tennis on it. Let us say that in order to duplicate the services from a tennis court on one's property, the family would have to fork over $1,000 a year to a private club around the corner. Thus, the implicit income stream or yield on the investment in the tennis court is approximately $1,000 a year. However, that income is not reported to the IRS. According to current IRS rulings and tax statutes, the implicit income or service flow from owner-used consumer durable goods, such as tennis courts, is nontaxable. The rate of return, then, of investing in a tennis court will be higher for this family than investing in bonds, for example.

Looked at in this manner, it is not surprising that individuals are buying more and bigger boats, more tennis courts, more expensive stereos, more luxury cars, and larger houses. This is particularly true for high-income individuals who face high tax rates.

THE LEISURE WORLD

Finally, one of the easiest and perhaps most pleasureful way to avoid paying income taxes is to work less and therefore not earn as much income. Taking a longer vacation, choosing a job with fewer hours, quitting a second job, retiring at an earlier age, are all ways that individuals can reduce their tax burden. Essentially, they substitute taxable income for leisure, which is a form of implicit income and as yet is nontaxed. We can predict that as more individuals are pushed into higher income tax brackets, work effort will fall accordingly.

SPECIAL INTEREST GROUPS

When any of us analyze the behavior of persons in business, we generally assume that they will do whatever is in their own best interests. Of course, there are exceptions, but it is best not to count on them. If we look at individual economic behavior, we generally will not go too far astray if we assume that people act in their own best interests and not necessarily in those of society. This is not to say that people are inherently bad; it is just human nature. If we take these same ideas about human behavior and apply them to how politicians and government officials will act, we realize that it will *not* be in their best interests to look out *only* for general welfare. You and I as consumers are a diffuse group made up of millions and millions of people with millions and millions of different tastes, wants, and needs. How could politicians satisfy all of us? Impossible, right? They can, however, satisfy **special interest groups**. That is what our political system is all about —special interest groups have very defined, clear-cut interests in specific pieces of government legislation. They can see the direct benefit and measure it in dollars and cents. They therefore know how much it is worth for them to spend in order to get that legislation passed. If we were to analyze the legislation now on the books, we would find that most of it was indeed sponsored by special interest groups, and in fact benefits special interest groups only.

When it was discovered, for example, that various milk associations contributed perhaps $2 million to the reelection campaign of President Nixon, it was also discovered that just before this contribution was given, milk support prices were raised, benefiting the dairy industry by about $600 million. This kind of behavior should not surprise you, however. That is exactly what you would expect, because special interest groups are going to look out for their own interests; and if it means influencing government actions, that is what they will do. As long as you are aware of this, then you as a citizen can guard against it by carefully considering all propositions and referenda up before you to vote on. If you first ask the question, "What special interest group is this legislation for?" then see if it in fact benefits you, you will be on your way to a good analysis. If, however, you start reading the slogans attached to the proposed or passed legislation, you are going to get lost in contradictory and often meaningless arguments. The same is true if you want to decide whether or not to vote for a particular incumbent candidate. You can look at his or her legislative record and find out what special interest groups he or she has catered to. This does not mean, however, that you as an individual will not benefit by special interest legislation. We showed, for example, that usury laws will benefit all those people with very good credit ratings who will continue to get credit at the lower interest rate. If you happen to be a plumber, you are obviously going to benefit from very strict building codes that require sophisticated plumbing for all new houses.

It should also not surprise you that regulatory agencies in general end up working on behalf of the regulated firms instead of on behalf of you the consumer. You the consumer generally know nothing about the industry in question because the technical details are too complicated and it would not be worth your while to learn anything about them. However, the firms themselves know the most about their own industry and have the most incentive to influence the regulators. Hence, few are shocked to find out that the Interstate Commerce Commission has worked to preserve noncompetition in the transportation industry; it should not surprise you that the Civil Aeronautics Board fights tooth and nail against competition in the industry; it should not surprise you that just about all regulatory agencies act to dampen instead of encourage competition. You the consumer generally lose out by this government/business marriage. However, in some cases you may win out. It is up to you to decide by seeing the benefits and the costs of different types of regulatory activities.

CAN WE IMPROVE OUR TAX SYSTEM?

Any of you who have tried to fill out a federal income tax form know that our tax system is incredibly complicated. When one President's life-long valet asked him to help out with his taxes, the President could not. It was too complicated to figure out. It is estimated that the cost of filling out forms, measured in people's time, is somewhere between $3 billion and $5 billion a year! Additionally, there is all the money spent on accountants and lawyers. Why has this all happened? Just as you would expect, because of special interest groups getting special benefits for themselves and thus adding complications to our tax laws.

One of the reasons special interest groups find it worthwhile to attempt to get special legislation that reduces their tax burden are the high progressive income tax rates. The higher the rate you pay, the greater incentive you have to find a loophole or, as a member of a group with other people in the same situation, to influence tax legislation to benefit your group. If all taxes were only 2 percent, nobody would try very hard to find loopholes. But if you are in the 70 percent tax bracket, you had better believe it is worthwhile to find one. Every dollar of income you can have declared nontaxable nets you 70¢ in cash, for that is the tax you do not have to pay. With the incredible numbers of loopholes and complexities, our so-called progressive tax system really is not progressive at all, or at least not very much, as evidenced by Table 18-4. Given this fact, there are some obvious tax reforms that could benefit the majority of Americans. When we talk here about tax reform, we certainly do not mean the kind that goes through Congress every few years. A tax reform act was passed in 1969, as we previously mentioned. Only lawyers and accountants benefited. Just about everybody else lost. As we already pointed out, another tax reform act was passed in 1976 that eliminated many of the loopholes, but it is so complicated that again mainly lawyers and accountants will benefit.

The only meaningful way to talk about tax reform is to forget about all special interest groups and do something drastic but simple, such as the following proposal that I have put forth for a number of years now:

1. Eliminate all deductions except an absolute minimum number of bona fide business expenses.
2. Increase the exemption, say, to the poverty line of income, meaning that the first $3,000 or $4,000 of income is not taxed at all.
3. Establish a uniform 15 to 20 percent proportionate tax rate on all income, no matter where it is from and no matter who earns it.

This is certainly drastic in comparison with what we now have. Notice, however, that the tax rate of 15 to 20 percent is lower than the actual taxes paid as a percentage of total income right now in the United States. How could this be, you might ask. Easy: if you eliminate the high, complicated progressive tax system, you eliminate people's wasted efforts trying to avoid taxes. There would be a proportionately higher degree of work effort and higher national income on which to base our taxes. That is how we could actually lower the overall tax rate and still get as much revenue as we now get.

Believe it or not, many rich people would be against lowering tax rates because they know that with all of the loopholes now, they pay very few taxes anyway. Some pay much less than 15 or 20 percent of their total income.

Few observers of the tax system acknowledge the virtue in simplicity of a tax system. It could avoid so many complications, perhaps make life so much easier for all of us, reduce the incentive for any of us to cheat, and increase the amount of work that many of us want to do because our tax rates would be lower. Because we do not have a progressive tax system anyway, it is ridiculous to argue against a uniform nonprogressive tax system on the basis of the "need" for "soaking the rich." We do not soak them anyway, so why should all of us suffer for some imaginary reasoning?

Unfortunately, you and I still have to suffer. Pure tax reform is a long way off. Until then, it behooves you to know the ins and outs of tax reporting and tax payments. There is nothing wrong with your taking advantage of every single legal way to reduce the taxes you owe your government. You have a right to spend what is legally yours. After all, you earned it.

SUMMARY

1. The three most often discussed principles of taxation are the benefits principle, the ability-to-pay principle, and the sacrifice principle.
2. In both the benefits and ability-to-pay principles, an additional assumption is necessary to use them to justify a system of progressive taxation in which progressively more is taken away from those who earn higher incomes. This additional assumption is that benefits and the ability to pay increase *more* than in proportion to income.
3. It is important to realize that in a progressive tax system you pay a higher tax rate only on the last dollars earned. For example, that you are someone in the 50 percent tax bracket in our progressive tax system does *not* mean that you pay 50 percent of your income in taxes. Rather, you pay 50 percent on the last tax bracket of income only.
4. The personal federal income tax is the most important source of government revenues in this country. It accounts for over 40 percent of all federal revenues.
5. Tax loopholes or shelters are usually available only for higher income earners. In other words, the benefit of a tax loophole is directly proportional to your marginal tax bracket. And unless you are making a high income, your marginal tax bracket isn't very high.
6. Capital gains tax rates are usually lower than tax rates on income. That is why it is beneficial to have any of your income received as a capital gain.
7. In spite of our progressive tax system, money income differences have not narrowed in the United States since World War II.
8. In analyzing any prospective government legislation, you must realize that it has probably been influenced by special interest groups. Therefore, informed voters must analyze the legislation to see who will benefit and who will pay. Very little legislation proposed and supported by special interest groups is made with the general welfare in mind. In fact, most of this legislation by necessity must hurt the consumer. Many restrictions on economic activities are of this nature, as well as the subsidies that are legislated for particular industrial and agricultural groups in our society.
9. It would be possible to improve our tax system by true reform in which all loopholes were eliminated, a large exemption was instituted, and a flat proportional tax of 15 to 20 percent was used in place of our very complicated system today.
10. Individuals are now avoiding taxes by: engaging in barter, taking more leisure, expanding the amount of do-it-yourself activities in which they engage, and purchasing more consumer durable goods whose implicit income stream is not taxed.

QUESTIONS FOR THOUGHT AND DISCUSSION

1. Why do you think the concept of progressive taxation is so popular in the United States?
2. Which aspect of government expenditures do you think is most important for your own well-being?
3. Which principle of taxation do you think best justifies progressive taxation?
4. Would you prefer to have most taxes collected from individuals or from corporations?
5. Who really pays the corporate income tax?
6. How do tax loopholes hurt or help you as a consumer?
7. Do you think that tax loopholes should exist?
8. Why has our progressive tax system failed to eliminate income differences in the United States since World War II?
9. Is there any way to prevent special interest groups from affecting government legislation?

THINGS TO DO

1. Get a copy of next year's individual income tax schedule from your local office of the Internal Revenue Service. Compare it with one from 10 years ago. Is there any difference?
2. Call up a local stockbroker and ask if he or she has any recommendations about tax shelters. Have that stockbroker send you copies of information on any tax shelters for sale. Do you think they would be beneficial for you if you were making $5,000 a year? $50,000 a year? $500,000 a year?
3. Write a letter to your senator or representative asking for copies of legislation that he or she has supported during the last year. Try to figure out why such legislation was supported by that legislator. If you are in doubt, write another letter asking why. Try to discover where special interests might be affecting his or her decision. Write your other senator or another representative in your area asking how a bill is proposed and eventually passes in Congress. Try to figure out at what point the bill's initiation or chance for passage can be affected by special interest groups.

SELECTED READINGS

Dietsch, R. W. "How Private Is Your Tax Return?" *Nation's Business*, December 1973, pp. 66–67.

Pechman, Joseph A., and Okner, Benjamin A. *Who Bears the Tax Burden?* Washington, D.C.: Brookings Institution, 1974.

People and Taxes. Washington, D.C.: Ralph Nader's Research Group (monthly newspaper).

"State and Local Taxes: How Do Yours Compare?" *Changing Times*, July 1976.

Stern, Phillip M. *The Rape of the Taxpayer*. New York: Random House, 1973.

Thurow, Lester C. *The Impact on the American Economy*. New York: Frederick A. Praeger, 1971.

Easing Your Tax Burden

Supreme Court Judge Learned Hand once said, "Anyone may so arrange his affairs that his taxes shall be as low as possible; he is not bound to choose that pattern which will best pay the Treasury; there is not even a patriotic duty to increase one's taxes." In other words, you have every right as a taxpayer to minimize the taxes that you pay. In this short consumer issue it will be impossible to give you a complete course in how to ease your tax burden. If you are really interested in getting all the details, you might want to buy one of the various tax books such as Lasser's *Tax Guide*, or H&R Block's *Income Tax Workbook*, or The Research Institute of America's *Individual Tax Return Guide*, all of which are published yearly. You can also get *Your Federal Income Tax* free from the Internal Revenue Service in your area. You can get numerous booklets from the Internal Revenue Service for every imaginable loophole that you might be eligible for. If that is not enough for you, you can buy the services of sophisticated tax lawyers or certified public accountants.

THE DO'S AND DON'TS OF HIRING TAX HELP

There are literally hundreds of thousands of individuals who sell their services as tax return preparers. Many of them work out of national franchises that advertise heavily. As tax laws become more complicated, the tax preparation business is bound to grow. The way to avoid deception in buying these services is to follow these rules:

1. Be wary of tax preparers who promise to give you a check for your refund immediately. The preparer is probably offering you a loan that you will pay interest on.

2. Never sign a blank return.

3. Never a sign a return prepared in pencil because it can be changed later.

4. Never allow your refund check to be mailed to the preparer.

5. Be wary of tax advisers who "guarantee" refunds, who want a percentage of the refund, or who supposedly know "all" the angles.

6. Avoid a tax preparer who advises you to overstate deductions, omit income, or claim fictitious dependants.

7. Make sure that the tax preparer signs the return that he or she prepares, together with his or her address and tax identification number. (You, however, are legally responsible for virtually all errors on your return, no matter who fills it out, unless there is a blatant case of fraud brought against the tax preparer.)

8. Be wary of preparers who claim they will make good any amounts due because of a mistake on your return. Usually the preparer means that he or she will pay the penalty charge, for the tax money due must come from you.

9. Find out the educational background of the preparer. Has that person a degree in accounting?

10. Use only preparers who have permanent addresses so that you will have no difficulty finding that person a few months later if problems develop.

TAKING THE ZBA

If you have no expenses that qualify as legitimate deductions, you will merely take the zero bracket amount, or ZBA, as a deduction. The 1977 Tax Reduction and Simplification Act allows that a flat $2,200 for single persons and a flat $3,200 for married persons filing joint returns as a standard deduction. (This replaces the previous 16 percent standard reduction that had minimum and maximum limits.) Thus, starting in 1977, a minimum tax rate of 14 percent is applied to the first $1,000 over the ZBA.

EXHIBIT P-1   Possible Income Deductions That Can Lower Your Tax Liability

Accounting and auditing expenses paid for preparation of tax returns

Alterations and repairs on business or income-producing property

Attending conventions (new laws only allow two conventions abroad a year and travel must be coach class)

Attorneys' fees in connection with your trade or employment

Automobile expenses incurred during business trips, trips for charitable organizations, and trips for medical care

Automobile expenses if used for your business, pro-rated

Automobile license

Burglary losses

Business expenses of employees in excess of amounts received as reimbursements

Campaign contributions

Charitable contributions (cannot exceed 50 percent of your income)

Child care expenses (now applies to divorced and separated people, as well as couples in which there is one full-time worker and the other is either part

time, going to school full-time, or looking for a job. A maximum of a $400 tax credit, $800 for two or more children)

Condominium owners' interest and realty taxes

Depreciation of property used in business

Dues for professional societies and organized labor unions

Educational expenses if required to keep your employment or professional standards

Fees paid to secure employment

Home office (only for individuals who have a separate place used only as an office and also a place where the individual receives clients. Greatly restricted by the 1976 Tax Reform Act.)

General sales taxes (state and local)

Income tax, state and city

Interest you paid or finance charges for any loans or retail installment contracts

Medical expenses in excess of 3 percent of adjusted gross income

Moving expenses

Property taxes

Safe deposit box expenses

RECORD KEEPING

But if your legitimate deductions are greater than the ZBA, you must keep good records to support those deductions. This is one minimum thing you must do to take advantage of all of the benefits in the tax laws. If the IRS conducts a tax audit and you cannot adequately substantiate the deductions you have taken on your tax returns, they will be disallowed and you may have to pay a penalty or, at a bare minimum, interest on the taxes that are now overdue. You have to keep supporting documents for at least three years after the date your return was filed, or at least three years from the date your tax was paid, whichever occurred later. In fact, it is a good idea to keep them even longer, just in case you want to make sure what you did, although they cannot legally be subpoenaed by the IRS after three years unless fraud is involved.

What Kind of Records

A good rule to remember is: when in doubt, keep a record.

EXHIBIT P-2   **Average Deductions Claimed on Adjusted Gross Income, 1976**

Type	$5,000-$6,000	$9,000-$10,000	$15,000-$20,000	$30,000-$50,000	$100,000 and up
Medical expenses	$671	$435	$ 305	$ 402	$ 654
Taxes	588	801	1,386	2,935	13,192
Contributions	277	298	412	945	10,825
Interest	570	800	1,178	1,799	9,423

You should have records for all medical expenses, for all business expenses, for all taxes paid —everything that could possibly be used to reduce your effective tax burden. The best way to keep records, of course, is to write checks. If you do any amount of business for which the expenses are tax deductible, you also should keep a complete diary of those expenses. If you move because of a change of job, you are allowed to deduct moving expenses. Make sure you have records for all of those. When you sell your house keep a record of that transaction.

The best way to keep records, of course, is to do it regularly. Every month when you go through your check stubs to balance your statement, separate the checks into individual envelopes, marked business expenses, telephone, medical expenses, and so on. If in fact you can prove that you use part of your home as a place of business, then you must keep records on all the expenses on your house: rental or mortgage payments, heating bills, light bills, telephone bills, electricity bills. Again, the best way to do this is to pay everything by check. The next best way is to keep a receipt for everything you pay for in cash. Here is where charge cards are also useful. You get a receipt every time a charge is made on your card. If it is a receipt for a tax deductible item, it will be useful in your record-keeping endeavors.

Other Pointers on Record Keeping

Here are some other pointers that are helpful in the tax field:

1. Always identify your sources of income.

2. Keep adequate records in order to take advantage of capital gain and loss provisions. This would apply to the purchase and sale of any asset, such as stocks and bonds.

3. Make sure that you explain to yourself on a piece of paper all of the items reported in an income tax return, so that you will be ready in case of an audit.

4. You must keep records indefinitely on the purchase, sale, and expenses of remodeling a home. Eventually you may have to pay capital gains taxes when you sell a house and don't buy a new one, say, when you retire.[1] In order to reduce those capital gains taxes, you must be able to prove that you spent money in remodeling or making additions to your house.

5. Retain copies of your filed tax returns as part of your records. They can help you in preparing future returns, particularly if you engage in income averaging, a method used to reduce your taxes.

What If You Are Uncertain?

Whenever you are uncertain about the acceptability of the deduction, it is not always unwise to take a chance. Many of the deductions are subject to interpretation by the IRS—that is, they are not cut and dried, and if you are audited you stand as good a chance of winning your case as of not winning it. At the most, because this action does not involve fraud or anything illegal, you only pay an interest rate penalty on the taxes due. At least until 1977, that interest rate was somewhat less than the rate of inflation, so you

[1]Currently, though, you are exempted from taxes on the first $35,000 of such gains if you are over 65.

really did not lose out by owing the government money for back taxes. However, it might prove inconvenient to pay any interest fine in one lump sum. You have to keep that in mind, too.

If, in fact, you do not think that you have many deductions at all, it is generally not worth your while to do anything except the simplest amount of work on your tax form. That is, you take a standard ZBA deduction, fill in the rest of the lines, and pay your taxes. That way you do not have to keep any records except those of the income you made. That certainly simplifies life, but it may not ease your tax burden. It only eases your tax work.

KEEPING DOWN YOUR TAXES

Exhibit P-1 lists possible deductions that you can use to help reduce your federal income taxes. You, of course, may find others in many of the excellent guides to filling out your tax forms. But remember, it certainly is not worthwhile for you to spend weeks filling out your tax forms that might save you another $25. You must figure out at what point you should *stop* trying to figure out ways to reduce your tax burden. This, of course, is a function of your marginal tax bracket. If you are in the 14 percent bracket, every extra dollar that you can find as a legal deduction saves you only 14¢. The incentive is not very much: if it takes you an extra hour to find $10 more of deductions, the benefit to you of those $10 of deductions is only $1.40. Is your time worth more than $1.40 an hour?

AMERICANS ARE HONEST

Americans in general are very honest. The IRS estimates that fully 95 percent pay their lawful due to the government. Being honest, though, does not prevent you from taking advantage of what is legally your right. That is, you can be very honest and report all income, but at the same time make sure that you take all deductions that are due. You owe that to yourself and to your family.

SUMMARY

1. As a basic reference for doing your own taxes, it would be useful to obtain one of the better known tax guides, such as Lasser's *Tax Guide*, or H&R Block's *Income Tax Workbook*. At the first of every year, a number of these tax guides become available in most bookstores throughout the country.

2. If you have complicated tax problems, it is best to get a certified public accountant and/or the advice of a tax lawyer. However, weigh the cost with the potential benefits—good tax advice does not come cheap.

3. If in fact you do not anticipate being able to deduct a large number of items from your income before you pay taxes, it may be cost saving for you to use the standard ZBA deduction and a short form for filling out your taxes.

4. If you decide to keep records and fill out a long form, you must have a record for everything you decide is a legitimate deduction.

5. The easiest way to keep records is to write checks for everything. Note, however, that in many cases you must substantiate those checks with receipts.

6. If you decide to take business expenses, you must keep a diary of expenses for which you do not obtain receipts, such as meals with business colleagues.

7. Whenever you are uncertain about the legitimacy of a deduction, it is best to decide in your own favor, for generally it is a matter of interpretation by the IRS agent who might audit your returns. And his or her interpretation could be the same as your own.

8. You can call your local office of the Internal Revenue Service and have many free booklets sent to you explaining all facets of our taxing system. Additionally, for small fees you can have some of the more complete tax guides written by the IRS sent to you directly. If there is no local IRS office nearby, write the nearest major city for these booklets.

QUESTIONS FOR THOUGHT AND DISCUSSION

1. When would it not pay to be careful about keeping records for tax purposes?

2. When is it definitely a waste of time to have a CPA fill out your tax returns?

3. What is the cost to you of deducting an expense from your income before paying taxes if upon a tax audit it is determined that that is not a legitimate deduction?

4. "It is cheaper to give things to charity than to sell them." How could this be true?

THINGS TO DO

1. Send away for all the free booklets from the Internal Revenue Service. See if you can find information that will be useful for your own tax planning.

2. Try to find out from the IRS what percentage of taxpayers are audited every year.

3. Buy one of the best-selling tax guides. Read through it to see if you can get a general feeling for how our tax system works. Do you think we have a complicated system or not?

4. Write down a list of reforms you think would make ours a better tax system.

SELECTED READINGS

Carper, J. "How to Fight the I.R.S.—and Win." *American Home*, May 1977, p. 16.

How to Prepare Your Personal Income Tax Return. Englewood Cliffs, N.J.: Prentice-Hall (published annually).

"If the IRS Calls You for a Tax Audit." *U.S. News*, April 11, 1977, pp. 96–98.

Janssen, Peter A. "Loosening the Grip of the IRS." *Money*, April 1977.

Lasser, J. K. *Your Income Tax*. New York: Simon and Schuster (published annually).

"Time to Think about Next Year's Tax Return." *Changing Times* April 1977.

"When the IRS Gets Your Tax Return." *U.S. News*, March 28, 1977, pp. 78–80.

"When IRS Gets Your Tax Return," *U.S. News*, March 28, 1977, pp. 78-80.

"Where to Go for Tax Help." *Consumer Reports*, March 1976, pp. 130–137.

Your Federal Income Tax. Washington, D.C.: Superintendent of Documents (published annually).

GLOSSARY OF TERMS

Substitute

Something that can be used or done in place of something else.

Complement

Something that is used along with something else, such as recreational equipment used along with leisure.

Leisure, Recreation, and Travel

CHAPTER PREVIEW

☐ What are the complements of leisure activities?

☐ How have Americans used their increased leisure time?

☐ What is the true cost of owning a recreational vehicle?

☐ How does one obtain information on possible leisure activities?

19 America has been called the consumer society, but another name that might be equally applicable is the leisure society. We see in Figure 19-1 the dramatic reduction in the number of hours worked per week for the average wage earner in the United States for the last 120 years. It wasn't that many years ago when individuals actually worked seven days a week, ten hours a day. There still may be those who work that long and even more, although the average American puts in not much more than 35 hours a week 50 weeks a year, at best. What does that mean? That means that there are a larger number of hours available in which recreational activities can be pursued.

SUBSTITUTES AND COMPLEMENTS

Leisure time activities or leisure time per se is a **substitute** for something else—work time. Given that there is a time constraint in everyone's existence, the more someone works, the less someone has for leisure. Hence, a decision to have more leisure time is necessarily also a decision to work less and therefore to have less money income. That means that as a nation, we have chosen to substitute leisure for money income. If the average work week in the United States were 50 hours a week, individuals could take home more money income, but would have less time to themselves for leisure activities.

Increased leisure time has brought with it the increased expenditure of consumer dollars on recreational activities. In Figure 19-2 we show the dramatic rise in recreational expenditures as a percent of gross national product. This is occurring because recreational equipment and services are **complements** to leisure time. They are used together. If individuals have more leisure time and wish to

**Figure 19-1
Hours Worked
Overtime**

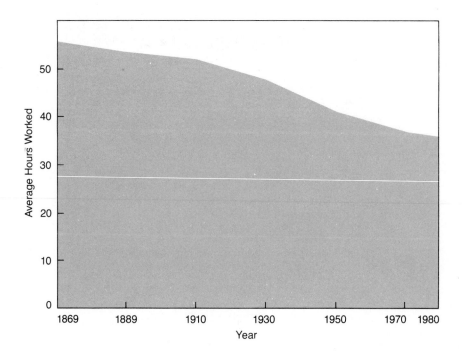

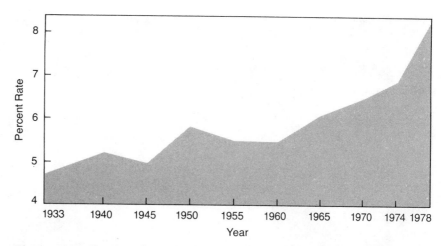

Figure 19-2 Percent of Personal Consumption Expenditures Devoted to Recreation

Back in 1933, only 4.7 percent of personal consumption expenditures were devoted to recreation. This percent has been rising ever since, today reaching 7 percent or more. (The 1978 figure is an estimate.)
Source: *Survey of Current Business.*

spend it skiing, playing tennis, playing golf, or doing photography, they will purchase the complementary items associated with those activities. We can predict, therefore, that as we become a more leisure-oriented society, expenditures on recreation will be an increasing part of total consumer spending.

VACATIONS

In 1874, the average American worked 338 days out of every year. Today, the average American only works 240 days. The number of legal holidays and the amount of paid vacation time have increased dramatically in the last century. Vacations have become a part of every American's life style. However, we still have a ways to go to catch up with some of our European counterparts. Even though Americans have been richer than, for example, people living in France, we have not yet fully accepted the idea of everyone taking one month's vacation every summer. Traditionally, in France, all factories close down during the month of August. Paris in that month is filled mainly with tourists. There has been some change to avoid crowding at resort areas; now, some French people take their vacations in July and a few even take them in September. Two weeks has been standard vacation time for Americans for a number of years, although that is changing slowly. It appears that we have preferred to take our vacation time in smaller doses—four-day weekends and the like—as opposed to taking it all at once in the middle of the summer.

Expanding leisure time and expanding vacations go hand in hand. We can, therefore, predict that vacations will become an increasingly important part of family decision making.

REDUCING THE NUMBER OF DAYS WORKED

In the beginning of the 1970s, many sociologists and labor market experts predicted that there would be an end to the five-day work week, just as there was an end to the seven-day and then the six-day work week. They pointed out that more and more workers were going to be willing to work ten hours a day for four days,

rather than eight hours a day for five days. A number of companies actually attempted an experiment by offering their workers the four-day work week. Some of them still have it and their workers are satisfied; others found that they did not like having an extra full day to fill up during the working part of the year. Thus, we might predict that rather than taking longer weekends, workers are going to be opting for regular work weeks with longer vacations so that they get all of their leisure activity in an intensive period, without interruptions.

VACATIONS AND RVs   Expanding vacation opportunities for Americans have led to a boom in the sales of recreational vehicles. At the end of the 1970s, the trend continues upward in the ownership of RVs, as they are popularly called. This trend did flatten out and even sank during the energy crisis in 1973–1974; but now it seems that so long as Americans believe that gas will be available, even though at a higher price, they prefer the independence of an RV and the call of the open road. An interesting consumer decision-making problem is faced when a family contemplates the purchase of a new or used RV. It is a consumer durable, which we discussed in Chapter 13 and Issue K. We also discussed decisions about buying an automobile in Chapter 14 and Issue L. All of the principles laid out in those chapters and issues are applicable here; however, there is a special attribute of RVs that must be considered in doing a cost-benefit analysis of buying one.

RVs Are Left Idle Much of the Time.   The important difference between an RV and many home appliances or the family automobile is that the RV is only used during vacation times or long weekends. Generally, it is too bulky and consumes too much gas to be used as a second car in a family. Thus, the "down" time may be so considerable as to make an investment in an RV quite uneconomical. Consider the extreme case where an RV sits in the driveway depreciating for 50 weeks out of the year and is then used for the family's annual 2-week vacation into the woods. The benefits of owning that RV consist of the service flow during a 2-week period, rather than a 52-week period. It is possible to count as part of the service flow the pleasure of seeing the RV in the driveway for the remaining 50 weeks, but for most people that pleasure is not tremendously valuable.

Depreciation and Opportunity Cost.   The RV depreciates whether it is being used or not, just like an automobile or a stereo or a refrigerator. During the first year, the depreciation is the greatest; thus, the purchase of a new RV means that the new owner will find that the RVs resale value may be lowered 25 percent or more one year hence. This is a true and actual cost of owning that RV for its first year and must be included in the cost-benefit calculations.

Equally important, particularly given that the RV will not be used very much during the year, is the opportunity cost of owning it. We talked about opportunity cost in Consumer Issue C when we referred to the time that parents must spend in raising children. We also talked about opportunity cost when we discussed doing cost-benefit analysis before making a decision to buy an appliance (see page 301). When deciding on purchasing an RV for $14,000, the potential owner must realize that even if he or she pays cash for that RV, there is an implicit interest charge every year. That $14,000 could earn interest in a savings and loan account at 6 percent per year. Thus, the opportunity cost for owning the RV for the first year is going to be $840 (6 percent times $14,000). Of course, the opportunity cost becomes explicit if the $14,000 had to be borrowed at some specific interest rate. Instead of opportunity cost, we call it interest on the loan, but it is actually giving you the same information.

THE ALTERNATIVES TO OWNING RECREATIONAL EQUIPMENT OR PROPERTY

The discussion about an RV is important because it highlights the expenses involved in purchasing that vehicle. The same is true for any other item that is purchased and used only infrequently. The owner incurs depreciation and opportunity cost irrespective of how much the item is used; thus, it may not make sense to own an RV, or scuba equipment, or a vacation home. As an alternative, the wise consumer might consider renting whatever is needed. It is possible, for example, to rent a recreational vehicle for two weeks, three weeks, or a month, provided that it is reserved ahead of time. The charge for an RV that will hold a family confortably may seem outrageously high, say, $500 for one week; however, that does not mean it would be cheaper to purchase one. Again consider the example where the RV would sit in the driveway for 50 weeks and be used only 2 weeks. Let's look at the first year's cost of that RV. We'll say that it cost $14,000.

First year's expenses

Depreciation	$3,500
Opportunity cost	840
Insurance	200
Maintenance	200
TOTAL	$4,740

If it is only used two weeks a year, then the implicit cost per week of use is equal to $2,370. Now this might be an exaggeration, particularly if the RV is used on weekends, but it does point out that the relevant way to make the calculation is to include depreciation and opportunity cost and then divide by the actual time the RV will be used.

It is easier and easier for Americans to rent not only RVs, but full camping and backpacking equipment, scuba equipment, golfing equipment, boats, skiing equipment, and the like. Whenever you find yourself in a situation where you very infrequently will use a piece of recreational equipment, the alternative of renting it should be considered. When making your calculation, do not be immediately shocked at the high rental rate per day or per week; rather, compare that seemingly high rental rate with the implicit cost you would be incurring if you decided to purchase the equipment on your own.

There are disadvantages to renting. You have to plan in advance to make sure that you will be able to obtain the item. Often you have to put down a deposit, which you will lose if you change your mind. Further, you cannot customize the rented piece of equipment as you would if you owned it. And, something that we cannot forget is pride in ownership. Individuals get value from actually owning something that they can take care of personally and show off personally as their own. This may turn out to be the most important reason for some individuals to buy their own recreational equipment rather than rent it.

MAKING TIME FOR RECREATION

Recreation is basically a technique by which you refresh your body and your mind after work. It means literally "to be re-created." This is done through activity and play. In a sense, then, we can distinguish between recreation and simply leisure, or free time. When you are engaged in recreation, you are actually doing something that is a diverting activity. True recreational activity involves free choice where you can say to yourself, this is what I like to do, rather than this is what I have to do.

NEVER FINDING TIME FOR RECREATION

Some individuals never seem to find "time" for recreation. When they are not working on a job for pay, they are engaged in doing tasks around the house. This may be the way in which an individual has to run his or her life; however, for those who never seem to have time for recreation and feel guilty about it, then, indeed, time must be found. Work will always expand to fit the time allowed; thus, unless a positive approach is taken to develop more time for recreational activities, it will never be found.

THE VALUE
OF INCREASED
RECREATION

Sociologists and psychologists contend that when recreation is freely chosen and allows the individual to get in touch with him- or herself, it allows individuals to find out and respond to their own personal needs and desires. Moreover, recreational activities that are undertaken with family and friends increase the bonds between the individual and those around him or her.

THINKING ABOUT
NECESSARY
RECREATION

Perhaps the best way to go about the search for your recreational needs is to start thinking. Think about yourself, your free time, the cost involved, and your alternatives.

Thinking about Yourself. If you can take time out to try to discover what your interests really are, you may also discover what types of recreation will be best for you. Does playing tennis really not satisfy you? Is it because you really don't want to engage in such a highly competitive sport? If so, then maybe something else less competitive would be better for you. Do you really need time away from everyone else? If so, then perhaps you should switch from sports in which you are with others to activities in which you are alone, such as bird watching, fishing, or nature photography.

Thinking Realistically about Your Leisure Time. Are you ever going to get three weeks away from your job to take that course in mountain climbing you've dreamed about? If you are being unrealistic in your dreams and you know it's never going to happen, then perhaps your energies would be better directed toward some other recreational activity that you can actually fit into your available free time. Do you really like to read but keep telling yourself that you need a large block of time in order to do so? Why not try to read just a chapter a night in novels that you have always wanted to savor. You might be amazed at how much you can do recreationally if you do it in very small time slots. A basic principle is to fit in the recreation you want in the time slots available rather than wishing that you had more leisure time or leisure time in different amounts than you now are able to arrange.

Thinking about Recreational Expenses. One must continue to be realistic in terms of the recreation desired, for much recreation requires expenses on complementary items. To become an avid skier may require more than just relatively inexpensive rented equipment. To do serious photography may require a complete darkroom at a price that exceeds your budget. You may have to substitute. There are numerous recreational activities that do not require any out-of-pocket expenses. Seeing free movies at the library or checking out books doesn't cost a cent. In fact, in many major cities, there are free activities provided by different groups every weekend and often during the week.

THE RANGE OF RECREATIONAL ACTIVITIES

It would be impossible to list the numerous recreational activities that are open to any individual in any part of the country. What we can do here is point out the activities that are most popular in the United States with respect to those that are physically demanding, those that take place outdoors, those that are creative, and those that are done at home.

ACTIVITIES THAT KEEP YOU FIT

Badminton, bicycling, bowling, calisthenics, hockey, jogging, skating, skiing, softball, swimming, tennis, and volleyball.

ACTIVITIES THAT KEEP YOU OUTDOORS

Birdwatching, boating, camping, fishing, gardening, hiking, hunting, and picnics.

CREATIVE ACTIVITIES

Acting, dancing, jewelrymaking, playing musical instruments, needlework, painting, pottery, refinishing furniture and houses, sewing, singing, and writing.

ACTIVITIES DONE RIGHT AT HOME

Collecting stamps, shells, antique bottles; games—cards, Scrabble; gourmet cooking, reading, indoor gardening.

GETTING INFORMATION ON RECREATION

There is really no problem in getting information on the alternatives for recreational activities. The problem is sorting out all of the possibilities! In most cities, newspapers give a list of many recreational activities and the whereabouts of clubs that can be contacted. YMCAs and YWCAs offer a plethora of recreational options.

Local colleges and universities can be a source of possibilities. There are newspapers and bulletin boards that can be consulted. Parks in your area probably have recreation programs throughout the year, both for yourself and other members of your family.

Your local library will undoubtedly have numerous sections on different types of sports, arts, and so on. You can learn about thousands of possibilities with just a small investment of your time.

Go to the largest newsstand in your area. You will find magazines dedicated to numerous different recreational activities, from gardening to rock collecting to model airplanes to boating to sewing—the list goes on and on.

INFORMATION NECESSARY WHEN YOU BUY

If you are deciding to buy something to be used as part of your recreational program, you want to apply the same buying principles as with anything else. You first want to acquire as much information as is reasonable for the purchase you are making. This can be done by querying friends and colleagues as to whether they have any information on the place to buy what you need, what brand you should buy, what quality and so on. Another way you can get information about something you might want to buy is to first rent, use it awhile, and then make a decision. This is often done by individuals, for example, who are trying to decide which brand of skis to purchase. They rent different brands and decide after having used each brand a day or two. Are you thinking about buying a recreational vehicle? Rent one first to see if it's really for you; thus, renting can be not only a convenient way to use an expensive piece of equipment, but it is also a way to obtain information about the advisability of owning that piece of equipment.

Your yellow pages can also offer a wealth of information as to where products are available. The salespeople in the stores you go to will certainly have information that will be helpful for you.

SUMMARY

1. Leisure and money income (that is, work) are substitutes.
2. Time and leisure activities are complements.
3. Hours worked overtime by the average American have fallen from what they were one hundred years ago. We have bought more leisure. As more Americans have purchased more leisure, they have also purchased more complementary products, such as recreational vehicles and sporting equipment.
4. Purchasing any consumer durable good involves looking at opportunity cost and depreciation. An RV that is used only two weeks a year may be much more expensive to own than to rent for those two weeks.
5. There is a vast range of recreational activities, and information may be obtained readily on all of them from YMCAs, YWCAs, local colleges and universities, parks, libraries, and so on.

QUESTIONS FOR THOUGHT AND DISCUSSION

1. Why do you think that hours worked have leveled off over the last 15 years in the United States?
2. Would rich people tend to take longer vacations than poor people? (Hint: Remember opportunity costs.)

3. If the price of tennis rackets and tennis balls fell, do you think people would play more tennis?

4. What can explain the increased amount of physical recreational activity that Americans are now doing?

THINGS TO DO

1. Go to your local or college library and find the section on sports activities. Do you find any books on activities that were unknown or unthought of by your parents when they were your age?

2. Visit a local recreational vehicle sales lot. Ask the salesperson to explain to you the full cost per year of owning an RV. Did that salesperson include the opportunity cost of the down payment you would have to provide in order to obtain a loan for the RV.

SELECTED READINGS

Brock, D. "Lessons for the Restless." *Esquire*, November 1976, pp. 103–107.

"Mobile Homes and RV's." *Consumers' Research Magazine*, October 1976, pp. 144–145.

Owen, John D. "Work Weeks and Leisure: An Analysis of Trends 1948-75." *Monthly Labor Review*, August 1976, p. 3.

Before You Spend Your Vacation Dollar

GETTING INFORMATION ON POSSIBLE VACATIONS

It would be impossible to list all of the available information sources on vacations. As we become a more vacation conscious society, we also find that there are more and more sources of information on what type of vacation we should take. Here are just a few suggestions.

1. Travel books: All you need do is go to your local library or a large bookstore in your area. You will find in the travel section books for every possible type of vacation you might want to take, from inexpensive camping trips to grand tours of Europe. For many years now, individuals traveling on a limited budget have been using the $5, $10 and $15 a day books put out by Eric Frommer (Simon and Shuster, publishers). You will find, however, that those books as well as any other can't seem to keep up with inflation in this country and elsewhere, so that you usually have to add 10 to 20 percent to all the prices given in the books to come up with what you will actually pay.

2. Write for travel information to tourist offices throughout the world. Every country in the world has a tourist office and will provide information free of charge. If you live in a large city, you can look in the yellow pages under "Tourist Information" and "Consulates and Other Foreign Government Representatives." A short telephone call will usually result in a wealth of free information via the mail.

3. If you are planning any camping trips, you can write the U.S. National Park Service, Department of the Interior, 18th and East Streets, Washington, D.C. 20240.

4. Each state has a Tourist Information Bureau. Write it directly to obtain needed information.

5. If you are a member of the American Automobile Association, you can obtain travel guides on the United States, Canada, Mexico, and elsewhere.

6. Airlines often have free or low-cost information on traveling to various parts of the world.

7. Read the travel section in your local newspaper to find out about alternative travel ideas.

8. Subscribe to a travel magazine, such as *Travel and Leisure*.

9. Check your local bus depot and/or railway for information on low-cost tickets that are good for travel anywhere for a set period of time.

Using a Travel Agent

You can also get information, brochures, and suggestions from a travel agent in your area. More important perhaps, a travel agent can take care of all of your reservations for transportation lodging, and tours. You can expect a travel agent to do the following for you:

1. Have all schedules and costs of planes, trains, and boats.

2. Be able to provide you with details on group arrangements and tours.

3. Be able to provide you with the dates of special events and festivals.

4. Be able to provide you with motel/hotel room rates and availability.

5. Help you obtain a passport and/or visa and tell you which shots you might need to have.

6. Make reservations for you for tours, planes, trains, motels, hotels, and special events.

7. Tell you the different seasons and how rates vary depending on those seasons.

8. Give you advice on tipping customs, clothing, and restaurants.

9. Make up a tour for you and/or your family that fits your

How to Pick a Travel Agent

Friends can be the greatest source of information about a good travel agent. The company you work for may also have a specific agent that it uses. This might be advantageous to you because the agent will want to keep good relations with the company and therefore may give you some special service. You may wish to speak with travel agents who are members of the American Society of Travel Agents. Any agency displaying the ASTA symbol has been in business at least three years and meets certain financial and ethical standards set up by the ASTA.

In order to get the most out of the travel agent you choose, you must make him or her aware of your budget and your tastes and preferences. Let the agent know if you truly can't stand a stuffy or a very relaxed atmosphere. That way he or she will not book you in that type of hotel or tell you to go to that type of restaurant. The more the agent gets to know you personally, the more you can be sure that he or she will be better able to cater to your desires.

IF YOU DECIDE TO DO IT ALONE

Do-it-yourself vacation planning is not all that difficult, particularly if you have a definite idea of where, when, and how you are going to travel.

Transportation Reservations

All airlines have their own booking office with agents who

tastes, interests, and available budget. In the travel trade, this is called an independent inclusive tour.

How You Pay a Travel Agent

Generally, the travel agent is paid for his or her services via commissions paid by airlines, hotels, and restaurants. In other words, you are not directly billed but implicitly pay for the agent's services when you pay your plane, train, and hotel bills. However, you may be expected to be charged for any extras such as certain reservations in foreign hotels, reticketing, and long distance telephone calls and telegrams.

can help you with fares and schedules over the telephone. You can reserve tickets and pick them up at the airport, charging them to one of your credit cards. If you decide to use the rail system in the United States, you can call Amtrak. The toll-free number throughout the United States for reservations and information is 800-523-5720. If you plan to go by rail into Canada, contact the Canadian National Railways, 630 Fifth Avenue, New York, New York 10020; and the Canadian Pacific Railways, 581 Fifth Avenue, New York, New York 10017.

If you desire to go by bus, contact either your local office of Greyhound or Continental Trailways, or write them at the New York Port Authority Bus Terminal at 8th Avenue and 41st Street, New York, New York 10014.

If you are planning to drive in the United States or elsewhere, you can obtain maps from gas stations. The Mobil Guides are useful for this endeavor. If you plan to drive in a foreign country, you should look into details on international driver's licenses and international automobile registration. Do this by writing or calling the American Automobile Association, 28 East 78th Street, New York, New York 10021. It is important to check whether your automobile insurance will cover you everywhere you plan to visit. If you are planning to go into Canada, your insurance company must provide you with a Canadian nonresident interprovince motor vehicle liability insurance card. In Mexico, United States insurance is

usually not valid for more than 48 hours after entry. The main point is to settle your car insurance problems *before you leave home*.

If you plan a day-by-day itinerary, you can write in advance for hotel/motel reservations. Most major chains of motels have toll-free numbers that can be found in your yellow pages. If you are planning a trip with your family, find out if there is a "family plan" in the hotel/motels that you plan to use. Often for a small fee or nothing at all, a motel will give you an extra bed in your room, thus saving you the charge of two rooms.

CUTTING VACATION COSTS

Proper planning and a willingness to cut some corners may save you a significant amount of money that you can spend for either a longer vacation or for something else. Here are some ideas. A travel agent or some of

the many budget travel books may present others.

1. Take vacations off season. Sometimes rates are 50 percent less in the hotels during the off-season months. A European holiday in October is considerably less expensive than in July. Not only are hotels cheaper, but so, too, are plane fares. A travel agent or airline representative can give you the exact differences between high season and off season. Thus, timing becomes crucial to saving money on vacations. You might even consider splitting your vacation into two holidays, taking advantage of bargain rates at the beginning or end of each season.

2. Take advantage of airfare bargains. Ask if there is a special "K" class with no meal on the flight you wish to take. Find out if there are any special tour fares. Some may require that you purchase a minimum amount of ground accommodations, but the saving can be well

worth your while. Charter flights are often quite a bargain; these must be planned in advance, however, and some of them leave many hours after they are scheduled to leave, thus imposing much discomfort on families waiting for the flight. If you have small children, this may be an important factor for you in deciding against a charter flight. Also, consider the fact that charter flights are usually sold by the seat, irrespective of the person's age. Thus, if you are traveling with small children, you will be charged the full charter flight fare for each of them. Compare this with a regularly scheduled airline that might offer significant savings for children under twelve.

3. Look into "stopover" possibilities on your travel arrangements. Sometimes for a small additional charge you may be able to visit several cities at once.

4. Try to go where the crowds are not. Head away from the jammed resorts; go to the more remote and less well known areas.

5. Get a copy of the "Traveler's Directory" from 51-02 39th Avenue, Woodside, New York 11277. It provides a listing in the United States and abroad of hundreds of people and places that will put you up for free, provided that you offer the same hospitality to others. You must also offer a "donation" of several dollars for the book.

6. If you are a student, obtain an international student identity card from the Council on International Educational Exchange, 777 United Nations Plaza, New York, New York 10017. Many hotels, restaurants, and cultural events will give you reduced rates.

7. Consider a Eurail pass in Europe, which gives you unlimited first-class rail travel. It must be purchased in the United States; ask your travel agent or write Eurail Pass, c/o French National Railroad, 610 Fifth Avenue, New York, New York 10020.

8. In the United States, consider a similar type of pass offered by the major bus companies. Greyhound has an Ameripass, and Continental Trailways has an Eaglepass.

9. If you decide on a vacation tour, shop around. When comparing prices, make sure you compare tours that provide similar services. Do you pay for porters and tour guides? Do you pay for theater tickets? What is included and what isn't? What type of accommodations will you get?

10. Hosteling is possible. Throughout the world there is a network of youth hostels that are inexpensive dormitory style accommodations. Fees in the United States range from $1.50 to $2.50 per day for lodging. In other countries, the fees are lower. In almost 50 countries, there are 4,500 hostels available. For information on trips and applications for youth hostel passes, write American Youth Hostels, AYH National Campus, Delaplane, Virginia.

11. Consider camping as an alternative to hotels. Look at Rand-McNally's *Guidebook for Campgrounds* in which some 16,000 United States and Canadian campgrounds are listed. If you plan to stay in National Parks throughout the country, the purchase of a golden eagle passport for $10 will save money. Write the U.S. Superintendent of Documents, Washington, D.C. 20402, for the following brochures: "Camping in the National Park System," "Boating in the National Park System," and "Fishing in the National Park System."

12. You can write some private organizations, too, such as: the Sierra Club, 1050 Mills Tower, 220 Bush Street, San Francisco, California 94104; American River Touring Association, 1016 Jackson Street, Oakland, California 94607; and Wilderness Society, Western Regional Office, 4260 Evans Avenue, Denver, Colorado 80222.

13. If you are driving your car, try to find hotels that do not charge for overnight parking.

14. Consider older, downtown hotels that have had to reduce their rates in recent years to compete with airport and suburban hotels and motels.

15. Consider house-swapping. Several clubs have been established to help you in this very inexpensive way to have lodging in another part of the country or the world. Write Holiday Home Exchange Bureau, Inc., P.O. Box 555, Grants, New Mexico 87020; or Vacation Exchange Club, Inc., 350 Broadway, New York, New York 10013. These clubs' annual directories list individuals interested in exchanging homes. There is a brief explanation of the home and facilities.

IF YOU DECIDE TO RENT A CAR

Often on vacations renting a car is extremely convenient. The first thing you want to do if you know where you are going is start some comparison shopping on the telephone. All national car rental agencies have toll-free numbers that you can call for information and reservations. These agencies will be listed in your yellow pages. Here are some pointers on how to get the most out of your rental dollar.

1. See if there is an additional drop fee if you leave the car in another city.

2. Reserve the car at least a week in advance to avoid last minute disappointments in selection and the necessity of renting a larger, more expensive car than you had desired.

3. Find out if you are eligible for a discount. There are discounts given to executives, employees of educational institutions, and so on. It is relatively easy to obtain a discount.

4. Sometimes in major airports in other countries, it is possible to bargain with the various rental agencies that are lined up as you leave the baggage checkout counter.

5. Find out what happens if the car is returned late. Are you allowed a few hours "grace" period?

6. Verify that the mileage written on your contract is the mileage on the rental car's odometer.

7. Check the insurance coverage. Often your own insurance will not cover rental cars, particularly in foreign countries. It may be worthwhile to pay the extra daily fee to have full comprehensive insurance so that even in minor accidents you don't have to worry.

8. If your health and medical insurance covers all accidents, then it is not worthwhile paying for the extra medical coverage when you rent a car.

9. See if car rental can be included in a fly-drive package plan. It may be much cheaper that way.

10. Avoid renting a car at the airport. Rates from car rental agencies that will come to pick you up are often significantly lower than rentals in many airports.

11. If you are planning an extended stay in Europe, consider a longer term lease arrangement with a European company or a sell-buy agreement, where they buy back the car at the end of the summer. It is no longer true that the purchase of a foreign car in another country saves you enough money to make it worthwhile. When you add insurance costs, shipping fees, and the amount of time you have to wait for the car to be delivered from Europe, you don't really save much, if anything.

12. Rent the smallest car that is convenient for you and your family.

13. Inquire about alternative rental arrangements. Most companies have special excursion plans.

USING CREDIT CARDS

Even if you decide that you do not want to borrow in order to go on vacation, it still may be advisable for you to have several major credit cards. These provide positive identification when renting an automobile and can be used for the deposit. The bills will constitute an accurate record of all hotel, plane, train, and restaurant expenses. The use of credit cards avoids the necessity of carrying large amounts of cash, purchasing large amounts of traveler's checks and keeping track of them, or attempting to use personal checks in places other than your own locality.

Many major credit cards provide an instant cash service in case you run out of money. American Express, for example, has set up machines in major airports in which you can purchase traveler's checks using your American Express card.

The question as to whether or not it is advisable to go into debt to take a vacation is, of course, an entirely separate issue. One often sees the suggestion that only consumer durable goods, such as cars, houses, and appliances should be purchased on time, but not vacations. We will mention a point made throughout this text. What is important is that you do not exceed your safe debt limit by going into debt to take a vacation. It is perfectly rational for some people to go into debt to take a vacation and thereby be unable to replace an old washing machine or get a new refrigerator. At the time that they make the decision, they believe it is more important that a restful and/or exciting vacation be consumed so that they will feel better the rest of the year. Looking forward to a vacation may provide a necessary inducement when undertaking tasks that are not always that much fun. Vacations can and are for some people just as important as having enough to eat, warm clothes, and a roof over their heads.

SUMMARY

1. Information on possible vacations can be obtained from travel books, national tourist offices, the U.S. National Park Service, state tourist information bureaus, the American Automobile Association, major airlines, travel sections of local newspapers, and travel magazines.

2. A travel agent can provide you with all schedules, details on group arrangements and tours, dates of special events and festivals, passport and visa details, etc. Travel agents are paid by the companies for which they sell tickets or book reservations. You do not pay agents directly.

3. Ways to reduce travel costs include taking vacations off season, taking advantage of airfare bargains, going to uncrowded resorts, using student discounts when possible, taking bus tours, and house-swapping.

QUESTIONS FOR THOUGHT AND DISCUSSION

1. Look at the suggestions in this issue for reducing travel costs. What benefits do you lose if you follow any of these suggestions?

2. How do travel agents make their income? Why would you ever want to use a travel agent?

3. Why do students get special discounts if they have student ID cards?

THINGS TO DO

If you have never done so, visit a travel agency to see what types of information are available.

SELECTED READINGS

"Learn-To-Do-Something-New Vacation." *Better Homes & Gardens*, April 1977, p. 200.

"When Traveling Is Easiest and Cheapest." *Changing Times*, March 1977, p. 4.

"Where to Go." See issues of *Outdoor Life*.

"Where Vacation Bargains Are." *U.S. News*, March 14, 1977, p. 175.

Retirement and the Golden Years

CHAPTER PREVIEW

☐ What percentage of the population is over sixty-five?

☐ Should there be mandatory retirement at any specified age?

☐ Is there any trend toward early retirement?

☐ What are the financial risks of early retirement?

20 One major change in our society concerns the percentage of the population that is 65 or over. That percentage is now rising. Why? Because we are approaching zero population growth. Thus, we will no longer be a nation of young people, a nation as enamored of the youth culture as it used to be. We will gradually see a reversal in the trend to younger and younger presidents of major corporations, universities, and foundations. We will become more like such countries as France, where the unknowing American immediately remarks how many "old" people there are in that country. Today the median age of the population is 29. Today 11 percent of the population is 65 or over. In the year 2000, that figure will have risen to 12½ percent.

Thus, the problems of aging and retirement are going to become increasingly important for this nation. Geriatric problems—problems of the aged—face us from three different directions:

1. We must individually face the problems of our own aging and retirement.
2. Often we must face the problems of aging of our parents.
3. From a societal point of view, we may wish to consider policy changes to improve the cultural, moral, and economic lot of the aged.

THE PLIGHT OF THE ELDERLY TODAY

In the latter part of the 1970s, there were 23 million individuals 65 or over. Of these, 3 million officially were below the money income poverty line. Poverty, at least on the surface, appears to be a major problem facing older people in America. In Figure 20-1 we show the distribution of income of older people in the United States in 1977. Fully 15 percent were earning less than $3,000 a year. There are a number of explanations for this phenomenon.

NOT PROVIDING FOR THE FUTURE

To some extent, we must admit that there are individuals who are poor when they are older because they did not save enough when they were younger. They did not start a retirement plan at an early enough age so that they could be comfortable in their older years. Those who rely on Social Security alone for retirement years can never expect to lead a comfortable life. Social Security was never envisioned to be a full retirement income program, but rather only a supplement to private savings.

BEING CRIPPLED BY MEDICAL BILLS

Many older individuals find themselves unable to make ends meet because they suffer from chronic illnesses that require constant attention and medical expenses. However, since the introduction of Medicare and Medicaid, this problem has been ameliorated for a large number of senior citizens. Further, many others take advantage of extensive private medical insurance in order to avoid being saddled with extraordinary expenses in case of extraordinary medical problems.

THE INABILITY TO FIND WORK EVEN WHEN IT IS DESIRED

Mandatory retirement systems in many companies and other work places make it extremely difficult for senior citizens to work even when they want to. Union restrictions and minimum wage laws further make it difficult, if not impossible, for senior citizens to find full- or part-time work in lower paying jobs that they might be perfectly happy to do if it weren't for the restrictions. Also, the Social Security program actually discourages retired people from making extra income. As of 1978, for every $2 that a Social Security recipient earns up to $3,000, he or she loses $1 of Social Security benefits. That is an effective tax rate of 50 percent, plus additional taxes, such as federal income tax, Social Security contributions, and state income taxes.

STATISTICS MAY NOT TELL THE FULL STORY

Unfortunately, the government statistics on income of older people is a very inaccurate measure of what their true standard of living is. The government statistics only look at money income; they ignore the value of all in-kind transfers from the government, such as food stamps, Medicare and Medicaid, public housing, and the like. Furthermore, money income data ignore completely the value of the services that older people obtain from any homes that they own. A large number of retired people own their own homes and indeed may have paid for them completely. If you are 70 years old and live in a $40,000 house, you are implicitly receiving a stream of services from that house equal to what it would cost you to rent the same type of accommodations in the housing market. If, hypothetically, such a house could be rented for $300 a month, then the value of the housing services received by the owner-occupier of the house is $3,600 a year. This would be part of a retired couple's true or real income. Thus, to the extent that money income excludes the value of owner-occupied housing and the value of food stamps from the government, those money income figures overstate the poverty problem of the aged.

Figure 20-1 Distribution of Income for People over Age 65

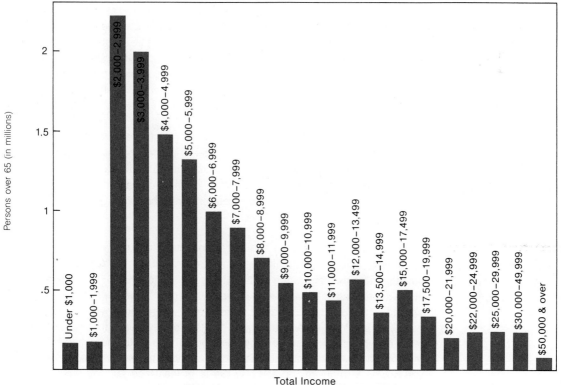

THE THORNY QUESTION OF MANDATORY RETIREMENT

A large number of businesses, universities, and school systems have a mandatory retirement age, which may be 65 or, in some cases, a little older. This has created bitterness on the part of senior citizens who do not wish to leave the job market. Employers contend that mandatory retirement is beneficial to society because it leaves room for younger workers to enter the labor market, and it allows them to legally get rid of unproductive workers who would otherwise stay on for years at high pay because of seniority.

Is there any truth in such contentions? Perhaps some, but certainly not very much with respect to the first comment. Workers 65 and over do not have to be mandatorily retired from the labor force in order to provide jobs for other workers. In a dynamic economy such as ours, the labor market can work well—there doesn't have to be a growing rate of unemployment over time—if there are no restrictions. The second comment that employers make about mandatory retirement does, in some situations, have some validity. If strict labor union or government regulations limit the ability of employers to fire unproductive employees or to lower their wage rates when they become less productive because of aging, then mandatory retirement is a way out of the dilemma. However, from the senior citizen's point of view, it would appear that a change in government and union regulations would be more advantageous; thus, the older person could be given a choice if he or she is indeed less productive to accept a lower wage rate, a different type of job, or to retire. This seems preferable to mandatory retirement.

In the past decade or so, employers have come up with a new reason to require mandatory retirement. They contend that health insurance premiums, which they must offer as a fringe benefit to their employees, would skyrocket if workers stayed on until they were much older and therefore were incurring numerous medical expenses due to chronic illnesses. There is an alternative to the current situation, however. Employers could offer over-65 employees separate health insurance at a higher rate than younger employees, consistent with their higher level of medical expenses. In this manner, younger employees would not be discriminated against by being forced to pay part of the cost of health insurance for older employees.

One thing is certain—if your company has an inflexible mandatory retirement age and you wish to continue working after that age, you must do something in preparation. You must either change jobs so that you work in a company that does not have such a policy or line up another job that you can immediately switch to when you are forced to retire from your current employment.

THE TREND TOWARD EARLY RETIREMENT

For many people the problem is not in continuing to work after age 65, but in knowing what to do upon early retirement, that is, at an age earlier than 65. The average retirement age in the United States is 63½. In 1890, 68 percent of all men in the country aged 65 were working; by 1976, only 21 percent of those aged 65 worked. The trend toward earlier retirement is increasingly evident.

The trend toward early retirement points to one certainty: those who decide to retire early must obviously have planned for that early retirement many years ago by providing for sufficient income to cover all those nonworking years. After all, if you decide to retire at 55, and you live to at least age 70, you need 15 years

of retirement income. You would have had to build up a pretty big nest egg in the form of a pension plan or some other retirement scheme. If you have any desire whatsoever to retire early (before 65 for men, 62 for women), there is no escaping the fact that to do so you will have to save more today. Do not plan on Social Security as a help to you: first, it would not start at age 55; and second, it does not provide you with a very comfortable living standard (or at least it has not in the past).

To fully enjoy a long retirement period, you have to be equipped to take advantage of 100 percent leisure time. You might be ill equipped if all of your working years were spent without developing outside interests. Hence, it could be important for your happiness in retirement to lead some sort of balanced life before retirement. That is, at least moderate amounts of leisure activities should have been worked into your working time periods. The man or woman who spends 65 hours a week working until age 55 and hopes to truly enjoy a long retirement period on a large pension plan may be sadly disappointed, for their only interest will have been in work, not play. (A person can, however, develop new interests *after* retirement.) It is not surprising that some people who work their heads off while they are young end up working their entire lives because they become addicted to the excitement of a full day of work, at least five and sometimes six or seven days a week. Of course, there is nothing necessarily wrong with this: each of us has the right to pursue our own values and preferences. But if work is not what you think you want to do the rest of your life, it is wise to start young in figuring out a balanced diet of work and play. If you always put off doing what you would like to do during leisure time you will probably never do it. Hobbies may sound corny to some, but they are an integral part of a life style that leads to a happy retirement that seems fulfilling, whether it be early or late.

In sum, then, successful early retirement requires two ingredients:

1. An exceptionally large saving program while you are working.
2. A personal development program for acquiring interests outside of work activities, to be expanded when retirement comes around.

ALTERNATIVES TO EARLY RETIREMENT

Obviously, there are many alternatives to early retirement. You can work less and retire later in life. You do not have to work 50 weeks a year every year until you retire at age 65. You can work 40 weeks a year, or 35, or even 6 months. It takes a very special job for that to be possible, but if that is really what you want in life, you can start your search right now to find the appropriate situation. You generally will not make as much money, but you will have more leisure time, which is a good in itself for most people. It has a value just as income does. Of course, here again you have to get just the right mix to suit yourself. For if you work too little, you have too little money to make your leisure time satisfying, such as by purchasing records, books, movie tickets, boats, restaurant meals, skis, and trips.

STARTING A SECOND CAREER

Rather than retiring early and only engaging in leisure activities thereafter, many individuals seek a second career. This has been standard practice for individuals who join the armed forces at a very young age and retire after 20 to 30 years of service on a full pension. Many start a new career in perhaps an entirely different field than the one they worked on for the past 20 or 30 years. More than half of all federal government employees who retire as early as age 55 are gainfully employed thereafter, usually part time. In deciding on a second career, it is necessary to do proper advance planning to avoid the kind of jobs associated with working pensioners—helper in the local store or being a night watchman. In other words, a long lead time is recommended for seeking a regular second job.

Many individuals in the business community will often retire and then work part time as consultants to other business persons. Such jobs can be on a retainer or a contract basis. Those who never were in business but always wanted to be can contact the United States Small Business Administration, Washington, D.C., to find out the risks and the possible benefits of going into business for oneself after an early retirement. A typical small business venture that many older people go into is the purchase of a dry cleaning franchise or some other such franchise where much of the advance planning has been taken care of by the national franchise management.

FINANCIAL RISKS IN EARLY RETIREMENT

If you seek early retirement from your current career before private and public pension rights will give you a satisfactory standard of living, you clearly must seek a second career. However, be aware of the financial hazards that you face.

Older employees, particularly those part time, are usually the first to be fired or layed off during a business downturn. You may also find that your physical strength is not as great as you had anticipated and that the job you took is too demanding. Your desire to move to a more pleasant climate may become increasingly acute as you become less interested in your second career.

Hence, for most people, a second career is most enjoyable when it is undertaken for pleasure rather than financial necessity.

A SECOND CAREER WITHOUT PAY— VOLUNTEER WORK

Individuals who find themselves financially secure but desirous of continuing working may find tremendous satisfaction in the hundreds, indeed thousands, of volunteer programs throughout the nation. Some of them even pay modest amounts of money to the participants. The federal government has several major volunteer groups directed through an agency called ACTION. ACTION includes the Peace Corps, for overseas service; VISTA, for service in the United States; and a number of other smaller organizations. SCORE is of particular importance to senior citizens. It is a service corps of retired executives. It helps small business-persons out when they are in trouble. Participants receive a modest expense allowance, but no pay. To get information, write ACTION, Washington, D.C. 20525.

The Administration on Aging, Department of Health, Education, and Welfare, Washington, D.C. 20201, serves as a general source of information for volunteer groups. It keeps tabs on state and local agencies. You can send for useful publi-cations. In addition, most states have their own agencies affiliated with the Admin-istration on Aging that direct public volunteer programs.

A listing of other possible volunteer organizations would include colleges and universities, organizations of the aged, senior citizens centers, neighborhood improvement centers, boards of education, churches, hospitals, and the Red Cross.

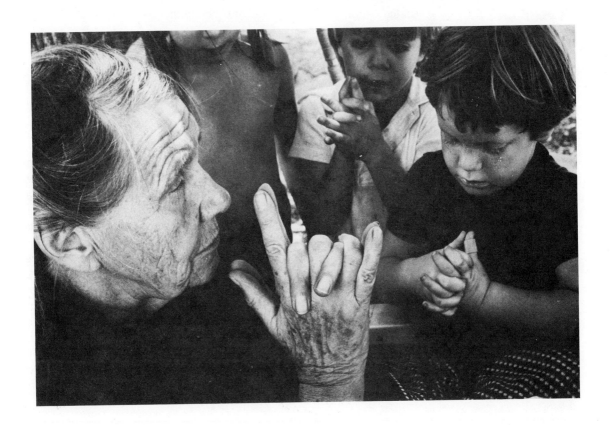

THE COSTS OF RETIREMENT

The decision to retire requires adequate knowledge of what expenses will be during retirement years. Those, of course, will also be a function of where one desires to live. Living costs vary from place to place, but in general are relatively the same except when the individual desires to live in a relatively warm climate in an environment associated with a resort area, such as south Florida, Hawaii, and parts of California. Actually, most retired people stay in the community where they spent their working years. This makes sense because that is where they have established relationships with the greatest number of people for the longest time period. It is quite disruptive to move to a totally new environment where one knows no one and is unfamiliar with the physical surroundings. Most retired people live in urban areas; the vast majority live in large cities or their suburbs; and, although few retired persons want to live in their children's household, a significant percent live within driving distance of their offspring.

THE DECISION AS TO WHERE TO LIVE

Even if a decision is made to remain in a familiar community, there are still further decisions that must be faced. They include:

1. Should you stay in the family home even if it is too big?
2. Should you move to a smaller house or to an apartment that would require less expense and less upkeep?
3. Should you share a living arrangement with other retired people?

If the decision is made to relocate, then further decisions must be faced:

1. Should you seek sunshine, even at a higher expense?
2. Would a planned community for retired persons be appropriate?
3. Would you like to go back to your old hometown?
4. Do you want to be within walking or driving distance of an offspring's house?
5. Do you want to move to a rural area?
6. Is a mobile home for you?

ESTIMATED BUDGET FOR A RETIRED COUPLE

Every year the Bureau of Labor Statistics, Department of Labor, puts out estimated annual budgets for retired couples in urban areas of the United States. In Table 20-1, we re-create the BLS's lower, intermediate, and higher budgets, which are given exclusive of income taxes. You must realize that these budgets are only averages; moreover, if you wanted to estimate what your own retirement budget would be some years from now, you would have to use a multiplication factor to account for anticipated inflation. For example, if we have an average of 5 percent inflation per year, in 15 years you would have to double the estimated annual budget figures for retired couples given in Table 20-1. In order to adjust a retirement budget to a particular location, you can consult Table 7-1 presented in Chapter 7. Here we show multiplication factors for different cities. If you are planning to live in urban United States—places with population of 2,500 or more—no adjustment is necessary. If you are planning to live in metropolitan areas, the index is 105; thus, you must increase the estimated budget by 5 percent. If you plan to retire in nonmetropolitan areas with populations between 2,500 and 50,000, then the index falls to 86. You can reduce the estimated budget by 14 percent.

SOME MYTHS ABOUT OLD AGE

The notion that as a person gets older, that person becomes less creative and less able to enjoy life has been contradicted through thousands of years of experience. A recent study of 738 successful individuals in arts and sciences who lived to be well over 78 years old revealed the following results:

1. Historians and philosophers reached their peak in their sixties.
2. Botanists are most productive in their forties and sixties.
3. Inventors develop most of their patents in their sixties.
4. Historians, botanists, philosophers, geologists, and inventors achieve more in their seventies than they did in their thirties.

Pablo Casals died at the age of 97. He played the cello until the end and retained his vigor and creativity all along. When once asked what his recipe for growing old youthfully was, he stated, "The secret of my good old age is this— I live. Very few people live." If you wish to get an idea of how other older individuals have continued to be creative and youthful well into their nineties, a reading of Dr. Alex Comfort's *A Good Age* (New York: Crown, 1976) will prove revelatory. Comfort's book probably marks the beginning of a new series of serious discussions on how individuals do not have to grow old "disgracefully." Very important in the premise of this book is that the notion of agism is fallacious. Agism is no different than sexism or racism. Individuals should not be discriminated against by virtue of having lived a specified number of years.

Table 20-1
Retirement Couple Budgets

Source: *Monthly Labor Review*, U.S. Department of Labor, Bureau of Labor Statistics, October 1976.

COMPONENT	LOWER		INTERMEDIATE		HIGHER	
	Budget	Percent Change 1974-75	Budget	Percent Change 1974-75	Budget	Percent Change 1974-75
Total budget[1]	$4,501	6.5	$6,465	7.0	$9,598	7.0
Total family consumption	4,308	6.5	6,076	7.0	8,863	7.1
Food	1,427	7.0	1,912	8.3	2,398	8.5
Housing	1,514	7.4	2,192	7.3	3,430	7.2
Transportation	297	9.2	577	9.5	1,059	9.1
Clothing	198	1.5	334	1.8	514	1.6
Personal care	128	6.7	188	6.8	275	6.6
Medical care[2]	552	3.4	555	3.4	559	3.5
Other family consumption	191	5.5	317	5.3	628	5.6
Other items	194	6.6	389	7.2	736	6.4

[1]For autumn 1973, 1974, and 1975, the total budget is defined as the sum of "total family consumption" and "other items." Income taxes are not included in the total budget.
[2]The autumn 1975 cost estimates for medical care contain a preliminary estimate for "out-of-pocket" costs for Medicare.
Note: Because of rounding, sums of individual items may not equal totals.

A few of Comfort's ideas defy the standard notions about senior citizens:

1. **Leisure.** "Leisure is a con, it should mean time when you do what you yourself want to do. It gets sold as part of the unperson package, as time in which you are expected to do trivial and useless things for which you have to pay money."
2. **Retirement.** "Two weeks is about the ideal length of time to retire."
3. **Doctors.** "If you find one who thinks that you have to be infirm, crazy, impotent, or the like, by virtue of chronological age, change doctors."
4. **Brain.** "The human brain does not shrink, wilt, perish, or deteriorate with age. It normally continues to function well through as many as nine decades."

Comfort points out that there is an incredible amount of inaccurate data relating to older people. He confronts the attitude that most older people are constantly in bed because of illness. His statistics show that older people suffer fewer acute illnesses than younger ones—1.3 illnesses per year as opposed to 2.1 for all ages. He does agree that 81 percent of persons over 65 have some chronic problem as against 54 percent of all below that age; however, the average chronic problem might be nothing more serious than hay fever or myopia. Further, a Duke University study found that 44 to 48 percent of those over 65 had no detectable deterioration in physical condition. In fact, some had improved over periods of from 3 to 13 years.

The basic cause of physical deterioration in older people appears to be boredom, inactivity, and the belief that infirmity was to be expected. What is Comfort's conclusion about older people becoming physically handicapped? "Most of the handicaps of oldness in our society are social, conventional, and imaginary."

SUMMARY

1. The percentage of the population over 65 has been rising as the nation's population growth rate has slowed down.
2. There may be discrimination against people over 65 in the job market.
3. Mandatory retirement seems to work against older citizens being able to lead productive lives.
4. There is, on the other hand, a trend toward earlier retirement for a significant part of the population.
5. Many individuals start second careers in their fifties and sixties.
6. There are many costs associated with retirement, not the least being the psychic costs of changing communities if a new environment is sought.
7. There are many myths about age, not the least of which is that older people cannot be creative or productive.

QUESTIONS FOR THOUGHT AND DISCUSSION

1. Why is the age distribution in the United States changing?
2. Will society be any different with an older population?
3. Discuss Alex Comfort's idea that "two weeks is about the ideal length of time to retire."

THINGS TO DO   Read Alex Comfort's *A Good Age.*

SELECTED   Butler, Robert N. "Helping the Aged and Their Families." *National Observer*,
READINGS   March 5, 1977.

Hoven, V. "Where Should You Live in Retirement?" *Retirement Living*, December 1976, pp. 20–22.

Mayer, A., et al. "Graying of America," *Newsweek*, February 28, 1977, pp. 50–52.

Miller, L. A. "10 Questions Retirees Ask Most about the New Tax Laws." *Retirement Living*, March 1977, pp. 22–25.

Schulz, James H. *The Economics of Aging.* Belmont, Calif.: Wadsworth, 1976. ing, 1976.

Shapiro, H. D. "Do Not Go Gently . . .; Compulsory Retirement." *New York Times Magazine*, February 6, 1977, pp. 36–38.

"Time to Rethink Compulsory Retirement." *Money* 6 (April 1977).

Woodward, K. L. "Growing Old Happy." *Newsweek*, February 28, 1977, pp. 56–57.

When the Alternative Is a Nursing Home

Today there are almost 1½ million nursing home patients. At some point in your life, you may be faced with helping a parent or loved one make a decision about which nursing home to choose. In this consumer issue, we look at how to solve some aspects of the nursing home problem.

THE RANGE OF INSTITUTIONAL CARING

Nursing homes are generally thought of as long-term care institutions that provide shelter, food, and usually supervised nursing care. The alternative long-term care facilities available today may be classified according to the services they render. Basically, a nursing home is a generic term that can be applied to sheltered living, convalescent centers, retirement centers, homes for the aged, skilled nursing facilities, and intermediate care facilities. Today there are almost 30,000 nursing homes of one type or another throughout the country. They provide a broad range of resident supervision and services, as well as recreational and rehabilitative programs.

Because the level of nursing care offered ultimately determines the Medicaid/Medicare classification of a nursing home, we will define more specifically some of the terms mentioned above:

1. Skilled nursing facility: The home has a medical staff and continuous professional nursing service and can provide in-patient care and serve convalescent patients who are not acutely ill. Skilled nursing facilities can be certified by the Joint Commission on Accreditation of Hospitals Council. The name that used to be applied to this type of institutional arrangement was an extended care facility. An individual covered by Medicaid and Medicare would be covered in such an institution.

2. Intermediate care facility: It differs from a skilled nursing facility with respect to the absence of a medical staff being able to provide in-patient service. When continuous medical care is not desired, an intermediate care facility can be used. If the intermediate care facility is licensed by the state, it will be recognized by the state's Medicaid program.

The Necessity of Matching the Patient to the Home

Given the array of nursing homes available, it is important to make sure that the person goes to the right type of home. In Exhibit R-1 we reprint a method of evaluating required level of care for older persons.

LOOKING FOR THE RIGHT HOME AWAY FROM HOME

Once you have decided on the level of care necessary, you must compile a list of possible alternative care facilities.

Obtaining Information on Different Homes

You can obtain the names of nursing homes from a variety of sources:

1. Your local health department.

EXHIBIT R-1   **Continuum of Care and Facilities Providing Care for the Elderly**

MAXIMUM CARE

24-HOUR CONTINUOUS SKILLED NURSING CARE

Medical director   Medicaid/Medicare certification   Medical consultants

Special equipment for cardiac care, respiratory   Physician on call
assistance, etc.

D

C

SUPERVISED NURSING CARE

Medicaid reimbursement   Physical therapy

CUSTODIAL CARE
Speech therapy

Daily assistance in self-care

B

Special diets

Occupational therapy

ASSISTANCE IN PERSONAL CARE

Counseling   Recreational programs and activities

Companionship   A   Reality orientation

Organized activities   Behavior therapy

Rehabilitative therapy

MINIMUM CARE

A	B	C	D
SUPPORTIVE CARE	**CUSTODIAL CARE**	**SUPERVISED NURSING CARE**	**CONTINUOUS NURSING CARE**
Senior Citizens' Residence	Homes for the Aged	Intermediate Care Facility	Skilled Nursing Facility
Day Care Centers			
Home Care Services			

The diagram of the continuum of care and services illustrates the four levels of care and services available to patients with different abilities and needs; the four are:

  A. Supportive care at home or in the community
  B. Custodial care at a home for the aged
  C. Supervised nursing care at an intermediate care facility
  D. Continuous nursing care at a skilled nursing facility.

The diagram is constructed to illustrate movement from minimum to maximum care depending on the individual's profile of abilities and needs. If an elderly individual needs all the services in the A block plus those in B, he requires custodial care. However, if he needs all the services in A, B, C, and D, he definitely should be placed in a home which provides all the services of a skilled nursing facility. Simply by looking at the diagram and identifying the services required by the patient, you can determine

EXHIBIT R-1 Continued

the level of care presently needed and project what he may need in the near future.

If the responses to the multiple-choice questions evaluating the patient are primarily the A descriptions then the patient probably needs minimum care within the community. However, if the best patient descriptions are those of the C responses, then an intermediate care facility should be considered. Borderline cases between two levels of care generally dictate choosing the facility with the more intensive level of care since elderly individuals generally move on the continuum from minimum to maximum care.

Evaluating Elderly Patients' Required Level of Care

Ability to Attend to Personal Care

A. Cares adequately for self with minimum assistance, e.g., beautician
B. Needs daily supervision in personal care and assistance in some tasks requiring agility, e.g., bathing, tying shoes, buttoning
C. Needs daily supervision in personal care and assistance in many aspects of grooming and dressing
D. Requires daily assistance in all areas of personal care

EVALUATION: ⸺

Ability to Move About

A. Can move about on his own with minimum assistance, e.g., cane or walker
B. Requires some assistance in walking or getting in and out of wheelchair, bed, or chair
C. Must be attended at all times when walking and moving about
D. Bedridden or confined to chair

EVALUATION: ⸺

Ability to Think Clearly and Make Decisions

A. Able to reason soundly and make responsible decisions, is attentive and responsive
B. Periods of confusion, less attentive and responsive, impaired judgment, and reduced ability or desire to make decisions
C. Slowed thought processes, lack of concentration, poor judgment, and reduced comprehension

D. Clouded thought processes and severely impaired judgment, long periods of unresponsiveness and lapses of memory

EVALUATION: ⸺

Ability to Perceive Time and Identify Places and Persons

A. Well oriented to time and place, normal self-identification and recognition of familiar places and persons
B. Confuses directions to his room, the dining room; forgets it's time to take medications or that it's Wednesday and clinic day
C. Doesn't know day of week or month, confuses time of day, mistakes strangers for friends
D. No awareness or concern about time, place, self, or other people   EVALUATION: ⸺

Ability to Initiate and Complete Tasks and Routine Duties

A. Spontaneously initiates doing household duties, caring for self; motivated to start and complete simple projects
B. Rarely initiates tasks but can be motivated to do things for self and others; completes projects only if encouraged and assisted
C. Lacks spontaneous initiative, resistant to motivation, requires constant urging to accomplish even routine tasks
D. Lack of any motivation or initiative to care for self, eat, move about, even talk

EVALUATION: ⸺

EXHIBIT R-1 Continued

Ability to Show Proper Emotional Response

A. Stable and appropriate emotional responses to situations, events, people
B. Periods of overreaction to minor incidents, times when no response is given to an emotional situation
C. Frequent inappropriate periods of laughing or crying. Seemingly stressless events cause undue reactions
D. Totally inappropriate emotional responses, or even none at all, to any situation or event

EVALUATION: ———

Patient's Ability to Feed Himself/Special Diets

A. Individual can feed himself and eats regularly, may require vitamin supplements and participation in meals-on-wheels program
B. Individual may need supervision and assistance in feeding himself, meal preparation by others, dietary supplements, and daily encouragement to eat properly
C. Individual requires assistance in feeding himself, special diets prepared, and possibly supervised intake of all foods and beverages
D. Individual must be fed; requires special diets, possibly intravenous feeding; and careful supervision of daily intake of fluids

EVALUATION: ———

Patient's Behavior Patterns

A. Individual has adjusted well to aging and developed appropriate behavior patterns while maintaining his level of sociability, cooperativeness, and interest in life
B. Individual has adjusted somewhat negatively to aging, acquired some inappropriate behavior patterns, lost some of his interest and modified his personality, becoming more difficult to reach

C. Individual has not adjusted well to aging and has become a behavior problem either being irritable, hostile, and aggressive or dejected, despondent, and hopeless
D. Individual has either completely withdrawn or become extremely anxious and aggressive, is extremely difficult to deal with because of abnormal behavior patterns

EVALUATION: ———

Patient's Recent Medical History

A. Basically good health, chronic conditions controlled with medications taken on own initiative, no serious disorders or handicaps
B. Fairly good health, may need supervision in taking medications, may be handicapped but would require personal assistance rather than nursing care, e.g., blindness, loss of hearing
C. Declining health, has had an acute episode requiring hospitalization and more serious chronic conditions requiring some nursing supervision
D. Failing health, has had several acute episodes and numerous hospitalizations and requires continuous skilled nursing care

EVALUATION: ———

Patient's Special Therapy Requirements

A/B Those needed therapies are readily accessible, given at home by visiting nurse or at a clinic or acute hospital which the individual can easily visit on his own or with assistance
C/D Individual requires daily or frequent therapies involving special equipment and highly trained personnel, e.g., physical therapy, speech therapy, rehabilitative therapy, and behavior therapy

EVALUATION: ———

Reprinted with the permission of Sandoz Pharmaceuticals, East Hanover, New Jersey.

2. Your local medical hospital and/or nursing home association.

3. Senior citizens and social work groups.

4. Your religious affiliation.

5. Your state commission on geriatric care.

6. Your state nursing home association or association of homes for aging.

7. The Social Security office in your area.

8. Your physician.

9. The yellow pages.

10. Friends and relatives.

Narrowing Down the List

The easiest way to narrow down the list is to make telephone calls to find out if the home satisfies the minimum requirements you have decided upon in terms of convalescent care, recreation, and so on. Also, you will presumably have a budget limitation. Certain more expensive homes can be crossed off the list immediately.

Once you have narrowed down your possible choices, write letters of inquiry to the homes' administrators. Ask about accreditation; services; admission requirements; and costs of basic rate and *all* extra charges.

Checking Out the Home in Person

When you have finally narrowed down your choices, visit the homes either in the late morning or at midday so you can observe the noon meal being served. There are some homes that allow you to inspect them during visiting hours. When you are there, check out certain physical considerations.

1. **Accident prevention.** Many good homes emphasize accident prevention. See if all areas are clear of low, small objects that can cause a patient to trip. Are there throw rugs or small area rugs that can slip? Are the chairs sturdy and not easily tipped? Are there handrails in the hallways and grab bars in the bathrooms?

2. **Fire safety.** Ask to see the home's last fire safety inspection, showing that it meets federal and state requirements. Good housekeeping is important in fire prevention. Do you see evidence of it? Are all exits and paths to exits clearly marked and unblocked? Does the home put residents through frequent fire drills so that they know the easiest way of leaving the building? Does the home have a written emergency evacuation plan available to show you? Are there sufficient staff members to accompany patients who cannot walk by themselves?

3. **Location.** Is the home near a hospital? If the patient wants to see his or her personal doctor, is the home near the hospital where the doctor practices? Is the location near family and friends? Is it in the country, if that is what the patient wants; or in the city, if that is what he or she wants?

4. **General feeling.** Do you get the general feeling that your loved one or friend who might spend the rest of his or her life there will be in a pleasant, clean, happy surrounding? Is there a sufficiently developed recreational program so that boredom will not set in? Do the nurses seem to treat the patients like human beings rather than robots? Can the patients participate in planning their own treatment? Do they have privacy? Are the administrators frank and unafraid of answering all questions? Can the residents wear their own clothing and decorate their rooms with personal belongings?

The list of additional things to look out for could go on, but what is most important perhaps is that after visiting a nursing home, you have a sense of well-being and feel that this is a place where you might be happy if some day you needed continuous care.

STAYING AT HOME

An older person who is sick does not necessarily have to go to a nursing home to get better. There is the option of home health care. Many state public health departments have home care nursing consultants who recommend such care as an alternative to staying in a hospital or going to a skilled care facility.

The majority of health care agencies are affiliated with the health department. There are also agencies that are hospital based and sponsored by the Visiting Nurse Association in different states.

One of the reasons home health care for the aged has not had much success is because of restricted rulings on whether or not Medicare can reimburse the expenses. Medicare only reimburses for "skilled" services, and there is a fine line between what a home health aid or visiting nurse does that qualifies as skilled care. In 1976, expenditures on home health care accounted for about 1 percent of the total spending of the Social Security Administration. It turns out that in most instances, a Medicare patient needs only one skilled service to qualify for home care; and the service may be skilled nursing, physical therapy, or speech therapy. It would seem that home health care is a viable alternative for individuals who wish to continue to lead as normal a life as possible, even after a serious illness. Undoubtedly, as more individuals become informed about the availability of Medicare paying for home health care, we will see a rise in the percentage of total Social Security expenditures on such care.

WHAT TO DO WHEN YOU HAVE A COMPLAINT ABOUT A NURSING HOME

If you have a serious complaint about a nursing home, you can attempt to have your complaint redressed by doing the following:

1. Talk to the nursing home administrator directly.

2. Consult your local Social Security office, which acts as a clearinghouse for complaints about all nursing homes whether or not they receive government funds.

3. If the patient is covered by Medicaid, contact the patient's caseworker or county welfare office.

4. Make a formal complaint about treatment of a nursing home patient by writing to your State Health Department, Licensing and Certification Agency. You can send a copy of your letter also to the U.S. Senate Special Committee on Aging, New Senate Office Building, Washington, D.C. 20001.

5. Still not satisfied? You may wish to write your member of Congress or Senator or your state and/or local elected representative.

6. If the nursing home has a Joint Commission on Accreditation of Hospitals certification, then write the JCAH, 815 North Michigan Avenue, Chicago, Illinois 60611.

7. If the home is a member of the American Health Care Association, write them at 1200-15th Street, N.W., Washington, D.C. 20004.

9. Contact your local Better Business Bureau and/or Chamber of Commerce.

10. Finally, if all else fails, contact a lawyer or go to the Legal Aid Society.

SUMMARY

1. There are approximately 1½ million nursing home patients today.

2. The range of nursing home care is vast, going from a basic sheltered living arrangement to one in which there is full medical care available.

3. It is necessary to match the needs of the older person to the care facilities available.

4. The names of nursing homes can be obtained from such places as your local health department, your Social Security office, your physician, or your yellow pages.

5. When checking out a nursing home, you must look at accreditation, services, admission requirements, and cost. If you have a complaint about a nursing home, you should talk to the nursing home administrator directly, consult your Social Security office if not satisfied, and make a formal complaint to your state Health Department, Licensing and Certification Agency.

QUESTIONS FOR THOUGHT AND DISCUSSION

1. Can you think of reasons older people should not be put in a nursing home?

2. When would you decide that your parent would be better off going to a nursing home?

3. Do you think there is competition among nursing homes so that their prices are not excessive?

THINGS TO DO

Write to the American Association of Homes for the Aging, 529 14th Street, N.W., Washington, D.C. 20004, for information on its services.

SELECTED READINGS

Burger, Sarah Greene, and D'Erasmo, Martha. *Living in a Nursing Home: A Complete Guide for Residents, Their Families and Friends.* New York: Seabury Press (latest edition).

Bush, S. "Changing of Scene Can Be Fatal; Nursing-Home Patients." *Psychology Today,* February 1977, p. 32.

"Caring for the Elderly in Your Family." *Business Week,* February 7, 1977, pp. 83–85.

"Paying the Bills for Nursing Home Care." *Changing Times,* January 1977, pp. 41–42.

Appendix A
Estate Planning: Wills, Trusts, and Taxes

Estate planning is an attempt to analyze an individual's present and future assets, liabilities, and desires relative to the event of his or her death. The commonest goal in estate planning is to minimize the inheritance taxes levied on a person's estate at death. An additional goal is to lower the nontax costs associated with dying, such as legal and accounting fees.

Estate planning can be done by the individual, but attorneys have traditionally handled the bulk of the more sophisticated estate plans. However, trust companies, banks, and even life insurance salespersons will offer estate planning advice.

ESTATE PLANNING IS NOT JUST FOR THE RICH

Of course, it is imperative that very rich persons engage in estate planning to minimize the tremendous inheritance taxes due upon death. But the average individual fails to undertake some form of estate planning, and therefore the heirs endure the hardship of unnecessary costs and problems, all because he or she failed to seek professional advice.

THE BASICS

It is difficult to get into the mood to plan for your death because it is such an undesirable topic of thought or discussion. It is also difficult to plan for what happens after your death because you will not be around to absorb the gratitude of your heirs or dependents. But anyone who is the head of a household or who lives in a state where married individuals have equal rights to all property of the family should in fact engage in some form of estate planning.

What Is Your Estate?

A person's estate can be defined as those material assets existing at his or her death. Homes, cars, cash, securities, and the like make up your estate. It is how these assets are taxed and given to your heirs that you must worry about. Therefore, it is important that you designate who is to inherit your estate and to do it in such a way that it minimizes the cost and the bother. In general, you designate who inherits your estate by making up a will, which we describe below. If you do not have a will when you die, all of your estate—your assets—will be subject to state laws governing inheritance. These laws, instead of your own desires, will decide who gets your property and what procedures (called probate) must be followed in the distribution of your estate. In most instances, the state laws would distribute and administer your estate in a manner that you would not have anticipated. Thus, by executing a will, the most basic element of an estate plan, you can designate who gets which assets and in which manner.

BASIC WILLS

Every state has a maze of rules and regulations pertaining to the proper content and execution of a will, so it is generally recommended that you contact an attorney, at least to advise you what formalities exist. Most people have an attorney draft their will. The following are the basic wills:

1. If you are not married, the commonest scheme divides your estate among your mother, father, brothers and sisters.

2. If you are married and without children, the disposition is generally to your spouse.

3. If you have children, you will want to provide for them in the event that you and your spouse die in a common disaster. This latter event is usually handled through a trust.

4. If you are divorced with children, you might also consider leaving your estate to a trust with your children as beneficiaries. This would eliminate any worry that your ex-spouse might obtain resources you had wished to go to the children.

What Makes a Will Valid?

In most states, the following are necessary to make a will legally valid:

1. Signature: Each page of the will must be signed by the maker or testator, and it must be signed in the presence of witnesses.

2. Witnesses: Usually two or three witnesses are required for a will to be valid. The will should state that all witnesses signed in the presence of each other; the addresses of all witnesses might profitably be included in the document.

3. Alterations: Sometimes alterations or erasures cause a will to be deemed invalid. Therefore, any time these have to be made it is usually worthwhile to have the entire will redrafted.

4. Terms: The will should specifically state how the estate should be distributed.

Wills Should Be Reviewed

A will can be changed whenever you want. That you decided on one aspect in your will a few years ago does not mean you cannot change it today. In fact, you can change your will right up to the time of your death. You can supplement it or modify it with an amendment or codicil.

It is not unwise to reread and reconsider your will each year or so. You would want a different will if you had additions to your family or a change in marital status. You might want a different will if you suddenly became poorer or richer. You might want a different will if you changed your mind about wanting to support your children through college.

The will should be reviewed in the presence of the attorney who drew it up, or a new one if you have moved.

WHERE TO PUT YOUR WILL

As with all valuable documents, the safest place for a will would be in a safe deposit box. But because a safe deposit box may be sealed for a while after your death, it is preferable to place the original will with the trust company or with your attorney.

LETTER OF LAST INSTRUCTION

In addition to a will, you should have a separate letter of last instruction. The letter, which is opened at death, should contain the following information:

1. The location of your will.

2. Instructions about how you should be buried.

3. The location of all of your relevant documents, such as your Social Security card, marriage certificate, and birth certificate.

4. The location of all safe deposit boxes.

5. A list of your life insurance policies and where they are deposited.

6. Pension statements.

7. A list of all stocks and bonds, real and other property, and bank accounts and their locations.

8. Any instructions concerning a business you might be engaged in.

9. A statement of reasons for not giving part of your estate to someone who would normally be expected to receive it.

Note that a letter of last instruction is not a legal document. It does not replace a will and therefore should be considered as a substitute for a valid will that would be accepted by a probate court in the state of domicile.

TRUSTS

In its commonest form, a trust is an arrangement whereby you leave your property to an individual, a bank, or a trust company to manage for the benefit of your heirs. Most trusts are set up because there are minor children surviving a parent or parents. The funds are usually invested by the trustee (the designated holder of the trust) in order to support and educate the children. After a given period of time, which is designated in the will or trust agreement, the remaining assets are distributed, usually to the beneficiaries of the trust.

Trusts can be created for anyone's benefit, including your spouse or a charity, and are not necessarily designed for the protection of children. For example, a surviving spouse may not have the interest or ability to manage the deceased spouse's estate after death, and therefore a trust agreement may be the most desirable method of arranging for use of the assets.

It should be kept in mind that a trust can also be established while you are still living, and these can provide at least as many benefits as a trust created at death. Below we list a number of the more popular trusts available today.

Life Insurance Trust

A life insurance trust is administered by a bank or any other trustee, but not an insurance company. The trustee is named to manage the insurance proceeds after death for any heirs inexperienced in handling large sums of money.

Funded Trusts

The funded trust is a method by which funds or assets other than life insurance can be put under the same expert management that the life insurance trust is under. This way, estate administrative expenses can be reduced and taxation can be averted. That is, taxes do not have to be paid first by a surviving parent and then by the children who would inherit the same funds from her or him.

Testamentary Trust

A testamentary trust is one that is tailor-made for you. In your will, for example, you can create a testamentary trust that makes certain your property will be managed expertly and used as you desire. The trustee, which is usually a bank, is given broad investment powers.

Living Trust

A living trust is a legal instrument in which you make the income from your assets payable to yourself while you are alive, or have them reinvested for your future benefit. This type of trust is not subject to probate (legal procedures for deciding the disposition of your estate at death). But if the living trust can be revocable—that is, altered or canceled at any time —then it will be subject to estate taxes.

THE TAXATION OF ESTATES

Prior to 1976, this section on estate taxes would have included various methods by which those taxes could have been minimized. However, the Tax Reform Act of 1976 virtually rewrote the estate and gift tax code. Specifically, the deductions and credits granted in the 1976 Tax Reform Act make all but the extremely rich not subject to federal estate taxes. Thus,

one of the basic reasons for setting up trusts has been eliminated for almost all individuals in the United States. Moreover, it used to be that gift taxes—that is, taxes imposed on the grantor of the gift—were less than estate taxes. Thus, it was beneficial for older individuals to gift parts of their estates to their future heirs to reduce the total taxes on the estate. Now this is no longer the case. The tax rate is the same on gifts and estates.

Comparing the Old Law with the New

It is interesting to compare the old federal estate tax laws with the new one. Under the old law, you could leave one-half of your estate to your spouse tax free; then an additional $60,000 was exempt from taxes. Now you have the option of leaving one-half of your estate or up to $250,000 (whichever is greater) to your spouse tax free. The $60,000 additional exemption is increased by means of a tax

Table A-1
Federal Estate Taxes in 1981

ADJUSTED GROSS ESTATE (after subtracting debts, funeral expenses, administrative costs, etc.)	TAXES DUE AT FIRST PARTNER'S DEATH (includes marital deduction)	TAXES DUE AT DEATH (single person)
$ 60,000	$ 0	$ 0
$ 80,000	0	0
100,000	0	0
200,000	0	6,600
300,000	0	37,200
400,000	0	68,000
500,000	21,400	98,900
1,000,000	98,800	265,600

credit to $175,000 by 1981. In Table A-1, we show taxes due at the first partner's death, which includes the marital deduction. These figures are given for 1981 and beyond. The taxes due are slightly more in 1979 and 1980. We also show the taxes due on the estate of a single person.

THE NUMBERS ARE SMALL

In 1981, 98 percent of all estates will have paid no federal estate tax. That is not surprising when you realize that estates up to $425,000 can be passed on to heirs free of any estate and gift taxes.

THERE ARE STATE TAXES, ALSO

We have just been discussing federal estate and gift taxes. Fifteen states have their own estate taxes, 34 plus the District of Columbia have inheritance taxes (Nevada has neither). They range from 1 percent to 23 percent of the estate.

GLOSSARY OF TERMS

Administrator
The person who administers an estate during probate. He or she is appointed by a probate court judge when no executor has been named by a will or is unable to perform his or her duties.

Bequest
A gift of money or personal property included in a will.

Codicils
Additions to a will that become a part of that will.

Corpus
The body of a trust.

Decedent
The deceased person.

Divise
A gift of real property included in the last will and testament of the donor.

Domicile
The permanent home of a person.

Donor
The legal owner of trust property.

Estate
The total property of whatever kind that is owned by a decedent prior to the distribution of that property in accordance with the terms of a will (or when there is no will, by the laws of inheritance in the state of domicile of the decedent).

Executor
The personal representative of the person who made a will. The executor takes charge of the estate, pays the debts, etc.

Fiduciary
The institution or person who manages a trust.

Holographic Will
A handwritten will.

Inter Vivos Gift
A gift made among living people.

Inter Vivos Trust
A trust made during the lifetime of the grantor.

Intestate
Having no will.

Legacy
Usually a specific item of value gifted under a will.

Lineals
Blood relatives of a decedent.

Per Stirpes
The distributional method of assets of a grant after the death of the original beneficiary. Children or grandchildren thereby share in the same proportions of the grant that their parents did or would have.

Probate
Proving a will before a court having jurisdiction over the administration of the estate.

Testamentary Instrument
A legal instrument, for example, a will or trust that bestows specific rights to specific individuals after the death of the person who created the instrument.

Testate
A decedent who left a will.

Testator
A person who has made a will or left a will.

Trustee
The person holding legal title to trust property.

Here is where you can find all of the new terms used throughout this book.

Index
of
Glossary
Terms

Index